D0183501

STREET ATLAS

Norfolk

First published 2003 by

Philip's, a division of
Octopus Publishing Group Ltd
2–4 Heron Quays, London E14 4JP

First edition 2003
First impression 2003

ISBN 0-540-08333-X (pocket)

© Philip's 2003

This product includes mapping data licensed
from Ordnance Survey® with the permission
of the Controller of Her Majesty's Stationery
Office. © Crown copyright 2003. All rights
reserved. Licence number 100011710

Ordnance Survey and the OS Symbol are
registered trademarks of Ordnance Survey,
the national mapping agency of Great Britain

Post Office is a trade mark of Post Office Ltd
in the UK and other countries.

Printed and bound in Spain
by Cayfosa-Quebecor

Contents

III **Key to map symbols**

IV **Key to map pages**

VI **Route planning**

VIII **Administrative and Postcode boundaries**

1 **Street maps** at 1¼ inches to 1 mile

132 **Street maps** at 2½ inches to 1 mile

170 **Street map of Norwich city centre** at 5 inches to 1 mile

179 **Town maps** of Bury St Edmunds and Lowestoft

180 **Index** of towns and villages

183 **Index** of streets, hospitals, industrial estates, railway stations, schools, shopping centres, universities and places of interest

Digital Data

The exceptionally high-quality mapping found in this atlas is available as digital data in TIFF format, which is easily convertible to other bitmapped (raster) image formats.

The index is also available in digital form as a standard database table. It contains all the details found in the printed index together with the National Grid reference for the map square in which each entry is named.

For further information and to discuss your requirements, please contact Philip's on 020 7531 8439 or ruth.king@philips-maps.co.uk

Key to map symbols

Motorway with junction number	
Primary route – dual/single carriageway	
A road – dual/single carriageway	
B road – dual/single carriageway	
Minor road – dual/single carriageway	
Other minor road – dual/single carriageway	
Road under construction	
Tunnel, covered road	
Rural track, private road or narrow road in urban area	
Gate or obstruction to traffic (restrictions may not apply at all times or to all vehicles)	
Path, bridleway, byway open to all traffic, road used as a public path	
Pedestrianised area	
DY7 Postcode boundaries	
County and unitary authority boundaries	
Railway, tunnel, railway under construction	
Tramway, tramway under construction	
Miniature railway	
Walsall Railway station	
Private railway station	
South Shields Metro station	
Tram stop, tram stop under construction	
Bus, coach station	

♦	Ambulance station
♦	Coastguard station
♦	Fire station
♦	Police station
✚	Accident and Emergency entrance to hospital
H	Hospital
⊢	Place of worship
𝑖	Information Centre (open all year)
P	Parking
P&R	Park and Ride
PO	Post Office
Ⴟ	Camping site
⊟	Caravan site
⊳	Golf course
✕	Picnic site
Prim Sch	Important buildings, schools, colleges, universities and hospitals
River Ouse	Tidal water, water name
	Non-tidal water – lake, river, canal or stream
	Lock, weir, tunnel
	Woods
	Built up area
Church	Non-Roman antiquity
ROMAN FORT	Roman antiquity

Acad	Academy	Inst	Institute	Recn Gd	Recreation Ground
Allot Gdns	Allotments	Ct	Law Court		
Cemy	Cemetery	L Ctr	Leisure Centre	Resr	Reservoir
C Ctr	Civic Centre	LC	Level Crossing	Ret Pk	Retail Park
CH	Club House	Liby	Library	Sch	School
Coll	College	Mkt	Market	Sh Ctr	Shopping Centre
Crem	Crematorium	Meml	Memorial	TH	Town Hall/House
Ent	Enterprise	Mon	Monument	Trad Est	Trading Estate
Ex H	Exhibition Hall	Mus	Museum	Univ	University
Ind Est	Industrial Estate	Obsy	Observatory	Wks	Works
IRB Sta	Inshore Rescue Boat Station	Pal	Royal Palace	YH	Youth Hostel
		PH	Public House		

87	Adjoining page indicators and overlap bands
228	The colour of the arrow and the band indicates the scale of the adjoining or overlapping page (see scales below)

■ The small numbers around the edges of the maps identify the 1 kilometre National Grid lines

■ The dark grey border on the inside edge of some pages indicates that the mapping does not continue onto the adjacent page

| The scale of the maps on the pages numbered in blue is 3.92 cm to 1 km • 2½ inches to 1 mile • 1: 25344 | 0   ¼   ½   ¾   1 mile |
| | 0   250m   500m   750m   1 kilometre |

| The scale of the maps on pages numbered in green is 1.96 cm to 1 km • 1¼ inches to 1 mile • 1: 50688 | 0   ¼   ½   ¾   1 mile |
| | 0 250m 500m 750m 1kilometre |

| The scale of the maps on pages numbered in red is 7.84 cm to 1 km • 5 inches to 1 mile • 1: 12672 | 0   220 yards   440 yards   660 yards   ½ mile |
| | 0   125m   250m   375m   ½ kilometre |

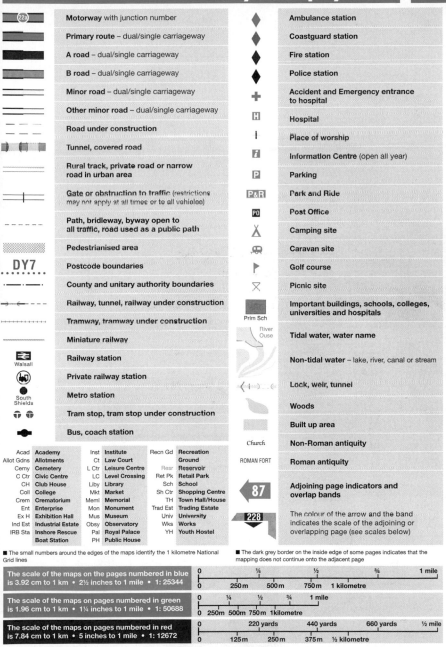

Wrangle

1

Thornham
Brancaster

Old Hunstanton
132
2 A149
3
Burnham Market
135
Wells-next-the-Sea
4
Burnham
Thorpe
5
136
6
Warham

Hunstanton
Ringstead
North Creake
Binham

133
134 Docking
South Creake
Little Walsingham
Hindringham

Heacham
Sedgeford
13
14
15
Syderstone
16
17

12
Snettisham
Shernborne
Great
Bircham
Sculthorpe
Little Snoring
141 Fakenham

140
Dersingham

Wolferton
West Rudham
East Rudham
Stibbard

25
26
27
Flitcham
28
29 A148
30
Colkirk
31
Great Ryburgh

Ongar Hill
148
North Wootton
Grimston
Great
Massingham
West Raynham
Whissonsett
32

Long Sutton
South Wootton

Sutton Bridge
Terrington
St Clement
King's Lynn
Gayton
Rougham
Tittleshall
North
Elmham

41
144 145
146 147
45
46
47
48
49

Walpole
St Peter
42
43
East Winch
Litcham
Beeston
Gressenhall

Ingleborough
St John's
Highway
West Winch
Middleton
East Walton
A47 East Winch
Castle Acre
Great
Dunham

Walton Highway
Tilney St
Lawrence
Watlington
Wormegay
Narborough
Sporle
Wendling
Dereham
154

Wisbech
59
60
61
62
63
Marham
64
153
65
Necton
66
67
Yaxham

152
Marshland St
James
Stowbridge
Shouldham
Swaffham
Bradenham
Shipdham

Emneth
North Pickenham

Friday Bridge
77
Outwell
78 Downham Market
79
Crimplesham
Cockley Cley
South
Pickenham
Ashill
Carbrooke

Upwell
Nordelph
172
80
81
Oxborough
82
83
84
85

Three Holes
A1122
Wereham
A134
Goodestone
Watton

March
Fordham
Whitington
Foulden
Little
Cressingham
Merton
Griston

Christchurch
Ten Mile Bank
Northwold
Thompson

95
96
Southery
97
Methwold Hythe
Ickburgh
Stanford
102
103

Welney
98
99
100
101
Shropham

Brandon
Creek
Mundford
West Tofts
Great Hockham

Feltwell

Brandon Bank
Hockwold
Cum Wilton
Weeting
Santon Downham
Croxton
116
118

Chatteris
Littleport
112
113
114
175
115
117
East
Harling

Brandon
Bridgham

Lakenheath
176
Shadwell

Ely
Thetford
Garboldisham

Barnham
Euston
Hopton

A1101
A1065
125
126
127

Barnham

Isleham
Mildenhall
Barningham

Soham
Honington
Hepworth

Cottonham
Burwell
Great Barton

Histon
Waterbeach
Newmarket
179
Bury St Edmunds

Cambridgeshire
STREET ATLAS

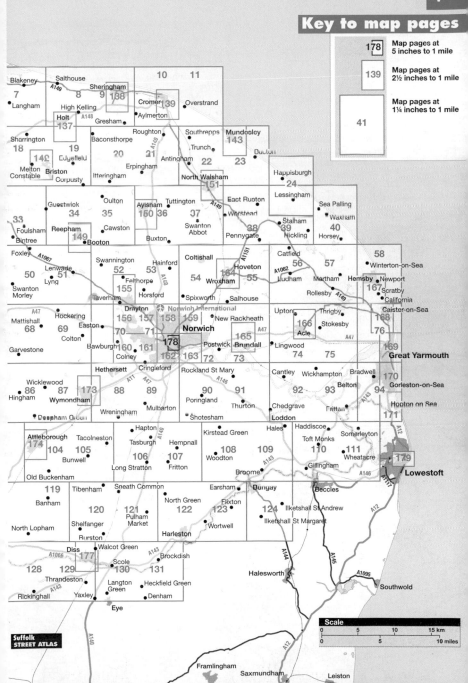

V

Map pages at
5 inches to 1 mile

Map pages at
2½ inches to 1 mile

Map pages at
1¼ inches to 1 mile

178

139

41

Blakeney
7
Langham

Salthouse
A149
8
High Kelling

Sheringham
9
188
Cromer 39
Overstrand

10   11

Holt
137
A148 Gresham
Aylmerton

Sharrington
18
142
Melton
Constable
Briston
Corpusty

Edgefield
Baconsthorpe
20
Roughton
21
Southrepps
Trunch
Antingham
22

Mundesley
143
Ruston
23

Foulsham
Bintree
33

Guestwick
34
Reepham
149
Booton

Oulton
35
Cawston

Aylsham
150 36
Tuttington
37
Swanton
Abbot
Buxton

East Ruston
Worstead
Pennygate

Lessingham
Sea Palling
Waxham
Horsey

Stalham
39
Hickling
40

Foxley
A1067
Lenwade
50   51
Lyng

Swannington
52   53
Felthorpe
155
Horsford

Hainford
54
Wroxham

Coltishall
164
Hoveton
55

Catfield
A1062 56
Ludham

57

Martham
Rollesby A149
Hemsby
Newport
167 Scratby
California
Caister-on-Sea

58
Winterton-on-Sea

Swanton
Morley

Taverham
Spixworth
Salhouse

Mattishall
68
Hockering
69
Easton
Colton

Drayton
156 157 158 159
Bawburgh 160 161
Colney

Norwich International

Norwich

New Rackheath

Upton
166
Acle
Stokesby

Thrigby
A47

Caister-on-Sea
168
76

Garvestone

162 163
72 73
Postwick Brundall
165

Lingwood
74 75

169
Great Yarmouth

Wicklewood
86 87
Hingham
173
Wymondham
88 89

Hethersett
A11
Cringleford
Mulbarton
Wreningham
Shotesham

Rockland St Mary
A146
90 91
Poringland
Thurton

Cantley
92
Chedgrave
Loddon

Wickhampton
93
Belton

Bradwell
94

Gorleston-on-Sea

170

Hopton on Sea
171

A12

Attleborough
174
104 105
Bunwell

Tacolneston

Hapton
A140
Tasburgh
106 107
Long Stratton Fritton

Hempnall

Kirstead Green
108 109
Woodton
Broome
A143

Hales
Toft Monks

Haddiscoe
Somerleyton
110 111
Gillingham
Wheatacre

Frittan

179

Lowestoft

Old Buckenham

119
Banham

Tibenham
120
Shelfanger
121
Pulham
Market
Burston

Sneath Common

North Green
122

Earsham

Flixton
123

Bungay

124
Ilketshall St Andrew
Ilketshall St Margaret

Beccles
A146

North Lopham
Harleston
Wortwell

A12

A145

Southwold

North Lopham

Diss
A1066
177
128 129
Thrandeston
A143
Rickinghall Yaxley

Walcot Green
Scole
130 131
Langton
Green
Denham

Brockdish
Heckfield Green

Eye

Halesworth
A1095

A144

A140

Suffolk
STREET ATLAS

A12

Framlingham
Saxmundham
Leiston

Scale

0   5   10   15 km
0   5   10 miles

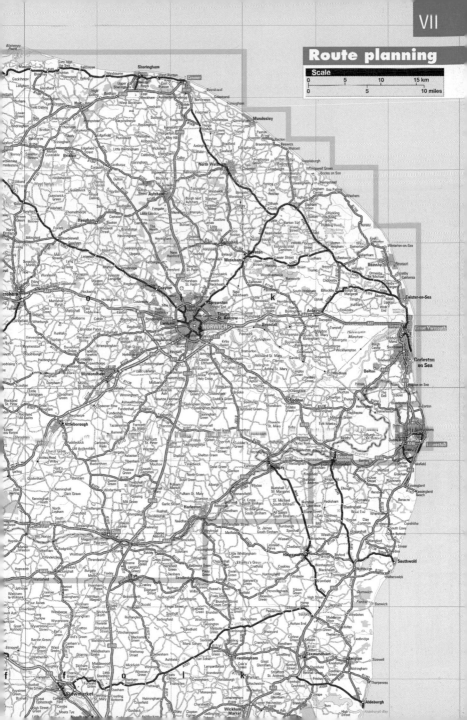

Route planning

Scale

0 ____ 5 ____ 10 ____ 15 km

0 ____ 5 ____ 10 miles

Administrative and Postcode boundaries

Scale

0	5	10	15	20	25	30km
0	5	10	15	20 miles

County and unitary authority boundaries

District boundaries

Postcode boundaries

Area covered by this atlas

Lincolnshire

Cambridgeshire

Suffolk

Norfolk

Great Yarmouth

Norwich

Broadland

North Norfolk

Brecklands

King's Lynn and West Norfolk

South Norfolk

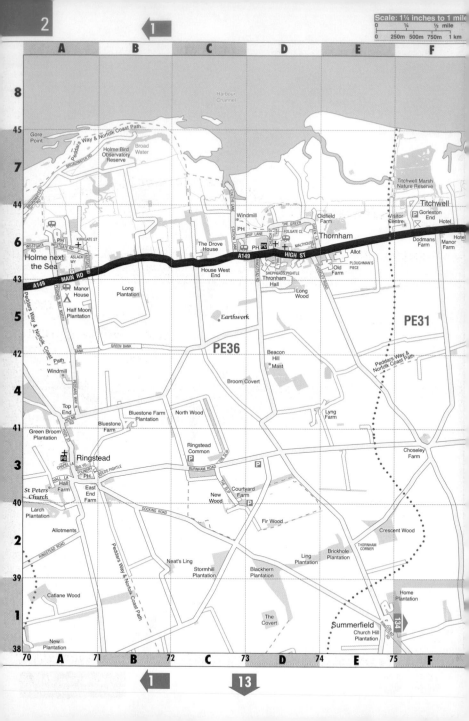

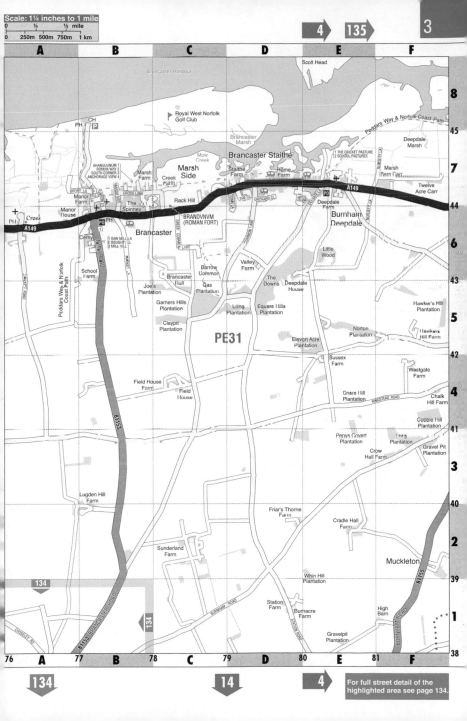

A   B   C   D   E   F

8

Brancaster Harbour

Scolt Head

45

Royal West Norfolk
Golf Club

PH CH P

Deepdale
Marsh

Mow
Creek

Peddars Way & Norfolk Coast Path

7

Brancaster Staithe

Deepdale
Marsh

BRANUUNIUM 1
ROMAN WAY 2
SOUTH CORNER 3
ANCHORAGE VIEW 4

Marsh
Farm

Marsh
Side

Staithe
Farm

Home
Farm

1 THE CRICKET PASTURE
2 SCHOOL PASTURES

Marsh
Barn Carr

Creek Farm

Cross Lane

The Spinney

Rack Hill

THE DL

ORCHARD DL

A149

Twelve
Acre Carr

44

PH Cross

Manor
House

Manor
Farm

A149

Cemy

Brancaster

BRANDVNVM
(ROMAN FORT)

GREEN COMMON LANE

Deepdale
Farm

PO

Burnham
Deepdale

RUSHER LA

6

1 SAW MILL LA
2 BOUGHEY DL
3 MILL HILL

School
Farm

Peddars Way & Norfolk Coast Path

Barrow
Common

Joe's
Plantation

Brancaster
Hall

Gas
Plantation

Valley
Farm

The
Downs

Deepdale
House

Little
Wood

43

Garners Hills
Plantation

Long
Plantation

Square Hills
Plantation

Hawker's Hill
Plantation

5

Claypit
Plantation

PE31

Elevon Acre
Plantation

Norton
Plantation

Hawkers
Hill Farm

42

Sussex
Farm

Westgate
Farm

Field House
Farm

Field
House

Snare Hill
Plantation

RINGSTEAD ROAD

Chalk
Hill Farm

4

Cobble Hill
Plantation

41

Penys Covert
Plantation

Long
Plantation

Gravel Pit
Plantation

Crow
Hall Farm

3

Lugden Hill
Farm

B1153 BRANCASTER ROAD

Muckleton

B1155 BURNHAM ROAD

Friar's Thorne
Farm

Cradle Hall
Farm

40

Sunderland
Farm

2

Whin Hill
Plantation

39

134

Station
Farm

Burnacre
Farm

High
Barn

BURNHAM ROAD

STAITH ROAD

134

Gravelpit
Plantation

1

38

76   A   77   B   78   C   79   D   80   E   81   F

134

14

4

For full street detail of the
highlighted area see page 134.

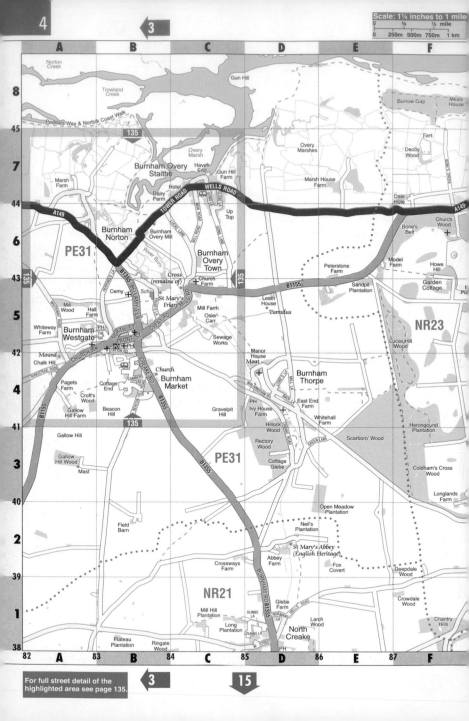

Scale: 1¼ inches to 1 mile

0   ¼   ½ mile
0   250m 500m 750m 1 km

A   B   C   D   E   F

Norton
Creek

8
Trowland
Creek

Gun Hill

Burrow Gap

Meals
House

45
Peddars Way & Norfolk Coast Walk

135

Overy
Marsh

Overy Marshes

Fort

Decoy
Wood

7
Burnham Overy
Staithe

Haven
End

Marsh House
Farm

Marsh
Farm

Hotel

Gun Hill
Farm

Dale
Hole

44
A149

Dairy
Farm

TOWER ROAD

WELLS ROAD

Up
Top

Bone's Belt

A149

Church
Wood

6
PE31

Burnham
Norton

Burnham
Overy Mill

NEW ROAD

GONG LANE

Burnham
Overy
Town

135

Peterstone
Farm

Model
Farm

Howe
Hill

River Burn

B1155

Garden
Cottage

135

43
BURNHAM RD

CHURCH LANE

Cross
(remains of)

Church
Farm

B1155

Leath
House

Sandpit
Plantation

5
Mill
Wood

Cemy

Sch

St Mary's

Friary Mill

ST LADYS LA

OVERY RD

Mill Farm

Osier
Carr

Tumulus

NR23

Lucas Hill
Wood

Whiteway
Farm

Halt
Farm

NORTH ST

FRONT ST

Sewage
Works

42
Mound

Chalk Hill

Burnham
Westgate

PH
THE
SUN

PO

PH

PH

STATION RD

Manor
House
Moat

Burnham
Thorpe

RINGSTEAD ROAD

CHURCH RD

CREAKE RD

LAMBERTS LA

WALSINGHAM RD

LOWES LA

MILL LA

4
B1155

Pagets
Farm

Croft's
Wood

Cottage
End

Church

Burnham
Market

East End
Farm

BACK ST

Whitehall
Farm

Beacon
Hill

Gallow
Hill Farm

B1355

Gravelpit
Hill

PH
Ivy House
Farm

Herongound
Plantation

41
135

Hillock
Wood

GREEN LANE

Scarboro' Wood

3
Gallow Hill

PE31

Rectory
Wood

Coldham's Cross
Wood

Gallow
Hill Wood

Mast

B1355

Cottage
Glebe

Longlands
Farm

40
Open Meadow
Plantation

2
Field
Barn

Neil's
Plantation

St Mary's Abbey
(English Heritage)

Deepdale
Wood

39
Crossways
Farm

Abbey
Farm

Fox
Covert

WELLS ROAD

Crowdale
Wood

1
NR21

Mill Hill
Plantation

DUNNS
LA

Glebe
Farm

NORMANS RD

Larch
Wood

Chantry
Hills

BURNHAM RD B1355

Long
Plantation

DUNNS LA

North
Creake

Plateau
Plantation

Ringate
Wood

W STREET

PH

82 A 83 B 84 C 85 D 86 E 87 F

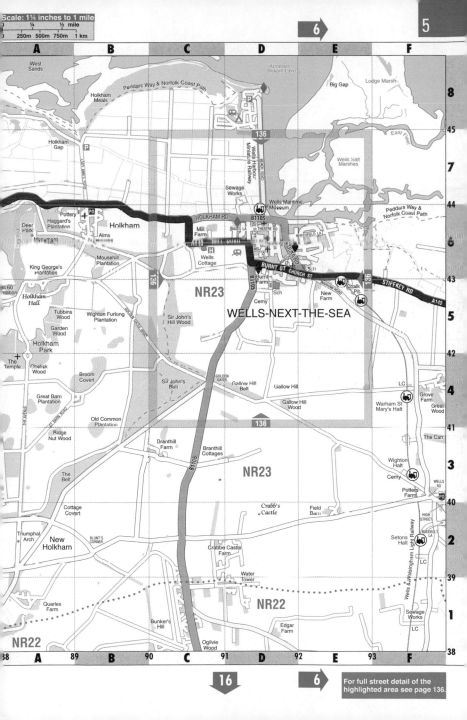

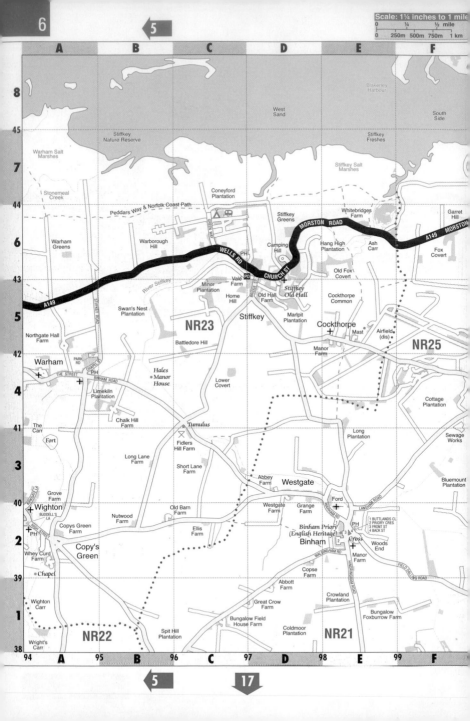

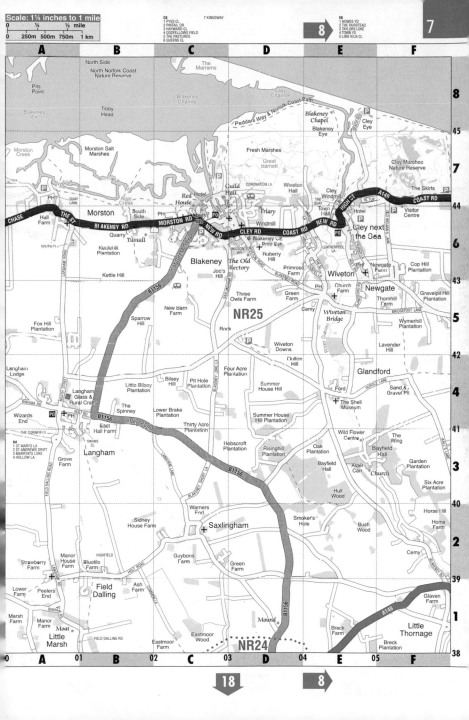

10

F5
1 CHARLOTTE'S CL
2 BRITON'S LA CL
3 ROBYNS RD
4 REGIS AVE

A   B   C   D   E   F

8

45

7

44

Peddars Way & Norfolk Coast Path

National Trust

Robin
Friend

SHERINGHAM

138

6

Dead
Man's Hill

North Norfolk Railway

Sheringham
Golf Course

CH

Mus

St Nicholas

Beeston
Spinney

LC

CHURCH LA

43

A149 WEYBOURNE ROAD

Corny

Leisure
Centre

CLIFF RD

NELSON ROAD

BEESTON ROAD

Priory
Farm

Priory Maze
& Gardens

The Grove

A149

Dale
Wood

Upper
Sheringham

NORFOLK

CROMER ROAD

BROOK

LC

Beeston
Hall Sch

NR27

Oak
Wood

HOLT ROAD

PLANTATION

Beeston
Regis

Shire Horse
Ctr

5

Sheringham
Hall

High Sch

Com Prim Sch

NR26

Nuttall's
Plantation

Davidson's
Plantation

White Barn
Covert

Osier Carr

Sheringwood

CLAYTON CL

Osier Carr

National
Trust

42

Sheringham Park
(National Trust)

The Old
House

Heath
Farm

PARK RD

A1082

WOODLANDS RISE

Long
Plantation

Pretty Corner
Farm

Stone
Hill

Row
Heath

Old Game Bag
Plantation

Weybourne
Wood

The
Dales

Sheringham
Wood

LODGE HILL

Osier Carr

HOLWAY RD

Brick Kiln
Plantation

Sheringham
Wood

Silver Fox
Plantation

Wellsdale
Farm

Iron
Workings

Row
Plantation

Laurel
Row

4

Bulman's
Plantation

Visitor Centre

Howe's Hill
(Tumulus)

Sheringham Wood

CAMPFIELD ROAD

Broadwood's
Dale

Old
Wood

Row
Plantation

41

HOLT ROAD

Mill
Farm

Gibbet
Plantation

Marlpit
Plantation

A148

Home
Farm

Glebe
Farm

Holt
End

Leisure
Centre

Bodham Covert

A148

ALLOTMENT LA

GIBBET LANE

NR11

Bennington's Lance

Wood
Dene Sch

3

Laburnham
Farm

NR25

High Wood

Bodham

WEYBOURNE RD

THE DELL

Street
Farm

BACK LA

SHERINGHAM RD

NR25

Oak Hills Plantation

138

East Beckham

Manor
Farm

40

HOLT RD

Lower
Farm

-Abbey-
Farm

PENNINGTON LA

Hill
Plantation

Mill Lane

Moor
Plantation

Rookery
Farm

Avenue
Farm

Gable
End

THE STREET

West Beckham

Hall
Farm

2

Allots

1 ROSEACRE ESTATE
2 SAYER CT

Manor Farm

CHURCH ROAD

PH

Church
Farm

Rounce's Coverts

The
Highborough
Farm

Walnut
Farm

Chestnut
Farm

Church
Farm

Low
Wood

Black Acre
Plantation

Lower
Bodham

Franklins
Farm

Highland
Farm

Cemy

Coneyfare
Wood

Gresham
Village Sch

Lower
Gresham

39

Hill
Farm

Mast

Camp
Farm

RED BARN LANE

Caspars
Copse

WATERMILL CL

Baconsthorpe
Wood

Pond
Farm

Bodham
Hill

OSIER LANE

NEW ROAD

Mill Common
Plantation

Chaucers
Farm

Gresham

CHURCH LA

CHEQUERS ST

Brick Kiln
Farm

1

Baconsthorpe
Castle
(English Heritage)

Alder Carr

PLUM LANE

MILL ROAD

Stonepit
Hill

BENNINGTON LA

Loke
End

HOLT RD

Castle
Farm Castle

38

2   A   13   B   14   C   15   D   16   E   17   F

20   10   For full street detail of the
highlighted area see page 138.

E1
1 BEECH CL
2 THE LOKE
3 CASTLE CL
4 PASTON CL
5 BRESSINGHAM RD

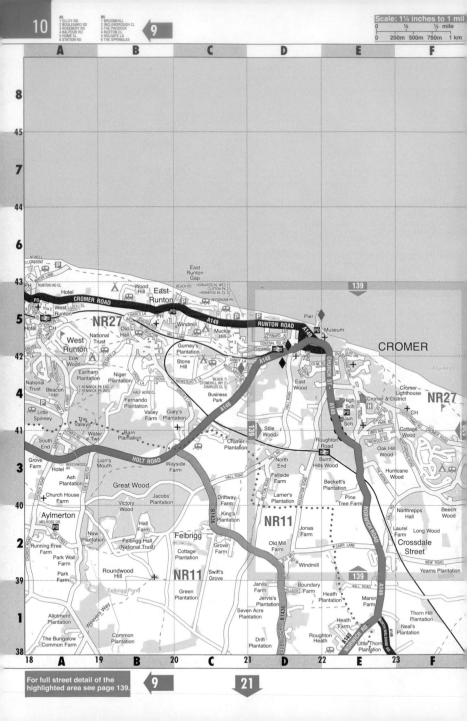

Scale: 1¼ inches to 1 mile
¼   ½ mile
250m 500m 750m 1 km

A   B   C   D   E   F

8
45
7
44
6
43
5
42
4
41

Overstrand

ILLINGDON PK
Sports Club
Belfry
VA Prim Sch
1 CHURCH CL
2 THE GLADE
Toll's Hill Wood
Long Broom Covert

PROMENADE
THORPE
HIGH STREET
PO
ORANGE AVE
MUNDESLEY ROAD
CLIFTON WY

Manor Farm
TOWER LANE
Mast

3
40

Hungry Hill
Sidestrand

STARLING RI

Northrepps
Shrublands Farm

Football Gd
Northrepps Prim Sch
PH
CHURCH ST

1 BROADGATE CL
2 SILVER CT
3 FOUNDRY CL

HUNGRY HILL

Shrieking Pits Plantation

NR27

Ivy Farm

Osier Carr

Pond Plantation

NR11

Trimingham

Hall Farm
CHURCH ST

BROADWOOD CL

2
39

Bizewell Farm
Rome Plantation

COAST ROAD

GATE WAY

STATION RD

Furyhill Plantation
BRETTON
RECTORY RD

PIT RD

India Wood

Fox Hills

Hill Covert
The Carr

Osier Carr

BLACK'S HEATH LA

Ballast Plantation

BLACKBERRY HALL LA

MIDDLE ST

MUNDESLEY RD

Water Tower Farm

Beacon Hill

BEACON RD

Mast

Marl Point

1
38

Lower Plantation

Frogshall

Little Marl Point

A   25   B   26   C   27   D   28   E   29   F

22

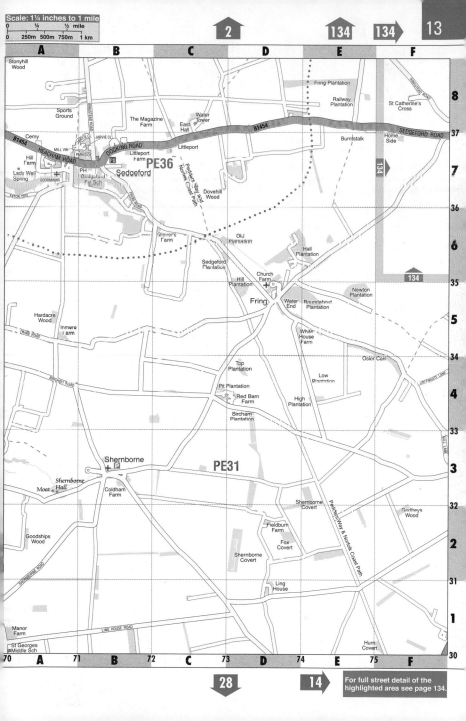

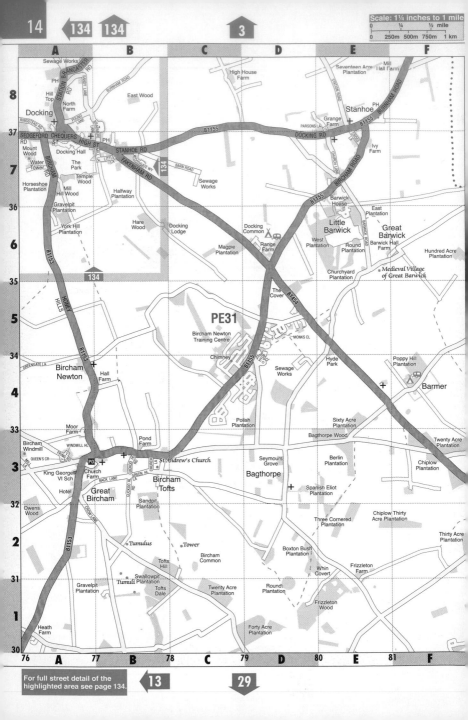

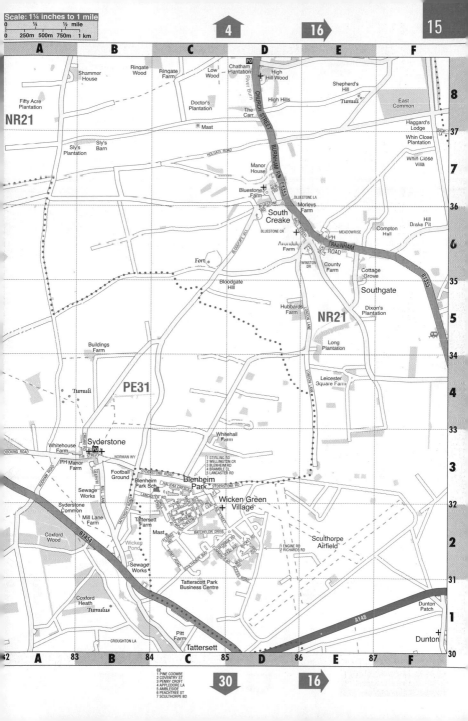

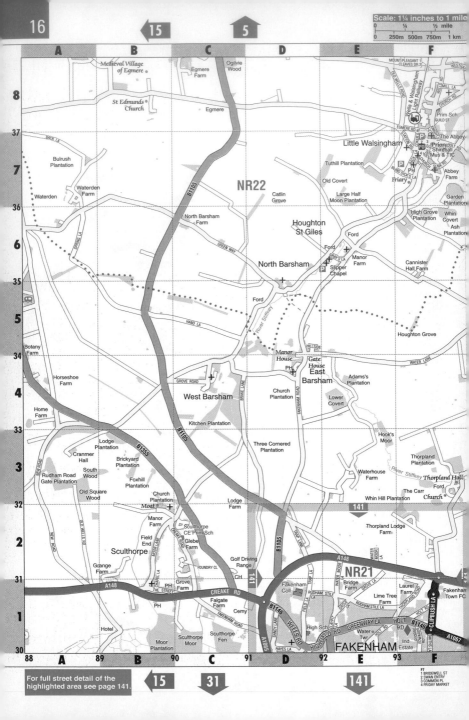

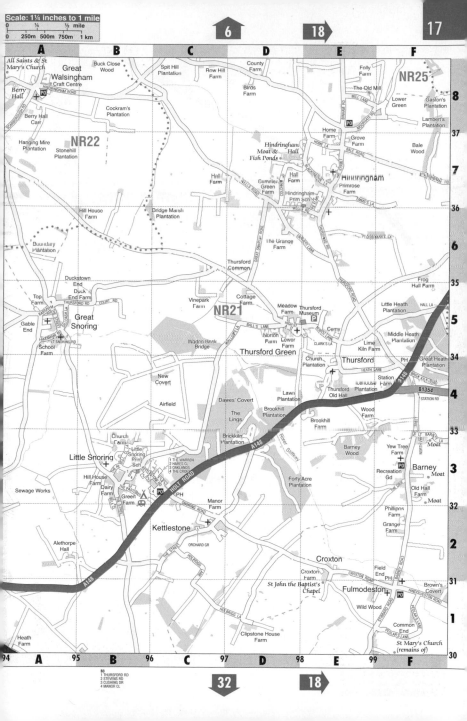

Scale: 1¼ inches to 1 mile

A **B** **C** **D** **E** **F**

All Saints & St Mary's Church

Great Walsingham
Craft Centre

Berry Hall

Buck Close Wood

Spit Hill Plantation

Row Hill Farm

County Farm

Folly Farm

NR25

The Old Mill

Lower Green

Gaston's Plantation

Berry Hall Carr

Cockram's Plantation

Birds Farm

Home Farm

Lambert's Plantation

Bale Wood

Hanging Mire Plantation

Stonehill Plantation

NR22

Grove Farm

Hindringham Moat & Fish Ponds

Hall Farm

Hindringham

Primrose Farm

Hill House Farm

Dridge Marsh Plantation

Hall Farm

Summer Green Farm

Hindringham Prim Sch

Boundary Plantation

The Grange Farm

Thursford Common

Duckstown End

Duck End Farm

Vinepark Farm

Cottage Farm

Meadow Farm

Thursford Museum

Little Heath Plantation

Frog Hall Farm

Top Farm

Great Snoring

NR21

Norton Farm

Lower Farm

Middle Heath Plantation

Gable End

Wadon Bank Bridge

Thursford Green

Clark's La

Lime Kiln Farm

School Farm

Church Plantation

Thursford

Great Heath Plantation

Icehouse Plantation

Station Farm

New Covert

Airfield

Dawes' Covert

The Lings

Lawn Plantation

Brookhill Plantation

Thursford Old Hall

Wood Farm

B1354

Church Farm

Little Snoring Prim Sch

1 THE WARREN
2 HARES CL
3 OAKLANDS
4 THE CROSS

Brickkiln Plantation

River Stiffkey

Brookhill Farm

Barney Wood

Yew Tree Farm

Moat

Barney

Little Snoring

Hill House Farm

Dairy Farm

Green Farm

Forty Acre Plantation

Recreation Gd

Old Hall Farm

Moat

Moat

Sewage Works

PH

Manor Farm

Phillips Farm

Kettlestone

ORCHARD GR

Grange Farm

Alethorpe Hall

Croxton

Field End

Croxton Farm

St John the Baptist's Chapel

Fulmodeston

Brown's Covert

Wild Wood

Heath Farm

Clipstone House Farm

Common Farm

St Mary's Church (remains of)

A 94 **B** 95 **C** 96 97 **D** 98 **E** 99 **F**

B3
1 THURSFORD RD
2 STEVENS RD
3 CUSHING DR
4 MANOR CL

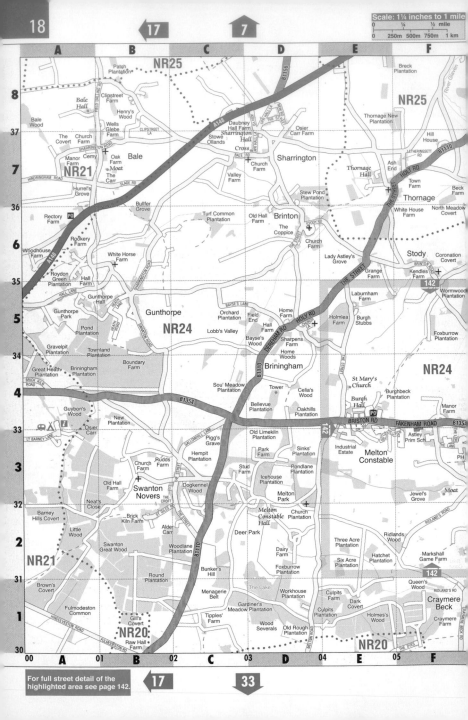

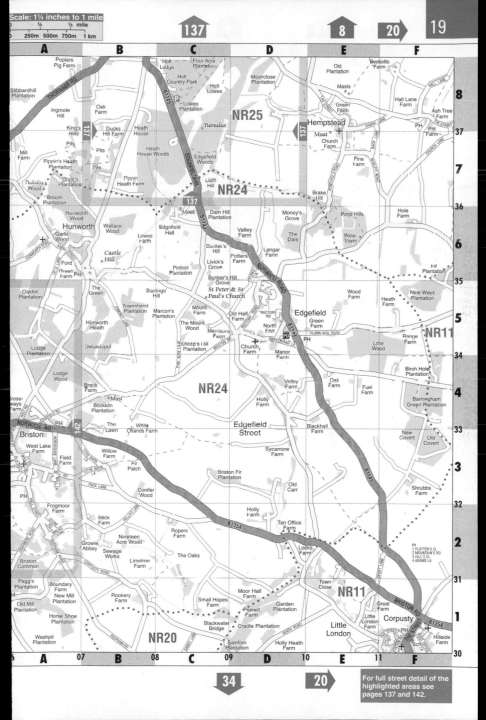

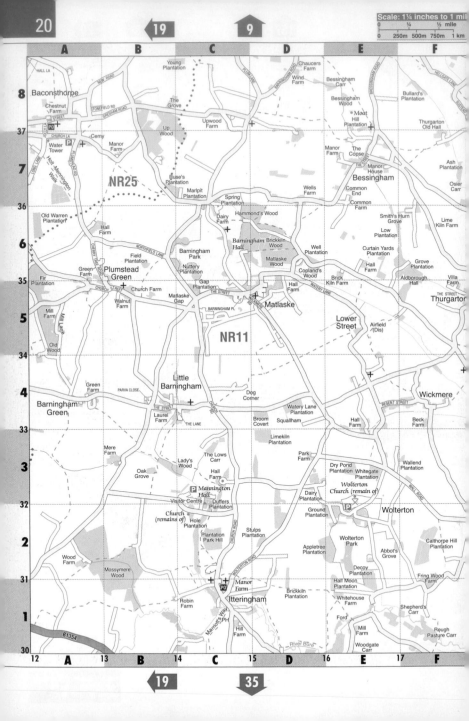

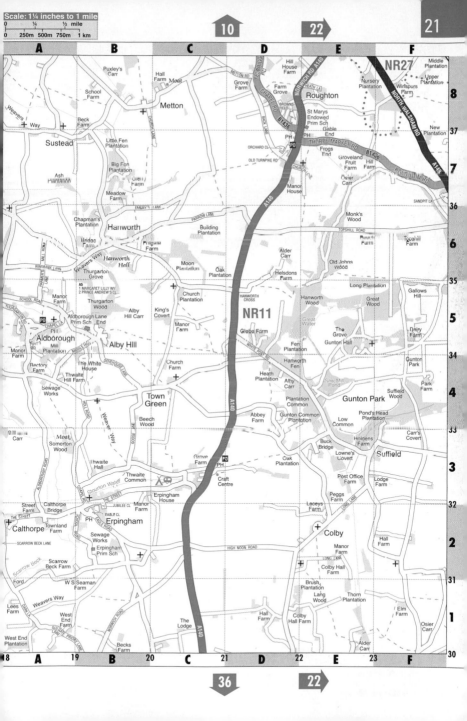

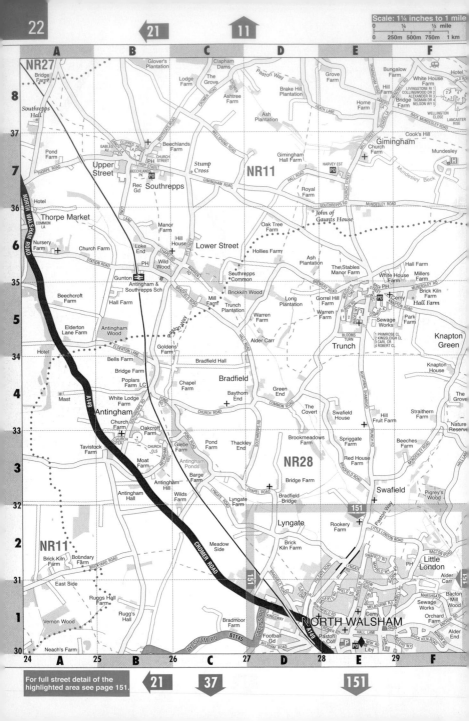

143

38   24   For full street detail of the highlighted area see page 143.

A | B | C | D | E | F

Hull
Sand

8

29

7

28

Diezst
Sand

6

27

Peter Scott Walk

5

26

Boet Creek

4

Peter Scott Walk

Admiralty
Point

25

New Inclosed
Marsh

Admiral's
Farm

PE34

Admiral's
Marsh

Ongar
Hill

3

SILT ROAD

Wingland Marsh

Horseshoe
Hole Farm

New
Marsh

24

Walkers
Marsh

Terrington
Marsh

Pierrepont
Farm

Bankside
Farm

Balaclava
Farm

2

Sharpes
Bank Farm

Burman
Farm

Governor's
Marsh

The Laurels
Farm

Grove
Farm

Fern House
Farm

23

New Common
Marsh Farm

Myrabella
Farm

Old New
Marsh

Weatherall
Farm

Creek
Farm

LOKE ROAD

Green
Marsh

Bentinck
Farm

1

Sycamore
Farm

Marshland
Farm

Bungalow
Farm

Bentinck
Marsh

Welbeck
Marsh

Tommyshop
Farm

G MARSH RD

HICK RD

22

A | 53 | B | 54 | C | 55 | D | 56 | E | 57 | F

Scale: 1¼ inches to 1 mil

0   ¼   ½ mile

0   250m   500m   750m   1 km

Bull Dog Sand

PE31

Estuary Farm

MARSH ROAD

PE30

Wooton Marsh

Marsh Farm

MARSH ROAD

PH

148

Orchard End

Vinegar Middle

KILHAMS WAY

MARSH ROAD

Lynn Channel

Peter Scott Walk

P

Ongarhill Marsh

PE34

South Outmarsh

KILHAMS WAY

Ma

Bank Farm

Point Farm

East Anglian Farm

Next Point Farm

Banklands

Sewage Works

River Great Ouse

South Wootton Sch

EDWARD   A1078

58   A   59   B   60   C   61   D   62   E   63   F

For full street detail of the highlighted area see page 148.

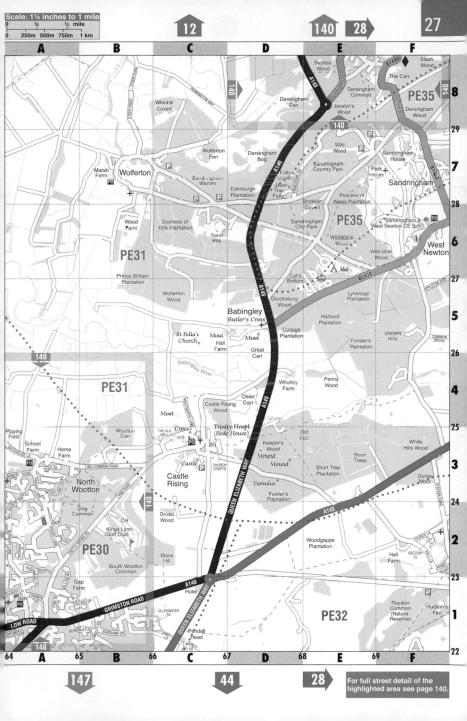

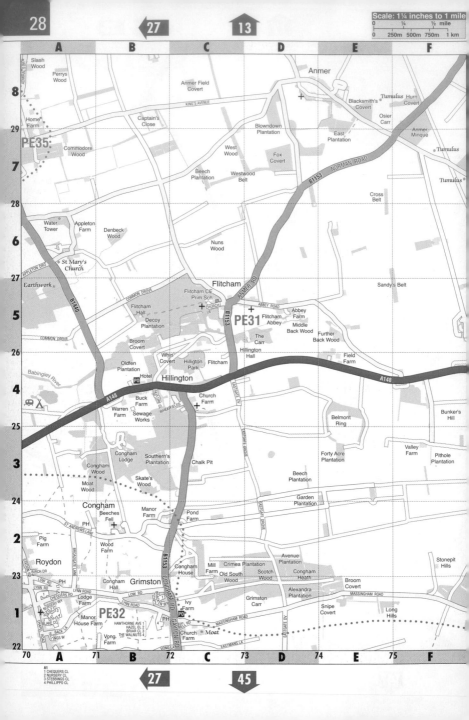

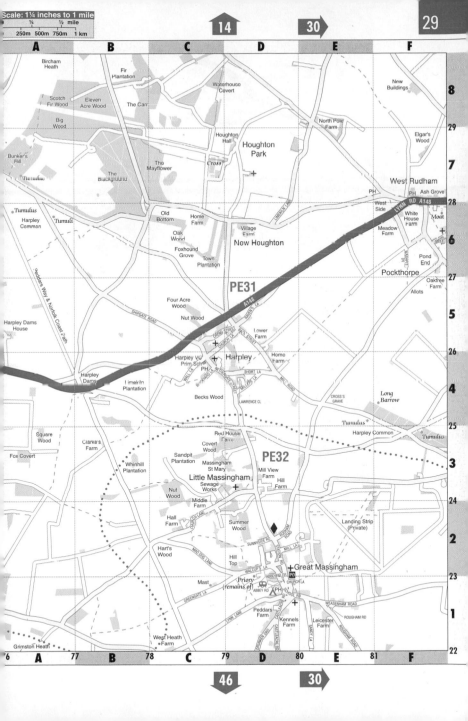

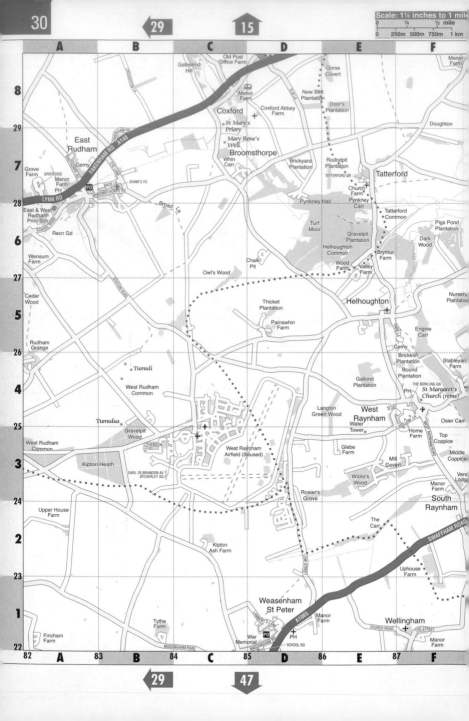

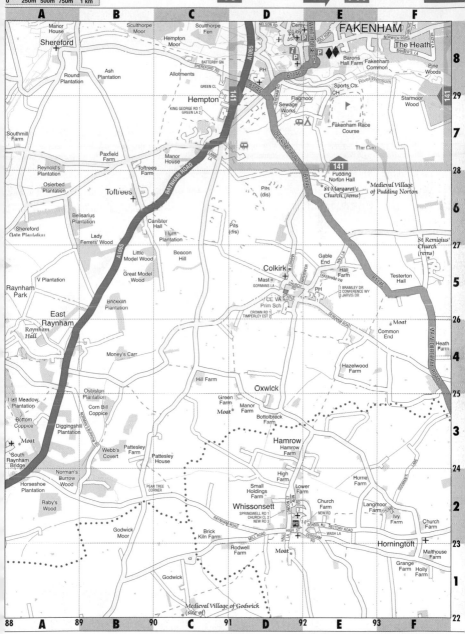

FAKENHAM

The Heath

Pine Woods

Shereford

Manor House

Sculthorpe Moor

Sculthorpe Fen

Hempton Moor

NELSON RD

WHIT HORSE LA

HOLT ROAD

Barons Hall Farm

Fakenham Common

BARBER'S LA

KEATLE

Round Plantation

Ash Plantation

Allotments

SHEREFORD RD

BATTERBY GN

GREEN CL

PH

B1146

A1065

Starmoor Wood

Sports Ctr.

CH

River Wensum

DEREHAM ROAD

Hempton

KING GEORGE RD 1
GREEN LA 2

Manor House

Flagmoor Sewage Works

Fakenham Race Course

The Gall

Southmill Farm

Paxfield Farm

Reynold's Plantation

Osierbed Plantation

Toftrees Farm

RAYNHAM ROAD

LANE

Pudding Norton Hall

St Margaret's Church (rems)

Medieval Village of Pudding Norton

Toftrees

Belisarius Plantation

Shereford Gate Plantation

Lady Ferrers' Wood

Canister Hall

Ilum Plantation

Pits (dis)

St Remigius' Church (rems)

V Plantation

Little Model Wood

Great Model Wood

Beacon Hill

Pits (dis)

Colkirk

Gable End

Hall Farm

Testerton Hall

Mast

GORMANS LA

CHURCH RD

WRONGWAY

FAKENHAM WY

MILL RD

PH

1 BRAMLEY DR
2 CONFERENCE WY
3 JARVIS DR

Raynham Park

A1065

Brickkiln Plantation

East Raynham

Raynham Hall

Money's Carr

CE VA Prim Sch

CROWN RD 1
TIMPERLEY EST 2

DEREHAM ROAD

Moat

Common End

Heath Farm

VA DEREHAM ROAD

Hall Meadow Plantation

Osbiston Plantation

Corn Bill Coppice

Hill Farm

Green Farm

Moat

Manor Farm

Oxwick

Hazelwood Farm

Bottom Coppice

Moat

Diggingshill Plantation

Bottolbreck Farm

Hamrow

Hamrow Farm

Horne Farm

South Raynham Bridge

Webb's Covert

Pattesley Farm

Pattesley House

High Farm

Lower Farm

Langmoor Farm

Ivy Farm

Church Farm

Horseshoe Plantation

Norman's Burrow Wood

PEAR TREE CORNER

Small Holdings Farm

Church Farm

NEW RD

DOORMANS LANE

Raby's Wood

Whissonsett

SPRINGWELL RD 1
CHURCH CL 2
NEW RD 3

PO

HIGH ST

SCHOOL RD

MILL ROAD

RECTORY ROAD

WASH LA

Horningtoft

Church Farm

Malthouse Farm

Godwick Moor

Brick Kiln Farm

RAYNHAM ROAD

Rodwell Farm

DEREHAM RD

Moat

Grange Farm

Holly Farm

Godwick

Medieval Village of Godwick
(site of)

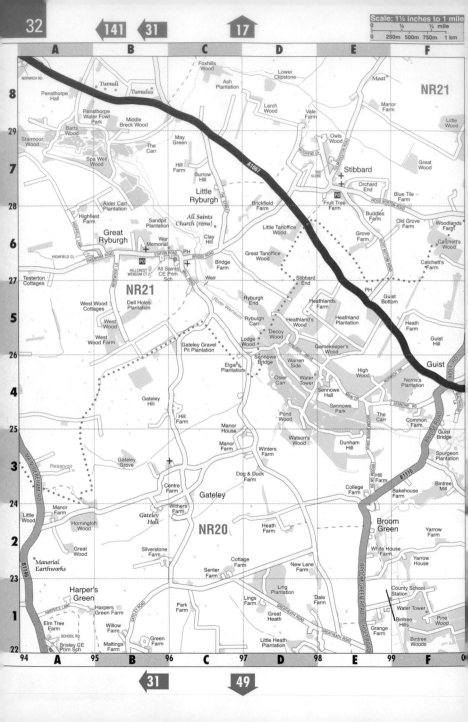

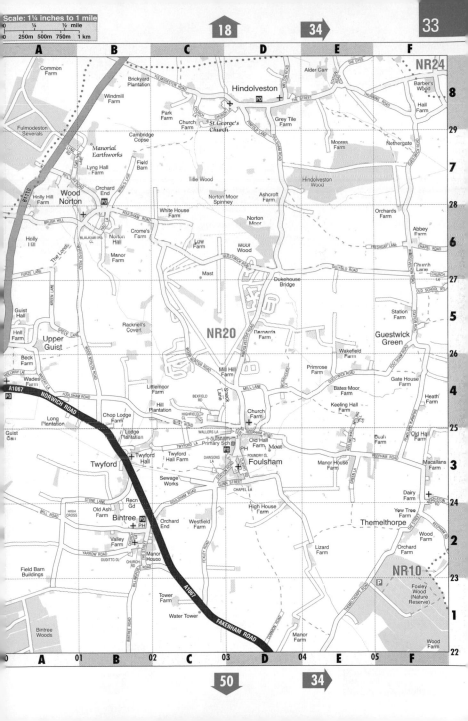

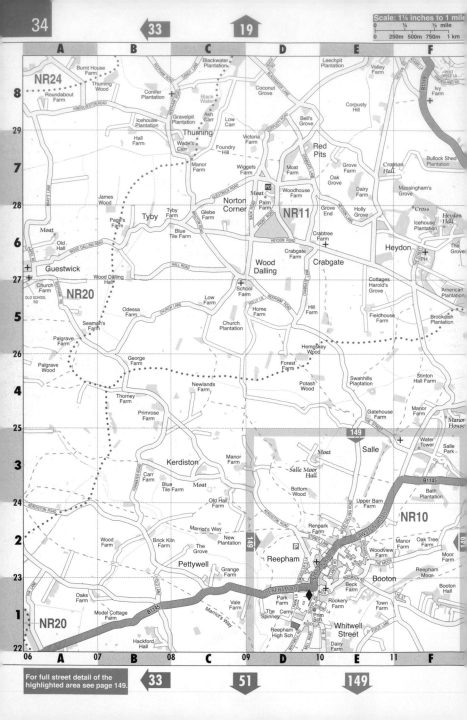

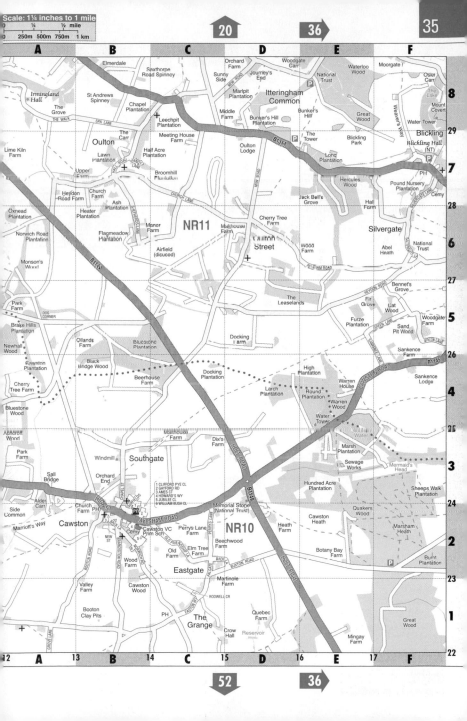

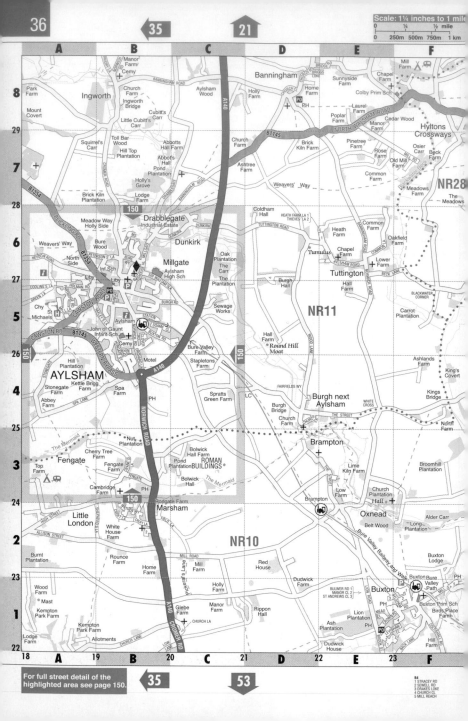

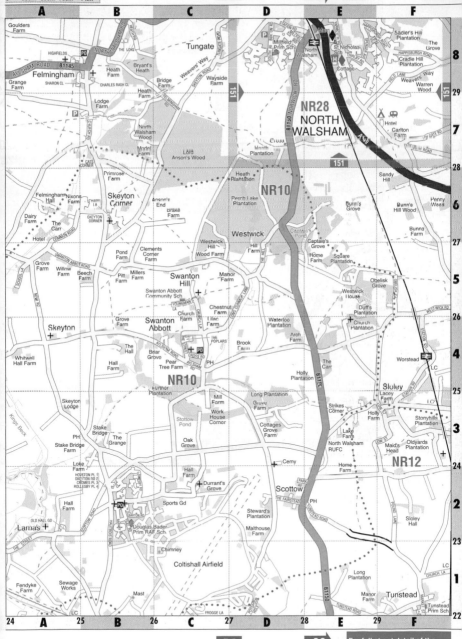

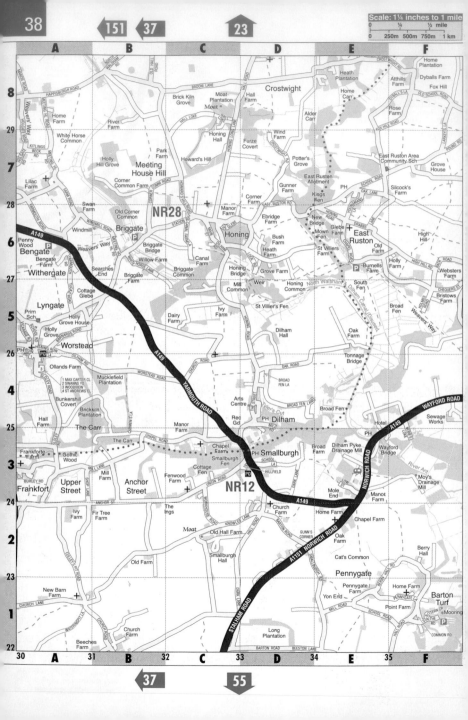

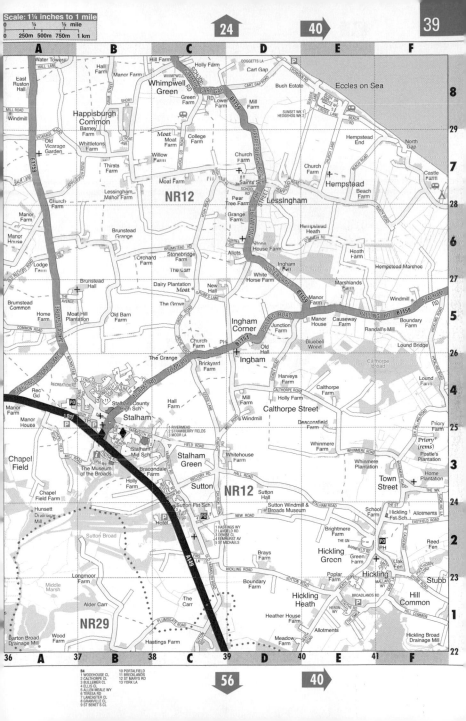

Scale: 1¼ inches to 1 mile

| A | B | C | D | E | F |

8

29

7

28

Keith Farm

6

CLINK RD

Sea Palling

PH

CHAPEL RD

Northend Farm

PO

27

THE STREET

STALHAM RD B1159

CHURCH CL

The Hall

PH

Rec Gnd

Sewage Works

WAXHAM ROAD

5

The Hall

WAXHAM CT 1
ST MARGARETS PL 2

Waxham

Lambridge Covert

CHURCH RD

26

Old Alder Carr

Frenchs Farm

Marram Hills

Great Moss Fen

4

New Cut

Decoy Covert

Lambrigg Mill

Brograve Farm

Poplar Farm

Long Gore Marsh

25

B1159

North Hills Marsh

Hickling Wall

Walnut Farm

Warren Farm

3

NR12

Brograve Level

Home Plantation

Bells Marsh

Fir Tree Farm

Waxham New Cut

Horsey Corner

24

EASTFIELD ROAD

Mill Marsh

Eastfield Farm

Brograve Drainage Mill

Delph Farm

2

Reed Fen

Horsey

The Hall

NR29

23

Commissioners' Drain

Willow Copse

Eye Farm

Hall Farm

PH

Street Farm

THE STREET

Brayden Marshes

Bramble Hill

1

Willow Farm

STUBB ROAD

Stubb Farm

Visitor Centre

Moorings

Fords Farm

North Wood

Stubb Mill

Horsey Mere

Horsey Windpump (NT)

B1159

22

| 42 A | 43 B | 44 C | 45 D | 46 E | 47 F | 48 |

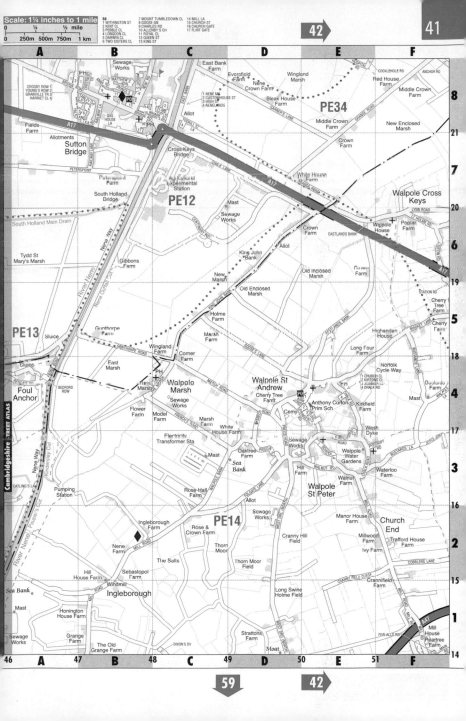

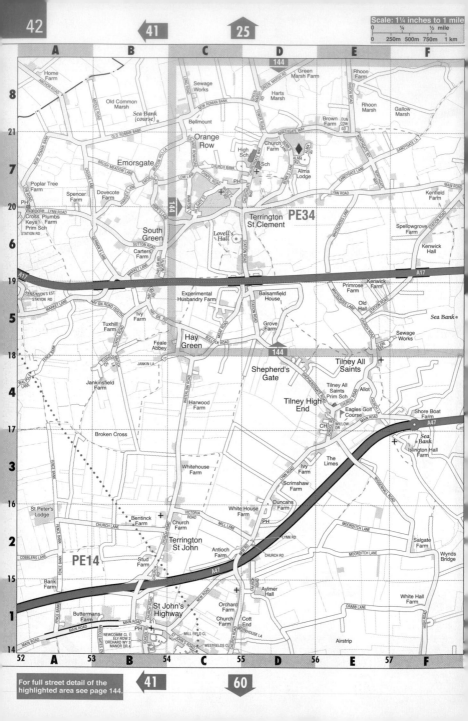

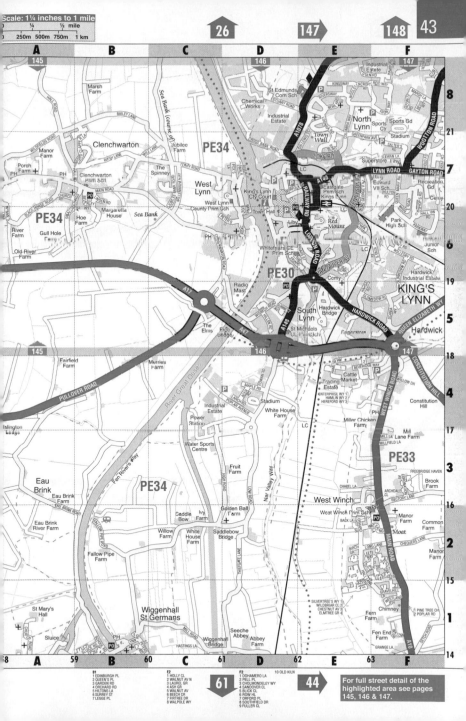

B1
1 EDINBURGH PL
2 QUEEN'S PL
3 GARDEN RD
4 ORCHARD RD
5 HILTONS LA
6 SURREY ST
7 LEGGE PL

E2
1 HOLLY CL
2 WALNUT AV N
3 LAUREL GR
4 ASH GR
5 WALNUT AV
6 BEECH CR
7 FIRTREE DR
8 WALPOLE WY

F2
1 DOHAMERO LA
2 PELL PL
3 CHOLMONDELEY WY
4 SANDOVER DR
5 BLICK CL
6 ROW HL
7 ORPFORD PL
8 SOUTHFIELD CL
9 FULLER CL

10 OLD KILN

For full street detail of the highlighted area see pages 145, 146 & 147.

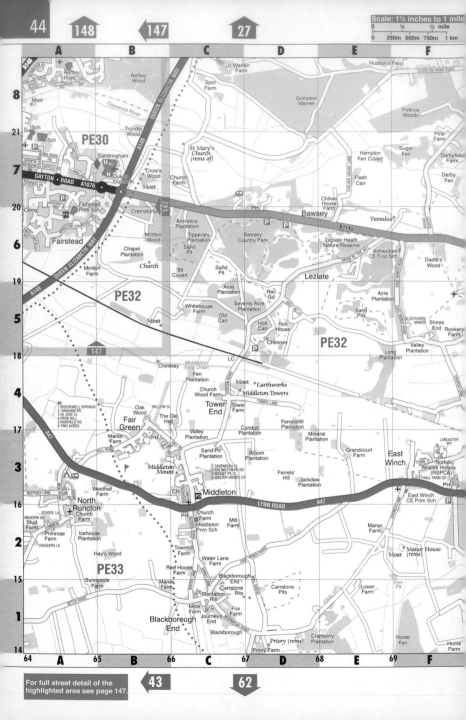

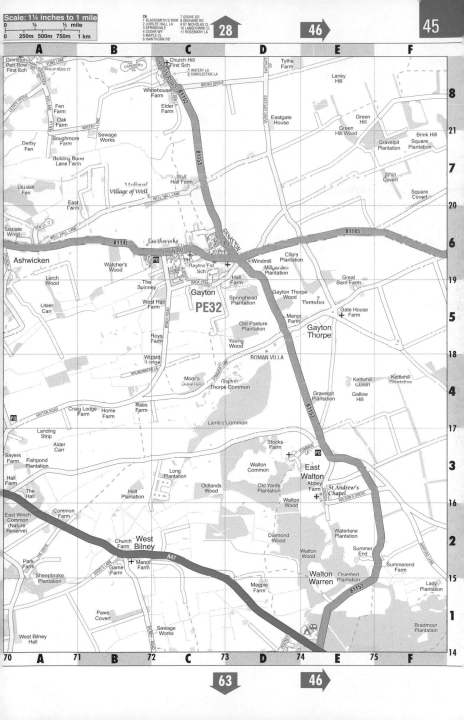

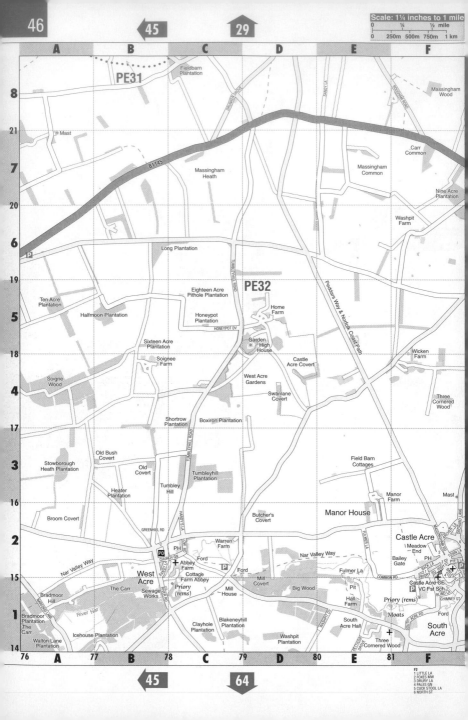

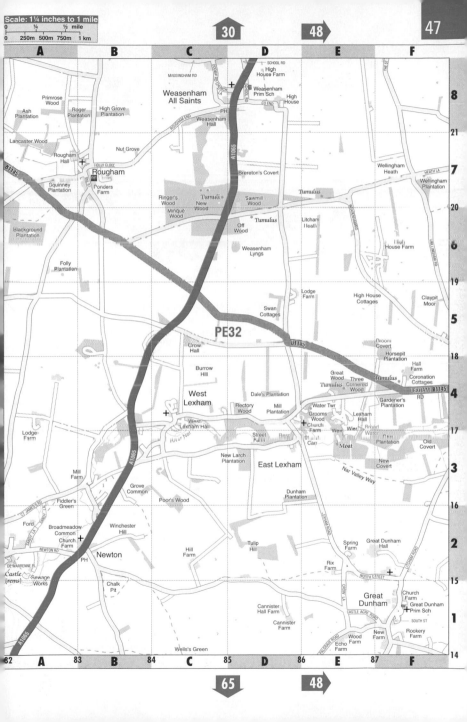

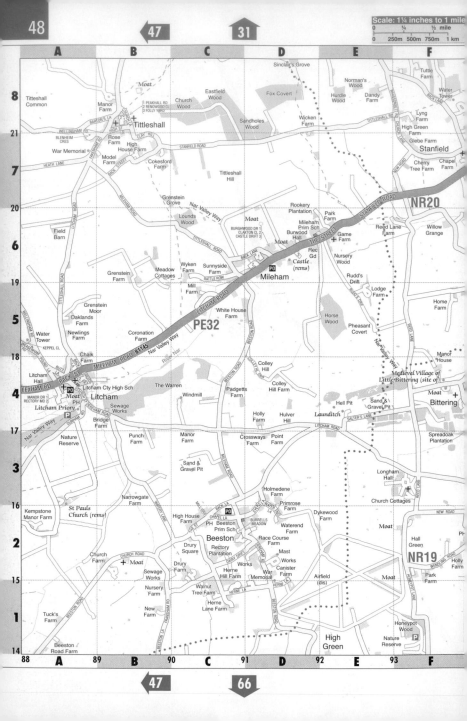

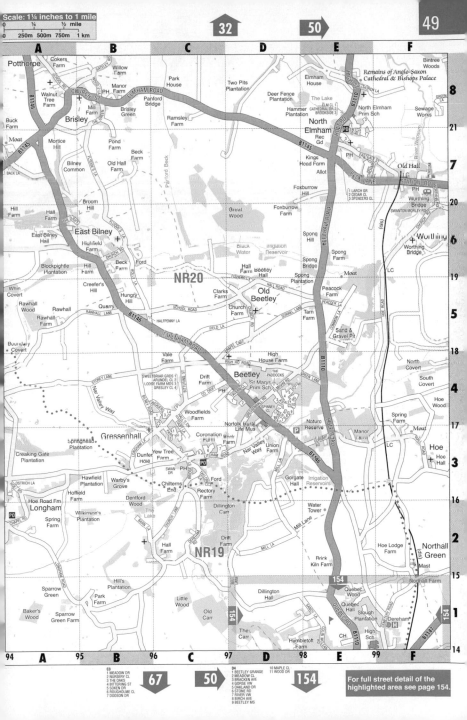

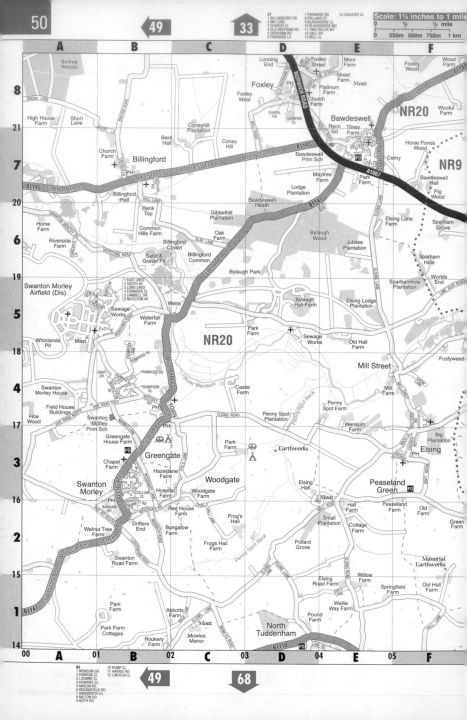

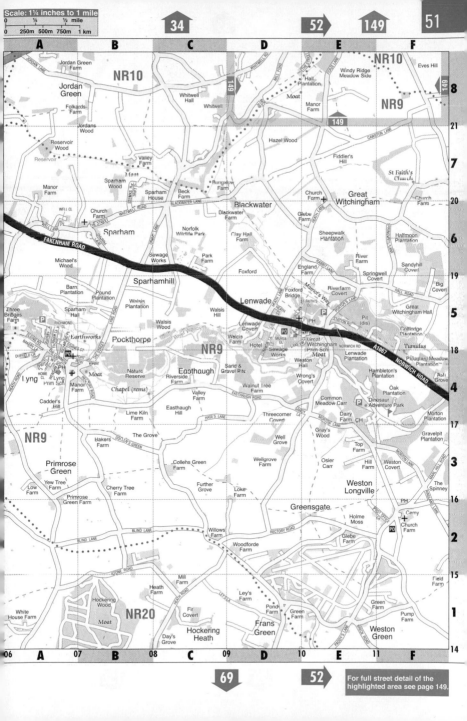

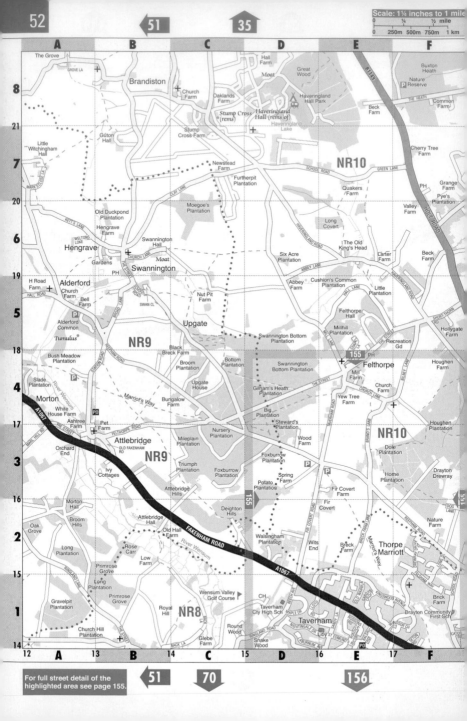

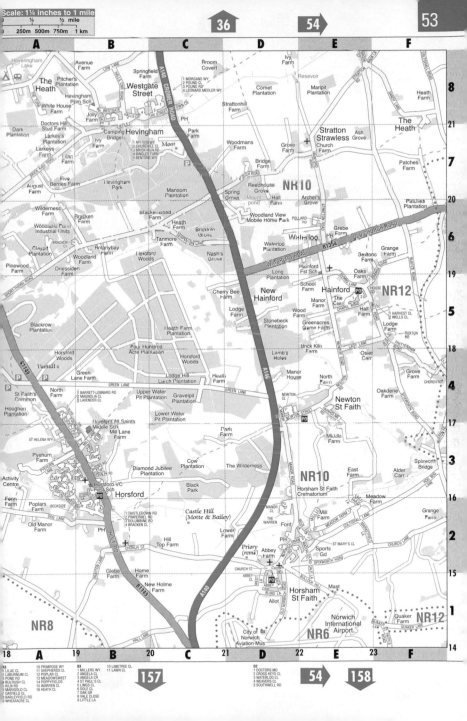

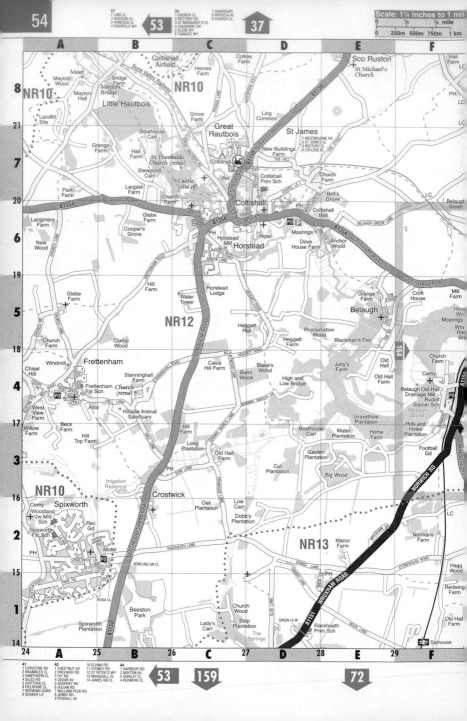

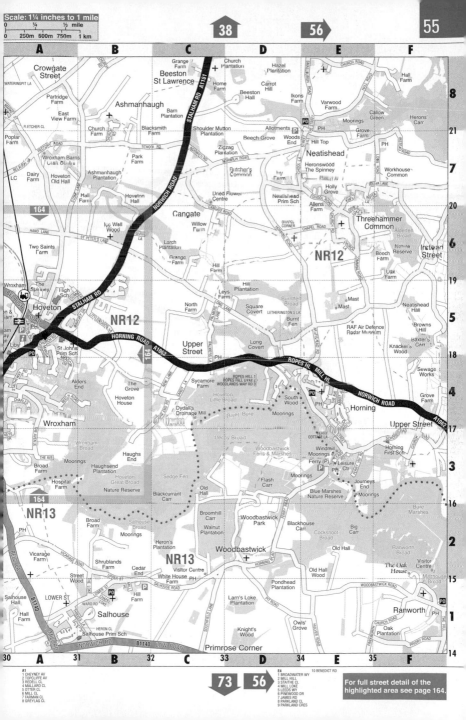

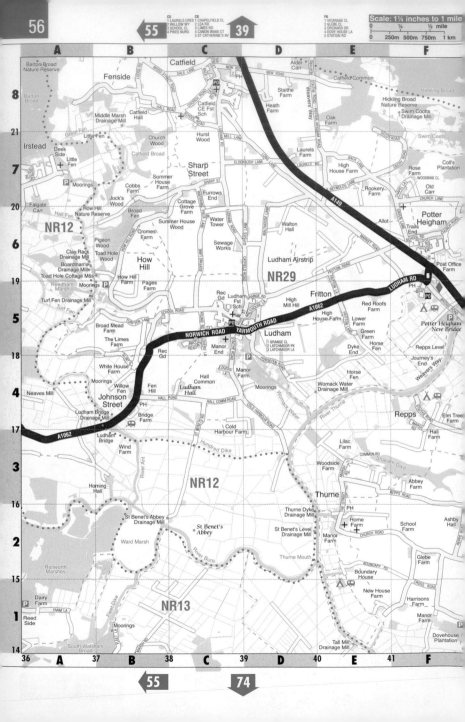

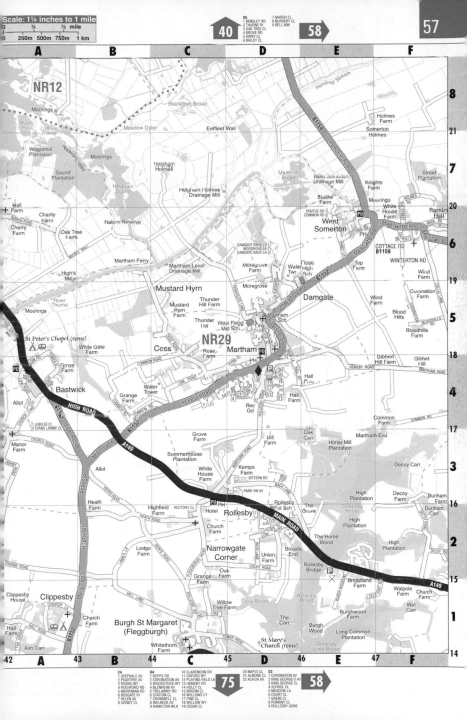

Scale: 1¼ inches to 1 mile

40

58

D5
1 BENSLEY RD
2 THURNE RD
3 OAK TREE CL
4 GROVE RD
5 KIRBY CL
6 BAILEY CL
7 MARSH CL
8 NURSERY CL
9 BELL MW

NR12

Blackfleet Broad

Moorings

Rush Hill

White Slob

Meadow Dyke

Eelfleet Wall

Holmes Farm

Somerton Holmes

Wagonhill Plantation

Moorings

Heigham Holmes

Martham Broad

West Somerton Drainage Mill

Street Plantation

Sound Plantation

Heigham Sound

Heigham Holmes Drainage Mill

Knights Farm

Moorings

White House Farm

Burnley Hall

Hall Farm

Charity Farm

Nature Reserve

Oak Tree Farm

Slaithe Farm

STAITHE RD 1
COMMON RD 2

West Somerton

COTTAGE RD
B1159

Cherry Farm

High's Mill

Martham Ferry

Martham Level Drainage Mill

DAMGATE BACK LA 1
MORGROVE LA 2
DAMGATE BACK LA 3

Morgrove Farm

Flegg High Sch

Top Farm

WINTERTON RD

Wind Farm

Mustard Hyrn

Moregrove

Water Twr

Damgate

Wind Farm

Coronation Farm

Moorings

Mustard Hyrn Farm

Thunder Hill Farm

Thunder Hill

West Flegg Mid Stn

Martham Fst Sch

Blood Hills

Bloodhills Farm

St Peter's Chapel (rems)

White Gate Farm

Cess

NR29

Rose Farm

Martham

Gibbert Hill Farm

Gibbet Hill

Grove Farm

Bastwick

Grange Farm

Water Tower

Common Road

Hall Fm

Hall Farm

Hemsby Road

Martham Road

Allot

1 JUBILEE CL
2 EVANS LOMBE CL

Red Gd

Manor Farm

Summerhouse Plantation

Grove Farm

Hill Farm

Oak Carr

Horse Mill Plantation

Martham End

Allot

White House Farm

BITTERN RD

Kemps Farm

Common Rd

Decoy Carr

Heath Farm

Highfield Farm

PARK VW AV

RECTORY CL

Rollesby Fst Sch

The Grove

High Plantation

Decoy Farm

Dunham Farm

Dunham Carr

Hotel

Rollesby

MAIN ROAD

Ormesby Broad

High Plantation

Church Farm

Narrowgate Corner

Union Farm

The Home Wood

High Plantation

Lodge Farm

Grange Farm

Oak Farm

Broads End

Rollesby Bridge

Broadland Farm

Walpole Farm

Church Farm

Clippesby House

Clippesby

Willow Tree Farm

Ley Broad

Rollesby Broad

Burghwood Farm

Wet Carr

Hall Farm

Church Farm

Burgh St Margaret (Fleggburgh)

Whitethorn Farm

The Carr

Burgh Wood

Long Common Plantation

Ormesby Little Broad

Ash Carr

St Mary's Church (rems)

C4
1 DEEPDALE AV
2 PEARTREE AV
3 RISING WY
4 ROCHFORD RD
5 MERRIMAN RD
6 BOSGATE RI
7 HELEN AV
8 SIDNEY CL

D4
1 REPPS RD
2 CORONATION AV
3 WOODSTOCK WY
4 BLENHEIM AV
5 TRELAWNY RD
6 STATION CL
7 CROMWELL CL
8 WELBECK AV
9 HAMILTON WLK

10 CLARENDON DR
11 OXFORD WY
12 PLAYING FIELD LA
13 HARVEY RD
14 HOLLY CL
15 BROOM CL
16 HOLLOWS CT
17 PINE CL
18 WILLOW WY
19 CEDAR CL

20 MAPLE CL
21 ALMOND CL
22 ACACIA CL

D2
1 CORONATION AV
2 KING GEORGE'S AV
3 KING GEORGE CL
4 SCHOOL CL
5 MEADOW LA
6 COURT CL
7 GREBE CL
8 ROMANY CL
9 ROLLESBY GDNS

B6
1 BACK PTH
2 OLD CHAPEL RD
3 BACK RD
4 THE LOKE
5 THE LA
6 WINMER AV

7 ACKLAND CL
8 GEORGE BECK RD
9 THE COBBLEWAYS
10 GREENCOURTS
11 SPINDRIFT CL
12 LAVENDER CT

57

North Wood
Winterton Ness

South Wood

Decoy Wood

Winterton Dunes (Nature Reserve)

Home Covert

Manor Farm
East Somerton
St Mary's Church (rems)
The Spinney
Winterton First Sch
Lokes End
Church Farm
Winterton-on-Sea
WINTERTON RD
SOMERTON RD
BACK RD
PH
King St
Hermanus Leisure Centre

High Barn Farm
Rainbows End
Mill Farm

Hemsby
Martham Road
Fengate Farm
PH
Sch
B1159
KINGS WAY
Kings Loke
Beach Road
P
PH
167
Hemsby Hole

BRIDGECOURT 1
BRIDGE MD 2
SUMMERFIELD CL 4
SPRINGFIELD CL 4
SPRINGFIELD RD 5
SPRINGFIELD N 6
The Spinney
PO
Cross (rems)
Newport Road
Newport
NR29
Swimming Pool
Dowe Hill Farm
167
Dowe Hill
Scratby

Pettingills Farm
Home Farm
Mill Farm
Scratby Hall
Thoroughfare Lane
Ormesby St Margaret
Heather Av
Beach Road

Barn Farm
Manships Farm
Manor Farm
Sch
PO
Gables Farm
Station Road
California
California Rd
PH

MAIN RD
A149
Ormesby St Michael
Manship's Plantation
Ormesby Hall
Willow Farm
Yarmouth Road
B1159
California Farm
PH
Hotel

For full street detail of the highlighted area see page 167

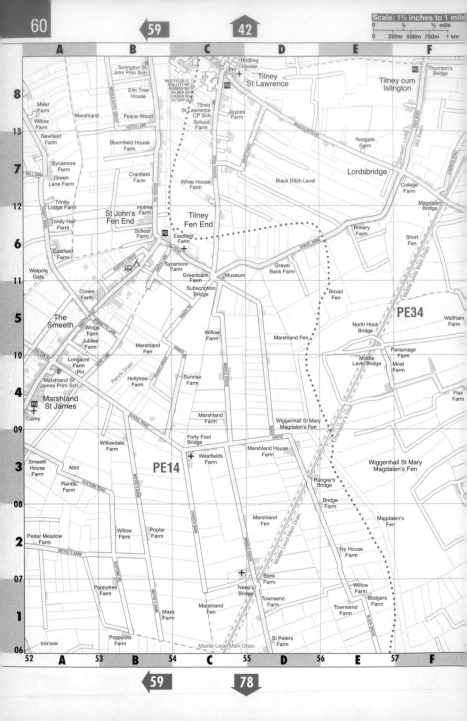

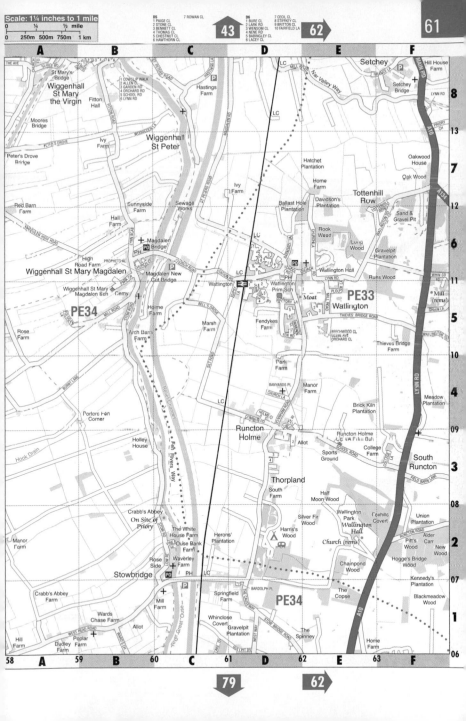

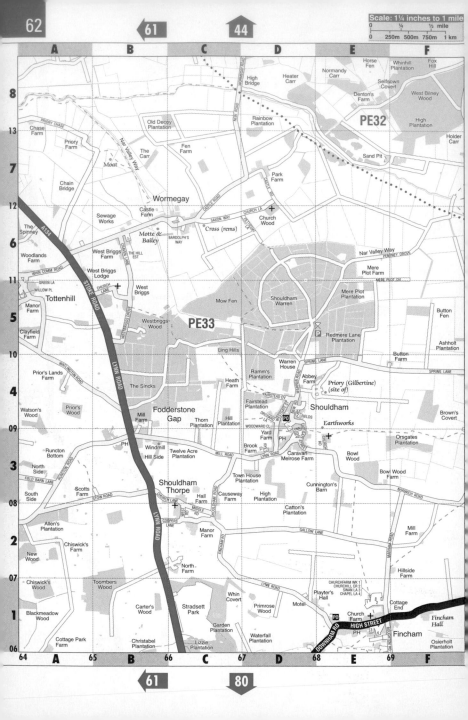

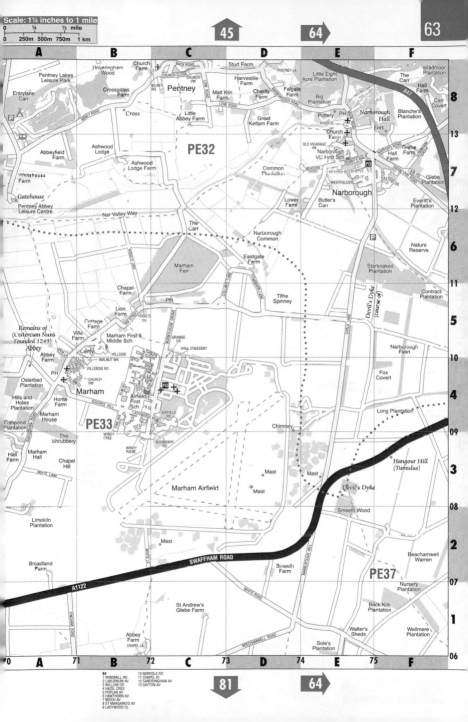

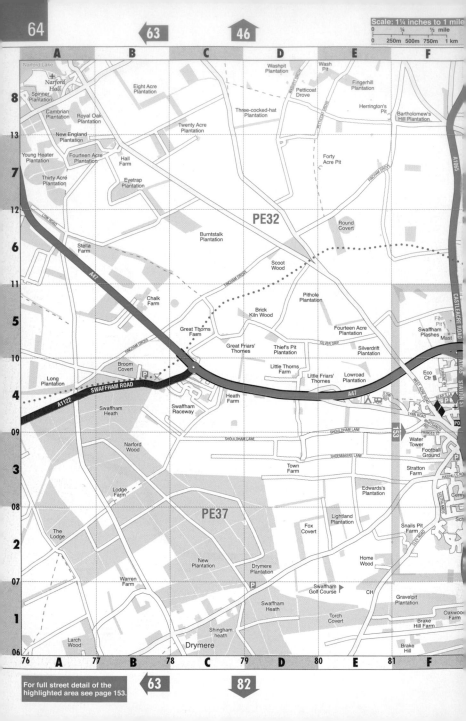

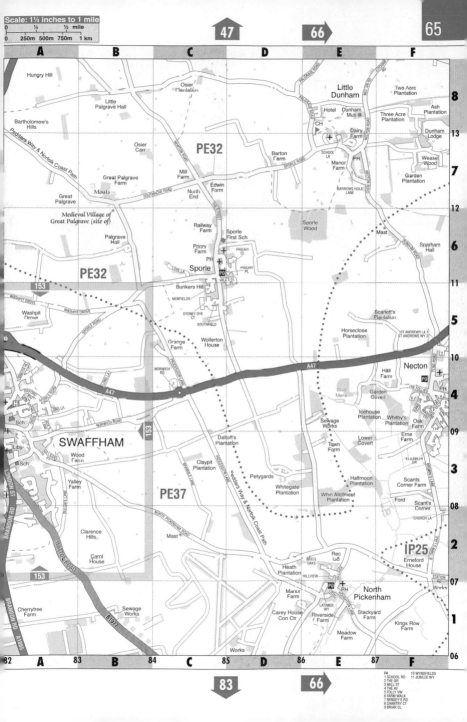

A B C D E F

8

Hungry Hill

Little Palgrave Hall

Osier Plantation

Little Dunham

Two Acre Plantation

Hotel Dunham Mus

Three Acre Plantation

Ash Plantation

13

Bartholomew's Hills

CH

Dunham Lodge

Osier Carr

PE32

Barton Farm

Dairy Farm

SCHOOL LA

PH

Weasel Wood

Garden Plantation

7

Peddars Way & Norfolk Coast Path

Great Palgrave Farm

Mouts

Mill Farm

North End

Edwin Farm

SOUTHACRE ROAD

Manor Farm

BARROWS HOLE LANE

12

Great Palgrave

Medieval Village of Great Palgrave (site of)

Palgrave Hall

Railway Farm

Sporle First Sch

Sporle Wood

Mast

6

Priory Farm

PH

PRIORY CL

Snarham Hall

PE32

LOVE LA

Sporle

PO

PRIORY PL

153

Bunkers Hill

HILL'S CL

11

WASHPIT DROVE

NEWFIELDS

Scarlett's Plantation

5

Washpit Drove

WASHPIT DROVE

SYDNEY DYE CT

SOUTHFIELD

Horseclose Plantation

ST ANDREWS LA 1
ST ANDREWS WY 2

SPORLE ROAD

Grange Farm

Wolferton House

A47

Necton

10

NORWICH RD

PROCESSION LANE

Hall Farm

PO

PH

THE FOLLIES

4

Wild Mere

Garden Covert

SWAFFHAM

A47

153

NORWICH ROAD

Dalton's Plantation

Sewage Works

Icehouse Plantation

Whitby's Plantation

Oak Farm

09

Wood Farm

Town Farm

Lower Covert

Erne Farm

ELIZABETH DR

Yalley Farm

PE37

Claypit Plantation

Petygards

Whitegate Plantation

Halfmoon Plantation

Scants Corner Farm

3

BRANDON RD

WATTON ROAD

NORTH PICKENHAM ROAD

Whin Allotment Plantation

Ford

Scant's Corner

CHURCH LA

08

Clarence Hills

Mast

Peddars Way & Norfolk Coast Path

IP25

Erneford House

2

Carol House

Rec Gd

WHITE OAKS

STATION RD

Works

07

153

Heath Plantation

HILLVIEW

PO

PH

North Pickenham

Cherrytree Farm

B1077

Sewage Works

Manor Farm

LATIMER WY

Stackyard Farm

Kings Row Farm

1

BRANDON RD
A1065

Carey House Con Ctr

Riverside Farm

Meadow Farm

Works

06

A 82 B 83 C 84 D 85 E 86 F 87

F4
1 SCHOOL RD
2 THE GR
3 MILL ST
4 THE AV
5 FOLLY VW
6 FARM WALK
7 BENGEY'S RD
8 CHANTRY CT
9 BRIAR CL
10 WYNDFIELDS
11 JUBILEE WY

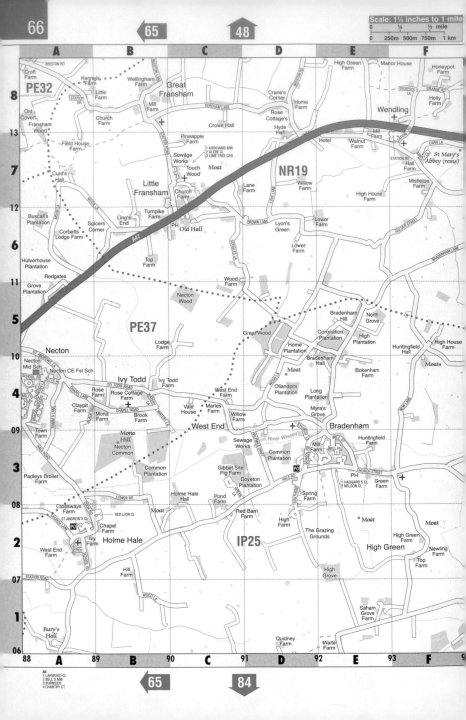

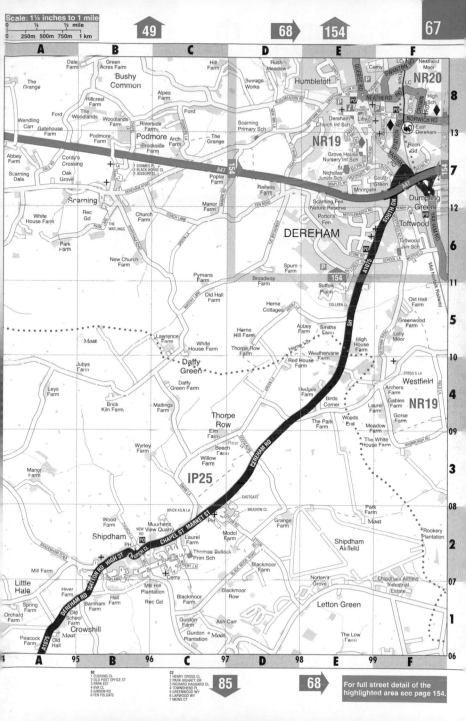

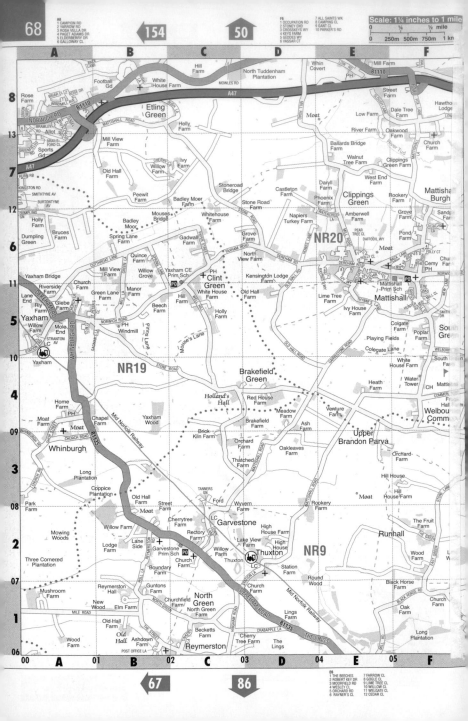

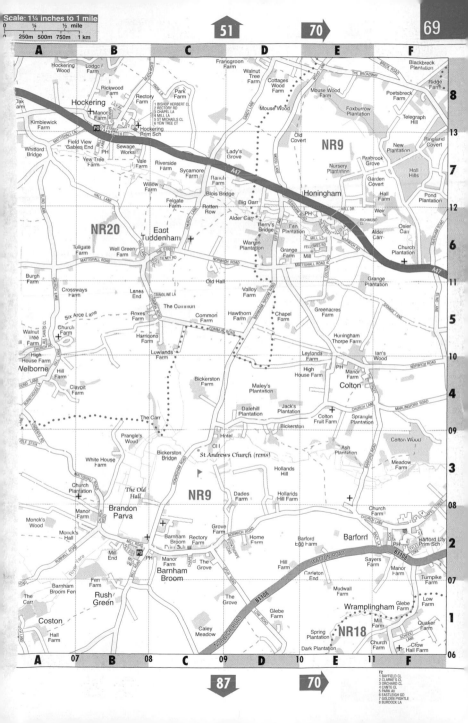

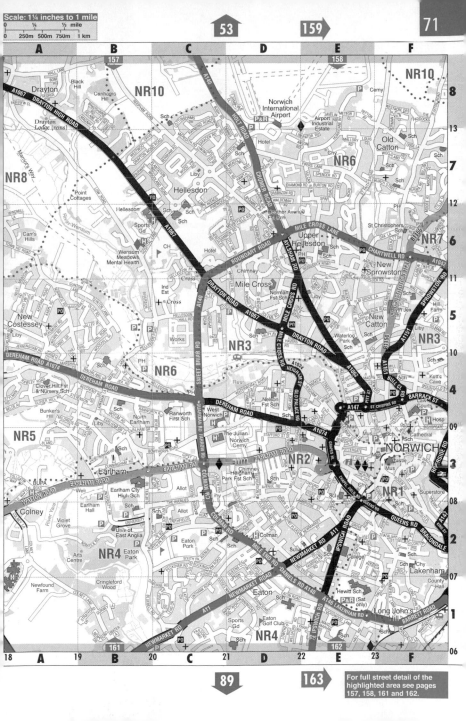

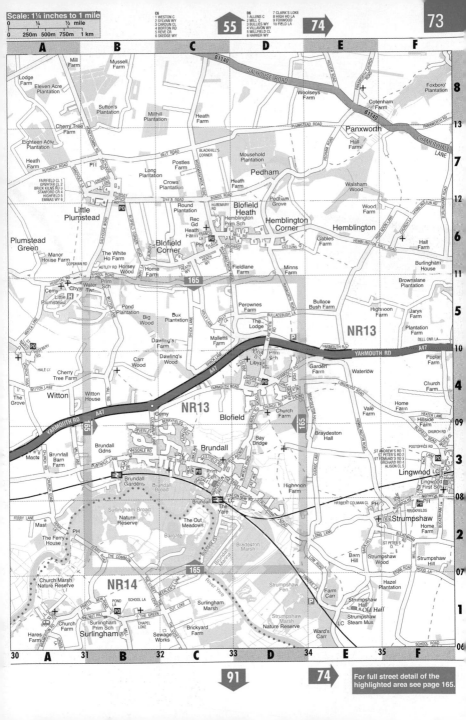

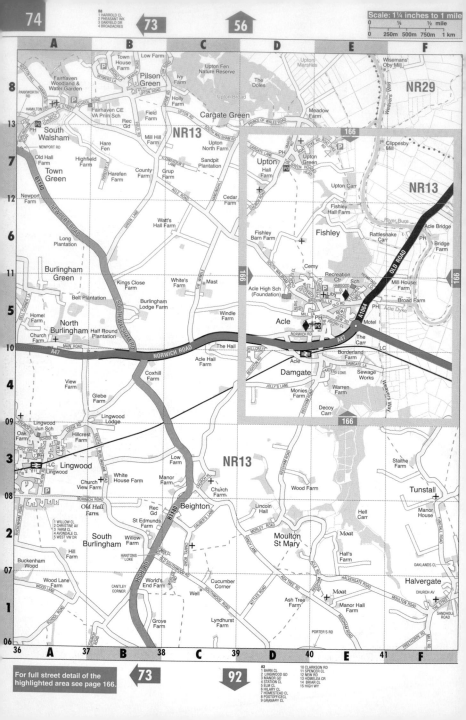

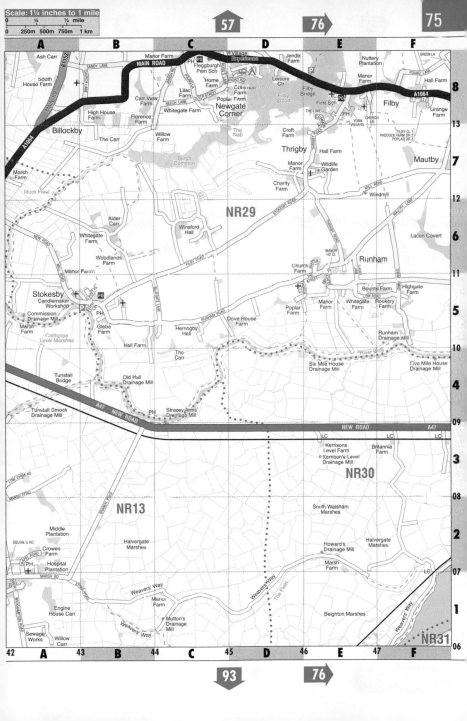

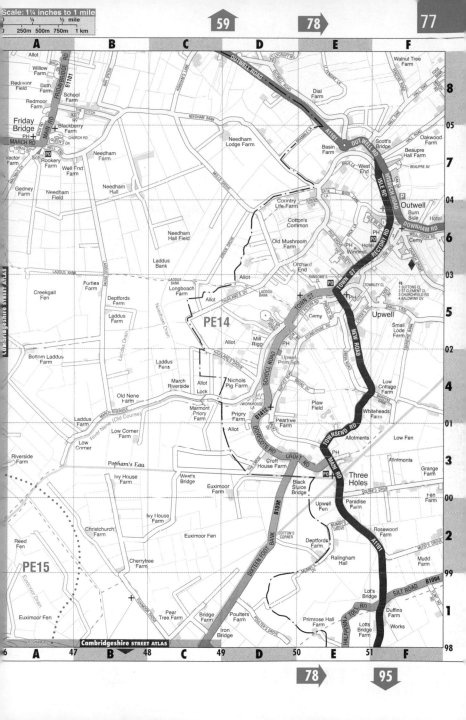

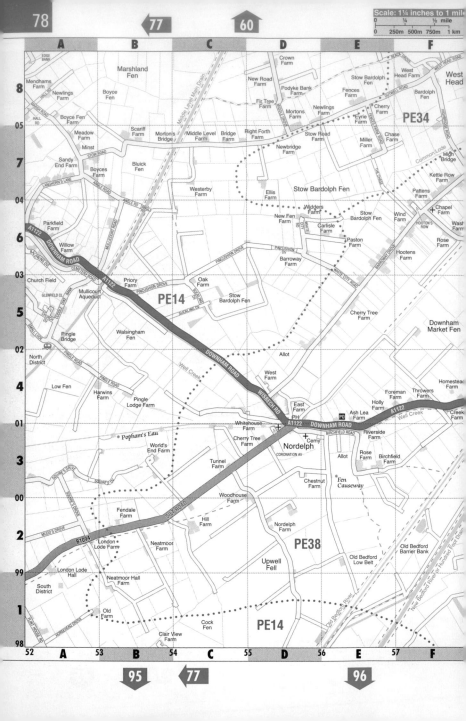

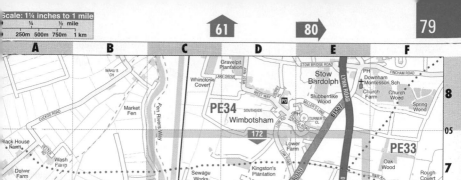

Scale: 1¼ inches to 1 mile
¼   ½   mile
250m 500m 750m 1 km

A   B   C   D   E   F

Wash's CH

Market Fen

Fen Rivers Way

Gravelpit Plantation

STOW BRIDGE ROAD

Stow Bardolph

Whinclose Covert

LAKE DROVE

WEST WAY

Slubberlike Wood

FINCHAM ROAD

PH
Downham Montessori Sch

Church Farm

Church Wood

Spring Wood

8

Black House Farm

CUCKOO ROAD

PE34
Wimbotsham

SOUTHSIDE
172

Lower Farm

MILLER'S LANE
TURNER'S RD

B1507

PE33

05

Dolver Farm

Wash Farm

Wayside Farm

Meadow End

Downham Market Fen

Kingston's Plantation

Sewage Works

Broomhill

Oak Wood

Rough Covert

Mast

7

04

PE38

Downham Market Fen

Bridge Farm

Downham Market

Ind Estate

MILL

LC

Hillcrest Prim Sch

Bexwell

BEXWELL ROAD

A10

Mast
Res

Mast

Gatehouse

A1122

Bexwell Hall Farm

Mast

6

Redgate Farm

Armstrong Siddeley Car & Aero Mus
Hermitage Hall

Downham Market

High Sch

DOWNHAM MARKET

172

03

Tile Farm

Poplar Farm

Slate Farm

Orchard Farm

Whitegate Farm

Slate Farm

Downham Bridge

A1122

LC

Industrial Estate

Library
PO

Cemy

Cemy

HOWDALE RD

High School

Rouses Farm

5

02

Chapel Farm

KEMP'S CL

Salters Lode

Poplar Farm

WATERMAN'S WY

Locks

Denver Sluice

MUND TOWN

High Hatter's Wood

A1122

Denver

West Hall Farm

Moat
PO

Prim Sch

PH

Moat

ELY RD

CH

Reservoir Plantation

Ryston Park Golf Club

Stonehills Farm

Stonehills Wood

Home Wood

Sandpit Spinney

Brick Kiln Wood

Bullstrong Plantation

4

01

White Hall Farm

PH

Fen Causeway

Middle Drove Farm

SLICE ROAD

LC

Hollies Farm

Windmill

COW LANE

Mill Farm

Glebe Common

Ash Plantation

Whin Common

172

Ryston Hall

Ryston Park

Oak Wood

Common Wood

Home Farm

Simkin's Spinney

Crossways Farm

TILGAY ROAD

Crossways Covert

3

Whitehouse Farm

Fen Rivers Way

Cut-off Channel

Ronkery Covert

Rookery Farm

PE38

Oval Plantation

School Plantation

Pheasant Wood

Roxham Farm

00

Denver Fen

Silt Fen Farm

Silt Fen

Sewage Works

Fordham

High House Farm

Oak Wood

Snowre Hall

Cut-off Channel

A10

Four Acre Covert

2

Ouse Bridge Farm

Wissey Bridge

Harold Covert

Khartoum Wood

Twelve Acre Covert

Church Farm

WHITTOME MILL 1
HOLTS LA 2
WATERMAN'S LA 3
POWER'S PL 4
MANOR RD 5
FORESTER'S AV 6
TOWER RD 7

Hill End

Hilgay Bridge

Meadow Side

Skipwith Corner

Roxham Fen

Two Acre Covert

Roxham Fen

99

Fordham Fen

Ouse Bridge

Ouse Bridge Farm

Willow Farm

STEEL'S DROVE

Great West Fen

Corner Farm

New Manor Farm

Sunny Side

PH

EAST END

Hilgay

Manorial Earthworks

HILL'S CT 2
LAWRENCE'S LA 3
AVENUE CL

HUBBARD'S DROVE

CHURCH RD

Hilgay Fen

Rose Hill Farm

HUBBARD'S DROVE

1

A   59   B   60   C   61   D   62   E   63   F   98

For full street detail of the highlighted area see page 172.

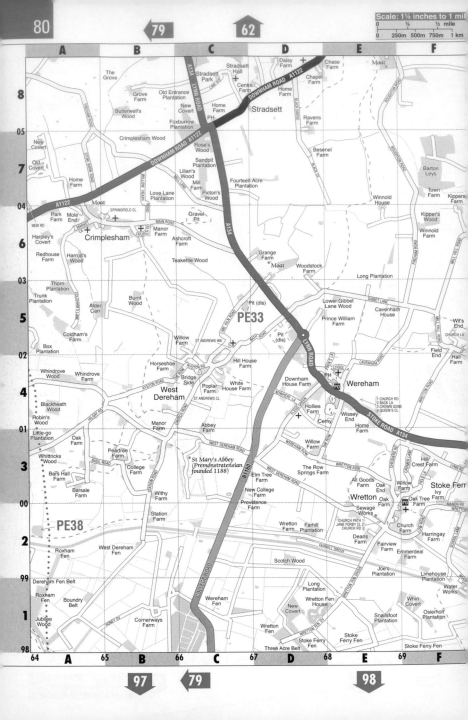

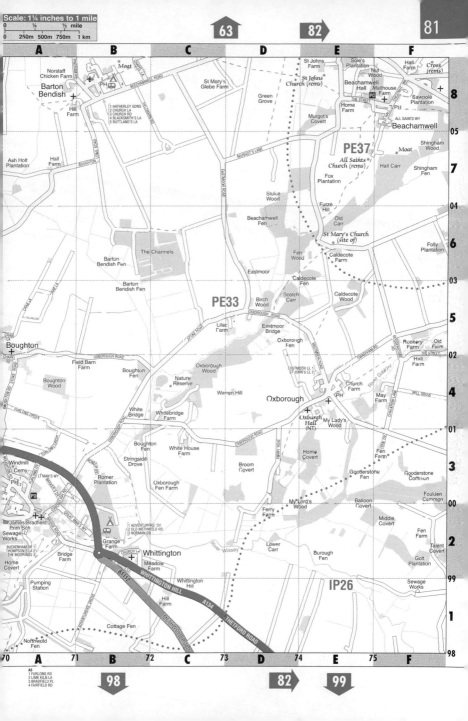

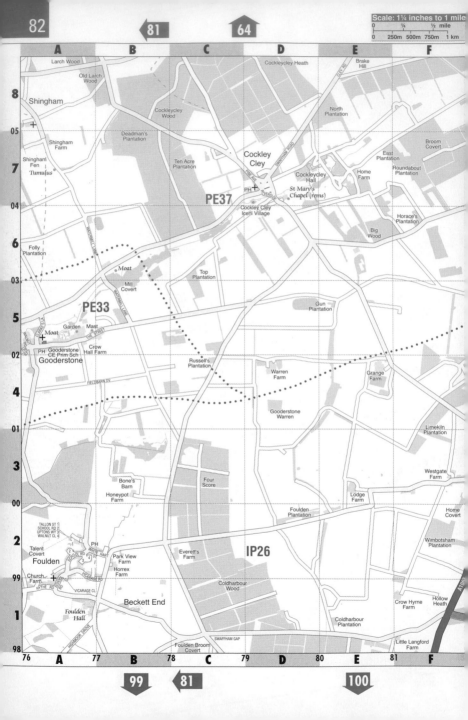

Scale: 1¼ inches to 1 mile

0   ¼   ½ mile
0   250m 500m 750m 1 km

A   B   C   D   E   F

Larch Wood
Old Larch Wood
Cockleycley Heath
Brake Hill

8

Shingham
Cockleycley Wood
North Plantation
Broom Covert

05
Shingham Farm
Deadman's Plantation
East Plantation
Roundabout Plantation

7
Shingham Fen
Tumulus
Ten Acre Plantation
Cockley Cley
PE37
Cockleycley Hall
St Mary's Chapel (rems)
Home Farm

PH

04
Cockley Cley Iceni Village
Horace's Plantation

6
Folly Plantation
Big Wood

03
Moat
Top Plantation

Mill Covert
Gun Plantation

5
PE33
Garden Mast
Crow Hall Farm

Moat
THE STREET

02
PH Gooderstone CE Prim Sch
Gooderstone
Russell's Plantation
Warren Farm
Grange Farm

FIELDBARN DV

4
Gooderstone Warren
Limekiln Plantation

01

3
Bone's Barn
Four Score
Westgate Farm

Honeypot Farm

00
Foulden Plantation
Lodge Farm
Home Covert

2
TALLON ST 1
SCHOOL RD 2
UPTONS WY 3
WALNUT CL 4
PH
WHITE HART
Park View Farm
Everett's Farm
IP26
Wimbotsham Plantation

Talent Covert
Foulden
Horrex Farm

99
Church Farm
Coldharbour Wood
Crow Hyrne Farm
Hollow Heath

VICARAGE CL

1
Beckett End
Foulden Hall
Coldharbour Plantation
Little Langford Farm

SWAFFHAM GAP

98
Foulden Broom Covert

76   A   77   B   78   C   79   D   80   E   81   F

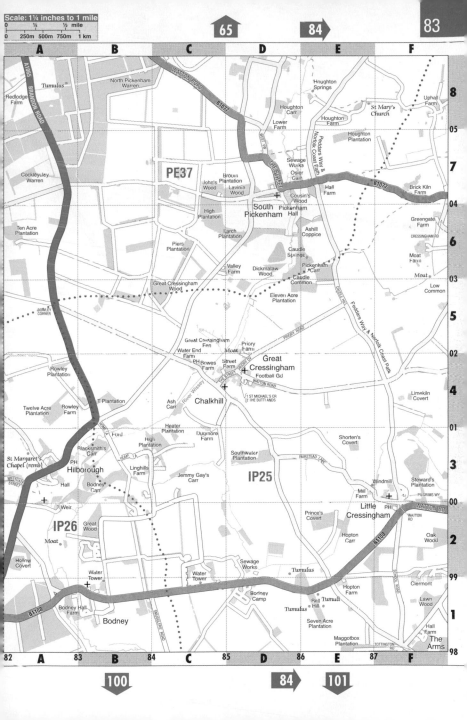

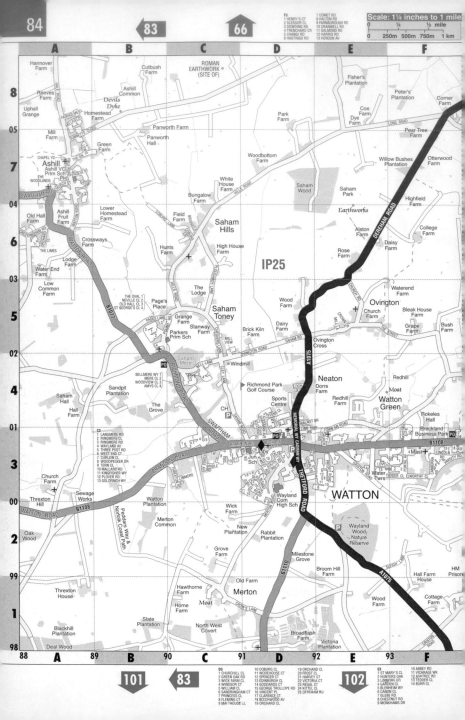

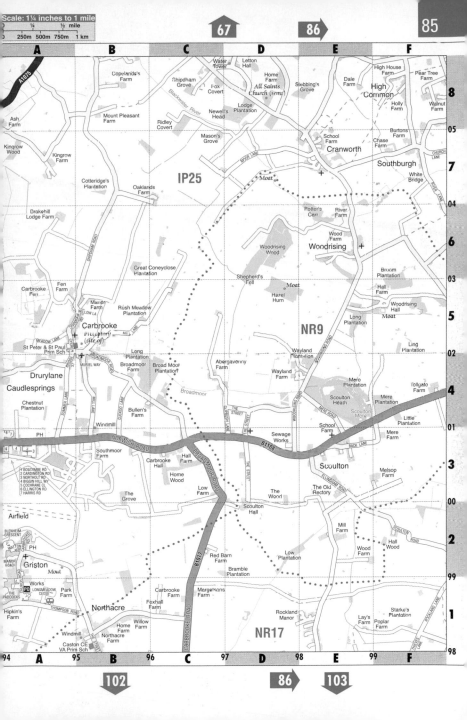

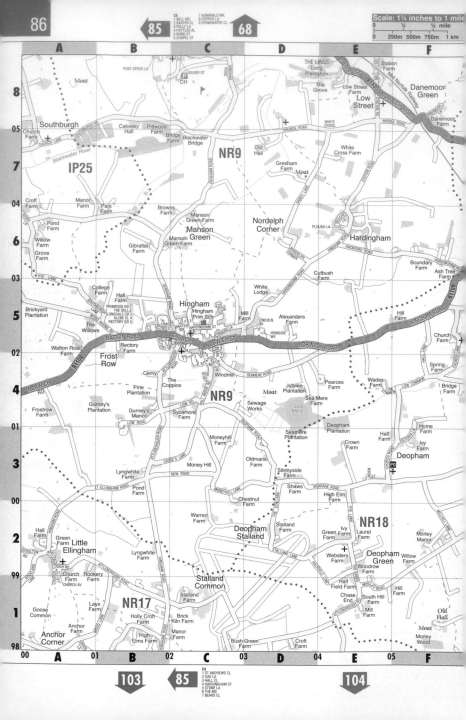

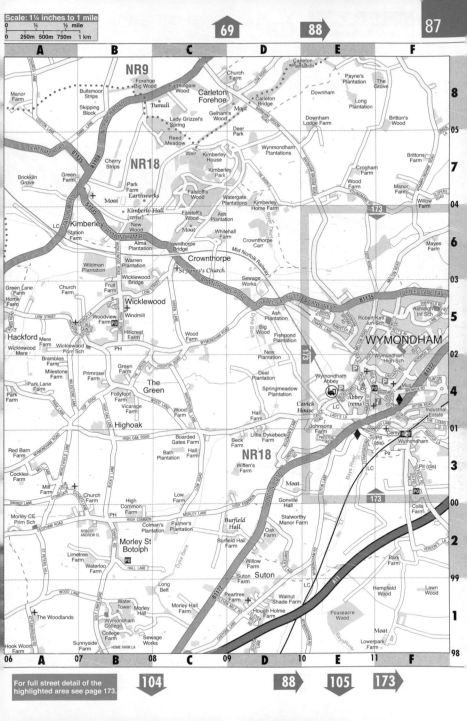

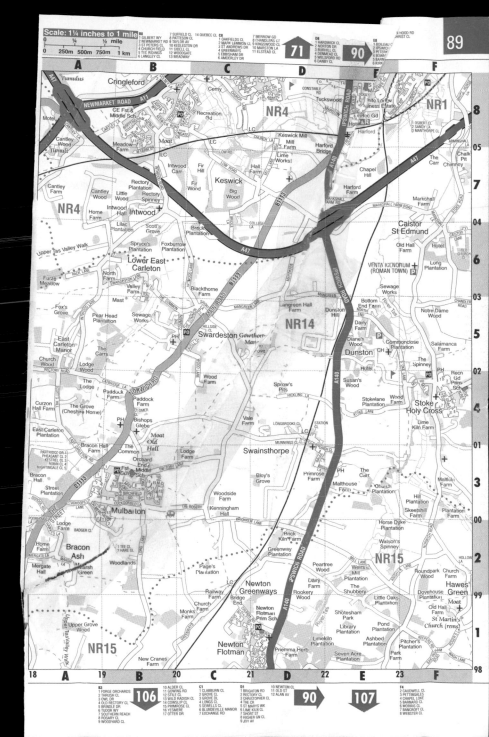

Scale: 1¼ inches to 1 mile

0   ¼   ½ mile
0   250m 500m 750m 1 km

D8
1 GILBERT WY
2 NEWMARKET RD
3 ST PETERS CL
4 CHURCH FIELD
5 THE RIDINGS
6 LANGLEY CL

B8
1 SUFFIELD CL
2 PATTESON CL
3 TAYLOR AV
10 KOSLESTON DR
11 SIDELL CL
12 WOODGATE
13 MEADWAY

14 QUEBEC CL

C8
1 OAKFIELDS CL
2 MARK LEMMON CL
3 ST ANDREWS DR
4 GREENWAY'S
5 EBBISHAM DR
6 AMDERLEY DR

7 MERROW GD
8 CHANDLERS CT
9 KINGSWOOD CL

D8
1 HARDWICK CL
2 NORTON DR
3 BURRILL CL
4 DENMEAD CL
5 WELSFORD RD
6 DANBY CL

10 MARSTON LA
11 ELSTEAD CL

71   90

E8
1 BOILEAU CL
2 IPSWICH RD
3 PETER...
4 BOWN...
5 BARN...
6 KIRN...

B3
1 FORGE ORCHARDS
2 THRUSH CL
3 OWL DR
4 OLD RECTORY CL
5 BRINDLE DR
6 TUDOR WY
7 SOUTHERN REACH
8 ROSARY CL
9 WOODYARD CL

10 ALDER CL
11 GOWING RD
12 STILE CL
13 WILD RADISH CL
14 COWSLIP CL
15 PRIMROSE CL
16 YESMERE
17 OTTER DR

C1
1 CLABBURN CL
2 GROVE CL
3 GROVE DL
4 LONGS CL
5 SEWELLS CL
6 BLUNDEVILLE MANOR
7 EXCHANGE RD

D1
1 BRIGHTON RD
2 RECTORY CL
3 CHRISTOPHER CL
4 THE CN
5 ST MARYS WK
6 LIME KILN CL
7 SHORT ST
8 HIGHER GN CL
9 JOY AV

10 NEWTON CL
11 OLD ST
12 ALAN AV

90   107

F4
1 CAUDWELL CL
2 PETTINGALES
3 CHAPEL LOKE
4 BARNARD CL
5 MORRIS CL
6 BANCROFT CL
7 WEBSTER CL

106

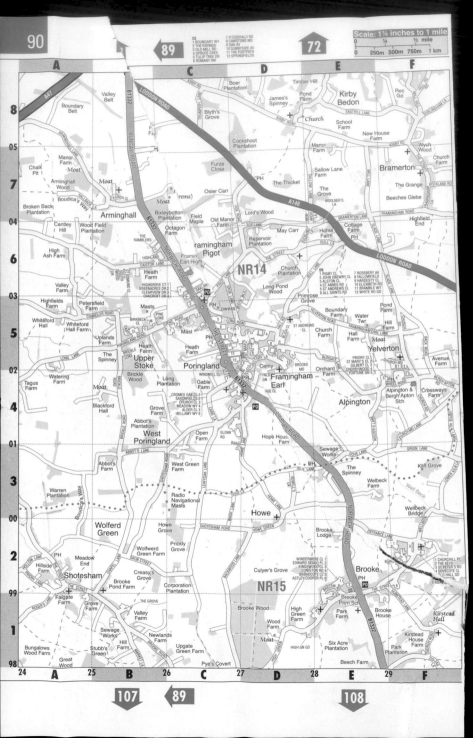

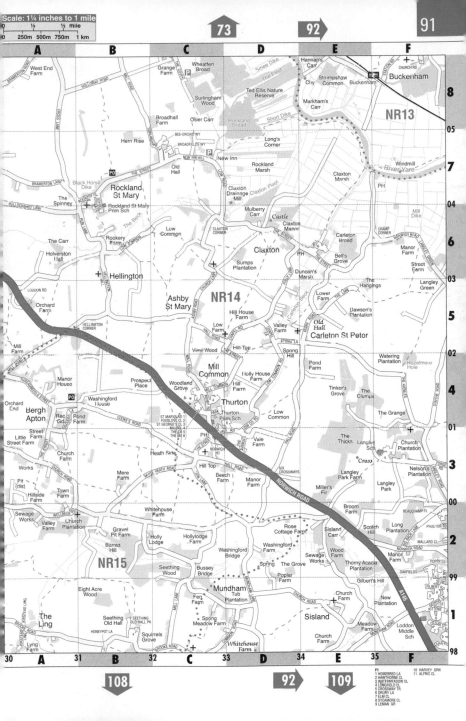

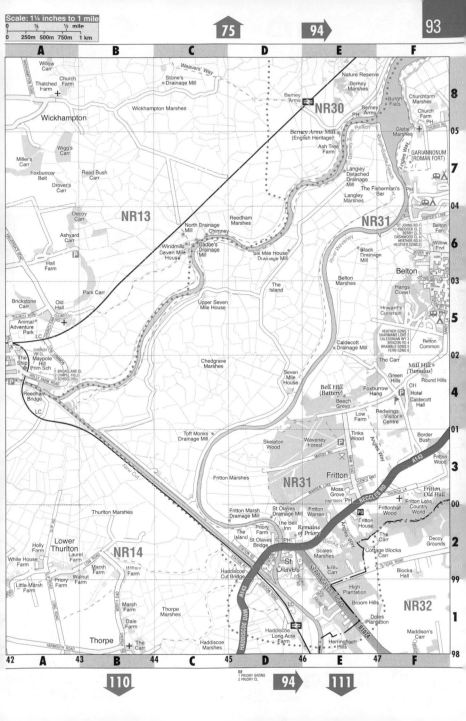

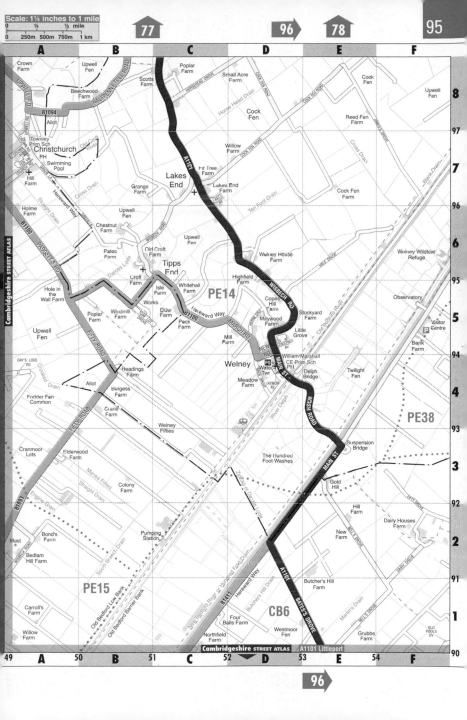

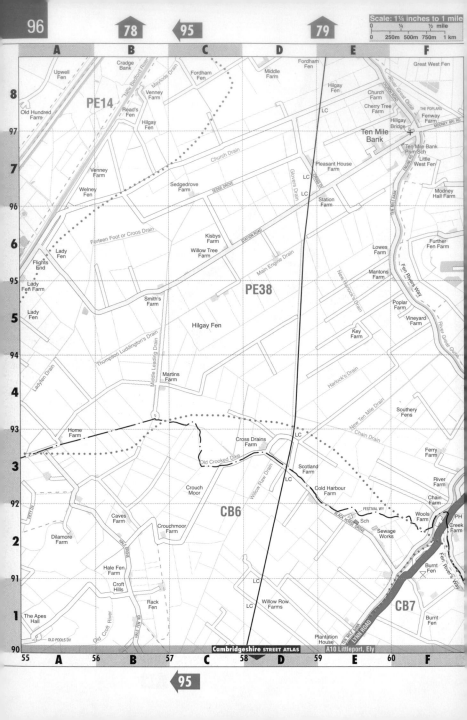

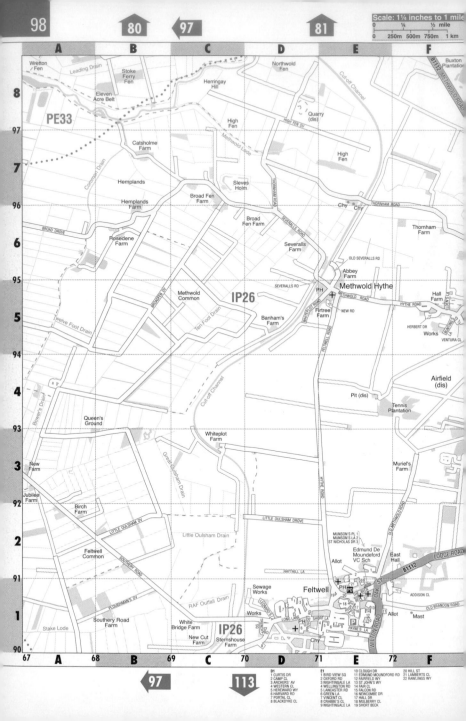

Scale: 1¼ inches to 1 mile

0   ¼   ½ mile
0   250m 500m 750m 1 km

A   **B**   **C**   **D**   **E**   **F**

Wretton / Fen

Leading Drain

Stoke Ferry Fen

Eleven Acre Belt

Herringay Hill

Northwold Fen

Curcoff Channel

B1112 METHWOLD ROAD

Buxton Plantation

PE33

8

Catsholme Farm

High Fen Dv

Quarry (dis)

HIGH FEN DV

High Fen

97

Common Drain

Methwold Lode

7

Hemplands

Sleves Holm

Hemplands Farm

Broad Fen Farm

THORNHAM ROAD

THORNHAM ROAD

Chy   Chy

Thornham Farm

96

Rosedene Farm

BROAD DROVE

Broad Fen Farm

Severalls Farm

SEVERALLS ROAD

OLD SEVERALLS RD

6

BROADER DV

Methwold Common

IP26

Yen Foot Drain

SEVERALLS RD   PH

Abbey Farm

UNITED LT ROAD

Methwold Hythe

METHWOLD ROAD

HYTHE ROAD

Hall Farm

95

Twelve Foot Drain

Banham's Farm

Firtree Farm

NEW RD

HERBERT DR

Works

VENTURA LA

5

Bower's Drain

Whiteplot Farm

Curcoff Channel

FELTWELL ROAD

Pit (dis)

Airfield (dis)

94

Tennis Plantation

4

Queen's Ground

Great Oulsham Drain

HYTHE ROAD

Muriel's Farm

93

New Farm

Whiteplot Farm

3

Jubilee Farm

Birch Farm

LITTLE OULSHAM DV

Little Oulsham Drain

LITTLE OULSHAM DROVE

OLD METHWOLD ROAD

92

SOUTHERY ROAD

2

Feltwell Common

MUNSON'S PL 1
MUNSON'S LA 2
ST NICHOLAS OR 3

Edmund De Moundeford VC Sch

East Hall

B1112

LODGE ROAD

91

PLOUGHMAN'S DV

RAF Outfall Drain

HAYHILL LA

Allot

PH

PO

OAK ST

ADDISON CL

OLD BRANDON ROAD

1

Stake Lode

Southery Road Farm

White Bridge Farm

IP26

Sternshouse Farm

New Cut Farm

Sewage Works

Works

LONG LANE

LEONARD'S CL

Feltwell

SHORT LA

PAYNE'S LA

Allot

Mast

WHITE CITY ROAD

Chy

90

67   **A**   68   **B**   69   **C**   70   **D**   71   **E**   72   **F**

D1
1 CURTIS DR
2 CAMP CL
3 ARCHERS AV
4 WESTERN CL
5 HEREWARD WY
6 HARVARD RD
7 PORTAL CL
8 BLACKDYKE CL

E1
1 BIRD VIEW SQ
2 OXFORD RD
3 NIGHTINGALE LA
4 WELLINGTON RD
5 LANCASTER RD
6 GREEN LA
7 VINCENT CL
8 CRABBE'S CL
9 NIGHTINGALE LA

10 CLOUGH DR
11 EDMUND MOUNDFORD RD
12 FAIRFIELD RD
13 ST JOHN'S WY
14 FAIR CL
15 FALCON RD
16 NEWCOMBE DR
17 HALL DR
18 MULBERRY CL
19 SHORT BECK

20 HILL ST
21 LAMBERTS CL
22 RAWLINGS WY

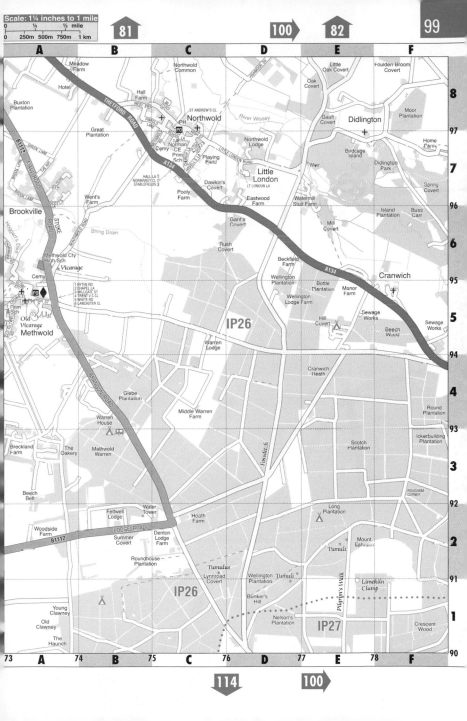

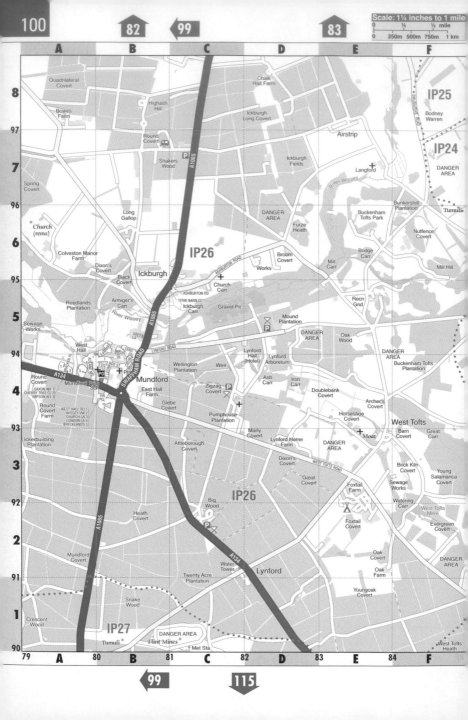

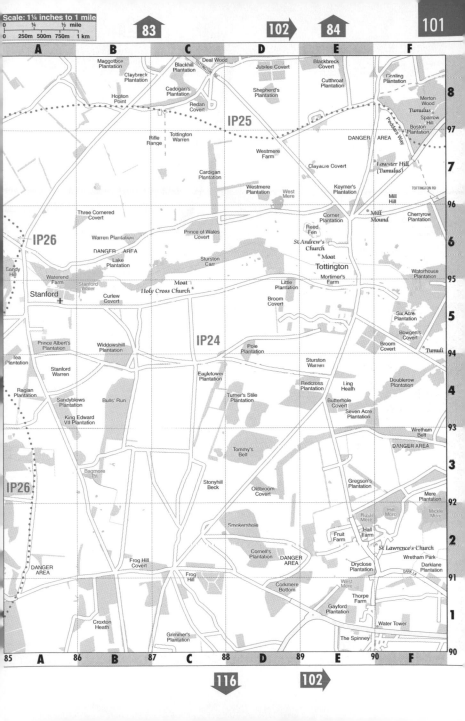

A   B   C   D   E   F

Maggotbox
Plantation

Claybreck
Plantation

Blackhill
Plantation

Deal Wood

Jubilee Covert

Blackbreck
Covert

Cutthroat
Plantation

Ginsling
Plantation

Merton
Wood

8

Hopton
Point

Cadogan's
Plantation

Redan
Covert

Shepherd's
Plantation

DANGER AREA

Tumulus

Sparrow
Hill

Boston
Plantation

97

IP25

Rifle
Range

Tottington
Warren

Westmere
Farm

Clayacre Covert

Lowster Hill
(Tumulus)

Peddars Way

7

Cardigan
Plantation

Westmere
Plantation

West
Mere

Keymer's
Plantation

Mill
Hill

TOTTINGTON RD

Three Cornered
Covert

Prince of Wales
Covert

Corner
Plantation

Mill
Mound

Cherryrow
Plantation

96

IP26

Warren Plantation

DANGER AREA

Lake
Plantation

Sturston
Carr

Reed
Fen

St Andrew's
Church

Tottington

6

Sandy
Hill

Waterend
Farm

Stanford
Water

Moat
Holy Cross Church

Moat

Mortimer's
Farm

Waterhouse
Plantation

95

Stanford

Curlew
Covert

Little
Plantation

Broom
Covert

Six Acre
Plantation

5

Prince Albert's
Plantation

Widdowshill
Plantation

IP24

Pole
Plantation

Bowgen's
Covert

Broom
Covert

Tumuli

94

Tea
Plantation

Stanford
Warren

Eagletower
Plantation

Sturston
Warren

Redcross
Plantation

Ling
Heath

Doublerow
Plantation

Raglan
Plantation

Sandyblows
Plantation

Bulls' Run

Turner's Stile
Plantation

Butterhole
Covert

Seven Acre
Plantation

Wretham
Belt

93

King Edward
VII Plantation

DANGER AREA

Tommy's
Belt

4

Bagmore
Pit

Stonyhill
Beck

Oldbroom
Covert

Gregson's
Plantation

Mere
Plantation

92

IP26

Smokershole

Rush
Mere

Hill
Mere

Mickle
Mere

DANGER
AREA

Frog Hill
Covert

Frog
Hill

Cornell's
Plantation

DANGER
AREA

Fruit
Farm

Hall
Farm

St Lawrence's Church

Wretham Park

2

Croxton
Heath

Grimmer's
Plantation

Corkmere
Bottom

Gayford
Plantation

Dryclose
Plantation

West
Mere

Thorpe
Farm

Water Tower

The Spinney

Darklane
Plantation

DARK LA

91

1

85   A   86   B   87   C   88   D   89   E   90   F   90

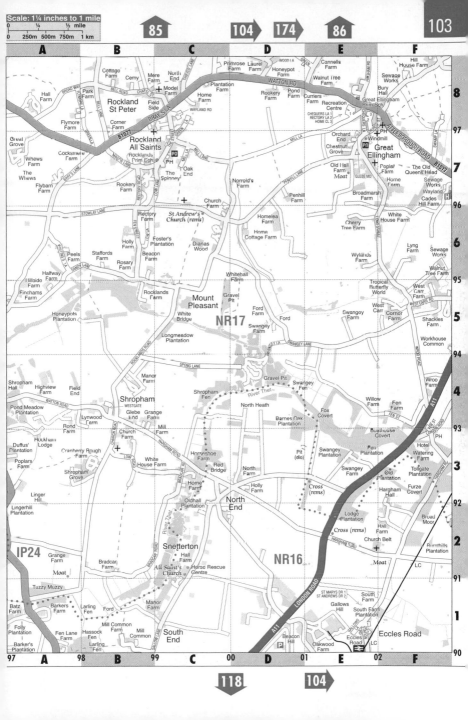

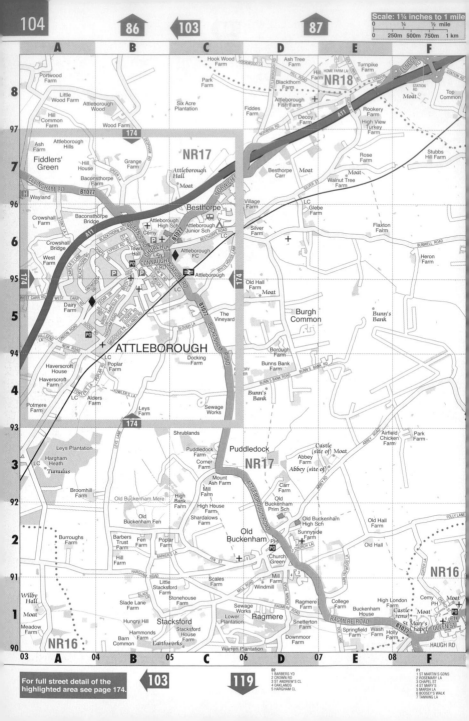

86
103
87

Scale: 1¼ inches to 1 mile

| 0 | ¼ | ½ mile |
| 0 | 250m | 500m | 750m | 1 km |

A · **B** · **C** · **D** · **E** · **F**

Portwood Farm

Little Wood Farm

Attleborough Wood

Hook Wood Farm

Ash Tree Farm

HOME FARM LA

Turnpike Farm

NR18

STATION RD

Moat

Top Common

Hill Common Farm

Wood Farm

174

Park Farm

Blackthorn Farm

Attleborough Fish Farm

A11

Rookery Farm

High View Turkey Farm

Six Acre Plantation

Fiddes Farm

Decoy Farm

Stubbs Hill Farm

Ash Farm

Attleborough Hills

Hill House

Grange Farm

NR17

Attleborough Hall

Moat

Besthorpe Carr

Moat

Rose Farm

Walnut Tree Farm

Fiddlers' Green

Baconsthorpe Farm

ELLINGHAM RD

Wayland

B1077

Baconsthorpe Bridge

Besthorpe

Village Farm

LC

Glebe Farm

Flaxton Farm

Crowshall Farm

Attleborough High Sch

Attleborough Junior Sch

Silver Farm

Crowshall Bridge

West Farm

Town Hall

CONNAUGHT RD

CHURCH ST

Attleborough FC

Heron Farm

174

Attleborough

Old Hall Farm

Moat

Burgh Common

Bunn's Bank

Dairy Farm

ATTLEBOROUGH

The Vineyard

Haverscroft House

Poplar Farm

Docking Farm

Borough Farm

Bunns Bank Farm

Bunn's Bank

Haverscroft Farm

Alders Farm

174

Leys Farm

Sewage Works

Bunn's Bank

Potmere Farm

Shrublands

Puddledock

Castle (site of) Moat

Airfield Chicken Farm

Park Farm

Leys Plantation

Hargham Heath

Tumulus

Puddledock Farm

Corner Farm

NR17

Abbey Farm

Abbey (site of)

Broomhill Farm

Old Buckenham Mere

High Bank Farm

Mill Farm

Mount Ash Farm

High House Farm

Carr Farm

Old Buckenham Prim Sch

Old Hall Farm

FOLLY LANE

Old Buckenham Fen

Shardalows Farm

Old Buckenham High Sch

Sunnyside Farm

Old Hall Farm

Burroughs Farm

Barbers Trust Farm

Fen Farm

Poplar Farm

Old Buckenham

Church Green

Old Hall

NR16

Wilby Hall

Moat

Hill Farm

Little Stacksford Farm

Scales Farm

Mill Farm Windmill

Ragmere Farm

College Farm

High London Farm

Cemy

Moat

Meadow Farm

Slade Lane Farm

Stonehouse Farm

Sewage Works

Stacksford

Lower Plantation

Ragmere

Snetterton Farm

Springfield Farm

Buckenham House

Wash Farm

Castle (rems)

Holly Farm

St Mary's Chapel

Hungry Hill

Hammonds Barn Common

Stacksford House Farm

Downmoor Farm

RAGMERE ROAD

HAUGH RD

NR16

Warren Plantation

For full street detail of the highlighted area see page 174.

103
119

D2
1 BARBERS YD
2 CROWN RD
3 ST ANDREW'S CL
4 OAKLANDS
5 HARGHAM CL

F1
1 ST MARTIN'S GDNS
2 ROSEMARY LA
3 CHAPEL ST
4 ST MARY'S
5 MARSH LA
6 BOOSEY'S WALK
7 TANNING LA

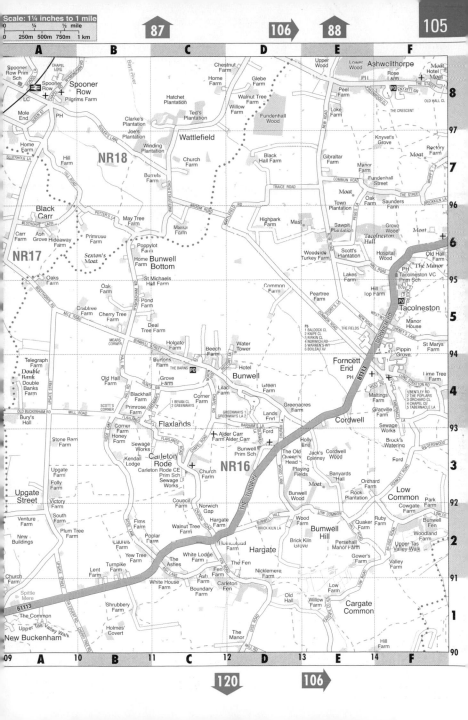

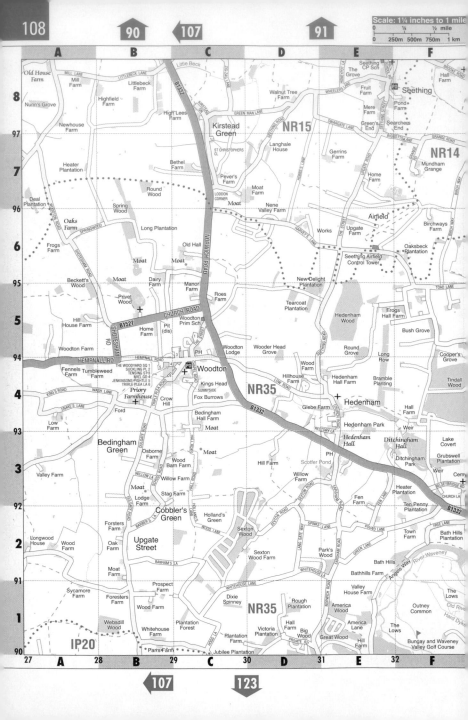

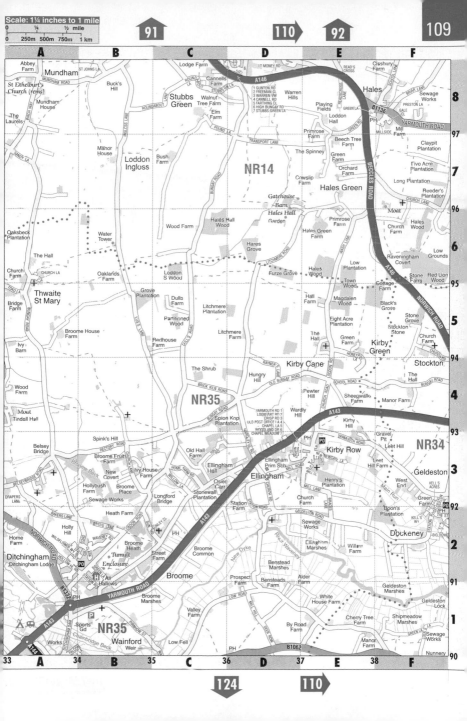

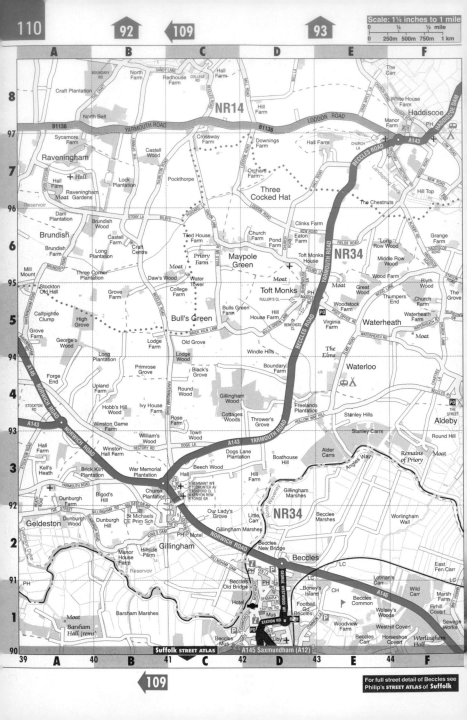

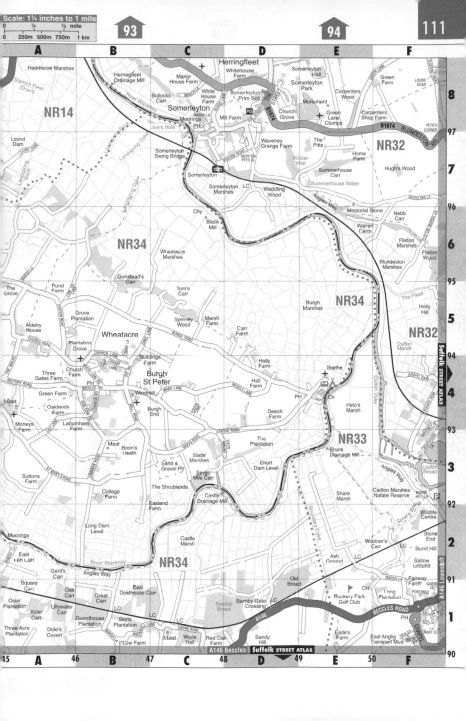

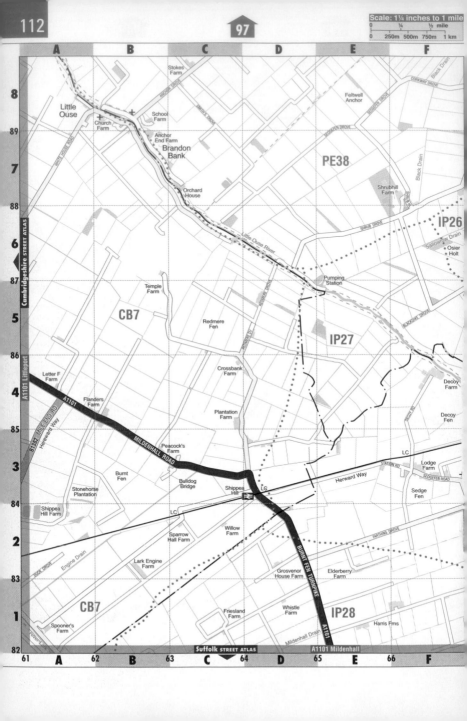

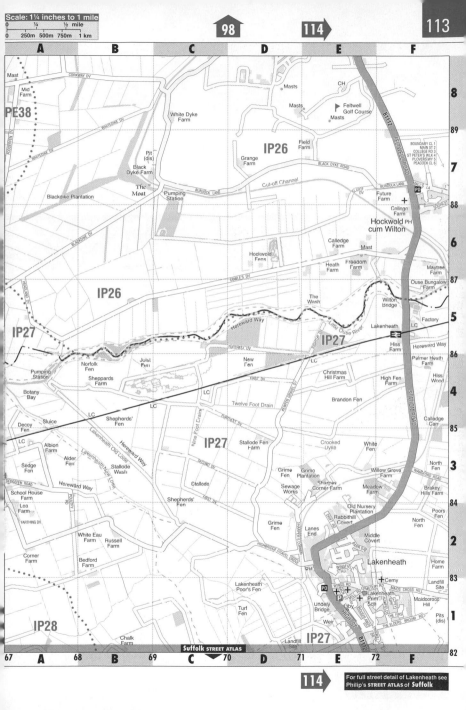

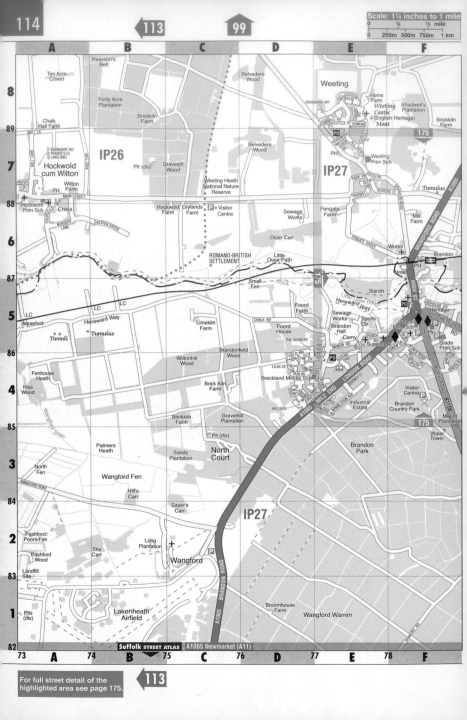

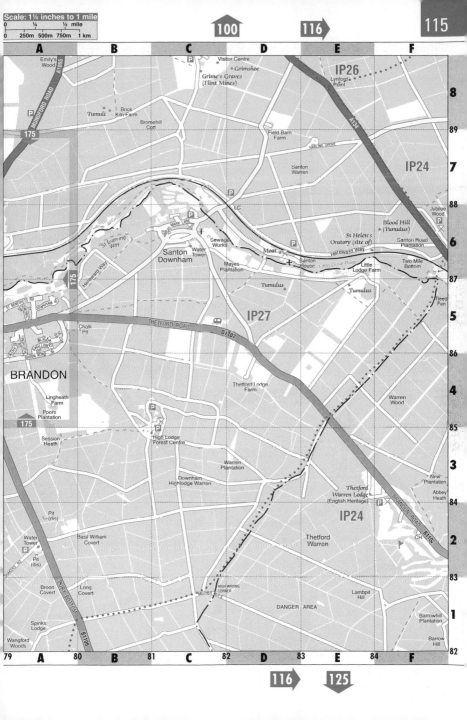

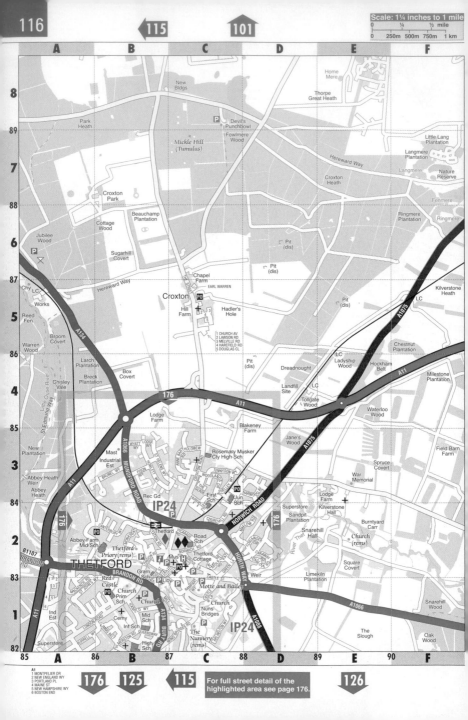

Scale: 1¼ inches to 1 mile

0   ¼   ½   mile
0   250m 500m 750m   1 km

A1
1 MONTPELIER DR
2 NEW ENGLAND WY
3 PORTLAND PL
4 MAINE ST
5 NEW HAMPSHIRE WY
6 BOSTON END

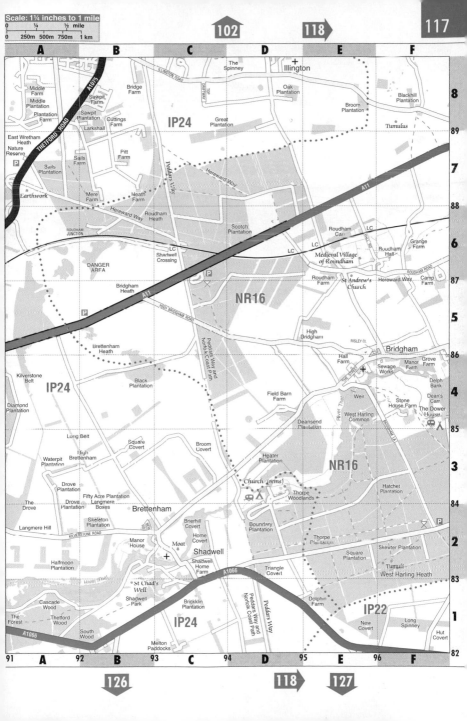

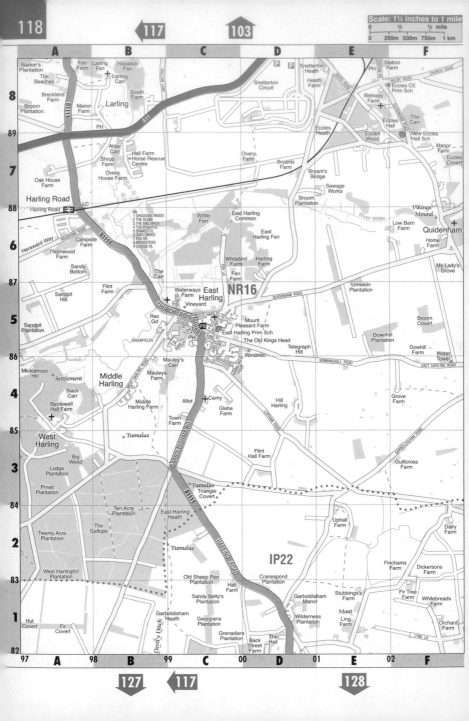

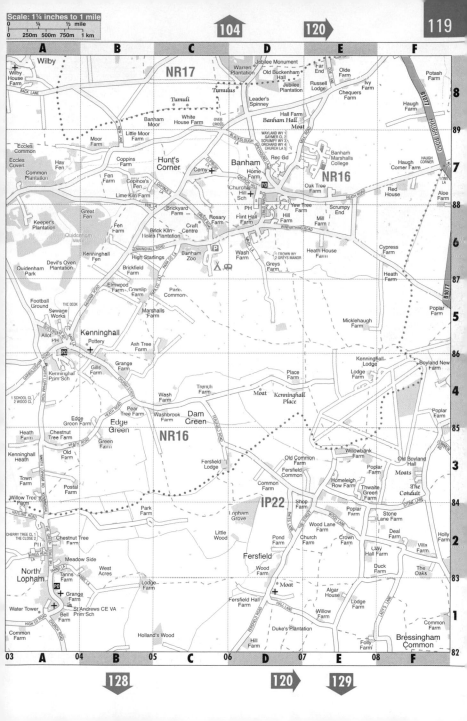

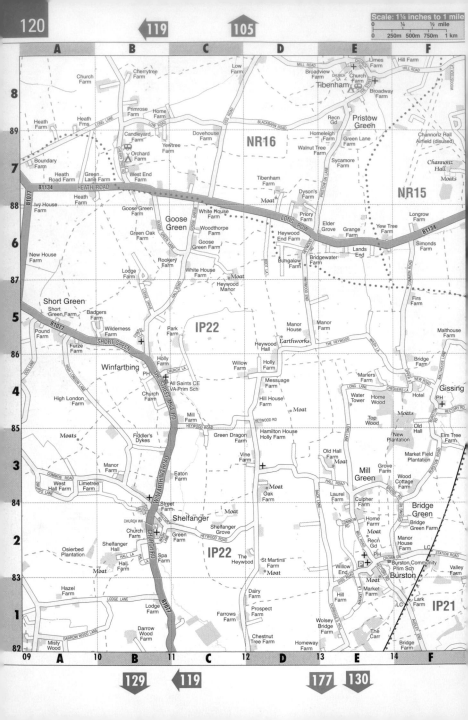

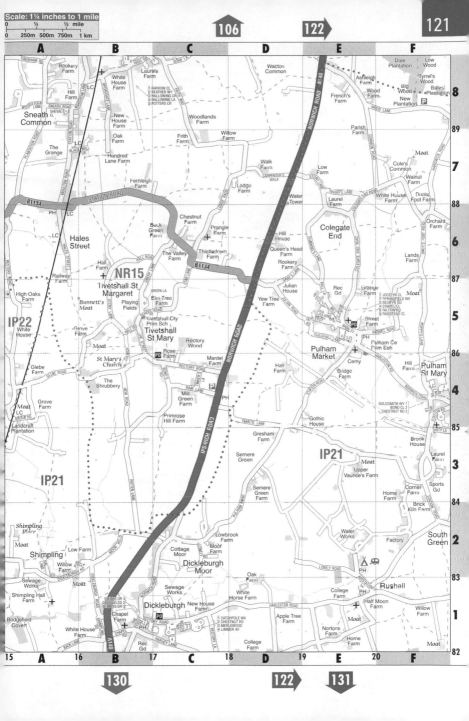

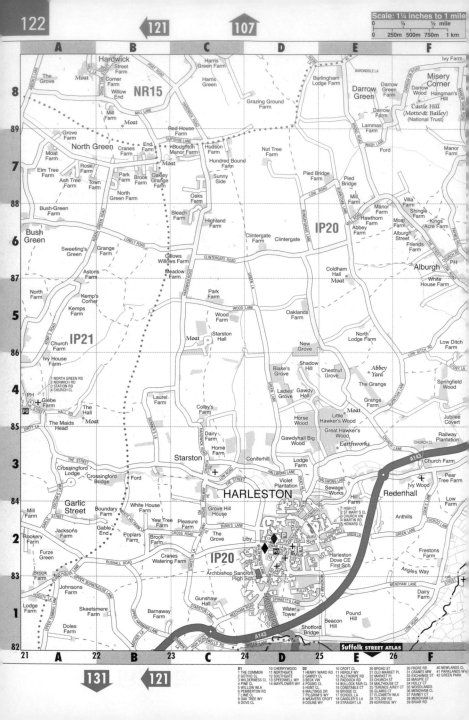

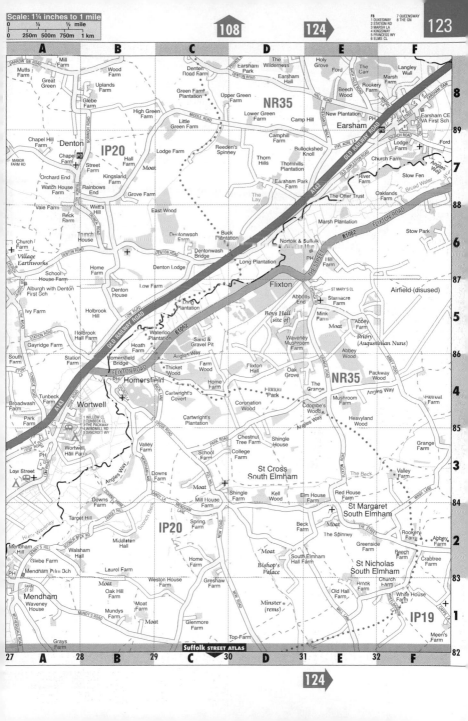

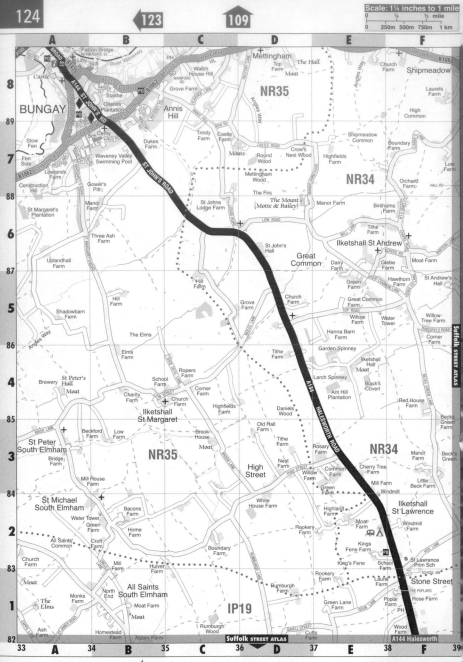

Scale: 1¼ inches to 1 mile

0   ¼   ½ mile
0   250m 500m 750m   1 km

115   116 126   176

125

F6 / WINDSOR CL
1 SALMOND DR
2 ELLINGTON RD
3 NEWALL RD
4 PORTAL CL
5 TEDDER CL
6 EDINBURGH CL

A   B   C   D   E   F

Rifle Range

Forest Retail Park

176

BURRELL WY

Playing Field

8

Olleys Farm

A11 LONDON ROAD

Barnhamcross Common

176

Water Tower

Elveden Gap

St Edmund Way

Nature Reserve

P

81

Parson's Slip Wood

Mileston Plantation

Boundary Belt

Barnham Cross (rems)

Great Snare Hill

Stonepit Wood

Redneck Farm

LONDON ROAD

Sketchfar Wood

Aughton Spinney

IP24

7

Elveden

Marmansgrave Wood

Icknield Way

Barnham Camp

80

Millhill Wood

Glebe Wood

Gorse Industrial Estate

Water Tower

Pig Farm

Little Ouse River

Elveden Hall

Water Tower

Home Wood

Larch Covert

Princess Mary's Plantation

Sewage Works

Thetford Heath

ELVEDEN ROAD

PH

WATER LA 1
ST MARTIN'S LA 2
MILL LA 3
BLACKSMITH LA 4

St Martin's Church (rems)

CHURCH LA

Barnham

6

Sandgault Plantation

North Farm

STATION RD

Works

Tumuli

THE STREET

East Farm

79

Basin Wood

Hunwellspring Plantation

Triangle Plantation

Barnham CE Prim Sch

Pit (dis)

Summerpit Farm

Albemarle Plantation

Furze Hill Plantation

Cranchill Spinney

Blackbird Spinney

5

Old Middlegouch Plantation

Coronation Covert

Works

Little Heath

Tumulus

78

St Edmund Way

Old Barnham Slip

Duke's Ride

Ixworth Spinney

Tumulus

BARROW'S CORNER

Barrow Clump Buildings

Icknield Way Path

West Calthorpe Heath

Breck Plantation

Bottom Plantation

Fox Pin

4

SHELTERHOUSE CORNER

Monument

Icknield Way Path

IP24

West Farm

77

Four Corners

New Zealand Cotts

Icknield Way Path

3

B1106

Works

76

D House

Field Barn

IP28

Warren Covert

Pits (dis)

Lodge Farm

Rymer Farm

2

P

Tumulus

Warren New Covert

Wordwell Barn

75

Belchamps Plantation

Ash Covert

Rubbinghouse Covert

Culfordheath

IP31

A134

Rymer Barn

1

Traveller's Hill (Tumuli)

Traveller's Hill Plantation

CHALK LA

Ling Covert

Seven Hills House

126   For full street detail of the highlighted area see page 176.

Suffolk STREET ATLAS

A11 Newmarket

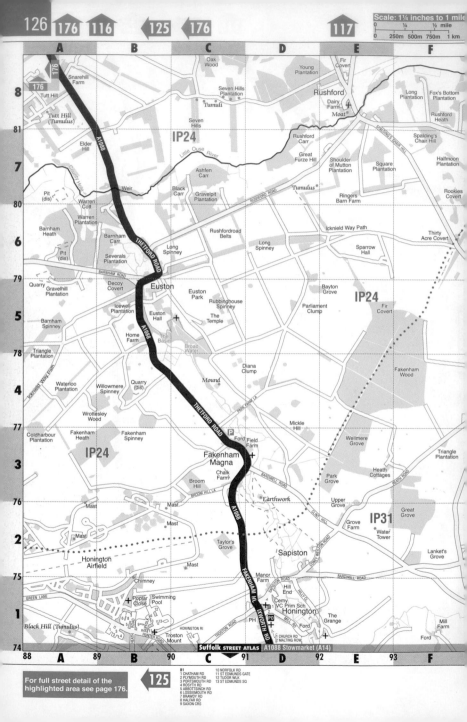

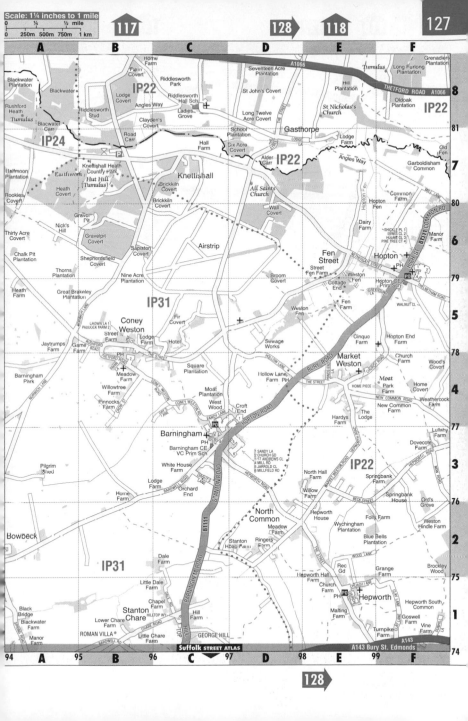

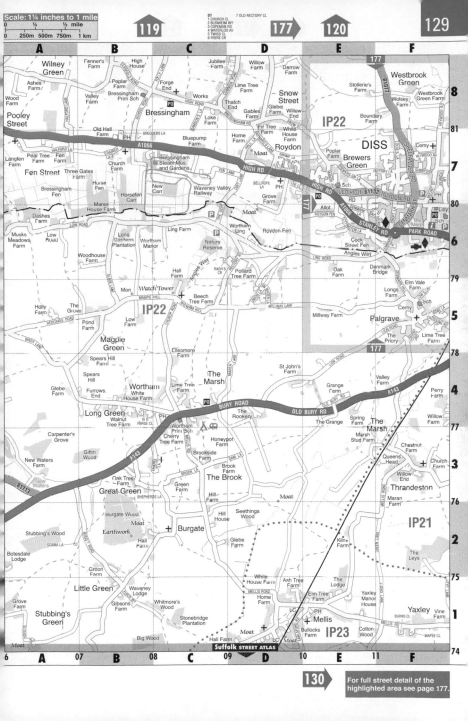

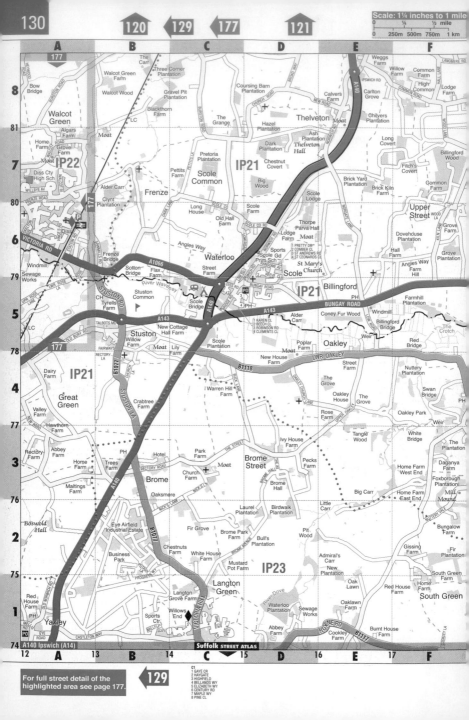

Scale: 1¼ inches to 1 mile

For full street detail of the highlighted area see page 177.

129

C1
1 GAYE CR
2 HAYGATE
3 HIGHFIELD
4 BELLANDS WY
5 ELIZABETH WY
6 CENTURY RD
7 MAPLE WY
8 PINE CL

Suffolk STREET ATLAS

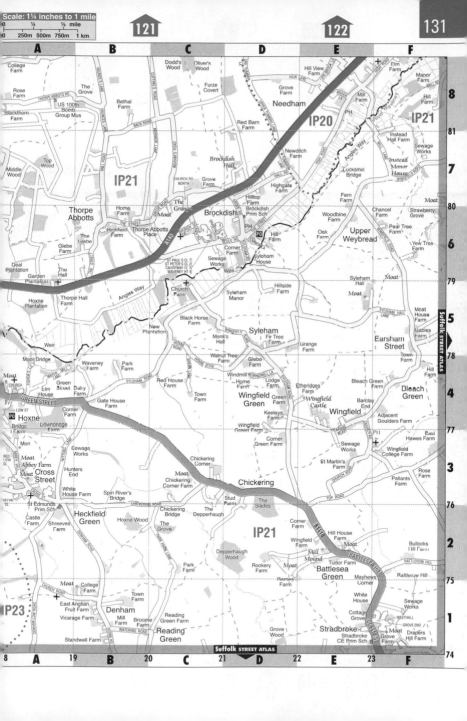

1 1 1

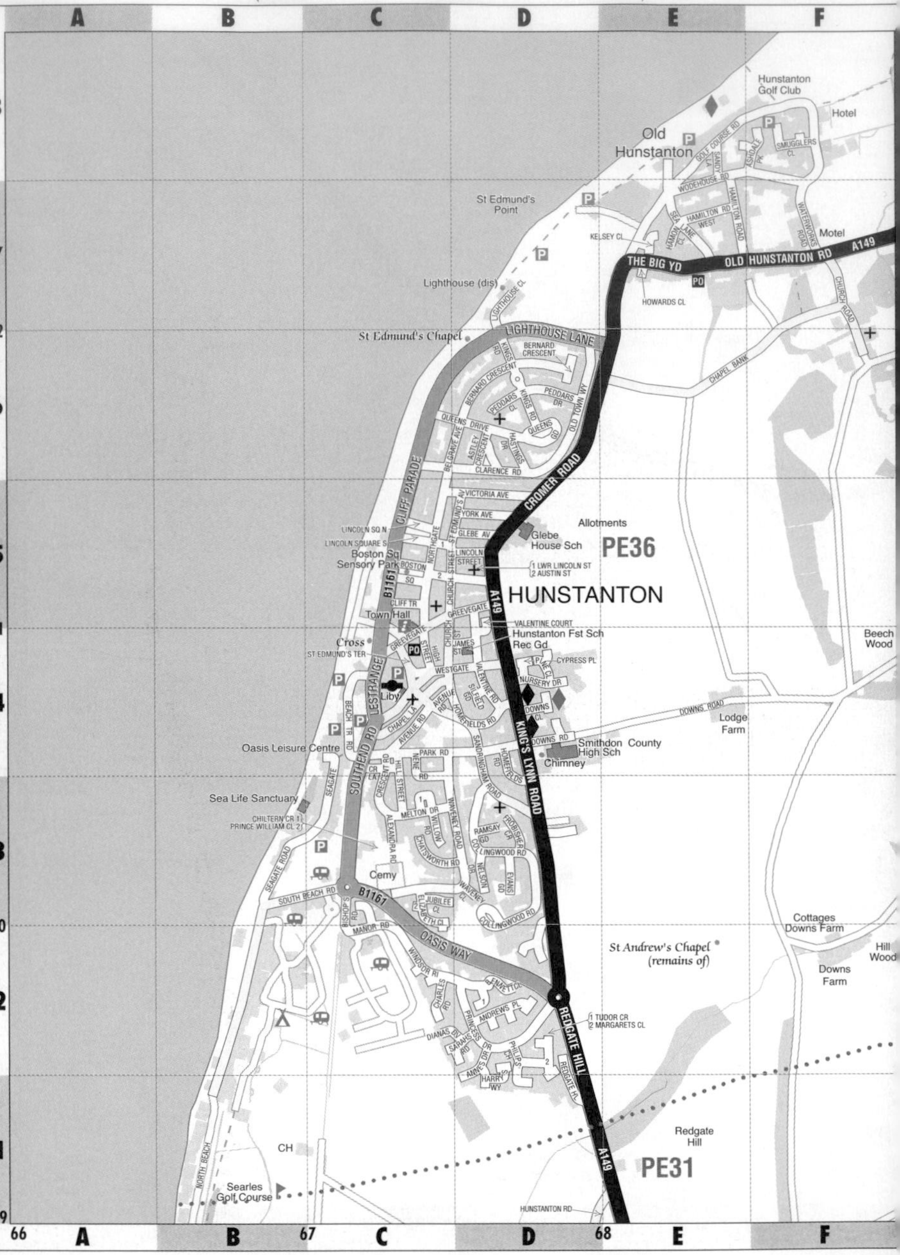

A B C D E F
8 7 42 6 5 41 4 3 40 2 1 39
66 67 68
Hunstanton Golf Club
Hotel
Old Hunstanton
GOLF COURSE RD
SANDY LA
ASHDALE PK
SMUGGLERS CL
WODEHOUSE RD
HAMILTON ROAD
HAMILTON RD WEST
SEA LANE
HAMON CL
WATERWORKS ROAD
Motel
St Edmund's Point
KELSEY CL
THE BIG YD
OLD HUNSTANTON RD
A149
PO
HOWARDS CL
CHURCH ROAD
Lighthouse (dis)
LIGHTHOUSE CL
St Edmund's Chapel
LIGHTHOUSE LANE
BERNARD CRESCENT
CHAPEL BANK
KINGS RD
BERNARD CRESCENT
PEDDARS CL
PEDDARS DR
OLD TOWN WY
QUEENS DRIVE
QUEENS GD
BELGRAVE AVE
ASTLEY CRESCENT
HASTINGS DR
CLARENCE RD
CROMER ROAD
CLIFF PARADE
VICTORIA AVE
YORK AVE
GLEBE AV
ST EDMUND'S AV
Allotments
Glebe House Sch
PE36
LINCOLN SQ N
LINCOLN SQUARE S
Boston Sq Sensory Park
NORTHGATE
LINCOLN STREET
1 LWR LINCOLN ST
2 AUSTIN ST
B1161
BOSTON SQ
CHURCH STREET
A149
HUNSTANTON
CLIFF TR
GREEVEGATE
Town Hall
VALENTINE COURT
Hunstanton Fst Sch
Rec Gd
Cross
ST EDMUND'S TER
JAMES ST
CYPRESS PL
Beech Wood
LESTRANGE
HIGH STREET
WESTGATE
PINE CL
NURSERY DR
Liby
AVENUE RD
VALENTINE RD
SILFIELD GD
DOWNS CL
DOWNS ROAD
Lodge Farm
BEACH TR RD
CHAPEL LA
HOMEFIELDS RD
DOWNS RD
KING'S LYNN ROAD
Smithdon County High Sch
Oasis Leisure Centre
PARK RD
SANDRINGHAM ROAD
Chimney
SOUTHEND RD
CR LA
CRESCENT RD
HILL STREET
NENE RD
HOMEFIELDS RD
SEAGATE
Sea Life Sanctuary
MELTON DR
WAVENEY ROAD
CHILTERN CR 1
PRINCE WILLIAM CL 2
ALEXANDRA RD
WILLOW RD
RAMSAY GD
FROBISHER CR
CHATSWORTH RD
COOK CL
LINGWOOD RD
SEAGATE ROAD
Cemy
NELSON DR
EVANS GD
WAVENEY CL
SOUTH BEACH RD
B1161
BISHOP'S RD
JUBILEE CL
ELIZABETH CL
COLLINGWOOD RD
MANOR RD
Cottages Downs Farm
OASIS WAY
St Andrew's Chapel (remains of)
Hill Wood
Downs Farm
WINDSOR RI
CHARLES RD
KENNEDY CL
REDGATE HILL
1 TUDOR CR
2 MARGARETS CL
PRINCESS DR
ANDREWS PL
DIANAS BL
SARAHS RD
PHILIPS CL
ANNE'S DR
HARRY WY
REDGATE PL
Redgate Hill
CH
PE31
NORTH BEACH
Searles Golf Course
HUNSTANTON RD

1 133 1

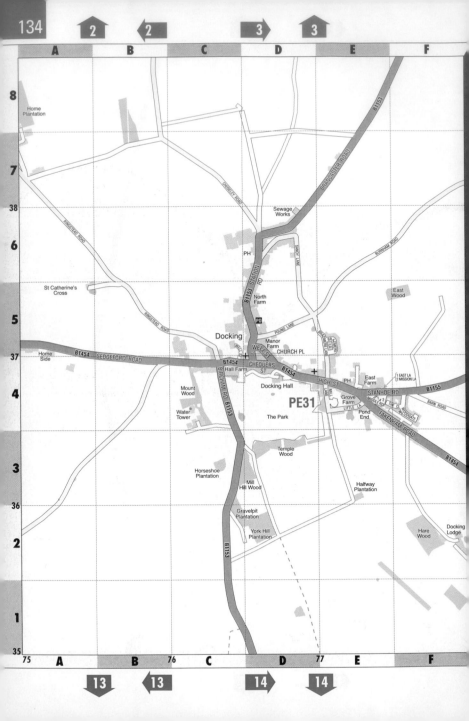

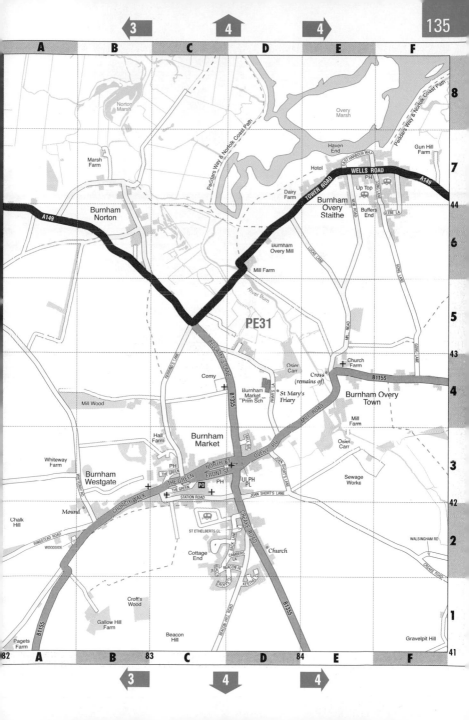

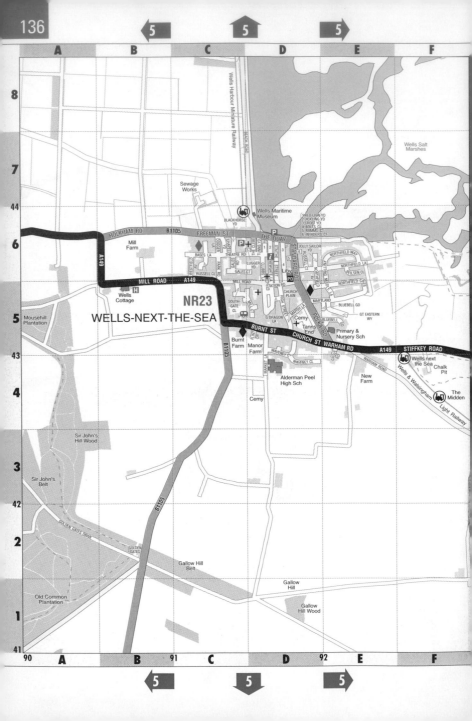

NR23
WELLS-NEXT-THE-SEA

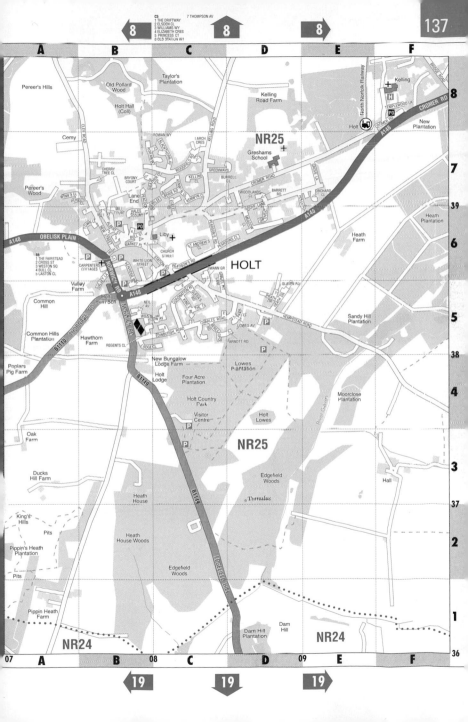

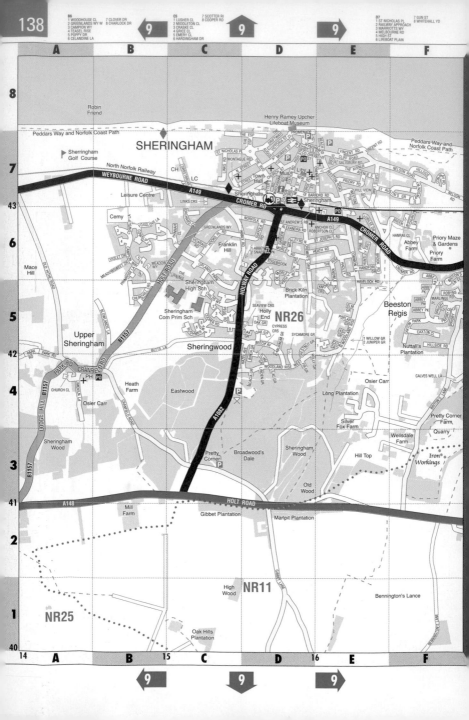

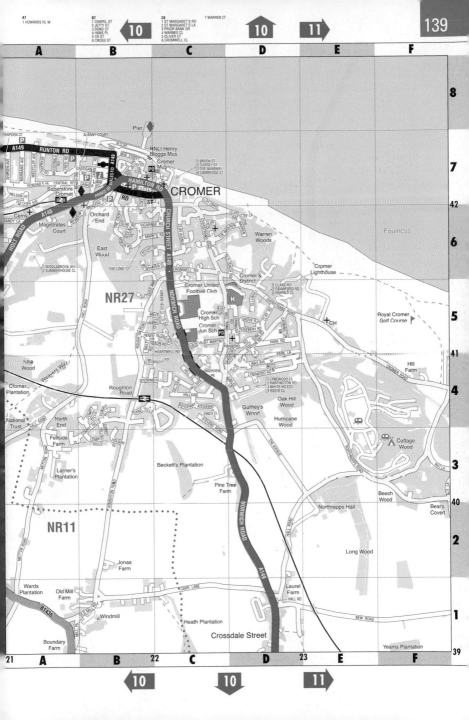

A7
1 HOWARDS HL W

B7
1 CHAPEL ST
2 JETTY ST
3 BOND ST
4 HANS PL
5 OR ST
6 CROSS ST

C6
1 ST MARGARET'S RD
2 ST MARGARET'S LA
3 PRIOR BANK OR
4 WARNES CL
5 OLIVER CT
6 CROMWELL CL

7 WARREN CT

CROMER

NR27

NR11

Crossdale Street

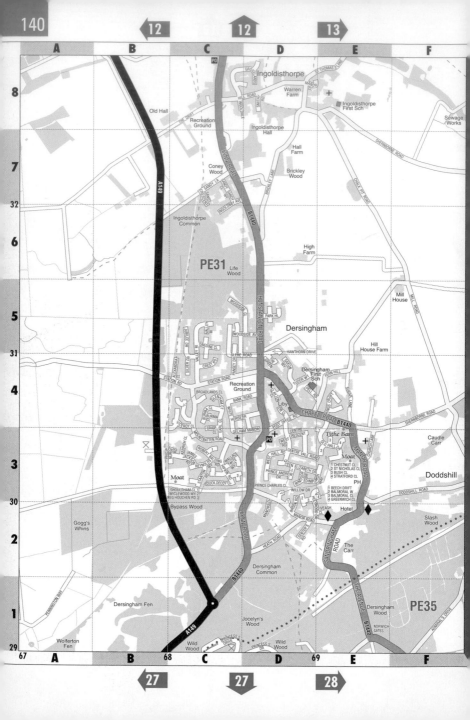

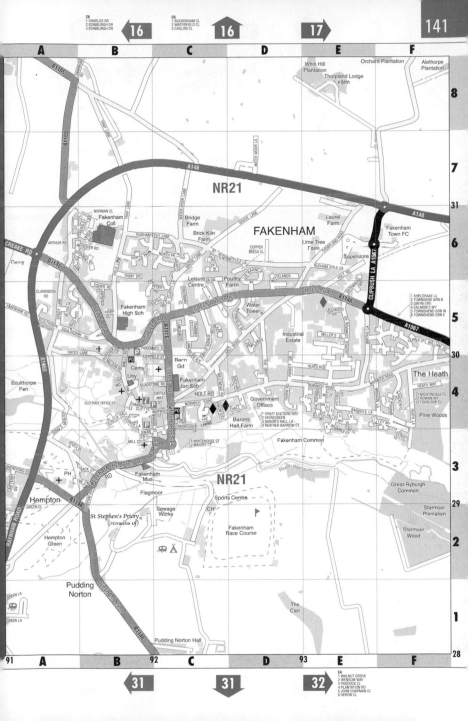

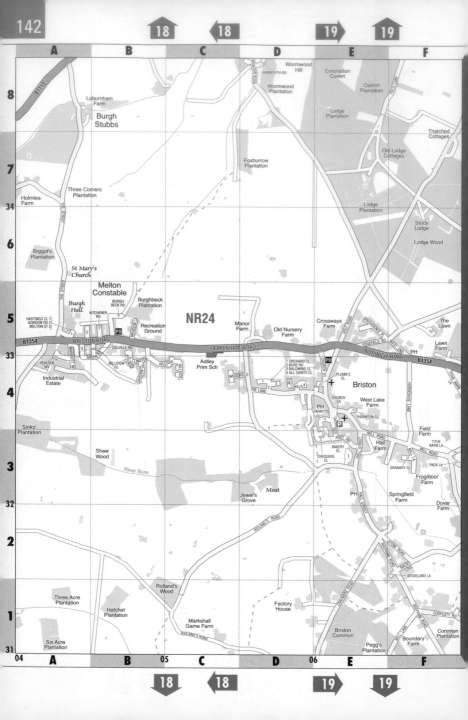

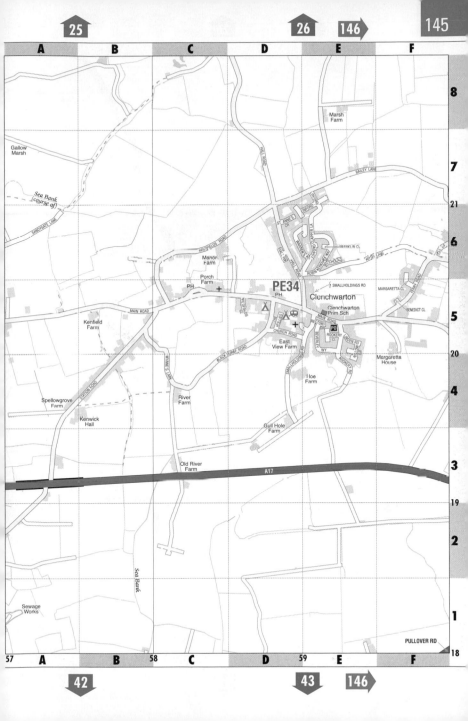

Marsh Farm

Gallow Marsh

Sea Bank (course of)

SANDGATE LANE

BAILEY LANE

ST ANNE'S CH

WOLFERLEE ROAD

Manor Farm

Porch Farm

PH

Kenfield Farm

MAIN ROAD

East View Farm

CHURCH ROAD

BLACK HORSE ROAD

River Farm

Spellowgrove Farm

STATION ROAD

Kenwick Hall

I loe Farm

Gull Hole Farm

Old River Farm

A17

Sea Bank

Sewage Works

PULLOVER RD

PE34

Clenchwarton

PH

Clenchwarton Prim Sch

SMALLHOLDINGS RD

1 SMALLHOLDINGS RD

MARGARETTA CL

BENEDICT CL

PO

ROCKERY CL

Margaretta House

ROCKERY RD

FRANKLIN CL

WALNUT CL

HALL ROAD

A B C D E F
8 7 21 6 5 20 4 3 19 2 1 18

57 58 59

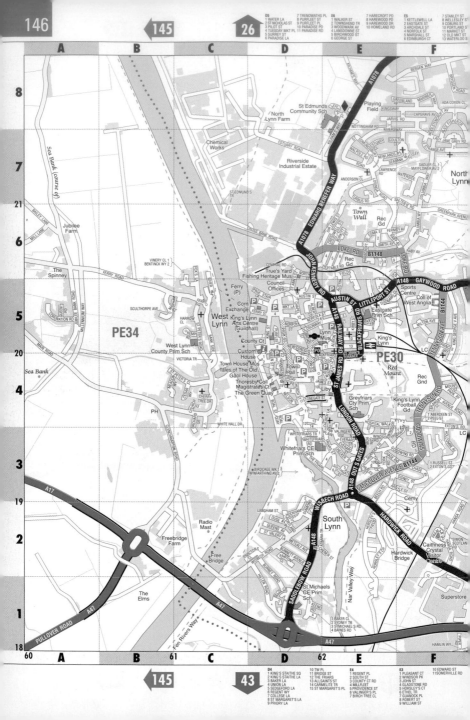

PE31

PE30

North Wootton

South Wootton

Wootton Carr

Wootton Carr

Ling Common

Ling Common Road

Ling Common Road

South Wootton Common

Kings Lynn Golf Club

Reffley Wood

Spring Wood

Playing Field

School Farm

Church Farm

Orchard End

North Wootton Prim Sch

South Wootton Fst Sch

South Wootton Junior Sch

Superstore

MARSH ROAD

STATION ROAD

MANOR ROAD

BATEHOUSE LANE

CARLTON DRIVE

PRIORY ROAD

WOODLAND RD

HEATHER CL

CRANMER AV

WHEATLEY DR

BLACK HORSE

RYALLA DRIFT

NURSERY LANE

BRYONY CT

THETFORD WY

ST AUGUSTINES WY

CASTLE RISING ROAD

AVON RD

BRIAR CL

RUSHMEADOW

BRACKEN

MEADOW

GREENWAY

CHURCH LA

COMMON LA

OAK AVENUE

BEECH AVE

ELM CL

ASH DR

PINE ROAD

POLLY

MAPLE DR

SYCAMORE CL
LARCH CL

WINDERMERE RD

GRIMSTON RD

GRIMSTON ROAD

A148

ENNERDALE DRIVE

CONISTON CLOSE

SANDY LANE

LOW ROAD A1078

LOW ROAD

EDWARD BENEFER WAY

A1078

A148 WOOTTON ROAD

BERGEN WAY

CARTER'S CL 1
FESTIVAL CL 2
CLIFTON RD 3
BALDOCK DR 4
WILLOW PK 5

OLD MANOR LA

THE BOYTONS

ELMHURST DR

HALL RD

SPENCER RD

SUFFIELD RD

DAWNAY AVE

ARUNDEL DR

DRIFTWAY

SPRING LANE

HOUGHTON AV

BEETLEY DR

GOLF

CROXLEY WY

BURGHLEY RD

EUSTON WAY

MANNINGTON

BARSHAM DR

THORPE

WELDOVER

BURGH

C5
1 GREGORY CL
2 WILTON CR
3 MEADOW CL
4 CUTHBERT CL

C4
1 STOCK LEA RD
2 RYELAND RD
3 ST AUGUSTINES WY
4 WINTERN GR
5 FINCHDALE CL
6 BECKETT CL

C3
1 ROSEBAY
2 CASTLE ACRE CL
3 ST BOTOLPH'S CL
4 BINHAM RD
5 HAZEL CL

1 SANDRINGHAM CR
2 CAMBRIDGE RD
3 EXETER DR
4 DEVON CR

1 SYCAMORE CL
2 LARCH CL

1 TICKWORTH CL
2 HINCHINGBROOK CL

F1
1 BLICKLING CL
2 KIRKSTONE GR
3 ULLESWATER AV
4 ULLSWATER AV

63 | 64 | 65

A | B | C | D | E | F

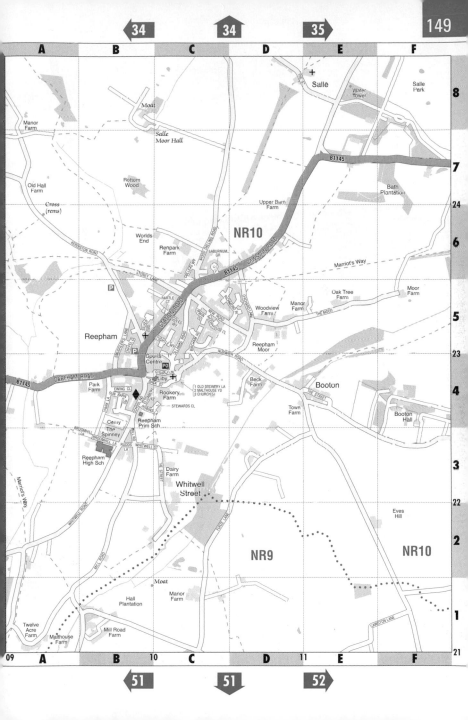

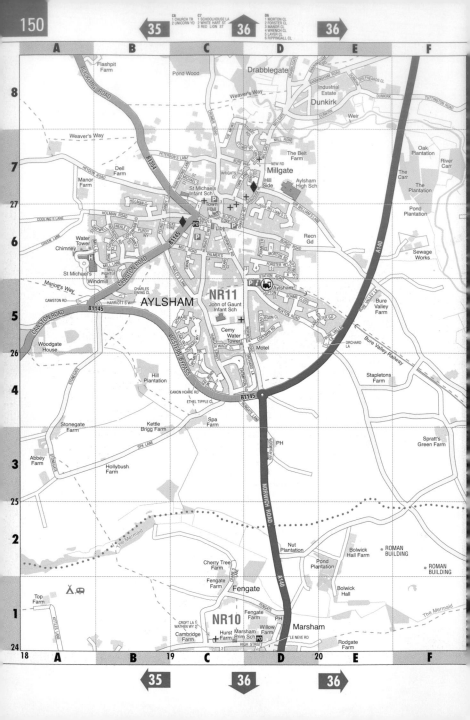

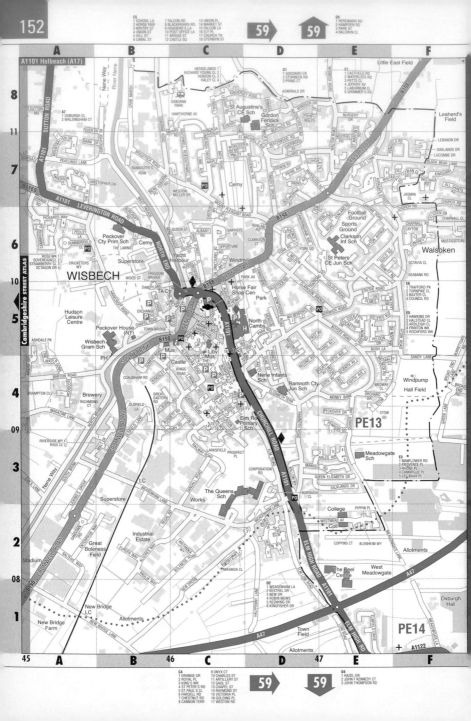

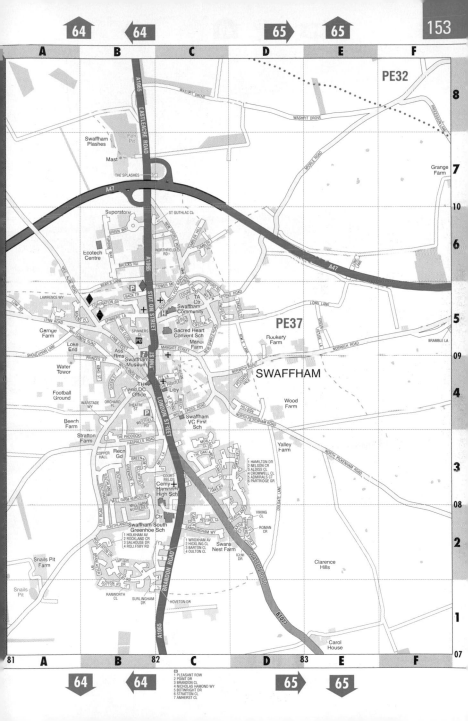

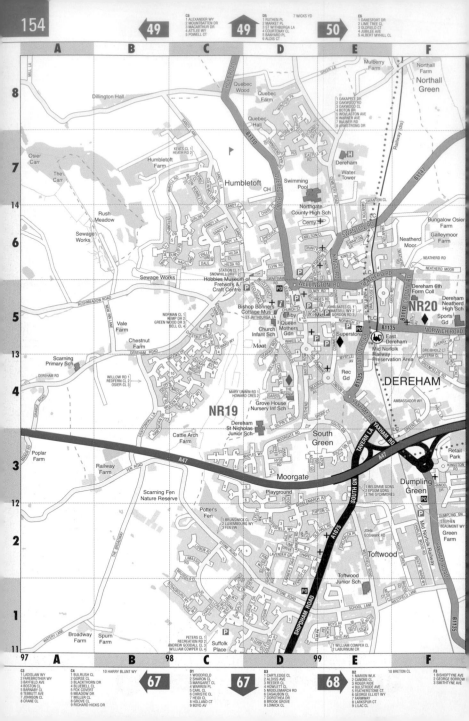

49
49
50

C6
1 ALEXANDER WY
2 MOUNTBATTEN DR
3 MACARTHUR DR
4 ATTLEE WY
5 POWELL CT

D5
1 RUTHEN PL
2 MARKET PL
3 ST WITHBURGA LA
4 COURTENAY CL
5 BANYARD PL
6 ALDIS CT

7 WICKS YD

E6
1 DANESFORT DR
2 LIME TREE CL
3 OLDFIELD CT
4 JUBILEE AVE
5 ALBERT MYHILL CL

Dillington Hall

Osier
Carr

The
Carr

Rush
Meadow

Sewage
Works

Vale
Farm

Chestnut
Farm

Scarning
Primary Sch

DEREHAM ROAD

Cattle Arch
Farm

Poplar
Farm

Railway
Farm

Scarning Fen
Nature Reserve

Potter's
Fen

Broadway
Farm

Spurn
Farm

Mill La

Quebec
Wood

Quebec
Farm

Quebec
Hall

Mulberry
Farm

Northall
Farm

Northall
Green

Humbletoft
Farm

Humbletoft

CH

Swimming
Pool

Northgate
County High Sch

Cemy

Dereham
Water
Tower

Sewage Works

Hobbies Museum of
Fretwork &
Craft Centre

Bishop Bonners
Cottage Mus

Church
Infant Sch

Moat

Queen
Mothers
Gdn

Wellington Rd

Mkt

JOHN BATES CL 1
MATSELL WY 2
GORDON RD 3

Superstore

East
Dereham

Mid Norfolk
Railway
Preservation Area

Rec
Gd

DEREHAM

Dereham 6th
Form Coll

Dereham
Neatherd
High Sch

Sports
Gd

NR20

Bungalow Osier

Galleymoor
Farm

Neatherd
Moor

NEATHERD RD

Neatherd
Moor

NORWICH ROAD

NR19

Grove House
Nursery Inf Sch

Dereham
St Nicholas
Junior Sch

MARY UNWIN RD 1
HOWARD CRES 2

South
Green

Moorgate

Playground

The
Grove

Ambassador Wy

Retail
Park

Kingston

Dumpling
Green

Stephen
Beaumont
Wy

Green
Farm

South Gn

Mid Norfolk
Railway

Toftwood

Toftwood
Junior Sch

SHIPDHAM ROAD

VAXHAM RD

A47

TAVERN LA

1 BELGRAVE GDNS
2 EPSOM GDNS
3 THE SYCAMORES

JOHN
GOSHAWK RD

STATION CL 1
SNOWHILL DRIFT 2

NORMAN CL 1
KEMP CL 2
GREEN WOOD DR 3
BELL CL 4

WILLOW RD 1
REDFERN CL 2
OSIER CL 3

Suffolk
Place

PETERS CL 1
RECREATION RD 2
ANDREW GOODALL CL 3
WILLIAM COWPER CL 4

1 WILLIAM COWPER CL
2 LABURNUM CR

67
67
68

10 HARRY BLUNT WY
10 BRETON CL

C3
1 LADISLAW WY
2 FAREBROTHER WY
3 BAYFIELD AVE
4 BOSTON CL
5 BARNABY CL
6 TEBBUTT AVE
7 JOHNSON CL
8 CRANE CL

C4
1 BULRUSH CL
2 GORSE CL
3 BLACKTHORN DR
4 BLUEBELL CL
5 FOX COVERT
6 MEADOW DR
7 MILLER CL
8 GROVE CL
9 RICHARD HICKS DR

D1
1 WOODFIELD
2 SHARON CL
3 MARGARET CL
4 WARREN PL
5 CARL CL
6 CHRISTIE CL
7 HEIDI CL
8 HOLLAND CT
9 BOYD AV

D3
1 CARTLEDGE CL
2 ALDISS AVE
3 REEDER CL
4 HOWLETT CL
5 MIDDLEMARCH RD
6 CASSABON CL
7 DOROTHEA DR
8 BROOK GROVE
9 LOWICK CL

D2
1 MARION WLK
2 CANIONS CL
3 ROGER RIDE
4 BULSTRODE AVE
5 FEATHERSTONE CT
6 GEORGE ELLIOT WY
7 FARRWAY
8 LARKSPUR CT
9 LILAC CL

F3
1 BISHOPTYNE AVE
2 GEORGE BORROW
3 SMITHYNE WE

B2
1 BAROLPHS CT
2 MULBERRY CT
3 BUCKTHORN CL
4 SNOWBERRY CL
5 BARBERRY CL
6 OAKLANDS

C1
1 WOODSIDE CL
2 ST EDMUND'S RI
3 VICTORIA RD

D2
1 HEDGEMERE
2 FOREGATE CL
3 THE FALLOWS
4 MARLAND RD
5 GARDYN CFT
6 THE SEATES
7 COWDEWELL MS
8 MONT CROSS

E2
1 ABER FURLONG
2 BECKS FUR
3 BISHOP RI
4 BRAMBLE CL
5 ASHGROVE

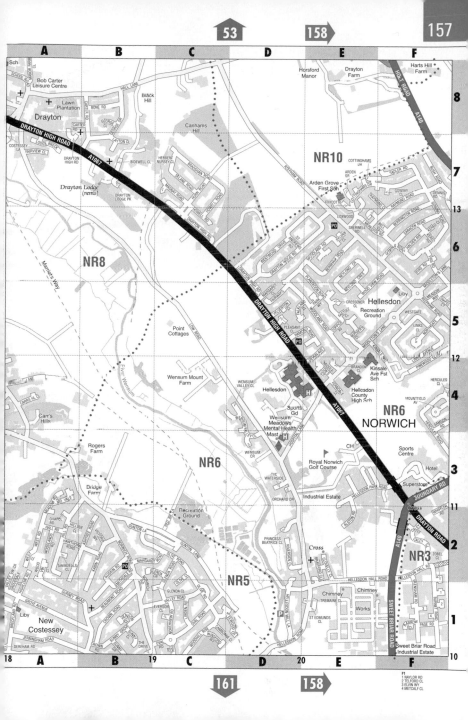

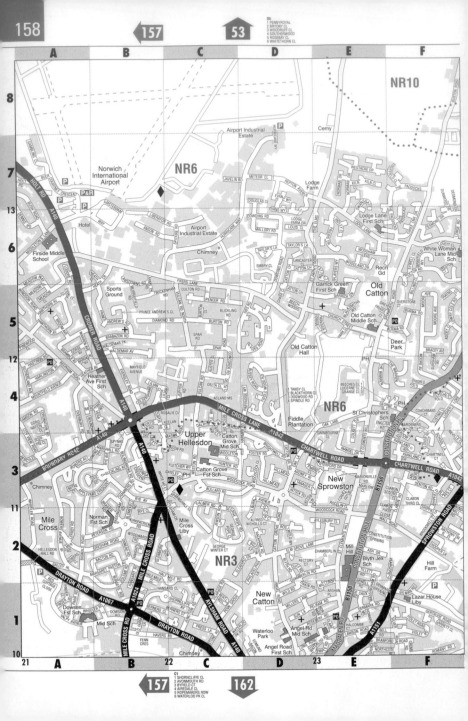

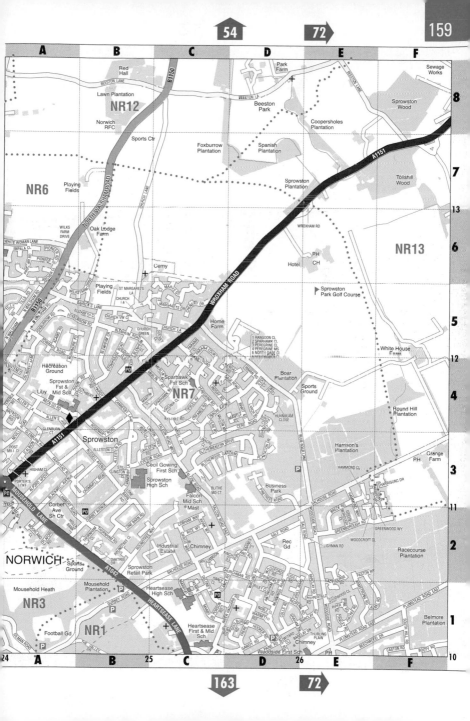

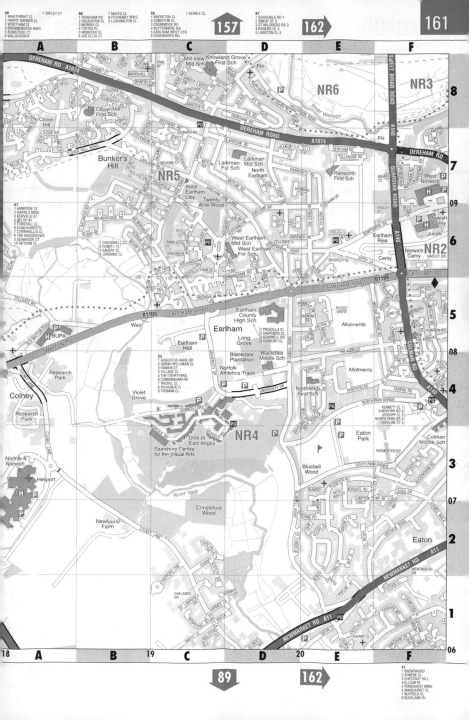

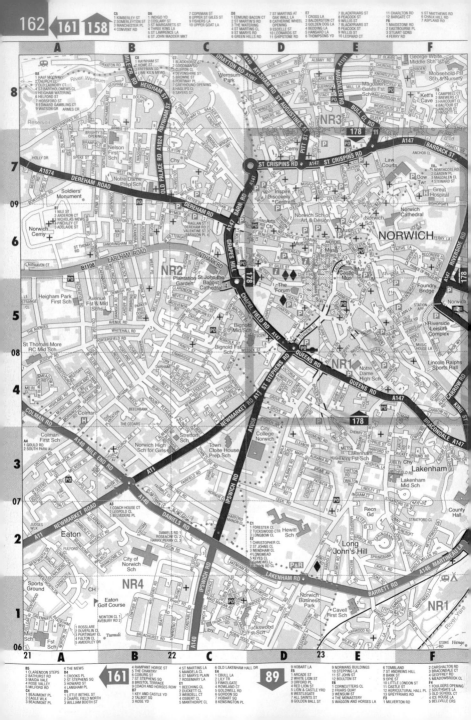

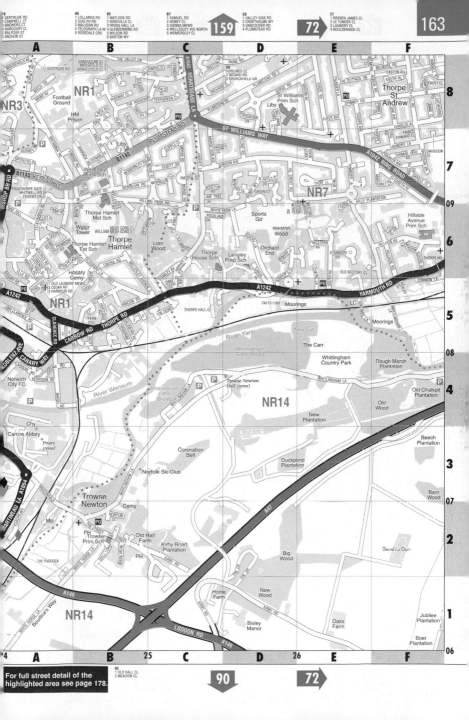

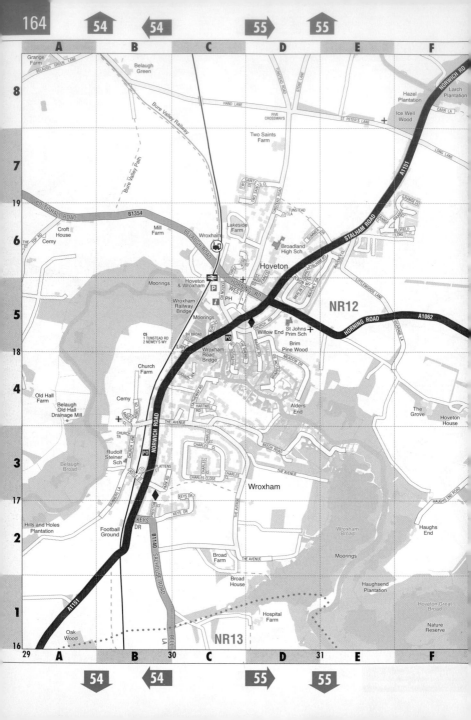

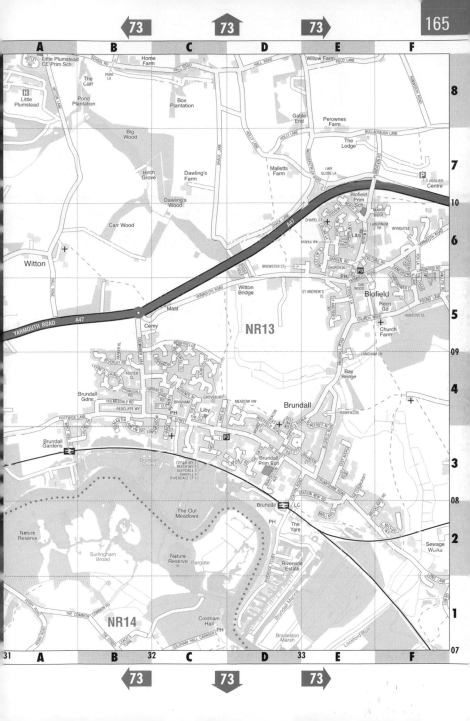

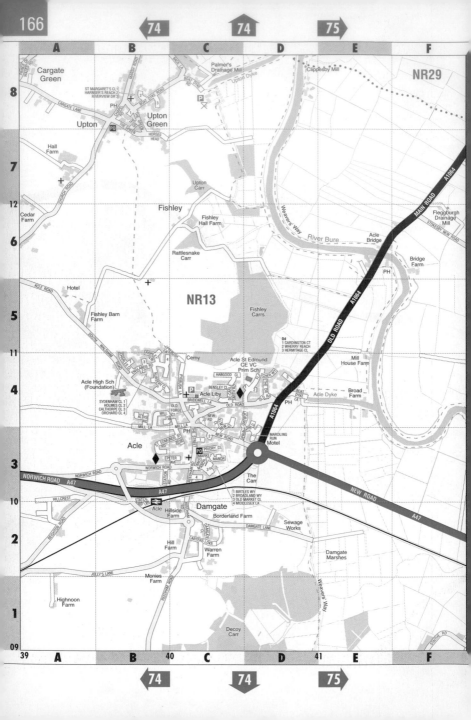

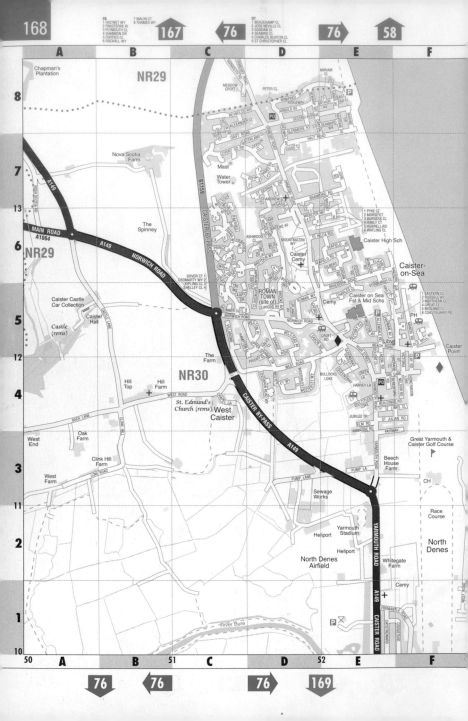

C6
1 BURE RD
2 ARCHER'S RD
3 MOAT RD
4 SCHOOL RD BACK
5 BRIDGE RD
6 LAUGHING IMAGE CORNER

7 WHITEHORSE PLAIN

D6
1 GRENVILLE PL
2 CUNNINGHAM AV
3 TENNYSON RD

D5
1 MIDLAND CL
2 HAMMOND RD
3 STEPHENSON CL
4 NORTH RD
5 MAYGROVE RD
6 WEST RD
7 FERRIER CL
8 TOTTENHAM ST

B4
1 COLLEGE CT
2 TYRRELL'S RD
3 MISSION RD
4 ST LUKE'S TR
5 CUBHOLM RD
6 LADY HAVEN RD
7 SAW MILL LA
8 BEAVANS CT
9 LUCAS RD

E3
1 TRAFALGAR SQ
2 STANDARD RD
3 EDINBURGH PL
4 YORK RD
5 PORTLAND PL

E4
1 BRITANNIA RD
2 MARLBOROUGH TR

E2
1 SOUTH BEACH PL
2 WATERLOO RD
3 BRANDON TR

D1
1 TRINITY SQ
2 FISH WHARF
3 MIDDLE RD W
4 MIDDLE RD E

C4
1 LIMEKILN WLK
2 BOWLING GREEN WLK
3 QUAY MILL WLK
4 PATTERSON CL
5 FISHERS' QUAY
6 CORONATION TR
7 HERRIES CL
8 FITZALAN CL
9 HOWARD ST N
10 FULLER'S HILL
11 PRIORY ROW
12 PRIORY GDNS
13 PRIORY PLAIN

D2
1 BURLEIGH CL
2 SIDNEY CL
3 FRIARS' LA
4 MALAKOFF RD
5 VICTORIA RD
6 DUNCAN RD
7 VICTORIA GDNS
8 MELROSE TR
9 MALAKOFF CL
10 HAVELOCK PL
11 CAMPERDOWN
12 DAGMAR MWS
13 ALBERT SQ
14 CLARENCE RD
15 LOUISE CL
16 SHADINGFIELD CL
17 ALBERT RD
18 WEST ST
19 SELBY PL

20 SEAFIELD CL

D3
1 DENE SIDE
2 TRAFALGAR RD
3 TOWNSHEND CL
4 DORSET CL
5 ORFORD CL
6 CLARENDON CL
7 BATH HILL
8 ST JOHN'S TR
9 NAPOLEON PL
10 STANDARD PL
11 WILSHERE CT

D4
1 CONISTON SQ
2 SILKMILL RD
3 THE EAGLES
4 OLIVER MWS
5 COBB'S PL
6 SWIRLE'S PL
7 UNION RD
8 MARKET GATES
9 REGENT RD
10 REGENT RD
11 EXMOUTH PL
12 WELLINGTON PL
13 SAXON RD
14 NETTLE HILL W
15 NETTLE HILL E
16 SOUTHAMPTON PL
17 BERMONDSEY PL W
18 BERMONDSEY PL E
19 BERMONDSEY PL S
20 ROMAN PL
21 ARTILLERY SQ
22 SOMERSET PL
23 RUSSELL RD
24 RUSSELL SQ

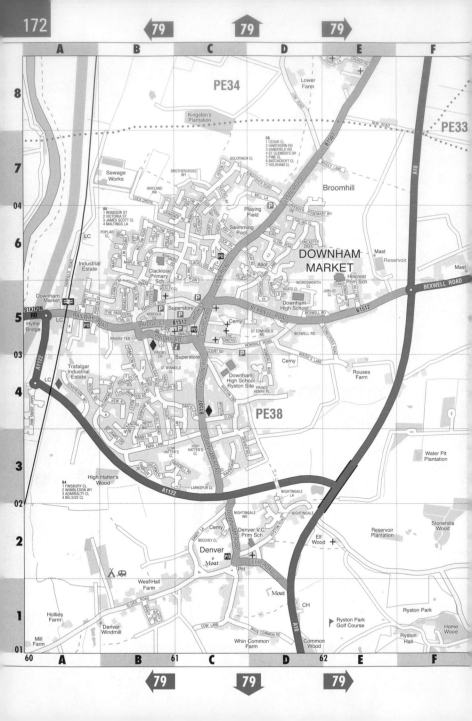

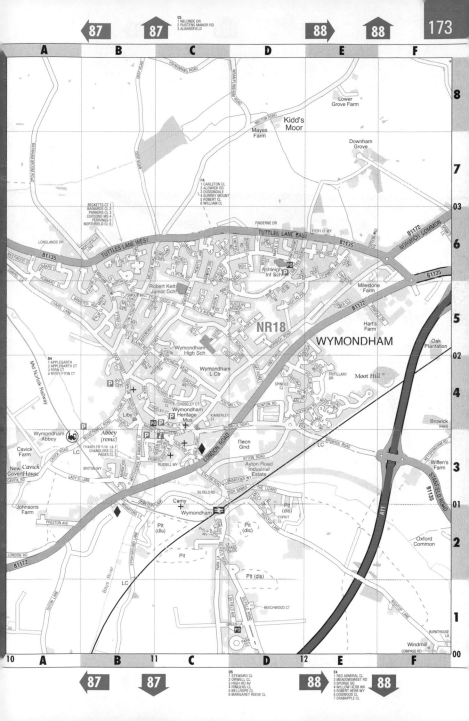

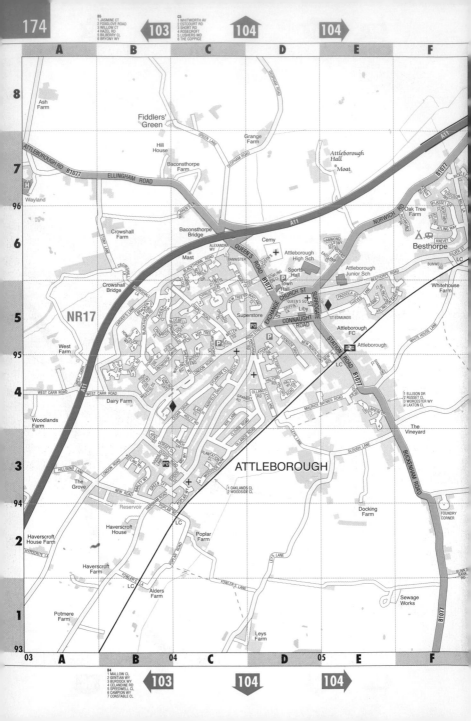

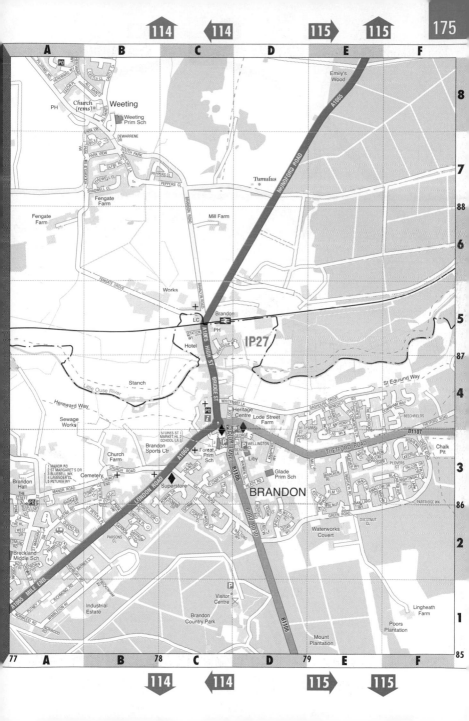

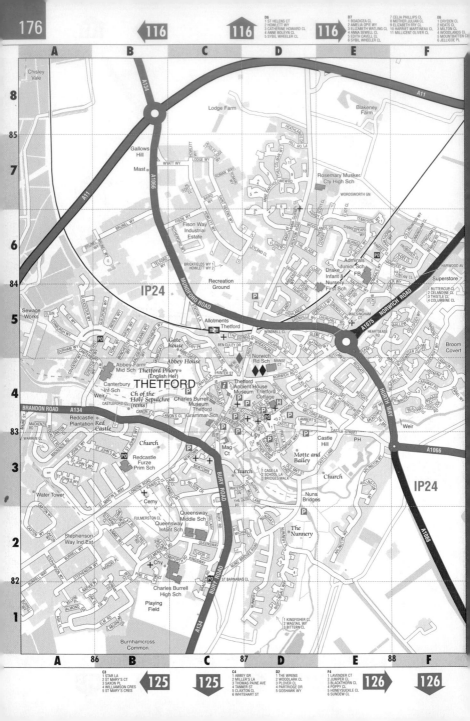

116 116 116

D6
1 ST HELENS CT
2 HOWLETT WY
3 CATHERINE HOWARD CL
4 ANNE BOLEYN CL
5 SYBIL WHEELER CL

D7
1 BOADICEA CL
2 AMELIA OPIE WY
3 ELIZABETH WATLING CL
4 ANNA SEWELL CL
5 EDITH CAVELL CL
6 SYBIL WHEELER CL

7 CELIA PHILLIPS CL
8 MOTHER JULIAN CL
9 ELIZABETH FRY CL
10 HARRIET MARTINEAU CL
11 MILLICENT OLIVER CL

E6
1 DRYDEN CL
2 KEATS CL
3 MILTON CL
4 WOODLANDS CL
5 MOUNTBATTEN CRE
6 JELLICOE PL

C3
1 STAR LA
2 ST MARY'S CT
3 SAXON PL
4 WILLIAMSON CRES
5 ST MARY'S CRES

125 125

C4
1 ABBEY GR
2 MILLER'S LA
3 THOMAS PAINE AVE
4 TANNER ST
5 CLAXTON CL
6 WHITEHART ST

D2
1 THE WRENS
2 WOODLARK CL
3 PLOVER CL
4 PARTRIDGE DR
5 GOSHAWK WY

F4
1 LAVENDER CT
2 JUNIPER CL
3 BLACKTHORN CL
4 POPPY CL
5 HONEYSUCKLE CL
6 SUNDEW CL

126 126

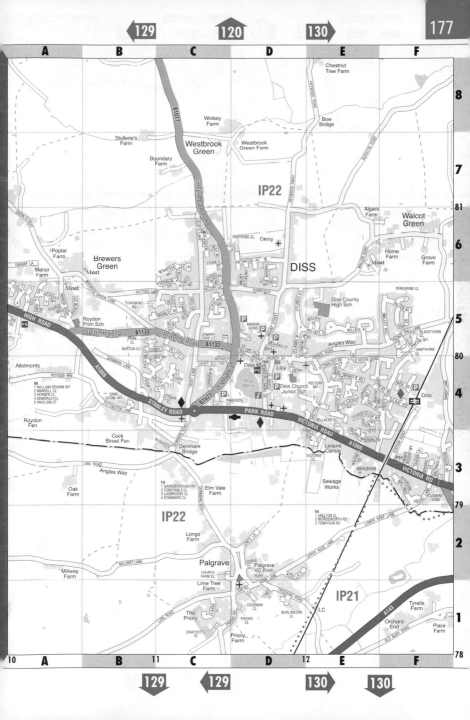

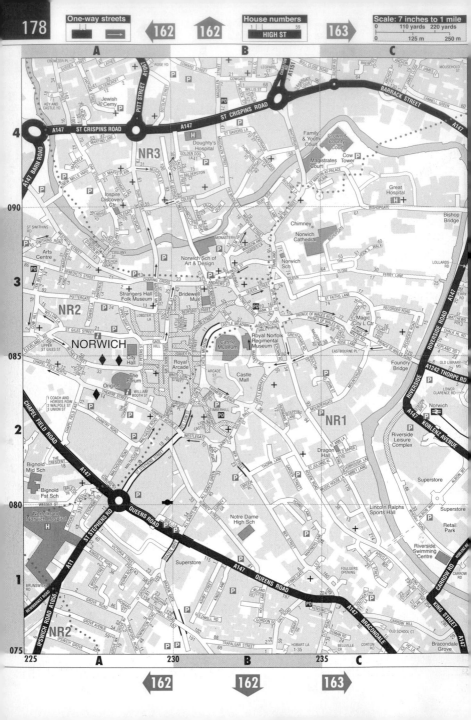

Bury St Edmunds

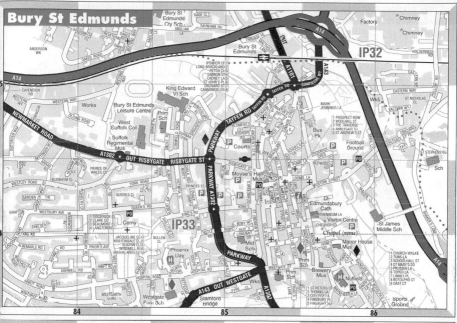

IP32

IP33

Lowestoft

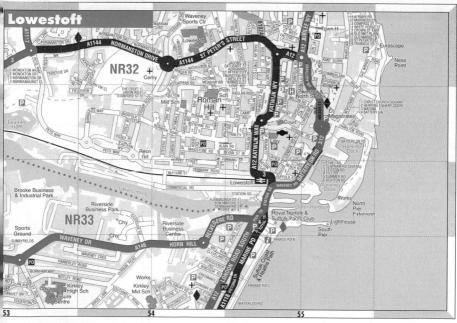

NR32

NR33

Roman Hill

Index

Church Rd **6** Beckenham BR2..........**53** C6

Place name	**Location number**
May be abbreviated on the map	Present when a number indicates the place's position in a crowded area of mapping
Locality, town or village	**Postcode district**
Shown when more than one place has the same name	District for the indexed place
Page and grid square	
Page number and grid reference for the standard mapping	

Public and commercial buildings are highlighted in magenta. Places of interest are highlighted in blue with a star★

Abbreviations used in the index

Acad	**Academy**	Comm	**Common**	Gd	**Ground**	L	**Leisure**	Prom	**Promenade**
App	**Approach**	Cott	**Cottage**	Gdn	**Garden**	La	**Lane**	Rd	**Road**
Arc	**Arcade**	Cres	**Crescent**	Gn	**Green**	Liby	**Library**	Recn	**Recreation**
Ave	**Avenue**	Cswy	**Causeway**	Gr	**Grove**	Mdw	**Meadow**	Ret	**Retail**
Bglw	**Bungalow**	Ct	**Court**	H	**Hall**	Meml	**Memorial**	Sh	**Shopping**
Bldg	**Building**	Ctr	**Centre**	Ho	**House**	Mkt	**Market**	Sq	**Square**
Bsns, Bus	**Business**	Ctry	**Country**	Hospl	**Hospital**	Mus	**Museum**	St	**Street**
Bvd	**Boulevard**	Cty	**County**	HQ	**Headquarters**	Orch	**Orchard**	Sta	**Station**
Cath	**Cathedral**	Dr	**Drive**	Hts	**Heights**	Pal	**Palace**	Terr	**Terrace**
Cir	**Circus**	Dro	**Drove**	Ind	**Industrial**	Par	**Parade**	TH	**Town Hall**
Cl	**Close**	Ed	**Education**	Inst	**Institute**	Pas	**Passage**	Univ	**University**
Cnr	**Corner**	Emb	**Embankment**	Int	**International**	Pk	**Park**	Wk, Wlk	**Walk**
Coll	**College**	Est	**Estate**	Intc	**Interchange**	Pl	**Place**	Wr	**Water**
Com	**Community**	Ex	**Exhibition**	Junc	**Junction**	Prec	**Precinct**	Yd	**Yard**

Index of localities, towns and villages

A

Acle 166 B3
Alburgh 122 F6
Alby Hill 21 B5
Aldborough 21 A5
Aldeby 110 F4
Alderford 52 A5
All Saints
  South Elmham ...124 B1
Alpington 90 E4
Anchor Corner 86 A1
Anchor Street 38 B3
Anmer 28 E8
Annis Hill 124 C8
Antingham 22 B4
Arminghall 90 B7
Ashby St Mary 91 C5
Ashill 84 A7
Ashmanhaugh 55 B8
Ashwellthorpe 105 F8
Ashwicken 45 A6
Aslacton 106 A2
Attleborough 174 D3
Attlebridge 52 B3
Aylmerton 10 A2
Aylsham 150 B5

B

Babingley 27 D5
Baconsthorpe 20 A8
Bacton 23 E5
Bacton Green 23 D5
Bagthorpe 14 D3
Bale 18 B7
Banham 119 D7
Banningham 36 D8
Barford 69 E2
Barmer 14 F4
Barney 17 F3
Barnham 125 F6
Barnham Broom 69 C2
Barningham 127 C3
Barningham Green ..20 A4
Barton Bendish 81 A8
Barton Turf 38 F1
Bastwick 57 A4
Battlesea Green ...131 E2
Bawburgh 160 B6
Bawdeswell 50 E8

Bawsey 44 D6
Beachamwell 81 F8
Beccles 110 D2
Beckett End 82 B1
Beckhithe 160 A1
Bedingham Green ..108 B3
Beeston 48 C2
Beeston Regis 138 F5
Beeston St Lawrence ..55 C8
Beetley 49 D4
Beighton 74 C2
Belaugh 54 E5
Bellmount 144 A7
Belton 93 F6
Bengate 38 A6
Bergh Apton 91 A4
Bessingham 20 E7
Besthorpe 174 F6
Bexwell 79 F6
Billingford 50 B7
Billingford
  Dickleburgh and Rushall ..130 E5
Billockby 75 A7
Binham 6 E2
Bintree 33 B2
Bircham Newton 14 A4
Bircham Tofts 14 B3
Bittering 48 F4
Blackborough End ..44 C1
Black Carr 105 A6
Blackwater 51 D6
Blakeney 7 C6
Bleach Green 131 F4
Blenheim Park 15 C3
Blickling 35 F7
Blofield 165 F5
Blofield Corner ...73 C6
Blofield Heath 73 D6
Blo' Norton 128 B6
Bloodman's Corner ..171 A4
Bobby Hill 128 A1
Bodham 9 A3
Bodney 83 B1
Booton 149 E4
Botesdale 128 F2
Boughton 81 A5
Bowbeck 127 A2
Bowthorpe 160 F7
Bracon Ash 89 A2
Bradenham 66 E4
Bradfield 22 C4
Bradwell 94 C7
Bradwell Great Yarmouth ..170 A4

Brakefield Green ..68 D4
Bramerton 90 F7
Brampton 36 D3
Brancaster 3 B6
Brancaster Staithe ..3 D7
Brandiston 52 B8
Brandon 175 D3
Brandon Bank 112 B7
Brandon Creek 97 A2
Brandon Parva 69 B2
Breckles 102 E5
Bressingham 129 C8
Bressingham Common ..119 F1
Brettenham 117 B2
Brewers Green 177 B6
Bridge Green 120 F2
Bridgham 117 F5
Briggate 38 B8
Briningham 18 D4
Brinton 18 D6
Brisley 49 A8
Briston 142 C4
Brockdish 131 C6
Brockholm 24 E4
Broome 109 C2
Broom Green 32 E2
Broomhill 172 E7
Broomholm 24 E4
Broomsthorpe 30 C7
Browston Green 94 C4
Brundall 165 D4
Brundish 110 A6
Buckenham 91 F8
Bull's Green 110 C5
Bumwell Hill 105 E2
Bungay 124 A8
Bunker's Hill Lound ..94 C3
Bunker's Hill Norwich ..161 B7
Bunwell 105 D4
Bunwell Bottom ...105 C6
Burgate 127 C2
Burgh Castle 94 A7
Burgh Common 104 D5
Burgh next Aylsham ..36 D4
Burgh St Margaret
  (Fleggburgh) 57 C1
Burgh St Peter ...111 C4
Burgh Stubbs 142 B8
Burlingham Green ..74 A5
Burnham Deepdale ...3 E6

Burnham Market ...135 C3
Burnham Norton ...135 B6
Burnham Overy Staithe ..135 E6
Burnham Overy Town ..135 E4
Burnham Thorpe 4 D4
Burnham Westgate ..135 B3
Burston 120 F2
Bush Green 122 A6
Bushy Common 67 B8
Bustard's Green ..106 C3
Buxton 36 E1

C

Caister-on-Sea ...168 F6
Caistor St Edmund ..89 F6
California 167 E3
Calthorpe 21 A2
Calthorpe Street ..39 C4
Candle Street 128 D1
Cangate 55 C6
Cantley 92 B7
Carbrooke 85 B5
Cargate Common ...105 E1
Cargate Green 166 A8
Carleton Forehoe ..87 C8
Carleton Rode 105 C3
Carleton St Peter ..91 E5
Castle Acre 46 F2
Castle Rising 27 C3
Caston 102 E8
Catfield 56 C8
Caudlesprings 85 A4
Cawston 35 B2
Cess 57 C5
Chalkhill 83 C4
Chapel Field 39 A3
Chedgrave 92 A7
Chickering 131 D3
Christchurch 95 A7
Church End 41 F2
Claxton 91 D6
Clenchwarton 145 E5
Cley next the Sea ..7 E6
Cliftonville 143 B7
Clint Green 68 C6
Clippesby 57 A1
Clippings Green ...68 C2
Cobbler's Green ..108 B2
Cobholm Island ...169 A4
Cockley Cley 82 D7
Cockthorpe 6 E5

Colby 21 E2
Colegate End 121 E6
Colkirk 31 D5
Colney 161 A4
Coltishall 54 C4
Colton 69 C4
Coney Weston 127 B5
Congham 28 B2
Copy's Green 6 A2
Cordwell 105 E4
Corpusty 19 F1
Costessey 56 F4
Costessey Park ...156 D3
Coston 69 A1
Coxford 30 C8
Crabgate 34 D6
Crackthorn Corner ..128 D5
Cranwich 99 F6
Cranworth 85 E7
Craymere Beck 18 F1
Crimplesham 80 B6
Cringleford 89 B8
Cromer 139 C7
Crossdale Street ..139 D1
Cross Street 131 A3
Cross Ways 94 B4
Crostwick 54 B3
Crostwight 38 D8
Crowgate Street ...55 A8
Crownthorpe 87 C6
Crowshill 67 A1
Croxton 32 D1
Croxton Fulmodeston ..17 E2
Cuckoo Green 171 A4
Culfordheath 125 D1

D

Daffy Green 67 C4
Damgate Acle 166 C2
Damgate Martham ..57 E5
Dam Green 119 C4
Danemoor Green 86 B3
Darrow Green 122 E8
Denham 131 B1
Denton 123 A7
Denver 79 E5
Deopham 86 E3
Deopham Green 86 E2
Deopham Stalland ..86 D2
Dereham 154 F4
Dersingham 140 D5

Dickleburgh 121 C1
Dickleburgh Moor 121 C2
Didlington 99 E8
Dilham 38 D4
Diss 177 D6
Ditchingham 109 A2
Dockeney 109 F2
Docking 134 C5
Doddshill 140 F3
Dowe Hill 167 C5
Downham Market 172 E6
Drabblegate 150 D8
Drayton 157 A8
Drurylane 85 A4
Drymere 64 C1
Dumpling Green 154 F3
Dunkirk 150 E8
Dunston 89 C5
Dunton 15 F1
Dussindale Park 72 E4

E

Earlham 161 D5
Earsham 123 E8
Earsham Street 131 F5
East Barsham 16 D4
East Bilney 49 B6
East Carleton 88 F4
Eastgate 35 C2
East Harling 118 C5
Easthaugh 61 C4
East Ferham 47 D3
Easton 70 B5
East Raynham 31 A4
East Rudham 30 A7
East Runton 10 B5
East Ruston 38 E6
East Somerton 56 A6
East Tuddenham 69 C6
East Walton 45 E3
East Winch 44 F3
East Wretham 102 A1
Eaton 161 F2
Eau Brink 43 A3
Eccles on Sea 24 E4
Eccles Road 103 F1
Edgefield 19 D5
Edgefield Street 19 D4
Edge Green 119 B4
Edingthorpe 23 C3
Edingthorpe Green 23 A2
Ellingham 109 D3
Elm 59 B1
Elsing 50 F3
Elveden 125 A7
Emneth 59 D2
Emneth Hungate 59 F2
Emorsgate 42 B7
Erpingham 21 B2
Etling Green 68 B8
Euston 126 B5

F

Fair Green 44 B4
Fairstead 147 D4
Fakenham 141 D6
Fakenham Magna 126 F3
Felbrigg 10 C2
Felmingham 37 A8
Felthorpe 155 C8
Feltwell 98 D1
Fengate 150 C1
Fenside 56 B8
Fen Street Hopton 127 E6
Fen Street Redgrave 128 F6
Fersfield 119 D2
Fiddlers' Green 174 B8
Field Dalling 7 F3
Filby 75 F8
Filby Heath 76 B8
Fincham 62 F1
Fishley 166 C6
Flaxlands 105 C4
Flitcham 28 C5
Flixton 123 D5
Flordon 106 D8
Fodderstone Gap 62 C4
Fordham 79 D2
Forncett End 105 E4
Forncett St Mary 106 B4
Forncett St Peter 106 B4
Foul Anchor 41 A4
Foulden 82 A2
Foulsham 33 D3
Foxhole 107 A7
Foxley 50 D8
Framingham Earl 90 D4
Framingham Pigot 90 C6
Frankfort 38 A3
Frans Green 51 D1
Freethorpe 92 E8
Frenze 130 B7
Frettenham 54 A4
Friday Bridge 77 A7
Fring 13 D5
Fritton Fritton and St Olaves 93 E3
Fritton Ludham 56 E5
Fritton Morning Thorpe 107 B3
Frogshall 11 B1

Frost Row 86 B4
Fulmodeston 17 F1
Fundenhall 106 A7

G

Garboldisham 128 A8
Garlic Street 122 A2
Garvestone 68 C2
Gasthorpe 127 D7
Gateley 32 C5
Gayton 45 C5
Gayton Thorpe 45 E5
Gaywood 147 B6
Geldeston 109 F3
Gillingham 110 C2
Gimingham 22 E7
Gissing 120 F4
Glandford 7 E4
Gooderstone 82 A4
Goose Green 120 C6
Gorleston-on-Sea 170 E4
Great Barwick 14 E6
Great Bircham 14 B3
Great Common 124 D6
Great Cressingham 83 D4
Great Dunham 47 E1
Great Ellingham 103 E7
Great Fransham 66 B8
Great Green Burgate 129 B3
Great Green Thrandeston 130 A4
Great Hockham 102 C3
Great Massingham 29 D2
Great Melton 70 B1
Great Moulton 106 B1
Great Plumstead 72 F5
Great Ryburgh 32 B6
Great Snoring 17 B3
Great Walsingham 17 A8
Great Witchingham 51 E7
Great Yarmouth 169 A5
Greengate 50 B3
Greensgate 50 C6
Gresham 9 I1
Gressenhall 49 B3
Grimston 28 B1
Griston 85 A2
Guestwick 34 A6
Guestwick Green 33 A5
Guist 32 F4
Gunthorpe 18 B5

H

Hackford 87 A5
Haddiscoe 110 F8
Hainford 53 E5
Hales 109 F8
Hales Green 109 C7
Hales Street 121 A6
Halvergate 74 F1
Hamrow 31 D3
Hanworth 21 B6
Happisburgh 24 C5
Happisburgh Common 24 B4
Hapton 106 C7
Hardingham 86 E6
Hardley Street 92 C4
Hardwick North Norfolk 147 B1
Hardwick Shelton 122 B8
Hargate 105 D2
Harleston 122 D3
Harling Road 118 A7
Harper's Green 32 A1
Harpley 29 D4
Hassingham 92 B8
Hawes' Green 89 F2
Hay Green 144 A1
Heacham 133 E4
Heckfield Green 131 D2
Heckingham 92 C1
Hedenham 108 F4
Helhoughton 30 E5
Hellesdon 157 F5
Hellington 91 B6
Hemblington 73 E6
Hemblington Corner 73 D6
Hempnall 107 D5
Hempnall Green 107 D4
Hempstead 37 D8
Hempstead Lessingham 24 E3
Hempton 141 A3
Hemsby 167 A7
Hengrave 52 A6
Hepworth 127 E1
Herringfleet 111 D8
Hethel 88 F3
Hethersett 88 C8
Hevingham 53 B7
Heydon 34 F6
Hickling 39 E2
Hickling Green 39 E2
Hickling Heath 39 E1
High Common 85 F8
High Green Bradenham 66 E2
High Green Fransham 48 E1
High Green Mattishall 88 B8
High Kelling 8 E3
Highoak 87 B4
High Street 124 D3

Hilborough 83 A3
Hilgay 79 E1
Hill Common 39 F1
Hillington 28 B4
Hinderclay 128 C3
Hindolveston 33 D8
Hindringham 17 E7
Hingham 86 C5
Hockering 69 B8
Hockering Heath 51 C1
Hockwold cum Wilton 114 A7
Hoe 49 F3
Holkham 5 B6
Holly End 59 D1
Holme Hale 66 B2
Holme next the Sea 2 A6
Holt 137 D6
Homersfield 123 B4
Honing 38 C6
Honingham 69 E7
Honington 126 D1
Hopton 127 F6
Hopton on Sea 171 D6
Horning 55 E4
Horningtoft 31 F1
Horsey 40 D2
Horsey Corner 40 D2
Horsford 53 B3
Horsham St Faith 53 D1
Horstead 54 C6
Houghton St Giles 16 E6
Hoveton 164 D6
Howe 90 D3
How Hill 56 B4
Hoxne 131 A4
Humbletoft 154 C7
Hunstanton 132 D5
Hunt's Corner 119 C7
Huntworth 19 A6
Hyltons Crossways 36 F8

I

Ickburgh 100 B6
Ilketshall St Andrew 124 E6
Ilketshall St Lawrence 124 F2
Ilketshall St Margaret 124 B4
Illington 117 D8
Ingham 39 D4
Ingham Corner 24 D2
Ingleborough 41 B3
Ingoldisthorpe 140 D8
Ingworth 36 B8
Intwood 89 B7
Irstead 56 A7
Irstead Street 55 A8
Itteringham 20 C1
Itteringham Common 35 D8
Ivy Todd 66 B4

J

Johnson Street 56 B4
Jordan Green 51 A8

K

Kelling 8 D5
Kenninghall 119 B5
Kerdiston 34 C3
Keswick Bacton 23 F4
Keswick 89 C7
Ketteringham 88 E6
Kettlestone 17 C2
Kidd's Moor 173 D8
Kimberley 87 B6
King's Lynn 147 A5
Kirby Bedon 90 E8
Kirby Cane 109 E4
Kirby Green 109 F5
Kirby Row 109 E3
Kirstead Green 108 C8
Knapton 143 B1
Knapton Green 22 F5
Knettishall 127 C7

L

Lakenham 162 F3
Lakenheath 113 E2
Lakes End 95 C7
Lamas 37 A2
Langham 7 B3
Langley Street 92 B4
Langton Green 130 C1
Larling 118 B8
Lenwade 51 D5
Lessingham 24 D3
Letheringsett 8 A1
Letton Green 67 E3
Leziate 44 C6
Limpenhoe 92 D6
Lingwood 73 F3
Litcham 48 A4
Little Barningham 20 C4
Little Barwick 14 E6
Little Cressingham 83 E2
Little Dunham 65 F8
Little Ellingham 86 A2

Little Fransham 66 B7
Little Green 129 B1
Little Hale 67 A1
Little Hautbois 54 B8
Little London Corpusty 19 E1
Little London Marsham 36 A2
Little London
Little London North Walsham 151 E7
Little London Northwold 99 D7
Little Marsh 7 A1
Little Massingham 29 C3
Little Melton 160 C2
Little Ouse 112 A8
Little Plumstead 73 B6
Little Ryburgh 32 C7
Little Snoring 17 B3
Little Thornage 7 F1
Little Walsingham 16 F7
Loddon 92 A1
Loddon Ingloss 109 B7
Long Green 129 B4
Longham 49 A2
Long John's Hill 162 E2
Long Stratton 106 E3
Lordsbridge 60 E7
Lound 94 C1
Low Common 105 F3
Lower Bodham 9 A2
Lower East Carleton 89 B6
Lower Gresham 9 F1
Lower Stow Bedon 102 F5
Lower Street Southrepps 22 C6
Lower Street Wickmere 20 L5
Lower Tasburgh 106 F7
Lower Thurlton 93 A2
Low Street 86 E8
Low Tharston 106 D6
Ludham 56 D5
Lundy Green 107 D3
Lynford 100 D2
Lyng 51 A4
Lyngate North Walsham 151 A8
Lyngate Worstead 38 A5

M

Magpie Green 129 B5
Manor House 46 E2
Manson Green 86 C6
Marham 63 B4
Market Weston 127 E4
Marlingford 70 A4
Marsham 150 D1
Marshland St James 60 A4
Marsh Side 3 C7
Martham 57 D5
Matlaske 20 D5
Mattishall 68 E5
Mattishall Burgh 68 F7
Mautby 75 F7
Maypole Green 110 C6
Meeting House Hill 38 B7
Mellis 129 F2
Melton Constable 142 B5
Mendham 123 A1
Merton 84 C1
Methwold 99 A5
Methwold Hythe 98 E5
Mettingham 124 E8
Middle Harling 118 B4
Middleton 44 C3
Mile Cross 158 A2
Mileham 48 D6
Mill Common 91 C4
Mill Green 120 E3
Mill Street 50 E4
Misery Corner 122 F8
Moorgate 154 D3
Morley St Botolph 87 B2
Morningthorpe 107 A3
Morton 7 B6
Morton 52 A4
Moulton St Mary 74 D2
Mount Pleasant 103 C5
Muckleton 3 F2
Mulbarton 89 B3
Mundesley 143 B5
Mundford 100 B4
Mundham 91 C1
Mustard Hyrn 57 C5

New Sprowston 158 E3
Newton 47 B2
Newton Flotman 89 C3
Newton Greenways 89 D2
Newton St Faith 53 E4
Newtown 169 D7
Nogdam End 92 D3
Nordelph 78 D3
Nordelph Corner 86 D6
Northacre 85 B1
Northall Green Dereham 154 F8
Northall Green Hoe 49 F2
North Barsham 16 D6
North Burlingham 74 A5
North Common 127 D2
North Court 114 C3
North Creake 4 D1
North Denes 168 F2
North Elmham 49 B8
North End 103 C3
North Green Garvestone 68 C1
North Green Pulham St Mary 122 A7
North Lopham 119 A2
North Lynn 146 F7
North Pickenham 65 E1
Northrepps 11 A2
North Runcton 44 A2
North Tuddenham 50 D1
North Walsham 151 E6
Northwold 99 C8
North Wootton 148 C5
Norton Corner 34 C7
Norton Subcourse 92 E1
Norwich 178 A3

O

Oakley 130 C5
Old Beetley 49 D5
Old Buckenham 104 D2
Old Catton 158 E5
Old Hall Street 23 A4
Old Hunstanton 132 E8
Orange Row 144 A6
Ormesby St Margaret 167 B3
Ormesby St Michael 58 A1
Ostend 24 A7
Oulton 35 B7
Oulton Street 35 C6
Outwell 77 F6
Overstrand 11 A4
Ovington 84 E5
Oxborough 81 D4
Oxnead 36 E2
Oxwick 31 D4

P

Palgrave 177 C2
Panxworth 73 E7
Paston 143 D2
Paston Green 143 D1
Peaseland Green 50 F3
Pedham 73 D7
Pennygate 38 E2
Pentney 63 C8
Pettywell 34 C2
Pilson Green 74 B8
Plumstead Green Great and Little Plumstead 73 B6
Plumstead Green Plumstead 20 B6
Pockthorpe Sparham 51 B5
Pockthorpe Thompson 102 A7
Pockthorpe West Rudham 29 F6
Podmore 67 B7
Pollard Street 23 D3
Pooley Street 129 A8
Poringland 90 C5
Postwick 72 E2
Pottergate Street 106 B2
Potter Heigham 56 F6
Potthorpe 49 A8
Primrose Corner 55 C1
Primrose Green 51 A3
Pristow Green 120 E8
Pudding Norton 141 B1
Puddledock 104 C3
Pulham Market 121 E5
Pulham St Mary 121 F4

Q

Quidenham 118 F6

R

Rackheath 72 E8
Ragmere 104 D1
Ranworth 55 F1
Ratten Row 59 F8
Raveningham 110 A7
Reading Green 131 C1
Redenhall 122 F3
Redgrave 128 E4
Red Pits 34 D7
Reedham 92 E5
Reepham 149 B5

Repps 56 F4
Reymerston 68 C1
Rickinghall 128 E2
Ridlington 23 C1
Ridlington Street 23 C1
Ringland 70 B8
Ringstead 2 A3
Road Green 107 E4
Rockland All Saints 103 B7
Rockland St Mary 91 B7
Rockland St Peter 103 B8
Rollesby 57 D2
Rougham 47 B7
Roughton 21 E8
Roydon 129 D7
Roydon 28 A2
Runcton Holme 61 D3
Runhall 68 F2
Runham Great Yarmouth .169 B5
Runham Mautby 75 E6
Rushall 121 F1
Rushford 126 E8
Rush Green 69 B1

S

Saham Hills 84 C6
Saham Toney 84 C5
St Cross South Elmham .123 D3
St James 54 D7
St John's Fen End 60 B6
St John's Highway 42 B1
St Margaret South
    Elmham 123 E2
St Michael South
    Elmham 124 A2
St Nicholas South
    Elmham 123 E2
St Olaves 93 D2
St Peter South Elmham .124 A3
Salhouse 55 B1
Salle 149 E8
Salters Lode 79 A4
Salthouse 8 B7
Sandringham 27 F7
Santon Downham 115 C6
Sapiston 126 D2
Saxlingham 7 C2
Saxlingham Green 107 D7
Saxlingham Nethergate .107 C8
Saxlingham Thorpe 107 A8
Scarning 67 B7
Scole 130 D6
Scole Common 130 C7
Sco Ruston 54 E8
Scottow 37 D2
Scoulton 85 E3
Scratby 167 E4
Sculthorpe 16 B2
Sea Palling 40 A6
Sedgeford 13 B7
Seething 108 F8
Setchey 61 E8
Shadwell 117 C2
Sharp Street 56 C7
Sharrington 18 D7
Shelfanger 120 C2
Shelton 107 B1
Shepherd's Gate 42 D4
Shepherd's Port 12 B4
Shereford 31 A8
Sheringham 138 C7
Sheringwood 138 C5
Shernborne 13 B3
Shimpling 121 A2
Shimpham 82 A8
Shipdham 67 B2
Shipmeadow 124 F8
Short Green 120 A5
Shotesham 90 A2
Shouldham 61 F1
Shouldham Thorpe 62 C3
Shropham 103 B4

Sidestrand 11 C2
Silfield 88 A2
Silvergate 35 F6
Silver Green 107 E3
Sisland 91 E1
Skeyton 37 A4
Skeyton Corner 37 B6
Sloley 37 F4
Smallburgh 38 D3
Smallworth 128 A7
Sneath Common 121 A8
Snetterton 103 C2
Snettisham 12 E5
Snow Street 129 D8
South Acre 46 F1
South Burlingham 74 B2
South Creake 15 D6
South Denes 170 E5
South End 103 C1
Southery 97 B5
Southgate Cawston 35 B3
Southgate South Creake . . .15 E5
South Green East Dereham .154 E3
South Green Hoxne 130 F1
South Green Mattishall . . .68 F5
South Green
    Pulham St Mary 121 F2
South Green
    Terrington St Clement . .42 B6
South Lopham 128 D8
South Lynn 146 E2
South Pickenham 83 D6
South Raynham 30 F3
Southrepps 22 B7
South Runcton 61 F3
Southtown 169 A1
South Walsham 74 A7
Southwood 92 D8
South Wootton 148 D2
Spa Common 23 A1
Sparham 51 B6
Sparhamhill 51 C5
Spixworth 54 A2
Spooner Row 105 A8
Sporle 65 C6
Sprowston 159 B3
Stacksford 104 C1
Stalham 39 B4
Stalham Green 39 C3
Stalland Common 86 C1
Stanfield 48 F7
Stanford 101 A5
Stanhoe 14 E8
Stanton Chare 127 B1
Starston 122 C3
Stibbard 32 E7
Stiffkey 6 D5
Stockton 109 F4
Stody 18 F6
Stoke Ferry 80 F3
Stoke Holy Cross 89 F4
Stokesby 75 A5
Stonebridge 102 B1
Stone Street 124 F1
Stow Bardolph 79 E8
Stow Bedon 102 E7
Stowbridge 61 B2
Stradbroke 131 E1
Stradsett 80 D8
Stratton St Michael 106 F4
Stratton Strawless 53 E7
Strumpshaw 73 F2
Stubb 39 F1
Stubbing's Green 129 A1
Stubbs Green 109 C8
Stuston 130 B5
Suffield 21 F3
Summerfield 2 E1
Summerhill 133 C3
Surlingham 73 B1
Sustead 21 A7
Suton 87 D2
Sutton 39 C3

Sutton Bridge 41 B7
Swaffham 153 D4
Swafield 22 E3
Swainsthorpe 89 D3
Swannington 52 B6
Swanton Abbott 37 C4
Swanton Hill 37 C5
Swanton Morley 50 B3
Swanton Novers 18 B3
Swardeston 89 C5
Syderstone 15 B3
Syleham 131 D5

T

Tacolneston 105 F5
Tasburgh 106 F7
Tatterford 30 E7
Tattersett 15 C1
Taverham 155 C1
Ten Mile Bank 96 E7
Terrington St Clement . . .144 B4
Terrington St John 42 C2
Tharston 106 E5
The Arms 83 F1
The Brook 129 C3
The Grange 35 C1
The Green 87 B4
The Heath Fakenham 141 F4
The Heath Hevingham 53 A8
The Heath
    Stratton Strawless 53 E8
The Limes 59 C5
The Ling 91 A1
Thelnetham 128 B5
Thelveton 130 D8
The Marsh Thrandeston . . .29 F3
The Marsh Wortham 129 C4
Themelthorpe 33 F2
The Smeeth 60 A5
Thetford 176 B4
Thompson 102 A8
Thornage 18 F7
Thornham 2 D6
Thorpe 93 B1
Thorpe Abbotts 131 B6
Thorpe End 72 D6
Thorpe Hamlet 163 B6
Thorpe Market 22 A6
Thorpe Marriott 155 F2
Thorpe Row 67 C4
Thorpe St Andrew 163 F8
Thorpland 61 D3
Thrandeston 129 F3
Three Cocked Hat 110 D7
Threehammer Common . .55 E6
Three Holes 77 E3
Thrigby 75 D7
Thurgarton 20 F5
Thurlton 92 F1
Thurne 56 E3
Thurning 34 C7
Thursford 17 E4
Thursford Green 17 D5
Thurton 91 D4
Thuxton 68 D2
Thwaite St Mary 109 A5
Tibenham 120 E8
Tilney All Saints 144 F1
Tilney cum Islington 60 F8
Tilney Fen End 60 C6
Tilney High End 42 D4
Tilney St Lawrence 60 D8
Tipps End 95 C6
Titchwell 2 F7
Tittleshall 48 B8
Tivetshall St Margaret . .121 B5
Tivetshall St Mary 121 B5
Toft Monks 110 D5
Toftrees 31 B6
Toftwood 154 E2
Topcroft 107 F3
Topcroft Street 107 F2

Toprow 88 E1
Tottenhill 62 A5
Tottenhill Row 61 E7
Tottington 101 E6
Tower End 44 C4
Town Green
    Alby with Thwaite 21 C4
Town Green
    South Walsham 74 A7
Town Street 39 F3
Trimingham 11 D2
Trowse Newton 163 B3
Trunch 22 E5
Tungate 37 C8
Tunstall 74 F3
Tunstead 37 F1
Tuttington 36 E6
Twyford 33 B3
Tyby 34 B6

U

Upgate 52 C5
Upgate Street Bedingham .108 B2
Upgate Street
    Old Buckenham 105 A3
Upper Brandon Parva 68 E3
Upper Guist 33 A5
Upper Hellesdon 158 C3
Upper Sheringham 138 A5
Upper Stoke 90 B5
Upper Street
    Dickleburgh and Rushall .130 F6
Upper Street Horning 55 F4
Upper Street Hoveton 55 C5
Upper Street Southrepps . . .22 B7
Upper Street Tunstead 38 A3
Upper Weybread 131 E6
Upton 166 A8
Upton Green 166 B8
Upwell 77 F5

W

Wacton 106 C2
Wainford 109 B1
Walcot Green 177 F6
Walcott 24 A7
Walpole Cross Keys 41 C7
Walpole Highway 59 F8
Walpole Marsh 41 B4
Walpole St Andrew 41 D4
Walpole St Peter 41 E3
Walsoken 152 F6
Walton Highway 59 D8
Walton Warren 45 E2
Wangford 114 C2
Warham 6 A4
Waterheath 110 E5
Waterloo Aldeby 110 E4
Waterloo
    Dickleburgh and Rushall .130 C6
Waterloo Hainford 53 E6
Watlington 61 E5
Wattisfield 128 B1
Wattlefield 105 C7
Watton 84 E3
Watton Green 84 E4
Waxham 40 C5
Weasenham All Saints . . .47 C8
Weasenham St Peter 30 D1
Weeting 175 B8
Welborne 69 A4
Welborne Common 68 F4
Wellingham 30 F1
Wells-Next-The-Sea 136 C5
Welney 95 D4
Wendling 66 F8
Wereham 80 E4
West Acre 46 B2
West Barsham 16 C4
West Beckham 9 C2

West Bilney 45 B2
Westbrook Green 177 C7
West Caister 168 C4
West Dereham 80 B4
West End Necton 66 C4
West End West Caister . . .76 B6
Westfield 67 F4
Westgate 6 D3
Westgate Street 53 B8
West Harling 118 A3
West Head 78 F8
West Lexham 47 C4
West Lynn 146 C5
West Newton 27 F6
Weston Green 51 E1
Weston Longville 51 E3
West Poringland 90 B4
West Raynham 30 E4
West Rudham 29 F7
West Runton 10 A5
West Somerton 57 E6
West Tofts 100 F4
West Walton 59 B8
Westwick 37 D6
West Winch 43 E3
Weybourne 8 F5
Wheatacre 111 B5
Whimpwell Green 24 C4
Whinburgh 68 A3
Whissonsett 31 D2
Whittington 81 B2
Whitwell Street 149 C3
Wicken Green Village . . .15 D2
Wickhampton 93 A8
Wicklewood 87 B5
Wickmere 20 F4
Wiggenhall St Germans . .43 C1
Wiggenhall
    St Mary Magdalen 61 B6
Wiggenhall
    St Mary the Virgin 61 A8
Wiggenhall St Peter 61 C7
Wighton 6 A2
Wilby 119 A8
Wilney Green 129 A8
Wimbotsham 79 D8
Winfarthing 120 B4
Wingfield 131 E4
Wingfield Green 131 D4
Winterton-on-Sea 58 C6
Wisbech 152 A6
Withergate 38 A6
Witton 165 A6
Witton Bridge 23 C2
Wiveton 7 E6
Wolferd Green 90 B2
Wolferton 27 B7
Wolterton 20 E2
Woodbastwick 55 D2
Wood Dalling 34 D6
Woodgate 50 C3
Wood Green 106 F2
Wood Norton 33 A7
Woodrising 85 E6
Woodton 108 C4
Wormegay 62 C7
Worstead 38 A5
Wortham 129 B4
Worthing 49 F6
Wortwell 123 B4
Wramplingham 69 E1
Wreningham 88 D1
Wretton 80 E3
Wroxham 164 D3
Wymondham 173 E5

Y

Yaxham 68 A3
Yaxley 130 A1
Yelverton 90 E5

Abbey Cl
Horsham St Faith &
Newton St Faith NR10 .....53 D1
Sheringham NR26 ....138 D6
Wendling NR19 ....66 F7
Abbey Farm Mid Sch
IP24 ....176 B4
Abbey La IP24 ......176 C4
Abbey Hill 1 IP24 ...131 A3
Abbey La
Haveringland NR10 ....52 D6
Norwich NR1 ....178 C2
Abbey Mr NR26 ....138 F5
Abbey Rd
Flitcham with Appleton
PE31 ....28 C5
Flixton NR35 ....123 F4
Great Massingham PE32 ...29 D1
Horsham St Faith NR10 ....53 D1
Old Buckenham NR17 .....104 D3
Pentney PE32 ....63 B8
Sheringham NR26 ....138 C6
10 Watton IP25 ....84 E3
Abbey St NR22 ....23 E6
Abbey The NR22 ......23 E6
Abbeyfields PE32 .....29 D1
Abbeygate IP24 ....176 C5
Abbot Cl NR18 ....173 C5
Abbot Rd Horning NR12 ..55 E4
Norwich NR1 ....178 C1
Abbot's Ct NR17 .....150 D7
Abbot's La NR14 ......90 B3
Abbots Way NR12 .....24 E4
Abbottsinch Rd 5 IP31 ..126 B1
Aberdeen St NR30 ....146 F4
Abinger Way NR4 .....89 B8
Abington Gr 4 PE14 ...59 A1
Abyssinia Rd NR20 ...169 D2
Acacia Ave Ashill IP25 ..84 A7
East Dereham NR19 ......154 E1
2 Martham NR29 ....57 D4
Wisbech PE13 ....152 C8
Acacia Gr NR26 ....138 D4
Acacia Rd NR7 ....163 E8
Access Rd NR12 ....15 C2
Acer Rd PE34 ....4 A3
Ackland Cl 7 NR29 ....58 B6
Acland Mews NR6 .....158 C4
Acle High Sch (Foundation)
NR13 ....166 B4
Acle New Rd NR30 ....169 C5
Acle Rd Beighton NR13 ..74 E2
South Walsham NR13 .....74 C7
Upton with Fishley NR13 ..166 A5
**Acle St Edmund CE VC Prim
Sch** NR13 ....166 B2
Acle Sta NR13 ....166 B2
Aconite Rd PE30 ......147 B7
Acorn Dr PE32 ....45 B6
Acorn Rd PE28 ....151 D6
Acorn Way NR19 ......154 D7
Acres Way NR8 ....155 E2
Ada Coxon Cl PE30 ...146 F8
Adam Cl PE30 ....147 C5
Adams La
4 Corpusty NR11 ....19 F1
Corpusty NR11 ....34 F8
Adams Rd NR7 ....159 A5
Adastral Pl PE37 ......153 C5
Addey Cl NR6 ....158 F5
Addison Cl
2 Coltishall NR12 ....54 C7
Feltwell IP26 ....98 F1
Addison Rd 2 NR31 ...170 C7
Adeane Mdw IP26 ....100 A4
Adelaide Ave PE30 ...147 B7
Adelaide St 5 NR2 ...162 B7
Admiral's Ct PE37 ....153 D3
Admiral's Dr
Sandringham PE31 ....28 A8
Sandringham PE35 ....140 F1
Admirals Dr PE13 ....152 D8
Admirals Jun Sch
IP24 ....176 E6
Admirals Quay NR31 ..169 C1
Admirals Way
Hethersett NR9 ....88 D8
Thetford IP24 ....176 E5
Admirals Wlk 7 NR9 ...86 C5
Admiralty Cl 3 PE38 ..172 B4
Admiralty Rd NR30 ...169 D1
Adventurers' Dro 81 B1
Aerodrome Cres NR7 ..163 D8
Afghan Pl NR3 ....158 C1
**Agricultural Experimental
Sta** PE12 ....41 C7
Agricultural Hall Plain
NR1 ....178 B3
Ailmar Cl PE30 ....147 A4
Ainsworth Cl 7 NR20 ..50 B3
Airedale Cl 4 NR3 ....158 C1
Airfield Rd NR8 ....63 C4
Airport Ind Est NR6 ..158 C6
Airstation La IP21 ...121 E2
Alan Ave NR31 ....94 C7
Alan Are NR15 ....89 D1
Alan Jarvis Way PE34 .144 D6
Alan Rd NR1 ....178 C1
Alban Rd PE30 ....148 C5
Alansfield 3 NR18 ....173 C5
Albany Cl NR31 ....169 C2
Albany Ct NR17 ....139 B7
Albany Rd
Great Yarmouth NR31 ....169 C2
Norwich NR3 ....162 D8

Albany Rd continued
Wisbech PE13 ....152 C6
Albemarle Rd
Great Yarmouth NR30 ....169 D5
Great Yarmouth NR31 ....170 C4
Norwich NR2 ....162 B3
Albert Myhill Cl 5
NR20 ....154 E6
Albert Pl NR1 ....163 A6
Albert Rd 17 NR30 ....169 D2
Albert Sq 18 NR30 ....169 D2
Albert St Holt NR25 ...137 B6
King's Lynn PE30 ....146 D5
Albert Terr NR2 ....162 C4
Albion Dr NR7 ....159 A3
Albion Rd
Great Yarmouth NR30 ....169 D4
Mundesley NR11 ....143 A7
Trunch NR28 ....22 E5
Albion St PE30 ....146 E5
Albion Way
Norwich NR1 ....178 C1
Wroxham/Hoveton
NR12 ....164 D6
Albourgh Loke 6 NR9 ..88 C7
Alburgh Rd NR13 .....107 D4
Alburgh with Denton Fst Sch
IP20 ....123 A5
Alby Croft Ctr* NR11 ...21 B5
Aldborough Prim Sch
NR11 ....21 B5
Aldborough Rd NR11 ...21 A3
Aldeby Rd NR34 ....110 F6
Alder Cl
Great Yarmouth NR31 ....94 C7
10 Mulbarton NR14 ......89 B3
North Walsham NR28 ....151 D7
Poringland NR14 ....90 D4
Alder Way NR8 ....155 B1
Alderman Peel High Sch
NR23 ....136 D4
Alderman Swindell Fst Sch
NR30 ....169 D8
Alderson Rd NR30 ....169 C5
Aldis Ct 8 NR14 ......154 D5
Aldis Rd NR13 ....166 B4
Aldiss Ave NR19 ......154 D3
Aldiss Cl PE37 ....153 D3
Aldryche Rd NR1 ......163 B8
Aldwick Rd 2 NR18 ...173 C6
Alex Moorhouse Way
NR5 ....156 A3
Alexander Cl 3
Caister-on-Sea NR30 ....168 C8
16 Long Stratton NR15 ..106 E3
Alexander Rd NR11 ....22 F8
Alexander Way 1 NR14 ..154 C6
Alexandra Cl PE31 ....140 C4
Alexandra Rd
Cromer NR27 ....139 B4
Great Yarmouth NR30 ....169 D4
Hunstanton PE36 ....132 C3
Mundesley NR11 ....143 A8
Norwich NR2 ....162 B6
Sheringham NR26 ....138 D6
Wisbech PE13 ....152 C5
Alexandra Way ....
Attleborough NR17 ......174 C6
Downham Market PE38 ...172 B3
Alford Gr NR7 ....159 A3
Alfred Nicholls Ct
NR3 ....158 D2
Alfred Rd NR27 ....139 A7
Alfred St NR1 ....91 F1
Algores Way PE13 ....152 B2
Alice Fisher Cres
PE30 ....146 F7
Alison Cl 1 NR13 ......73 F3
All Hallows' Hospl
NR35 ....109 B2
All Saints Dr PE30 ...175 B8
All Saints Gn NR1 .....178 B2
All Saints CE Prim Sch
NR21 ....32 C6
All Saints CE VA Prim Sch
IP22 ....120 B4
All Saints Cl
Briston NR24 ....142 D4
Runhall NR20 ....69 A5
2 Weybourne NR25 ....8 F5
Wicklewood NR18 ....87 B5
1 Wisbech PE14 ....59 A1
All Saints Dr PE30 ...148 C4
All Saints Gn NR1 .....178 B1
All Saints Rd NR14 ....90 D5
All Saints Sch NR12 ...24 C2
All Saints St 18 PE30 ..146 D4
All Saints Way
Beachamwell PE37 ....81 F8
Mundesley NR11 ....143 C6
All Saints Wlk 7 NR20 ..50 B3
Allanadale Rd NR14 ...162 C1
Allen Cl PE34 ....61 B8
Allen Meale Way 5
NR12 ....39 B4
Allenbrooks Way
NR18 ....173 C3
Allenby's Chase 16 PE12 ..41 B8
Allendale Rd NR18 ....168 E5
Allen's Ave NR7 ....159 A4
Allen's Cl 1 NR13 .....162 C4
Allens La NR11 ....162 C4
Allen's La NR7 ....159 A4
Allerton Cl NR7 ....159 B3
Allerton Rd NR7 ....159 B3
Alley The PE32 ....44 C1

Allison St NR10 ....36 A2
Allotment La NR25 ......9 B3
Allthorpe Rd 12 IP20 ..122 D2
Allwood Ave NR19 .....154 C5
Alma Ave NR30 ....144 D6
Alma Chase PE34 .....144 D6
Alma Rd
Great Yarmouth NR30 ....169 D2
Snettisham PE31 ....12 E4
Alma Terr NR3 ....162 D8
Almond Cl 2 NR29 .....57 D4
Almond Gr NR20 ......176 A1
Almond Rd NR31 ......170 B6
Alpha Rd NR31 ....170 C8
Alpington & Bergh Apton Sch
NR14 ....90 F4
Alston Cl 3 NR4 ....90 D5
Alston Rd NR6 ....157 E2
Altongate 1 NR13 .....132 D6
Ambassador Way
NR20 ....154 F4
Ambleside
13 Hethersett NR9 ....88 D8
5 Sculthorpe Airfield NR21 ..15 C2
Ambleside Cl NR5 .....161 C6
Ambrose Cl 1 NR5 ....161 A7
Ambrose Rd NR30 ....169 A1
Amderley Dr
6 Norwich NR4 ....89 C8
Norwich NR4 ....161 F1
Amelia Opie Way 2
PE24 ....176 D7
Ames Ct NR10 ....35 B2
Amethyst Cl NR31 .....94 C7
Amherst Cl 7 PE37 ....153 C3
Amhurst Gdns NR31 ...94 A5
Amsterdam NR31 ......158 D5
Amyson Ct IP25 ....84 C4
Anchor Cl Norwich NR3 ..178 D4
Sheringham NR26 ....138 E6
Anchor Ct NR3 ....169 C2
Anchor Dro PE38 ......112 B8
Anchor Quay NR2 .....178 A3
Anchor Rd
North Walsham NR28 ....151 F5
Sutton Bridge PE34 ......41 F8
Anchor St
Coltishall NR12 ....54 D6
3 Norwich NR3 ....162 F8
Tunstead NR12 ....38 B2
Anchor Way NR33 .....111 F1
Anchorage View PE31 ...3 B6
Anderson Cl
King's Lynn PE30 ....146 E7
Wisbech PE13 ....152 A5
Andrew Goodall Cl
NR19 ....154 C1
Andrews Pl PE36 ......132 D2
Angel Rd NR3 ....158 D1
Angel Rd Fst Sch NR3 ..158 E1
Angel Rd Mid Sch
NR3 ....158 D1
Angela Cl NR10 ....53 B3
Angela Cres 1 NR10 ...53 B3
Angela Rd NR10 ....53 B3
Angerstein Cl IP27 ....114 E8
Angle Rd PE14 ....78 A7
Anglia Way NR11 ......152 B2
Anglian Way 3 NR11 ...171 D5
Animal Adventure Pk*
NR13 ....93 A5
Anmer Cl NR5 ....161 C6
Anmer Rd PE31 ....28 D3
Anna Gurney Cl IP24 ...176 D6
Anna Sewell Cl 4 PE24 ..176 D7
Anne Bartholomew Rd
IP24 ....176 D6
Anne Boleyn Cl 4 IP24 ..176 D6
Anne Cl PE30 ....144 D6
Anne Rd PE12 ....41 B8
Anne Stannard Way
NR12 ....23 F4
Annes Cl PE30 ....148 D1
Annes Rd PE36 ....132 D1
Annis Hill NR35 ....124 C8
Anson Cl
5 Hethersett NR9 ....88 E8
Mundesley NR11 ....143 A7
Anson Rd
Great Yarmouth NR31 ....169 C2
Norwich NR6 ....158 B6
Anson's La PE14 ......122 A3
Anthony Curton Prim Sch
PE14 ....41 E4
Anthony Dr NR3 ....158 D1
Antingham & Southrepps Sch
NR11 ....22 B8
Antingham Dr NR28 ...151 D6
Antingham Hill NR28 ...22 B3
Antingham Rd NR7 ....159 D1
Apollo Wlk NR30 .....169 C5
Appledore Cl NR30 ....168 C6
Appledore La PE14 ....15 C2
Applegarth 1 NR18 ....88 A5
Applegarth 2 NR18 ....173 B4
Appleton Dr NR20 .....27 F5
Appleton Dro NR17 ....27 F5
Appletree Cl PE31 ....133 C6
Appletree La IP22 ....177 C5
Appleyard Cres NR4 ...161 F1
Apsley Cl NR5 ....161 F6
Apsley Rd NR10 ....53 B2
Arbor Rd NR27 ....139 B6
Arcade St NR1 ....178 B2
**Archbishop Sancroft High
Sch** IP20 ....122 D2

Archdale Cl PE33 ......43 F3
Archdale St 3 PE30 ...146 E5
Archer Cl NR6 ....159 A5
Archer La 46 F2
Archer's Ave 3 IP26 ...98 D1
Archer's Rd 3 NR30 ...169 C5
Archibald Rd NR12 ....24 A7
Arden Cl NR27 ....11 A3
Arden Gr NR10 ....157 E7
Arden Gr Fst Sch .....
Arderon Ct 2 NR2 .....162 B7
Ardleigh Cl 2 PE13 ...152 E5
Ardney Rise NR3 ....158 D3
Argyle St
King's Lynn PE30 ....146 E3
Norwich NR1 ....178 C2
Argyll Cres NR18 .....156 E8
Aries Ave PE13 ....152 E3
Arlington Cl NR17 .....174 E5
Arlington La NR2 ......162 C4
Arlington Pk Rd PE32 ..44 C3
Arlington Way PE24 ...176 E3
Armada Cl PE13 ......152 D8
Armes Cres NR2 ......162 A8
Armes St NR2 ....162 B7
Arminghall Cl NR5 ....162 A8
Arminghall La NR14 ....89 F8
Armitage Ct NR4 ......89 B8
Arms Pk Rd NR6 ....158 B6
Armstrong Dr NR19 ...154 E7
Armstrong Rd NR7 ....159 E2
**Armstrong Siddley Car &
Aero Mus*** PE38 ....79 B6
Army Rd NR11 ....157 E7
Arnfield La NR5 ....161 A5
Arnold Ave NR30 ......168 D8
Arnold Miller Rd NR1 ..162 F7
Arnott Ave NR31 ......170 D1
Arnott Rd NR25 ....137 D5
Arnside Cl 22 NR9 .....88 D8
Arthur Ave NR30 ......168 E8
Arthur Rd NR21 ....141 A4
Arthurton Rd NR10 ....54 A1
Artillery Sq 21 NR30 ..169 D4
Artillery St 11 PE30 ..171 D5
Arundel Cl NR20 ......49 C4
Arundel Dr PE30 ......148 C1
Arundel Rd
Great Yarmouth NR30 ....169 D1
Wymondham NR18 ....173 C6
Ascot Gdns NR19 .....154 D3
Ash Cl Brandon IP27 ...175 E3
Downham Market PE38 ...172 C6
10 Hethersett NR9 ....88 D8
Swaffham PE37 ....153 B3
Thetford IP24 ....176 A1
Ash Dr IP21 ....121 C6
Ash Gr King's Lynn PE30 ..148 D2
Norwich NR3 ....158 D2
2 West Winch PE33 ......43 E2
Ash La NR16 ....105 C5
Ash Rd PE33 ....63 B4
Ash Tree Cl NR17 .....174 C5
Ash Tree Rd NR17 .....74 D1
Ashburton Rd PE30 ...100 C5
Ashby Rd
Ashby St Mary NR14 ....91 C5
Repps with Bastwick
NR29 ....57 A3
Ashby St NR1 ....178 B1
Ashdale Pk
Old Hunstanton PE36 ....132 F8
Wisbech PE13 ....152 A5
Ashdown Cl NR13 .....166 A4
Ashfield Cl PE34 ......144 D6
Ashfield Hill PE30 .....147 C4
Ashfield Rd NR31 ......94 A5
Ashford Cl NR14 ......110 C7
Ashgrove 1 NR8 ....155 E2
Ashill VC Prim Sch
IP25 ....84 A7
Ashleigh Gdns NR18 ..173 E6
Ashleigh Inf Sch ....
NR18 ....173 D6
Ashley Ct PE30 ....49 D4
Ashtree Rd
Norwich NR5 ....157 B2
12 Watton IP25 ....84 E3
Ashwellthorpe Rd
NR16 ....88 D1
Ashwicken CE Fst Sch
PE32 ....44 F6
Ashwicken Rd PE32 ...45 C6
Ashwood Cl NR30 .....168 D6
Aslack Way PE36 ....2 E6
Aslacton Prim Sch
NR15 ....106 A1
Aspen Way NR7 ....159 A1
Aspland Rd NR1 ....178 C3
Association Way 2 NR7 ..72 D4
Astell Rd NR1 ....89 F8
Astley Cooper Pl NR15 ..90 E1
Astley Cres PE30 ......147 A5
Astley Prim Sch NR24 ..142 C4
Astley Rd
Great & Little Plumstead
NR13 ....73 B6
Little Plumstead NR13 ...146 F1
Norwich NR5 ....160 F8
Atbara Terr PE30 .....146 E2

Atcherley Sq PE31 .....30 B3
Atkinson Cl NR5 ......160 E8
Atling Ct NR17 ....174 F6
Atling Way NR17 .....174 F6
Atmer Cl 2 NR4 ....161 F1
Atthill Rd NR2 ....162 A7
Attleborough FC
NR17 ....174 E5
Attleborough High Sch
NR17 ....174 D6
Attleborough Jun Sch
NR17 ....174 E6
Attleborough Rd
Caston NR17 ....102 F8
Deopham NR18 ....86 E1
Great Ellingham NR17 ...103 F8
Little Ellingham NR17 ....86 A2
Morley NR17 ....87 A1
Attleborough Sta
NR17 ....174 E5
Attlee Way 4 NR19 ...154 C6
Audley Ct IP24 ....176 C7
Audley End IP21 ......120 F1
Audley St NR30 ....169 D5
Augusta Cl NR30 .....138 U/
Augustus Hare Dr 1 ....
PE13 ....161 C5
Aurania Ave NR1 .....162 D3
Auster Cl NR6 ....158 C4
Austin Fields PE30 ....146 E5
Austin Rd NR31 ....169 B3
Austin St
Hunstanton PE36 ....132 C5
King's Lynn PE30 ....146 D5
Autumn Cl 1 IP24 .....176 F4
Autumn Dr NR5 ....161 B8
Avebury Rd NR4 ......162 B1
Avenue Cl PE38 ....79 E1
Avenue Fst & Mid Schs
NR2 ....162 B5
Avenue Rd
Great Yarmouth NR31 ....170 D6
High Kelling NR25 ....8 E2
Hunstanton PE36 ....132 C4
King's Lynn PE30 ....146 F4
Norwich NR3 ....162 D6
Wymondham NR18 ....173 C3
Avenue The
Brome & Oakley IP23 ....130 D3
Brookville IP26 ....99 A7
Brumstead NR12 ....24 A1
Dersingham PE35 ....140 E1
Hemsby NR29 ....167 A7
Holkham NR23 ....5 A4
4 Necton PE37 ....65 F4
Northrepps NR27 ....139 D3
Sheringham NR26 ....138 E7
Snettisham PE31 ....12 D4
Wiggenhall St Germans
PE34 ....61 A8
Wroxham NR12 ....164 C2
Wroxham/Hoveton
NR12 ....164 B4
Wymondham NR18 ......87 D7
Avenues The
Langley with Hardley
NR14 ....91 F4
Norwich NR1 ....161 E4
Thurton NR14 ....91 D3
Avian Way NR7 ....72 D4
Avon Rd PE30 ....148 C2
Avondale Cl NR13 .....74 A2
Avondale Rd NR13 ....170 D3
Avonmouth Rd 2 NR3 ..158 C1
Aylesbury Cl NR3 .....158 D2
Aylmer Dr PE14 ....60 C8
Aylsham Cres NR3 ....158 D2
Aylsham High Sch ......
NR11 ....150 D7
Aylsham Rd
Burgh & Tuttington NR11 ..36 E5
Cawston NR10 ....35 B2
Felmingham NR28 ....37 A8
North Walsham NR28 .....22 C1
Oulton NR11 ....158 C1
Swanton Abbott NR10 ...37 C4
Aylsham Sta NR11 ....150 D5
Ayre Way PE30 ....147 D8
Ayton Rd NR18 ....173 D3
Ayton Rd Ind Est
NR18 ....173 D3

Babingley Cl 5 PE33 ...61 D6
Bachelor's La NR28 ...23 E2
Back Chapel La NR31 ..170 D6
Back Dro Upwell PE14 ...77 D4
Welney PE14 ....95 D4
Back La Barford NR9 ...69 F2
Beeston with Bittering
PE32 ....48 C2
Bircham PE31 ....14 B3
Blakeney NR25 ....7 C7
Burgh Castle NR31 ......94 A8
Burnham Market PE31 ...135 D2
Burnham Thorpe PE31 ...4 D4
Buxton with Lammas
NR10 ....53 E8

Back La *continued*
Castle Acre PE32 46 F2
Catfield NR29 56 C8
Cawston NR10 35 B2
Dereham NR20 68 A8
Diss IP22 120 D3
East Rudham PE31 30 B7
East Ruston NR12 24 A3
Elsing NR20 50 F3
Happisburgh NR12 23 F2
Hempstead NR25 19 E7
Hethersett NR9 88 E8
Kenninghall NR16 119 A5
Litcham PE32 48 A4
Lound NR32 94 C2
Martham NR29 57 D5
Mattishall NR20 68 E6
Mileham PE32 48 C6
North Elmham NR20 49 E7
Outwell PE14 77 E7
Potter Heigham NR29 56 E7
Quidenham NR16 119 A8
Rackheath NR13 54 D1
Ringland NR8 52 C1
Rollesby NR29 57 D3
Roughton NR11 21 D8
Roydon PE32 28 A1
St Mary, South Elmham otherwise Homersfield IP20 123 B4
Scole IP21 121 A1
Scoulton NR9 85 E3
South Creake NR21 15 E6
Stanfield NR20 48 F8
Upton with Fishley NR13 166 C8
Walsingham NR22 16 F7
Wereham PE33 80 E4
West Beckham NR25 9 B3
West Caister NR30 168 A4
West Winch PE33 43 E2
Wymondham NR18 173 C4
Back Mkt La NR29 167 B7
Back Mundesley Rd NR11 22 F8
Back Path 1 NR29 58 B6
Back Pier Plain NR31 170 D4
Back Rd Brockdish IP21 131 B8
East Ruston NR12 38 F6
Elm PE14 77 A8
Pentney PE32 63 C8
Somerton NR29 57 F6
Wisbech PE14 77 A7
Wood Dalling NR11 34 D6
Yelverton NR14 90 F5
Back St Binham NR21 6 E2
Fakenham NR21 141 B3
Garboldisham IP22 128 A8
Gayton PE32 45 C5
Harpley PE31 29 D5
Horsham St Faith NR10 53 D1
Lakenheath IP27 113 E1
Litcham PE32 48 A4
Mundesley NR11 143 C5
Reepham NR10 149 B4
South Creake NR21 15 D6
Tittleshall PE32 48 B7
Trunch NR28 22 E5
Back Terr PE37 153 B5
Backwood La
Howe NR15 90 C2
Shotesham NR15 107 F8
Bacon Rd NR4 161 F5
Baconsthorpe Castle (English Heritage)* NR25 9 A1
Bacton Cl PE30 148 D3
Bacton Rd Bacton NR12 23 D5
North Walsham NR28 151 D6
Norwich NR3 158 B2
Paston NR28 143 E2
Witton NR28 23 C1
Bacton-on-Sea Fst Sch NR12 23 E4
Bader Cl PE30 147 D4
Badger Cl NR14 89 A2
Badgers Brook Rd NR8 155 F2
Bagge Rd PE30 147 A5
Bagthorpe Rd PE31 30 A7
Bailey Cl
4 Hethersett NR9 88 D7
6 Martham NR29 57 D5
Bailey La PE34 145 E7
Bailey Rd NR27 139 B5
Bailey St PE32 46 F2
Bailiwick The 3 NR16 118 C5
Bainard Rise NR15 107 C6
Bainards Cl NR18 173 B6
Baines Rd 4 PE30 146 D1
Baines Way 2 NR5 160 E8
Baird Way IP24 176 C7
Baker Cl
King's Lynn PE30 146 D1
North Walsham NR28 151 D3
Baker La 3 PE30 146 D4
Baker St NR31 170 D5
Bakers La NR35 109 A2
Baker's Rd NR13 75 A1
Bakers Rd NR3 162 D8
Bakery Cl NR24 142 E3
Bakery La NR9 51 A5
Balderston Ct NR3 178 B4
Baldock Cl 1 NR16 105 F5
Baldock Dr PE30 147 B8
Baldric Rd NR8 155 D1
Baldwin Cl 4 PE13 152 D5
Baldwin Rd PE30 147 C6
Baldwins Cl NR24 142 D4
Baldwins Dro 4 PE14 77 F6
Bale Rd Brinton NR24 18 C7
Hindringham NR21 17 E7
Balfour Rd 4 NR27 10 A5
Balfour St 4 NR3 162 F8
Baliol Rd NR31 170 C5
Ball's La NR21 17 D5
Ballygate NR34 110 C1
Balmoral Ave NR30 169 D7
Balmoral Cl PE31 140 D3
Balmoral Cres PE31 133 C5
Balmoral Rd PE30 147 C7
Balmoral W PE31 140 D3
Bambers La PE14 59 C2
Bancroft Cl 7 NR14 89 F4
Banham Barn Craft* NR16 119 C6
Banham Dr NR20 50 B2
Banham Marshalls Coll NR16 119 E7
Banham Rd NR16 119 B5
Banham Zoo* NR16 119 C6
Banham's La NR35 108 B2
Banister Way NR18 173 A5
Bank Dr PE13 152 A7
Bank Loke 6 NR28 151 C5
Bank Rd PE31 140 C4
Bank Side PE34 146 C5
Bank St Norwich NR2 178 B3
Pulham Market IP21 121 E5
Bankside PE31 133 B6
Banningham Ct NR28 151 A4
Banningham Rd NR11 150 D8
Bannister Cl NR17 174 C6
Bannister's Row PE13 152 B7
Banters La NR34 124 F6
Banyard Pl 5 NR19 154 D5
Banyards Pl PE33 61 D4
Baptist Rd PE14 77 D4
Bar Dro PE14 77 B8
Barberry Cl 5 NR8 155 B2
Barber's La
Bedingham NR35 108 B2
Fakenham NR21 141 E4
Barbers Yd 1 NR17 104 D2
Barclay Gn NR7 159 D1
Barclay Rd NR7 159 E1
Bard Hill NR25 8 B6
Bardolph Pl PE34 61 D1
Bardolph's Way PE33 62 C6
Bardwell Rd
Barningham IP31 127 C3
Fakenham Magna IP24 126 D3
Stanton IP31 127 B1
Bardyke Bank PE14 77 F4
Barford Cty Prim Sch NR9 69 F2
Barford Rd
Marlingford NR9 69 E3
Sheringham NR26 138 D7
Topcroft NR35 107 E2
Bargate Ct NR3 178 B4
Barham Ct NR31 170 D5
Barham's La NR16 105 D4
Barker St NR2 162 C8
Barker Way 5 NR13 72 D6
Barker's Dro PE33 81 A3
Barker's La
Norwich NR7 159 A5
Old Buckenham NR17 104 B2
Barkis Rd NR30 169 D1
Barley Way
Attleborough NR17 174 B3
Thetford IP24 176 D6
Barleycroft NR29 167 B7
Barleyfield Rd 8 NR10 53 A3
Barn Cl
2 Hopton on Sea NR31 171 E5
1 Lingwood NR13 74 A3
Barn Hill NR13 73 E2
Barn La
Gressenhall NR19 49 B2
Mautby NR29 75 E6
Barn Mdw NR14 163 B2
Barn Rd Docking PE31 134 F4
Norwich NR2 178 A4
Barnaby Cl 5 NR19 154 C3
Barnard Ave NR30 169 D7
Barnard Cl 5 NR14 89 F4
Barnard Cres NR30 169 C7
Barnard Rd NR5 160 E8
Barnards La PE33 61 D6
Barnards Rd NR28 38 A5
Barnby Rd NR10 37 B2
Barnes Cl
Brandon IP27 175 A2
Norwich NR7 159 D2
Barnes' Rd IP21 121 E5
Barnesdale Rd 5 NR4 89 E8
Barney Rd NR21 17 F2
Barnfield Rd NR12 39 E2
Barnham Broom Prim Sch NR9 69 C2
Barnham Broom Rd
East Tuddenham NR20 69 D5
Wymondham NR18 173 A7
Barnham CE Prim Sch IP24 125 E5
Barnham Rd IP24 126 B6
Barningham CE VC Prim Sch IP31 127 C3
Barningham Pl NR11 20 C5
Barningham Rd
Gresham NR11 20 D8
Stanton IP31 127 C1
Barns The NR16 105 C4
Barnwell Rd PE30 147 B6
Barolphs Ct 1 NR8 155 B2
Barondole La
Alburgh IP20 122 E8
Topcroft NR35 107 E2
Baron's Cl NR21 141 C4
Baron's Hall La NR21 141 D4
Barr Dr IP27 113 E2
Barrack Rd
Great Yarmouth NR30 169 D1
Norwich NR1 163 B7
Barrack St NR3 178 C4
Barrett Cl PE30 147 E5
Barrett Rd Holt NR25 137 D7
Norwich NR1 162 E1
Barrett-Lennard Rd NR10 53 A4
Barri Cl NR14 90 C3
Barrow Cl NR3 157 F1
Barroway Dro PE38 78 E6
Barrow's Cnr IP24 125 A4
Barrows Hole La PE32 65 E7
Barsham Dr PE30 148 E1
Barsham Rd NR21 17 A5
Bartle Ct NR10 149 C5
Barton Broad Nature Reserve* NR12 56 A8
Barton Cl
North Walsham NR28 151 A4
Swaffham PE37 153 C2
Barton Ct PE30 147 D5
Barton Rd
Ashmanhaugh NR12 38 D1
Coltishall NR10 37 B2
Wisbech PE13 152 A4
Barton Way
6 Norwich NR1 163 B5
Ormesby St Margaret NR29 167 B3
Barton's La PE32 48 A8
Barwick Rd PE31 14 E6
Bases La NR23 136 C6
Basey Rd NR13 72 E8
Basham St IP22 177 B4
Basil Rd PE33 80 A3
Bassingham Rd NR3 158 B2
Batchcroft Cl 6 PE38 172 C6
Batchelor Dr NR21 15 C2
Bately Ave NR31 170 D1
Bateman Cl 3 NR5 160 F7
Bates Gn NR5 161 C8
Bates La IP22 119 D2
Bates's Dro CB6 95 D1
Bath Ave NR20 154 F5
Bath Hill 7 NR30 169 D3
Bath Hill Terr NR30 169 D3
Bath Hills Rd NR35 123 E8
Bath Rd
West Dereham PE33 80 D5
Wisbech PE13 152 C7
Bathurst Rd 2 NR2 162 B5
Batterby Gn
Fakenham NR21 141 A3
Hempton NR21 31 C8
Battery Rd NR30 170 D8
Battlesea Hill IP21 131 E2
Bawburgh Cl NR5 156 D1
Bawburgh La NR5 156 D1
Bawburgh Prim Sch NR9 160 B6
Bawburgh Rd NR9 70 B5
Bawdeswell Prim Sch NR20 50 E7
Bawdeswell Rd NR20 50 C7
Bawsey Ctry Pk* PE32 44 D6
Baxter Cl 2 Hingham NR9 86 C5
3 Wisbech PE13 152 E6
Baxter Ct NR3 158 B3
Baxter Rd NR9 86 C5
Baxter Row NR19 154 D4
Baxter's La NR15 107 F8
Bayes La NR16 106 C6
Bayfield Ave 3 NR19 154 C3
Bayfield Cl
1 Ixworth NR9 69 F2
King's Lynn PE30 147 D4
Baynard's La IP22 129 D7
Bayse's La NR24 18 C5
Bayspole Rd 5 NR15 106 E3
Beach Cl Hemsby NR29 167 E3
Mundesley NR11 143 C6
Overstrand NR27 11 A4
Beach Dr NR29 167 E4
Beach La NR25 8 E6
Beach Rd Bacton NR12 23 E5
Caister-on-Sea NR30 168 E5
Cley next the Sea NR25 7 E8
Cromer NR27 139 B7
Eccles on Sea NR12 24 E4
3 Great Yarmouth NR31 170 D4
Happisburgh NR12 24 C5
Hemsby NR29 167 C7
Hemsby NR29 167 D3
Holme next the Sea PE36 1 F6
Hopton on Sea NR31 171 E4
Lessingham NR12 24 E3
Mundesley NR11 143 C6
Runton NR27 10 C5
Salthouse NR25 8 C6
Sea Palling NR12 40 A6
Sheringham NR26 138 E7
Snettisham PE31 12 A4
Wells-next-the-Sea NR23 136 C7
Winterton-on-Sea NR29 58 B6
Beach Terr Rd PE36 132 C4
Beacon Hill PE31 135 C2
Beacon Hill La PE34 144 A6
Beacon Hill Rd PE31 135 C1
Beacon Rd NR11 11 F1
Beaconsfield Rd
Great Yarmouth NR30 169 D6
Norwich NR3 162 E8
Bears Cl 7 NR9 86 C4
Bears La NR9 86 C5
Bear's La PE37 153 B5
Bears Rd NR28 143 D2
Beatrice Ave NR19 154 D4
Beatrice Cl 6 NR28 151 C6
Beatrice Rd
Norwich NR1 163 A6
Wisbech PE13 152 D7
Beatty Cl
Great Yarmouth NR30 169 D8
Thetford IP24 176 E5
Beatty Rd
Great Yarmouth NR30 169 D8
Norwich NR4 162 B1
Beauchamp Cl
1 Caister-on-Sea NR30 168 D7
Chedgrave NR14 91 F2
Beauchamp Rd 2 NR14 92 A2
Beaumont Pl 1 NR2 162 C4
Beaumont Rd NR5 157 B1
Beaumont Way PE30 147 C5
Beaupre Ave PE14 77 F7
Beavans Ct 8 NR31 169 B4
Beavor La IP27 175 C4
Beccles Mus* NR34 110 C1
Beccles Rd
Aldeby NR34 110 F4
Aldeby, Wheatacre, Burgh St Peter NR34 111 B4
Belton with Browston NR31 94 A5
Bungay NR35 124 B8
Carlton Colville NR33 111 F1
Fritton & St Olaves NR31 93 E3
Great Yarmouth NR31 170 A5
Great Yarmouth NR31 170 C7
Haddiscoe NR14 110 E7
Hales NR14 109 E7
Loddon NR14 92 A1
Raveningham NR14 110 A7
Thurlton NR14 92 F1
Beccles Sta NR34 110 D1
Becclesgate NR19 154 D6
Beck Ave NR29 167 A4
Beck Cl 5 NR25 8 F5
Beck La
Burgh & Tuttington NR11 36 E6
Horsham St Faith & Newton St Faith NR10 53 D2
Beck St IP22 127 E3
Beck The Feltwell IP26 98 E1
Kenninghall NR16 119 A5
Beck View 3 IP20 122 D2
Beck Way NR14 91 F1
Becketswell Rd NR18 173 B3
Beckett Cl 6 PE30 148 C4
Becketts Ct NR18 173 B6
Beckmeadow Way NR11 143 C5
Becks Fur 2 NR8 155 E2
Becks Gn La NR34 124 F4
Beckside NR10 53 A2
Bedding La NR3 178 B4
Bede Cl PE30 148 C4
Bedford Dr PE30 148 B1
Bedford Row PE14 41 A4
Bedford St
Norwich NR2 178 B3
Wisbech PE13 152 C6
Bedingfield Rd 6 NR20 50 B3
Beech Ave
Attleborough NR17 174 C4
King's Lynn PE30 148 D2
7 Marham PE33 63 B4
Sheringham NR26 138 D5
Taverham NR8 155 B1
Beech Cl 1 Gresham NR11 9 E1
High Kelling NR25 8 E2
6 Loddon NR14 92 A1
Scole IP21 130 C5
Swaffham PE37 153 C4
Thetford IP24 176 B2
Wymondham NR18 173 D6
Beech Cres 6 PE33 43 E2
Beech Dr
East Dereham NR19 154 E1
Norwich NR6 158 C4
Norwich NR2 162 B4
Norwich NR1 163 A8
Strumpshaw NR13 73 F3
Beech Drift PE31 140 D3
Beech La NR29 75 C8
Beech Rd Beetley NR20 49 D4
Downham Market PE38 172 B6
King's Lynn PE30 146 E3
Wroxham/Hoveton NR12 164 D3
Beech Rise 23 NR31 94 C7
Beech Way
Brundall NR13 165 C3
Dickleburgh IP21 121 C1
Beech Wlk NR14 90 D5
Beechamwell Rd PE33 81 B8
Beechbank NR2 162 B4
Beechbank Dr 6 NR13 72 D6
Beechcroft NR5 156 F1
Beecheno Rd NR5 161 C8
Beeches Cl NR6 158 E4
Beeches La NR9 86 E6
Beeches The 1 NR20 68 E6
Beechey Cl PE38 172 C2
Beechfields IP27 175 F4
Beeching Cl 1 NR1 162 E1
Beeching Rd NR1 162 E2
Beechlands NR8 155 B1
Beechlands Pk NR11 22 B7
Beechwood Ave
Aylmerton NR11 10 A3
18 Watton IP25 84 D3
Beechwood Ct PE33 61 E5
Beechwood Cl NR18 173 D1
Beechwood Dr NR7 159 E1
Beechwood Rd
Hemsby NR29 167 A8
Wisbech PE13 152 D7
Beechwoods NR6 158 D5
Beehive Yd IP22 177 C4
Beeleigh Way NR30 168 C7
Bee-Orchid Way NR14 91 C7
Beerlick's Loke NR14 73 B1
Beeston Hall Sch NR27 9 F5
Beeston La
Barton Turf NR12 38 D1
Beeston St Andrew NR12 159 B8
Fransham NR19 66 B8
Beeston Prim Sch PE32 48 C2
Beeston Rd
Beeston with Bittering PE32 48 D1
Great Dunham PE32 66 A8
Mileham PE32 48 D5
Sheringham NR26 138 E7
Beevor Rd NR30 170 E7
Begdale Rd PE14 59 A1
Beighton Rd NR13 166 A2
Bek Cl NR4 161 E2
Belaugh Gn La
Belaugh NR12 164 A8
Coltishall NR12 54 E6
Belaugh La NR12 55 A7
Belaugh Rd NR12 164 C6
Belgrave Ave PE36 132 C6
Belgrave Gdns NR19 154 E3
Bell Cl
13 Bawdeswell NR20 50 E7
East Dereham NR19 154 C5
Little Snoring NR21 17 B3
Norwich NR6 157 F6
Taverham NR8 156 E8
Bell La Rocklands NR17 103 B8
Saham Toney IP25 84 C4
Salhouse NR13 164 B1
Bell Mdw 1 Hingham NR9 86 C5
9 Martham NR29 57 D5
Bell Rd
Barnham Broom NR9 69 B2
Grimston PE32 28 C1
Norwich NR3 158 E1
Rocklands NR17 103 B8
Bell St IP26 98 E1
Bellacre Cl IP22 177 E4
Bellamy Way NR14 90 C4
Bellamy's La
Burnham Norton PE31 135 C5
West Walton PE14 59 A8
Bellands Way 4 IP23 130 C1
Bellmere Way IP25 84 C4
Bellomonte Cres NR8 156 F8
Bellrope Cl 5 NR18 173 D5
Bellrope La
Roydon IP22 129 D7
Wymondham NR18 173 D5
Bell's Dro Littleport CB6 95 E2
Runcton Holme PE33 61 C5
Bells La PE14 128 C4
Bell's Marsh Rd NR31 170 D5
Bell's Mdw 2 PE37 66 A4
Bells Rd NR31 170 D4
Bellview Cl NR24 142 B4
Bellville Cres NR1 178 C1
Belmore Cl NR7 163 E8
Belmore Rd NR7 163 F8
Beloe Ave 4 NR5 161 A7
Beloe Cres PE30 146 D1
Belseybridge Rd NR35 108 F3
Belsize Cl 4 PE38 172 B4
Belsize Rd NR1 163 B7
Belstead Ave NR30 168 D5
Belt Rd NR13 73 C7
Belvedere Pl 3 NR4 162 A3
Belvidere Rd NR30 169 D5
Belvoir St NR2 162 B6
Ben Culey Dr IP24 176 C5
Benbow Cl 6 NR9 88 E8
Benbow Rd IP24 176 F6
Bendish Ave NR31 170 D2
Bendish Way NR5 160 E7
Benedict Cl PE34 145 F5
Benedict Rd 10 NR12 55 E4
Benets View 3 NR28 151 E5
Bengey's Rd 7 PE37 65 F4
Bennett Cl
Hunstanton PE36 132 D2
3 Watlington PE33 61 D5
Bennett Rd NR20 50 B2
Bennett St PE38 172 A5
Bennington's La
Aylmerton NR11 138 F1
East Beckham NR11 9 D2
Benn's La PE34 144 C5
Ben's La PE33 80 E4
Bensley Cl NR13 166 C4
Bensley Rd
1 Martham NR29 57 D5
Norwich NR2 162 A4
Bentinck Way 2 PE34 146 C5
Bentley Rd NR16 105 F4
Bentley Way NR3 158 C4

Bentons Way NR10 53 B8
Ber St NR1 178 B1
Beresford Rd
Caister-on-Sea NR30 168 E4
Great Yarmouth NR30 169 D7
Holt NR25 137 C5
Bergamot Cl IP24 176 F4
Bergen Way PE30 146 F8
Bergh Apton Rd NR14 90 F4
Bermondsey Pl E 19 NR30 169 D4
Bermondsey Pl S 18 NR30 169 D4
Bermondsey Pl W 17 NR30 169 D4
Bernard Cl
High Kelling NR25 8 E2
11 New Rackheath NR13 72 E7
Bernard Cres PE36 132 D6
Bernard Rd
Cromer NR27 139 A7
Great Yarmouth NR31 170 D2
Berners Cl NR3 158 B1
Berners St NR3 158 B1
Berney Arms Sta NR30 93 D8
Berney Arms Windmill (English Heritage)* NR30 93 E7
Bernham Rd NR6 157 E6
Berrington Rd NR6 157 F6
Berry Cl NR31 93 F6
Berry Hall Rd NR12 38 E1
Berryfields NR13 165 C5
Berry's La NR9 69 D6
Bertie Rd NR3 158 C1
Bertie Ward Way NR19 154 F2
Bessemer Rd NR4 162 D1
Bessemer Way NR31 169 B1
Besthorpe Carr NR17 105 A6
Besthorpe Rd NR17 174 E5
Bestthorpe Rd NR16 105 A5
Bethel St NR2 178 A3
Beulah St PE30 147 B6
Bevan Cl
Carleton Rode NR16 105 C4
Norwich NR5 161 B6
Beveridge Way PE33 43 E4
Beverley Cl NR5 161 E6
Beverley Rd
Brundall NR13 165 B4
Norwich NR5 161 E6
Beverley Way
Clenchwarton PE34 145 E5
Taverham NR8 156 F8
Bevis Way PE30 147 B7
Bewfeld Rd 4 NR5 160 E8
Bewick Cl
11 Great Yarmouth NR31 94 C8
5 Snettisham PE31 12 E5
Bewit Rd NR7 159 D4
Bexfield Rd NR20 33 C4
Bexwell Rd
Downham Market PE38 172 D5
Ryston PE38 172 F5
Bickley Cl NR17 174 F7
Bidewell Cl NR8 157 B7
Bidwell Rd NR13 72 E8
Bier La IP22 128 F5
Big Back La
Chedgrave NR14 91 F2
1 Loddon NR14 92 A2
Big Row NR34 109 F2
Big Yd PE36 2 A3
Big Yd The PE36 132 E7
Biggin Hill Way IP25 85 A3
Biggotts La NR15 108 E7
Biggs Rd PE14 59 D4
Bignold Fst Sch NR2 178 A2
Bignold Mid Sch NR2 178 A2
Bignold Rd NR3 158 A2
Bilberry Cl 5 NR17 174 B5
Bilbys NR14 110 B6
Bill Todd Way NR8 155 C2
Billing Cl NR6 158 F5
Billingford Rd
1 Bawdeswell NR20 50 E7
Bintree NR20 33 B1
Bilney La NR10 155 E8
Bilney Rd Beetley NR20 49 B4
East Winch PE32 45 B1
Pentney PE32 63 C8
Bingles Turn NR10 53 B7
Binham Rd
Field Dalling NR25 7 A1
Hindringham NR21 17 E8
4 King's Lynn PE30 148 C3
Langham NR25 7 A4
Warham NR23 6 A4
Bintree Rd NR20 50 B8
Birbeck Cl PE30 148 B2
Birbeck Rd NR1 162 E2
Birch Cl
East Dereham NR19 154 C4
Little Melton NR9 160 D2
North Walsham NR28 151 D6
6 Snettisham PE31 12 E4
Birch Ct NR7 159 D4
Birch Dr
Attleborough NR17 174 C3
Roydon PE32 28 A2
Birch Gr
Sheringham NR26 138 D4
West Winch PE33 43 E2
Wisbech PE13 59 B1
Birch Rd Gayton PE32 45 C6
11 Hethersett NR9 88 D8
Birch Tree Cl 7 PE30 146 E4
Birch Way NR14 108 F6
Bircham Newton Training Ctr PE31 14 C5
Bircham Rd
Docking PE31 134 C4
Reepham NR10 149 C5
Snettisham PE31 13 A4
Stanhoe PE31 14 E7
Birches The PE30 148 D4
Birchfield Gdns NR14 89 B3
Birchfield La NR14 89 B3
Birchfield Rd PE38 78 E3
Birchgrove Rd PE30 147 C4
Birchwood 4 NR7 72 D3
Birchwood St 5 PE30 146 E6
Birchwood Way PE38 172 B6
Bird View Sq 1 IP26 98 E1
Birdcage Wlk PE30 146 D3
Birds Cnr IP25 67 E4
Birds Rd NR28 151 B3
Birkbeck Cl NR14 90 B5
Birkbeck Way NR7 163 F7
Birkdale NR4 162 A2
Birkin Cl 3 NR16 105 F5
Birtles Way NR13 166 C3
Biscay Gdns NR30 168 C6
Bishop Bonners Cottage Mus* NR19 154 D5
Bishop Bridge Rd NR1 163 A6
Bishop Herbert Cl NR20 69 B8
Bishop Rise 3 NR8 155 E2
Bishopgate NR1 178 C3
Bishop's Cl NR7 163 D5
Bishop's Rd
Hunstanton PE36 132 C2
King's Lynn PE30 147 B4
Bishops Wlk 6 NR31 171 D5
Bishoptyne Ave 1 NR19 154 F3
Bishy Barnebee Way NR5 160 F6
Bittering St NR20 49 C4
Bittern Cl IP24 176 D1
Bittern Cres NR12 38 F1
Bittern Rd NR29 57 D3
Bixley Cl NR5 161 D6
Black Bear La PE13 152 F7
Black Drif PE37 66 A4
Black Dro
Downham West PE38 79 B6
Feltwell PE38 97 F2
Fincham PE33 80 D7
Marshland St James PE14 60 D4
Stow Bardolph PE34 78 E8
Black Dyke Rd IP26 113 E7
Black Horse Cl NR19 67 B7
Black Horse Dro CB6 96 E2
Black Horse Rd
Clenchwarton PE34 145 C4
Runhall NR9 68 F1
Black Mill La NR15 121 A7
Black Moor Rd IP25 67 D2
Black St Hemsby NR29 58 B6
Martham NR29 57 D5
Blackbarn Rd NR16 120 D8
Blackberry Gr NR27 10 C4
Blackberry Hall La NR11 11 D1
Blackbird Ave IP27 175 F3
Blackbird Cl 17 NR31 94 C8
Blackdale Mid Sch NR4 161 D4
Blackdike Dro IP27 112 F5
Blackdyke Cl 8 IP26 98 D1
Blackford PE30 147 D8
Blackfriars' Rd NR30 169 D2
Blackfriars Rd
King's Lynn PE30 146 E5
8 Wisbech PE13 152 C5
Blackfriars St
King's Lynn PE30 146 D4
Norwich NR3 178 B4
Blackhills Cnr NR13 73 C7
Blackhorse Cl 9 NR20 50 E7
Blackhorse Mdw 10 NR20 50 E7
Blackhorse St 1 NR2 162 C7
Blackhorse Yd NR23 136 C6
Blackmoor Row IP25 67 D1
Blackslough La NR16 119 D7
Blacksmith La IP24 125 E6
Blacksmiths Cl NR20 33 B6
Blacksmiths La NR16 106 B8
Blacksmith's La PE33 81 B8
Blacksmiths La
Happisburgh NR12 24 B6
Hindringham NR21 17 E7
Blacksmith's La NR15 107 A2
Blacksmith's Loke NR32 94 C2
Blacksmith's Row 1 PE32 45 C6
Blacksmiths Way NR6 158 E5
Blackthorn Ave NR25 137 C7
Blackthorn Cl
Diss IP22 177 F5
Norwich NR6 158 D4
3 Thetford IP24 176 F4
Blackthorn Dr 3 NR19 154 C4
Blackthorn Rd
Attleborough NR17 174 B5
King's Lynn PE30 148 C3
Wymondham NR18 173 D4
Blackwall Reach NR31 170 D5
Blackwater Cnr NR11 36 F5
Blackwater La
Great Witchingham NR9 51 C6
Heydon NR11 34 D8
Blackwell Ave NR7 159 A3
Blake Cl PE32 28 A1
Blake Dr NR31 170 A7
Blake Rd NR30 169 D7
Blakeney CE Prim Sch NR25 7 D6
Blakeney Cl NR4 161 E2
Blakeney Long La NR25 7 C4
Blakeney Rd
Letheringsett with Glandford NR25 7 F2
Morston NR25 7 B6
Blakeney Short La NR25 7 C3
Blakes Ct NR3 158 F3
Blakestone Dr NR7 163 D7
Bland Rd NR5 161 B6
Blatchford Way PE31 133 B5
Blenheim Ave 4 NR29 57 D4
Blenheim Cl
12 Long Stratton NR15 106 E3
Norwich NR7 159 B5
Blenheim Cres
Beeston with Bittering PE32 48 D2
Griston IP25 85 A2
Norwich NR7 159 B5
Tittleshall PE32 48 A7
Blenheim Dr NR17 174 E4
Blenheim Pk Sch NR21 15 C3
Blenheim Rd
King's Lynn PE30 147 C8
Norwich NR7 159 B5
Sculthorpe Airfield NR21 15 C3
Blenheim Way
Emneth PE14 152 E2
2 Roydon IP22 129 D7
5 Watton IP25 84 E3
Blick Cl 5 PE33 43 F2
Blickling Cl 1 PE30 148 F1
Blickling Hall (National Trust)* NR11 35 F7
Blickling Rd
Blickling NR11 150 A8
Norwich NR6 158 C5
Bligh Cl NR14 90 D5
Blind Dick's La NR22 16 E7
Blind La
Castle Acre PE32 46 F1
Hockering NR9 51 A2
Honingham NR9 69 F5
Horsham St Faith NR10 53 D1
Mattishall NR20 69 A7
Blithe Mdw Ct NR7 159 C3
Blithemeadow Dr NR7 159 C3
Blithewood Gdns NR7 159 C3
Blo' Norton Rd IP22 128 C7
Blocka Rd NR32 93 F2
Blofield Cnr Rd NR13 73 B6
Blofield Loke NR12 164 E6
Blofield Prim Sch NR13 165 E7
Blofield Rd
Brundall NR13 165 E3
Lingwood & Burlingham NR13 73 F3
Blofields Loke NR11 150 C6
Blomefield Rd
Diss IP22 177 D4
Norwich NR3 158 D2
Bloodgate Hill NR21 15 D6
Bloodhills Rd NR29 57 F5
Bloodslat La NR12 23 D4
Bloomfield Rd NR30 170 E7
Blooms Turn NR28 22 E5
Bloomstile La NR25 8 B6
Bloomstiles NR25 8 B6
Blowlands La NR26 138 B5
Blue Boar La NR7 159 D3
Blue Doors Loke NR31 94 C3
Blue Marshes Nature Reserve* NR13 55 E3
Bluebell Cl
Attleborough NR17 174 B5
4 East Dereham NR19 154 C4
Thetford IP24 176 F4
Bluebell Cres NR4 161 D2
Bluebell Gdns NR23 136 E5
Bluebell Rd
Mulbarton NR14 89 B3
North Walsham NR28 151 D6
Norwich NR4 161 D3
Bluebell Way 19 NR31 94 C6
Bluebell Wlk IP27 175 A2
Bluegate La NR29 75 B5
Bluestone Cres NR21 15 D6
Bluestone La NR21 15 D7
Bluestone Rd NR21 15 D6
Blundeston Rd NR32 111 F8
Blundeville Manor 6 NR15 89 C1
Blunt's Cnr NR23 5 B2
Blyth Cres NR26 138 D6
Blyth Jex Sch NR3 158 E2
Blyth Rd NR3 158 D2
Boadicea Cl 1 IP24 176 D7
Boal Quay PE30 146 D4
Boal St PE30 146 D4
Boat Dyke La NR13 166 D4
Boat Dyke Rd NR13 166 B8
Boathouse La NR32 111 F3
Bob Carter Leisure Ctr NR8 157 A8
Bodleian Ct NR31 170 B2
Boileau Ave 6 NR16 105 F5
Boileau Cl 1 NR4 89 E8
Boleness Rd PE13 152 C2
Bolingbroke Rd NR3 158 B3
Boltons The PE30 148 C1
Bolts Cl NR23 136 D6
Bond Cl IP21 121 F4
Bond St 4 Cromer NR27 139 B7
5 Hingham NR9 86 C5
Norwich NR2 162 A7
Bonds Rd NR13 73 C7
Bond's Rd NR15 121 C4
Bone Rd NR8 157 B8
Bone's Dro NR23 4 F7
Boniface Cl NR4 162 C1
Bonnetts La PE14 60 B5
Boosey's Wlk 6 NR16 104 F1
Boot La IP22 120 D6
Booton Rd NR10 35 B2
Booty Rd NR7 159 F1
Borage Cl IP24 176 F4
Border La NR32 94 B2
Borough Cl PE13 152 D3
Borrowdale Dr NR1 163 B8
Borton Rd 4 NR13 73 C6
Boscombe Rd IP25 85 A3
Bosgate Rise 6 NR29 57 C4
Boston Cl 4 NR19 154 C3
Boston End 6 IP24 116 A1
Boston Sq PE36 132 C5
Boston Sq Sensory Pk* PE36 132 C5
Boston St NR3 158 D2
Botolph St NR3 178 A4
Boton Dr NR19 154 D7
Bottom Breck Cl NR5 156 F2
Botwright Dr 5 PE37 153 C3
Boudica's Way NR14 163 A1
Boughey Cl PE31 3 B6
Boughton Long Rd PE33 81 B7
Boughton Rd
Fincham PE33 62 E1
Stoke Ferry PE33 81 A3
Boulderside Cl 4 NR7 163 F7
Boulevard Rd 2 NR27 10 A5
Boulton Rd NR7 163 C7
Boulton St NR1 178 B2
Boundary Ave NR6 158 A4
Boundary Cl IP26 113 F7
Boundary La
Norwich NR7 72 E3
Paston NR28 23 B3
Boundary Rd
Ashby with Oby NR29 56 E2
Great Yarmouth NR31 169 B1
1 Hockwold cum Wilton IP26 114 A7
Marham PE33 63 C3
Norton Subcourse NR14 92 D1
Norwich NR6 157 F3
Raveningham NR14 110 B8
Boundary Way 1 NR14 90 C5
Bourne Cl
King's Lynn PE30 148 C2
Long Stratton NR15 106 E3
Bow Hill NR9 70 A3
Bowers Ave NR3 158 A2
Bowers Cl NR3 158 A2
Bowlers Cl NR13 92 E7
Bowling Gn Cl
Attleborough NR17 174 D6
Crostwick NR12 54 B2
Bowling Gn The NR21 30 F4
Bowling Gn Wlk 2 NR30 169 C4
Bowman Rd 4 NR4 89 E8
Bowthorpe Hall Rd NR5 160 F7
Bowthorpe Rd
Norwich NR5 161 D6
Wisbech PE13 152 D5
Box's La PE37 153 D5
Boyces Rd PE13 152 E5
Boyd Ave 9 NR19 154 D1
Boylandhall La NR15 107 B4
Brabazon Rd NR6 158 B5
Bracecamp Cl NR29 167 C2
Braces La NR35 109 E3
Bracey Ave NR6 158 F5
Bracken Ave
Norwich NR6 158 A4
Overstrand NR27 11 A3
Bracken Cl
Fakenham NR21 141 F4
Horsford NR10 53 B2
Stratton Strawless NR10 53 A6
Bracken Dr NR17 174 B5
Bracken Rd
King's Lynn PE30 148 C2
Thetford IP24 176 C1
Bracken Rise
Brandon IP27 175 E3
Mundford IP26 100 A4
Bracken Way PE32 28 B1
Brackenwoods PE37 66 A4
Bracon Rd NR31 93 F5
Bracondale NR1 178 C1
Bracondale Ct 3 NR1 162 F3
Bradcar Rd NR17 103 B2
Braddock Rd NR30 168 E5
Bradeham Way NR4 162 A1
Bradenham La NR19 66 F6
Bradenham Rd IP25 67 A2
Bradfield Cl NR28 151 A6
Bradfield Pl 3 PE33 81 A3
Bradfield Rd
Antingham NR11 22 C5
North Walsham NR28 151 A6
Bradfield Rd *continued*
Swafield NR28 22 E3
Bradman's La NR18 87 D3
Bradmere La PE31 134 E5
Bradshaw Rd NR8 157 C7
Bradwell Ave
19 Great Yarmouth NR31 94 C7
3 Great Yarmouth NR31 170 A5
Brady Cl PE38 172 B1
Brady Gdns PE38 172 B1
Braeford Cl NR6 157 E2
Brailsford Cl NR20 68 A7
Braithwait Cl 1 NR5 161 A8
Brake La NR21 16 C4
Bramble Ave NR6 158 A5
Bramble Cl
Sculthorpe Airfield NR21 15 C2
4 Taverham NR8 155 E2
Bramble Ct NR21 141 E4
Bramble Dr PE30 148 C2
Bramble Gdns NR31 93 F5
Bramble La
Outwell PE14 77 D7
Swaffham PE37 153 F5
Bramble Way
11 Poringland NR14 90 D5
Wymondham NR18 173 E4
Brambles Cl 2 NR10 54 A1
Bramerton La
Framingham Pigot NR14 90 E7
Rockland St Mary NR14 91 A7
Bramerton Rd NR14 91 A8
Bramfield Cl NR2 162 A7
Bramley Dr NR21 31 E5
Bramley Rd
Dereham NR20 68 A8
Diss IP22 177 C5
Wisbech PE13 152 C7
Brampton Cl PE13 152 A4
Brampton Sta NR10 36 E3
Brancaster Cl
King's Lynn PE30 147 C8
1 Taverham NR8 155 F3
Brancaster Rd PE31 134 E7
Brancaster Way PE37 153 B2
Branch Rd NR13 75 B2
Brandiston Rd NR10 35 B2
Brandon Cl
Norwich NR6 157 E4
3 Swaffham PE37 153 C3
Brandon Ct NR13 165 E3
Brandon Her Ctr* IP27 175 D1
Brandon Rd
Cockley Cley PE37 83 A8
Methwold IP26 99 B4
Saham Toney IP25 84 B3
Swaffham PE37 65 A1
Thetford IP24 176 A4
Wangford IP27 114 C1
Watton IP25 84 C3
Weeting-with-Broomhill IP27 175 C5
Brandon Sports Ctr IP27 175 B3
Brandon Sta IP27 175 C5
Brandon Terr NR30 169 E2
Brand's La
Felthorpe NR10 155 D6
Tharston & Hapton NR15 106 F5
Brandvnvm (Roman Fort) (Branodunum)* PE31 3 C6
Branford Rd
Caister-on-Sea NR30 168 D7
Norwich NR3 158 E1
Branksome Cl NR4 162 B2
Branksome Rd NR4 162 A2
Branodunum PE31 3 B7
Bransby Cl PE30 146 F4
Brasenose Ave NR31 170 B3
Brasier Rd NR3 158 D2
Brawdy Rd 7 IP31 126 B1
Braydeston Ave NR13 165 D3
Braydeston Cres NR13 165 D3
Braydeston Dr NR13 165 F6
Braydeston Hall La NR13 73 E4
Brayfield Way NR6 158 F6
Braymeadow NR9 160 C2
Braymeadow La NR9 160 D2
Bray's La
Guestwick NR20 34 A6
Rocklands NR17 103 A7
Brazen Gate NR1 178 A1
Breck Farm Cl NR8 155 C2
Breck Farm La NR8 155 C2
Breck Rd Norwich NR7 159 E2
Weston Longville NR9 51 E1
Breckland Bsns Pk IP25 84 F3
Breckland Mid Sch IP27 175 A2
Breckland Rd NR5 157 A1
Brecklands
Mundford IP26 100 B4
11 Stalham NR12 39 B4
Brecklands Rd NR13 165 E2
Brecon Rd NR15 90 E2
Brellows Hill PE34 144 A5
Brenda James Cl 1 NR7 163 E7
Brennewater Mews 4 NR5 161 A8

Brent Ave PE31 . . . . .12 E5
Brentwood ■ NR4 . . . . .161 F1
Brereton Cl ■ NR5 . . . . . . .161 C6
Bressingham Prim Sch
IP22 . . . . .129 B8
Bressingham Rd
  ⑤ Gresham NR11 . . . . .9 E1
  Roydon IP22 . . . . .129 C8
  Sustead NR11 . . . . .20 E8
Bressingham Steam Mus &
  Gdns* IP22 . . . . .129 C7
Breton Cl ⑩ NR19 . . . . . . .154 D2
Brett Ave NR31 . . . . .170 D1
Brett Way NR30 . . . . .169 C4
Brettingham Ave NR4 . . .89 B8
Brewers Ct
  ② Norwich NR3 . . . . .162 F8
  Norwich NR3 . . . . .178 C4
Brewers Gn La IP22 . . . . .177 B6
Brewery La NR18 . . . . .173 C3
Brewery Rd NR28 . . . . .22 D5
Brewery St NR30 . . . . .169 C4
Brewster Ct NR13 . . . . . . .165 D6
Brewsters ⑧ NR16 . . . . . .118 C5
Breydon Dr N NR8 . . . . . .156 C4
Breydon Dr N NR8 . . . . . .156 C5
Breydon Junc NR30 . . . . . .76 C3
Breydon Rd
  Great Yarmouth NR31 . . . .169 B4
  King's Lynn PE30 . . . . .147 D5
  Norwich NR7 . . . . .159 A4
Breydon Way NR30 . . . . . .168 D6
Brian Ave NR1 . . . . .162 D3
Briar Ave NR11 . . . . .94 C7
Briar Cl Dereham NR20 . . . .68 A8
  Grimston PE32 . . . . .28 B1
  King's Lynn PE30 . . . . .148 C3
  ⑯ Lingwood NR13 . . . . . . .74 A3
  ⑬ Methwold PE37 . . . . . . .65 F4
Briar La
  Heckingham NR14 . . . . . . .109 F8
  Rickinghall Inferior
  IP22 . . . . .128 C1
  Swainsthorpe NR14 . . . . . . .89 D3
Briar Rd ⑩ IP20 . . . . .122 D2
Briars Ct NR5 . . . . .161 F7
Brick Kiln La
  Mundesley NR16 . . . . .105 D2
  Gillingham NR34 . . . . .110 C5
  Long Stratton NR15 . . . . . .107 A5
  Shipdham IP25 . . . . .67 C2
Brick Kiln Rd
  Hethersett NR9 . . . . .109 C4
  Hevingham NR10 . . . . .53 A2
  North Walsham NR28 . . . . .151 E5
  Thursford NR21 . . . . .17 F4
Brick Kilns Rd NR13 . . . . .73 B7
Brick La NR27 . . . . .10 B5
Brickfield Loke NR8 . . . . .156 C5
Brickfields NR13 . . . . .73 F2
Brickfields Way IP24 . . . .176 D3
Brickkiln La
  Ashwellthorpe NR16 . . . . .105 F7
  Mulbarton NR14 . . . . .89 C2
  South Lopham IP22 . . . . . .128 F7
Brickle Loke NR14 . . . . . . .90 B5
Brickle Rd NR14 . . . . .90 B4
Brickley La PE31 . . . . .140 D7
Brickyard La PE31 . . . . . . .29 C4
Brickyard Rd NR28 . . . . . . .22 A2
Bridewell La
  Acle NR13 . . . . .166 C4
  Botesdale IP22 . . . . .128 E3
Bridewell Mus* NR2 . . . .178 B3
Bridewell St
  ■ Little Walsingham NR22 . .16 F7
  Wymondham NR18 . . . . . . .173 C3
Bridge Broad Cl NR12 . . .164 C5
Bridge Cl
  ⑯ Harleston IP20 . . . . . . .122 D2
  Heacham PE31 . . . . .133 E5
Bridge Farm La NR44 . . . .161 C6
Bridge Gdns NR19 . . . . . .154 F1
Bridge La IP25 . . . . .84 C6
Bridge Mdw NR29 . . . . .58 A4
Bridge Rd
  Brome & Oakley IP21 . . . .130 C5
  Bunwell NR16 . . . . .105 C4
  Burston & Shimpling
  IP22 . . . . .120 E3
  Colby NR11 . . . . .36 D8
  Downham Market PE38 . . . .79 B5
  Great Ryburgh NR21 . . . . . .32 C6
  ⑤ Great Yarmouth NR30 . .169 C5
  Great Yarmouth NR31 . . . .170 C2
  High Kelling NR25 . . . . .137 F8
  North Elmham NR20 . . . . . .32 F3
  Potter Heigham NR29 . . . . .56 F5
  Stoke Ferry PE33 . . . . .81 A2
  Sutton Bridge PE12 . . . . . . .41 A8
  Wymondham NR18 . . . . . . .88 B2
Bridge St Brandon IP27 . .175 C4
  Carbrooke IP25 . . . . .85 A4
  Downham Market PE38 . . . .172 B5
  Fakenham NR21 . . . . .141 B3
  Gressenhall NR20 . . . . .49 C3
  Hilgay PE38 . . . . .79 D7
  ■ King's Lynn PE30 . . . . .146 D4
  Loddon NR14 . . . . .92 A2
  Stiffkey NR23 . . . . .6 D5
  Thetford IP24 . . . . .176 C4
Bridgecourt NR29 . . . . .58 A4
Bridgefoot La NR25 . . . . . . .7 F5
Bridges Wlk IP24 . . . . . . .176 D3

Bridgford Cl NR31 . . . . . . .170 C2
Bridgham La NR16 . . . . . . .117 F4
Bridle La
  Downham Market PE38 . . .172 D7
  Keswick NR4 . . . . .89 C7
Bridle Rd IP25 . . . . .84 C3
Brigg St NR1 . . . . .178 B2
Briggs Loke NR21 . . . . .36 D8
Brigham Cl NR13 . . . . .165 C4
Brighton Rd ■ NR15 . . . . . .89 C1
Brightwell Rd NR3 . . . . . . .158 D3
Brighty's Opening
  NR2 . . . . .162 B7
Brigstock Rd PE13 . . . . . . .152 B7
Brimbelow Rd NR12 . . . . .164 D4
Brindle Dr ⑤ NR14 . . . . . .89 B3
Brinell Way NR31 . . . . .170 B8
Brinton Rd NR24 . . . . .142 D8
Brisley CE Prim Sch
  NR20 . . . . .32 A1
Bristol Terr NR2 . . . . .178 A2
Bristol Rd
  Briston NR24 . . . . .142 A5
  Corpusty NR11 . . . . .19 F1
  Edgefield NR24 . . . . .19 C5
  Wood Dalling NR11 . . . . . . .34 C6
Britannia Rd
  ■ Great Yarmouth NR30 .169 E4
  Norwich NR1 . . . . .163 A7
Britannia Way PE13 . . . . .152 C2
Britch La PE34 . . . . .42 B4
Briton Way NR18 . . . . .173 B3
Briton's La
  Beeston Regis NR26 . . . . .138 F4
  Sheringham NR26 . . . . .9 F5
Briton's La Cl
  ② Beeston Regis NR27 . . . . .9 F5
  Sheringham NR26 . . . . . . .138 F5
Britten Cl ⑤ PE33 . . . . . . .61 D6
Broad Dro Emneth PE14 . .59 C2
  Grimston PE32 . . . . .45 C8
  Methwold IP26 . . . . .97 F6
  Upwell PE14 . . . . .77 D4
Broad End La PE13 . . . . . .152 F4
Broad End Rd PE14 . . . . . .152 F4
Broad Fen La NR28 . . . . . . .38 D4
Broad La Brancaster PE31 . . .3 A7
  Great & Little Plumstead
  NR13 . . . . .72 F6
  South Walsham NR13 . . . . .74 B8
  Swannington NR9 . . . . .52 B5
Broad Rd Alburgh IP20 . . .122 E8
  Fleggburgh NR29 . . . . .75 C8
Broad Reaches NR29 . . . . .56 C5
Broad St Bungay NR35 . . .124 A8
  ⑳ Harleston IP20 . . . . . . .122 D2
  King's Lynn PE30 . . . . .146 D5
Broad View ⑨ NR13 . . . . . .72 D6
Broad Way
  Dickleburgh & Rushall
  IP21 . . . . .130 D8
  Rocklands NR17 . . . . .103 A8
Broadacres ⑤ NR13 . . . . .74 B8
Broadcote Cl NR15 . . . . . . .90 E1
Broaden La NR15 . . . . .107 C6
Broadfen Dro IP26 . . . . . . .98 B5
Broadfields Way NR4 . . . . .91 C7
Broadgate NR8 . . . . .155 B2
Broadgate Cl NR27 . . . . . . .11 A2
Broadgate La
  Great Moulton NR15 . . . . .121 B8
  Roydon PE32 . . . . .28 A2
Broadhurst Rd NR4 . . . . . .162 B1
Broadland Cl NR13 . . . . . . .93 A4
Broadland Dr NR13 . . . . . .72 D6
Broadland High Sch
  NR12 . . . . .164 D6
Broadland Sports Club
  NR29 . . . . .75 D8
Broadland Way
  Acle NR13 . . . . .166 C3
  Postwick with Witton NR7 . .72 C3
Broadlands PE38 . . . . .172 B5
Broadlands Cl PE31 . . . . .140 C4
Broadlands Rd NR12 . . . . . .39 E1
Broadmead Gn NR13 . . . . .72 E6
Broadmoor Rd IP25 . . . . . .85 B4
Broadwater La PE32 . . . . . .45 B4
Broadwater Rd PE36 . . . . . .1 F7
Broadwater Way ■ NR12 . .55 E4
Broadway Cl ⑤ NR15 . . . . .107 C5
Broadway The
  Heacham PE31 . . . . .133 D5
  Honingham NR9 . . . . .69 E8
  Scarning NR19 . . . . .154 B2
Broadwood Cl NR11 . . . . . .11 E1
Brockdish Prim Sch
  IP21 . . . . .131 D6
Brocks Rd PE37 . . . . .153 B6
Brockwell Ct NR3 . . . . . . .158 F2
Brome Ave IP23 . . . . .130 C2
Brome Hall La IP23 . . . . . .130 D3
Brook Gr ⑧ NR19 . . . . . . .154 D3
Brook La Brookville IP26 . . .99 A7
  Burgate IP22 . . . . .129 C3
  Needham IP20 . . . . .131 E8
  St Margaret, Ilketshall
  NR35 . . . . .124 C3
Brook Pl NR1 . . . . .178 B2
Brook Rd
  Dersingham PE31 . . . . .140 D2
  Sheringham NR26 . . . . . . .138 E6
Brook St
  Buxton with Lammas
  NR10 . . . . .36 E1
  Cromer NR27 . . . . .139 C7
  Lamas NR10 . . . . .53 E8
Brooke Ave NR30 . . . . . . .168 D5

Brooke Prim Sch NR15 . . . .90 E1
Brooke Rd
  Kirstead NR15 . . . . .91 A1
  Mundham NR14 . . . . .108 F8
  Seething NR15 . . . . .91 C1
  Shotesham NR15 . . . . .107 F8
Brookes Dr NR28 . . . . .151 A4
Brooks Dr NR19 . . . . .154 B4
Brooks Mdw NR14 . . . . .90 D5
Brooks Rd NR10 . . . . .53 B3
Brookside NR20 . . . . .49 E8
Brookwell Springs ■
  PE32 . . . . .44 B3
Broom Ave
  Norwich NR6 . . . . .158 A5
  Norwich NR6 . . . . .163 E8
Broom Rd
  ⑯ Marthan NR29 . . . . .57 D4
  Norwich NR6 . . . . .162 F3
  Taverham NR8 . . . . .155 C3
Broom Gn Dr NR20 . . . . . . .32 E4
Broom Gn Rd NR20 . . . . . . .32 E2
Broom Hill La IP24 . . . . . .126 C3
Broom La Easton NR9 . . . . .70 B5
  Witton NR28 . . . . .38 C8
Broom Rd
  Lakenheath IP27 . . . . .113 F1
  Wymondham NR18 . . . . . . .105 C6
Broome Gdns ■ NR11 . . .150 C2
Broomhall ■ NR27 . . . . . . .10 B5
Broomhill La NR19 . . . . . .149 B3
Broomsthorpe Rd PE31 . . .30 A7
Brothercross Way
  PE38 . . . . .172 C7
Brow of the Hill PE32 . . . .44 E6
Browick Rd NR18 . . . . .173 C4
Browne St ⑤ NR2 . . . . . . .162 C7
Brown's La
  Holme Hale IP25 . . . . .65 F2
  Mautby NR29 . . . . .76 B7
  Necton PE37 . . . . .65 F3
  Saxlingham Nethergate
  NR15 . . . . .107 B8
Brownsfield NR11 . . . . .21 D8
Brownshill NR27 . . . . .139 B4
Browston Hall Golf Club
  NR31 . . . . .94 C4
Browston La NR32 . . . . . . .94 B3
Browston Rd NR31 . . . . . . .94 B3
Brumstead Rd
  Brumstead NR12 . . . . .24 A1
  Stalham NR12 . . . . .39 A4
Brundall Gdns Sta
  NR13 . . . . .165 A3
Brundall Low Rd NR13 . . .72 F3
Brundall Prim Sch
  NR13 . . . . .165 D3
Brundall Rd NR13 . . . . . . .165 E4
Brundish St NR15 . . . . . . .123 B8
Brundish Rd NR14 . . . . . . .110 A6
Brunel Way IP24 . . . . .176 B6
Brunswick Cl NR9 . . . . . . .154 C2
Brunswick Rd NR2 . . . . . . .178 A1
Brush Mdw La PE34 . . . . . .42 B7
Brushmakers Way
  IP22 . . . . .177 C6
Brussels Cl NR19 . . . . .154 C2
Bryars La IP27 . . . . .177 F3
Bryggen Rd NR30 . . . . . . .169 A4
Bryony Cl ■ NR6 . . . . .158 D5
Bryony Cour NR25 . . . . . . .137 B7
Bryony Ct NR25 . . . . .148 C3
Bryony Way ⑥ NR17 . . . . .174 B5
Buccaneer Way ⑧ NR9 . . .88 D8
Buck Courtney Cres
  NR6 . . . . .158 A7
Buck La IP21 . . . . .130 C4
Buckenham Cl ■ NR21 . . .141 C5
Buckenham Dr NR21 . . . . . .81 A2
Buckenham La NR13 . . . . . .73 F2
Bucket Rd NR21 . . . . .15 D2
Buckingham Cl ID 148 C5
Buckingham Dr ■ NR7 . . .88 C7
Buckingham Rd NR4 . . . . .161 F3
Buckland Rise ⑧ NR4 . . . .161 F1
Buck's Heath La NR11 . . . .11 D1
Buck's La NR18 . . . . .87 B3
Buckshott Rd PE14 . . . . . . .59 B7
Buckthorn Cl ⑧ NR8 . . . .155 B2
Buddell's La NR27 . . . . .9 E2
Buggs Hole La IP22 . . . . . .128 A6
Bugg's Rd IP22 . . . . .129 B2
Buildings Rd NR30 . . . . . .168 E4
Bull Cl
  East Tuddenham NR20 . . . . .69 C6
  ⑷ Holt NR25 . . . . .137 B6
  Norwich NR3 . . . . .178 B4
Bull Cl La NR17 . . . . .17 B3
Bull Cl Rd Norwich NR3 . .162 E8
  Norwich NR3 . . . . .178 B4
Bull La NR1 . . . . .178 A1
Bull St NR25 . . . . .137 B6
Bullace Rd NR5 . . . . .156 F2
Bullacebush La NR13 . . . .165 E7
Bullard Rd NR3 . . . . .158 C3
Bullen Cl ■ NR12 . . . . .39 B4
Bullies Way ⑧ NR13 . . . . . .73 D6
Bullman's Cross La
  NR20 . . . . .69 A6

Bullock Fair Cl ⑭ IP20 . .122 D2
Bullock Hill NR10 . . . . .53 E1
Bullock Rd PE14 . . . . .144 B1
Bullocks Loke NR30 . . . . .168 E4
Bullockshed La NR14 . . . . .91 A7
Bulls Gn La NR34 . . . . .110 D5
Bulls Gn Rd NR34 . . . . . . .110 C6
Bull's La NR31 . . . . .94 A6
Bull's Row NR27 . . . . .11 A2
Bulmer La NR29 . . . . .58 B6
Bulmer Rd NR3 . . . . .158 A2
Bulrush Cl
  ■ East Dereham NR19 . . . .154 C4
  ⑷ Horsford NR10 . . . . .53 A3
Bulstrode Ave ⑷ NR13 . . .74 A3
Bultitudes Loke NR30 . . .168 E4
Bulwer Rd
  East Dereham NR19 . . . . . .154 E7
  Lamas NR10 . . . . .36 E1
Bumstede Cl ⑤ NR5 . . . . .161 A8
Bungalow La NR7 . . . . .72 D3
Bungay & Waveney Valley
  Golf Course NR35 . . . . . .108 F1
Bungay High Sch
  NR35 . . . . .124 B7
Bungay Rd Bixley NR14 . . .90 B8
  Dickleburgh & Rushall
  IP21 . . . . .130 E5
  Ellingham NR35 . . . . .109 C4
  Hempnall NR15 . . . . .107 D5
  Loddon NR14 . . . . .109 C7
  Poringland NR14 . . . . .90 D4
  Scole IP21 . . . . .130 D5
  Stockton NR34 . . . . .109 F4
  Thwaite NR35 . . . . .109 A5
Bungaygrave La IP20 . . . .122 D6
Bunkel Rd NR13 . . . . .72 E8
Bunnett Ave PE30 . . . . . . .146 D2
Bunnewell Ave NR31 . . . .170 A4
Bunn's Bank Rd
  Attleborough NR17 . . . . . .174 F2
  Old Buckenham NR17 . . . .104 A8
Bunn's La
  Great Yarmouth NR31 . . . .169 C3
  Starston IP20 . . . . .122 C2
Bunting's La IP26 . . . . .98 F5
Buntings The ⑱ NR16 . . .106 D2
Bunwell Hill NR16 . . . . . .105 D2
Bunwell Prim Sch
  NR16 . . . . .105 D3
Bunwell Rd
  Aslacton NR16 . . . . .106 A2
  Attleborough NR17 . . . . . .174 F6
  Besthorpe NR17 . . . . .104 F6
  Bunwell St NR16 . . . . .105 B5
  Bunyan Cl ■ NR13 . . . . . . .72 E4
BUPA Hospl (Private)
  NR4 . . . . .161 A5
Burch Cl NR30 . . . . .147 E4
Burcroft Rd PE13 . . . . .152 B6
Burdett Rd PE13 . . . . .152 B6
Burdock La
  Hockwold cum Wilton
  IP26 . . . . .113 C7
  ⑧ Wramplingham NR9 . . . .69 F2
  Wramplingham NR9 . . . . . .70 A2
Burdock Way ⑧ NR14 . . .174 B4
Bure Cl ⑨ Belton NR31 . . .94 A6
  Caister-on-Sea NR30 . . . .168 D6
  Great Yarmouth NR30 . . . .169 C6
  King's Lynn PE30 . . . . .147 E5
  ⑧ Watlington PE33 . . . . . .61 D6
  Wroxham/Hoveton
  NR12 . . . . .164 C5
Bure Rd Briston NR24 . . . .142 D4
  ⑦ Great Yarmouth NR30 .169 C5
Bure Valley La NR11 . . . . .150 C5
Bure Way NR11 . . . . .150 C7
Burgate La NR14 . . . . .90 E5
Burgess Cl NR30 . . . . .168 D6
Burgess Rd NR3 . . . . .158 A2
Burgess Way NR15 . . . . . . .90 E2
Burgh Beck Rd NR24 . . . . .142 B5
Burgh Hall Leisure Ctr
  NR31 . . . . .94 B7
Burgh La NR20 . . . . .68 F6
Burgh Rd
  Aylsham NR11 . . . . .150 D6
  Burgh St Peter NR34 . . . . .111 C5
  Great Yarmouth NR31 . . . .170 B7
  Burgh Wood Rd NR29 . . . .57 E1
Burghley Rd PE30 . . . . . . .148 E1
Burghwood Dr PE32 . . . . .48 D6
Burhill Cl ■ NR4 . . . . .161 F1
Burkitt St PE30 . . . . .146 E6
Burleigh Cl ■ NR30 . . . . .168 D2
Burley Rd NR12 . . . . .38 A3
Burlingham Rd NR13 . . . . .73 F8
Burlington Cl IP22 . . . . . . .177 D1
Burma Cl PE31 . . . . .140 C4
Burman Rd PE34 . . . . .61 B4
Burnet Rd
  Great Yarmouth NR31 . . . . .94 C6
  Norwich NR3 . . . . .157 F1
Burney Rd PE30 . . . . .146 D2
Burnham Ave NR30 . . . . . .147 C8
Burnham Mkt Prim Sch
  PE31 . . . . .135 D4
Burnham Rd
  Docking PE31 . . . . .134 E6
  Downham Market PE38 . . .172 B4
  North Creake NR21 . . . . .4 D2
  Ringstead PE36 . . . . .2 C2
  South Creake NR21 . . . . . . .15 D7
Burns Cl
  East Dereham NR19 . . . . . .154 C2
  Thetford IP24 . . . . .176 E6
  Yaxley IP23 . . . . .129 F1

Burnside ⑧ PE37 . . . . .66 A4
Burnt Fen Turnpike
  IP28 . . . . .112 D2
Burnt Hill NR13 . . . . .111 F3
Burnt Hills NR27 . . . . .139 B4
Burnt House Rd NR13 . . . .92 B6
Burnt La
  Great Yarmouth NR31 . . . .170 C7
  Wiggenhall St Mary Magdalen
  PE34 . . . . .61 A4
Burnt St NR23 . . . . .136 D5
Burnthouse Cres PE33 . . .63 B4
Burnthouse Dro PE33 . . . .63 C5
Burnthouse La
  Hethersett NR9 . . . . .160 C1
  Runhall NR20 . . . . .69 A4
  Scole IP20 . . . . .122 A1
  Toft Monks NR34 . . . . .110 D5
  Wymondham NR18 . . . . . .173 F1
Burntoak La IP20 . . . . .122 E4
Burntwood La NR12 . . . . . .54 C4
Burr Cl NR25 . . . . .84 E3
Burrell Cl NR25 . . . . .137 A7
Burrell Way NR4 . . . . .176 A1
Burrett Gdns PE13 . . . . . . .59 C5
Burrett Rd PE13 . . . . .59 C5
Burrettgate Rd PE13 . . . .152 F5
Burrows Gn NR34 . . . . . . .110 F5
Burston Com Prim Sch
  IP22 . . . . .120 E2
Burston Rd
  Dickleburgh & Rushall
  IP21 . . . . .130 C8
  Diss IP22 . . . . .177 E7
  Gissing IP22 . . . . .120 F3
Burton Ave NR28 . . . . .151 B4
Burton Cl
  North Walsham NR28 . . . . .151 B4
  Norwich NR6 . . . . .158 C5
  Roydon IP22 . . . . .177 B5
Burton Dr ⑨ NR13 . . . . . . .72 E7
Burton Rd NR6 . . . . .158 C5
Burtontyne Ave NR19 . . . .68 A7
Bury Bottom IP27 . . . . . . .115 A1
Bury Rd Botesdale IP22 . . .128 F3
  Brandon IP27 . . . . .175 D2
  Market Weston IP22 . . . . . .127 E4
  Rickinghall Inferior
  IP22 . . . . .128 D1
  Thetford IP24 . . . . .176 C1
  Wortham IP22 . . . . .129 C4
Bury St NR27 . . . . .162 B4
Bush Cl PE31 . . . . .140 E3
Bush Dr NR12 . . . . .24 E4
Bush Est NR12 . . . . .24 D4
Bush La Dereham NR20 . . . .68 B8
  Wisbech PE13 . . . . .152 E5
Bush Rd Hemsby NR29 . . . .58 B5
  Norwich NR6 . . . . .157 F7
Bussey Rd NR6 . . . . .158 D4
Bussey's La NR31 . . . . . . .170 D5
Bussey's Loke
  Great Yarmouth NR31 . . . .170 A5
  Hempnall NR15 . . . . .107 D5
Bustards' La PE14 . . . . . . .41 F3
Butcher's La NR21 . . . . . . .141 B4
Butt La Belton NR31 . . . . . .94 A6
  Litcham PE32 . . . . .48 A4
Butter La NR14 . . . . .92 D1
Buttercup Cl IP22 . . . . . . .176 F5
Buttercup Dr NR31 . . . . . . .94 C6
Buttercup Way NR5 . . . . . .160 F6
Buttermere ■ NR29 . . . . .167 B7
Buttermere Rd ⑷ NR5 . . .161 C6
Butterwick ⑧ PE30 . . . . .147 C5
Buttlands Cl NR21 . . . . .6 E2
Buttland's La PE33 . . . . . . .81 B8
Buttlands The IP25 . . . . . . .83 D4
Buttle's La NR15 . . . . .106 D3
Butts La NR26 . . . . .138 B5
Butts The NR5 . . . . .160 F8
Buxton Ave NR31 . . . . .170 D1
Buxton Cl ⑷ NR27 . . . . . . .10 B5
Buxton Prim Sch NR10 . . .36 F1
Buxton Rd
  Aylsham NR11 . . . . .150 D5
  Cawston NR10 . . . . .53 F3
  Frettenham NR12 . . . . .53 F3
  Hainford NR10 . . . . .53 F5
  Horstead with Stanninghall
  NR12 . . . . .54 B6
  North Walsham NR28 . . . . .151 B4
  Norwich NR3 . . . . .162 D8
  Spixworth NR10 . . . . .158 F8
Buxton Sta NR10 . . . . .36 F2
Bvd The
  Sheringham NR26 . . . . . . .138 D7
  Thorpe End NR13 . . . . .72 E6
Byfield Cl ⑧ NR31 . . . . . . .94 C6
Byron Rd
  Great Yarmouth NR30 . . . .169 C8
  Taverham NR8 . . . . .156 D8
Byron Way NR30 . . . . .168 D6

C

Cabbell Rd NR27 . . . . .139 B7
Cabin Cl NR33 . . . . .111 F1
Cadge Cl NR5 . . . . .161 D7
Cadge Rd NR5 . . . . .161 D7
Cadge's La NR9 . . . . .86 B3
Cadle's Way NR13 . . . . . . .171 E4
Cadman Way NR25 . . . . . . .84 D3
Cadogan Rd NR27 . . . . . . .139 B5
Caernarvon Rd NR2 . . . . .162 B6
Cage La IP24 . . . . .176 D3

Cains The NR8 ....155 C2
Caister By-Pass NR30 .168 C4
Caister High Sch
 NR30 ....168 E6
Caister on Sea Fst & Mid
 Schs NR30 ....168 E5
Caister Rd NR30 ....169 C7
Caister Sands Ave
 NR7 ....168 E8
Caister Castle Car
 Collection* NR30 ...168 A5
Caistor La
 Caistor St Edmund NR14 ....89 F6
 Poringland NR14 ....90 A6
Caithness Crystal Visitor
 Ctr* PE30 ....146 F2
Caius Cl PE31 ....133 C5
Calamint Rd PE30 ....147 A8
Caledonian Way NR31 ..94 A5
Caley Cl NR3 ....133 D5
Caley St PE31 ....133 D5
Calf La NR10 ....53 E2
California Ave NR29 ....167 E4
California Cres NR29 ...167 F2
California Rd NR29 ......167 E2
Calkewood La IP22 ....128 C1
Calthorpe Cl
 Acle NR13 ....166 B4
 2 Stalham NR12 ....39 B4
Calthorpe Rd
 Ingham NR12 ....39 C4
 Norwich NR5 ....161 B6
Calvert St NR3 ....178 B4
Calves Well La
 Beeston Regis NR26 ...138 E4
 Sheringham NR27 ......10 A5
Camargue Pl PE13 ......152 E3
Cambell Dr NR20 ....50 B5
Camberley Rd NR4 ......162 A2
Cambers La PE31 ....135 D2
Camberton Ct NR5 ......157 C1
Cambridge Ave NR41 ..170 A3
Cambridge Dr PE13 ....152 A6
Cambridge Rd PE30 ...148 D5
Cambridge St
 Cromer NR27 ....139 C7
 Norwich NR2 ....162 C4
Camden Rd NR30 ....169 D2
Cameron Cl NR1 ....133 C4
Cameron Gn NR8 ....156 E8
Camp Cl 2 IP26 ....98 D1
Camp La NR9 ....163 A6
Camp La Ind Est* 154 D3
Camp Rd NR8 ....155 C1
Campbell Cl 1 NR3 ....162 F8
Camperdown 1 NR20 .169 D2
Camping Cl 3 NR20 ...NR20 ..68 A1
Camping Field La NR12 ..39 B4
Campion Ave NR31 ......170 B3
Campion Cl 4 NR25 ....151 E5
Campion Pl PE38 ....172 B3
Campion Rd
 1 Dereham NR20 ....68 A8
 Thetford IP24 ....176 F4
Campion Way
 6 Attleborough NR17 ..174 B4
 3 Sheringham NR26 ...138 B6
Campsey Rd PE38 ....97 B6
Canada Cl PE13 ....12 E5
Canada Rd NR27 ....139 B7
Canal Farm La PE38 ....38 C6
Canal St 6 PE13 ....152 C5
Canary Way NR1 ....163 A4
Canberra Rd IP25 ......104 F2
Candle Stick NR3 ....69 A3
Candlemaker Workshop*
 NR29 ....75 A5
Candler's La 1 IP20 ...122 D2
Candlestick La PE31 ...122 C4
Canfor Rd 7 NR13 ......72 E7
Cangate Rd NR12 ....55 C6
Cannell Gn NR3 ....178 C4
Cannell Rd
 1 Loddon NR14 ....92 A1
 Loddon NR14 ....109 D8
Cannerby La NR7 ....159 B3
Cannon St PE13 ....152 C4
Cannon Terr 8 PE13 ...152 C4
Canon Cl 3 NR15 ....88 D7
Canon La 1 NR29 ....88 D7
Canon House Rd NR1 .150 C4
Canon Pickering VC Jun Sch
 IP20 ....122 D2
Canon Wake Ct 4 NR29 ..56 C8
Canons Cl 2 NR19 ......154 D2
Canon's Cl IP24 ....176 B4
Canterbury Inf Sch
 IP24 ....176 B4
Canterbury Way IP24 .176 B5
Cantley Cnr NR13 ....74 B1
Cantley Fst Sch NR13 ..92 B7
Cantley La
 Cringleford NR4 ....89 A8
 Ketteringham NR18 ....88 F6
Cantley Rd NR13 ....92 D7
Cantley Sta NR13 ....92 B6
Cants Cl 3 NR1 ....69 F2
Capgrave Ave PE30 ...146 F8
Capps La IP19 ....123 F1
Caraway Dr 22 NR31 ...94 C6
Caraway Rd IP24 ....176 F4
Carbrooke Rd
 Caston NR17 ....85 C1
 Caston NR17 ....102 F8
 Griston IP25 ....85 A2
Cardiff Rd NR2 ....162 B5
Cardington Cl 1 NR13 .166 D4
Cardington Rd IP25 ....85 A3

Cardun Cl 3 NR13 ....73 C6
Carey House Con Ctr
 PE37 ....65 D1
Cargate Comm Rd
 NR16 ....105 E1
Cargate La
 Saxlingham Nethergate
 NR15 ....107 A8
 Upton with Fishley NR13 .166 A8
Carl Cl 5 NR19 ....154 D1
Carl Cres NR28 ....22 E5
Carleton Cl 1 NR18 ...173 C6
Carleton Rd NR7 ....159 B3
Carleton Rode CE Prim Sch
 NR16 ....105 C3
Carlton Cl 1 NR19 ......154 D4
Carlton Dr PE30 ....148 D5
Carlton Marshes Nature
 Reserve* NR33 ....111 F3
Carlyle Rd NR1 ....162 F3
Carmelite Terr 4 NR30 .146 D4
Carmen's La NR28 ....38 B3
Carn Cl NR13 ....74 B2
Carnoustie NR4 ....162 A1
Carol Cl NR14 ....90 B5
Caroline Ct NR4 ....161 F4
Carpenters Cotts
 NR25 ....137 B6
Carpenter's Wlk NR15 .121 F7
Carr La
 Great Moulton NR15 ..106 B1
 Hoveton NR12 ....164 F8
 Northrepps NR27 ....139 C1
 Overstrand NR27 ....11 A3
 Poringland NR14 ....90 C4
 Wendling NR19 ....66 F7
Carrington Rd NR27 ...139 D5
Carrow Abbey NR1 ....163 A3
Carrow Hill NR1 ....178 C1
Carrow Rd NR1 ....178 C1
Carrs Hill Cl NR8 ....157 A4
Carrs Rd NR13 ....92 B8
Carshalton Rd 4 NR1 .162 F3
Cart Gap Rd NR12 ....24 C4
Carter Cl
 Caister-on-Sea NR30 .168 D8
 Swaffham PE37 ....153 C2
Carter Rd NR8 ....157 A8
Carterford Dr NR6 .....158 C3
Carter's Cl NR18 ....148 B1
Carter's La NR20 ....50 A6
Carters Loke NR13 ....166 C2
Cartledge Cl 3 NR19 ..154 D3
Cartmel 8 NR9 ....88 D8
Carver's La NR17 ....174 B5
Casaubon Cl 8 NR19 ..154 D3
Casion Cl 3 NR21 ......141 C5
Castell Rd NR19 ....154 D7
Castle Acre Castle*
 PE32 ....47 A2
Castle Acre Cl 2 PE30 .148 B1
Castle Acre Rd PE32 ...47 E1
Castle Cl 3 Gresham NR11 ..9 F1
 King's Lynn PE30 ......147 C8
 Weeting IP27 ....175 B8
Castle Drift PE32 ....148 A5
Castle La Bungay NR35 .124 A8
 Thetford IP24 ....176 D3
 West Caister NR30 ....168 B5
Castle Mdw NR1 ....178 B2
Castle Rd
 Mettingham NR35 .....124 D7
 Wormegay PE33 ....62 C6
Castle Rise NR8 ....155 E3
Castle Rising Castle*
 PE31 ....27 C3
Castle Rising Rd PE30 .148 D3
Castle Sq 6 PE13 ......152 C5
Castle St Norwich NR2 .178 B3
 Wroxham/Hoveton
 NR12 ....164 B3
Castleacre Rd
 Great Massingham PE32 ..29 D1
 Swaffham PE37 ....153 B8
Castleford Cl IP24 ......176 B4
Castleton Cl 4 NR5 ....160 F8
Castleton Way PE13 ...130 A1
Caston CE VA Prim Sch
 NR17 ....85 B1
Caston Cl 5 NR25 ......137 B6
Caston Rd NR7 ....163 F8
Cat bridge La NR14 .....89 A4
Catchpole Wlk NR1 ...121 C1
Catfield CE Fst Sch
 NR29 ....56 C8
Catfield Rd NR29 ....56 D6
Cathedral Dr NR20 ......49 E7
Cathedral St NR1 ....178 C2
Catherine Howard Cl 3
 IP24 ....176 D6
Catherine Wheel Opening 8
 NR3 ....162 D8
Catling's La PE13 ......141 A1
Catmere Herne NR14 ..89 A3
Cator Rd NR5 ....155 F1
Catriona Ct NR25 ....37 B7
Cats Cnr NR10 ....37 B7
Cattle Mkt PE33 ....43 E4
Cattle Mkt St
 Fakenham NR21 ....141 C4
 Norwich NR1 ....178 B2
Catton Chase NR6 .....158 D5
Catton Ct NR6 ....158 E6

Catton Gr Fst Sch
 NR3 ....158 C3
Catton Gr Mid Sch
 NR3 ....158 C2
Catton Gr Rd NR3 ......158 D2
Catton View Ct NR3 ..158 D3
Caudle Hill IP25 ....83 E5
Coudwell Cl 8 NR14 ...89 F4
Causeway Cl
 Brockdish IP21 ....131 C6
 Norwich NR2 ....162 C8
Causeway Dr 4 NR12 ..54 C6
Causeway The
 Heigham Bridge NR29 ..57 A5
 Hickling NR12 ....39 F2
 Stow Bardolph PE34 ..61 E1
Cavalier Cl 8 NR7 ....72 D4
Cavell Cl NR14 ....89 C5
Cavell Fst Sch NR1 ....162 E1
Cavell Rd NR1 ....162 E2
Cavendish Cl PE32 .....44 C3
Cavenham Rd PE33 ....80 E4
Cave's Cl PE34 ....144 B5
Cavick Rd NR18 ....173 A3
Cawston La
 Great Witchingham NR9 ..51 E7
 Little Witchingham NR9 .149 E1
Cawston Rd
 Aylsham NR11 ....150 A8
 Reepham NR10 ....149 D6
Cawston VC Prim Sch
 NR10 ....35 B2
Cawstons Mdw 8 NR1 ..90 C5
Caxton Cl NR26 ....138 F5
Caxton Cl NR30 ....147 D4
Caxton Rd NR26 ....138 F5
Caxton Way NR34 .....110 D1
Laystreward NR30 .....168 E1
Cecil Cl 7 PE33 ....61 D6
Cecil Gowing Fst Sch
 NR7 ....159 C3
Cecil Rd
 East Dereham NR20 ..154 F5
 Norwich NR1 ....162 D3
Cedar Ave NR14 ....54 A2
Cedar Cl
 8 Downham Market
 PE38 ....172 C6
 12 Great Yarmouth NR31 ..94 C7
 19 Martham NR29 ....57 D4
 19 Mattishall NKZU 68 E6
 Wisbech PE13 ....152 A4
 Wymondham NR18 ...173 B5
Cedar Cr NR18 ....173 D6
Cedar Dr
 Attleborough NR17 ...174 C4
 10 Loddon NR14 ....92 A1
Cedar Gr
 North Runcton PE33 ...44 A3
 Sheringham NR26 .....138 C5
Cedar Rd
 Hethersett NR9 ....88 C8
 Norwich NR28 ....63 B4
 Norwich NR1 ....163 A5
Cedar Rise NR20 ....68 E6
Cedar Springs PE31 ..133 B6
Cedar Way
 Brandon IP27 ....175 D2
 9 Gayton PE32 ....45 C6
 King's Lynn PE34 ......146 C4
Cedars The NR7 ....162 B4
Ceders The PE31 ....12 B4
Celandine Cl IP24 .....176 F5
Celandine La 8 NR14 ..90 C4
Celandine Rd 1 NR17 .174 B4
Celia Phillips Ct 7
 IP24 ....176 D7
Cemetery La NR18 .....173 B3
Cemetery Rd
 East Ruston NR12 .....154 F7
 Lakenheath IP27 ....113 E1
 Outwell PE14 ....77 E4
Centenary Way PE12 ..41 C6
Central Ave NR7 ....72 D3
Central Cl 1 NR1 ....88 D7
Central Cres 2 NR9 ...88 D7
Central Dr NR30 ....168 D3
Central Rd
 Cromer NR27 ....139 A7
 King's Lynn PE30 .....146 D6
Centre Cres PE31 .....140 D3
Centre Vale Rd PE31 .140 D3
Century Rd 6 Eye IP23 .130 C1
 Great Yarmouth NR31 .169 B3
Century Way NR8 ......155 F3
Cere Rd NR7 ....159 C4
Cess Rd NR29 ....57 B6
Chalk Hill Rd NR1 ......178 C3
Chalk La Culford IP31 .125 C1
 Narborough PE32 ....63 E5
 Stoke Ferry PE33 ....41 C7
Chalk Pit Rd NR1 ......162 E2
Chalk Rd Brandon IP27 .114 D5
 Walpole St Andrew PE14 ..41 E4
Chalkpit Rd NR1 ....162 E2
Chalkrow La PE33 ......81 F4
Chamberlin Cl NR3 ...158 E2
Chamberlin Ct NR3 ...165 E6
Chamberlin Rd NR3 ..158 D3
Chambers Rd NR3 .....158 D3
Chamerryhall La NR13 ..73 F7
Champney's Rd IP27 ..177 C4
Chancel Cl NR13 ....165 C3
Chancellors Dr NR4 ...161 C4
Chandler Rd NR14 ......89 F5
Chandlers Cl NR18 .....89 C8
Chandlers Ct 8 NR4 ...89 C8

Chandler's Hill La
 NR18 ....173 B3
Changi Rd 5 IP25 ......84 F3
Channonz Hall Airfield (dis)
 NR15 ....120 F7
Chantry Cl 8 Necton PE37 ..65 F4
 4 Necton PE37 ....66 A4
Chantry La PE37 ....66 A4
Chantry Rd NR2 ....178 A2
Chantry The NR2 ....178 A2
Chapel Bank NR15 ....106 E3
Chapel Bank PE36 .....132 E6
Chapel Break Fst Sch
 NR5 ....160 F8
Chapel Break Rd NR5 .160 E7
Chapel Cl
 Barnham Broom NR9 ..69 C2
 Pulham Market IP21 ..121 E5
 Reepham NR10 ....149 B5
 Tacolneston NR16 ....105 F4
 Winfarthing IP22 ......120 B5
Chapel Cnr NR12 ....55 C6
Chapel Ct Blofield NR13 ..165 E6
 Norwich NR6 ....157 F5
Chapel Field NR13 ......93 A4
Chapel Field E NR2 ...178 A2
Chapel Field N NR2 ...178 A2
Chapel Field Rd
 Norwich NR2 ....162 C5
 Norwich NR2 ....178 A2
 Stalham NR12 ....39 A3
Chapel Hill
 Aldborough NR11 ......21 A5
 Ashby St Mary NR14 ..91 D5
 Barton Bendish PE33 ..81 B8
 Beeston with Bittering
 PE32 ....48 C2
 Bootley NR20 ....49 C4
 Botesdale IP22 ....128 E2
 Burgate IP22 ....129 C3
 Coltishall NR12 ....54 D7
 East Dereham NR19 ..154 D2
 Fincham PE33 ....59 B2
 Felthorpe NR10 ....155 F7R
 Fincham PE33 ....62 E1
 Foulsham NR20 ....33 D3
 8 Great Yarmouth NR31 ..94 C6
 Hempstead NR25 ....19 E8
 Hockering NR20 ....69 B8
 Hunstanton PE36 .....132 C14
 Kirby Row NR35 ....109 E3
 Methwold IP26 ....99 A5
 Norwich NR2 ....162 A4
 Norwich NR7 ....66 A4
 Potter Heigham NK2U ..56 F7
 Ringstead PE36 ....2 A3
 Scarning NR19 ....67 B7
 Sculthorpe NR21 ....16 B1
 Shelton NR15 ....90 C1
 Shotesham NR15 ....90 B2
 Skeyton NK10 ....37 B6
 West Caister NR30 ...168 C4
 West Winch PE33 ....43 E3
 Wimbotsham PE34 ....72 E6
 Wiveton NR25 ....7 E6
 Wymondham NR10 ...173 A5
Chapel Loke
 Lessingham NR12 ......24 C2
 Salhouse NR13 ....55 B1
 8 Stoke Holy Cross NR14 ..89 F4
 Surlingham NR14 ....73 H1
 Wymondham NR18 ...105 A8
Chapel Mdw NR35 .....109 E3
Chapel Rd
 Ally with Thwaite NR11 ..21 B3
 Ashby St Mary NR14 ..91 D5
 Attleborough NR17 .....74 C2
 Beighton NR13 ....74 C2
 Boughton PE33 ....81 A4
 Carleton Rode NR16 .105 C3
 Denning PE31 ....140 D4
 Dilham NR28 ....38 B3
 East Ruston NR12 ....38 F8
 Foxley NR20 ....50 D8
 Grimston PE32 ....28 A1
 Guestwick NR20 ....33 D3
 Hainford NR10 ....53 E5
 Halvergate NR13 ....75 A2
 Lingwood NR13 ....73 F3
 Longham NR19 ....49 A2
 Lowestoft NR33 ....111 F1
 Morley NR18 ....87 B2
 Neatishead NR12 ....55 E6
 Necton PE37 ....66 B4
 North Walsham NR28 ..22 D8
 Paston NR28 ....143 D1
 Potter Heigham NR29 ..56 E7
 Roydon PE32 ....28 A1
 St Andrew, Ilketshall
 NR34 ....109 F7
 Scole IP21 ....121 B1
 Southrepps NR11 ....22 B6
 Swafield NR28 ....22 B6
 Terrington St Clement
 PE34 ....144 B5
 Upton with Fishley NR13 .166 B8
 Wisbech PE13 ....152 B5
 Woodton NR35 ....108 A8
 Wymondham NR18 ...105 A8
Chapel Rise 11 PE33 ..83 B4
Chapel St Barford NR9 .70 A3
 3 Cromer NR27 ....139 B7
 Diss IP22 ....177 D4
 6 Hingham NR9 ....86 C5
 Ixworth NR9 ....105 E3
 King's Lynn PE30 .....146 D5

Chapel St continued
 8 Old Buckenham NR16 ..104 F1
 Rocklands NR17 ....103 B8
 Shipdham IP25 ....67 C2
 Warham NKE3 ....6 A4
 18 Wisbech PE13 ......152 C4
Chapel Yd Ashill IP25 ..84 A7
 Wells-next-the-Sea
 NR23 ....136 C6
Chapelfield Cl 1 NR29 ..56 C8
Chapman Ave NR30 ..168 E5
Chapnall Cl PE13 ....152 E5
Chapnall Rd PE13 ......152 E6
Chare Rd IP31 ....127 B1
Charing Cross NR2 ...178 A3
Charles Ave
 Norwich NR7 ....163 F8
 Watton IP25 ....83 B4
Charles Burrell High Sch
 IP24 ....176 C1
Charles Burrell Mus*
 IP24 ....176 C4
Charles Burton Cl 5
 NR3 ....168 D7
Charles Cl Wisbech PE13 .166 E4
 Caister-on-Sea NR30 .168 E5
 Cromer NR27 ....10 C4
 Dereham NR19 ....154 C1
 Wroxham/Hoveton
 NR12 ....164 C3
Charles Ewing Cl
 NR11 ....150 B5
Charles Rash Cl NR20 ..37 B8
Charles Rd
 Bootley NR18 ....141 C4
 Holt NR25 ....137 C5
 Hunstanton PE36 .....132 C2
 8 Sutton Bridge PE12 ..41 B8
Charles St
 Great Yarmouth NR30 ..169 C2
 King's Lynn PE30 .....146 E3
 10 Wisbech PE13 ......152 C4
Charles Watling Way 1
 NR5 ....160 E8
Charles Wood Rd
 NR19 ....154 F2
Charlock Dr 8 NR26 ..138 B6
Charlotte's Cl 1 NR27 ..9 F5
Charlton Rd NR1 ....178 B4
Charter Cl NR31 ....170 B4
Chartwell Ct NR7 ......158 F3
Chartwell Rd NR5 ......158 F4
Chase Ave PE30 ....146 E3
Chase Cl NR6 ....158 D5
Chase Ct NR19 ....154 D6
Chase St PE13 ....152 C5
Chase The
 Brandon IP27 ....175 E2
 Brundall NR13 ....165 F6
 Stow Bardolph PE34 ..78 E7
 Upwell PE14 ....77 D3
 Watlington St Andrew PE14 ..41 E4
 Wisbech PE13 ....152 A7
Chatham Rd 1 IP31 ...126 B1
Chatham St NR3 ....178 A4
Chatsworth Rd PE36 .132 C3
Chaucer Cl 11 NR20 ...50 B7
Chaucer Rd NR30 .....169 D8
Checker St PE30 ....146 C3
Cheese Hill 9 NR16 ..118 C5
Chenery Dr NR7 ....159 C5
Cheney Cres PE31 ....133 D4
Cheney Hill PE31 ......133 D4
Cheney's La NR16 .....105 F5
Chepore La NR18 ....87 C1
Chequers Cl
 Briston NR24 ....142 F3
 2 Long Stratton NR15 .106 D3
 1 Roydon PE32 ....28 A1
Chequers La
 Bressingham IP22 ....129 B7
 Burston & Shimpling
 IP22 ....120 E4
 Great Ellingham NR17 ..103 E8
 Gressenhall NR20 ......49 B4
 North Runcton PE33 ...44 A2
 Saham Toney IP25 ....84 C5
Chequer's La NR15 ...107 D8
Chequers La 2 NR19 ..43 F2
 Roydon PE32 ....28 A1
 Tharston & Hapton
 NR15 ....106 D3
 Wretton PE33 ....80 E3
Chequers St
 Docking PE31 ....134 D4
 East Ruston NR12 ......38 F5
 Gresham NR11 ....9 E1
Cherry Cl
 1 Great Yarmouth NR31 .94 C7
 Marham PE33 ....63 A4
 Norwich NR1 ....162 E3
Cherry La
 Belton with Browston
 NR31 ....94 A4
 Dereham NR20 ....68 B7
Cherry Orch NR20 ....154 F5
Cherry Rd
 Great Yarmouth NR31 ..170 B6
 Wisbech PE13 ....152 C8
Cherry Tree Cl
 Holt NR25 ....137 B7
 Mundford IP26 ....100 A4
 North Lopham IP22 ..119 A2
 Wretham IP24 ....102 B1

Cherry Tree Ct IP22 .... **177** C5
Cherry Tree Dr PE34 .... **146** C4
Cherry Tree La NR28 .... **151** B5
Cherry Tree Rd
Carleton Rode NR16 .... **105** A1
Plumstead NR11 .... **20** A6
Snettisham PE31 .... **12** E5
Tibenham NR16 .... **120** B7
Cherrywood
Alpington NR14 .... **90** F4
10 Redenhall with Harleston
IP20 .... **122** D1
Cherrywood Ave NR21 .... **15** C2
Chester PI NR2 .... **162** C6
Chester Rd NR2 .... **162** C6
Chester Way IP24 .... **176** A4
Chestnut Ave
Great Yarmouth NR31 .... **170** A5
North Walsham NR28 .... **151** E4
Sculthorpe Airfield NR21 .... **15** C2
1 Spixworth NR10 .... **54** A2
Welney PE14 .... **95** D5
West Winch PE33 .... **43** E1
Chestnut Cl
Brandon IP27 .... **175** E4
Dersingham PE31 .... **140** E3
East Dereham NR19 .... **154** E1
Norwich NR5 .... **156** E2
5 Watlington PE33 .... **61** D5
Chestnut Gr NR26 .... **138** D4
Chestnut Hill **8** NR4 .... **161** F1
Chestnut Loke NR15 .... **107** A6
Chestnut Rd
Dickleburgh IP21 .... **121** C1
East Dereham NR19 .... **154** C5
Pulham St Mary IP21 .... **121** F4
5 Snettisham PE31 .... **12** E4
15 Tasburgh NR15 .... **106** F6
8 Watton IP25 .... **84** E3
7 Wisbech PE13 .... **152** C6
Chestnut Terr PE12 .... **41** B8
Chestnut Wlk PE37 .... **81** F8
Chestnuts The IP22 .... **128** E2
Chew Ct PE30 .... **147** E8
Cheyham Mount NR4 .... **161** F1
Cheyney Ave **8** NR13 .... **55** A1
Chickering Rd IP21 .... **131** B2
Childs Rd NR9 .... **88** C8
Childs Way NR26 .... **138** C5
Chiltern Cres PE34 .... **136** C2
Chilver House La PE32 .... **44** E7
Chimney Springs
NR29 .... **167** A3
Chimney St PE32 .... **46** F1
Chipperfield Rd NR7 .... **159** E1
Chirick Cl **5** NR10 .... **54** A1
Cholmondeley Cl 3
PE3 .... **43** F2
Choseley Ct NR18 .... **173** C4
Choseley Rd
Docking PE31 .... **134** C7
Thornham PE36 .... **2** D6
Christ Church Rd
NR31 .... **170** A4
Christchurch Rd NR2 .... **162** A4
Christie Cl **6** NR19 .... **154** D1
Christine Ave NR13 .... **74** A2
Christine Rd **11** NR10 .... **54** A1
Christopher Cl
3 Newton Flotman NR15 .... **89** D1
1 Norwich NR1 .... **162** E2
Christopher Dr PE13 .... **152** A7
Church Alley NR13 .... **165** E6
Church Ave
Croxton IP24 .... **116** C5
Halvergate NR13 .... **74** F1
Little Ellingham NR17 .... **86** A1
Norwich NR4 .... **162** B3
Church Ave E
Marshland St James PE14 .... **60** C2
Terrington St Clement
PE34 .... **144** B6
Church Cl
Antingham NR28 .... **22** B3
3 Bawdeswell NR20 .... **50** E7
Beeston Regis NR27 .... **9** F5
Bixley NR14 .... **90** B7
Brandon IP27 .... **175** B3
Caister-on-Sea NR30 .... **168** D5
Cantley NR13 .... **92** C7
Colby NR11 .... **36** D8
9 Coltishall NR12 .... **54** C6
Grimston PE32 .... **45** B8
Hepworth IP22 .... **127** E1
1 Horstead with Stanningfall
NR12 .... **54** C6
King's Lynn PE34 .... **146** C4
Lamas NR10 .... **36** F1
16 Loddon NR14 .... **92** A7
2 Norwich NR2 .... **162** B8
Overstrand NR27 .... **11** A3
Pentney PE32 .... **63** C8
Poringland NR14 .... **90** C4
Pulham St Mary IP21 .... **122** A4
1 Roydon IP22 .... **129** D7
Sea Palling NR12 .... **40** B5
Shipdham IP25 .... **67** B2
South Walsham NR13 .... **74** A8
Swainsthorpe NR14 .... **89** D4
Upper Sheringham
NR26 .... **138** A4
Walpole St Andrew PE14 .... **41** E4
Whissonsett NR20 .... **31** D2

Church Cl continued
Wiggenhall St Mary Magdalen
PE34 .... **61** B6
Wortwell IP20 .... **122** F3
Church Cotts NR14 .... **48** E3
Church Crofts PE31 .... **27** C3
Church Dam NR13 .... **93** A5
Church Dro PE14 .... **77** F6
Church End IP27 .... **175** B3
Church Farm Cl
Palgrave IP22 .... **177** C2
1 Weybourne NR25 .... **8** F5
Church Farm Cres
NR29 .... **167** B6
Church Farm La NR19 .... **154** C5
Church Farm Rd PE33 .... **113** F7
Church Field **4** NR4 .... **89** B8
Church Gate **18** PE12 .... **41** B8
Church Gdns IP31 .... **127** C3
Church Gn
Norwich NR7 .... **159** B5
West Acre PE32 .... **46** B2
Church Hill
Banham NR16 .... **119** D7
Beighton NR13 .... **74** C3
Hoxne IP21 .... **131** A4
Reepham NR10 .... **149** C4
Saxlingham Nethergate
NR15 .... **107** B8
Starston IP20 .... **122** C3
Church Hill Fst Sch
PE32 .... **45** C8
Church Hill Sch NR19 .... **119** D7
Church La Aldeby NR24 .... **110** F5
Aldeby, Wheatacre,
Burgh St Peter NR34 .... **111** B5
Antingham NR28 .... **22** B3
Ashwellthorpe NR16 .... **106** A7
Baconsthorpe NR25 .... **19** F7
Bacton NR28 .... **23** C3
Banham NR16 .... **119** D7
Barnham IP24 .... **125** F6
Barton Bendish PE33 .... **81** B8
Belaugh NR12 .... **54** E5
Belton with Browston
NR31 .... **94** A5
Billingford NR20 .... **50** B7
Bintree NR20 .... **33** B2
Bircham PE31 .... **14** B3
Blo' Norton IP22 .... **128** B6
Boughton PE33 .... **80** F5
Bracon Ash NR14 .... **88** F3
Bradenham IP25 .... **66** D4
Bressingham IP22 .... **129** B7
Briningham NR24 .... **18** D5
Briston NR24 .... **142** E4
Brockdish IP21 .... **131** C6
Broome NR35 .... **109** B3
Brundall NR13 .... **165** D3
Burgh & Tuttington NR11 .... **36** D4
Claxton NR14 .... **91** C5
Cley next the Sea NR25 .... **7** E6
Corton NR32 .... **171** F1
Cranworth IP25 .... **67** B8
Deopham NR18 .... **86** F4
Dersingham PE31 .... **140** E3
Ditchingham NR35 .... **108** F3
East Tuddenham NR20 .... **69** C6
East Walton PE32 .... **45** E3
East Winch PE32 .... **44** F2
Easton NR9 .... **70** B6
Felthorpe NR10 .... **155** D7
Filby NR29 .... **75** E8
Fleggburgh NR29 .... **57** A1
Flitcham with Appleton
PE31 .... **28** C5
Frettenham NR12 .... **54** A5
Fritton & St Olaves NR31 .... **93** F3
Great Massingham PE32 .... **29** D1
Great Yarmouth NR31 .... **170** C5
Gresham NR11 .... **9** C3
Gressenhall NR19 .... **49** C2
Guestwick NR20 .... **33** F6
Haddiscoe NR14 .... **110** E7
Hales NR14 .... **109** F7
Harpley PE31 .... **29** C5
Heacham PE31 .... **133** E6
Heckingham NR14 .... **92** C1
Hemblington NR13 .... **73** F6
Hepworth IP22 .... **127** E1
Hevingham NR10 .... **36** B1
Hindolveston NR20 .... **33** C8
Hockwold cum Wilton
IP26 .... **114** A6
Holme Hale PE37 .... **65** F2
Ixworth NR9 .... **69** E2
Ketteringham NR18 .... **88** E5
King's Lynn PE30 .... **146** E4
King's Lynn PE30 .... **148** C2
Langley with Hardley
NR14 .... **92** C3
Lessingham NR12 .... **24** A2
Leziate PE32 .... **44** F4
Little Ellingham NR17 .... **86** A1
Little Massingham PE32 .... **29** C2
Long Stratton NR15 .... **106** F4
Lound NR32 .... **171** A3
Marham PE33 .... **63** A4
Marlingford NR9 .... **69** E4
Marsham NR10 .... **36** B2
Mattishall NR20 .... **68** F6
Mautby NR29 .... **75** D5
Morley NR18 .... **87** A3
Mundesley NR11 .... **143** C6
Mundford IP26 .... **100** B4
Neatishead NR12 .... **55** B6
North Elmham NR20 .... **49** E8
Northwold PE33 .... **81** B2

Church La continued
Northwold IP26 .... **99** C7
Norwich NR7 .... **159** C5
Norwich NR4 .... **161** E1
Old Buckenham NR17 .... **104** D2
Oulton NR11 .... **35** B6
Potter Heigham NR29 .... **56** F7
Redenhall with Harleston
IP20 .... **122** E3
Rickinghall Superior
IP22 .... **128** E1
Royston PE32 .... **27** F2
Runcton Holme PE33 .... **61** D4
Runhall NR20 .... **69** A6
Runhall NR9 .... **87** A8
St Mary, South Elmham
otherwise Homersfield
IP20 .... **123** B4
Sheringham NR26 .... **138** F6
Shipdham IP25 .... **67** B2
Shouldham Thorpe PE33 .... **62** B3
4 Southery PE38 .... **97** B5
Sparham NR9 .... **51** B6
Spixworth NR10 .... **53** F2
Sprowston NR7 .... **159** B5
Stanhoe PE31 .... **14** E7
Stanhoe PE31 .... **1** E7
Stuston IP21 .... **130** B4
Surlingham NR14 .... **73** A1
Sustead NR11 .... **21** B8
Swannington NR9 .... **52** B6
Swanton Abbott NR10 .... **37** C5
Terrington St John PE14 .... **42** B2
Thelnetham IP22 .... **128** B5
Thompson IP24 .... **102** C7
Thwaite NR35 .... **109** A6
Tibenham NR16 .... **120** B8
Tilney All Saints PE34 .... **42** E4
Tittleshall PE32 .... **48** B8
Tivetshall St Mary NR15 .... **121** B4
Tunstead NR12 .... **37** F1
Watlington PE33 .... **61** E6
Weasenham All Saints
PE32 .... **47** C8
Wicklewood PE34 .... **87** B5
Winfarthing IP22 .... **120** B4
Wood Dalling NR11 .... **34** B5
Wormegay PE33 .... **62** B5
Wormegay PE33 .... **62** D6
Wroxham/Hoveton
NR12 .... **164** B3
Yaxham NR19 .... **68** A5
Church Loke NR11 .... **21** D7
Church Marsh Nature
Reserve* NR14 .... **73** A1
Church Mdw
Rickinghall Inferior
IP22 .... **128** D2
Rockland St Mary NR14 .... **90** E5
Church Mdw La NR14 .... **90** F4
Church of the Holy Sepulchre
(rems)* IP24 .... **176** B4
Church Path PE33 .... **80** E2
Church PI PE31 .... **134** D5
Church Plain NR23 .... **136** D5
Church Rd
Alburgh IP20 .... **122** F6
Alpington NR14 .... **90** F4
Aslacton NR15 .... **106** A2
Aylmerton NR11 .... **10** A3
Bacton NR12 .... **23** D4
Barningham IP31 .... **127** C3
Barton Bendish PE33 .... **81** B8
Barton Turf NR12 .... **55** E8
Beeston with Bittering
PE32 .... **48** B2
Beetley NR20 .... **49** B6
Beetley NR20 .... **49** D5
Bergh Apton NR15 .... **91** A3
Bintree NR20 .... **33** B2
Brandon IP27 .... **175** B3
Bridgham NR16 .... **118** B5
Brockdish IP21 .... **131** C6
Brundall NR13 .... **165** E5
Burgh Castle NR31 .... **93** F8
Cantley NR13 .... **92** D7
Carleton Rode NR16 .... **105** C2
Catfield NR29 .... **56** C8
Christchurch PE14 .... **95** A7
Clenchwarton PE34 .... **145** D5
Colby NR11 .... **36** D8
Colkirk NR21 .... **31** D5
Crimplesham PE33 .... **80** B6
Denham IP21 .... **131** A1
Deopham NR18 .... **86** E3
Dickleburgh & Rushall
IP21 .... **130** D8
Dilham NR28 .... **38** C4
Downham Market PE38 .... **172** C5
Earsham NR35 .... **123** F7
Ellingham NR35 .... **109** D3
Elm PE14 .... **77** F8
Elsing NR20 .... **50** E3
Felmingham NR28 .... **37** B7
Flixton NR35 .... **123** E5
Fordham PE38 .... **79** B1
Freethorpe NR13 .... **92** F8
Frettenham NR10 .... **53** F4
Garboldisham IP22 .... **128** A8
Gillingham NR34 .... **110** C3
Great & Little Plumstead
NR13 .... **73** A4
Great Yarmouth NR31 .... **170** C7
Griston IP25 .... **85** A1
Haddiscoe NR14 .... **110** E8
Hardingham NR9 .... **86** D7
Hedenham NR35 .... **108** E4
Hilgay PE38 .... **79** E1

Church Rd continued
Hilgay PE38 .... **96** E8
Hoe NR20 .... **49** F6
Holme Hale IP25 .... **66** A2
Honington IP31 .... **126** D1
Horning NR12 .... **55** F3
Hunstanton PE36 .... **132** F7
Itteringham NR11 .... **20** C2
Ketteringham NR18 .... **88** D5
Kirby Cane NR35 .... **109** E4
Kirstead NR15 .... **90** F1
Leverington PE14 .... **59** C2
Leverington PE13 .... **152** F7
Lingwood & Burlingham
NR13 .... **73** F3
Little Barningham NR11 .... **20** C4
Market Weston IP22 .... **127** E4
Marlingford NR9 .... **70** A3
Neatishead NR12 .... **55** B6
Newton Flotman NR15 .... **89** C1
North Lopham IP22 .... **119** A1
Norton Subcourse NR14 .... **92** E1
Ovington IP25 .... **84** E5
Postwick with Witton
NR13 .... **72** F3
Potter Heigham NR29 .... **56** F6
Quidenham NR16 .... **118** F8
Reedham NR13 .... **93** A5
Repps with Bastwick
NR29 .... **57** A4
Runhall NR9 .... **69** A1
Runhall NR20 .... **69** A5
Sea Palling NR12 .... **40** A5
Shelfanger IP22 .... **120** B2
Shouldham PE33 .... **62** E3
Shropham NR17 .... **103** B3
Sisland NR14 .... **91** D1
Snettisham PE31 .... **12** E5
Somerton NR29 .... **57** F6
South Lopham IP22 .... **128** D8
Stockton NR34 .... **109** F5
Stoke Ferry PE33 .... **80** E2
Strumpshaw NR13 .... **91** F8
Sutton NR12 .... **39** C3
Swafield NR28 .... **22** C4
Tasburgh NR15 .... **106** F6
Terrington St John PE14 .... **42** B1
Tharston & Hapton
NR15 .... **106** D5
Thompson IP24 .... **102** B7
Thurlton NR14 .... **92** F1
Thurne NR29 .... **56** E2
Tibenham NR16 .... **120** E8
Tilney All Saints PE34 .... **144** F1
Tilney St Lawrence PE34 .... **42** D2
Tilney St Lawrence PE34 .... **60** C8
Toft Monks NR34 .... **110** D6
Topcroft NR35 .... **107** F3
Tunstead NR12 .... **55** B8
Upton with Fishley NR13 .... **166** A6
Wacton NR15 .... **106** C2
Walpole St Andrew PE14 .... **41** E3
Walsingham NR22 .... **16** F8
Watlington PE34 .... **61** C6
Watton IP25 .... **84** E3
Wellingham PE32 .... **30** E1
Wereham PE33 .... **80** E4
West Beckham NR25 .... **9** C2
West Dereham PE33 .... **80** B4
Wheatacre NR34 .... **111** A5
Whinburgh & Westfield
NR19 .... **68** A3
Wiggenhall St Germans
PE34 .... **61** B6
Wimbotsham PE34 .... **172** E8
Wingfield IP21 .... **131** E3
Woodton NR35 .... **108** B5
Wortham IP22 .... **129** C5
Wreningham NR16 .... **88** E1
Wroxham/Hoveton
NR12 .... **164** D5
Yelverton NR14 .... **90** F5
Church Rd N IP21 .... **131** C7
Church St Ashill IP25 .... **84** A7
Attleborough NR17 .... **174** D5
Bawburgh NR9 .... **160** A6
Bradenham IP25 .... **66** E3
Brisley NR20 .... **49** A8
Briston NR24 .... **142** E4
Carbrooke IP25 .... **85** A5
Coltishall NR12 .... **54** C6
Cromer NR27 .... **139** C6
Diss IP22 .... **177** D4
East Dereham NR19 .... **154** D5
Elsing NR20 .... **50** F3
Gimingham NR11 .... **22** E7
Great Ellingham NR17 .... **103** F7
23 Harleston IP20 .... **122** D2
Hingham NR9 .... **86** C5
Holt NR25 .... **137** C6
Horsford NR10 .... **53** B2
Hunstanton PE36 .... **132** C4
Kenninghall NR16 .... **119** B4
King's Lynn PE30 .... **146** D4
Litcham PE32 .... **48** A4
Little Walsingham NR22 .... **16** F7
New Buckenham NR16 .... **104** F1
North Creake NR21 .... **15** D8
North Lopham NR16 .... **119** A1
Northrepps NR27 .... **11** A2
Norwich NR6 .... **158** E5
Plumstead NR11 .... **20** A6
Reepham NR10 .... **149** C4
Sheringham NR26 .... **138** D7
Southrepps NR11 .... **22** B7
Stiffkey NR23 .... **6** D5
18 Sutton Bridge PE12 .... **41** B8
Thornham PE36 .... **2** D6

Church St continued
Trimingham NR11 .... **11** D1
Wells-next-the-Sea
NR23 .... **136** D5
Wymondham NR18 .... **173** B4
Church Terr
1 Aylsham NR11 .... **150** C6
17 Wisbech PE13 .... **152** C5
Wroxham NR12 .... **164** B3
Church View
Harleston IP20 .... **122** E2
Marham PE33 .... **63** B4
Ormesby St Margaret
NR29 .... **167** B2
Pentney PE32 .... **63** C8
Church View Cl
Norwich NR7 .... **159** B5
Reedham NR13 .... **93** A5
Church Wlk
Burnham Market PE31 .... **135** B8
Great Yarmouth NR31 .... **94** C6
Shelfanger IP22 .... **120** B2
Churchfarm Wlk PE33 .... **62** E1
Churchfield Gn **3** NR7 .... **163** D8
Churchfield Rd **8** PE14 .... **77** F6
Churchfields NR19 .... **88** D8
Churchfields Rd NR15 .... **106** F4
Churchgate St **2** PE38 .... **97** B5
Churchgate Way PE34 .... **144** C5
Churchill Cl
Hevingham NR10 .... **53** B8
1 Watton IP25 .... **84** D3
Churchill Cres
Fincham PE33 .... **62** E1
Sheringham NR26 .... **138** B5
Churchill PI NR15 .... **90** F2
Churchill Rd
Great Yarmouth NR30 .... **169** D6
Norwich NR3 .... **162** E8
Thetford IP24 .... **176** E5
Wisbech PE13 .... **152** D6
Churchill Way PE38 .... **172** B4
Churchman Rd NR7 .... **159** C2
Churchway IP22 .... **128** F5
Cider Cl NR17 .... **174** E4
Cinder La NR14 .... **111** B4
Cintra Rd NR1 .... **163** B6
Cirrus Way NR7 .... **159** C2
City Coll Norwich
NR2 .... **162** D3
City of Norwich Aviation
Mus* NR6 .... **53** D1
City of Norwich Sch
NR4 .... **162** B2
City Rd NR1 .... **178** C1
City View Rd NR6 .... **158** A4
Civic Gdns NR3 .... **158** B3
Civray Ave PE38 .... **172** D5
Clabburn Cl **13** NR15 .... **89** C1
Clabon Fst Cl NR13 .... **158** F2
Clabon Rd NR13 .... **158** F2
Clabon Second Cl
NR3 .... **158** F3
Clabon Third Cl NR3 .... **158** F3
Clackclose Rd PE38 .... **172** C6
Clackclose Prim Sch
PE38 .... **172** B6
Clancy Rd NR7 .... **159** C1
Clare Ave NR31 .... **170** B2
Clare Cl NR3 .... **158** E1
Clare Dr Cromer NR27 .... **139** D5
King's Lynn PE30 .... **148** C3
Claremont Rd
Norwich NR4 .... **162** A2
Wisbech PE13 .... **152** E5
Clarence Ct **17** IP25 .... **84** D3
Clarence Rd
14 Great Yarmouth NR30 .... **169** D2
Great Yarmouth NR31 .... **170** D3
Hunstanton PE36 .... **132** D6
Norwich NR1 .... **163** A5
Wisbech PE13 .... **152** D6
Clarendon Cl **6** NR30 .... **169** D2
Clarendon Dr **10** NR29 .... **57** D4
Clarendon Rd
Norwich NR2 .... **162** C5
Sculthorpe NR21 .... **141** A5
Clarendon Stps **1** NR2 .... **162** B5
Clark Rd NR35 .... **109** B2
Clark Terr Cl IP22 .... **177** C1
Clarke Rd NR3 .... **162** D8
Clarke's Cl **2** NR9 .... **69** F2
Clarke's La
Barsham NR34 .... **124** F7
Gooderstone PE33 .... **82** A5
Clarkes Rd NR30 .... **169** B5
Clarke's Rd NR11 .... **170** C5
Clark's La NR21 .... **17** E5
Clark's Loke **7** NR13 .... **73** D6
Clarkson Ave PE13 .... **152** D5
Clarkson Ct PE13 .... **152** D6
Clarkson Inf Sch PE13 .... **152** D6
Clarkson Rd
16 Lingwood NR13 .... **74** A3
Norwich NR1 .... **161** C7
Claxton Castle* NR14 .... **91** C6
Claxton Cl Mileham PE32 .... **48** D6
5 Thetford IP24 .... **176** C4
Claxton Cnr NR14 .... **91** C6
Clay Hill PE32 .... **48** B7
Clay La Bacton NR28 .... **23** B4
Blundeston NR32 .... **94** C5
Hepworth IP22 .... **127** F1
Saxlingham Nethergate
NR15 .... **107** A7
Swannington NR9 .... **52** C7
Clay Rd NR30 .... **168** F5
Claydon Gr NR31 .... **170** B7

Cla - Cro 189

Claymore Gdns NR29 . . .167 B2
Claypit La NR21 . . . . .141 C5
Claypit Rd NR20 . . . . .33 D3
Clayton Cl
Dersingham PE31 . . . . . . .140 D4
Wisbech PE13 . . . . .152 F6
Clearview Dr NR14 . . . . . .90 C5
Cleaves Dr NR22 . . . . .16 F8
Clebe The NR23 . . . . .136 D6
Clement Gdns IP22 . . . . .177 F3
Clements Cl IP21 . . . . . . .130 C5
Clenchwarton Prim Sch
PE34 . . . . .145 E5
Clenchwarton Rd
PE34 . . . . .146 B4
Clere Cl NR18 . . . . .173 C5
Cleveland Rd NR2 . . . . . . .178 A3
Cleves Way NR8 . . . . .156 E4
Cley La IP25 . . . . .84 C4
Cley Marshes Nature Reserve* NR25 . . . . .7 F7
Cley Rd Blakeney NR25 . . . . .7 D6
Bradwell NR31 . . . . .94 C7
Cockley Cley PE37 . . . . .82 E8
Holt NR25 . . . . .137 B8
Swaffham PE37 . . . . .153 B2
Cliff Ave Cromer NR27 . . . .139 C6
Great Yarmouth NR31 . . . .170 D3
Cliff Cl NR13 . . . . .92 F4
Cliff Dr NR27 . . . . .139 C7
Cliff Hill 4 NR31 . . . . . . .170 D4
Cliff La Cromer NR27 . . . .139 C6
Great Yarmouth NR31 . . . .171 D8
Cliff Par PE36 . . . . .132 C5
Cliff Pk Com Mid Sch
NR31 . . . . .170 D2
Cliff Pk Fst Sch NR31 . .170 D2
Cliff Pk High Sch
NR31 . . . . .170 D1
Cliff Rd Cromer NR27 . . . .139 D5
Overstrand NR27 . . . . .11 A3
Sheringham NR26 . . . . .138 E7
Cliff Terr PE36 . . . . .132 C5
Cliffe-en-Howe Rd
PE32 . . . . .44 F8
Clifford Ave NR30 . . . . . .168 D5
Clifford Burman Cl
PE30 . . . . .148 A1
Clifford Pye Cl NR10 . . . . .35 B2
Clifton Cl 3 NR2 . . . . . . .162 C7
Clifton Pk NR27 . . . . .10 C5
Clifton Rd
King's Lynn PE30 . . . . .148 B1
Wymondham NR18 . . . . . . .173 C6
Clifton St NR2 . . . . .162 B7
Clifton Way NR27 . . . . .11 B3
Clink Hill NR20 . . . . .168 B4
Clink Rd NR12 . . . . .40 A6
Clint Hill IP31 . . . . .126 D2
Clint St NR29 . . . . .56 B5
Clintergate Rd IP20 . . . .122 C6
Clipbush La
Banham NR16 . . . . .119 C7
Fakenham NR21 . . . . .141 E5
Scoulton NR9 . . . . .85 C4
Clipped Hedge La NR11 . .22 B7
Clipstreet La NR21 . . . . . . .18 B8
Close The
Brancaster PE31 . . . . .3 D7
Brundall NR13 . . . . .165 C4
Docking PE31 . . . . .134 E4
Great Yarmouth NR31 . . . . .170 A5
Hemsby NR29 . . . . .167 B7
Holt NR25 . . . . .137 C5
Little Melton NR9 . . . . .160 D2
North Lopham IP22 . . . . . .119 A2
North Walsham NR28 . . . . .151 D4
Norwich NR1 . . . . .178 C3
Rackheath NR13 . . . . .72 D8
Roydon IP22 . . . . .177 A5
Stow Bedon NR17 . . . . .102 D7
Clough Dr 10 IP26 . . . . .98 E1
Clough La PE30 . . . . .146 D4
Clovelly Cl NR6 . . . . .157 E2
Clover Dr 7 NR26 . . . . . . .138 B6
Clover Hill Fst Sch
NR5 . . . . .161 B8
Clover Hill Rd NR5 . . . . .160 F8
Clover Rd
Attleborough NR17 . . . . . . .174 C3
Aylsham NR11 . . . . .150 D5
Norwich NR7 . . . . .158 F3
Clover Way
Fakenham NR21 . . . . .141 E4
12 Great Yarmouth NR31 . . .94 C6
Great Yarmouth NR31 . . . . .170 A4
Thetford IP24 . . . . .176 D5
Cloverland Dr 6 NR29 . . .167 B7
Clubbs La NR23 . . . . .136 D6
Clydesdale Rise NR31 . . . .94 C8
Coach & Horses Row
NR2 . . . . .178 A2
Coach House Ct 1 NR4 .162 A3
Coach La NR19 . . . . .67 C6
Coachmans Ct NR7 . . . . .158 F4
Coalwharf Rd PE13 . . . . .152 B4
Coast Rd Bacton NR12 . . . . .23 F4
Cley next the Sea NR25 . . . . . .7 F7
Corton NR32 . . . . .171 F1
Happisburgh NR12 . . . . .23 F3
Hopton on Sea NR31 . . . . . .171 D4
Overstrand NR27 . . . . .11 B3
Salthouse NR25 . . . . .8 A7
Wiveton NR25 . . . . .7 D6
Coastguard Rd NR30 . . .168 F5
Coates Ct 5 PE14 . . . . .59 D2
Cob Cl 7 NR31 . . . . .94 C8
Cobblers La PE14 . . . . .41 F2
Cobbleways The 9 NR29 . .58 B6
Cobbold St IP22 . . . . . . .177 B5
Cobb's Pl 5 NR30 . . . . . .169 D4
Cobham Way NR7 . . . . . . .159 C2
Cobholm Fst Sch
NR31 . . . . .169 B4
Cobholm Rd 5 NR31 . . . .169 B4
Coburg Cl 10 IP25 . . . . . . .84 D3
Coburg La IP25 . . . . .84 B6
Coburg St
9 King's Lynn PE30 . . . . . .146 E5
Norwich NR2 . . . . .178 A2
Cochrane Cl IP25 . . . . .85 A3
Cock Dro PE38 . . . . .172 B7
Cock Fen Rd PE14 . . . . . . .95 D7
Cock Rd NR14 . . . . .92 A3
Cock St Ixworth NR9 . . . . . .69 F2
Wymondham NR18 . . . . . . .173 B5
Cocketts Dr PE13 . . . . . . .152 E5
Cocklehole Rd PE34 . . . . .41 F8
Codling's La NR11 . . . . . .150 A6
Coigncroft The NR13 . . .165 E3
Coke Rd NR1 . . . . .162 E1
Coker's Hill NR22 . . . . .16 F7
Colby Prim Sch NR11 . . . . .36 E8
Cold Harbour Rd NR29 . . .56 D4
Coldershaw Rd NR6 . . . . .158 B4
Coldham Cl NR29 . . . . . .167 B3
Coldham Hall Carnser
NR14 . . . . .165 C1
Coldham Rd NR21 . . . . .17 D7
Coldham's La PE33 . . . . . .80 A5
Coldhorn Cres PE13 . . . .152 D7
Coleburn Rd NR1 . . . . .89 E8
Colegate NR3 . . . . .178 A3
Colegate End Rd IP21 . .121 E6
Coleman Cl
Palgrave IP22 . . . . .177 D1
Taverham NR8 . . . . .155 F2
Coleridge Cl NR8 . . . . . . .156 D8
Coleridge Rd IP22 . . . . .177 E4
Coles Way NR10 . . . . .149 C5
Colin Mclean Rd
NR19 . . . . .154 C7
Colindeep La NR7 . . . . . .159 A4
Colkett Dr NR6 . . . . .158 E3
Colkirk CE VA Prim Sch
NR21 . . . . .31 D5
Coll of W Anglia PE30 . .146 F5
Colleen Cl
Dereham NR19 . . . . .67 E5
East Dereham NR19 . . . . . .154 D1
College Cl NR12 . . . . .54 D7
College Ct 1 NR31 . . . . . .169 B4
College Dr PE31 . . . . . . .133 C4
College La Keswick NR4 . . .89 C7
7 King's Lynn PE30 . . . . . .146 D4
Runcton Holme PE33 . . . . . . .61 F3
College Rd
Hockwold cum Wilton
IP26 . . . . .113 F7
Norwich NR2 . . . . .162 A5
Thompson IP24 . . . . .102 C7
Thurlton NR14 . . . . .110 C8
Wereham PE33 . . . . .97 F8
Collen's Gn NR9 . . . . .51 B3
Collers Way NR10 . . . . . .149 C6
Collett's Bridge La
PE14 . . . . .59 C1
Colley Hill Drif PE32 . . . . .48 D4
Collingwood Cl
Heacham PE31 . . . . .133 D3
25 Hethersett NR9 . . . . .88 D7
Collingwood Dr NR11 . . . .22 F8
Collingwood Rd
Downham Market PE38 . . .172 B4
Great Yarmouth NR30 . . . .169 E7
Hunstanton PE36 . . . . .132 D3
Collingwood Way
IP24 . . . . .176 F6
Collins La PE31 . . . . .133 D5
Collin's La PE33 . . . . .63 C5
Collis La NR29 . . . . .57 F5
Colls Rd NR7 . . . . .159 D1
Colman Ave 1 NR14 . . . . . .89 F4
Colman Fst Sch NR4 . . . .162 A3
Colman Hospl NR2 . . . . .162 A4
Colman Mid Sch NR4 . . .161 F3
Colman Rd NR4 . . . . .161 F5
Colne Pl NR27 . . . . .139 B6
Colne Rd NR27 . . . . .139 B6
Colney La Colney NR4 . . .161 A3
Cringleford NR4 . . . . .161 B2
Hethersett NR9 . . . . .160 D1
Colney Rd PE30 . . . . .147 D5
Colomb Rd NR31 . . . . . . .170 C6
Coltishall Airfield NR10 . .54 B8
Coltishall La NR10 . . . . . . .53 E2
Coltishall Prim Sch
NR12 . . . . .54 D7
Coltishall Rd
Belaugh NR12 . . . . .164 A6
Buxton with Lammas
NR10 . . . . .53 F8
Coltishall Sta NR12 . . . . . .54 C7
Colton Rd NR9 . . . . .69 E6
Coltsfoot Way IP24 . . . . .176 F5
Columbia Way PE30 . . . . .146 F6
Columbine Cl IP24 . . . . .176 F5
Columbine Rd NR10 . . . . . .53 B2
Columbine The NR5 . . . . .160 E7
Colvile Rd PE13 . . . . .152 E5
Colville Rd NR24 . . . . . . .142 B5
Combe Way 6 NR13 . . . . . .72 E7
Comber Cl IP21 . . . . .130 D6
Comet Rd 7 IP25 . . . . .84 F3
Commercial Rd NR19 . . . .154 E5
Common Drift NR20 . . . . . .49 C4
Common Dro
Flitcham with Appleton
PE31 . . . . .27 F5
Southery PE38 . . . . .97 B5
Common End PE32 . . . . . . .47 D8
Common La
Beccles NR34 . . . . .110 D1
Beetley NR20 . . . . .49 E5
Brancaster PE31 . . . . .3 D6
Brockdish IP21 . . . . .131 D6
Burgh & Tuttington NR11 . . .36 E6
East Walton PE32 . . . . .45 E3
Field Dalling NR25 . . . . .7 B1
Filby NR29 . . . . .75 E8
Gayton PE32 . . . . .45 C4
Great Witchingham NR9 . . .51 D6
King's Lynn PE30 . . . . .148 C2
North Runcton PE33 . . . . . . .44 A2
Norwich NR7 . . . . .163 F5
Sheringham NR26 . . . . .138 E6
6 Southery PE38 . . . . .97 B5
Thorpe Market NR11 . . . . . . .22 A6
Common Loke NR14 . . . . . .92 A2
Common Pl 3 NR22 . . . . . . .16 F7
Common Rd
Aldeby NR34 . . . . .111 B3
Ashwellthorpe NR16 . . . . . .105 E7
Barton Turf NR12 . . . . .38 F1
Botesdale IP22 . . . . .128 F1
Bressingham IP22 . . . . .129 C8
Brumstead NR12 . . . . .24 A1
Burston & Shimpling
IP22 . . . . .120 E2
Castle Acre PE32 . . . . .46 E1
East Tuddenham NR20 . . . . .69 B5
Forncett NR16 . . . . .105 E5
Foxley NR20 . . . . .33 D1
Gissing NR15 . . . . .120 F5
Great Yarmouth NR31 . . . . .170 C8
Hemsby NR29 . . . . .57 F4
Hopton IP22 . . . . .127 F6
Lessingham NR12 . . . . .24 E2
Martham NR29 . . . . .57 B4
Mundham NR14 . . . . .91 C1
Neatishead NR12 . . . . .55 E6
Pulham Market IP21 . . . . . .121 E7
Runcton Holme PE33 . . . . . .61 D4
Runhall NR20 . . . . .68 F4
Scole IP21 . . . . .130 F8
Shelfanger IP22 . . . . .119 F3
Shelton NR15 . . . . .107 B1
Skeyton NR10 . . . . .37 A6
Snettisham PE31 . . . . .12 D4
Somerton NR29 . . . . .57 E6
Surlingham NR14 . . . . .165 B1
Swafield NR28 . . . . .22 D1
Thurne NR29 . . . . .56 D3
Wacton NR15 . . . . .106 D2
West Walton PE14 . . . . .59 D7
Wiggenhall St Germans
PE34 . . . . .60 F7
Common The
Freethorpe NR13 . . . . .92 E7
1 Harleston IP20 . . . . .122 D1
Lyng NR9 . . . . .51 A4
Surlingham NR14 . . . . .165 A1
Swardeston NR14 . . . . .89 B6
Commonwealth Way 12
NR7 .72 D4
Compass Rd NR18 . . . . . .173 F1
Compit Hills NR27 . . . . . .139 B3
Concorde Rd NR6 . . . . . .158 C5
Conesford Dr NR1 . . . . . .162 F3
Coney Weston Rd
Barningham IP31 . . . . .127 C4
Sapiston IP31 . . . . .126 D2
Conference Way NR21 . . . .31 E5
Conge The NR30 . . . . . . .169 C4
Congham Rd PE32 . . . . . . .28 B1
Conifer Cl NR29 . . . . .167 A3
Coniston Cl
2 Hethersett NR9 . . . . .88 E8
King's Lynn PE30 . . . . .148 F1
2 Norwich NR5 . . . . .161 C6
Coniston Rd NR15 . . . . . . .90 E1
Coniston Sq 1 NR30 . . . .169 D4
Connaught Ave NR31 . . .170 C3
Connaught Rd
Attleborough NR17 . . . . . .174 D5
Cromer NR27 . . . . .139 D5
Norwich NR2 . . . . .162 B7
Constable Cl
7 Attleborough NR17 . . . .174 B4
2 Diss IP22 . . . . .177 C4
Constable Ct 15 IP20 . . .122 D2
Constable Dr 4 NR31 . . .170 A7
Constable Rd
Norwich NR4 . . . . .89 D8
Norwich NR4 . . . . .162 C1
Constitution Hill
North Runcton PE33 . . . . . . .43 F4
Norwich NR6 . . . . .158 E3
Constitution Opening
NR3 . . . . .158 E2
Convent Rd 4 NR2 . . . . .162 C5
Conway Rd
Great Yarmouth NR31 . . . .170 D6
Sheringham NR26 . . . . . . .138 F7
Conyers NR18 . . . . .173 C6
Cook Rd IP25 . . . . .66 A3
Cooke Cl NR5 . . . . .160 E7
Cooke's Rd NR15 . . . . .91 B4
Cookley La IP23 . . . . . . .130 F1
Cook's La IP20 . . . . .122 F2
Cooper La NR1 . . . . .89 F8
Cooper Rd
North Walsham NR28 . . . . .151 D6
8 Sheringham NR26 . . . . .138 C5
Co-operative St NR26 . .138 D7
Coopers Cl NR8 . . . . .155 E3
Coopers La PE33 . . . . .62 B2
Copeman Rd
Aylsham NR11 . . . . .150 D5
Great & Little Plumstead
NR13 . . . . .73 A6
3 Roydon IP22 . . . . .129 D7
Copince's La NR16 . . . . .119 C7
Copper Beech Cl
NR21 . . . . .141 D6
Copper Hall PE37 . . . . . .153 B3
Copper La 8 NR9 . . . . .86 C5
Copperfield 4 PE30 . . . .147 C5
Copperfield Ave
Great Yarmouth NR30 . . . .169 D1
1 Great Yarmouth NR30 . .170 D8
Coppice Ave NR6 . . . . . . .157 E5
Coppice The 6 NR17 . . . .174 C5
Coppins Ct PE14 . . . . . . .152 E2
Corbet Ave NR7 . . . . .159 B2
Corbett Rd 2 NR28 . . . . .151 C6
Corbyn Shaw Rd PE30 . .147 C4
Cordon St PE13 . . . . .152 C4
Coriander Dr IP24 . . . . . .176 F4
Corie Rd NR4 . . . . .161 F4
Corkway Dro PE38 . . . . . . .97 E1
Cormorant Way 10 NR31 . .94 C8
Corncutters Cl NR3 . . . . .178 B3
Corner Comm Rd NR28 . . .38 B7
Corner La NR10 . . . . .53 B3
Corner St 5 NR27 . . . . . .139 B7
Cornfield The NR25 . . . . . . .7 A3
Cornfields IP21 . . . . .121 B1
Cornish Ave NR28 . . . . . . .22 E5
Cornish Way NR28 . . . . .151 C7
Cornwallis Cl 7 NR5 . . . .161 A7
Coronation Ave
3 Martham NR29 . . . . .57 D4
Nordelph PE38 . . . . .78 D3
1 Rollesby NR29 . . . . .57 D2
West Winch PE33 . . . . .43 F3
Coronation Cl NR6 . . . . .158 A4
Coronation Cotts PE32 . . .47 F4
Coronation Cres
NR15 . . . . .107 D5
Coronation Gn NR31 . . . .169 B3
Coronation Gr PE37 . . . .153 B5
Coronation La
Blakeney NR25 . . . . .7 D7
Somerton NR29 . . . . .57 F5
Coronation Pl IP27 . . . . .175 B2
Coronation Rd
Clenchwarton PE34 . . . . . .146 A5
Great Yarmouth NR31 . . . .169 B3
Holt NR25 . . . . .137 C5
Norwich NR6 . . . . .158 A4
Coronation Terr
Caston NR17 . . . . .102 F8
6 Great Yarmouth NR30 . .169 C4
Corporation Rd PE13 . . .152 D3
Corpusty Prim Sch
NR11 . . . . .19 F1
Corpusty Rd
Briston NR24 . . . . .142 F1
Thurning NR24 . . . . .19 B2
Wood Dalling NR11 . . . . .34 D7
Corton Rd NR1 . . . . .178 C1
Coslany St NR3 . . . . .178 A3
Costessey High Sch
NR5 . . . . .156 F2
Costessey Jun Sch
NR5 . . . . .156 F1
Costessey La
Drayton NR8 . . . . .156 E6
Ringland NR8 . . . . .70 B8
Taverham NR8 . . . . .157 A7
Coston La NR18 . . . . .87 A8
Cotman Cl IP22 . . . . .177 C4
Cotman Dr NR31 . . . . . . .170 A7
Cotman Rd NR1 . . . . .163 B5
Cotoneaster Cl 4 NR31 . .170 B6
Cottage Dr The NR7 . . . .163 E8
Cottage Farm Abbey
PE32 . . . . .46 C2
Cottage Rd NR29 . . . . .57 E6
Cottinghams Dr NR10 . . .157 E7
Cotton Rd NR9 . . . . .70 A4
Cotton's Cnr PE14 . . . . . . .77 D2
Cotts La PE34 . . . . .144 F1
Coughtrey Cl NR7 . . . . . .159 B5
Couhe Cl PE37 . . . . .153 C5
Coulton Cl PE30 . . . . . . .146 E7
Council Rd 4 PE13 . . . . .152 E6
County Ct Rd 3 PE30 . . .146 E4
Court Cl 6 NR29 . . . . .57 D2
Court Dr NR27 . . . . .139 B6
Court Gdns PE38 . . . . . . .172 C5
Court Hill NR12 . . . . .54 A4
Court Rd
Great Snoring NR21 . . . . . . .17 B5
Rollesby NR29 . . . . .57 D2
Courtenay Cl
4 East Dereham NR19 . . .154 D5
2 Norwich NR5 . . . . .160 F8
Courtfields PE37 . . . . . . .153 B3
Courtnell Pl PE30 . . . . . .147 D5
Courtyard The 5 NR4 . . .161 C5
Covent Gdn Rd NR30 . . . .168 C7
Coventry St 2 NR21 . . . . . .15 C2
Coventry Way IP24 . . . . .176 A4
Covert The IP24 . . . . .176 E6
Covey The
Surlingham NR14 . . . . .91 C8
Taverham NR8 . . . . .155 D2
Covey Way IP27 . . . . .113 F1
Cow Hill NR2 . . . . .178 A3
Cow La Denver PE38 . . . . .172 C1
Cow La *continued*
Tharston & Hapton
NR15 . . . . .106 C7
Cow Lake Dro PE14 . . . . . .59 D5
Cow Mdw Rd NR13 . . . . . . .92 C8
Cow Tro NR29 . . . . .57 D3
Cowdewell Mews 7
NR8 . . . . .155 D1
Cowgate NR3 . . . . .178 B4
Cowle's Dro IP26 . . . . . . .113 D5
Cowper Cl NR11 . . . . .143 C5
Cowper Rd NR19 . . . . . . .154 E5
Cowslip Cl 14 NR14 . . . . . .89 B3
Cowslip La NR26 . . . . . . .138 B6
Cowslip Wlk PE34 . . . . . . .61 B8
Cox's La PE13 . . . . .152 A3
Coxswain Read Way
NR30 . . . . .168 D4
Cozens Rd NR1 . . . . .163 A4
Cozens Hardy Rd NR7 . .159 D4
Crab Apple La NR14 . . . .110 E8
Crab La Boughton PE33 . . .81 A5
Great Yarmouth NR31 . . . . .170 A5
Crab Marsh PE13 . . . . . . .152 B8
Crabapple Cl 7 NR18 . . .173 E4
Crabapple La NR9 . . . . . . .68 D1
Crabb La PE34 . . . . .42 E1
Crabbe's Cl 8 IP26 . . . . . .98 E1
Crabb's Abbey PE34 . . . . .61 B2
Crabgate La NR11 . . . . . . .34 D5
Crabtree La NR34 . . . . . .110 F4
Crabtree Rise IP21 . . . . .131 C6
Cradle Wood Rd NR28 . .151 E3
Cradock Ave NR30 . . . . .169 D8
Craft La NR27 . . . . .11 A1
Craft The
Raveningham NR14 . . . . . .110 B8
Winterton-on-Sea NR29 . . . .58 B6
Cramp Cnr NR14 . . . . .91 F6
Cranage Rd NR1 . . . . . . .162 E1
Crane Cl 8 NR19 . . . . . . .154 C3
Crane's La NR10 . . . . . . .150 C1
Cranes Mdw 31 IP20 . . . .122 D2
Cranes Rd NR14 . . . . .88 F3
Cranfield Rd NR26 . . . . .138 A4
Cranleigh Rise NR4 . . . . .161 F1
Cranley Rd NR7 . . . . .72 E4
Cranmer Ave PE30 . . . . .148 C4
Cranmer Ct NR21 . . . . . . .141 C5
Cranny Field Chase
PE14 . . . . .41 E1
Cranwell Rd 10 IP25 . . . . .84 F3
Craske Cl 10 NR26 . . . . . .138 C5
Craske Dr NR13 . . . . .72 E7
Craske La PE34 . . . . .42 A7
Craske Mews 6 NR5 . . . .160 E8
Craven La PE33 . . . . .62 D6
Crawford Rd NR27 . . . . .139 D5
Craymere Beck Rd
NR24 . . . . .18 F1
Craymere Rd NR24 . . . . .142 E1
Creake Rd
Burnham Market PE31 . . . .135 D2
Burnham Thorpe PE31 . . . .135 F2
Sculthorpe NR21 . . . . .141 A6
Sculthorpe Airfield PE31 . . . .15 B3
Creance Rd NR7 . . . . . . .159 C4
Crecen La PE36 . . . . .132 C4
Cremer Cl 14 PE31 . . . . . . .12 E4
Cremer St NR26 . . . . .138 D7
Cremer's Drift NR26 . . . .138 D6
Cremorne La NR1 . . . . . .163 B5
Crescent Rd PE36 . . . . . .132 C3
Crescent The
Ashwellthorpe NR16 . . . . . .105 F8
Bacton/Walcott NR12 . . . . . .24 A7
East Dereham NR19 . . . . . .154 C1
East Harling NR16 . . . . . . .118 C4
Hemsby NR29 . . . . .167 D7
Hethersett NR9 . . . . .88 C7
4 Newton Flotman NR15 . . .89 D1
Norwich NR2 . . . . .178 A2
Taverham NR8 . . . . .156 F8
Thurton NR14 . . . . .91 C4
Wisbech PE13 . . . . .152 C4
Cressener Cl NR6 . . . . . .157 E5
Cressingham Rd IP25 . . . . .83 F6
Cresswell Cl NR5 . . . . . . .161 B6
Cresswell St PE30 . . . . . .146 E6
Crest Rd PE31 . . . . .140 C4
Cricket Cl NR8 . . . . .155 E3
Cricket Gd Rd NR1 . . . . .162 E3
Cricket Pasture The
PE31 .3 F7
Cricketers Way PE13 . . . .152 A6
Cricketer's Wlk NR13 . . . .92 E7
Crick's Wlk IP22 . . . . . . .177 A5
Crimp Cramp La NR34 . . .111 B4
Cringleford CE Fst & Mid Sch
NR4 . . . . .89 B8
Cringleford Chase
NR4 . . . . .161 C1
Crinoline La NR20 . . . . . . .69 C5
Crisp Cl PE31 . . . . .140 C3
Crisp Rd NR35 . . . . .109 E3
Critten's Rd NR31 . . . . . .169 B4
Croft Cl Diss IP22 . . . . . .177 C4
10 Harleston IP20 . . . . . . .122 D2
Croft Hill NR29 . . . . .75 B5
Croft La Corpusty NR11 . . . .19 F2
Diss IP22 . . . . .177 C4
Marsham NR10 . . . . .150 C1
Croft Rd
Caister-on-Sea NR30 . . . . .168 E5
Norton Subcourse NR14 . . . .92 E1

Croft Rd continued
Upwell PE14 ....77 D3

Croft The
Costessey NR8 ....156 F4
Cromer NR27 ....139 B6
Little Snoring NR21 ....17 C3
Swanton Novers NR24 ..18 E3
Croft Yd NR23 ....136 D6
Croftholme Way 2 NR7 .163 C8
Crofts Cl PE31 ......135 C4
Crofts The NR5 ......160 F7
Cromarty Way NR30 ..168 D5
Crome Cl IP22 ......177 B4
Crome Rd NR3 ......162 F8
Cromer NR27 ....139 D6

Cromer High Sch
NR27 ....139 C5
Cromer Jun Sch NR27 .139 C5
Cromer Rd PE33 ....80 F3
Cromer Mus* NR27 ..139 C7

Cromer Rd
Aylsham NR11 ......150 C8
Blickling NR11 .....36 B7
Hevingham NR10 ...36 B1
Holt NR25 ....137 D7
Hunstanton PE36 ..132 D5
Mundesley NR11 ...143 B7
North Walsham NR28 .151 A6
Norwich NR6 ......158 A5
Ormesby St Margaret
  with Scratby NR29 .167 A2
Overstrand NR27 ...139 F4
Runton NR27 ......10 A5
Sheringham NR26 ..138 E6
Southrepps NR11 ..22 C8
Trimingham NR11 ..11 C2
Cromer Sta NR27 ..139 A7
Cromes Oak Cl NR14 .90 C4
Cromes Pl NR10 ...37 B2
Crompton Rd NR11 .150 C4

Cromwell Cl
Cromer NR27 ......139 C6
5 Hethersett NR9 ..88 D8
7 Marthan NR29 ...57 D4
Swaffham PE37 ....153 D3

Cromwell Rd
Cromer NR27 ......139 C6
Great Yarmouth NR31 .169 C1
Norwich NR7 ......159 B3
Weeting-with-Broomhill
IP27 ....114 E8
Wisbech PE13 .....152 A2
Crooks Pl NR1 ....178 A1
Crosby Row PE12 ..41 A8
Cross Bank Rd PE30 .146 C6
Cross Dro Hilgay PE38 .96 D7
Southery PE38 ....97 B3
Cross Keys Cl 2 NR10 .53 D2
Cross La Brancaster PE31 .3 B7
Lessingham NR12 ..24 E4
Northwold IP26 ...99 C7
Norwich NR3 .....178 A4
Runton NR27 .....10 B4
Stanhoe PE31 ....14 E7
Surlingham NR14 ..91 A8

Cross Rd
Ashby with Oby NR29 .56 F1
Great Yarmouth NR31 .170 D6
Starston IP20 ....122 C2
Cross St 6 Cromer NR27 .139 B6
Harpley PE31 ....29 C5
2 Holt NR25 .....137 B6
Hoxne IP21 ......131 A3
Salthouse NR25 ..8 B6
Cross Stone Rd NR14 .92 B3
Cross Way PE31 ..133 C5
Crossing Rd IP22 .177 D1
Crosskeys Way 3 NR20 .68 F6
Crossroad NR10 ..37 C4
Cross's Grave PE31 .29 E4
Crosstead NR20 .169 D8
Crossway Terr 5 NR14 .91 F1
Crossways 4 NR29 .167 A2
Crostwick La NR10 .54 A2
Crostwight Rd NR28 .38 D7
Croughton La PE31 .30 B8
Crow Hall Gn NR31 .170 C2
Crow La Bircham PE31 .14 A2
Elsing NR20 ......50 F6
Great Dunham PE32 .47 E1
Crow Rd NR20 ....151 D6
Crow St IP31 .....127 B4
Crowden Rd NR12 .24 D4
Crowes Loke NR13 .73 B7
Crown Ave PE14 ..59 E5
Crown Cres IP25 ..84 E6
Crown Gdns PE33 .80 F4
Crown Gn IP22 ...120 C2

Crown La
Coney Weston IP31 .127 A4
Hindringham NR21 .66 D6

Crown Rd
Christchurch PE14 .95 A7
Colkirk NR21 .....31 D5
East Dereham NR20 .154 F5
Great Yarmouth NR30 .169 D7
Horsham St Faith NR10 .53 D2
Lamas NR10 .....36 E1
Mundford IP26 ...100 B4
Norwich NR5 ....157 B1
Norwich NR1 ....178 B3
2 Old Buckenham NR17 .104 D2

Crown St
Banham NR16 ....119 D7

Crown St continued
Brandon IP27 ....175 A2
Methwold IP26 ...99 A5
Crown Way NR16 .119 D6
Crownthorpe Rd NR18 .87 C6
Crow's La IP25 ...84 C1
Crowshall La NR17 .174 B5

Croxton Rd
Fulmodeston NR21 .17 E2
Thetford IP24 ...176 D4
Crummock Rd 3 NR5 .161 C6
Cubitt Rd NR1 ...163 C7
Cuck's Lode Rd PE14 .95 A4
Cuck Stool La 5 PE32 .46 F2
Cuckoo Hill Rd PE31 .14 B3

Cuckoo La
Brundall NR13 ...73 E3
Carbrooke IP25 ..85 B4
Redenhall with Harleston
IP20 ....122 F2
Cuckoo Rd PE34 .79 A8
Cuckoofield La NR14 .89 A3
Cucumber La NR13 .165 B5
Cuddle Dike Bank PE14 .78 A5
Cuffer La NR16 ..104 F2
Culey Cl PE30 ...146 F7
Culley's Pit Rd NR12 .38 A2
Culling's Hill NR13 .72 F2
Cullum Cl NR20 ..50 B3
Culverin Cl 3 NR7 .72 D4
Cummings Byd NR21 .15 C2
Cunningham Ave 2
NR30 ....169 D8
Cunningham Cl IP24 .176 F6
Cunningham Rd 6 NR5 .161 C5
Curd's Hall NR19 .66 A7
Curlew Cl 7 IP25 .84 C3
Curlew Way NR31 .170 A6
Curson Cl 11 NR9 .88 C7
Curson Rd 8 NR15 .106 F6
Cursons Mews NR18 .173 B6
Curtis Dr 1 IP25 .98 D1
Curtis La NR26 ..138 E7
Curtis Rd NR3 ...158 B4
Cushing Cl 1 IP25 .67 B2
Cushing Dr 3 NR1 .72 D3
Custom House (TIC)*
PE30 ....146 D5
Customhouse St PE12 .41 C8
Cut Loke NR14 ..73 C1

Cuthbert Cl
4 King's Lynn PE30 .148 C5
Norwich NR7 ....159 B4
Cutler Way NR5 ..160 E8
Cutthroat La NR19 .68 A6
Cutting's Rd IP21 .131 C8
Cuttons Cnr NR13 .73 D6
Cypress Cl NR8 ..156 E8
Cypress Cres NR26 .138 D5
Cypress Pl NR29 .132 D4
Cyprus Rd NR17 .174 C5
Cyprus St NR1 ...162 E3
Cyril Rd NR7 ....163 F7

D

Dacre Cl NR4 ....161 E1
Dades La PE14 ...60 B6
Daffodil Way NR20 .68 E6
Dagmar Mews 12 NR30 .169 D2
Dairy Drift PE22 .48 C2
Dairy Dro PE36 ..95 F2
Dairy Farm Cl NR21 .141 C6
Dairy La NR11 ...9 E1
Dakenham Cl NR13 .72 F8
Dakin Rd NR3 ...150 C4
Dalbier Cl 2 NR13 .72 E4
Dale End PE31 ...3 D7
Dale La NR29 ....56 C8

Dale Rd
East Dereham NR19 .154 C6
Scarning NR19 ..67 A7
Dales Cl 6 NR13 .94 C8
Dales La NR14 ...163 D5
Dales The NR13 .165 D3
Dalrymple Way NR3 .158 C4
Dam La IP22 ....129 D3
Damate Back La NR29 .57 D6
Damgate Cl NR13 .166 C2
Damgate La Acle NR13 .166 D2
Martham NR29 ..57 D6
Damgate St NR18 .173 B3
Danby Cl 3 NR4 .89 D8
Danby Rd NR13 ..170 C6
Dane Cl IP24 ....176 B3
Danemoor La NR9 .86 F8
Danesbower Cl NR13 .165 F6
Danesbower La NR13 .165 F6
Danesfort Dr 1 NR19 .154 E6
Daniels Rd NR4 ..162 B2

Dark La
Ashmanhaugh NR12 .38 C1
Dickleburgh & Rushall
IP21 ....130 B6
Erpingham NR11 .21 A1
Kimberley NR18 ..87 B7
Smallburgh NR12 .38 D3
Swardeston NR14 .88 F4
Wretham IP24 ...101 F2
Darrell Pl NR5 ...161 D7
Darrow Wood NR20 .122 F8
Darrow Wood La (National
Trust)* NR20 ...122 F8
Darrow Wood La IP22 .120 A1
Darwin Cl 3 PE12 .41 B8
Daseley's Cl PE30 .148 A1

Dashwood Cl NR31 .93 F6
Dauber's La NR13 .74 C2
Davey Rd NR2 ...178 B3
Davidson Cl NR7 .163 F7
Davidson Rd NR7 .163 F7
Davy Pl Heacham PE31 .133 C5
2 Loddon NR14 ..92 A1
Dawber Cl NR10 .149 B6
Dawes La 8 PE31 .12 E4
Dawnay Ave NR29 .148 B1
Dawsons La NR4 .33 C3
Day's La IP21 ....127 C4
Day's Lode Rd PE14 .95 A4
De Caux Rd NR3 .158 E1
De Grey Rd PE30 .147 B5
De Hague Rd NR4 .161 F4

De Havilland Rd
Hethersett NR9 ..154 C6
Wisbech PE13 ...152 C6
De Lucy Cl IP22 .177 C5
De Morley Cl 4 IP22 .177 A5
De Morley Garth
NR26 ....138 D6
De Warrenne Pl PE32 .47 A2
Deacon Cl NR13 .165 D4
Deacon Dr 14 NR9 .88 D8
Deben Dr 14 NR31 .94 A6
Debenne Rd NR28 .151 C6
Deepdale NR13 ..166 C3
Deepdale 1 NR31 .57 C4
Deer Row NR35 ..109 D1
Delane Rd NR8 ..157 C7
Delgate La PE31 .3 E7
Dell Cl NR15 ....106 F8
Dell Cnr La NR13 .165 F6
Dell Cres NR5 ...161 D7
Dell Loke NR14 ..163 B2
Dell The Bodham NR25 .9 A3
Hingham NR9 ...86 B5
Delta Cl NR6 ....158 C4
De-Narde Rd NR19 .154 D7
Denbigh Rd NR7 .159 C2
Dene Ave NR29 ..167 A3
Dene Side NR30 .169 C4
Denes The NR1 ..163 C5
Denham Low Rd IP21 .131 A1
Denham Rd IP21 .131 B2
Denmark Hill IP22 .177 C3
Denmark Rd IP22 .177 B4
Denmark Opening
NR3 ....158 E1

Denmark Rd
Beccles NR34 ....110 D1
2 King's Lynn PE30 .147 B6
Norwich NR3 ....158 E1
Denmark Rise IP22 .177 C3
Denmark St IP22 .177 C3
Denmead Cl 4 NR4 .89 D8
Denney Rd PE30 .147 A4
Dennis Rd NR6 ..158 D1
Denny's Hill NR10 .123 A2
Denny's Wlk PE32 .63 E7

Denton Rd
Denton IP20 .....123 C6
Norwich NR8 ....158 F3
Denver Hill PE38 .172 C3
Denver VC Prim Sch
PE38 ....172 D2

Deopham Rd
Attleborough NR17 .174 C7
Scarning NR19 ..86 C4
Morley NR9 .....87 A2
Derby St NR2 ...162 C2
Dereham 6th Form Coll
NR20 ....154 F5
Dereham Church Inf Sch
NR19 ....154 D5
Dereham Hospl NR19 .154 E7
Dereham La NR19 .154 C8
Dereham Neatherd High Sch
NR20 ....154 F5

Dereham Rd
5 Bawdeswell NR20 .50 E7
Beeston with Bittering
PE32 ....48 D2
Brinningham NR24 .18 D5
Bylaugh NR20 ...50 C6
Colkirk NR21 ....31 E5
Costessey NR5 ..156 D1
Dereham NR20 ..50 B2
East Dereham NR19 .154 B5
Easton NR9 .....70 C5
Garvestone NR9 .69 E3
Gressenhall NR19 .49 C2
Hempton NR21 ..141 B2
Hingham NR9 ...86 B5
Honingham NR9 .69 F6
Kimberley NR18 .87 A7
Litcham PE32 ...48 A4
Mattishall NR20 .68 D6
North Elmham NR20 .49 E6
Norwich NR5 ....157 A1
Ovington IP25 ...84 E6
Pudding Norton NR21 .141 B1
Reepham NR10 ..149 A4

Dereham Rd continued
Scarning NR19 ..154 A4
Shipdham IP25 ..67 A1
28 Watton IP25 .84 D3
Whinburgh & Westfield
NR19 ....67 F5
Whissonsett NR20 .31 E2
Worthing NR20 ..68 A5
Dereham St Nicholas Jun Sch
NR19 ....154 D4
Dersingham Fst Sch
PE31 ....140 D4
Dersley Ct NR5 ..160 F6
Derwent Ave PE30 .148 F2
Desborough Way NR13 .72 D4
Desmond Dr NR6 .158 F6
Devon Ave NR6 ..157 E4
Devon Cres PE30 .148 D5
Devonshire Rd NR2 .162 A4
Devonshire St 4 NR2 .162 C7
Dewarrene Dr IP27 .175 B7
Dewing Rd NR13 .72 E8
Dexter Rd NR19 .154 C6
Dial Cl PE38 ....172 B5
Diamond Rd NR6 .158 B5
Diamond St NR26 .146 D2
Dian Rd NR13 ...165 E3
Diana Cl NR19 ..154 C1
Diana Way NR30 .168 D6
Dianas Dro PE36 .132 C2
Dibden Rd NR3 ..162 F8
Dickens Ave NR30 .169 D1
Dickfool's La NR19 .66 F8
Dickleburgh Rd NR21 .121 A1
Dicks Mount NR34 .111 D3
Dicky Hill IP20 ..122 D3
Digby Dr NR31 ..148 C6
Dilham Arts Ctr* NR28 .38 E4
Dilham Rd Honing NR28 .38 A4
Worstead NR28 ..38 A4
Dilldash La NR21 .17 A5
Dinosaur Adventure Pk*
NR9 ....51 E4

Dirty La
North Tuddenham NR20 .50 E1
Pulham St Mary IP21 .121 F3
Diss Church Jun Sch
IP22 ....177 D6
Diss Cty High Sch
IP22 ....177 E5
Diss Mus* IP22 ..177 D4

Diss Rd
Burston & Shimpling
IP22 ....120 E1
Garboldisham IP22 .128 A8
Scole IP21 ......130 C5
South Lopham IP22 .128 F8
Tibenham NR16 ..120 C8
Wattisfield IP22 .128 B1
Diss Sta IP22 ...177 F4
Ditchingham Dam
NR35 ....109 A1
Dix Cl PE31 .....133 E5
Dixon Rd Cromer NR27 .139 B5
North Walsham NR28 .151 D5
Norwich NR7 ....159 A4
Dixon's Dro PE14 .59 C8
Dixon's Fold NR6 .158 F4
Dobbs' La NR13 .54 D2
Dock Tavern La NR31 .170 D5

Docking Rd
Ringstead PE36 ..2 B2
Sedgeford PE36 .13 B7
Stanhoe PE31 ...15 A3
Syderstone PE31 .15 A3
Doctor's La IP21 .122 A2
Doctors Mdw 1 NR10 .53 D2
Doctors Rd NR13 .165 E6
Dodd Cl NR30 ...168 D7
Dodderman Way NR5 .160 F6
Dodds Cl NR17 ..174 B3
Dodds La PE32 ..45 B2
Dodds Rd NR17 .174 B3
Doddshill Rd PE31 .140 F3
Dodgers La NR15 .91 A3
Dodma Rd PE32 .47 C8
Dodoma Rd 1 PE33 .43 F2
Doit La IP22 ....129 D7
Doit The IP27 ...114 B7
Dolphin Gr NR2 .162 B8
Doman Rd NR1 ..178 C1
Donchurch Cl 6 NR7 .161 A7
Doris Rd NR2 ...162 B4
Dorking Rd NR31 .171 B4
Dorothea Dr 7 NR19 .154 C7
Dorothy Ave NR31 .94 C7

Dorset Cl
Attleborough NR17 .174 B3
4 Great Yarmouth NR30 .169 D3
Dougall's Hospl NR5 .178 A2
Douglas Bader Cl
NR28 ....151 C7

Douglas Bader Prim RAF Sch
NR10 ....37 B2

Douglas Cl
Croxton IP24 ....116 C5
Norwich NR6 ....158 D7
Douglas Haig Rd NR5 .161 B6
Doune Way 9 IP20 .122 D2
Douro Pl NR2 ...162 C6

Dove Cl
1 Great Yarmouth NR31 .170 A6
3 Harleston IP20 .122 D1
Dove House La 4 NR29 .56 F6
Dove La NR15 ...90 C3
Dovecote Cl NR13 .50 F2
Dovecote Rd PE14 .77 D3
Dovedale Rd NR16 .105 F5
Dovedales Fold NR7 .158 F4
Dovehouse La NR11 .21 B4
Dover Cir NR30 ..168 D5
Dover St NR2 ...162 B5
Dow La 54 C3

Dowding Rd
Norwich NR5 ....158 D6
2 Watton IP25 ..84 F3
Downham Cres NR18 .173 B6
Downham Dro PE32 .63 F7
Downham High Sch
PE38 ....172 D5
Downham High Sch Ryston
Site PE38 ......172 C4
Downham Mkt Sta
PE38 ....172 C4
Downham Montessori Sch
PE34 ....79 E8

Downham Rd
Crimplesham PE33 .80 B7
Denver PE38 ....172 C2
Fincham PE33 ...62 E1
Nordelph PE38 ..78 D3
Outwell PE14 ...77 F6
Runton Holme PE33 .61 D4
Stradsett PE33 ..80 B8
Downham Way IP27 .175 F4
Downing Mews NR5 .160 D8
Downing Rd NR31 .170 C5
Downs Cl PE36 ..132 D4
Downs Farm La IP20 .123 B3
Downs Rd PE36 .132 D4
Dowsing Ct 6 NR12 .72 D5
Dowson Fst Sch NR3 .158 A1
Dowson Rd NR3 .158 B1
Drabblegate NR11 .150 D8
Drabbs La NR12 .38 E6
Dragon Hall NR1 .178 C2
Dragoon Cl 27 NR7 .72 D4
Drake Ave NR30 .169 D7
Drake Cl 1 NR10 .53 D2
Drake Inf & Nursery Fst Sch
IP24 ....176 E6
Drake Rd 2 PE14 .176 E5
Drakes Cl 18 NR16 .118 C5
Drakes Loke NR10 .36 F1
Draper Way NR5 .160 D8
Drapers La NR35 .109 A3
Draycote Cl PE30 .147 D8
Draycotts Rise IP22 .177 C1
Drayton Com Fst Sch
NR8 ....155 F1
Drayton Gr NR8 .156 F4
Drayton High Rd NR8 .157 A8
Drayton La NR10 .53 B1
Drayton Lodge Pk
NR8 ....157 B7
Drayton Rd NR3 .157 F2
Drayton Wood Rd
NR6 ....157 D6
Draytonhall La NR19 .154 B3
Dreibholz Ct NR31 .171 D8
Drewray Dr NR8 .156 E5
Dried Flower Ctr*
NR12 ....55 C7

Drift The
Bawdeswell NR20 .50 E6
Fulmodeston NR21 .17 F3
Drift La NR29 ...49 C3

Drift Rd
Caister-on-Sea NR30 .168 C7
Lakenheath IP27 .113 E2
Drift The Beetley NR20 .49 A6
Botesdale IP22 ..128 E3
Fakenham NR21 .141 D4
Heacham PE31 ..133 D6
Ingoldisthorpe PE31 .140 C8
Swardeston NR14 .89 B5
Driftlands NR21 .141 D5
Driftway PE30 ..148 C1

Driftway The
1 Holt NR25 ....137 C5
Sheringham NR26 .138 D8
Drill St NR21 ...15 C3
Drinkwater Cl 9 NR3 .158 B1
Drive The Acle NR13 .166 D4
East Winch PE32 .45 A2
Norwich NR5 ....161 B8
Trowse with Newton
NR14 ....163 D1
Drout's La IP31 .127 C3

Drove The
Brandon IP27 ...114 D4
Raynham NR21 ..30 E4
Taverham NR8 ..155 C2
Drudge Rd NR31 .170 D4
Druids La Litcham PE32 .48 A4
Shelfanger IP22 .120 B2
Druids' La IP22 .120 A3
Drunken Dro PE32 .46 C8

Drury La
3 Castle Acre PE32 .46 F2

Drury La continued
  6 Loddon NR14 ....91 F1
Dryden Cl 1 IP24 ......176 E6
Dryden Rd NR8 ....156 D8
Duck Decoy Cl PE31 ...140 C3
Duck Dro CB7 ....112 A2
Duckett Cl 2 NR1 .....162 E1
Duck's Foot Rd IP21 ...121 F6
Duff Rd NR3 ....158 D2
Duffield Cres NR9 ......51 A4
Dugard Ave NR1 ....163 B8
Duke Rd NR31 ....170 D6
Duke St Norwich NR3 ..178 A4
  Wisbech PE13 ....152 D4
Duke's La NR17 ....102 E8
Dukesway 1 NR35 .....123 F8
Dulgate La PE37 ....153 D2
Dulgate Rd NR35 ......108 B3
Dull's Rd NR21 ....109 C5
Dumbs La NR10 ....53 E5
Dumpling Gn
  Dereham NR19 ....68 A6
  East Dereham NR19 ...154 F2
Dun Cow Gdns PE34 ...144 E7
Dun Cow Rd NR34 .....111 E8
Dunburgh Rd NR34 ....110 A2
Duncan Cl IP24 ....176 F6
Duncan Rd 6 NR30 ....169 D2
Dunford La IP24 ....102 A2
Dunham Mus* PE32 .....65 E8
Dunham Rd
  Litcham PE32 ....48 A4
  Necton PE37 ....65 F6
Dunhill La IP22 ....127 F1
Dunkirk NR11 ....150 E8
Dunlop Rd NR19 ......154 D6
Dunnet Cl NR17 ....174 E5
Dunnetts Cl IP25 ....84 A7
Dunning's La IP21 .....121 E6
Dunns La NR21 ....4 D1
Dunwood Dr NR6 .....158 F7
Durbidge's Hill IP22 ...108 C2
Durham Ave NR11 ....170 B2
Durham St NR2 ....162 B4
Durham Way IP24 ....176 A5
Dussindale 3 NR18 ...173 C6
Dussindale Dr 16 NR7 ..72 D4
Duverlin Cl 2 NR4 ....162 A1
Dyball's La* 38 F8
Dyers Yd NR3 ....178 A3
Dye's Rd NR13 ....73 C7
Dyes The NR20 ....33 E8

E

Eade Rd NR3 ....162 D8
Eagle Cl NR11 ....21 B2
Eagle Rd NR11 ....21 B2
Eagle Wlk 2 NR2 .....162 C4
Eagles Golf Course
  PE34 ....42 E4
Eagles The 3 NR30 ...169 D4
Earl Cl PE31 ....140 C3
Earl of Brandon Ave
  PE31 ....30 B3
Earl Rd NR13 ....72 E8
Earl Warren IP24 .....116 C5
Earlham City High Sch
  NR4 ....161 D5
Earlham Gn La NR5 ...161 B7
Earlham Gr NR5 ......161 D6
Earlham Rd NR4 ......161 C5
Earlham W Ctr 5 NR5 .161 C6
Carls' St IP24 ....176 D4
Earlsford Rd IP23 ....129 C1
Earsham CE VA Fst Sch
  NR35 ....123 F8
Earsham Dam NR35 ...123 F8
Earsham Dr PE30 .....147 D8
Earsham Rd NR35 ....108 E2
Earth La NR32 ....94 C1
East & W Rudham Prim Sch
  PE31 ....30 A6
East Anglia Transport Mus*
  NR33 ....111 C3
East Anglian Way
  NR21 ....170 C6
East Ave NR13 ....165 E3
East Bank PE12 ....41 C8
East Bilney Hall NR20 .49 A6
East Carleton Rd NR14 .89 A4
East Cres NR20 ....50 B5
East Dereham Sta
  NR20 ....154 E5
East End PE38 ....79 E1
East End Cl NR30 .....168 E8
East Farm La NR10 ....53 E3
East Gn NR9 ....68 F2
East Gr NR27 ....139 C5
East Harbour Way
  PE31 ....135 E7
East Harling Prim Sch
  NR16 ....118 C5
East Harling Rd NR16 .118 F4
East Hills Rd NR5 ....156 E1
East La PE31 ....134 E4
East Norfolk 6th Form Coll
  NR30 ....169 D5
East Rd
  Great Yarmouth NR30 .169 D5
  Watton IP25 ....84 D3
East Ruston Area Com Sch
  NR12 ....38 F7
East Ruston NR28 .....38 D6
East Winch CE Prim Sch
  PE32 ....44 F3

East Winch Rd
  Leziate PE32 ....44 F5
  Middleton PE32 ....44 C2
East Winchcommon (Nature
  Reserve)* PE32 ....45 A2
Eastbourne Pl NR1 ...178 C3
Easterley Way NR29 ..167 A7
Eastern Ave
  Caister-on-Sea NR30 .168 E6
  Norwich NR7 ....72 D4
Eastern Cl
  Caister-on-Sea NR30 .168 E5
  Norwich NR7 ....72 D4
Eastern Rd NR7 ....72 D4
Eastfen Dro IP26 .....114 B6
Eastfield NR8 ....156 D8
Eastfield Rd
  Hickling NR12 ....39 F2
  Long Stratton NR15 ..106 F4
  1 Wisbech PE13 .....152 E7
Eastfield Way PE13 ..152 C6
Eastfields Cl PE30 ...147 A6
Eastgate NR25 ....67 D3
Eastgate Dro
  Congham PE31 ....28 D2
  Grimston PE32 ....45 D8
  Hillington PE31 ....28 C3
Eastgate Prim Sch
  PE30 ....146 E5
Eastgate Rd PE36 .....2 A6
Eastgate St
  3 King's Lynn PE30 ..146 E5
  North Elmham NR20 ...49 E2
  Shouldham PE33 ......62 D4
Easthaugh Rd NR9 ....51 D4
Easthill La NR14 ......90 E8
Eastland Cl NR17 ....174 C6
Eastlands Bank PE14 ..41 E5
Eastleigh Gdns 6 NR9 .69 F2
Eastmans La PE32 ....38 E4
Eastmoor Cl PE33 .....81 E4
Eastmoor Rd PE33 ....81 C7
Eaton Coll NR4 ....70 C4
Eaton Way NR10 ......35 C1
Eaton Chase NR4 ....161 E2
Eaton Dro
  Sedgeford PE36 ....13 A7
  Snettisham PE31 .....12 F5
Eaton Gdns NR19 ....154 F3
Eaton Golf Course
  NR4 ....162 B1
Eaton Rd NR4 ....162 B2
Eaton St Cringleford NR4 .89 B8
  Norwich NR4 ....161 E1
Eau Brink Rd PE34 ....43 A2
Ebbisham Dr
  5 Norwich NR4 ......89 C8
  Norwich NR4 ....161 F1
Ebble Cl PE30 ....148 C2
Ebenezer Pl NR3 ....178 A4
Eccles CE Prim Sch
  NR16 ....118 F8
Eccles Rd NR17 .....137 C7
Eccles Rd Sta NR16 ..103 E1
Ecclestone Cl NR31 ..170 A4
Eckersley Dr NR21 ...141 A6
Ecotech Ctr* PE37 ..153 B6
Ecton Gr 6 PE14 .....59 A1
Eden Cl
  Bacton/Walcott NR12 .23 E4
  Norwich NR7 ....163 C6
Edenside Dr NR17 ...174 D5
Edge Bank PE14 ....77 F8
Edgebrook Rd PE30 ..138 D6
Edgefield Cl NR6 ....158 F7
Edgefield Hill NR25 ..137 C2
Edgefield Rd NR24 ...142 E5
Edgehill 4 NR7 ....72 E4
Edges La 2 NR15 ....106 E3
Edge's La NR15 ......107 A3
Edgeworth Rd 6 NR5 .161 C6
Edinburgh Ave
  Great Yarmouth NR31 .170 B2
  King's Lynn PE30 ....147 C7
Edinburgh Cl
  6 Barnham IP24 .....125 F6
  2 Barnham IP24 .....125 F6
  Caister-on-Sea NR30 .168 E5
  10 Watton IP25 ....84 D3
Edinburgh Cl 8 PE30 .146 E5
Edinburgh Dr
  Fakenham NR21 .....141 C6
  Wisbech PE13 ....152 C8
Edinburgh Pl
  Great Yarmouth NR30 .169 E3
  1 Wiggenhall St Germans
    PE34 ....43 B1
Edinburgh Rd
  Holt NR25 ....137 C5
  Norwich NR2 ....162 A6
Edinburgh Way
  Dersingham PE31 ....140 D3
  Thetford IP24 ....176 A5
Edison Way NR31 ....170 A8
Edith Cavell Cl 8 IP24 .176 D7
Edma St PE30 ....146 E6
Edmund Bacon Ct 1
  NR3 ....162 D8
Edmund De Moundeford VC
  Sch IP26 ....98 E2
Edmund Moundford Rd 11
  IP26 ....98 E1
Edmund Rd IP27 .....175 A2
Edrich Cl NR13 ......165 E6
Edrich Way NR5 .....160 E7
Edward Benefer Way
  King's Lynn PE30 ....146 D6

Edward Benefer Way continued
  North Wootton PE30 ...26 E1
Edward Gambling Ct 8
  NR3 ....162 B8
Edward Rd NR29 ......58 B5
Edward Seago Pl NR15 .90 E2
Edward St
  8 King's Lynn PE30 ..146 E3
  Norwich NR3 ....178 B4
Edward Worlledge Mid Sch
  NR31 ....169 C2
Edwards Cl NR20 ......50 B5
Edwards Rd NR7 .....159 A5
Edwin Cl NR18 ....173 B5
Eels Foot Rd NR29 ....57 E1
Egmere Medieval Village of*
  NR22 ....26 E8
Egmere Rd NR22 .....16 F8
Egremont Rd IP22 ...177 B5
Eighth Ave PE13 .....152 E4
El Alamein Way NR31 .94 C8
Elan Cl NR18 ....173 D3
Elden's La IP26 ....98 F5
Elder La PE32 ....45 C8
Elderberry Dr 5 NR20 .68 A8
Elderbush La NR29 ...56 C7
Elders The IP27 .....113 F1
Eldorton La NR28 .....22 B5
Eleanor Rd NR1 .....162 D3
Eleven Mile Rd NR18 .87 C1
Elgin IP24 ....176 A5
Eliot Cl IP24 ....176 E6
Elise Way NR18 .....173 D2
Elizabeth Ave
  Downham Market PE38 .172 B5
  Fakenham NR21 ....141 C6
  Norwich NR7 ....163 F7
Elizabeth Cl
  Attleborough NR17 ...174 C6
  East Dereham NR19 .154 D1
  Hunstanton PE36 ....132 C3
  Norwich NR7 ....159 A5
  Reepham NR10 .....149 B4
Elizabeth Cres
  Caister-on-Sea NR30 .168 E6
  4 Holt NR25 ....137 C5
Elizabeth Dr PE37 ....65 F3
Elizabeth Fry Cl 9
  IP24 ....176 D7
Elizabeth Rd
  Brandon IP27 ....175 C3
  10 Poringland NR14 ...90 C5
Elizabeth Terr PE13 ..152 D4
Elizabeth Way 8 IP23 .130 C1
Elizabeth Wlk IP20 ..122 D2
Elizabethan House Mus*
  NR30 ....169 C3
Elkins Rd NR18 .....173 B5
Ella Rd NR1 ....163 A6
Ellcar Rise 4 NR4 ...161 F1
Ellenhill NR27 ......139 D5
Eller Dr PE13 ....43 E2
Ellingham Prim Sch
  NR35 ....109 D3
Ellingham Rd
  Attleborough NR17 ..174 B7
  Scoulton NR9 ....85 E3
Ellington Rd
  2 Barnham IP24 .....125 F6
  Great Yarmouth NR30 .169 D6
Ellmor Rd NR28 .....151 D4
Ellis Cl 4 NR12 ....39 B4
Ellison Dr NR17 .....174 E4
Elm Ave NR31 ....170 C4
Elm CE Jun Sch PE14 .59 B1
Elm Cl Acle NR13 ....166 C4
  Brandon IP27 ....175 E3
  Downham Market PE38 .172 B6
  King's Lynn PE30 ...148 D2
  5 Hingham NR9 ....51 A3
  7 Ludham NR29 ......56 C4
  7 Hinxton NR14 ......91 F1
  Mulbarton NR14 ......89 B3
  North Elmham NR20 ..49 E8
  Norwich NR5 ....156 F2
  Yaxham NR19 ....68 A5
Elm Gr
  Garboldisham IP22 ..128 A8
  Sheringham NR26 ...138 E5
Elm Gr La NR13 ......158 D2
Elm High Rd PE14 ...152 E1
Elm Hill NR3 ....178 B3
Elm La NR13 ....30 D8
Elm Low Rd PE14 ...152 D2
Elm Pk NR19 ....154 E1
Elm Rd
  Caister-on-Sea NR30 .168 E4
  Lingwood NR13 ....74 A3
  Marham PE33 ....68 F3
  Thetford IP24 ....176 B1
  Wisbech PE13 ....152 D3
Elm Rd Prim Sch
  PE13 ....152 D4
Elm's La NR15 ....107 A8
Elmfield Dr PE14 ....152 E1
Elmgrove Rd NR31 ..170 C3
Elmham Rd
  Beetley NR20 ....49 D4
  Brisley NR20 ....48 F8
  North Elmham NR20 ..49 E8
Elmhurst Ave NR12 ..39 C2
Elmhurst Dr NR12 ...170 C3
Elms Cl 6 NR35 ......123 F8
Elms Rd NR34 ....110 E5

Elms The
  Hindringham NR21 ....17 E6
  Norwich NR6 ....158 E6
Elmside PE14 ....59 D1
Elmstead Rd PE30 ...147 C4
Elmtree Gr PE33 ......43 E1
Elsden Cl 2 NR25 ...137 C5
Elsie Rd NR31 ....169 B3
Elsing Dr PE30 ......148 C1
Elsing La
  Bawdeswell NR20 .....50 E6
  Dereham NR20 ....50 C1
Elsing Rd Lyng NR9 ...51 A5
  North Tuddenham NR20 .50 E2
  Swanton Morley NR20 .50 C6
Elsteed Cl 11 NR4 ....89 C8
Elveden Cl NR4 ......161 F1
Elveden Rd IP24 .....125 D6
Elvin Rd NR19 ....154 D6
Elvin Way 8 NR3 ....157 F1
Elvina Rd 10 NR10 ....54 A2
Elvington PE30 ......147 D5
Elworthy Cl IP25 .....84 F3
Elwyn Rd 7 NR1 ....162 E2
Ely Pl 10 PE13 ......152 C5
Ely Rd Denver PE38 ..172 D2
  Hilgay PE38 ....97 B8
Ely Row NR4 ....42 B1
Ely St NR2 ....162 C7
Ely Way IP24 ....176 A5
Embry Cl NR6 ....158 D6
Emelson Cl NR19 ....154 D6
Emery Cl 5 NR26 ...138 C5
Emery's La NR11 .....21 B6
Emmanuel Ave NR31 .170 B2
Emmas Way NR13 ....73 B6
Emms's La NR27 .....10 D2
Emneth Prim Sch PE14 .59 D2
Emorsgate PE34 ......42 E7
Empire Ave PE30 ...147 B8
Empress Rd NR31 ...169 B3
Empsons Loke NR29 ..58 B6
End Lodge PE31 .....133 C5
Enfield Rd NR5 .....161 C6
Engine Rd Hilgay PE38 .96 F7
  Sculthorpe Airfield NR21 .15 D2
England's La NR31 ..170 D4
Englands Rd NR13 ..166 B4
English Rd NR6 .....158 E4
Ennerdale Dr PE30 ..148 F2
Enterprise Way
  Fakenham NR21 ....141 E3
  King's Lynn PE30 ....43 E4
  Wisbech PE13 ......152 A2
Entrance La NR15 .....90 E2
Entry The IP22 ......177 D4
Enue 16 PE30 ....63 B4
Eppingham Cl IP24 ..176 F6
Epsom Gdns NR9 ....69 F2
Erica Way NR17 ....170 B6
Erlswell Dr IP27 ....113 E1
Erpingham Prim Sch
  NR11 ....21 B2
Estelle St 9 NR3 ....162 D8
Esplanade NR27 ....139 B7
Esplanade The
  Hemsby NR29 ......167 E5
  Sheringham NR26 ...138 C7
Esprit Cl NR18 ......173 D2
Essex St NR2 ....162 A5
Estcourt Rd
  2 Attleborough NR17 .174 C5
  Great Yarmouth NR30 .169 D6
Estelle Way NR18 ...173 E6
Estuary Cl PE30 .....146 F2
Estuary Rd PE30 ....146 D2
Ethel Colman Way
  NR30 ....169 B7
Europa Way
  Norwich NR1 ....163 A2
  Wisbech PE13 ....152 B2
Euston Hall* IP24 ...126 B5
Euston Rd NR30 .....169 D4
Euston Way PE30 ...148 D1
Euximoor Dro PE14 ..77 A1
Eva Cl 4 IP25 ....67 B2
Eva Rd NR13 ....72 E7
Evans Gdns PE36 ...132 D3
Evans Lombe Cl NR7 .57 A4
Evans Way NR6 .....158 D6
Evelyn Cl IP21 ....131 A3
Evelyn Way 4 IP20 ..147 A8
Eversley Rd NR6 ...158 B4
Everson Cl
  Norwich NR5 ....157 C1
  10 Tasburgh NR15 ...106 F6
Ewing Cl NR10 ......149 B4
Exchange Rd 7 NR15 .89 C1
Exchange Sq PE13 ..152 B5
Exchange St
  Attleborough NR17 ..174 D5
  32 Harleston IP20 ...122 D2
  Norwich NR2 ....178 A3
Exeter Cres PE30 ...148 D5
Exeter Rd NR31 .....170 A4
Exeter St NR2 ....162 C7
Exeter Way IP24 ....176 A5
Exmouth Cl 25 NR9 ..88 D8
Exmouth Pl 11 NR30 .169 D4
Exmouth Rd NR30 ..169 D1
Exton's Gdns PE30 ..146 F3
Exton's Pl PE30 .....147 A3

Dru - Fal 191
Exton's Rd PE30 .....146 F4
Eye Airfield Ind Est
  IP23 ....130 B2
Eye La PE31 ....30 B7
Eye Rd IP23 ....130 A1

F

Factory La IP22 .....177 B5
Factory Rd NR30 ....169 D5
Faeroes Dr NR30 ....168 C6
Fair Cl Beccles NR34 .110 D1
  14 Feltwell IP26 .....98 E1
Fairfax Dr 6 NR7 .....72 D4
Fairfax Rd NR4 ......161 F4
Fairfield
  Great & Little Plumstead
    NR13 ....73 B7
  Mundesley NR11 ....143 C6
Fairfield Dr NR17 ...174 C4
Fairfield La 10 PE33 ..61 D6
Fairfield Rd
  Downham Market PE38 .172 A5
  2 Middleton PE32 ....44 B3
  Norwich NR2 ....162 C2
  4 Stoke Ferry PE33 ..81 A3
Fairfield Way 12 IP26 .98 E1
Fairfields Cawston NR10 .35 B2
  Thetford IP24 ....176 D5
Fairhaven CE VA Prim Sch
  NR13 ....165 B3
Fairhaven Way 1 NR31 .36 D4
Fairhill Dro PE33 .....80 E2
Fairholme Cl IP25 ....84 A8
Fairholme Rd NR10 ...53 E4
Fairlee Dr NR30 .....168 E5
Fairland St NR18 ...173 C3
Fairmile Cl NR2 .....162 B3
Fairstead Cl
  North Walsham NR28 .151 A3
  Pulham Market NR21 .121 E5
Fairstead Dro PE33 ..62 D4
Fairstead La
  Hempnall NR15 .....107 A5
  Little Cressingham IP25 .83 D3
Fairstead Prim Sch
  PE30 ....147 D4
Fairstead Rd NR7 ...159 A3
Fairstead The
  Botesdale IP22 ......128 E3
  2 Cley next the Sea NR25 .7 E6
  3 Holt NR25 ....137 B6
  Scottow NR10 ....37 D2
Fairview Cl NR8 .....157 A7
Fairview Dr NR31 .....31 E5
Fairview Rd NR28 ...151 E4
Fairway NR30 ....168 E3
Fairway Fst Sch NR4 .162 A1
Fairway Mid Sch NR4 .162 A1
Fairway The NR31 ...171 D8
Fairways Norwich NR5 .157 D5
  Stuston IP21 ....130 B5
Fakenham Coll NR21 .141 A6
Fakenham High Sch
  NR21 ....141 B5
Fakenham Hill IP31 ..126 C2
Fakenham Jun Sch
  NR21 ....141 C4
Fakenham Mus* 141 B3
  NR21
Fakenham Race Course
  NR21 ....141 D2
Fakenham Rd
  Attleborough NR9 ....52 C2
  Briston NR24 ....142 C5
  Docking PE31 ....134 E4
  East Rudham PE31 ...30 A7
  Foxley NR20 ....33 C1
  Great Snoring NR21 ..17 A5
  Ryburgh NR21 ....32 A6
  Sculthorpe NR21 ....141 A5
  South Creake NR21 ..15 E6
  Sparham NR9 ....50 A4
  Taverham NR8 ......155 B2
  Tittleshall PE32 ......48 A7
Fakenham Town FC
  NR21 ....141 F6
Fakenham View NR21 .31 E3
Fakes Rd NR29 ......167 D6
Falcon Ave IP22 ....177 E5
Falcon Dr IP27 .....175 F3
Falcon La Bungay NR35 .109 A1
  16 Wisbech PE13 ...152 C5
Falcon Mews NR7 ...159 C3
Falcon Rd E NR7 ...159 C3
Falcon Rd W NR7 ...159 C4
Falgate NR10 ....35 C2
Falkland Cl NR6 ....157 D5
Falkland Rd NR31 ...94 C6
Falklands Dr PE13 ..152 E3
Falklands Rd PE14 ..41 A8
Fall Gn NR14 ....90 D4
Fallow Pipe Rd PE34 ..43 B2
Fallowfield
  4 Hemsby NR29 ....167 B7

Fallowfield continued
 Poringland NR14 ....90 D5
Fallowfield Cl NR1 ....163 B8
Fallows The NR8 ....155 D2
Faraday Pl IP24 ....176 B2
Faraday Rd NR31 ....170 A8
Fardell Rd PE31 ....152 C4
Fardell Rd PE31
NR19 ....154 C3
Farm Cl Lingwood NR13 ......74 A2
 Loddon NR14 ....92 A2
Farm La ST IP20 ....123 A1
Farm La NR13 ....56 A1
Farm Rd
Heckingham NR14 ....92 D1
Worstead NR28 ....38 A7
Farm View NR8 ....151 E5
Farm Wlk PE37 ....65 F4
Farman Ave NR28 ....151 D5
Farman Cl Belton NR31 ......94 A6
Lyng NR9 ....51 A5
 Salhouse NR13 ....55 A1
Farmers Ave NR1 ....178 B2
Farmland Rd NR5 ....156 F1
Farmway NR19 ....154 D2
Farnborough Rd IP25 ......84 F3
Farrow Cl
 Great Moulton NR15 ......106 B1
Great Moulton NR15 ....121 B8
 Mattishall NR20 ....68 C6
 Swanton Morley NR20 .....50 B3
Farthing Cl Diss IP22 ......177 D6
Loddon NR14 ....109 D8
Farthing Dro
Beck Row, Holywell
Row & Kenny Hill IP27 .....112 E2
Lakenheath IP27 ....113 A2
Southery PE38 ....97 A2
Farthing Rd PE38 ....79 B5
Fastnet Way NR18 ....168 C6
Fastolf Cl NR6 ....157 E5
Fastolff Ave NR31 ....170 B3
Fayregreen NR21 ....141 D4
Feale Abbey PE34 ....144 A1
Fearn's Ct NR27 ....139 D5
Feathercone Ct
NR19 ....154 D2
Felbrigg Cl PE30 ....148 F1
Felbrigg Hall (National
Trust)* NR11 ....10 B2
Felbrigg Hall Gdn & Pk
(National Trust)*
NR11 ....139 A4
Felbrigg Rd
Downham Market PE38 ......172 C6
Roughton NR11 ....21 D8
Fell Way NR14 ....94 C8
Fellowes Dr NR31 ....94 C6
Fellowes Rd NR9 ....69 E6
Fellows Cl NR5 ....156 D1
Felmingham Rd NR28 ....37 C7
Felsham Way NR8 ....155 E2
Felsted Ave PE13 ....152 E5
Felthorpe Rd NR9 ....52 B3
Feltwell Golf Club IP26 .....98 E1
Feltwell Golf Course
IP26 ....113 C8
Feltwell Rd
Hockwold cum Wilton
IP26 ....113 F7
Methwold IP26 ....98 E5
Southery PE38 ....97 D5
Fen Cl PE13 ....152 E6
Fen Dro PE33 ....81 F3
Fen Folgate IP25 ....67 B2
Fen La Banham NR16 ....119 B6
Beccles NR34 ....110 D2
Ditchingham NR35 ....108 E3
Garboldisham IP22 ....128 A7
Grimston PE32 ....45 A7
Harling NR16 ....118 C6
Leziate PE32 ....45 A6
Marham PE33 ....63 A5
Rickinghall Inferior IP22 ...128 E2
Roydon IP22 ....129 C2
Thelnetham IP22 ....128 B5
Fen Rd Blo' Norton IP22 ....128 C6
Carleton Rode NR16 ....105 C2
Marham PE33 ....63 B4
Scarning NR19 ....154 B3
Watlington PE33 ....61 D5
Fen St
Attleborough NR17 ....103 F3
Hinderclay IP22 ....128 C5
Old Buckenham NR17 ....104 C2
Redgrave IP22 ....128 F6
Rocklands NR17 ....103 B6
Fen View
Christchurch PE14 ....95 A7
East Dereham NR19 ....154 C2
Fen Way NR13 ....59 A1
Fence Bank PE14 ....42 A1
Fences Farm Rd PE34 ....78 E8
Fendyke Rd PE14 ....59 E2
Fengate Heacham PE31 ......13 C4
Marsham NR10 ....150 D1
Fengate Dro IP27 ....175 B6
Fengate Rd PE14 ....59 C5
Wereland Rd
King's Lynn PE30 ....147 C8
Wisbech PE13 ....152 E6
Fenland W Norfolk Aviation
Mus* PE14 ....59 C7
Fenn Cres NR3 ....158 B1
Fennel Way IP24 ....176 F4

Fenner Rd NR30 ....170 E7
Fenside PE31 ....133 C4
Fenway PE31 ....133 B3
Ferguson Way NR17 ....174 F7
Fern Ave PE30 ....146 E6
Fern Cl NR18 ....173 B4
Fern Dr NR28 ....151 E5
Fern Gdns NR13 ....93 F5
Fern Hill
Dersingham PE31 ....140 E4
Norwich NR1 ....163 B5
Ferndale Cl NR6 ....157 E4
Ferndene Rd NR14 ....147 C4
Ferrier Cl NR30 ....169 D5
Ferrier Cl NR30 ....167 B6
Ferrier Rd NR30 ....169 C5
Ferry Bank PE38 ....97 A4
Ferry Hill NR31 ....170 D7
Ferry La
Great Yarmouth NR31 ....169 C2
Norwich NR1 ....178 C3
Postwick with Witton
NR13 ....73 A2
Stokesby with Herringby
NR29 ....75 B5
Ferry Rd
Carleton St Peter NR14 ......91 E5
Clenchwarton PE34 ....145 F5
Horning NR12 ....55 E3
King's Lynn PE34 ....146 B6
Norton Subcourse NR14 .....92 D2
Norwich NR1 ....178 C3
Oxborough PE33 ....81 D3
Reedham NR13 ....92 E4
Surlingham NR14 ....165 A1
Woodbastwick NR13 ....55 D2
Ferry Sq PE34 ....146 C5
Ferry St PE30 ....146 D5
Ferry View Rd NR12 ....55 E3
Ferryboat La NR31 ....170 D7
Ferrygate La NR29 ....57 D5
Ferryside Rd
Bressingham IP22 ....129 B8
Kenninghall NR16 ....119 C4
South Lopham IP22 ....128 F8
Festival Cl PE32 ....148 B1
Festival Rd NR20 ....50 B7
Festival Way CB6 ....96 E2
Ffolkes Dr
King's Lynn PE34 ....148 C1
Terrington St Clement
PE34 ....144 B5
Ffolkes Pl NR5 ....61 D3
Fiddle Wood Rd NR6 ....158 D4
Field Acre Way NR15 ....106 E4
Field Barn Cotts PE32 ....46 E3
Field Barn La PE33 ....61 F3
Field Dalling Rd
Field Dalling NR25 ....7 A3
Gunthorpe NR21 ....18 B8
Field End Cl PE30 ....147 B6
Field House Gdns
IP22 ....177 E5
Field La Beetley NR20 ....49 C5
 Blofield NR13 ....73 D6
Blofield NR13 ....165 E8
Fakenham NR21 ....141 B6
Hempnall NR15 ....107 D3
King's Lynn PE34 ....147 B6
Marsham NR10 ....36 B2
North Walsham NR28 ....151 E3
Stody NR24 ....142 F8
Whinburgh & Westfield
NR19 ....67 F4
Wroxton PE33 ....80 F3
Field Rd Brandon IP27 ....114 D4
King's Lynn PE34 ....147 B5
Ringland NR8 ....70 B8
Stalham NR12 ....39 C3
Fieldbarn Dro PE33 ....82 A4
Fieldbarn Rd PE33 ....81 B8
Fieldfare Cl NR12 ....54 A1
Fields Rd NR14 ....110 E6
Fields The
Forncett NR16 ....105 E5
Hingham NR9 ....86 C5
Fieldview NR5 ....161 E6
Fiennes Rd NR7 ....72 D5
Fifers La NR6 ....158 C6
Fifth Ave PE13 ....152 E4
Fifty Dro CB6 ....95 F3
Fifty Rd PE14 ....95 A3
Filbert Rd NR14 ....91 F1
Filby Fst Sch NR29 ....75 E8
Filby La NR29 ....167 A1
Filby Rd Coltishall NR10 .....37 B2
Stokesby with Herringby
NR29 ....153 B2
Finch Cl Cromer NR27 ....139 C4
Norwich NR17 ....159 D2
Finch Way NR13 ....165 C3
Fincham Dro PE32 ....64 B5
Fincham Rd
Barton Bendish PE33 ....81 A8
Crimplesham PE33 ....80 A8
Fincham PE33 ....63 A1
Shouldham Thorpe PE33 .....62 C2
Stow Bardolph PE34 ....79 E8
Wereham PE33 ....80 F6
Finchdale Cl NR2 ....148 C4
Finchley Cl NR12 ....162 B7
Finderne Dr NR18 ....173 D6
Finisterre Rise NR30 ......168 C6
Finkelgate NR1 ....178 B1
Finningham Rd IP22 ....128 E1

Finsbury Pk PE38 ....172 B4
Fiona Cl NR18 ....173 E6
Fir Cl Heacham PE31 ....133 C6
Wymondham IP26 ....100 B4
Fir Covert Rd
Carleton Rode NR16 ....105 A1
Taverham NR10 ....155 B4
Fir Gr NR26 ....138 D4
Fir La NR10 ....34 A1
Fir Pk IP25 ....84 A7
Fir Rd IP24 ....176 B1
Fir Tree Dr NR31 ....43 E2
Firethorn Cl NR8 ....155 B2
Firs Ave NR29 ....167 A3
Firs La NR12 ....39 C2
Firs Rd Hethersett NR9 ......88 D7
Norwich NR6 ....157 F6
Firs The
Downham Market PE38 .....172 D6
Lakenheath IP27 ....113 F1
Firs Way IP27 ....175 C2
Firside Mid Sch NR6 ....158 A6
First Ave PE13 ....152 D5
First Dro PE33 ....113 C3
First Marsh Rd PE13 ....41 F6
Firtree Cl NR13 ....165 B4
Firtree Rd NR1 ....159 E1
Firwood Cl NR1 ....163 C8
Fish Wharf NR30 ....169 D1
Fisher Ave NR30 ....169 D8
Fisher Rd Diss IP22 ....177 E4
Fakenham NR21 ....141 B5
Fisher Row NR2 ....111 F4
Fisher Way IP24 ....176 E5
Fishergate NR3 ....178 B4
Fishers La NR14 ....49 C6
Fisher's La NR2 ....131 A4
Fishers La NR2 ....178 A3
Fishers' Quay NR30 ....169 C4
Fishley View NR13 ....166 B4
Fiske's Opening
NR1 ....170 D4
Fison Way IP24 ....176 C6
Fison Way Ind Est
IP24 ....176 C6
Fitton Rd PE14 ....61 B8
Fitzalan Cl NR30 ....169 C4
Fitzgerald Rd
Norwich NR1 ....162 E1
 Poringland NR14 ....90 C5
Fitzhenry Mews NR5 ....161 B8
Fitzwalter Rd IP27 ....175 B2
Five Acre La NR35 ....123 E7
Five Acres NR18 ....89 F4
Five Alls Rd PE14 ....41 F1
Five Crossways NR12 ....164 D8
Flag St NR21 ....15 C2
Flaxlands NR16 ....105 B4
Flaxlands Rd NR16 ....105 C3
Fleet La NR13 ....56 B1
Fleet Rd NR13 ....56 B1
Fleetwood Dr NR13 ....72 D4
Flegg Gn PE33 ....80 D4
Flegg High Sch NR29 ....75 C8
Fleggburgh Prim Sch
NR29 ....75 C8
Fleggburgh Rd NR29 ....57 C2
Fleming Ct PE25 ....84 D3
Fletcher Cl NR17 ....55 A8
Fletcher Way
Acle NR13 ....166 D4
Cromer NR27 ....139 B5
Flint Dr NR23 ....136 D5
Flint Gate PE12 ....41 B8
Flint House Gdns NR6 .....54 B2
Flint House Rd PE14 ....77 F1
Flitcham Abbey PE31 ....28 D5
Flitcham CE Prim Sch
PE31 ....28 C5
Flixton Marsh La
NR32 ....111 F6
Flixton Rd
Bungay NR35 ....124 A7
Flixton NR35 ....123 E6
Lound NR32 ....94 C1
St Margaret, South Elmham
IP20 ....123 E3
Somerleyton, Ashby &
Herringfleet NR32 ....111 F8
Flordon Rd
Bracon Ash NR14 ....88 F1
Flordon NR15 ....106 D8
Newton Flotman NR15 ......106 F8
Florence Barclay Cl
IP24 ....176 D1
Florence Rd NR1 ....163 A6
Florida Bvd NR21 ....15 C2
Flowerday Cl NR31 ....171 D5
Flowerdew Cl NR8 ....88 C7
Flowerdew's La NR13 ....24 B2
Flowerpot La NR15 ....106 D3
Fludge's La NR20 ....49 B6
Flymore La NR17 ....103 A8
Fodderfen Dro PE38 ....113 A7
Foldgate La PE34 ....61 A5
Folgate NR16 ....88 D1
Folgate Cl
Costessey NR8 ....156 F5
Thornham PE36 ....2 D6
Folgate La
Costessey NR8 ....156 F4
Walpole PE14 ....41 B2
Folgate Rd
Heacham PE31 ....133 C4
North Walsham NR28 ....151 B6
Folland Ct NR20 ....50 E7
Follies The PE37 ....65 F4

Folly Cl NR18 ....173 C5
Folly Ct
King's Lynn PE30 ....147 B7
Mattishall NR20 ....68 F6
Folly Gdns NR18 ....173 C5
Folly Gr PE30 ....147 B7
Folly La Beetley NR20 ....49 B6
Bressingham IP22 ....129 C8
Claxton NR14 ....91 D5
 Hingham NR9 ....86 C5
Old Buckenham NR17 ....104 F2
Folly Rd NR18 ....173 C5
Folly View PE37 ....65 F4
Folly Yd PE32 ....48 B7
Folwell Rd NR5 ....156 E1
Footpath The NR14 ....90 C5
Ford Ave PE30 ....148 D5
Ford St IP24 ....176 D3
Foregate Cl NR8 ....155 D2
Forest Cl IP27 ....175 C2
Forest Dr PE31 ....133 C6
Forest Mount NR1 ....73 C3
Forest Prim Sch IP27 ....175 C3
Forest Ret Pk IP24 ....125 D8
Forester Cl NR4 ....112 C1
Forester's Ave PE38 ....97 A8
Forge Cl Palgrave IP22 .....177 D2
Poringland NR14 ....90 D4
Forge Gr NR14 ....110 C2
Forge Orchards NR14 .....89 B3
Forge Rd NR14 ....91 F1
Forncett CE Prim Sch
NR16 ....106 B3
Forncett Ind Steam Mus*
NR16 ....106 B3
Forncett Rd
Bunwell NR16 ....105 F3
Tharston & Hapton
NR15 ....106 D4
Forster Cl NR11 ....150 D6
Forster Way NR11 ....150 D6
Forsythia Rd NR31 ....170 B5
Forth Cl NR30 ....168 C5
Forties Cl NR30 ....168 C6
Fortune Gn NR14 ....90 E4
Forum The ™ NR2 ....178 B3
Forwater Rd NR10 ....34 B3
Foster Cl Brundall NR13 ...165 B4
Ormesby St Margaret
NR29 ....167 C2
Foster Rd NR3 ....158 D3
Foulgers Opening
NR1 ....178 C1
Foulsham Prim Sch
NR20 ....33 D3
Foulsham Rd
Bintree NR20 ....33 C2
Guestwick NR20 ....33 D4
Guist NR20 ....33 A7
Hindolveston NR20 ....33 D7
Wood Norton NR20 ....33 D4
Foundry Cl
Foulsham NR20 ....33 D3
Northrepps NR27 ....11 A2
Sculthorpe NR21 ....16 C2
Foundry Cnr NR17 ....174 F2
Foundry La PE36 ....22 A3
Fountaine Gr PE30 ....148 C4
Fountains Rd NR4 ....89 A8
Fourth Ave PE13 ....152 E4
Fowell Cl NR5 ....161 B6
Fowler's La NR17 ....174 B2
Fox Gr NR15 ....118 C5
Fox Hill IP20 ....123 C3
Fox Hill Rd NR12 ....38 E7
Fox La Brundall NR13 ....165 F6
Framingham Pigot NR14 ....90 D6
North Tuddenham NR20 .....68 F8
Fox Rd NR14 ....90 D7
Foxburrow Rd NR7 ....159 A5
Foxcote Cl NR6 ....157 E7
Foxes Mdw PE32 ....46 F2
Foxglove Cl
Fakenham NR21 ....141 F4
North Walsham NR28 ....151 D5
Thurton NR14 ....91 C4
Foxglove Dr NR31 ....94 C6
Foxglove La NR26 ....138 B6
Foxglove Rd
 Attleborough NR17 ....174 B5
Thetford IP24 ....176 F4
Foxley Cl NR5 ....161 D6
Foxley Rd
Bawdeswell NR20 ....50 D8
Foulsham NR20 ....33 C2
Fox's La PE34 ....146 C6
Foxs Loke NR11 ....150 D6
Foxwood NR13 ....73 D6
Foxwood Cl NR5 ....155 E3
Framingham Earl High Sch
NR14 ....90 C6

Freedom Bridge PE13 ......152 B6
Freeland Cl NR5 ....155 E3
Freeland Cnr NR10 ....155 C6
Freeman Cl NR14 ....109 D8
Freeman Sq NR2 ....162 C8
Freeman St NR23 ....136 C6
Freethorpe Com Prim Sch
NR13 ....92 F7
Freethorpe Rd
Cantley NR13 ....92 D5
Freethorpe NR13 ....74 F1
Freiston PE30 ....147 C5
Fremantle Rd NR30 ....168 E1
French's Rd PE14 ....41 C4
Frensham Rd NR13 ....165 E4
Frenze Hall La IP22 ....177 F5
Frenze Rd IP22 ....177 F4
Frenze Rd IP22
Frere Cnr IP22 ....129 D2
Frere Rd
 Harleston IP20 ....122 D2
Norwich NR7 ....159 D1
Freshfield Cl NR5 ....161 C7
Freshgap La NR20 ....33 A3
Freshwater Way NR8 ....155 F3
Frettenham Fst Sch
NR12 ....54 A4
Frettenham Rd
Hainford NR10 ....53 F5
Horstead with Stanninghall
NR12 ....54 B5
Freyden Way NR1 ....54 A4
Friar Tuck Rd NR4 ....162 C1
Friar's La PE31 ....135 D4
Friars' La NR30 ....169 D2
Friars Quay NR3 ....178 B3
Friars St PE30 ....146 E3
Friars The PE30 ....146 D4
Friarscroft La NR18 ....173 B3
Friday Bridge Prim Sch
PE14 ....77 A7
Friday Mkt NR22 ....16 F7
Fridaybridge Rd
Elm PE14 ....77 A8
Wisbech PE14 ....59 A1
Friends Cl NR5 ....161 C5
Friends Rd NR4 ....161 C5
Fring Rd Bircham PE31 ......14 A3
Snettisham PE31 ....13 A5
Frinton Way PE13 ....152 E5
Frith Way NR5 ....106 B1
Fritillary Dr NR18 ....173 E4
Fritton Cl NR29 ....167 B3
Fritton La NR29 ....56 E5
Fritton Lake Ctry World*
NR31 ....93 F2
Fritton Rd NR29 ....56 E6
Frobisher Cl IP24 ....176 F6
Frobisher Cres PE36 ....132 D3
Frogge La
Coltishall NR12 ....54 C8
Scottow NR12 ....37 C1
Frogs Hall La NR1 ....163 B5
Frog's Hall La NR20 ....50 C2
Frogs Hole
Blofield NR13 ....165 D6
Somerleyton, Ashby &
Herringfleet NR32 ....93 F1
Front Rd
Tydd St Giles PE13 ....41 A4
Wood Dalling NR11 ....34 D6
Front St Binham NR21 ....6 E2
Burnham Market PE31 ....135 C3
Trunch NR28 ....22 E5
Front Way PE30 ....147 A7
Frost Cl Norwich NR7 ....163 F8
 Watton IP25 ....84 D3
Frost's La NR15 ....106 B1
Fugill Rd NR7 ....159 D1
Fulcher Ave NR27 ....139 A7
Fulford Cl NR4 ....162 A2
Fuller Cl
 Rackheath NR13 ....72 E7
 West Winch PE33 ....43 F2
Fuller Mews NR5 ....160 E8
Fuller Rd
North Walsham NR28 ....151 B4
Redenhall with Harleston
IP20 ....122 D1
Fuller's Cl NR30 ....110 D5
Furthest Dro IP27 ....113 C4
Furze Ave NR7 ....163 E8
Furze Hill NR27 ....139 C5
Furze Hill Dr NR28 ....151 E3
Furze La
Great Witchingham NR9 ....149 C2
Guist NR20 ....33 A6
Furze Rd NR7 ....163 E8
Furze Way NR29 ....167 B2
Fye Bridge St NR3 ....178 B4

G

Gablehurst Ct NR31 ...170 A4
Gables Ave NR11 ...22 B7
Gage Rd NR7 ...159 C4
Gagman's La NR19 ...68 A5
Gainsborough Ave
- 1 Diss IP22 ...177 C4
- Great Yarmouth NR31 ...170 A7

Gale Cl NR14 ...109 F8
Gales Ct NR23 ...136 D6
Gales Rd NR23 ...136 C6
Gallant's La NR16 ...118 C5
Galley Hill NR3 ...158 A2
Gallow Dr PE38 ...172 C7
Gallow Hill (Tumulus)* NR25 ...8 B5
Gallow La PE33 ...62 D2
Galloway Cl 6 NR20 ...68 A8
Gallowhill La NR24 ...18 C3
Gallows La NR16 ...103 E1
Galyon Rd PE30 ...147 B8
Gambling Cl NR6 ...158 A7
Gamewell Cl 6 NR1 ...162 E2
Gangway The NR27 ...139 C7
Ganners Hill NR8 ...155 E3
Gannet Rd NR29 ...167 E4
Gant Cl 9 NR20 ...68 F6
Gaol Hill NR2 ...178 A3
Gaol St 12 PE13 ...152 C4
Gapton Hall Ind Est NR31 ...170 A8
Gapton Hall Rd NR31 ...170 A8
Gapton Hall Ret Pk NR31 ...169 A1
Garboldisham Prim Sch IP22 ...128 A8
Garboldisham Rd
- Harling NR16 ...118 C3
- Kenninghall NR16 ...118 F3

Garden Cl Briston NR24 ...142 B4
- Bungay NR35 ...124 B8
- North Walsham NR28 ...151 C6
- 4 Watton IP25 ...84 E3

Garden Ct 1 NR14 ...92 A1
Garden La NR25 ...8 A1
Garden Pl 2 NR3 ...162 E8
Garden Rd
- Brundall NR13 ...165 E6
- Hemsby NR29 ...167 D7
- Sheringham NR26 ...138 D6
- 3 Wiggenhall St Germans PE34 ...43 B1
- Wiggenhall St Germans PE34 ...61 D8

Garden Row PE30 ...146 E3
Garden St
- Cromer NR27 ...139 B7
- Norwich NR1 ...178 B2

Gardeners Terr NR7 ...158 F4
Gardenhouse La IP22 ...128 E2
Gardyn Croft 5 NR8 ...155 D2
Garfield Rd NR30 ...169 D7
Gargle Hill NR7 ...163 F7
Gariannonum (Roman Fort)* NR31 ...93 F7
Garlic St IP21 ...122 A2
Garlondes 6 NR16 ...118 C5
Garner's La PE34 ...41 D8
Garnham Rd NR31 ...170 C7
Garrett Cl NR3 ...158 F1
Garrick Gn NR6 ...158 E5
Garrick Gn Fst Sch NR6 ...158 E5
Garrison Rd NR30 ...169 C5
Garrood Dr NR21 ...141 E5
Garvestone Prim Sch NR9 ...68 C2
Garvestone Rd NR20 ...68 E4
Garwood Cl PE30 ...147 E4
Gas Distribution Sta NR12 ...143 F2
Gas Hill NR1 ...163 A6
Gas House La PE12 ...41 B8
Gashouse Dro IP27 ...175 E4
Gashouse Hill NR11 ...150 D6
Gaskell Way PE30 ...148 C1
Gatacre Rd NR31 ...169 B3
Gatehouse La PE30 ...148 C6
Gateley Gdns NR3 ...158 B3
Gateley Rd NR20 ...49 B8
Gaultree Sq PE14 ...59 D2
Gavell St IP19 ...124 D1
Gawdy Cl 2 IP20 ...122 D2
Gawdy Rd NR7 ...159 D1
Gaye Cres 1 IP23 ...130 C1
Gayford Rd NR10 ...35 B2
Gaymer Cl NR16 ...119 D7
Gaymer's Way NR28 ...151 B6
Gaynor Cl NR18 ...173 B5
Gayton Fst Sch PE32 ...45 C6
Gayton Rd
- East Winch PE32 ...45 A4
- Grimston PE32 ...45 C8
- King's Lynn PE30 ...147 C5

Gaywood Cl NR30 ...168 D5
Gaywood Com Prim Sch PE30 ...147 C7
Gaywood Hall Dr PE30 ...147 B5
Gaywood Rd PE30 ...146 F5
Geddes Way 5 NR20 ...68 F6
Gedge Rd NR30 ...168 E6
Geldeston Hill NR34 ...109 F2
Geldeston Rd
- Ellingham NR35 ...109 D2
- Geldeston NR34 ...110 B2

Gelham Manor PE31 ...140 C3
Geneva Gdns NR31 ...171 E4
Gentian Way 2 NR17 ...174 B4
Gentlemans Wlk NR14 ...92 A3
Gentleman's Wlk NR2 ...178 A3
Gentry Pl NR5 ...161 C8
Geoffrey Rd 4 NR1 ...162 F3
George Beck Rd 8 NR29 ...58 B6
George Borrow Rd
- 2 East Dereham NR19 ...154 F3
- Norwich NR4 ...161 E5

George Cl NR8 ...157 B8
George Dance Pl NR5 ...161 C7
George Dr NR8 ...157 B7
George Edwards Rd NR21 ...141 E5
George Elliot Way 6 NR19 ...154 D2
George Fox Way NR5 ...161 B5
George Hill
- Norwich NR6 ...158 E4
- Stanton IP31 ...127 C1

George La 2 NR14 ...92 A1
George Pope Cl NR3 ...158 C2
George Pope Rd NR3 ...158 C2
George St
- Brandon IP27 ...175 D3
- Great Yarmouth NR30 ...169 C4
- 6 King's Lynn PE30 ...146 E6
- Sheringham NR26 ...138 D7

George Trollope Rd 15 IP25 ...84 D3
George Westwood Way NR34 ...110 D2
George White Mid Sch NR3 ...162 F8
George Winter Ct NR3 ...158 C2
Georges Rd NR19 ...154 D5
Georgia Rd NR21 ...15 C2
Gerald Cl NR1 ...163 C8
Germander Ct 8 NR31 ...94 C6
German's La PE34 ...42 A6
Gertrude Rd NR3 ...158 F1
Ghost Hill Fst Sch NR8 ...156 D8
Gibbet La
- East Beckham NR11 ...138 D2
- Wereham PE33 ...80 E5

Gibbs Cl NR9 ...160 B2
Gibson Rd 5 IP25 ...67 B2
Gidney Dr PE31 ...133 C5
Gilbard Rd NR5 ...161 C7
Gilbert Cl NR14 ...90 F4
Gilbert Rd NR30 ...168 F6
Gilbert Way
- 1 Cringleford NR4 ...89 B8
- Cringleford NR4 ...161 D1

Gilchrist Cl 8 NR4 ...89 E8
Gildencroft NR3 ...178 A4
Gilderswood NR16 ...105 F3
Giles Rd NR10 ...54 A1
Gillingham Rd NR34 ...110 A2
Gillingham Dam NR34 ...110 C2
Gilman Rd NR3 ...158 F1
Gilpin's Ride NR19 ...154 D4
Gilray Rd IP22 ...177 F4
Gimingham Rd
- Mundesley NR11 ...143 A6
- Southrepps NR11 ...22 C7

Gipsies' La NR25 ...9 A3
Gipsies La NR29 ...56 D6
Gipsy Cl NR5 ...161 D6
Gipsy La Norwich NR5 ...161 E5
- Watlington PE33 ...61 D5

Girling Rd NR19 ...154 C6
Girlings La NR7 ...163 E5
Girton Rd
- Great Yarmouth NR31 ...170 A3
- Norwich NR2 ...162 B4

Gissing Rd IP22 ...120 F2
Glade Prim Sch IP27 ...175 D3
Glade The
- Costessey NR8 ...156 F4
- Overstrand NR27 ...11 A3
- Thetford IP24 ...176 D6

Gladstone Rd
- Fakenham NR21 ...141 B4
- 4 King's Lynn PE30 ...146 E3

Gladstone St NR2 ...162 B6
Glamis Ct 26 IP20 ...122 D2
Glandford Rd NR25 ...7 E5
Glaven PE30 ...147 C5
Glaven Rd NR25 ...137 D5
Glebe Ave
- Hunstanton PE36 ...132 D5
- Watlington PE33 ...61 E5

Glebe Cl Fransham NR19 ...66 C7
- Hingham NR9 ...86 B5
- 19 Long Stratton NR15 ...106 E3
- Northwold IP26 ...99 C8
- 2 Potter Heigham NR29 ...56 F6
- Taverham NR8 ...155 F1
- Thetford IP24 ...176 D5

Glebe Est PE34 ...144 F1
Glebe House Sch PE36 ...132 D5
Glebe La PE31 ...135 F6
Glebe Mdw NR17 ...103 E7
Glebe Rd Acle NR13 ...166 C3
- Dersingham PE31 ...140 C4
- Downham Market PE38 ...172 D6
- Gissing IP21 ...121 A4
- Norwich NR2 ...162 A4
- 7 Watton IP25 ...84 E3
- Weeting IP27 ...175 B7

Glebe The
- 2 Harling NR16 ...118 C5

Glebe The *continued*
- Hemsby NR29 ...167 C8
- Honing NR28 ...38 C6
- Stibbard NR21 ...32 E7

Glebe Way 5 NR12 ...54 C6
Glebes The 13 NR31 ...94 A5
Glenalmond NR4 ...162 A1
Glenburn Ave NR7 ...159 A3
Glenburn Ct NR7 ...159 A3
Glenda Cl NR5 ...157 C1
Glenda Cres NR5 ...157 B2
Glenda Rd NR5 ...157 C1
Glendenning Rd 4 NR1 ...163 B5
Glenfield Cl PE14 ...78 A5
Glengarry Cl NR9 ...88 C8
Glenham Ct PE31 ...140 C4
Glenmore Ave NR30 ...168 D7
Glenmore Gdns NR3 ...158 B2
Glenn Rd NR14 ...90 C4
Globe La NR13 ...165 E6
Globe Pl NR2 ...162 C5
Globe St IP26 ...99 A5
Glosthorpe Manor PE32 ...44 F5
Gloucester Ave NR31 ...170 C4
Gloucester Rd PE30 ...147 B6
Gloucester St NR2 ...162 C4
Gloucester Way IP24 ...176 A5
Gobbett's Rd IP22 ...128 C4
Goddard Cres 1 PE13 ...152 D7
Goddards Ct 14 IP25 ...84 D3
Godfrey Rd 5 NR10 ...54 A2
Godric Pl NR2 ...161 F6
Godwick Medieval Village of* PE32 ...31 C1
Godwin Rd PE13 ...152 D7
Goffe Cl IP25 ...84 D4
Goffins La NR29 ...56 C6
Goggles La NR19 ...66 C6
Gogg's Mill Rd NR21 ...141 A3
Gogle Cl 8 NR20 ...68 E6
Golden Ball St NR1 ...178 B2
Golden Dog La NR3 ...178 B4
Golden Gates NR23 ...136 B2
Golden Gates Dr NR23 ...136 A2
Golden Pightle 7 NR9 ...69 F2
Goldfinch Cl PE38 ...172 C7
Goldfinch Way 13 IP25 ...84 C3
Golding Pl 15 PE13 ...152 C4
Golds Pightle PE36 ...2 D3
Goldsmith St NR2 ...162 C7
Goldsmith Way IP21 ...121 F4
Goldwell Rd NR1 ...178 B1
Golf Cl King's Lynn PE30 ...148 D1
- Runton NR27 ...10 A5

Golf Course Rd PE36 ...132 E8
Golf Links Rd
- Brundall NR13 ...165 D4
- Wymondham College NR18 ...104 E8

Gong La PE31 ...135 F6
Gonville Cl PE31 ...133 C5
Gonville Rd NR31 ...170 A4
Gooch Cl NR28 ...151 C6
Gooderstone CE Prim Sch PE33 ...82 A5
Gooderstone Rd PE33 ...81 F5
Goodhale Rd 1 NR5 ...161 B7
Goodman Sq 2 NR2 ...162 C7
Goodminns PE36 ...13 A7
Goodwin Rd NR11 ...143 C6
Goodwins Rd PE30 ...146 E3
Goodwood Cl NR7 ...159 F1
Goosander Cl 4 PE31 ...12 E5
Goose Gn
- 8 Sutton Bridge PE12 ...41 B8
- Winfarthing IP22 ...120 C6

Goose Gn La IP22 ...120 B6
Goose Gn Rd PE31 ...12 E4
Goose La
- Alby with Thwaite NR11 ...21 B3
- Stalham NR12 ...39 C4

Gooseacre La IP25 ...67 D3
Gooseberry Hill NR20 ...50 B3
Goose's La PE14 ...41 D5
Gordon Ave NR7 ...163 C7
Gordon Fendick Sch PE13 ...152 D8
Gordon Godfrey Way NR10 ...53 A3
Gordon Rd
- Briston NR24 ...142 A5
- East Dereham NR20 ...154 E5
- Great Yarmouth NR31 ...169 C2

Gordon Sq NR1 ...178 B1
Gordon Terr NR11 ...143 B4
Gore La NR15 ...121 C8
Gorgate Rd NR20 ...49 E3
Gorleston Golf Course NR31 ...171 E7
Gorleston La NR31 ...170 A2
Gormans La NR21 ...31 D5
Gorse Ave NR6 ...158 A5
Gorse Cl 4 Belton NR31 ...94 A5
- 2 East Dereham NR19 ...154 C4
- Fakenham NR21 ...141 F3
- Mundesley NR11 ...143 B5

Gorse Ind Est IP24 ...125 C6
Gorse Rd NR7 ...163 D8
Goshawk Way 5 IP24 ...176 D2
Gosmoor La PE14 ...59 B1
Gothic Cl 2 IP20 ...122 D1
Goulburn Rd NR7 ...159 D1
Gould Rd 1 NR2 ...162 A4
Gournay Ave NR31 ...170 D2
Gowing Cl NR6 ...157 F7
Gowing Ct NR3 ...158 B3
Gowing Rd
- 11 Mulbarton NR14 ...89 B3
- Norwich NR6 ...157 F6

Gowing Way NR15 ...107 B5
Grace Edwards Cl NR8 ...155 F2
Grafton Cl PE30 ...147 C8
Grafton Rd PE30 ...147 C8
Graham Dr 2 PE32 ...44 B3
Graham Sq NR7 ...159 D1
Graham St PE30 ...146 E3
Grammar Sch Rd NR28 ...151 C4
Granary Cl
- Briston NR24 ...142 F3
- Freethorpe NR13 ...92 E7
- 9 Lingwood NR13 ...74 A3

Granary Ct PE30 ...146 D4
Granary Rd NR17 ...174 C4
Grand Cl NR19 ...154 C4
Grange Ave NR27 ...11 B3
Grange Cl Ludham NR29 ...56 D5
- Norwich NR6 ...158 E4
- 10 Snettisham PE31 ...12 E4
- Wroxham/Hoveton NR12 ...164 E6

Grange Cres PE33 ...63 C5
Grange Ct NR28 ...151 C4
Grange La
- Honingham NR9 ...69 F5
- West Winch PE33 ...61 E8

Grange Rd
- Caister-on-Sea NR30 ...168 D5
- Cantley NR13 ...92 C6
- Flixton NR35 ...123 E4
- Hainford NR10 ...53 F5
- Ludham NR29 ...56 D5
- Mundham NR14 ...108 F7
- Norwich NR2 ...162 A4
- Scarning NR19 ...154 A4
- Sutton Bridge PE34 ...41 E8
- Wendling NR19 ...66 F8
- Wisbech PE13 ...152 A7

Grange Wlk NR12 ...164 C4
Granny Bard's La NR12 ...54 C3
Grant Rd NR10 ...54 A2
Grant St NR2 ...162 A7
Grantly Ct PE30 ...147 D5
Granville Cl 8 NR12 ...39 B4
Granville Rd NR31 ...169 B4
Granville Terr PE12 ...41 A8
Grapes Hill NR2 ...162 C6
Grasmere 19 NR9 ...88 D8
Grasmere Cl NR5 ...161 C6
Grassgate La PE14 ...59 B7
Gravel Bank PE14 ...60 D6
Gravel Dam NR32 ...111 F4
Gravel Hill NR14 ...89 F4
Gravel Pit La NR25 ...137 C5
Gravelfield Cl NR1 ...163 B8
Gravelhill La PE33 ...43 F1
Gravelpit Hill NR17 ...102 F6
Gray Dr NR20 ...50 B4
Grays Fair NR5 ...156 F1
Gray's La NR22 ...16 E6
Grays La PE14 ...59 C2
Gray's La IP21 ...121 D5
Grays Rd NR34 ...111 C3
Great Barn Rd NR23 ...5 A4
Great Barwick Medieval Village of* PE31 ...14 E6
Great Cl NR30 ...168 F5
Great Comm La NR34 ...124 E8
Great Dunham Prim Sch PE32 ...47 F1
Great Eastern Rd PE13 ...152 B4
Great Eastern Way
- Fakenham NR21 ...141 D4
- Wells-next-the-Sea NR23 ...136 E5

Great Ellingham Prim Sch NR17 ...103 E8
Great Hautbois Rd NR12 ...54 C7
Great Hockham Prim Sch IP24 ...102 E4
Great Hospl NR1 ...178 C4
Great Man's Way PE33 ...81 A2
Great Melton Rd
- Hethersett NR9 ...88 C8
- Little Melton NR9 ...160 A2

Great Northern Cl NR30 ...169 D6
Great Palgrave Medieval Village of* PE32 ...65 B6
Great Snoring Rd NR21 ...17 D6
Great Witchingham Prim Sch NR9 ...51 E5
Great Yarmouth & Caister Golf Course NR30 ...168 F3
Great Yarmouth Coll NR31 ...169 C1
Great Yarmouth High Sch NR30 ...169 E6
Great Yarmouth Sta NR30 ...169 B5
Greatheath Rd NR20 ...32 D1
Grebe Cl
- Great Yarmouth NR31 ...170 A7
- 7 Rollesby NR29 ...57 D2

Green Bank PE36 ...2 A5
Green Cl
- Hempton NR21 ...141 A2
- Norwich NR5 ...156 E1

Green Comm La PE31 ...3 C6
Green Croft NR17 ...174 B3
Green Ct
- Fakenham NR21 ...141 E4
- Norwich NR7 ...163 D7

Green Dragon La NR23 ...136 D5
Green Dro PE14 ...77 D6
Green Gr PE33 ...81 D8
Green Hill La PE31 ...14 B3
Green Hills Cl NR8 ...156 F3
Green Hills Rd 6 NR3 ...162 D8
Green House La PE37 ...153 E5
Green La Alpington NR14 ...90 F3
- Attleborough NR17 ...174 C7
- Aylsham NR11 ...150 A6
- Bawburgh NR9 ...160 C4
- Beetley NR20 ...49 D4
- Billingford NR20 ...49 F8
- Burgh St Peter NR34 ...111 C4
- Burnham Thorpe PE31 ...4 D3
- Caister-on-Sea NR30 ...168 F4
- Christchurch PE14 ...95 A7
- Coltishall NR12 ...54 C6
- Dereham NR19 ...154 E8
- Ditchingham NR35 ...109 B2
- Earsham NR35 ...108 E2
- 6 Feltwell IP26 ...98 E1
- Filby NR29 ...75 F8
- Foulsham NR20 ...33 E3
- Great & Little Plumstead NR13 ...72 E5
- Great Ellingham NR17 ...103 E8
- Great Moulton NR15 ...106 B1
- Great Yarmouth NR31 ...94 C6
- Guist NR20 ...33 A5
- Hales NR14 ...109 E8
- Haveringland NR10 ...52 F7
- Horsford NR10 ...53 B4
- King's Lynn PE30 ...148 E2
- Little Ellingham NR17 ...86 A1
- Methwold IP26 ...99 A7
- Mundford IP26 ...100 B5
- Postwick with Witton NR7 ...72 E4
- Potter Heigham NR29 ...56 F6
- Pudding Norton NR21 ...141 A1
- Redenhall with Harleston IP20 ...122 E2
- Rocklands NR17 ...103 C7
- Saxlingham Nethergate NR15 ...107 B7
- Shipdham IP25 ...67 D4
- Shipmeadow NR34 ...109 F1
- Somerleyton, Ashby & Herringfleet NR32 ...111 F8
- South Walsham NR13 ...74 B6
- Starston IP20 ...122 D4
- Stow Bedon NR17 ...103 B8
- Syleham IP21 ...131 C4
- Thelnetham IP22 ...128 A2
- Thetford IP24 ...176 E4
- Thornham PE36 ...2 D6
- Thrandeston IP21 ...129 F2
- Tivetshall St Margaret NR15 ...121 B5
- Toft Monks NR34 ...110 C6
- Tottenhill PE33 ...61 F5
- Troston IP31 ...126 A1
- Upwell PE14 ...95 B6
- Walsoken PE14 ...152 F4
- Wicklewood NR18 ...87 C5
- Wramplingham NR18 ...87 F7
- Wymondham NR18 ...173 D1
- Yaxham NR19 ...68 B6

Green La E NR13 ...72 E7
Green La N NR13 ...72 D5
Green La W NR13 ...72 D8
Green Man La NR15 ...108 C8
Green Marsh Rd PE34 ...144 C7
Green Oak Rd 2 IP25 ...84 D3
Green Pk 42 IP20 ...122 D2
Green Pk Rd NR10 ...53 B3
Green Quay The* PE30 ...146 D4
Green Rd Brandon IP27 ...175 E2
- Hales NR14 ...109 E8
- Upwell PE14 ...77 E4

Green St IP21 ...131 A4
Green The Ashill IP25 ...84 A7
- Belton with Browston NR31 ...94 A5
- Boughton PE33 ...80 F4
- Brisley NR20 ...49 B8
- Burnham Market PE31 ...135 C3
- Deopham NR18 ...86 E2
- Dersingham PE31 ...140 D4
- 8 Earsham NR35 ...123 F8
- Fakenham NR21 ...141 A3
- Freethorpe NR13 ...92 E8
- Hickling NR12 ...39 E2
- Hockham IP24 ...102 E3
- Lound NR32 ...94 C2
- North Lopham IP22 ...119 A2
- Runhall NR9 ...68 F2
- Saxlingham Nethergate NR15 ...107 D7
- Surlingham NR14 ...73 B1
- Thornham PE36 ...2 D6
- Upton with Fishley NR13 ...166 B8
- Wicklewood NR18 ...87 B4

Green Way
- Barsham NR22 ...16 C6
- Stiffkey NR23 ...6 C6
- Swaffham PE37 ...153 B6

Green Wood Dr NR19 ...154 C5
Greenacre Cl NR13 ...165 C4

Greenacre Fst & Mid Sch
NR30 ....169 D1
Greenacre Rd NR9 ....86 B5
Greenacres
Bradwell NR31 ....170 A3
Little Melton NR9 ....160 C2
Greenacres Cl PE30 ......148 B2
Greenacres Dr NR14 ....90 C5
Greenborough Cl NR7 ....159 E2
Greenborough Rd
NR7 ....159 E2
Greencourts 10 NR29 .....58 B6
Greenfield Cl NR15 ....156 D1
Greenfield Cl NR27 ....139 C5
Greenfields NR16 ....118 B5
Greenfields Rd NR20 ...154 F4
Greengate NR20 ....50 B2
Greengate La
Bircham PE31 ....13 F4
Great Massingham PE32 ..29 C1
Greenhill Ave NR30 ......108 D8
Greenhill Rd PE32 ....46 B2
Greenhoe Pl PE37 ....153 B3
Greenland Ave
King's Lynn PE30 ....146 E8
Wymondham NR18 ....173 E6
Greenlands Way NR26 ..138 C6
Greenlands Way W 2
NR26 ....138 B6
Greenpark Ave PE30 .....146 F6
Green's La NR27 ....10 C4
Greens Rd
East Dereham NR20 ......154 F3
North Walsham NR28 ....151 A5
Greenway Cl
Fakenham NR21 ....141 C5
2 North Walsham NR28 ..151 C5
Greenway La
Fakenham NR21 ....141 C5
Tharston & Hapton
NR15 ....106 D6
Greenways
Bunwell NR16 ....105 D4
Flordon NR15 ....106 E8
Holt NR25 ....137 C7
Newton Flotman NR15 .....89 C1
Norwich NR4 ....161 F1
Greenways Cl NR15 ......106 E8
Greenways La
Bunwell NR16 ....105 D4
Carleton Rode NR16 ......105 B4
Greenwich Cl
Dersingham PE31 ....140 E3
Downham Market PE38 ...172 B3
Greenwood Cl NR16 .....105 E8
Greenwood Rd NR4 ......162 C1
Greenwood Way
5 Shipdham IP25 ....67 C2
Thorpe St Andrew NR7 ...159 F2
Greevegate PE36 ....132 C4
Gregory Cl 1 PE30 ......148 C5
Gregs Cl NR20 ....68 F5
Grenville Cl 3 NR9 ....88 E8
Grenville Pl NR30 ....169 D8
Grenville Way IP24 ....176 C5
Gresham Cl
Great Yarmouth NR31 ....170 C2
Sheringham NR20 ....147 C8
Gresham Rd
Baconsthorpe NR25 ....20 B8
Norwich NR3 ....158 B2
Gresham Village Sch
NR11 ....9 E1
Greshams Sch NR25 ....137 D7
Gresley Cl NR20 ....49 C4
Gressenhall Rd NR20 ...49 D4
Greyfriars Cl NR6 ....158 E5
Greyfriars Cty Prim Sch
PE30 ....146 E4
Greyfriars Rd NR1 ....178 B3
Greyfriars Way NR30 ...169 C3
Greyhound La
Banham NR16 ....119 D7
Hopton IP22 ....127 E5
Greyhound Opening 7
NR2 ....162 C7
Greylag Cl 8 NR13 ....55 A1
Greys Manor NR16 ....119 D6
Grice Cl 4 NR26 ....138 C5
Griffin La
Attleborough NR17 ....174 D5
Thorpe St Andrew NR7 ...72 D3
Grigsons Wood 1
NR16 ....118 C5
Grime's Graves (English
Heritage)* IP27 ....115 C8
Grimmer La NR13 ....92 B7
Grimmer's Rd 6 PE13 ..152 E7
Grimshoe Rd PE38 ....172 B6
Grimston Pott Row Fst Sch
PE32 ....45 A8
Grimston Rd
Gayton PE32 ....45 C6
King's Lynn PE30 ....148 E1
Gristock Pl NR15 ....161 C8
Griston Rd
Thompson IP24 ....102 B8
Watton IP25 ....84 E3
Groomes Cl 4 NR31 .....171 D5
Grosvenor Rd
Norwich NR2 ....162 B5
Wisbech PE13 ....152 D7
Grouts La NR25 ....8 B6
Grove Ave
Norwich NR5 ....157 A1

Grove Ave continued
Norwich NR1 ....178 A1
Grove Cl
8 East Dereham NR19 ...154 C4
Holt NR25 ....137 D6
2 Newton Flotman NR15 ..89 C1
Grove Dale 8 NR15 ....89 C1
Grove End IP21 ....131 F1
Grove Gdns 2 PE32 ....45 C6
Grove House Nursery Inf Sch
NR19 ....154 D4
Grove La Booton NR10 ...52 A8
Fakenham NR21 ....141 C6
Forncett NR16 ....106 A3
Holt NR25 ....137 D6
Sparham NR9 ....51 B6
Tasburgh NR15 ....106 F7
Thetford IP24 ....176 D4
Grove Rd
Banham NR16 ....119 C6
Barsham NR21 ....16 C4
Brockdish IP21 ....131 C6
Cantley NR13 ....92 D8
Cromer NR27 ....139 D5
Gissing IP21 ....121 A4
Hethersett NR9 ....88 D8
Ingham NR12 ....24 C1
4 Marthan NR29 ....57 D5
Melton Constable NR24 ..142 A4
North Walsham NR28 ....151 D5
Norwich NR1 ....178 A1
Repps with Bastwick
NR29 ....57 A4
Starston IP20 ....122 C2
Wells-next-the-Sea
NR23 ....136 E4
Grove The
Coltishall NR12 ....54 D6
East Dereham NR19 ......154 D4
Fleggburgh NR29 ....57 A4
2 Necton PE37 ....65 F4
Roydon PE32 ....28 A1
Shotesham NR15 ....90 B1
Grove Way NR15 ....89 C1
Grove Wlk NR1 ....178 A1
Grovebury Cl NR13 ......165 C4
Grovedale Cl NR5 ....157 A1
Grovelands PE31 ....140 D8
Groveside PE31 ....30 A7
Growle Abbey NR24 ....19 B2
Grub La IP19 ....124 E1
Grub St
Happisburgh NR12 ....24 B4
Shotesham NR15 ....90 B2
Grubb's La NR11 ....24 C1
Grubb's Rd 7 PE30 ......146 E3
Guanock Terr PE30 ......146 E3
Guardian Rd NR5 ....161 F7
Guelph Rd 2 NR1 ....163 A6
Guernsey Rd NR3 ....162 E8
Guestwick Rd
Foulsham NR20 ....33 E4
Hindolveston NR20 ....33 F7
Wood Dalling NR11 ....34 C7
Wood Norton NR20 ....33 C6
Guild Rd PE13 ....152 A8
Guild St NR22 ....16 F8
Guildford Way IP24 ......176 B5
Guildhall La IP21 ....121 E5
Guildhall St NR3 ....176 D3
Guiler's La NR18 ....105 B8
Guist Cross Way PE38 ..172 C6
Guist Bottom Rd NR20 ..32 E6
Guist Rd NR20 ....33 C4
Gulgate La NR11 ....21 A1
Gull La NR14 ....90 C6
Gullpit Dro PE34 ....61 D1
Gun St 9 NR26 ....138 D7
Gunn Rd NR7 ....159 D1
Gunn St NR11 ....33 C3
Gunner Cl 3 NR7 ....72 D5
Gunn's Cnr NR12 ....138 D2
Gunthorpe Rd PE14 ....41 B5
Gunton La NR5 ....157 B2
Gunton Rd
Loddon NR14 ....109 C8
Norwich NR2 ....161 F5
Wymondham NR18 ....173 D4
Gunton Sta NR11 ....22 B6
Gurney Cl NR5 ....161 B8
Gurney Ct NR5 ....161 B8
Gurney Dr NR7 ....159 D3
Gurney La NR4 ....161 C2
Gurney Rd
Norwich NR5 ....157 A1
Norwich NR1 ....163 A7
Gwyn Cres NR21 ....141 F5
Gymkhana Way PE31 ...133 B5

Habgood Cl NR13 ....166 C4
Hackford Rd
Hardingham NR9 ....86 E6
Wicklewood NR18 ....87 A5
Haconsfield 6 NR9 ....88 D7
Haddiscoe Dam NR14 ...110 F8
Haddiscoe Rd NR14 ......110 F6
Haddiscoe Sta NR31 ......93 D1
Hadfield Rd NR28 ....151 B6
Hadley Cres PE31 ....133 C5
Hadley La NR25 ....8 D6
Hadley Rd NR28 ....151 C6
Hagbech Hall Cl 2 PE14 ..59 D2
Haggard's Cl IP25 ....66 E3
Haig Cl NR19 ....154 D3
Hainford Fst Sch NR10 ..53 E6

Hainford Rd NR10 ....53 E7
Halcombe Ct NR3 ....158 E1
Halden Ave NR6 ....157 F6
Hale Ct NR13 ....74 E4
Hale Dro Littleport CB6 ...96 B2
Welney PE14 ....95 E6
Hale Fen Rd CB6 ....96 B1
Hale Rd Ashill IP25 ....84 D4
Bradenham IP25 ....66 D3
Necton PE37 ....65 F4
Hales Cl NR30 ....168 D5
Hales Ct NR25 ....137 B6
Hales St NR15 ....121 A6
Halesworth Rd NR34 ....124 E4
Haley Cl 4 PE13 ....152 C8
Half Acre Cl NR27 ....10 B4
Half Mile Cl NR3 ....158 B2
Half Mile Rd NR3 ....158 B2
Half Moon La IP22 ....128 E4
Half Moon Way NR2 ....162 B8
Halfar Rd 8 IP31 ....126 B1
Hallfield La NR18 ....86 D2
Halfmile Drift IP25 ....66 D3
Halford La NR17 ....92 B3
Halford La IP27 ....129 A7
Halford Pl NR17 ....174 D4
Halford Rd NR17 ....174 D4
Halfpenny La
Beetley NR20 ....49 C5
Elm PE14 ....59 A2
Wisbech PE14 ....152 D1
Halfpenny Toll Rd PE14 ..95 B8
Halifax Cres NR15 ....15 C3
Hall Bridge Rd PE14 ....67 D6
Hall Cl Fakenham NR21 ..141 D4
Heacham PE31 ....133 D7
4 Hemsby NR29 ....167 A7
5 Hethersett NR9 ....88 D7
8 Hingham NR9 ....86 C4
8 Southery PE38 ....97 B5
Hall Comm Rd NR29 ....56 C4
Hall Cres PE33 ....63 C5
Hall Dike PE14 ....77 F7
Hall Dr Costessey NR5 ..156 D2
17 Feltwell IP26 ....98 E1
Honingham NR9 ....69 E6
North Runcton PE33 ....44 A3
Santon Downham IP27 ..115 C6
Hall Farm Gdns PE32 ....44 F3
Hall Farm Horse Rescue Ctr*
NR13 ....118 B7
Hall Farm Pl NR9 ....160 B6
Hall Hills IP22 ....177 C5
Hall La
Baconsthorpe NR25 ....19 F8
Bressingham IP22 ....119 D1
Burston & Shimpling
IP21 ....121 A2
Colkirk NR21 ....31 E5
Deopham NR18 ....86 F4
East Carleton NR14 ....88 B4
East Dereham NR20 ......154 F4
East Ruston NR12 ....24 A4
Felthorpe NR10 ....52 E5
Frettenham NR12 ....54 B3
Gunthorpe NR24 ....18 A5
Hingham NR9 ....86 C5
Horsford NR10 ....53 B1
King's Lynn PE30 ....148 B1
Knapton NR28 ....143 B1
Knapton NR28 ....151 F8
Long Stratton NR15 ....106 F3
Morley NR18 ....87 B2
North Tuddenham NR20 ...68 F8
North Walsham NR28 ....151 D5
Northwold IP26 ....99 C7
Postwick with Witton
NR13 ....72 F2
Redgrave IP22 ....128 E4
Ringstead PE36 ....2 A3
Roydon IP22 ....129 D7
Saxlingham Nethergate
NR15 ....107 C2
Scole IP21 ....130 F8
Shelfanger IP22 ....120 B2
Shelton NR15 ....122 A8
Taverham NR8 ....157 B8
Tharston & Hapton
NR15 ....106 D5
Thompson IP24 ....102 B7
Thornham PE36 ....2 D6
Thursford NR21 ....17 F5
Watton NR15 ....106 C1
West Winch PE33 ....43 E2
Whissonsett NR20 ....31 D2
Wiveton NR25 ....7 D6
Wood Norton NR20 ....33 B6
Hall Loke NR8 ....86 C4
Hall Moor Rd NR9 ....86 C4
Hall Orchards PE32 ....44 C3
Hall Plain NR30 ....169 C3
Hall Rd Alderford NR9 .....52 A5
Barsham NR34 ....124 F7
Barton Turf NR12 ....23 B1
12 Bawdeswell NR20 ......50 E7
Bedingham NR35 ....108 C3
Beetley NR20 ....49 D5
Blofield NR13 ....165 C8
Bracon Ash NR14 ....88 B4
Brockdish IP21 ....131 D7
Bunwell NR16 ....105 E2
Burston & Shimpling
IP22 ....120 E3
Carleton Rode NR16 .....105 B4
Catfield NR29 ....56 B8
Clenchwarton PE34 ....145 D6

Hall Rd continued
Cromer NR27 ....139 B5
Earsham NR35 ....123 E8
Easton NR9 ....70 E5
Ellingham NR35 ....109 C3
Elsing NR20 ....50 D2
Felbrigg NR27 ....139 A4
Fleggburgh NR29 ....57 A4
Framingham Earl NR14 ...90 D5
Gimingham NR11 ....22 D7
Great Melton NR9 ....88 B8
Great Witchingham NR9 ..51 F5
Hainford NR10 ....53 D3
Hemsby NR29 ....167 A7
Hoe NR20 ....49 F3
Honing NR28 ....38 D8
Hopton on Sea NR31 .....171 B6
King's Lynn PE30 ....148 C1
Ludham NR29 ....56 B4
Marthan NR29 ....57 D4
Mautby NR29 ....76 A6
Northrepps NR27 ....139 D2
Norwich NR5 ....157 A2
Norwich NR1 ....178 B1
Oulton NR11 ....35 B7
Outwell PE14 ....77 F7
Postwick with Witton
NR13 ....165 A5
Pulham St Mary IP21 ....122 A4
Reedham NR13 ....92 A3
Roudham NR16 ....117 E6
Runhall NR20 ....69 A4
Smallburgh NR12 ....38 D2
9 Stalham PE31 ....12 E5
Sutton NR12 ....39 D3
Swafield NR28 ....22 C5
Taconeston NR16 ....105 E6
Tharston & Hapton
NR15 ....106 E5
Thurton NR14 ....91 C3
Tivetshall St Margaret
NR15 ....121 B6
Toft Monks NR34 ....110 D7
Walpole Highway PE14 ...59 F8
Winfarthing IP22 ....120 C5
Wortwell IP20 ....131 A6
Hall St NR24 ....142 E3
Hall Staithe NR21 ....141 B4
Hall View Rd PE30 ....147 B4
Hall Wlk NR7 ....51 D5
Hallback La NR14 ....90 F1
Hallfield Rd IP24 ....102 A7
Hallfields PE33 ....62 D4
Hallgate 2 NR13 ....72 D6
Hallowing Cres 8 NR15 ..106 B1
Hallowing La NR15 ....121 B8
Halls Cnr NR10 ....53 B8
Halls Cnr Rd NR10 ....53 B8
Hall's Dr NR20 ....49 C4
Hallwong La IP20 ....122 D3
Halstead Cl 8 PE13 ......152 E5
Halt Rd NR30 ....168 D7
Halton Rd 8 IP25 ....84 F3
Halvergate Rd
Beighton NR13 ....74 E1
Reedham NR13 ....93 A6
Hambling's Piece
NR16 ....118 C4
Hamburg Way PE30 ......147 A8
Hamilton Cl
North Walsham NR28 ....151 C5
South Walsham NR13 .....74 A8
Hamilton Dr PE37 ....153 D3
Hamilton Rd
Cromer NR27 ....139 B7
Great Yarmouth NR30 ...169 D7
Old Hunstanton PE36 ....132 E7
Hamilton Rd W PE36 ....132 C7
Hamilton Way NR28 .....172 B5
Hamilton Wlk 9 NR29 .....57 D4
Hamlet Cl NR28 ....151 D7
Hamlin Way PE30 ....146 F1
Hammond Cl NR7 ....159 E3
Hammond Rd 8 NR20 ..169 D5
Hammond Way
Attleborough NR17 ....174 E6
Norwich NR7 ....159 E3
Hamond Cl NR36 ....132 E7
Hamond Rd NR5 ....157 D5
Hamonds High Sch
PE37 ....153 C3
Hampden Dr 19 NR7 ....72 D4
Hampden Rd 2 PE13 ....152 E6
Hampton Ave 8 NR14 ....92 F1
Hampton Cl NR30 ....168 C5
Hanbury Cl 4 NR5 ....161 D5
Hancock Cl 8 NR12 ....54 C7
Hancock Ct NR5 ....160 E7
Hand La Barsham NR21 ..16 C4
Hoveton NR12 ....164 C8
Handel Dr NR19 ....154 F3
Handford Dr NR26 ....138 C6
Hanginghill NR13 ....74 C6
Hankin Ct 8 NR4 ....161 C5
Hankinson's Est PE34 ....42 A5
Hanly Cl NR7 ....159 C2
Hanly Ct NR30 ....168 D6
Hannah Cl NR26 ....138 C6
Hannah Rd NR20 ....50 B4
Hannant Rd NR28 ....151 B6
Hanover Rd NR2 ....162 C4
Hanrae Cl PE30 ....138 F6
Hans Pl 3 NR27 ....139 B7
Hansa Rd PE30 ....146 F2
Hansard Cl NR3 ....158 B1
Hansard La NR3 ....178 B4
Hansard Rd 3 NR3 ....158 B1
Hansell Rd NR7 ....163 F8

Hantons Loke NR13 ....74 B2
Hanworth Cross NR11 ....21 D5
Happisburgh Fst Sch
NR12 ....24 D5
Happisburgh Rd
East Ruston NR12 ....24 A3
Lessingham NR12 ....24 D4
North Walsham NR28 .....151 D4
Witton NR28 ....23 E2
Hapton Prim Sch
NR15 ....106 C7
Harbord Cl 4 NR28 ....151 C5
Harbord Cres NR30 ......170 D8
Harbord Rd
Cromer NR27 ....139 C5
Norwich NR4 ....161 F5
Overstrand NR27 ....11 A3
Harbour La IP22 ....128 A7
Harbour Rd
8 Frettenham NR12 ....54 A4
Norwich NR3 ....163 A5
Harcourt Cl 3 NR1 ....162 F8
Hardesty Cl 9 NR14 ....90 D5
Hardingham Dr 6
NR26 ....138 C5
Hardingham Rd NR9 ....86 C4
Hardingham St 8 NR9 ....86 C4
Hardley Cross* NR14 .....92 E4
Hardley Hall La NR14 .....92 C3
Hardley Rd NR14 ....92 A3
Hardley St NR14 ....92 B3
Hardwick Cl 1 NR4 ....89 D8
Hardwick Ind Est
PE30 ....147 B2
Hardwick Rd
King's Lynn PE30 ....146 E2
Pulham Market IP21 ....121 F7
Shelton NR15 ....122 C8
Hardy Cl
Downham Market PE38 ..172 B4
1 North Walsham NR28 ..151 C5
Thetford IP24 ....176 D6
Hardy Rd NR1 ....163 A4
Hardy's La PE32 ....46 C2
Hare Cl 2 NR14 ....89 B2
Hare Rd NR5 ....72 F5
Harebell Rd NR18 ....173 B3
Harecroft Par 7 PE30 .....46 B4
Harecroft Rd PE13 ....152 B5
Hareton La NR13 ....74 B7
Harefield Rd IP24 ....116 C5
Hares Cl NR21 ....17 C3
Harewood Dr
9 King's Lynn PE30 ....146 E6
Taverham NR8 ....155 E3
Harewood Par 8 PE30 ..146 E6
Harford Manor Cl
NR2 ....162 C2
Harford St NR1 ....162 E3
Harfreys Ind Est NR31 ..169 B1
Harfrey's Rd NR31 ....170 B8
Hargate La PE34 ....42 B7
Hargham Cl 5 NR17 .....104 D2
Hargham Rd
Attleborough NR17 ....174 B2
Old Buckenham NR17 ....104 B2
Shropham NR17 ....103 C3
Harker Way 8 NR13 ....73 D6
Harleston Dove CE Fst Sch
IP20 ....122 D2
Harleston Mus* IP20 ....122 D2
Harleston Rd
Pulham Market IP21 ....121 E4
Scole IP21 ....121 D1
Harley Rd NR30 ....169 D6
Harling Dro IP27 ....115 E7
Harling Rd
Garboldisham IP22 ....118 C2
Hockham IP24 ....102 E3
North Lopham IP22 ....119 A4
Harling Rd Sta NR16 ....118 A6
Harlington Ave NR6 ......158 A4
Harlingwood La NR17 ...104 E1
Harman Cl 2 NR9 ....88 D8
Harman's La IP20 ....122 C1
Harmer Cl NR28 ....151 E5
Harmer Cres NR4 ....161 C1
Harmer La NR4 ....161 C1
Harmer Rd NR3 ....158 D3
Harmer's La NR14 ....90 A7
Harnser's Reach NR13 ..166 B8
Harold Cl PE21 ....141 B5
Harpe's La NR20 ....32 A1
Harpley VC Prim Sch
PE31 ....29 C4
Harp's Hall Rd PE14 ....59 E5
Harpsfield NR5 ....160 E8
Harriet Cl PE12 ....41 A8
Harriet Martineau Cl 10
IP24 ....176 D7
Harriott's Way NR11 .....150 D8
Harris Rd
11 Swanton Morley NR20 ..50 B3
Wymondham NR18 ....173 B5
Harrisons Dr NR7 ....159 C2
Harris Mews 2 NR5 ....161 A7
Harrold Cl
1 South Walsham NR13 ..74 A8
Taverham NR8 ....155 E2
Harrolds Cl PE13 ....59 C5
Harrow Cl PE34 ....146 C5
Harry Barber Cl 2 NR5 ..161 A7
Harry's La IP21 ....121 E7
Harry Blunt Way 10
NR19 ....154 C4
Harry Perry Cl NR4 ....162 C2
Harry's La IP21 ....121 E7

Harrys Way
Hunstanton PE36 ....132 D1
Wisbech PE13 ....152 C2
Harsnett Cl NR5 ....160 F8
Hart La NR25 ....9 A2
Hartington Rd NR27 ....139 D4
Hartmann Rd NR30 ....170 E6
Hart'a La NR0 ....160 A7
Harts La NR4 ....161 C1
Hartwell Rd NR12 ....164 C4
Harvard Rd 6 IP26 ....98 D1
Harvest Cl 1 NR10 ....53 E5
Harvest La NR21 ....17 D6
Harvey Cl
2 Hethersett NR9 ....88 C7
Norwich NR7 ....163 C7
Tasburgh NR15 ....106 E7
Harvey Dr NR28 ....151 C7
Harvey Est NR11 ....22 E7
Harvey Gn 10 NR14 ....91 F1
Harvey La
Caister-on-Sea NR30 ....168 E4
Dickleburgh IP21 ....131 C4
Norwich NR7 ....163 C6
Harvey St 21 IP25 ....84 D3
Harvey's La NR15 ....100 D6
Harwood Ave IP24 ....176 E6
Harwood Rd NR1 ....162 E1
Hase's La NR9 ....51 C6
Haslips Cl 3 NR2 ....162 C7
Haspalls Rd PE37 ....153 B3
Hassett Cl 6 NR3 ....162 F8
Hastings Ave NR6 ....158 A4
Hastings Cl
Briston NR24 ....142 A5
6 Tasburgh NR15 ....106 F6
Hastings Dr NR26 ....132 D6
Hastings La PE34 ....61 C8
Hastings Rd 4 IP25 ....84 F3
Hastings Way NR12 ....39 C3
Hatherley Gdns PE33 ....81 B8
Hatton Rd NR1 ....162 E3
Haugh Cnr NR16 ....119 F7
Haugh Rd NR16 ....119 F8
Haughs End Rd NR12 ....164 F2
Hautbois Rd NR10 ....37 B2
Havaker The NR13 ....92 F5
Havant Cl NR4 ....161 E1
Havelock Pl 10 NR30 ....169 D2
Havelock Rd
Great Yarmouth NR30 ....169 D2
Norwich NR2 ....162 B6
Sheringham NR26 ....138 E5
Havergate 2 NR12 ....54 C6
Haveringland Rd NR10 ....52 E6
Havers Rd NR1 ....162 B6
Haverscroft Cl NR8 ....155 D2
Hawk Cres IP22 ....177 F5
Hawkes La NR14 ....89 A2
Hawkins Ave NR30 ....169 C8
Hawkins Cl NR30 ....169 C8
Hawkins Dr 3 PE13 ....152 E5
Hawthorn Ave
6 Marham PE33 ....63 B4
Norwich NR6 ....158 A5
Hawthorn Cl Diss IP22 ....177 F5
5 Spixworth NR10 ....54 A1
6 Watlington PE33 ....61 D5
Hawthorn Cres NR31 ....94 C6
Hawthorn Dr
Dersingham PE31 ....140 D5
East Dereham NR19 ....154 B3
Hawthorn Rd
2 Downham Market
PE38 ....172 C6
Emneth PE14 ....59 D1
8 Gayton PE32 ....45 C5
Great Yarmouth NR31 ....170 B6
Norwich NR5 ....157 A2
Hawthorn Rise NR11 ....143 B5
Hawthorn Way IP24 ....176 E6
Hawthorne Ave
Grimston PE32 ....28 B1
Wisbech PE13 ....152 C8
Hawthorne Cl
2 Loddon NR14 ....91 F1
Wymondham NR18 ....173 D6
Hay Gn Rd PE34 ....144 A1
Hay Gn Rd N PE34 ....42 B6
Hay Gn Rd S PE34 ....42 A5
Haycroft 3 NR29 ....167 B7
Hayes La NR21 ....141 A5
Hayfield Rd PE30 ....148 C4
Haygate 2 IP23 ....130 C1
Haylett Cl NR30 ....168 E5
Haythill La IP20 ....98 D2
Hayward Cl 3 NR25 ....7 C6
Haywood End IP22 ....120 D6
Hazel Ave NR26 ....138 D4
Hazel Cl Grimston PE32 ....28 B1
8 King's Lynn PE30 ....148 C3
Taverham NR8 ....155 D1
West Winch PE33 ....43 E1
Wymondham NR18 ....173 D4
Hazel Cres 8 PE33 ....63 B4
Hazel Gdns 1 PE13 ....152 D4
Hazel Rd
4 Attleborough NR17 ....174 B5
Norwich NR5 ....156 F1
Hazel Way NR31 ....170 A6
Hazell Rd NR30 ....151 C7
Heacham Fst Sch
PE31 ....133 C5
Heacham Mid Sch
PE31 ....133 C4
Heacham Rd PE36 ....13 A7
Headington Cl NR31 ....170 A5
Headland Dro IP26 ....113 A5

Headley Dr NR28 ....151 C4
Hearne Cl 3 NR5 ....160 E8
Heartsease Fst & Mid Sch
NR7 ....159 C1
Heartsease High Sch
NR7 ....159 C1
Heartsease La NR7 ....159 B1
Heartsease Rd IP24 ....176 E6
Heartwell Rd NR7 ....139 C5
Heater La NR13 ....73 F4
Heath Cl 16 Horsford NR10 ....53 A3
Lenwade NR9 ....51 D5
Norwich NR6 ....158 A6
Heath Cres NR6 ....158 B5
Heath Dr NR15 ....137 D5
Heath Farm La NR11 ....36 E6
Heath La
Fakenham NR21 ....141 F4
Gimingham NR11 ....22 D8
Great Witchingham NR9 ....51 E6
Gunthorpe NR24 ....18 B5
Lenwade NR9 ....51 D5
Mundesley NR11 ....143 B5
Roughton NR11 ....22 C2
Thursford NR21 ....17 E4
Tittleshall PE32 ....47 F7
Heath Rd
Ashby with Oby NR29 ....57 R?
Banham NR16 ....119 E7
Brandon IP27 ....175 D3
Catfield NR29 ....56 D8
Corpusty NR11 ....19 D1
Dersingham PE31 ....140 D2
East Dereham NR19 ....154 C7
Felmingham NR28 ....37 B8
Fritton & St Olaves NR31 ....93 E1
Geldeston NR34 ....110 A3
Gunthorpe NR24 ....18 B5
Heydon NR11 ....34 D8
Hickling NR12 ....20 E8
Hockering NR20 ....69 B8
Honing NR28 ....23 E1
Kenninghall NR16 ....119 A3
Lessingham NR12 ....24 F2
Lyng NR9 ....51 A4
Norwich NR1 ....162 D8
Quidenham NR16 ....118 E8
Rollesby NR29 ....57 B2
Sapiston IP31 ....126 E3
Sheringham NR26 ....138 D6
Shotesham NR15 ....107 H8
9 Thorpe End NR13 ....72 D6
Troston IP31 ....126 B1
Winfarthing IP22 ....120 A7
Heath Rise
Fakenham NR21 ....141 E4
Sculthorpe Airfield PE31 ....15 B3
Heath The NR10 ....52 F8
Heath Way Blofield NR13 ....73 C6
Fakenham NR21 ....141 F4
Heather Ave
Hemsby NR29 ....167 D4
Norwich NR6 ....158 A4
Heather Ave Fst Sch
NR6 ....158 B4
Heather Barrow Ct
NR21 ....141 D4
Heather Cl PE30 ....148 D5
Heather Dr NR25 ....137 B7
Heather Gdns NR31 ....93 F6
Heather Rd 2 NR21 ....94 A6
Heather Way
Brandon IP27 ....175 E3
Great Massingham NR15 ....121 B8
Heatherwood Cl 7 NR13 ....72 D6
Heathfield Cl NR25 ....8 E3
Heathfield Rd NR25 ....8 E3
Heathgate NR3 ....163 A8
Heathlands 7 ....153 D2
Heathlands Dr IP24 ....176 D8
Heathside Rd NR1 ....163 B5
Hebrides Way NR30 ....168 C6
Heckingham Holes
NR14 ....92 B1
Hedgehog Wlk NR12 ....24 E4
Hedgelands 1 PE13 ....152 C8
Hedgemere 8 NR8 ....155 D2
Hedgerows The 8 NR5 ....160 E8
Hedley La NR13 ....111 F1
Heffer Cl NR19 ....154 D3
Heggatt Rd NR12 ....54 C5
Heidi Cl 7 NR19 ....154 D1
Heigham Gr NR2 ....162 C6
Heigham Pk Fst Sch
NR2 ....162 A5
Heigham Rd NR2 ....162 B6
Heigham St NR2 ....162 B8
Heigham Watering 5
NR2 ....162 B8
Helen Ave 7 NR29 ....57 C4
Helena Rd
Norwich NR2 ....162 B6
Witton NR12 ....23 F3
Helford St 8 NR2 ....162 B8
Hellesdon Cl NR6 ....161 D8
Hellesdon Cty High Sch
NR6 ....157 E4
Hellesdon Hall Rd
NR6 ....157 E1
Hellesdon Hospl NR6 ....157 D4
Hellesdon Mill La
NR6 ....157 D1
Hellesdon Pk Rd NR6 ....157 E3
Hellesdon Rd NR6 ....157 D2
Hellgate La NR11 ....20 F8
Hellington Cnr NR14 ....91 B5
Hellington Hill NR14 ....91 B6
Hellpit La NR24 ....19 B2

Helska Leisure Ctr
NR12 ....55 E3
Hemblington Hall Rd
NR13 ....73 E6
Hemblington Prim Sch
NR13 ....73 C6
Hemblington Rd NR13 ....73 E4
Hemington Cl NR0 ....147 DH
Hemlin Cl NR5 ....161 C6
Hemmant Way NR34 ....110 B3
Hemmings Cl 4 NR5 ....160 F7
Hempnall Rd NR35 ....108 A4
Hempnall Sch NR15 ....107 C5
Hempstead Rd
Holt NR25 ....137 D5
Lessingham NR12 ....24 D3
Hempsted Mews NR5 ....160 E7
Hempton Rd NR21 ....141 B3
Hemsby Fst Sch NR29 ....167 A7
Hemsby Rd
16 Marthan NR29 ....57 D4
Winterton-on-Sea NR29 ....58 B5
Henby Way NR7 ....159 C4
Henderson Rd NR4 ....161 F5
Hendon Ave 16 IP25 ....84 F3
Hendon Cl NR25 ....157 R1
Hendrie Rd NR25 ....137 C7
Henley Rd NR2 ....162 A4
Hennessey's Cl NR28 ....23 A3
Henry Bell Cl PE30 ....147 A5
Henry Blogg Rd NR27 ....139 B5
Henry Cross Cl 1 IP25 ....67 C2
Henry Preston Rd 1
NR15 ....106 F6
Henry Ramey Upcher
Lifeboat Mus* NR26 ....138 D8
Henry St PE13 ....152 C4
Henry Warby Ave 7
PE14 ....59 A1
Henry Ward Rd 1 IP20 ....122 D2
Henry's Ct 1 IP25 ....84 F3
Henson Cl 3 PE13 ....152 C8
Henstead Rd NR9 ....88 D8
Hepworth Rd IP31 ....127 D3
Herbert Colman Cl
NR13 ....73 E2
Herbert Dr IP26 ....98 F5
Herbert Nursey Cl
NR8 ....157 C7
Herbert Ward Way
PE34 ....144 D6
Hercules Cl NR6 ....157 F4
Hercules Rd NR6 ....157 F4
Hereford Way PE33 ....43 E4
Hereward Rd 1 PE13 ....152 D5
Hereward Way
8 Feltwell IP26 ....98 D1
Weeting IP27 ....175 A8
Weeting-with-Broomhill
IP27 ....114 E8
Herman Fst Sch NR31 ....170 A3
Herman Mid Sch
NR31 ....170 A3
Hermanus Leisure Ctr
NR29 ....58 B6
Hermitage Cl 3 NR14 ....89 A3
Herne Cotts NR12 ....67 D5
Herne Dro PE14 ....95 D5
Herne La
Beeston with Bittering
PE32 ....48 C1
Shipdham NR19 ....67 C2
Heroff Way 11 IP20 ....122 D2
Hcron Ave IP27 ....175 A3
Heron Cl
Downham Market PE38 ....172 C7
8 Fakenham NR21 ....141 E4
Great Yarmouth NR31 ....170 A7
Salhouse NR13 ....55 B1
Heron Gdns NR12 ....39 B3
Heron Rd PE13 ....152 D2
Heron Way NR12 ....39 B1
Herrick Rd NR8 ....156 E8
Herries Cl 7 NR30 ....169 C4
Herring La NR9 ....69 A1
Herringfleet Rd NR31 ....93 E2
Herring's La PE31 ....135 C4
Hertford Way NR13 ....170 B4
Hethel Rd NR16 ....105 A4
Hethersett High Sch
NR9 ....88 D7
Hethersett La NR4 ....160 F3
Hethersett Old Hall Sch
NR9 ....88 D7
Hethersett Rd
East Carleton NR14 ....88 F5
Great Melton NR9 ....88 B8
Hevingham Prim Sch
NR10 ....53 B8
Hewett Cl NR3 ....170 D2
Hewett Rd NR30 ....170 A8
Hewitt Sch NR1 ....162 D2
Hewitts Cl NR24 ....142 E4
Hewitts La NR18 ....173 C5
Hextable Rd PE30 ....146 E6
Heydon Hall* NR11 ....34 F6
Heydon La NR11 ....34 E7
Heydon Rd
Aylsham NR11 ....150 A7
Corpusty NR11 ....34 F8
Wood Dalling NR11 ....34 D6
Heywood Ave IP22 ....177 D6
Heywood Rd Diss IP22 ....177 D6
Shelfanger IP22 ....120 C2
Tibenham NR16 ....120 C4
Winfarthing IP22 ....120 C4
Heywood The IP22 ....120 D5

Hickling Broad Nature
Reserve* NR29 ....56 F8
Hickling Broad Visitor Ctr*
NR12 ....40 A1
Hickling Cl PE37 ....153 C2
Hickling Fst Sch NR12 ....39 F2
Hickling La NR14 ....89 D4
Hickling Rd
Sea Palling NR12 ....24 F1
Sutton NR12 ....39 C2
Hickling Way NR29 ....167 B3
Hickory Gdns 16 NR31 ....94 C7
Hickory Rd PE30 ....147 C5
High Ash Rd NR18 ....88 C5
High Banks NR18 ....173 C3
High Bridgham Rd
NR16 ....117 C5
High Bungay Rd NR14 ....109 D8
High Comm NR18 ....87 D2
High Common Rd IP22 ....128 C8
High Cross NR20 ....33 A2
High Ct IP20 ....122 E2
High Fen Dro IP26 ....98 D8
High Gn Brooke NR15 ....90 D1
Great Melton NR9 ....88 B8
5 Great Moulton NR15 ....106 B1
Great Moulton NR15 ....121 B8
High House Ave 3
NR18 ....173 D5
High House Cotts PE32 ....47 E5
High House La 6 NR13 ....72 D6
High House Rd NR20 ....49 C4
High Lodge Forest Ctr*
IP27 ....115 C3
High London La IP22 ....120 A4
High Mill Rd NR31 ....169 B3
High Noon La NR13 ....73 E6
High Noon Rd NR11 ....21 D2
High Oak La NR18 ....87 D3
High Oak Rd NR18 ....87 B3
High Rd Beighton NR13 ....74 B1
Bressingham IP22 ....129 B6
Burgh Castle NR31 ....94 B8
Cantley NR13 ....92 B8
Forncett NR16 ....106 B6
Great Yarmouth NR31 ....170 C8
Lessingham NR12 ....24 C2
Needham IP20 ....131 E7
Repps with Bastwick
NR29 ....57 A4
Roydon IP22 ....177 A5
Tilney St Lawrence PE34 ....60 F8
Wiggenhall St Germans
PE34 ....42 F1
Wiggenhall St Germans
PE34 ....43 D3
Wimbotsham NR20 ....123 A3
High St
Attleborough NR17 ....174 D5
Blakeney NR25 ....7 C6
Brandon IP27 ....175 C5
Caister-on-Sea NR30 ....168 E5
Castle Acre PE32 ....46 F2
Cawston NR10 ....35 B3
Cley next the Sea NR25 ....7 E6
Coltishall NR12 ....54 C7
Cromer NR27 ....139 B7
Docking PE31 ....134 E4
Downham Market PE38 ....172 C5
East Dereham NR19 ....154 D5
Feltwell IP26 ....98 E1
Fincham PE33 ....62 E1
Foulsham NR20 ....33 D3
Great Yarmouth NR31 ....170 D6
Heacham PE31 ....133 B5
Hilgay PE38 ....79 E1
Holt NR25 ....137 B6
Hopton IP22 ....127 F6
Hunstanton PE36 ....132 C4
Ketteringham NR18 ....88 D5
King's Lynn PE30 ....146 D5
Lakenheath IP27 ....113 E1
Loddon NR14 ....92 A1
Ludham NR29 ....56 C5
Marsham NR10 ....150 C1
Methwold IP26 ....99 A5
Mundesley NR11 ....143 C5
North Elmham NR20 ....49 E8
Northwold IP26 ....99 C7
Overstrand NR27 ....11 A3
Ringstead PE36 ....2 A3
St Margaret, Ilketshall
NR35 ....124 D3
5 Sheringham NR26 ....138 D7
Shipdham IP25 ....67 B2
Southrepps NR11 ....22 B7
Stalham NR12 ....39 B4
Stoke Ferry PE33 ....81 A2
Sutton Bridge PE12 ....41 C8
Thelnetham IP22 ....128 B4
Thornham PE36 ....2 D6
Thursford NR21 ....17 D5
Tittleshall PE32 ....48 B8
Walsingham NR22 ....16 F7
Watton IP25 ....84 D3
Wells-next-the-Sea
NR23 ....136 D5
Whissonsett NR20 ....31 D2
Wicklewood NR18 ....87 B5
Wighton NR23 ....5 F2
Wisbech PE13 ....152 C5
High View Dr NR13 ....72 D7
High Way 16 NR13 ....74 A3
High Wrong Cnr IP24 ....115 C1

Higham Cl NR7 ....159 A3
Highbridge Gravel Dro
IP27 ....113 D2
Highbridge Rd PE34 ....78 F8
Highbury Rd IP27 ....175 A2
Higher Gn Cl 2 NR15 ....89 U1
Highfield 3 Eye IP23 ....130 C1
Field Dalling NR25 ....7 B2
Great & Little Plumstead
NR13 ....73 B7
King's Lynn PE30 ....147 C5
Highfield Ave NR13 ....165 D3
Highfield Cl
Foulsham NR20 ....33 C4
1 Norwich NR7 ....72 D3
Ryburgh NR21 ....32 A6
Highfield La NR21 ....32 A6
Highfield Rd
East Dereham NR19 ....154 D8
Fakenham NR21 ....141 B5
Great Yarmouth NR31 ....170 D7
Taverham NR8 ....155 F1
Highfield Way 4 NR12 ....54 C7
Highfields
Felmingham NR28 ....37 A8
Lakenheath IP27 ....113 F1
Norwich NR5 ....156 D1
Highgrove Ct NR14 ....90 C6
Highland Ave NR14 ....90 B6
Highland Ave NR20 ....162 A4
Highland Cl NR13 ....90 C6
Highland Rd
Norwich NR2 ....162 A4
Taverham NR8 ....155 D1
Highlands
Costessey NR8 ....156 F4
Thetford IP24 ....176 D5
Highland Rd NR5 ....157 A1
Highmoor Dro IP26 ....99 D8
Highview Cl NR13 ....165 E6
Highway Pk NR27 ....139 C4
Hilary Ave NR11 ....143 B8
Hilary Cl 3 NR12 ....74 A3
Hilda Rd NR11 ....143 C6
Hilgay Rd Ryston PE38 ....79 F3
West Dereham PE33 ....80 A4
Hill Ave NR31 ....170 C1
Hill Cl NR27 ....139 C4
Hill Comm NR12 ....39 F1
Hill Crest Rd NR7 ....163 D7
Hill Est The PE33 ....62 B6
Hill Farm Rd NR15 ....106 F3
Hill Fields NR13 ....154 C1
Hill Fort Cl IP24 ....176 D7
Hill House La IP24 ....176 D7
Hill House Rd
Bramerton NR14 ....90 F8
Norwich NR7 ....163 D5
Hill La Nuthall NR20 ....69 A4
Sculthorpe Airfield NR21 ....15 C2
Hill Rd
Ingoldisthorpe PE31 ....140 C8
King's Lynn PE30 ....147 B8
Middleton PE33 ....44 B3
Morley NR18 ....104 D8
Norwich NR5 ....156 F2
Tibenham NR16 ....120 F8
Hill Side Cl 31 PE32 ....44 B3
Hill St 10 Fellwell IP26 ....98 C1
Hunstanton PE36 ....132 C4
Norwich NR2 ....162 C4
6 Wisbech PE13 ....152 C5
Hill The Brandon IP27 ....72 A2
Coltishall NR12 ....54 D7
Little Snoring NR21 ....17 B3
Shimpling NR21 ....17 B3
Shipmeadow NR34 ....124 F8
Westwick NR10 ....37 D5
Woodbastwick NR13 ....55 F1
Hill Top
Cley next the Sea NR25 ....7 E7
Stanton IP31 ....127 C1
Hill Top Dr NR8 ....156 F3
Hill View Rd NR26 ....138 E7
Hillary Rd IP24 ....176 D7
Hilburn Rd PE13 ....152 B4
Hillcrest Acle NR11 ....166 A3
Downham Market PE38 ....172 E5
Great Ryburgh NR21 ....32 B6
7 Loddon NR14 ....92 A1
Hillcrest Ave NR14 ....154 C1
Hillcrest Prim Sch
PE38 ....172 E6
Hillen Rd PE30 ....146 D2
Hillfield NR12 ....38 D3
Hillgate La PE34 ....144 A4
Hillingdon Pk NR27 ....11 A4
Hillmead NR3 ....158 D3
Hill's Cl 3 Corpusty NR11 ....19 F1
Sporle PE32 ....65 C6
Hill's Ct PE38 ....79 E1
Hills Rd IP25 ....84 C5
Hills The NR13 ....92 F4
Hillsend La NR17 ....174 A3
Hillside
Barnham Broom NR9 ....69 B2
Barsham NR21 ....16 D5
Brandon IP27 ....114 D4
Briston NR24 ....142 B4
Cromer NR27 ....139 C4
Loddon NR14 ....92 A2
Shouldham PE33 ....63 B5
North Pickenham PE37 ....65 E2

Hillside continued
Poringland NR14 ....90 C5
Roughton NR11 ....C6
Sheringham NR26 ......138 F7
Swaffham PE37 ....153 D4
Hillside Animal Sanctuary★
NR12 ....54 B4
Hillside Ave NR7 ......163 F6
Hillside Ave Prim Sch
NR7 ....163 F6
Hillside Cl
Norwich NR7 ....163 F6
Ormesby St Margaret
NR29 ....167 B2
Swardeston NR14 ......89 C5
Hillside Cres NR18 ....87 B5
Hillside Fst Sch NR31 ..94 C7
Hillside Rd
Horning NR12 ....55 E3
Norwich NR7 ....163 F6
Sheringham NR26 ......138 F5
Hillside Rd E NR35 ....124 B7
Hillside Rd W NR35 ...124 A7
Hilltop Way IP31 ......127 C1
Hillview PE37 ....65 E2
Hillview Dr NR29 ......58 B6
Hillvue Cl NR5 ....157 A2
Hilly Cl IP31 ....126 D1
Hilly Plantation NR7 ..163 F7
Hilton Cl PE37 ....153 C4
Hiltons La 5 PE34 .....43 B1
Hinchingbrook Cl
PE30 ....148 E1
Hinderclay La IP22 ...128 B5
Hinderclay Rd
Redgrave IP22 ....128 D5
Rickinghall Inferior
IP22 ....128 D3
Wattisfield IP22 ......128 D3
Hindolveston Rd
Foulsham NR20 ....33 D4
Fulmodeston NR21 .....17 F1
Guestwick NR20 ....33 F6
Thurning NR20 ....34 A8
Hindringham Prim Sch
NR21 ....17 D7
Hindringham Rd
Binham NR21 ....6 E2
Gunthorpe NR21 ......18 A7
Hindringham NR21 .....17 F7
Walsingham NR22 .....17 A8
Hingham Prim Sch
NR9 ....86 C5
Hingham Rd
Deopham NR18 ....86 F5
Garvestone NR9 ....86 C8
Great Ellingham NR17 .103 E8
Hardingham NR9 ....86 A6
Little Ellingham NR17 ..86 A2
Hingley Cl NR31 ....170 C8
Hinks Cl NR10 ....155 C3
Hinshalwood Way
NR8 ....156 E4
Hipkin Rd NR31 ....140 C3
Hipperson Cl 2 NR28 .151 C7
Hobart Cl NR18 ....173 C6
Hobart High Sch NR14 ..92 A1
Hobart La NR1 ....178 B1
Hobart Sq NR1 ....178 B1
Hobbies Mus of Fretwork &
Craft Ctr★ NR19 .....154 C5
Hobb's La NR13 ....92 D7
Hobbs's La NR15 ......108 D7
Hobland Rd
Belton with Browston
NR31 ....94 C4
Bradwell NR31 ....171 A7
Hobrough La NR1 ....178 C2
Hockering La NR9 ....160 B6
Hockering Prim Sch
NR20 ....69 B8
Hockham St PE30 .....146 E6
Hockwold Prim Sch
IP26 ....114 A6
Hockwold Rd IP27 ....175 B7
Hodgson Rd NR4 ......161 F5
Hoe Hall NR20 ....49 F3
Hoe Rd NR20 ....49 F5
Hoe Rd N NR20 ....50 A4
Hoe Rd S NR20 ....50 A2
Hog Bog La NR10 .....53 F3
Hog La NR34 ....124 F2
Hogarth Cl 18 NR31 ...94 C8
Hogg La NR35 ....108 C1
Hogg's Dro PE33 ......63 B5
Hogherd's La 9 PE13 .152 C5
Hogsty La IP21 ....122 A1
Holbrigg La NR21 ....17 C1
Holcombe Ave PE30 ..146 F3
Holders La IP26 ....99 A7
Holgate Hill NR25 .....8 D4
Holgate Rd 6 NR27 ...10 B5
Holgate Rd
North Walsham NR28 ..151 F1
South Creake NR21 ...15 C7
Holiday & Leisure Ctr
NR31 ....171 E3
Holiday Village NR31 ..94 C8
Holkham Ave PE32 ...13 B2
Holkham Cl 8 PE38 ..172 C6
Holkham Hall★ NR23 ...5 A5
Holkham Rd NR25 ...136 B6
Holl La Billingford NR20 ..50 B7

Holl La continued
Garvestone NR9 ....68 B1
Tharston & Hapton
NR15 ....106 C7
Holl Rd NR15 ....21 B4
Holland Cl 8 NR19 ...154 D1
Holland St NR15 ......108 C3
Hollies The
Clenchwarton PE34 ...145 D5
North Walsham NR28 .151 C5
Hollow Hill Rd NR35 ..109 A2
Hollow La
Barningham IP31 ......127 D4
4 Langham NR25 ......7 A4
Raynham NR21 ....30 F3
Shotesham NR15 ......89 F2
Hollow Way Hill NR14 ..110 D4
Holloway Rd NR14 ....91 B8
Holls La NR1 ....178 B1
Hollway La NR20 .....33 A4
Holly Ave NR31 ....94 C7
Holly Bank NR7 ......159 A2
Holly Blue Rd NR18 ..173 E4
Holly Cl
Downham Market PE38 ..172 B6
Holt NR25 ....137 D7
King's Lynn PE30 ....148 D2
16 Marthan NR29 .....167 C4
Mattishall NR20 ....68 E6
Rougham PE32 ....47 B7
1 West Winch PE33 ...43 E2
Holly Ct
34 Harleston IP20 ....122 D2
Wymondham NR18 ...173 E6
Holly Dr NR2 ....162 A7
Holly Farm Rd NR13 ..93 A4
Holly Gr NR26 ....138 D5
Holly Hill Rd NR13 ...165 D7
Wood Dalling NR11 ....34 D5
Holly Rd NR17 ....174 C4
Hollybush Rd NR18 ..151 F5
Hollycroft Cl NR14 ....59 D1
Hollycroft Rd PE14 ....77 D8
Holman Cl NR11 .....150 B7
Holman Rd NR11 .....150 B6
Holman's Chase 2 NR8 ..97 B6
Holme Cl Hopton IP22 ..127 F6
Runcton Holme PE33 ...61 D4
Holme Rd PE36 ....2 A4
Holmes Cl Acle NR13 ..166 B4
Norwich NR7 ....163 D8
Holmes Dr PE13 ......152 E5
Holmes Rd
East Ruston NR12 .....38 F5
Somerton NR29 ....7 F5
Holmesdale Rd NR13 .165 B4
Holmwood Rise NR7 .163 C6
Holt Cl PE14 ....41 E3
Holt Ctry Pk★ NR25 ..137 C4
Holt House La PE34 ...44 D5
Holt Prim Sch NR25 .137 B5
Holt Rd Aylmerton NR11 ..10 B3
Briston NR28 ....142 E5
Cawston NR10 ....35 D2
Cley next the Sea NR25 ..7 E6
Cromer NR27 ....139 A6
Fakenham NR21 ......141 C4
Felthorpe NR10 ....52 F6
Field Dalling NR25 .....7 B2
Gresham NR11 ....9 E1
Guist NR20 ....32 F4
Hoe NR19 ....154 C8
Langham NR25 ....7 A6
Letheringsett with Glandford
NR25 ....8 A1
Little Snoring NR21 ...17 C3
North Elmham NR20 ...49 E7
Norwich NR7 ....157 F8
Sheringham NR26 ....138 B5
Thornage NR25 ....18 F7
Upper Sheringham
NR26 ....138 C3
Walsingham NR22 ....16 F7
Weybourne NR25 .....8 E5
Holt Sta NR25 ....137 E8
Holt's La PE30 ....79 D1
Holway Cl NR27 ......139 B3
Holway Rd NR26 .....138 D5
Holway The NR29 .....58 B6
Holworthy Rd NR5 ...161 B8
Holy Rd NR24 ....18 D5
Holyrood Dr PE31 ....140 D3
Home Cl
Great Ellingham NR17 .103 E8
Lyng NR9 ....51 A4
3 Sheringham NR27 ...10 A5
Home Farm La NR18 .104 E8
Home Farm La NR18 .104 E8
Home Farm Rise NR35 ..109 C3
Home La
Hilborough IP25 ....83 B4
Hindringham NR21 ...17 E7
Home Piece IP22 .....127 E4
Home St NR2 ....162 C8
Homebred La 1 NR14 ..91 F1
Homefield Ave NR11 ..94 C7
Homefields Rd PE36 ..132 D4
Homeland Rd 10 PE30 ..146 E6
Homelea Cres 15 NR13 ..74 A3
Homestead Cl NR13 ...74 A3
Homestead Gdns
NR29 ....167 B7
Honey Cl 2 NR1 ......163 B7
Honey Dro PE33 ....80 B1
Honey Hill PE34 ....79 D8
Honey Hills PE31 .....14 A5
Honeycombe Rd PE31 ..73 B8

Honeymoon Loke
NR30 ....168 F4
Honeypot Dro PE32 ...46 C5
Honeypot La
Kirby Cane NR35 .....109 E5
Longham NR19 ....48 F2
Saething NR15 ....108 E8
Honeysuckle Cl
North Walsham NR28 .151 E4
5 Thetford IP24 ......176 F4
Honeysuckle Dr NR20 ..154 F4
Honeysuckle Way
NR17 ....174 B5
Honing Long La NR28 ..38 C7
Honing Rd NR28 ....38 D5
Honing Row NR28 ....38 A5
Honingham NR8 ....70 A8
Honingham Rd NR9 ...69 C3
Honington Airfield
IP31 ....126 A2
Honington Rise IP31 ..126 C1
Honington VC Prim Sch
IP31 ....126 B2
Hood Way IP24 ....176 E5
Hooker Rd NR7 ......159 D1
Hooks Hill Rd NR26 ..138 C6
Hook's Wlk NR1 ....178 C3
Hookwood La NR18 ..104 C8
Hooper La NR1 ....158 F2
Hooton's Row PE38 ...78 F6
Hope La PE14 ....60 A4
Hopton CE Prim Sch
IP22 ....127 F5
Hopton Cl 5 NR7 .....72 D4
Hopton Fst Sch NR31 .171 E4
Hopton Gdns NR31 ..171 D5
Hopton Rd
Barningham IP31 ......127 D4
Garboldisham IP22 ...128 A8
Thelnetham IP22 .....128 A5
Horizon Views NR12 ..64 C2
Hornbeam Cl
5 Great Yarmouth NR31 ..170 B6
Norwich NR7 ....159 D4
Horner Cl 8 IP22 ....127 C5
Horning Cl NR5 ......161 D7
Horning Fst Sch NR12 ..55 F3
Horning Rd
Hoveton NR12 ....164 E5
Neatishead NR12 ....55 D6
Woodbastwick NR13 ..55 D2
Horning Rd W NR12 ..164 C5
Hornor Cl NR2 ....162 C3
Horns La NR1 ....178 B2
Horsbeck Way NR10 ...53 A3
Horse Fair 2 PE13 ...152 C5
Horse Rescue Ctr★
NR16 ....103 C2
Horse Shoe Rd NR20 ..69 A4
Horsehead Dro PE14 ..56 D4
Horses Head NR11 ..166 B7
Horseshoe Cl NR5 ...156 E1
Horseshoe La NR24 ..142 F4
Horseshoe Terr PE13 .152 B7
Horsey Windpump (National
Trust)★ NR29 ....40 D1
Horsey's La NR11 ....170 D5
Horsford All Saints Mid Sch
NR10 ....53 B4
Horsford St 7 NR2 ...162 B8
Horsford VC Fst Sch
NR10 ....53 B3
Horsley's Chase PE30 .146 E2
Horsley's Ct 5 PE30 .146 E3
Horsley's Field PE30 .146 E2
Horton Rd PE30 ......147 D6
Hospital La
Hellesdon NR6 ....157 D3
Norwich NR1 ....162 E3
Hospital Rd
Great & Little Plumstead
NR13 ....73 A5
Sutton Bridge PE12 ...41 E8
Wicklewood NR18 ....87 C4
Hospital Wlk PE30 ...146 E4
Hotblack Rd NR2 .....162 A8
Hotch La PE14 ....60 B8
Hotson Cl 5 NR15 ...106 D3
Houghton Ave NR20 .148 D1
Houghton Cl 2 NR5 ..161 B8
Houghton La PE37 ....65 E1
House Gdns NR10 ....53 E5
Hovell's La IP26 ....99 C7
Hoveton & Wroxham Sta
NR12 ....164 C5
Hoveton Cl PE30 .....147 D5
Hoveton Dr PE32 .....153 D2
Hoveton Pl NR10 .....37 B2
How Hill Nature Reserve★
NR29 ....56 A6
How Hill Rd NR29 ....56 B6
Howard Cl
Harleston IP20 ....122 E2
Norwich NR7 ....163 D7
4 Swanton Morley NR20 ..50 B3
Terrington St Clement
PE34 ....144 B4
Howard Cres NR19 ..154 D4
Howard Jun Sch NR30 .147 B4
Howard Mews NR3 ..158 C1
Howard St N 6 NR30 .169 C4
Howard St S NR30 ...169 C4
Howard Way NR11 ...150 C5
Howards Cl PE36 ....132 E7
Howard's Hill NR27 ...139 A7

Howards Hill Cl NR27 ..10 C5
Howard's Hill Rd NR28 ..23 E8
Howards Hill W 1
NR27 ....139 A7
Howards The PE30 ...148 B4
Howard's Way NR10 ..35 B2
Howdale Rise PE38 ..172 C5
Howe Gn NR15 ....90 D2
Howe La NR15 ....90 D3
Howe Rd NR30 ....169 D7
Howell Rd NR8 ......157 C6
Howes Cl 10 NR9 .....88 D8
Howes La NR10 ......68 D6
Howes Yd 1 NR25 ....7 E6
Howlett Cl 4 NR19 ...154 D3
Howlett Dr NR5 ......161 A8
Howlett Way 2 IP24 ..176 D6
Howletts Hill NR13 ..152 C4
Hoxne Rd Denham IP21 ..131 B1
Eye IP23 ....130 E1
Syleham IP21 ....131 C4
Hubbard Cl
1 Long Stratton NR15 ..106 E3
Wymondham NR18 ...173 C6
Hubbard's Dro PE38 ...79 E1
Hudson Leisure Ctr
NR6 ....158 A6
Hudson Way NR5 ....160 E7
Hugh Cl PE30 ....148 E5
Hughenden Rd NR1 ..162 E3
Hughes Ct 15 NR19 ...88 D8
Hulton Rd PE30 ......147 A5
Hulver Rd NR13 ....73 E8
Hulver St NR13 ....66 F6
Humber Cl NR30 .....168 C5
Humberstone Rd 3
NR31 ....170 C7
Humbletoft Rd NR19 .154 C7
Humbleyard NR5 .....104 B2
Hungate La NR11 ....150 C4
Hungate St NR11 ....150 C4
Hungate Rd NR12 ....59 E2
Hungry Hill NR27 .....11 B2
Hunstanton Fst Sch
PE36 ....132 D4
Hunstanton Golf Club
PE36 ....132 F8
Hunstanton Hall★ PE36 ..1 F4
Hunstanton Rd
Dersingham PE31 ....140 D5
Heacham PE31 ....132 D1
Heacham PE31 ....133 D6
Hunstanton Sea Life
Sanctuary★ PE36 .....132 D6
Hunstead La NR15 ...90 F2
Hunt Cl 8 IP20 ......122 D2
Hunter Ave NR20 .....68 F5
Hunter Dr 4 NR31 ...94 C8
Hunter Rd
Norwich NR3 ....158 C3
Troston IP31 ....126 B1
Hunters Cl
Brundall NR13 ....165 F5
Terrington St Clement
PE34 ....144 F6
Hunter's Dro PE14 ...59 D8
Hunters Oak 2 IP25 ..84 E3
Huntley Cres NR26 ..138 E6
Hunts Gn NR16 ......105 B4
Hunworth Rd NR24 ..142 D8
Hurd Rd NR4 ....161 E3
Hurdle La NR25 ....7 E4
Hurn La NR16 ....106 A6
Hurn Rd Dereham NR20 ..68 A7
Hurrell Rd NR30 .....148 B8
Hurricane Way NR6 .158 C6
Hurst Rd 8 NR14 .....92 A2
Hurth Way IP24 ......176 E4
Hutchinson Rd NR5 .161 D6
Huxley Cl NR1 ....162 F2
Huxley Rd NR1 ......162 F2
Hyde Cl PE31 ....14 D4
Hyde Ct NR13 ....72 E5
Hyde Rd NR19 ......154 D5
Hypocrite La NR17 ..174 A2
Hyrne Cl NR20 ....57 D4
Hythe Rd Feltwell IP26 ..98 E5
Foulden IP26 ....82 A1
Methwold IP26 ....98 F5

Ingloss La NR14 .....109 B7
Ingoldale PE31 ....140 C8
Ingoldisthorpe Fst Sch
PE31 ....140 E8
Ingoldsby Ave NR11 .140 C6
Ingolside PE31 ....12 D4
Ingram Ct NR1 ....162 E3
Ingram's Rd IP21 ....131 C7
Inman Rd NR7 ....159 D4
Inner Link Rd NR19 .154 E5
Inspire Science Ctr★
NR3 ....178 A4
Intwood La
East Carleton NR14 ...89 A5
Swardeston NR14 ....89 C6
Intwood Rd NR4 .....89 B8
Invaders Ct NR23 ...136 D6
Ipswich Gr NR2 .....178 A1
Ipswich Rd
2 Norwich NR4 ......89 E8
Norwich NR2 ....178 A1
Pulham Market NR15 .121 E8
Saxlingham Nethergate
NR15 ....107 A7
Scole IP21 ....130 D5
Ireton Cl 25 NR7 .....72 D4
Iris Cl NR17 ....174 B5
Irmingland Rd NR11 ...34 F8
Ironside Way NR9 .....86 D5
Irstead Rd
Barton Turf NR12 .....55 F7
Norwich NR5 ....161 E6
Irving Rd NR4 ....162 C1
Irwin Cl NR10 ....149 C5
Isaac's Rd NR31 ....169 B4
Isbets Dale NR8 .....155 D2
Isis Cl NR11 ....170 B3
Isle Bridge Rd PE14 ..77 E6
Isle Rd PE14 ....77 F7
Iveagh Cl PE31 ......140 E2
Ives Cl IP22 ....177 E4
Ives Rd NR6 ....158 D5
Ivory Rd NR4 ....161 E4
Ivy Rd 31 NR10 ....54 A2
Ivy Todd Rd PE37 ....66 A4
Ivy Way NR20 ....68 E6
Ixworth Rd IP31 .....126 D1

J

Jaguar Rd 9 NR9 .....88 D8
James Bradfield Prim Sch
PE33 ....81 A2
James Cl PE30 ......148 B1
James Gn Cl 3 NR10 ..154 A2
James Jackson Rd
PE31 ....140 C3
James Paget Hospl
NR31 ....170 B1
James Rd 2 NR31 .....55 E4
James Scott Cl 3 PE38 ..172 A5
James St PE36 ....132 D4
James Watt Cl NR31 ..94 C8
Jamieson Pl NR5 ....161 C8
Jane Forby Cl PE33 ..88 E2
Jankin La PE34 ......144 A1
Jannys Cl NR11 .....150 B6
Jarrold Cl NR12 .....127 D3
Jarrold Way NR5 ....160 F8
Jarvis Cl NR14 ....53 A3
Jarvis Dr NR21 ....31 E5
Jarvis Rd PE36 ......146 E8
Jasmin Cl PE13 .....152 E7
Jasmine Cl
Thetford IP24 ....176 F4
Jasmine Ct 8 NR17 .174 B5
Jasmine Gdns 7 NR31 ..94 C7
Javelin Rd NR6 ......158 C2
Jay Gdns NR5 ......160 E8
Jay La NR32 ....171 C3
Jay's Gn IP20 ....122 E2
Jeffery Ave 4 PE13 ..152 E7
Jeffery Cl PE30 .....148 E8
Jegon Cl NR11 ......150 D5
Jellicoe Pl 6 IP24 ...176 F5
Jellicoe Rd NR30 ...169 D2
Jenkinsons Pightle
NR35 ....108 B4
Jennings Cl PE31 ...133 C5
Jennings Way IP22 ..177 D5
Jermyn Rd PE34 ....146 C6
Jermyn Way 3 NR15 .106 D3
Jerningham Rd NR5 .157 A1
Jessopp Cl
Norwich NR4 ....161 E7
Scarning NR19 ....67 B7
Jessopp Rd NR4 ....161 E7
Jetty Cl NR27 ....139 B7
Jetty St 2 NR27 .....139 B7
Jew's La 10 NR31 .....94 C6
Jewson Rd NR3 .....158 C2
Jex Ave NR5 ....161 D8
Jex La NR5 ....161 D8
Jex Rd NR5 ....161 D8
Jickling Yd NR23 ...136 D6
Joan Short's La PE31 .133 D3
Jocelyn Cl PE21 ....121 E5
Joe Ellis Ct 6 NR5 ...161 B8
John Bates Cl NR19 .154 E5
John Chapman Cl 5
NR21 ....141 E4
John Davis Way PE33 ..61 D5
John Drewry Cl 2 NR4 ..90 D5
John F Kennedy Ct 2
PE13 ....152 D4

John Goshawk Rd
 NR19 ....154 E2
John Hill Cl 6 NR15 ..106 E3
John Kennedy Rd
 PE30 ....146 D6
John O'Gaunt Cl
 NR11 ....150 C5
John O'Gaunt Cl NR11 ..150 B6
John Rd
 Caister-on-Sea NR30 ..168 F7
 Great Yarmouth NR31 ..170 D5
John St 3 PE30 ......146 E3
John Thompson Rd 3
 PE13 ....152 D4
Johnson Cl 7 NR19 ..154 C3
Johnson Cres PE31 ..133 C4
Jolly La NR25 ....20 A7
Jolly Sailor Yd NR23 ..136 D6
Jolly's La NR13 ....166 A2
Jones's Dro PE14 ......95 E8
Jordan Cl NR18 ....155 E4
Jordan La NR10 ....51 A8
Jordan Rd NR30 ......168 E6
Jordans Cl NR5 ......161 B6
Jose Neville Cl 2 NR30 ..168 D7
Josephina Cl NR1 ....162 D3
Joshua Ct NR31 ......171 D8
Joy Ave
 5 Newton Flotman NR15 ..89 D1
 1 Newton Flotman NR15 ..107 A8
Joyce La
 Heacham PE31 ....133 D5
 Walpole PE14 ....41 F3
Joyce Rd NR5 ....124 B8
Jubilee Ave
 4 East Dereham NR20 ..154 E6
 East Harling NR16 ....118 C5
 Fakenham NR21 ......141 C4
 Heacham PE31 ....133 B5
Jubilee Bank Rd 4 PE14 ..46 A5
Jubilee Cl Cawston NR10 ..35 B2
 Downham Market PE38 ..172 E5
 Erpingham NR11 ....21 B2
 Hunstanton PE36 ......132 C3
 Repps with Bastwick
  NR29 ....57 A4
 Weeting IP27 ....175 B7
Jubilee Dr
 Dersingham PE31 ....140 C5
 Sheringham NR26 ....138 E6
Jubilee Gdns 7 PE31 ..12 E4
Jubilee Hall La 2 PE32 ..45 C6
Jubilee La NR27 ......139 C4
Jubilee Rd
 Heacham PE31 ....133 A5
 Holt NR25 ....137 B6
 Watton IP25 ....84 D3
Jubilee Rise PE31 ......61 D3
Jubilee Terr
 Caister-on-Sea NR30 ..168 E4
 Norwich NR1 ....162 F3
Jubilee Way 1 PE37 ..65 F4
Judas La IP21 ....22 C3
Judges Dr NR4 ......161 F2
Judges Gdns NR8 ....155 E2
Judges Wlk NR4 ......161 F2?
Juler Cl 2 NR18 ......151 C6
Julian Hospl NR2 ....161 F6
Julian Rd
 King's Lynn PE30 ....148 C5
 Pulham Market IP21 ..121 D5
 6 Spixworth NR10 ......54 A2
Julian Way NR31 ....171 D5
Julians Way IP21 ....121 C5
Junction Rd NR3 ....158 C1
Juniper Cl 2 IP24 ....176 F4
Juniper Gr NR26 ....138 E5
Juniper Way NR8 ....155 B2
Jupiter Rd NR6 ......158 C4
Jury St NR30 ....169 D4

K

Kabin Rd NR5 ....157 B2
Kalmia Gn 3 NR31 ..170 B6
Karen Cl
 15 Hethersett NR9 ....88 C7
 Scole IP21 ....130 C5
Keable Cl 7 NR5 ....161 C6
Keats Cl
 Downham Market PE38 ..172 D5
 East Dereham NR19 ..154 C2
 2 Thetford IP24 ......176 E6
Keats Rd NR8 ....156 D8
Keble Cl PE30 ....148 B4
Keble Rd NR31 ......170 B3
Kedleston Dr 10 NR4 ..89 B8
Keel Cl NR18 ....111 F1
Keelan Cl NR6 ....158 B4
Keeling Hall La NR20 ..50 A5
Keeling Way NR17 ..174 B3
Keene Rd PE30 ......146 D1
Keepers Rd NR15 ....89 F1
Keepham Rd NR20 ....33 F2
Keith Rd 3 NR20 ......50 B3
Kelling Cl NR5 ......157 C7
Kelling Heath Pk Sta
 NR25 ....8 E4
Kelling Hospl NR25 ..137 F8
Kelling Prim Sch NR25 ..8 E6
Kelling Rd NR25 ....137 C7
Kell's Acres NR14 ..109 F3
Kell's Way NR34 ....109 F2
Kelsey Cl PE36 ......132 D7
Kelvin Pl IP24 ......176 A1
Kemp Gr NR19 ......154 C5
Kempe Cl NR7 ......159 C1

Kempe Rd PE34 ......146 C5
Kemp's Cl PE38 ......79 A4
Kemp's Rd IP21 ....122 A5
Kenan Dr NR17 ......174 F7
Kendal Cl 11 NR9 ....88 D8
Kendall Cl NR28 ....151 B6
Kendle Way PE30 ..147 E8
Konhill Cl 2 PE31 ....12 E5
Kenlan Rd PE13 ....152 D6
Kennedy Ave NR11 ..170 C1
Kennedy Cl NR19 ..154 D1
Kennel Loke NR31 ..171 D8
Kennett Cl NR4 ....161 F4
Kenninghall Prim Sch
 NR16 ....119 A4
Kenninghall Rd
 Banham NR16 ....119 B6
 Harling NR16 ....118 C4
 Kenninghall NR16 ..119 A3
Kenside Rd 8 PE31 ..12 E5
Kensington Cl NR15 ..107 C8
Kensington Pl NR1 ..178 B1
Kensington Rd
 Downham Market PE38 ..172 B4
 King's Lynn PE30 ....147 B6
Kent Ave NR1 ....170 C3
Kent Cl
 Attleborough NR17 ..174 B3
 2 Sutton Bridge PE12 ..41 B8
Kent Rd PE30 ....146 E3
Kent Sq NR30 ......169 D3
Kenwood Rd PE31 ..133 D5
Kenwood Rd S PE31 ..133 D5
Kenwyn Cl NR35 ..137 C7
Kenyon Row NR34 ..110 C2
Keppel Cl PE32 ......48 A5
Keppel Rd 3 NR31 ..170 D4
Kerdiston Rd
 Reepham NR10 ......149 A6
 Themelthorpe NR20 ..33 F2
Kerridge Way
 20 Harleston IP20 ....122 D2
 Holt NR25 ....137 B6
Kerridges NR16 ......118 D4
Kerridges The NR5 ..156 F1
Kerrison Rd NR1 ....163 A4
Kerville St 3 NR5 ..161 A7
Kestrel Ave PE38 ....172 C/?
Kestrel Cl
 Burnham Market PE31 ..135 D1
 Great Yarmouth NR31 ..170 A7
 Mulbarton NR14 ......89 A3
 Swaffham PE37 ......153 C2
Kestrel Dr
 Brandon IP27 ....175 F3
 2 Wisbech PE13 ....152 D2
Kestrel Rd NR7 ....159 C4
Koswick Cl NR4 ......89 B8
Keswick Rd Bacton NR12 ..23 F4
 Cringleford NR4 ......89 B8
Ketteringham La NR18 ..88 E6
Ketteringham Pk NR18 ..88 E6
Ketteringham Rd
 NR18 ....173 F7
Kettlestone Rd NR21 ..17 B3
Kettlewell La PE30 ..146 E5
Kett's Ave NR18 ....173 C5
Kett's Cl
 3 Hethersett NR9 ....88 D7
 Wymondham NR18 ..173 C5
Ketts Hill PE37 ......61 A6
Kett's Hill NR1 ......163 A7
Kett's La NR18 ....52 A6
Kett's Oak NR9 ......88 C6
Kett's Oak NR15 ....89 E5
Ketts Rd NR28 ......151 B4
Kevin Wlk NR19 ....154 D2
Kew Rd PE38 ....172 B4
Key & Castle Yd NR3 ..178 A4
Keyes Ave NR30 ....169 D7
Keyes Cl 5 NR30 ..169 D7
Keyes Rd NR1 ......162 E2
Keys Dr NR21 ......164 B2
Keys Farm 4 NR20 ..68 F6
Keys The NR15 ......90 F2
Kilham's Way
 King's Lynn PE30 ....146 E7
 North Wootton PE30 ..26 E1
Kiln Cl NR6 ....158 E7
Kiln Farm La IP22 ..128 E1
Kiln La
 Dickleburgh & Rushall
  IP21 ....130 F6
 Needham IP20 ......131 D8
Kiln Rd 8 NR10 ......53 A3
Kilverstone Rd IP24 ..117 A2
Kimberley Rd NR28 ..151 D5
Kimberley St
 1 Norwich NR2 ....162 C5
 Wymondham NR18 ..173 C4
Kimberley Terr NR19 ..169 E2
Kimms Belt IP24 ..176 B2
Kinderley Rd PE13 ..152 C8
King Edward VII Sch
 PE30 ....147 A5
King George Cl 3 NR29 ..57 D2
King George Rd NR1 ..31 C7
King George V Ave
 PE30 ....146 F5
King George VI Sch
 PE31 ....14 A3
King George's Ave 2
 PE31 ....14 A3
King John Ave PE30 ..147 A5
King John Bank PE14 ..41 C5

King St
 East Harling NR16 ..118 C5
 Great Yarmouth NR30 ..169 C4
 King's Lynn PE30 ..146 D5
 Neatishead NR12 ....55 E7
 Norwich NR1 ....178 C1
 10 Sutton Bridge PE12 ..41 B8
 Swaffham PE37 ......153 B4
 Thetford IP24 ....176 C4
 Winterton-on-Sea NR29 ..58 B6
 Wisbech PE13 ....152 C5
King William Cl PE34 ..144 C5
Kingfisher Cl
 7 Fakenham NR21 ..141 E4
 Great Yarmouth NR31 ..94 C7
 Thetford IP24 ....176 D1
Kingfisher Dr
 Brandon IP27 ....175 E3
 6 Wisbech PE14 ....152 B8
Kingfisher Rd PE38 ..172 C7
Kingfisher Way 11 IP25 ..84 C3
Kinghorn Rd NR2 ..161 F4
King's Arms St NR28 ..151 C5
King's Aver PE31 ......28 C8
King's Croft PE31 ....140 E4
King's Ct NR29 ......168 A8
King's Dam NR34 ..110 B2
Kings Head La
 Deopham NR18 ......87 A5
 North Lopham IP22 ..119 A2
King's Lane NR1 ....178 B1
Kings La NR1 ....178 B1
Kings Loke NR29 ..167 B8
King's Lynn Arts Ctr
 (Guildhall)* PE30 ..146 D5
Kings Lynn Golf Club
 PE30 ....132 D4
King's Lynn RFC PE36 ..132 D4
King's Lynn Sports Ctr
 PE30 ....148 F5
King's Lynn Sta PE30 ..146 E5
King's Pk NR19 ......154 C6
King's Rd
 Great Yarmouth NR30 ..169 D2
 Holt NR25 ....137 D6
 King's Lynn PE30 ..147 A5
 Topcroft NR35 ......108 A4
Kings Rd Bungay NR35 ..124 E7
 East Dereham NR19 ..154 F4
 Fakenham NR21 ......141 A5
 Hunstanton PE36 ....132 C4
 Wisbech PE13 ....152 C4
Kings St NR17 ......174 D5
King's Staithe La 2
 PE30 ....146 D4
King's Staithe Sq 3
 PE30 ....146 D4
Kings Way NR29 ....167 B7
King's Wk 8 PE13 ..152 C4
Kingsleigh Cl NR28 ..22 E5
Kingsley Ave PE13 ..152 B4
Kingsley Rd NR1 ..178 A1
Kingston Ave NR30 ..168 E5
Kingston Rd NR30 ..168 E5
Kingston Sq NR4 ..162 A3
Kingsway 7 Blakeney NR25 ..7 C6
 4 Earsham NR35 ....123 F8
 King's Lynn PE30 ..146 E8
 Leverington PE13 ..41 B8
 3 Newton Flotman NR15 ..107 A8
 North Walsham NR28 ..151 A6
 Norwich NR2 ....162 C8
 Thetford IP24 ....176 C5
Kingswood Ave NR8 ..155 C2
Kingswood Cl
 Brooke NR15 ....90 E1
 9 Norwich NR5 ......89 C8
Kingswood Cl NR5 ..157 E5
Kinsale Ave NR31 ..94 C7
Kinsale Ave Fst Sch
 NR6 ....157 E4
Kinver Cl NR4 ......162 B3
Kipling Cl NR30 ....168 D6
Kirby Rd PE31 ....57 D5
Kirby Rd Bixley NR14 ..90 D8
Kirby St PE30 ......146 E5
Kirk Rd PE14 ....41 D4
Kirkgate La NR23 ....4 D5
Kirkgate St
 Holme next the Sea PE36 ..2 A6
 Wisbech PE13 ....152 E7
Kirkham's La PE14 ..77 C8
Kirkhams Mdw NR19 ..66 C7
Kirklands NR18 ......156 E4
Kirklees 8 NR4 ......89 B8
Kirkpatrick Rd NR3 ..158 B5
Kirkstone Gr 2 NR30 ..168 F1
Kirstead Gn NR15 ..108 C8
Kirstead Ling NR15 ..91 A1
Kirtons Cl NR14 ......90 E2
Kitchener Rd
 Great Yarmouth NR30 ..169 D3
 Melton Constable NR24 ..142 B5
Kitchener St PE30 ..146 F3
Killings Beck Rd NR28 ..38 A7
Kittel Cl 2 NR20 ....68 A8
Kittens La NR14 ......91 F1
Kittiwake Cl 12 NR31 ..94 C7
Kittles La NR10 ......37 D3
Kittles Rd NR13 ......74 D1
Knappers Way IP27 ..175 A8
Knapton Rd
 Mundesley NR11 ....143 B4
 Trunch NR28 ....22 E5
Knevet Cl NR17 ......174 F6
Knight St NR2 ....162 C4
Knight's La NR15 ....89 E2

Knights Rd NR3 ....158 B2
Knipe Cl 2 NR15 ....105 F5
Knitting Needle La
 NR23 ....136 C5
Knowland Gr NR5 ..161 C8
Knowland Gr Fst Sch
 NR5 ....161 C8
Knowle Cres NR26 ..138 E5
Knowle Rd NR26 ..138 E5
Knowles' La NR12 ..38 C2
Knowsley Rd NR3 ..162 E8
Knox Ave NR1 ......163 B8
Knox Cl NR1 ....163 B8
Knox Rd NR1 ....163 B8
Knudsen Cl 4 NR15 ..107 C5
Knyvett Gn NR16 ..105 F8
Koblenz Ave NR1 ..178 C1
Kooreman Ave PE13 ..152 D7
Krons The NR15 ....107 C5

L

Laburnham Rd NR28 ..151 B4
Laburnum Ave
 13 Marham PE33 ......63 B4
 Taverham NR8 ......155 B1
Laburnum Cl
 8 Great Yarmouth NR31 ..94 C7
 2 Horsford NR10 ......53 A3
 Mundesley NR11 ......143 B5
Laburnum Cres 3 NR13 ..152 E7
Laburnum Dr NR13 ..165 F6
Laburnum Gr
 Reepham NR10 ......149 C6
 Sheringham NR26 ..138 D4
 Thetford IP24 ....176 B1
Lacey Cl 6 PE33 ......61 D6
Lacey Rd NR8 ....155 D1
Lackford Cl NR15 ..163 C4?
Ladbroke Cl 8 PE32 ..177 C4?
Laddus Bank PE14 ..77 A6
Laddus Dro PE14 ....77 D6
Ladislaw Way 1 NR19 ..154 C3
Lady Ann's Rd NR23 ..5 B7
Lady Haven Rd 6 NR31 ..169 B4
Lady Jane Grey Rd
 NR30 ....146 F7
Lady La NR10 ....53 E5
Lady Margaret's Ave
 NR31 ....170 D3
Lady Mary Rd NR1 ..162 D3
Lady's Dro 1 PE14 ..59 D2
Lady's La
 Bressingham IP22 ..119 F1
 Wymondham NR18 ..173 A3
Ladywood Cl 9 PE33 ..63 B4
Ladywood Rd PE33 ..63 B4
Lake Ave PE14 ......77 C8
Lake Cl PE13 ....152 D4
Lake View Cl NR3 ..162 F8
Lake View Dr NR13 ..165 B4
Lakeland 3 IP26 ....89 E8?
Lakeland Way 1 NR20 ..68 E8
Lakenfields NR1 ......162 E2
Lakenham Fst Sch
 NR1 ....162 E3
Lakenham Mid Sch
 NR1 ....162 F2
Lakenham Rd NR1 ..162 C2
Lakenheath Airfield
 IP27 ....114 B1
Lakenheath Prim Sch
 IP27 ....113 A1
Lakenheath Sta IP27 ..113 F5?
Lakes Ave NR14 ......89 B3
Lamb La NR21 ....31 C7
Lambert Cl NR2 ....159 A3
Lamberts Cl PE31 ..26 D1
Lamberts Cres 8 PE21 ..98 E1
Lambert's La PE32 ..30 D1
Lammas Rd 3 NR15 ..106 F6
Lammas The IP26 ..100 A4
Lamport Ct 3 PE30 ..147 D6
Lamsey La PE31 ....133 D3
Lancaster ave NR2? ..141 C5
Lancaster Cl
 Fakenham NR21 ....141 C5
 Methwold IP26 ....99 A5
 Norwich NR6 ....158 D6
Lancaster Cres 3 PE28 ..172 D6
Lancaster Gdns NR11 ..150 D5
Lancaster Pl PE31 ..12 E5
Lancaster Rd
 Great Yarmouth NR30 ..169 D3
 King's Lynn PE30 ..147 B4
 Sculthorpe Airfield NR21 ..15 C3
Lancaster Rise NR11 ..22 F8
Lancaster Way PE32 ..44 F3
Landlow La NR9 ....87 A6
Lane The Briston NR24 ..142 D4
 Carleton St Peter NR14 ..91 E5
 5 Hemsby NR29 ......58 B6
 Little Barningham NR11 ..20 C4
 Winterton-on-Sea NR29 ..58 B6
Lang Gate Way NR35 ..108 E6
Langham Glass & Rural
 Crafts* NR21 ....7 A4
Langham Gn 3 NR13 ..165 E4
Langham La NR25 ......7 C3
Langham Pl NR1 ....178 A1

Langham Rd
 Binham NR21 ....6 E2
 Blakeney NR25 ....7 C6
 Field Dalling NR25 ....7 A2
 Morston NR25 ....7 A4
Langham St PE30 ..146 D2
Langhorn's La PE14 ..78 A7
Langland PE30 ......147 D6
Langley Abbey NR14 ..92 A6
Langley Cl 6 NR4 ..89 B8
Langley Gn NR14 ....91 F6
Langley Prep Sch
 NR7 ....163 D6
Cantley NR13 ....92 C6
Chedgrave NR14 ......91 F3
King's Lynn PE30 ..147 E8
Loddon NR14 ....92 A2
Langley Sch NR14 ....91 F3
Langley St NR14 ......92 A4
Langmere Rd
 Thetford IP24 ....176 E7?
 1 Watton IP25 ....84 C3
Lansdowne Cl 5 NR5 ..161 B7
Lansdowne Rd NR6 ..158 B6
Lansdowne St PE30 ..146 E6
Lantern La NR12 ......24 B5
Lapwing Cl 3 NR13 ..170 A6
Larch Cl
 Attleborough NR17 ..174 C4
 King's Lynn PE30 ..148 D2
 North Walsham NR28 ..151 D4
Larch Cres NR13 ....137 C7?
Larch Dr
 10 Great Yarmouth NR31 ..94 C7
 Great Yarmouth NR31 ..170 A5
Larch Gr PE30 ......148 D2
Larch Rd PE14 ....43 U4
Larch Rd 3 NR13 ....89 E5?
Lark Cl IP27 ....175 F3
Lark Rd 2 PE33 ......61 D6
Lark Rise NR14 ......89 A3
Lark Way NR31 ......171 A8
Larkey's La NR14 ....38 F7
Larkman Fst Sch NR5 ..161 D7?
Larkman La NR5 ....161 C7?
Larksfield PE13 ....152 C3
Larkspur Cl 7 PE28 ..172 C3
Larkspur Cl 8 NR19 ..154 D2
Larners' Drift NR19 ..154 D1
Larners Rd NR19 ..154 D2
Larwood Cl 3 PE33 ..62 C4
Larwood Way 8 IP25 ..67 C4
Latchmoor La NR20 ..56 D5
Latchmoor Pk NR29 ..56 D5
Lathes The NR3 ....178 A4
Latimer Rd NR1 ....162 E2
Latimer Way 2 NR5 ..65 E1?
Laud Cl 2 NR4 ......72 D4
Laughing Image Cnr 6
 NR30 ....169 C5
Launditch Cres PE38 ..172 C6
Laundry Cl NR7 ....163 E7?
Laundry La Blofield NR13 ..73 B6
 Norwich NR7 ....163 F7
Laundry Loke NR28 ..151 B6
Laurel Dr
 Brundall NR13 ......165 B3
 Great Yarmouth NR31 ..94 C7
Laurel Gr 3 PE33 ....43 E2
Laurel Rd NR7 ......159 E1
Laurels Cl 1 NR29 ....56 C5
Laurels Rd PE33 ......36 D7
Laurels The NR21 ..171 D5
Lavender Cl
 Attleborough NR17 ..174 B5
 Brandon IP27 ....175 A2
 Heacham PE31 ......133 C5
 Horsford NR10 ....53 A4
Lavender Ct
 12 Hemsby NR29 ......58 B6
 5 King's Lynn PE30 ..147 B6
 1 Thetford IP24 ......176 F4
Lavender Dr PE38 ..172 C6
Lavender Gr NR12 ..154 D2
Lavender Rd PE30 ..147 B6
Lavengro Rd NR3 ..163 A8
Lawn Cl Horsford NR10 ..53 B3
 Roughton NR28 ......143 B1
Lawn Cres NR13 ....72 E6
Lawn's La
 Belton with Browston
  NR31 ....94 A5
 Terrington St Clement
  PE34 ....57 B2?
Lawns The
 Fakenham NR21 ....141 C4
 Great Yarmouth NR30 ..169 C7
 Wisbech PE13 ....152 B6
Lawnswood Dr NR30 ..168 D6
Lawrence Cl
 Fakenham NR21 ....141 B5
 Harpley PE31 ....29 C4
Lawrence Pl NR20 ..50 D8
Lawrence Rd PE30 ..146 E7
Lawrence Way PE37 ..153 A5
Lawrence's La PE38 ..79 E1
Lawson Rd
 Croxton IP24 ....116 C5
 Norwich NR3 ....158 E1
Lawson Way NR29 ..56 E4
Laxfield Way NR12 ..39 C3
Laxton Cl NR17 ......174 E4

Layer Cl
5 Aylsham NR11 .....150 D6
Norwich NR5 ....160 F7
Layton Cl NR8 ....157 B7
Le Neve Rd NR10 ....150 D1
Le Strange Ave PE30 146 F7
Le Strange Cl NR2 ...161 F5
Le Tunder Cl 2 NR7 .163 E7
Lea Rd 2 NR29 ....56 C8
Lea The NR30 ....169 C6
Lea Way PE30 ....147 A8
Leach Cl NR11 ....170 A4
Leach's Turn NR14 ...165 B1
Leafield Rd PE30 .....147 C3
Leafyoak La NR14 ....90 C3
Leaside PE31 ....133 B6
Leatherpool La NR25 ..7 E6
Leathway NR29 ......167 B2
Lebanon Dr PE13 ....152 F7
Lee Warner Ave NR21 141 D6
Leeder Hill NR13 .....72 F2
Leeds Way 5 NR12 ...55 E4
Leete Way PE33 ......43 E2
Leewood Cres NR5 ..157 C1
Lefevre Way NR1 .....94 C8
Lefroy Rd NR3 ....158 A2
Legge Pl 4 PE34 .....43 E1
Legrice Cres NR28 ...151 C3
Leicester Ave PE30 ..147 B5
Leicester Rd 1 NR31 .170 D4
Leicester St NR2 .....162 C4
Leigh Cl NR3 ....174 C5
Leman Cl 3 NR14 .....92 A1
Leman Gr 9 Loddon NR14 91 F1
9 Loddon NR14 ....92 A1
Leman Rd NR11 ......170 D2
Leng Cres NR4 ....161 E2
Lenthall Cl 16 NR7 ...72 D4
Leonard Cl 3 PE37 ..147 B6
Leonard Medler Way
NR10 ....53 B8
Leonard's La IP26 ....98 D1
Leopard Cl 5 NR3 ...162 D8
Leopard Ct NR1 ......178 B4
Leopold Cl NR4 ......162 A3
Leopold Rd NR4 ......162 A3
Lerowe Rd PE13 .....152 E7
Les Baux Pl 8 PE13 ..152 E3
Lesley Wlk NR19 .....154 D2
Lestrange PE36 ......132 C4
Letheringsett Rd NR25 ..18 F7
Letherington's La NR12 ..55 D5
Letton Rd IP25 ....67 C2
Leverington Rd PE13 152 A6
Levers Cl PE30 ......147 D8
Leveson Rd NR7 .....159 B3
Levine Cl NR13 ......165 B4
Levishaw Cl NR10 ...36 E1
Lewis Cl Ashill IP25 ..84 A7
Hopton IP22 ....127 F6
Lewis Dr Roydon IP22 ..177 A5
Wiggenhall St Germans
PE34 ....61 A8
Lexham Rd
Great Dunham PE32 ..47 E2
King's Lynn PE30 ....147 E8
Litcham PE32 ....47 F4
Lexington Cl NR29 ..167 A7
Leyland Cl IP24 .....176 D6
Leys Cl NR31 ....169 C1
Leys La NR17 ....174 D2
Ley's La NR20 ....51 C1
Leys La
Old Buckenham NR17 ..104 B3
Yaxley IP23 ....129 F1
Leziate Dro
Grimston PE32 ....45 A8
Leziate PE32 ....44 F6
**Leziate Heath Nature
Reserve*** PE31 ....44 E6
Liberator Cl NR13 ....72 E8
Liberator Rd NR6 ...158 B6
Lichfield Rd NR13 ...169 B3
Lichfield St NR21 ....141 B4
Licking's Dro PE13 ..152 A2
Lifeboat Plain 6 NR26 138 D7
Light La PE12 ....59 D6
Lighthouse Cl
Happisburgh NR12 ....24 C5
Hunstanton PE36 ....132 D7
Lighthouse La PE36 132 D6
Lilac Cl Brandon IP27 ..114 D4
2 East Dereham NR19 ..154 D2
20 Great Yarmouth NR31 ..94 C7
4 Great Yarmouth NR31 ..170 A5
1 Horsford NR10 .....53 A3
Wisbech PE13 ....152 F7
Lilac Dr NR6 ....138 D4
Lilac Wood PE30 ....147 B8
Lilburne Ave NR3 ...158 D2
Lilian Cl NR6 ....158 B4
Lilian Rd NR10 ......54 A2
Lily Ave NR20 ....68 A8
Lily La NR34 ....111 A3
Lily Terr NR1 ....178 B1
Limassol Rd NR19 ..154 C2
Lime Ave Stradsett PE33 ..80 C8
Wisbech PE13 ....152 C7
Lime Cl
7 Harleston IP20 ....122 D1
Marham PE33 ....63 A4
Lime Dr NR19 ....154 D2
Lime Gr Gayton PE32 ..45 C6
Sheringham NR26 ...138 D4

Lime Kiln Cl
6 Cley next the Sea NR25 ..7 E6
6 Newton Flotman NR15 ..89 D1
Lime Kiln La
2 Stoke Ferry PE33 ...81 A3
Thetford IP24 ....176 D4
Lime Kiln Mews NR3 162 C8
Lime Kiln Rd
Gayton PE32 ....45 C6
Sparham NR9 ....50 F5
West Dereham PE33 ..80 C5
Lime St PE12 ....41 C8
Lime Tree Ave
Costessey NR8 ......156 F4
Long Stratton NR15 ..106 E2
Norwich NR7 ....163 C7
Wymondham NR18 ..173 D6
Lime Tree Cl
24 East Dereham NR19 ..154 E6
2 Mattishall NR20 ....68 E6
Wymondham NR18 ..173 D5
Lime Tree Rd
North Walsham NR28 ..151 D5
Norwich NR2 ....162 B3
Lime Tree Wlk IP25 ..84 D3
Lime Way NR31 .....170 B5
Limekiln La
Houghton PE31 ....29 D6
Upper Sheringham
NR26 ....138 A4
Limekiln Wlk 1 NR19 169 C4
Limes Ave PE14 .....59 A1
Limes Cl IP22 ....177 D1
Limes The IP25 .....84 A6
Limetree Cl NR8 .....53 B3
Limetree Ct NR8 ....155 B2
Limmer Ave IP21 ...121 C1
Limmer Rd NR31 ...170 D4
Limpenhoe Rd
Cantley NR13 ....92 C7
Reedham NR13 ......92 E6
Linacre Ave NR7 ....159 C4
Linacre Cl NR7 ......159 C3
Linalls Dr NR8 ......156 C4
Lincoln Ave
Great Yarmouth NR31 ..170 C3
Hingham NR9 ....86 D5
Lincoln Cl 12 NR20 ..50 B3
Lincoln Ralphs Sports Hall
NR1 ....178 C1
Lincoln Rd IP25 .....84 D3
Lincoln Sq N PE36 ..132 C5
Lincoln Sq S PE36 ..132 C5
Lincoln St
Hunstanton PE36 ...132 D5
Norwich NR2 ....162 B5
Lincoln Way IP24 ...176 B5
Linden Cl NR18 .....86 E3
Linden Dr 5 NR9 ....88 C7
Linden Gr Diss IP22 ..177 C6
Sheringham NR26 ...138 D4
Linden Rd
Clenchwarton PE34 ..145 E5
Norwich NR5 ....157 C1
Linden Tree Gdns 15
NR31 ....94 C7
Lindford Dr NR4 ....89 C8
Lindley Cl NR8 ......158 E6
Lindley Rd 3 NR8 ...88 C7
Lindley St NR1 ......162 E3
Lindsay Rd NR7 ....159 C4
Linford PE34 ....145 D6
Linford Clapper La
PE34 ....145 E6
Ling Cl 1 NR12 .....54 C7
Ling Comm Rd NR10 ..148 D6
Ling House Rd PE31 ..13 B1
Ling Rd IP22 ....177 B3
Ling Way NR12 .....54 C7
Lingheath Rd IP27 ..175 E3
Lings Cl 5 NR31 .....53 B3
Lingwood Fst Sch NR13 ..73 F3
Lingwood Gdns 2 NR13 ..74 A3
Lingwood Jun Sch
NR13 ....74 A3
Lingwood Rd
Blofield NR13 ....73 E4
Brundall NR13 ......165 F6
Lingwood Sta NR13 ..74 A3
Link The 2 IP24 .....176 D4
Links Ave
Brundall NR13 ......165 C4
Cromer NR27 ....139 D4
Norwich NR6 ....157 F4
Links Cl
Caister-on-Sea NR30 ..168 E4
Norwich NR6 ....157 F5
6 Thurlton NR14 .....92 F1
Links Cres NR26 ....138 C7
Links Rd
Great Yarmouth NR31 ..171 D8
Mundesley NR11 ....143 B6
Sheringham NR26 ...138 C7
Links Way
Sheringham NR26 ....10 A5
4 Thurlton NR14 .....92 F1
Linmore Cres 3 IP25 ..84 E3
Linmore Ct IP25 .....84 E3
Linn Chilvers Dr NR1 133 B5
Linnet Cl 8 NR13 ....101 A6
Linnet Cres IP27 ....175 E3
Linnets The NR31 ...156 F1
Lintock Rd NR3 .....159 B3
Linton Cl NR7 ....159 B3
Linton Cres NR7 ....159 B4

Lion & Castle Yd NR1 ..178 B2
Lion La NR14 ....91 C3
Lion Rd
Buxton with Lammas
NR10 ....36 E1
Palgrave IP22 ....177 C1
Lion Wood Rd NR1 ..163 B7
Lion's Mouth NR11 ..10 A3
Lisbon Rd NR19 .....154 C2
Lisbon Rd IP27 .....159 C2
Lisle Rd NR5 ....160 F7
Lister's Rd 3 NR14 ..91 D2
Litcham Cty High Sch
PE32 ....48 A4
Litcham Hall PE32 ...48 A4
Litcham Rd
Beeston with Bittering
PE32 ....48 D4
East Dereham NR19 ..47 F2
Gressenhall NR20 ....48 D3
Little Dunham PE32 ..65 F8
Mileham PE32 ....48 E6
Tittleshall PE32 .....48 A6
Litchmere Rd NR14 ..109 D6
Litester Cl NR28 ....151 D4
Little Armes St NR2 162 A8
Little Barney La NR21 ..17 F3
Little Bethel St NR1 178 A2
**Little Bittering Medieval
Village of*** NR19 ....49 A3
Little Carr Rd PE30 ..148 D5
Little Dowgate PE13 ..152 A7
Little Ellingham Rd
NR9 ....85 E4
Little Fendike La PE14 ..77 E8
Little Hockham La
IP24 ....94 A1
Little Holme Rd PE34 ..41 F6
Little John Rd NR14 ..162 C1
Little La
1 Castle Acre PE32 ...46 F2
Docking PE31 ....134 E4
9 Horsford NR10 ....53 B3
Roydon PE32 ....28 A1
Stoke Ferry PE33 ....80 F3
Little London Rd
North Walsham NR28 ..151 D8
Northwold IP26 ......99 C7
Little London St NR2 ..178 B3
Little Man's Way PE33 ..81 A3
Little Melton Fst Sch
NR9 ....160 C2
Little Melton Rd NR9 160 B1
Little Money Rd NR14 ..109 D5
Little Oulsham Dro
IP26 ....98 B2
Little Plumstead CE Prim Sch
NR13 ....165 A8
Little Plumstead Hospl
NR13 ....165 A8
Little Scratby Cres
NR29 ....167 E4
Little Snoring Prim Sch
NR21 ....17 A5
Little Snoring Rd NR21 ..17 A5
Little Walsingham Cl
NR22 ....16 F7
Littlebeck La NR15 ..108 B8
Littlefields NR19 ....154 D5
Littleport St PE30 ...146 E5
Littlewoods La NR17 ..102 E2
Livingstone Rise NR11 ..22 F8
Livingstone St NR2 ..162 B7
Lizard The NR14 ....173 D3
Lloyd Rd Norwich NR1 ..163 B7
Taverham NR8 ......155 B2
Loanin The NR1 .....162 F3
Lobelia Cl NR14 ....178 A3
Loch La IP25 ....84 D4
Lock Rd NR28 ......38 D6
Lockhart Rd NR35 ..109 D3
Lock's La NR34 .....109 F1
Locksley Rd NR4 ....89 B8
Loddon Cnr NR15 ...108 C7
Loddon Fst Sch NR14 ..92 A1
Loddon Mid Sch NR14 ..91 F1
Loddon Rd
Ditchingham NR35 ..109 B2
Gillingham NR34 ....110 C8
Haddiscoe NR14 ....110 D8
Heckingham NR14 ...92 D1
Holverston NR14 ....91 A5
Kirby Cane NR35 ....109 F4
Norton Subcourse NR14 ..92 E1
Toft Monks NR14 ....110 D7
Yelverton NR14 .....90 E6

Lodge Rd continued
St John, Ilketshall
NR34 ....124 C6
St Margaret, South Elmham
NR35 ....124 A2
Lodge Way IP24 ....176 C7
Lodore Ave NR6 ....158 A6
Loggers La IP22 ....128 B5
Loke Rd PE30 ....146 E6
Loke The
Belton with Browston
NR31 ....93 F6
Briston NR24 ....142 D4
Brumstead NR12 ....204 A2
Cringleford NR4 .....89 C8
Cromer NR27 ....139 B6
East Beckham NR11 ..9 D2
Felmingham NR28 ...37 B8
Filby NR29 ....75 E8
Freethorpe NR13 ....92 E7
2 Gresham NR11 ....9 E1
4 Hemsby NR29 .....58 B6
Salhouse NR13 ......55 B2
Sparham NR13 ......73 F2
Loke Wiffens 2 NR19 ..88 D8
Lollards Rd
1 Norwich NR1 .....163 A6
Norwich NR1 ....178 C3
London La
Mundford IP26 ......100 B4
South Creake NR21 ..15 E5
London Rd
Attleborough NR17 ..174 B3
Brandon IP27 ....114 E3
Downham Market PE38 ..172 C4
East Dereham NR19 ..154 E4
Elveden IP24 ....125 B7
Harleston IP20 ......122 E2
King's Lynn PE30 ...146 E4
Snetterton NR16 ....105 C2
Thetford IP24 ....176 B3
Wymondham NR18 ..173 A2
London St
Brancaster PE31 .....3 B7
Norwich NR2 ....178 B3
Swaffham PE37 .....153 C4
Whissonsett NR20 ...31 D1
Londs The NR27 ....11 A3
Lone Barn Rd NR7 ..159 B2
Lonely Rd
Pulham St Mary IP21 ..122 B6
Scole IP21 ....121 C2
Long Barrow Dr IP24 ..176 D4
Long Comm La NR10 ..37 D4
Long Dale NR8 .....155 E2
Long Dro PE38 .....97 D2
Long John Hill NR1 ..162 E3
Long La
Baconsthorpe NR25 ..20 A7
Bawburgh NR9 .....156 D1
Bawburgh NR9 .....160 B8
Burston & Shimpling
IP22 ....120 E4
Catfield NR29 ....56 D7
Colby NR11 ....21 E2
Feltwell IP26 ....98 D1
Flordon NR15 ....106 E8
Great Yarmouth NR31 ..170 A4
Hoveton NR12 ......164 F7
Mulbarton NR14 ....89 B2
Saxlingham Nethergate
NR15 ....107 B8
Southrepps NR11 ...22 B7
Stoke Holy Cross NR14 ..89 F4
Strumpshaw NR13 ..165 F2
Swaffham PE37 .....153 E5
Thornage NR25 .....18 D4
NR15 ....106 D6
West Winch PE33 ....43 E2
Winfarthing IP22 ....119 F7
Long Lots PE14 .....59 F3
Long Rd
Barton Turf NR12 ...55 F7
Poringland NR14 ....90 C5
Saham Toney IP25 ..84 F8
Terrington St Clement
PE34 ....144 A8
Thurlton NR14 ......88 A1
Wymondham NR18 ..88 A1
Long Row Norwich NR1 ..153 B8
Tibenham NR16 .....120 D6
Long St NR17 ....103 E6
Longbow Cl 3 NR1 ..162 C1
Longbrooke Cl NR14 ..89 D4
Longdell Hills NR5 ..156 E2
Longdon Cl 2 PE12 ..41 B8
Longe Rd NR9 ......88 C7
Longfellow Rd NR30 168 D5
Longfield Cl 4 NR14 ..91 F1
Longfields PE37 ....153 C5
Longfields Rd NR7 ..72 C5
Longfulans La NR30 168 E4
Longham La NR20 ...49 A3
Longham Rd NR19 ..49 A6
Longlands Dr NR18 173 A6
Longmead NR1 .....162 E2

Longmeadow NR13 ..165 B3
Longmeadow Cl IP25 ..85 A1
Longs Cl 4 NR15 ....89 C1
Longview Cl NR23 ...72 C7
Longview 1 NR9 ....88 D8
Longview Cl 4 PE31 ..12 E4
Longwater La NR8 ..156 D3
Lonsdale Cres NR6 ..86 B5
Lonsdale St NR2 ....162 C5
Loom Ct 2 NR20 ....50 B3
Loop Rd NR1 ....11 D1
Lopham Rd NR16 ...118 D4
Lord Cres NR20 .....50 B5
Lord Rd IP22 ....177 E4
Lord Walsingham Ct
IP24 ....176 E5
Lord's La NR31 .....94 B7
Lords La PE31 ......133 C5
Lorraine Gdns NR3 ..158 E3
Losinga Cres NR3 ..158 E3
Losinga Rd PE30 ...146 E7
Lossiemouth Rd 6
IP31 ....126 B1
Lothian St NR1 .....162 B6
Lothingland Mid Sch
NR32 ....171 A3
Louden Rd IP22 ....139 B7
Louie's La IP22 .....177 C6
Louis Cl NR6 ....158 D6
Louis Dahl Rd 8 NR31 ..94 A6
Louise Cl 1 NR10 ...150 D2
Lound Dam NR11 ...111 A7
Lound Rd
Belton with Browston
NR31 ....94 B4
Norwich NR4 ....161 F5
Somerleyton, Ashby &
Herringfleet NR32 ...111 F8
Lovat Cl IP20 ....122 E2
Love La Fransham NR19 ..66 D7
Sporle with Palgrave
PE32 ....65 C4
Wisbech PE13 ....152 C4
Lovelace Rd NR1 ...161 E4
Lovell Gdns IP25 ...84 E3
Lovell Way PE34 ...144 B4
Lovers' La NR29 ....56 C4
Lovett Cl NR6 ......158 F6
Lovewell Rd NR11 ..170 D5
Low Bungay Rd NR14 ..92 A1
Low Comm
Aslacton NR16 ......106 A2
Bunwell NR16 ......105 E2
Deopham NR18 .....86 E4
Hellington NR14 ....91 B6
Reedham NR13 .....92 A5
South Lopham IP22 ..128 F7
Thurlton NR14 ......89 B6
Low Comm La NR34 ..111 A5
Low Comm Rd
South Lopham IP22 ..128 E7
Thurton NR14 ......91 D2
Low Ditch Rd IP20 ..122 F4
Low Farm Rd NR13 ..75 A3
Low Hatter's Cl PE38 ..172 B3
Low La Hevingham NR10 ..53 B8
Rocklands NR17 ....103 B6
Terrington St Clement
PE34 ....144 A5
Low Rd Alburgh IP20 ..122 F6
Bunwell NR16 ......105 E1
Denton IP20 ....123 B5
Dickleburgh & Rushall
IP21 ....130 C6
Dickleburgh & Rushall
IP21 ....130 E5
Forncett NR16 ......106 B5
Frettenham PE13 ...92 F7
Great & Little Plumstead
NR13 ....72 E5
Grimston PE32 .....28 B1
Haddiscoe NR14 ....110 F7
Hedenham NR35 ...108 D4
Hellesdon NR6 .....157 D7
Hingham NR9 ......86 B4
Keswick NR4 ....89 C7
Kimberley NR9 .....87 D8
King's Lynn PE30 ...148 C1
Mautby NR29 ......75 B1
Metringham NR35 ..109 D1
Narborough PE32 ...63 F7
North Tuddenham NR20 ..68 E8
Norton Subcourse NR14 ..92 F2
Pentney PE32 ....63 C8
Redenhall with Harleston
IP20 ....122 D7
Redenhall with Harleston
IP20 ....122 F1
Repps with Bastwick
NR29 ....57 A4
Rockland St Mary NR14 ..91 C7
Rollesby NR29 .....57 D2
Roydon PE32 ....28 A4
St John, Ilketshall
NR34 ....124 D6
St John's fen End PE14 ..60 B6
Scole IP21 ....130 C5
Shelton NR15 ......107 B1
Shropham NR17 ...103 B3
Southburgh NR19 ..68 A2
Stanton IP20 ....122 C3
Stow Badolph PE34 ..61 C1
Stow Bedon NR17 ..102 E5
Strumpshaw NR13 ..165 F1
Swaffham PE37 .....153 A1
Tasburgh NR15 .....106 F2
1 Thurlton NR14 ....92 F1

Low Rd *continued*
Tibenham NR16 ....93 B2
Thurlton NR14 ....120 B8
Walpole Cross Keys PE34 ..42 A7
West Acre PE32 ....46 C2
West Caister NR30 ..168 A3
Wicklewood NR18 ....87 C3
Wiggenhall St Germans PE34 ..43 D3
Wimbotsham PE34 ..172 D8
Winterton-on-Sea NR29 ..58 B6
Wisbech PE14 ....152 E1
Woodbastwick NR13 ..55 C1
Wortham IP22 ....129 A6
Wortwell IP20 ....123 A3
Low Side PE14 ....77 F6
Low St Hardingham NR9 ..86 E8
Hoxne IP21 ....131 A4
Ketteringham NR18 ..88 D6
St Margaret, Ilketshall NR35 ..124 B4
Sloley NR12 ....37 E3
Smallburgh NR12 ....38 E3
Weasenham St Peter PE32 ..30 D2
Wicklewood NR18 ....87 A5
Low Wr La IP22 ....129 D5
Lower Clarence Rd NR1 ....178 C2
Lower Cliff Rd NR31 ..170 D4
Lower Drag Way IP22 ..128 D8
Lower Espl NR31 ....170 D3
Lower Globe La NR13 ..165 E7
Lower Gn NR11 ....93 E8
Lower Hall La NR24 ..18 D7
Lower Hardley Rd NR14 ....92 A2
Lower Kiln La NR15 ..90 F3
Lower Lincoln St PE36 ....132 C5
Lower Oakley IP21 ..130 D4
Lower Rd IP25 ....66 B3
Lower Rose La IP21 ..177 E2
Lower Spink's La NR18 ..88 B4
Lower St Horning NR12 ..55 E4
Salhouse NR13 ....55 A1
Lowes Ave NR25 ....137 D5
Lowe's La PE31 ....4 D4
Lowes View IP22 ....177 E3
Lowestoft Rd
Gorleston NR31 ....170 C1
Great Yarmouth NR31 ..170 D4
Lowick Cl [9] NR19 ..154 D3
Lowry Cl [3] NR31 ..170 A7
Lowry Cole Rd NR6 ..158 F5
Low's La IP21 ....177 D2
Lowther Rd NR4 ....162 B1
Loxwood NR6 ....157 C6
Lubbock Cl NR2 ....161 F5
Lucas Ct [2] NR7 ....72 D5
Lucas La PE31 ....135 E6
Lucas Rd [8] NR31 ..169 B4
Lucerne Cl NR6 ....158 E4
Lucerne Rd [9] NR31 ..94 C6
Lucombe Dr PE13 ..152 F7
Luddenham Rd NR20 ..50 B2
Ludham Airstrip NR29 ..56 D5
Ludham Fst Sch NR29 ..56 C5
Ludham Rd
Catfield NR29 ....56 C6
Potter Heigham NR29 ..56 F7
Lugger Yd NR27 ....136 D6
Lug's La NR35 ....109 B5
Lusher Cl [1] NR26 ..138 C5
Lusher Rise NR5 ....161 D8
Lusher's Loke NR7 ..158 F4
Lushers Mdw [8] NR17 ..174 C5
Lushington Ct [3] NR5 ..161 B8
Luxembourg Way NR19 ....154 C2
Lydgate Cl NR19 ....154 D3
Lyhart Rd NR4 ....162 B1
Lynch Gn [3] NR9 ....88 D8
Lyndford Rd NR2 ....39 B4
Lynewood Cl NR27 ..139 D4
Lynewood Rd NR27 ..139 D4
Lynfield Rd NR28 ..151 C6
Lynford Rd IP26 ....100 B5
Lyng Hall La NR20 ....33 A7
Lyng La IP22 ....118 F1
Lyng Prim Sch NR9 ....51 A4
Lyng St Sparham NR9 ..51 B5
Wood Norton NR20 ....33 A9
Lyngate Cl [8] NR9 ....26 E3
Lyngate Rd NR28 ..151 B8
Lynn Gr NR31 ....170 A6
Lynn Gr High Sch NR31 ....170 A6
Lynn La NR12 ....29 D1
Lynn Mus & Art Gall* PE30 ....146 E5
Lynn Rd
Castle Rising PE30 ..148 F5
Clenchwarton PE34 ..144 C5
Dersingham PE31 ....140 C2
Downham Market PE38 ..172 C6
East Rudham PE31 ....30 A7
Gayton PE32 ....45 C6
Grimston PE32 ....28 D8
Heacham PE31 ....133 E3
Ingoldisthorpe PE31 ..140 C7
King's Lynn PE30 ..147 A5
Littleport CB7 ....96 E1
Middleton PE32 ....28 A1
Runcton Holme PE33 ..61 F4
Shouldham PE33 ....62 D3
Shouldham Thorpe PE33 ..62 B2

Lynn Rd *continued*
Southery PE38 ....97 A6
Stow Bardolph PE34 ..79 E8
Stradsett PE33 ....80 C8
Swaffham PE37 ....153 A5
Terrington St Clement PE34 ..42 A6
Tilney St Lawrence PE34 ..42 D2
Walpole Cross Keys PE34 ..41 F6
Walsoken PE14 ....59 A6
Watlington PE33 ....61 E6
Wereham PE33 ....80 D5
West Rudham PE31 ....29 F6
West Walton PE14 ....59 D8
West Winch PE33 ....61 F8
Wiggenhall St Mary Magdalen PE34 ..61 A6
Wisbech PE13 ....152 C6
Wretton PE33 ....80 F3
Lynn Rd Terr PE14 ....59 D8
Lynn St PE37 ....153 B4
Lynton Rd NR12 ....24 A7
Lytton Rd NR8 ....156 D8

M

Macarthur Dr [3] NR19 ..154 C6
Macdonald Rd NR27 ..139 A7
Mackenzie Rd NR24 ..176 A3
Mackintosh Rd NR13 ..72 E8
Mack's La NR8 ....156 D7
Macks Loke NR24 ....142 F2
Mad Dog La PE32 ....29 C2
Madden Ave NR30 ..169 D8
Maden Ct NR18 ....173 B5
Magazine Cl PE13 ..152 A4
Magazine La PE13 ..152 A4
Magdalen Gates Fst Sch NR3 ....162 E8
Magdalen High Rd PE34 ....61 A6
Magdalen Rd
Norwich NR3 ....162 E8
Tilney St Lawrence PE34 ..60 D0
Wiggenhall St Germans PE34 ..61 C7
Magdalen Sq NR31 ..170 B4
Magdalen St
Norwich NR3 ....178 B4
Thetford IP24 ....176 D4
Magdalen Way NR31 ..170 B4
Magic City Leisure Ctr NR1 ....178 C3
Magnay Rd NR6 ....157 C7
Magnolia Cl NR10 ....53 A4
Magpie Ct [3] IP20 ..122 D2
Magpie Hill IP22 ....129 B5
Magpie La NR17 ....103 B7
Magpie Rd NR3 ....162 D8
Maid Marian Rd NR4 ..162 C1
Maida Vale [3] NR2 ..162 B5
Maidens Cl [1] NR2 ..162 B5
Maids Cross Hill IP27 ..113 F1
Maidstone Rd NR1 ....178 B3
Main Cross Rd NR30 ..170 D8
Main Dereham Rd NR21 ....31 F4
Main Dr NR20 ....32 E4
Main Rd
Clenchwarton PE34 ..145 B5
Crimplesham PE33 ....80 B6
Filby NR29 ....76 A8
Fleggburgh NR13 ....166 F6
Holme next the Sea PE36 ..2 A5
Lingwood & Burlingham NR13 ..74 A5
Methwold IP26 ....99 A7
Narborough PE32 ....63 E8
Ormesby St Michael NR29 ..58 A1
Rollesby NR29 ....57 D2
Swardeston NR14 ....89 C5
Tilney All Saints PE34 ..42 E4
Upwell PE14 ....77 E3
Walpole Highway PE14 ..59 E8
West Caister NR30 ..168 A6
West Winch PE33 ....61 F8
Wisbech PE14 ....77 A7
Main St
Hockwold cum Wilton IP26 ..113 F2
Honing NR28 ....38 C6
Irstead NR12 ....95 D4
Maine St
[4] Thetford IP24 ....116 A1
Thetford IP24 ....176 A4
Malakoff Rd [4] NR30 ..169 D2
Malborough Gn Cres NR29 ....57 C4
Malbrook Rd NR5 ....161 B7
Maldon Rd PE13 ....152 E5
Maldon Ct [7] NR30 ..168 C6
Mallard Cl
Brundall NR13 ....165 E2
Chedgrave NR14 ....91 F2
[4] Loddon NR14 ....92 A2
[1] Salhouse NR13 ....55 A1
[1] Snettisham PE31 ..12 E6
Mallard Rd [10] IP25 ..84 C3
Mallard Way
Brandon IP27 ....175 E2
Great Yarmouth NR31 ..170 A6
Hickling NR12 ....39 E3
Mallory Rd NR6 ....158 D6
Mallow Cl [1] NR17 ..174 B4
Mallow Rd IP24 ....176 E4

Mallow Way NR18 ....173 D4
Malsters Cl IP26 ....100 B5
Malt Dr PE13 ....152 B3
Malthouse Cl [4] IP25 ..84 D2
Malthouse Cres PE31 ..133 E5
Malthouse Ct
East Dereham NR20 ..154 E5
[3] Redenhall with Harleston IP20 ..122 D2
[3] Snettisham PE31 ..12 E5
Thornham PE36 ....2 A2
Malthouse La
Cantley NR13 ....92 B6
Gissing IP22 ....120 F4
Great Yarmouth NR31 ..170 C8
Guist NR20 ....32 F4
Ludham NR29 ....56 D5
Malthouse Rd
[4] Hethersett NR9 ....88 C7
Norwich NR2 ....178 A2
Malthouse Yd NR13 ..149 C4
Malting Row NR21 ..126 D1
Maltings Cl IP22 ....177 F3
Maltings Dr [8] IP20 ..122 D2
Maltings La [4] PE38 ..172 A5
Maltmas Dro PE14 ....77 A7
Malt's La IP22 ....113 F7
Malvern Cl PE30 ....148 D3
Malvern Rd [1] NR1 ..161 A6
Manby Rd
Downham Market PE38 ..172 B3
Great Yarmouth NR30 ..169 D4
Great Yarmouth NR31 ..170 C7
Norwich NR7 ....159 C1
Manchester Pl [3] NR2 ..162 C5
Mandela Cl NR3 ....178 A4
Mangate St NR17 ....153 C5
Mangreen NR14 ....89 D6
Mangreen La NR14 ....89 C5
Manning's La IP22 ....128 B1
Mannington Hall* NR11 ....20 E4
Mannington Pl PE30 ..148 E1
Mann's La NR20 ....50 B4
Manor Chase NR8 ..156 E8
Manor Cl
[4] Aylsham NR11 ..150 D6
[1] Great Yarmouth NR31 ..170 C7
Hockering NR20 ....69 B8
Horsham St Faith & Newton St Faith NR10 ..53 D2
Ingoldisthorpe PE31 ..140 D8
Lamas NR10 ....36 E1
[4] Little Snoring NR21 ..17 B3
Tunstead NR12 ....37 F1
Manor Dr NR28 ....151 D5
Manor Gr Litcham PE32 ..48 A4
Roydon IP22 ....177 A5
Terrington St John PE14 ..42 B7
Manor Farm Rd NR8 ..157 A8
Manor Farm Rd
Denton IP20 ....122 F8
St John, Ilketshall NR34 ..124 D7
Somerton NR29 ....58 A6
Manor Gdns Diss IP22 ..177 D5
Hopton on Sea NR31 ..171 D8
[8] Lingwood NR13 ....74 A3
Wisbech PE13 ....152 A4
Manor House Cl NR7 ....75 E6
Manor La PE31 ....12 E5
Manor Pk Gdns [16] NR15 ....106 E3
Manor Rd
Brandon IP27 ....175 A3
Caister-on-Sea NR30 ..168 F5
Cantley NR13 ....92 B8
Dersingham PE31 ....140 D2
Great Yarmouth NR31 ..170 C7
Griston IP25 ....85 A2
Heacham PE31 ....133 D8
Hilgay PE38 ....79 D1
Hopton on Sea NR31 ..171 D4
Horsham St Faith & Newton St Faith NR10 ..53 D3
Hunstanton PE36 ....132 C2
King's Lynn PE30 ..148 C5
Salthouse NR25 ....8 B6
Shotesham NR15 ....107 E8
Somerleyton, Ashby & Herringfleet NR32 ....94 A1
Terrington St Clement PE34 ..41 F6
Walpole Cross Keys PE14 ..41 F5
Wells-next-the-Sea NR23 ..136 D5

Maple Gdns [17] NR31 ..94 C7
Maple Rd
Downham Market PE38 ..172 B6
King's Lynn PE30 ....43 D4
Maple Way [7] Eye IP23 ..130 C1
Great Yarmouth NR31 ..170 B6
Mapplebeck Cl NR30 ..147 E4
March La PE14 ....59 F8
March Rd Elm PE14 ....77 A7
Welney PE14 ....95 C5
March Riverside PE14 ..77 B4
Mardle Rd NR34 ....110 D5
Mardling Run NR13 ..166 D3
Marea Mdws PE31 ..133 C5
Margaret Cl
[3] East Dereham NR19 ..154 D1
Norwich NR6 ....157 D5
Margaret Cres NR7 ..163 F7
Margaret Lilly Way [4] NR11 ....21 A5
Margaret Paston Ave NR3 ....158 A2
Margaret Reeve Cl [6] NR18 ....173 D5
Margaret Rose Cl PE30 ....147 E4
Margarets Cl PE36 ..132 D2
Margaretta Cl NR24 ..145 F5
Margetson Ave NR7 ..163 C7
Marguerite Cl [1] NR18 ..94 C6
Margyle Way PE31 ..133 B6
Marham Airfield PE33 ..63 C3
Marham Airfield Fst Sch PE33 ....63 B4
Marham Cl PE34 ....146 B5
Marham Fst & Mid Sch PE33 ....63 B5
Marham Rd PE33 ....62 E2
Marie Cl NR13 ....92 B6
Marigold Cl [6] NR10 ..53 A3
Marina Leisure Ctr NR30 ....169 E3
Marina Rd NR30 ....143 C6
Marine Cl
Great Yarmouth NR31 ..170 D1
Great Yarmouth NR31 ..171 D8
Marine Cres NR30 ..169 E6
Marine Dr NR30 ....169 E8
Marine Par
Great Yarmouth NR30 ..169 E3
Gorleston NR31 ....171 D8
Mariner's Cl NR31 ..171 D8
Mariner's Compass NR3 ....171 C8
Mariners La NR1 ....178 B1
Mariners Pk Cl NR31 ..172 C3
Mariners' Rd NR30 ..169 D2
Mariners Way PE30 ..146 F8
Marion Cl NR18 ....173 C5
Marion Rd NR1 ....163 A6
Marion Wlk [1] NR18 ..173 C5
Marionville Rd NR3 ..158 E3
Maritime Mus for E Anglia* NR30 ....169 E4
Marjoram Rd NR28 ..151 E4
Marjoram Rd [2] NR31 ..94 C6
Mark Lemmon Cl [2] NR4 ..89 C8
Market Ave NR1 ....178 B3
Market Gates [8] NR30 ..169 D4
Market Hill
Brandon IP27 ....175 C3
Colkirk NR21 ....31 D5
Diss IP22 ....177 D4
Market La
Blundeston NR32 ....171 D1
Brancaster PE31 ....3 B6
Burston & Shimpling IP22 ..120 E1
Crimplesham PE33 ....80 A6
Filby NR29 ....76 B7
Great Melton NR9 ....70 C1
Great Moulton NR15 ..106 C1
King's Lynn PE30 ..146 D5
Little Melton NR9 ....160 A2
Market Manor NR13 ..166 C3
Market Mews PE13 ..152 C5
Market Pl
Aylsham NR11 ....150 C6
Diss IP22 ....177 D4
[3] East Dereham NR19 ..154 D5
Fakenham NR21 ....141 B4
Great Yarmouth NR30 ..169 C4
[22] Harleston IP20 ..122 D2
Holt NR25 ....137 B6
North Walsham NR28 ..151 C5
[1] Thetford IP24 ....176 D4
Wisbech PE13 ....152 C5
Market Rd
Burgh Castle NR31 ....94 B8
Potter Heigham NR29 ..56 E6
Market St
East Harling NR16 ..118 C5
[1] King's Lynn PE30 ..146 E5
Shipdham IP25 ....67 C2
Tunstead NR12 ....37 F1
[4] Wisbech PE13 ....152 C5
Wymondham NR18 ..173 B4

Market Weston Rd IP22 ..127 E3
Marketfield La NR10 ..53 E2
Mark's Cl La NR9 ....52 A7
Markshall Farm Rd NR14 ....89 E7
Marl La NR14 ....89 F7
Marl Hill Rd NR9 ....51 F3
Marl Pit La NR5 ....161 C8
Marland Rd [4] NR8 ..155 D2
Marlborough Rd NR3 ..162 E8
Marlborough Terr [2] NR30 ....169 E4
Marlinge Pl NR26 ..138 F5
Marlingford Rd
Easton NR9 ....70 B4
Easton NR9 ....160 A7
Marlingford NR9 ....69 F4
Marlingford Sports Club NR9 ....70 B4
Marlingford Way NR9 ..70 B5
Marlow Cl NR3 ....158 E3
Marlpit La NR13 ....106 F6
Marlpit Rd
Hempstead NR25 ....19 E7
Thompson IP24 ....102 A7
Marram Dr NR10 ....53 E3
Marram Way PE31 ..133 B6
Marrams Ave NR27 ..139 A7
Marriott Cl NR2 ....162 C7
Marriott Chase NR8 ..155 E1
Marriott Way NR24 ..142 A1
Marriotts Way NR26 ..138 D7
Marryat Rd NR7 ....159 C1
Marryats Loke [3] NR25 ..7 A4
Marsh La Aldeby NR34 ..111 A6
Bracon Ash NR14 ....89 A2
Burgh Castle NR31 ....94 A8
Carlton Colville NR33 ..111 F2
[3] Earsham NR35 ....123 F8
King's Lynn PE30 ..148 A1
[4] New Buckenham NR16 ..104 F1
North Cove NR34 ....111 B1
Somerleyton, Ashby & Herringfleet NR32 ....111 C8
Tharston & Hapton NR15 ..106 C8
Wells-next-the-Sea NR23 ..136 D5
Wiveton NR25 ....7 E6
Worlingham NR34 ....110 F1
Wortham IP22 ....129 D4
Marsh Loke NR28 ....23 D1
Marsh Rd Cantley NR13 ..92 D6
Fleggburgh NR13 ....75 C8
Fritton & St Olaves NR31 ..93 E3
Great Yarmouth NR31 ..169 B3
Halvergate NR13 ....75 A1
North Walsham NR28 ..148 A6
Outwell PE14 ....77 F8
Potter Heigham NR29 ..57 A6
Repps with Bastwick NR29 ..56 F4
South Walsham NR13 ..74 B8
Thurne NR29 ....56 E3
Upton with Fishley NR13 ..166 B8
Walpole PE14 ....41 C4
Wroxham/Hoveton IP22 ..164 D5
Marsh Side PE31 ....3 B7
Marsh The PE14 ....41 C4
Marshall Cl Norwich NR5 ..161 B8
Marshall Rd NR3 ....158 B3
Marshall St [5] PE30 ..146 E5
Marsham Prim Sch NR10 ....150 C1
Marsham Rd NR28 ..151 E6
Marshland High Sch PE14 ....59 B8
Marshland Smeeth & Fen Mus* PE14 ....60 C6
Marshland St [4] NR14 ..144 B5
Marshland St James Prim Sch PE14 ....60 A4
Marston La [6] NR4 ....89 C8
Marston Moor [7] NR7 ..72 D4
Martham Fst Sch NR29 ..57 D5
Martham Rd
Martham NR29 ....57 F4
Rollesby NR29 ....57 D3
Somerton NR29 ....57 E6
[5] Great Yarmouth NR31 ..94 C7
Martin Cl Diss IP22 ....175 E3
Martin Rd Diss IP22 ....177 E4
Harleston IP20 ....122 E2
Martineau La NR1 ....162 F1
Marwood Cl NR18 ....173 B3
Mary Chapman Cl [9] NR7 ....72 D4
Mary Unwin Rd NR19 ..154 D4
Maryland NR23 ....136 D5
Masefield Dr NR28 ..172 D5
Masefield Rd IP22 ....177 E5
Mason Rd Norwich NR6 ..158 B3
[5] Swanton Morley NR20 ..50 B3
Masons Ct NR31 ....65 F4
Masquers Cl NR31 ....94 C6
Massey Ct [2] NR21 ..141 C3
Massingham Rd
Castle Acre PE32 ....46 F2

Massingham Rd continued
Grimston PE31 ....28 C1
Norwich NR3 ....158 E1
Weasenham All Saints
PE32 ....30 B1
Mast Cl NR33 ....111 F1
Mather La JP20 ....122 B1
Matlock Rd 1 NR1 ....163 B5
Matthews Cl 4 NR15 ....106 F6
Mattishall Golf Club
NR20 ....68 F4
Mattishall La
Hockering NR20 ....69 A7
Mattishall NR20 ....68 F7
Mattishall Prim Sch
NR20 ....68 F5
Mattishall Rd
Dereham NR20 ....68 B8
East Tuddenham NR20 ....69 A4
Garvestone NR9 ....68 D2
Hockering NR20 ....69 A3
Runhall NR9 ....69 A3
Maud St NR2 ....162 B6
Maud Terr NR10 ....169 D6
Maurice Gaymer Rd
NR17 ....174 D4
Mautby La NR29 ....75 F6
Max Carter Cl NR28 ....38 A4
May Cl NR18 ....173 B5
Maybank NR28 ....151 D7
Mayes Cl 7 NR5 ....161 B8
Mayfield Ave NR6 ....158 B4
Mayfield Dr NR27 ....139 B5
Mayfield Way NR28 ....151 D7
Mayflower Ave PE30 ......146 F7
Mayflower Rd 1 PE13 ....156 F3
Mayflower Way 14 NR20 .122 D1
Maygrove Rd 8 NR30 ....169 D5
Mayton Ave 2 NR12 ....54 A4
Mead Cl NR17 ....36 E1
Meadow Way PE34 ....146 B4
Meadow Cl
Cromer NR27 ....139 A6
5 Hemsby NR29 ....167 A8
Hethersett NR9 ....88 C7
Holt NR25 ....137 D6
3 King's Lynn PE30 ....148 C5
Mundesley NR11 ....143 C5
Narborough PE32 ....63 E7
North Walsham NR28 .....151 C6
Norwich NR6 ....158 A5
2 Norwich NR14 ....163 B2
Shipdham IP25 ....67 D2
8 Thurlton NR14 ....92 F1
Meadow Cotts PE32 ....48 B6
Meadow Ct
Fakenham NR21 ....141 E4
Great Yarmouth NR31 ...171 C8
Meadow Dr
8 East Dereham NR19 ...154 C4
Mundesley NR11 ....143 C5
Wroxham/Hoveton
NR12 ....164 D4
Meadow Farm Dr NR4 ....80 F7
Meadow Farm La NR10 ...53 E2
Meadow Gdns NR6 ....158 F4
Meadow Gr PE33 ....44 A2
Meadow La
Briston NR24 ....142 B5
Carbrooke IP25 ....85 A5
Kelling NR25 ....8 D5
5 Rollesby NR29 ....57 D2
Meadow Loke 2 NR20 ....50 E7
Meadow Patch NR28 .....151 C6
Meadow Rd
Bungay NR35 ....124 B8
Cromer NR27 ....139 B6
Heacham PE31 ....133 D5
King's Lynn PE30 ....148 C2
Narborough PE32 ....63 E7
Norwich NR5 ....157 A2
Meadow Rise NR28 ....167 A8
Meadow Rise Ave
NR2 ....162 A4
Meadow Rise Cl NR2 ....162 A4
Meadow Rise Rd NR2 ...162 A4
Meadow Vale NR5 ....157 A3
Meadow View NR5 ....165 D4
Meadow Way
Attleborough NR17 ....174 C3
East Carleton NR14 ....88 F5
Horsford NR10 ....53 B3
Norwich NR6 ....157 F5
Poringland NR14 ....90 C4
Sheringham NR26 ....138 B6
Meadowbrook Cl 5
NR1 ....162 F3
Meadowcroft NR28 ....168 C8
Meadowgate La PE14 ....152 E2
Meadowgate Sch
PE13 ....152 E3
Meadowland Dr 17 NR11 .94 C6
Meadowrise IP22 ....15 E6
Meadows The
Aylsham NR11 ....150 C7
6 Hingham NR9 ....86 C4
South Wootton PE30 .....148 B2
Thetford IP24 ....176 E4
Thurton NR14 ....91 D4
Meadowside IP22 ....128 B6
Meadowsweet 11 NR10 ...53 A3
Meadowsweet Dr
NR26 ....138 B6

Meadowsweet Rd 2
NR26 ....173 E4
Meadowvale Gdns
PE30 ....147 B7
Meadway 13 NR4 ....89 B8
Mear Gdns NR11 ....163 B6
Mears Cnr NR16 ....105 B5
Medeswell 2 NR29 ....167 B7
Medeswell Cl NR13 ......165 C5
Medway Ct IP13 ....152 E4
Meer Dyke La PE14 ....59 D5
Meeting Hill Rd NR28 .....38 A7
Meeting House Hill Rd
NR28 ....38 B6
Melbourne Rd
North Walsham NR28 .....151 D6
4 Sheringham NR26 .....138 D7
Melford Bride Rd
NR3 ....176 D4
Melford Cl 8 NR10 ....148 E1
Melford Comm 4 NR17 ..176 D4
Melford Ct 3 IP24 ....176 D4
Mellis Rd
Thrandeston IP21 ....129 F2
Wortham IP22 ....129 C3
Yaxley IP23 ....130 A1
Melrose Dr NR11 ....10 A2
Melrose Rd NR4 ....162 A3
Melrose Terr 8 NR30 ....169 D2
Melton Cl NR13 ....173 B6
Melton Constable Hall*
NR24 ....18 D2
Melton Ct NR9 ....88 C8
Melton Dr
Hunstanton PE36 ....132 C3
Taverham NR8 ....155 E1
Melton Gate NR18 ....173 B5
Melton Rd
Hindolveston NR20 ....33 D8
Wymondham NR18 ....173 B5
Melville Cl IP24 ....116 C5
Memorial Way
Thorpe St Andrew NR7 ...72 E4
Watton IP25 ....84 D4
Mendham Cl
50 Harleston IP20 ....122 D2
3 Norwich NR1 ....162 E2
Mendham La
38 Harleston IP20 ....122 D2
St Mary, South Elmham
otherwise Homersfield
IP20 ....123 B3
Mendham Prim Sch
IP20 ....123 A2
Merchant Way NR4 ....158 A4
Mere Plot Dro PE33 ....62 E5
Mere Rd Scoulton NR9 ...85 E4
Stow Bedon NR17 ....102 E7
Mere St IP22 ....177 D4
Meredith Rd NR6 ....157 E6
Mereside NR15 ....90 E3
Mergate La NR14 ....89 A2
Meriewood IP21 ....121 C1
Merlin Ave NR7 ....159 B4
Merlin Mews NR7 ....159 C4
Merriman Rd 5 NR29 .....57 C4
Merrow Gdns 7 NR4 ......89 C8
Merryweather Cl 3
NR15 ....106 E3
Merton Ave NR31 ....170 A3
Merton Rd
Norwich NR2 ....162 A7
Watton IP25 ....84 D2
Metcalf Ave PE30 ....146 D2
Metcalf Cl 8 NR11 ....157 F1
Meteor Cl NR6 ....158 D7
Methuen Ave PE30 ....147 A6
Methwold Cty High Sch
IP26 ....99 A6
Methwold Prim Sch
IP26 ....99 A5
Methwold Rd
Methwold IP26 ....98 E5
Northwold IP26 ....98 F8
Northwold IP26 ....99 C7
Metton Rd
Felbrigg NR11 ....139 A2
Roughton NR11 ....21 D8
Mews Ct 7 IP25 ....67 C2
Mews The 4 NR2 ....162 C4
Micawber Ave 2 NR30 ..170 D8
Mid Norfolk Rly*
NR10 ....154 E5
Midden Sta NR12 ....136 F4
Middle Dro Denver PE38 .79 B4
Marshland St James PE14 .60 C2
Stow Bardolph PE14 ......78 D8
Middle Gates Dro 2
NR13 ....60 B8
Middle Hill
Alby with Thwaite NR11 ..21 A5
Reedham NR13 ....92 F4
Middle La NR34 ....111 D4
Middle Mkt Rd NR30 ....169 D4
Middle Rd
Blo' Norton IP22 ....128 C6
Docking NR13 ....134 E4
Earsham IP20 ....123 C8
Great & Little Plumstead
NR13 ....72 F5
Hardingham NR9 ....86 E8
Morning Thorpe NR15 ...107 B3
Shouldham Thorpe PE33 ..62 E2
Terrington St Clement
PE34 ....42 B8
Middle Rd E 4 NR30 .....169 D1

Middle Rd W 3 NR30 ....169 D1
Middle St NR11 ....11 E1
Middle Way NR29 ....57 A6
Middlebrook Way
Cromer NR27 ....139 A6
Runton NR27 ....10 C4
Middlegate NR30 ....169 D2
Middlemarch Rd 5
NR13 ....154 D3
Middlesex La NR13 ......166 C3
Middlestone Cl NR11 ....170 C4
Middleton Ave NR20 ......50 B4
Middleton Cl
NR3 ....158 C3
2 Sheringham NR26 ....138 C5
Middleton Cres NR13 ....156 E2
Middleton Cl 4 NR18 ....173 B4
Middleton Gdns NR13 ...170 C5
Middleton Prim Sch
PE32 ....44 C2
Middleton Rd NR31 ......170 C4
Middleton St NR18 ....173 B4
Middleton's Cl NR6 ......157 E4
Middleton's La NR6 ......157 F5
Midland Cl
Caister-on-Sea NR30 ....168 F5
1 Great Yarmouth NR30 .169 D5
Midland Rd NR28 ....151 C4
Midland St NR2 ....162 C7
Mikanda Cl NR14 ....162 C7
Mildenhall Rd CB7 ....112 B3
Mile Cross La NR6 ....158 C4
Mile Cross Mid Sch
NR3 ....158 B1
Mile Cross Rd NR3 ......162 B8
Mile End IP27 ....175 A1
Mile End Cl NR14 ....162 A3
Mile End Rd
Littleport CB7 ....112 A3
Norwich NR4 ....162 A3
Mile Rd
Carleton Rode NR16 .....105 A5
Garvestone NR9 ....68 A1
Mileham Prim Sch
PE32 ....48 D6
Mileham Rd
Beeston with Bittering
PE32 ....48 C3
Litcham PE32 ....48 A4
Tittleshall PE32 ....48 B7
Milford Rd 8 NR2 ....162 B5
Mill Bank PE14 ....59 F7
Mill Cl Aylsham NR11 ...150 A6
2 Blofield Heath NR13 ...73 D6
Hethersett NR9 ....88 C7
Hickling NR12 ....39 F2
Kirby Row NR35 ....109 E3
Mattishall NR20 ....68 F5
Norwich NR1 ....162 E3
Pulham Market NR15 ....121 E5
6 Salhouse NR13 ....55 A1
Thurton NR14 ....91 C4
Wisbech PE13 ....152 C6
Mill Cnr NR9 ....88 A4
Mill Comm NR14 ....91 C4
Mill Comm Rd NR28 .....23 E2
Mill Cres NR18 ....166 B4
Mill Croft NR5 ....156 E1
Mill Ct Fakenham NR21 .141 B3
Holt NR25 ....137 B6
Wells-next-the-Sea
NR23 ....136 D5
Mill Drif
Beeston with Bittering
PE32 ....48 C3
Hockwold cum Wilton
IP26 ....114 A7
Mill Dro
Gooderstone PE33 ....81 F4
Middleton PE32 ....44 D2
Southery PE38 ....97 A5
Mill Farm Nurseries
PE37 ....153 B2
Mill Field Cl PE14 ....42 C1
Mill Gdns
Blakeney NR35 ....88 F4
Horsford NR10 ....53 B3
Mill Gn
Burnham Market PE31 ..135 D3
Stoke Holy Cross NR14 ...89 E4
Mill Hill Bradenham IP25 .66 F6
Bramerton NR14 ....90 F6
Brancaster PE31 ....3 B6
Brandon IP27 ....175 E3
2 Horning NR12 ....55 E4
Mettingham NR35 ....108 C2
Norwich NR3 ....158 C2
Roughton NR11 ....139 A1
Salhouse NR13 ....55 B1
Strumpshaw NR13 ....73 F2
Mill Hill Rd
Boughton PE33 ....80 F5
Norwich NR2 ....162 B5
Mill La Acle NR13 ....166 C3
All Saints & St
Nicholas, South Elmham
IP20 ....123 E1
Aslacton NR15 ....121 B3
Attleborough NR17 ....174 F7
Aylsham NR11 ....150 B6
Bacton/Walcott NR12 .....23 E4
Barnham IP24 ....76 A3
Bircham PE31 ....13 F3
Blackborough End PE32 ..44 C1
Briston NR24 ....142 F1

Mill La continued
Briston NR24 ....142 F3
Brooke NR15 ....108 A8
Burnham Thorpe PE31 ....4 D4
Carbrooke IP25 ....85 B4
Catfield NR29 ....56 C7
Claxton NR14 ....91 E6
Clenchwarton PE34 ......145 F6
Crimplesham PE33 ....80 B7
Cromer NR27 ....139 B6
Dereham NR19 ....154 A8
Docking PE31 ....134 E4
Downham Market PE38 .172 D7
Ellingham NR35 ....109 A4
Felthorpe NR10 ....155 C8
Fleggburgh NR29 ....57 B1
Foulsham NR20 ....33 B6
Garboldisham IP22 ....128 A8
Great Ellingham NR17 ..103 D7
Great Massingham PE32 .29 D2
Great Yarmouth NR31 .....94 C7
Haddiscoe NR14 ....110 D8
Hindringham NR21 ....17 E8
Hockering NR20 ....69 B7
Hockwold cum Wilton
IP26 ....114 A7
Hoe NR20 ....49 D3
Honingham NR9 ....69 E6
Hopton IP22 ....127 F7
Horsford NR10 ....53 B3
Horsham St Faith &
Newton St Faith NR10 ....53 C2
Keswick NR4 ....89 D7
King's Lynn PE30 ....43 F3
King's Lynn PE30 ....147 B8
Kirby Bedon NR14 ....90 F7
Long Stratton NR15 ......106 F3
Morley NR18 ....87 A3
Newton Flotman NR15 ...89 E2
Norwich NR3 ....162 E8
Ormesby St Margaret
with Scratby NR29 ....58 A1
Ovington IP25 ....84 E5
Postwick with Witton
NR13 ....73 A3
Pulham Market IP21 .....121 E5
Redgrave IP22 ....128 E5
Repps with Bastwick
NR29 ....57 B3
Rickinghall Inferior
IP22 ....128 D2
Rocklands NR17 ....103 C7
St John, Ilketshall
NR34 ....124 E6
Seething NR15 ....91 C1
Shelton NR15 ....122 B8
1 Southery PE38 ....97 B5
5 Sutton Bridge PE12 ....41 B8
Syderstone PE31 ....15 B3
Thetford IP24 ....176 D3
Tilney St Lawrence PE34 .42 C2
Tunstead NR12 ....38 A3
Walpole Highway PE14 ...59 F7
Walsingham NR22 ....16 F8
West Walton PE14 ....59 C8
Weybread IP21 ....131 F7
Wreningham NR16 ....88 D1
Yaxham NR19 ....68 B4
Mill Loke 4 NR12 ....55 E4
Mill Orch IP21 ....121 E5
Mill Pightle NR14 ....150 B6
Mill Rd Alburgh IP20 ....122 E6
Aldborough NR11 ....21 A6
Ashby St Mary NR14 .....91 C4
Aylsham NR11 ....150 C6
Bacton NR28 ....119 D7
Banham NR16 ....119 D7
Barnham Broom NR9 .....69 B2
Barningham IP31 ....127 C3
Barton Turf NR12 ....38 E1
Bergh Apton NR14 ....91 A4
Mundesley
NR11 ....33 A2
Blofield Heath NR13 ....73 D6
Botesdale IP22 ....128 F2
Brancaster PE31 ....3 B6
Briston NR24 ....142 F3
Brockdish IP21 ....131 B7
Burgh Castle NR31 ....94 A7
Burgh St Peter NR34 ....111 B4
Burnham Market PE31 ..135 A6
Burston & Shimpling
IP22 ....120 E2
Carleton Rode NR16 .....105 A4
Colby NR11 ....36 F7
Cromer NR27 ....139 C5
Dersingham PE31 ....140 F5
Dilham NR28 ....24 A4
East Ruston NR12 ....24 D3
Emneth PE14 ....59 D2
Forncett NR16 ....106 B3
Foxley NR20 ....50 D8
Freethorpe NR13 ....92 F8
Frettenham NR12 ....54 A4
Great Yarmouth NR31 ....93 B3
Gresham NR11 ....9 D1
Halvergate NR13 ....74 F1
Hardingham NR9 ....86 E8
Hardley PE31 ....29 D7
Hempnall NR15 ....107 C5
Hemsby NR29 ....58 A4
7 Hethersett NR9 ....88 E8
Honington IP31 ....126 D1
Illington NR16 ....102 A3
Lakenham IP27 ....113 E1
Little Melton NR9 ....88 B2
Loddon NR14 ....92 A1

Mill Rd continued
Long Stratton NR15 ......107 A2
Marlingford NR9 ....70 A3
Marsham NR10 ....36 C2
Mattishall NR20 ....68 F5
Mautby NR29 ....75 E7
North Walsham NR28 ....151 D3
Old Buckenham NR17 ...104 C1
Potter Heigham NR29 .....56 F5
Reedham NR13 ....93 A5
Reepham NR10 ....149 B2
Repps with Bastwick
NR29 ....57 A4
Rybürgh NR21 ....32 C6
Saham Toney NR19 ....84 A7
Salhouse NR13 ....55 A1
Shelton NR15 ....122 B8
Shipdham IP25 ....67 B2
Shouldham Thorpe PE33 .62 C3
Stoke Holy Cross NR14 ...89 F4
Stokesby with Herringby
NR29 ....75 A6
Surlingham NR14 ....91 B8
Sutton NR12 ....39 C3
Terrington St John PE14 ..42 B1
Thelnetham IP22 ....128 B5
Thompson IP24 ....102 A7
Thurlton NR14 ....110 D8
Tibenham NR16 ....120 C8
Twetshall St Mary NR15 .121 B5
Topcroft NR35 ....107 E4
Walpole St Andrew PE14 .41 E3
Watlington PE33 ....61 D8
Watlington PE33 ....41 E3
Wattisfield IP22 ....167 C3
Wattlington PE33 ....55 D3
Wells-next-the-Sea
NR23 ....136 D3
West Walton PE14 ....59 B8
Weybread IP21 ....131 F8
Whissonsett NR20 ....31 D2
Wiggenhall St Germans
PE34 ....43 C1
Wiggenhall St Mary Magdalen
PE34 ....58 D4
Winfarthing IP22 ....120 B4
Mill Rd S IP22 ....128 F2
Mill Reach NR10 ....36 F1
Mill Row NR11 ....150 D7
Mill St Bradenham IP25 ..66 E3
Elsing NR20 ....49 E1
Gimingham NR11 ....22 E7
Holt NR25 ....137 B6
Horsham St Faith NR10 ..53 E2
Lamas NR10 ....36 F5
Mattishall NR20 ....68 F5
Necton PE37 ....65 F4
Soham Morley NR20 ......50 B4
Mill View
Barnham Broom NR9 .....69 B2
Saham Toney IP25 ....84 C5
Sedgeford PE36 ....13 A7
Mill View Mid Sch
NR5 ....161 C8
Mill Way PE14 ....77 B8
Millard Cl NR28 ....151 A6
Millcroft NR3 ....158 E1
Millennium Way PE34 ..146 A5
Miller Cl 17 NR19 ....154 C4
Miller Sq NR17 ....104 C1
Miller's Breck NR8 ....155 D1
Millers Dr NR21 ....121 B1
Millers La Harpley PE31 .29 D4
Norwich NR3 ....158 D1
Miller's La
2 Thetford IP24 ....176 C4
Wimbotsham PE34 ....79 E8
Millers Way 1 NR10 ......53 A8
Millfield 6 IP25 ....84 A8
Millfield Cl 5 NR13 ....73 D6
Millfield La PE33 ....43 F3
Millfield Prim Sch
NR28 ....151 B3
Millfield Rd
Barningham IP31 ....127 D3
North Walsham NR28 ....151 B4
Millfields 2 NR15 ....107 C5
Millfleet 8 PE30 ....146 E5
Millgate IP18 ....150 D7
Millgate St NR29 ....99 A5
Millhill NR18 ....86 E2
Millicent Oliver Cl 11
IP24 ....176 D7
Mills Cl NR8 ....155 C1
Millside Hales NR14 .....109 F8
Stalham NR12 ....39 B3
Millview NR29 ....167 A3
Millway NR18 ....173 B6
Millway Ave IP22 ....177 C6
Millway La
Palgrave IP22 ....177 B2
Wortham IP22 ....129 D5
Milner Rd PE13 ....152 C4
Milton Ave PE30 ....146 F5
Milton Cl
East Dereham NR19 ......154 C7
Norwich NR1 ....162 E3
3 Thetford IP24 ....176 E6
Milton Rd
Great Yarmouth NR30 ...169 D8
4 Swanton Morley NR20 .50 B3
Milverton Rd 1 NR1 .....162 F3
Mingay Rd IP24 ....176 B2
Minion Cl 3 NR27 ....94 A6
Minns Ct NR18 ....78 A7
Minster PE14 ....42 A2
Minstergate IP24 ....176 C4
Miriam Cl NR29 ....168 C8

Misburgh Way NR31 ...171 E4
Mission La
 Docking PE31 ....134 E4
 Fakenham NR21 ....141 E4
Mission Pl NR30 ....169 D6
Mission Rd Diss IP22 ...177 E3
 8 Great Yarmouth NR31 169 B4
 Rackheath NR13 ....72 E8
Mitchell Ct 4 NR5 .....180 H8
Mitre Ct NR3 ....158 A3
Mitre Tavern Yd 4
 NR28 ....151 C5
Moat Rd
 1 Great Yarmouth NR30 .169 C5
 Terrington St Clement
 PE34 ....144 B1
Modney Bridge Rd
 PE38 ....96 F8
Mokyll Croft NR8 ......155 D2
Moles La NR34 ....124 D5
Molls Dro PE14 ....77 C7
Monastery The NR3 .....178 B3
Money Bank PE13 ......152 E4
Moneyhill La NR9 ....86 C3
Moneypot La IP22 .....128 E5
Monkhams Dr 9 IP25 ...84 E3
Monks Cl PE31 ....14 D5
Monksgate IP24 ....176 D4
Muns Ave NR1 ....165 A8
Mont Cross 8 NR8 .....155 D2
Montagu Cl PE37 ......153 C3
Montague Rd NR26 ....138 C7
Montcalm Rd NR1 .....163 B6
Montgomery Cl 2 NR5 .160 F7
Montgomery Way
 PE30 ....147 D4
Montpelier Dr 1 IP24 ..116 A1
Montrose Ct 8 NR7 .....72 D4
Monument Rd NR10 ...170 F7
Moor La Cranworth IP25 ..85 D7
 Elsing NR20 ....50 F3
 Fransham NR19 ....66 A7
 Sculthorpe NR21 ....16 B2
 Stalham NR12 ....39 C3
Moor Rd
 Burston & Shimpling
 IP21 ....121 B2
 Stalham NR12 ....39 C3
Moor The NR10 ....149 E5
Moorditch La PE34 ......42 E2
Moore Ave NR6 ....158 F5
Moorend La NR21 ......32 D7
Moorfield Rd 8 NR20 ...68 E6
Moorgate Rd
 East Dereham NR19 ...154 D3
 Hintringham NR21 ......17 F7
Moorhouse Cl NR10 ...149 C5
Moorings The PE33 .....81 A2
Moorland Cl NR7 ......159 A2
Moorland Way 8 NR31 ..94 A5
Moors The NR8 ....155 F2
Morello Cl NR4 ....161 E5
Morgan Way NR5 .....160 F8
Morgans Way NR10 .....53 C8
Morgrove La NR29 .....57 D6
Morley CE Prim Sch
 NR18 ....87 A2
Morley La NR18 ....87 C2
Morley Rd
 Beighton NR13 ....74 D2
 Deopham NR18 ....86 E1
 Sheringham NR26 .....138 D6
Morley Rd N NR26 .....136 D6
Morley St NR3 ....162 F8
Morleyfield La NR18 ....87 A3
Mormor La IP21 ......131 C8
Mornington Rd NR2 ...162 A4
Morris Cl
 2 Norwich NR5 ....161 B8
 6 Stoke Holy Cross NR14 .89 F4
Morris St NR28 ....151 B4
Morris St NR28 ....138 D7
Morrison Cl NR28 .....151 B5
Morse Ave NR1 ....163 C7
Morse Cl
 Brundall NR13 ....165 D3
 Great Witchingham NR9 ..51 D5
Morse Ct NR30 ....168 C6
Morse Rd NR1 ....163 C7
Morston Chase NR25 ....6 F5
Morston Rd
 Blakeney NR25 ....7 C6
 Stiffkey NR23 ....5 D6
Mortimer Cl NR17 ....174 F6
Morton Cl 1 NR11 .....150 D6
Morton Cres 22 NR31 ...94 C7
Morton La NR9 ....63 E3
Morton Peto La NR32 ..111 D7
Morton Peto Rd NR31 ..170 B8
Morton Rd NR11 ......150 D6
Mossfield Cl NR1 ......163 B8
Mother Julian Cl 8
 IP24 ....176 D7
Mother Quy's IP24 ....115 C1
Mottram Cl NR5 ....161 D6
Motum Rd NR5 ....161 C7
Moulton Cl
 Beetley NR20 ....49 C4
 Norwich NR2 ....162 B4
Moulton La
 Tivetshall St Margaret
 NR15 ....121 A7
Mount Cl Brandon IP27 ..175 D2
 Swaffham PE37 ....153 A5
Mount Pl PE13 ....152 E4
Mount Pk Cl PE32 ......44 C3
Mount Pleasant
 Diss IP22 ....177 D5
 Little Walsingham NR22 ...16 FR
 Norwich NR2 ....162 B4

Mount Pleasant Rd
 PE13 ....152 C7
Mount St Cromer NR27 ..139 B7
 Diss IP22 ....177 D5
 King's Lynn PE30 .....146 F4
Mount Tumbledown Cl 7
 PE12 ....41 B8
Mountain's Rd 2 NR11 ...19 F1
Mountbatten Cl 5 IP24 .176 E6
Mountbatten Dr
 7 East Dereham NR19 .154 C6
 Wisbech PE13 ....152 A7
Mountbatten Rd
 Bungay NR35 ....124 A7
 Dersingham PE31 .....140 C3
Mountbatten Way
 NR30 ....168 D6
Mounteney Cl NR7 ....159 A4
Mountergate NR1 .....178 B2
Mountfield Ave
 Hellesdon NR6 ....157 F4
 Norwich NR6 ....158 A4
Mousehold Ave NR3 ..163 A8
Mousehold Fst Sch & Nursery
 NR3 ....162 F8
Mousehold La NR7 ....159 A3
Mousehold St NR3 ....178 C4
Mowles Rd NR20 ....68 C8
Moyse's Bank PE14 ....60 A2
Muck La NR13 ....72 F8
Muckleburgh Collection
 The* NR25 ....8 E6
Mud Rd NR21 ....15 D2
Mudd's Dro PE14 ......77 F2
Muir La NR15 ....106 B2
Mulbarton Mid Sch
 NR14 ....89 B3
Mulberry Cl 18 PE30 ...98 E1
Mulberry Ct NR10 ....155 D2
Mulberry Gr 4 NR31 ...94 C6
Mulberry La NR15 ....107 A3
Mulberry Rd PE30 ....147 D4
Mullicourt Rd PE14 ....78 B6
Mumby's Dro PE14 .....77 F1
Mundesley Hospl NR11 ..22 F7
Mundesley Jun Sch
 NR11 ....143 B5
Mundesley Maritime Mus*
 NR11 ....143 C6
Mundesley Rd
 Gimingham NR11 ......22 F7
 Knapton NR28 ....22 F3
 North Walsham NR28 .151 C6
 Overstrand NR27 ......11 A3
 Paston NR28 ....143 D3
 Trimingham NR11 ......11 E1
 Trunch NR28 ....22 F5
Mundford Prim Sch
 IP26 ....100 B4
Mundford Rd
 Thetford IP24 ....176 C6
 Weeting-with-Broomhill
 IP27 ....175 D7
Mundham La NR14 .....91 D2
Mundham Rd
 Loddon NR14 ....91 E1
 Mundham NR14 ....109 A8
Mundy's Rd IP20 .....123 A1
Munhaven Cl NR11 ...143 C5
Munnings Cl NR14 ....89 A7
Munnings Rd NR7 ....159 D1
Munson's La NR16 .....98 F2
Munson's Pl IP26 ......98 E2
Murgot's La IP24 .....116 A1
Muriel Kenny Ct 10 NR9 .88 C7
Muriel Rd NR2 ....162 A4
Muriel Way IP25 ....85 B4
Murrayfield Rd NR4 ...158 B5
Mus of the Broads The*
 NR12 ....39 B3
Music House La NR1 ...178 B2
Musketeer Way 22 NR7 ..72 D4
Muspole St NR3 ....178 A4
Musticott Pl PE13 ....152 F6
Myrtle Ave
 Costessey NR8 ....156 F3
 East Dereham NR19 ..154 E4
Myrtle Rd NR9 ....88 C8

N

Naber Furlong 1 NR8 .155 E2
Napier Cl NR28 ....147 C5
Napier Pl IP24 ....176 A1
Naples Cl NR31 ....171 E4
Napoleon Pl 9 NR30 ..169 D3
Narborough Hill PE33 ..62 E2
Narborough Rd PE32 ...63 D8
Narborough VC Fst Sch
 PE32 ....63 E7
Narford La PE32 ....45 F2
Narford Rd PE32 ....62 E3
Naseby Way 1 NR7 ....72 D4
Nash Rd NR10 ....155 C8
Nash's La PE32 ....23 E1
Nasmith Rd NR4 ......161 E3
Naylor Rd 4 NR1 .....162 E7
Neale Ct NR11 ....150 B6
Neatherd Moor NR20 .154 F6
Neatherd Rd NR19 ...154 F6
Neatishead Prim Sch
 NR12 ....55 D7
Neatishead Rd 4 NR12 .55 E5
Necton CE Fst Sch
 PE37 ....66 A4
Necton Mid Sch PE37 ..66 A4
Necton Rd PE32 ....65 E7

Needham Bank PE14 ....77 C8
Needham Rd IP20 ....122 C1
Neil Ave NR25 ....137 B5
Neilsen Cl NR23 ......136 E6
Nelonde Dr 1 NR18 ...173 C5
Nelson Ave PE38 .....172 B5
Nelson Cl
 Bradenham IP25 ......66 E3
 4 Hethersett NR9 .....88 E8
Nelson Cres
 Swaffham PE37 ....153 D3
 Thetford IP24 ....176 C3
Nelson Ct IP25 ....84 D4
Nelson Dr PE36 ....132 D3
Nelson Fst Sch NR27 ..162 B7
Nelson Gdns PE13 ....152 D6
Nelson Hts NR27 .....139 A7
Nelson Mus* NR30 ...169 C5
Nelson Rd
 Caister-on-Sea NR30 .168 F4
 Fakenham NR21 ......141 B4
 Great Yarmouth NR31 .169 C5
 North Walsham NR28 .151 D5
 Sheringham NR26 ....138 F7
Nelson Rd Central
 NR30 ....169 D3
Nelson Rd N NR30 ....169 D5
Nelson Rd S NR30 ....169 D2
Nelson St
 King's Lynn PE30 .....146 D4
 Norwich NR2 ....162 B7
Nelson Way
 Hevingham NR10 ......53 B8
 Mundesley NR11 ......143 A7
 Wiveton NR25 ....7 E6
 Wormegay PE33 ....62 C8
New Bank
 New Roxe PE31 ....133 D6
 New Sporle Rd PE32 .153 C5
 Terr St Cawston NR10 ..35 B2
 Cromer NR27 ....139 B7
 Holt NR25 ....137 B6
 King's Lynn PE30 .....147 B7
 Sheringham NR26 ....138 D7
Newall Rd 8 IP24 ....125 F6
Newark Cl NR14 ....90 E7
Newark Cl 22 NR7 .....72 D4
Newarp Way NR30 ...168 D6
Newbegin Cl NR1 ....163 C7
Newbegin Rd NR1 ...163 B7
Newbury Way 20 NR7 ..72 D4
Newby Rd 2 PE30 ....147 D6
Newcastle Cl 8 NR7 ...72 D4
Newcastle Rd NR30 ..169 D1
Newcombe Cl PE14 ....82 E1
Newcombe Dr 10 IP26 .98 E1
Newell Crescent NR27 .10 A6
Newey's Way 12 NR2 .164 C5
Newfen Gravel Dro
 PE27 ....113 D4
Newfields Cl NR4 .....161 C1
Newgate NR35 ....109 E3
Newgate La
 Kirby Cane NR35 .....109 E3
 Wells next the Sea
Newhaven Cl NR27 ...139 B6
Newland Rd PE36 ....146 E7
Newlands Cl 10 IP20 .122 D2
Newman Rd NR13 .....72 D7
Newmarket Rd
 2 Cringleford NR4 ....89 B8
 Norwich NR2 ....178 A1
Newmarket St NR2 ..162 C4
Newnham Grn NR31 .170 A4
Newport Rd
 Hemsby NR29 ....167 C6
 South Walsham NR13 ..74 A6
Newstead Wlk IP22 ..177 C6
Newstead's La NR27 ...10 C4
Newton Cl
 Hockham St Faith &
 Newton St Faith NR10 ..53 D4
 10 Newton Flotman NR15 .89 D1
 Norwich NR4 ....162 B1
Newton Flotman Prim Sch
 NR15 ....89 D1
Newton Rd
 Hainford NR10 ....53 E5
 Newton by Castle Acre
 PE32 ....47 A2
 Sporle with Palgrave
 PE32 ....65 C7
Newton St NR10 ....53 D4
Newtown IP24 ....176 C3
Neylond Cres NR6 ...157 C6
Nicholas Ave PE14 ...145 C6
Nicholas Hamond Way 4
 PE37 ....153 C3
Nicholas Mews 8 NR2 .162 B7
Nicholls Way IP22 ....177 A5
Nick's La IP23 ....130 B2
Nicolson Ave NR20 ....50 B5
Nightingale Cl
 Denver PE38 ....172 D2
 Fakenham NR21 .....141 F4
 Hemsby NR29 ....167 E4
 Mulbarton NR14 ......89 A3
Nightingale Dr NR8 ..155 B1
Nightingale La
 Denver PE38 ....172 D3
 8 Feltwell IP26 ....98 E1
 1 Feltwell IP26 ....98 E1
 Norwich NR3 ....162 E8

New Rd continued
 North Walsham NR28 .151 D5
 Northrepps NR27 ....139 E1
 Norton Subcourse NR14 ..92 E1
 Oulton NR11 ....35 D7
 Outwell PE14 ....77 E5
 Reedham NR13 ....92 F4
 Reepham NR10 ......149 C5
 St Cross, South Elmham
 IP20 ....123 D1
 Saxlingham Nethergate
 NR15 ....107 B8
 Sculthorpe NR21 ......16 A3
 Sheringham NR26 ....138 D7
 Shipdham IP25 ....67 B2
 Shouldham PE33 ......62 D4
 South Creake NR21 ...15 D7
 Stanfield NR20 ....48 F7
 Stokesby with Herringby
 NR29 ....75 A6
 Surlingham NR14 ......73 B1
 Sutton NR12 ....39 D2
 Sutton Bridge PE12 ...41 B8
 Taconeston NR16 ....105 E5
 Thelnetham IP22 ....127 F3
 Thetford IP24 ....176 C4
 Threxton IP24 ....117 A4
 Tilney St Lawrence PE34 ..42 C1
 Tivetshall St Mary NR15 .121 B4
 Toft Monks NR34 ....110 D6
 Welney PE14 ....95 D5
 Whissonsett NR20 ....31 D2
 Wimbotsham PE34 ...172 E8
 Wiveton NR25 ....7 E6
 Wormegay PE33 ....62 C8
New Roman Bank
 PE34 ....144 B7
New Row PE31 ....133 D6
New Sporle Rd PE32 .153 C5
New St Cawston NR10 ..35 B2
 Cromer NR27 ....139 B7
 Holt NR25 ....137 B6
 King's Lynn PE30 .....147 B7
 Sheringham NR26 ....138 D7
Newall Rd 8 IP24 ....125 F6
Newark Cl NR14 ....90 E7
Newark Cl 22 NR7 .....72 D4
Newarp Way NR30 ...168 D6
Newbegin Cl NR1 ....163 C7
Newbegin Rd NR1 ...163 B7
Newbury Way 20 NR7 ..72 D4
Newby Rd 2 PE30 ....147 D6
Newcastle Cl 8 NR7 ...72 D4
Newcastle Rd NR30 ..169 D1
Newcombe Cl PE14 ....82 E1
Newcombe Dr 10 IP26 .98 E1
Newell Crescent NR27 .10 A6
Newey's Way 12 NR2 .164 C5
Newfen Gravel Dro
 PE27 ....113 D4
Newfields Cl NR4 .....161 C1
Newgate NR35 ....109 E3
Newgate La
 Kirby Cane NR35 .....109 E3
 Wells next the Sea
Newhaven Cl NR27 ...139 B6
Newland Rd PE36 ....146 E7
Newlands Cl 10 IP20 .122 D2
Newman Rd NR13 .....72 D7
Newmarket Rd
 2 Cringleford NR4 ....89 B8
 Norwich NR2 ....178 A1
Newmarket St NR2 ..162 C4
Newnham Grn NR31 .170 A4
Newport Rd
 Hemsby NR29 ....167 C6
 South Walsham NR13 ..74 A6
Newstead Wlk IP22 ..177 C6
Newstead's La NR27 ...10 C4
Newton Cl
 Hockham St Faith &
 Newton St Faith NR10 ..53 D4
 10 Newton Flotman NR15 .89 D1
 Norwich NR4 ....162 B1
Newton Flotman Prim Sch
 NR15 ....89 D1
Newton Rd
 Hainford NR10 ....53 E5
 Newton by Castle Acre
 PE32 ....47 A2
 Sporle with Palgrave
 PE32 ....65 C7
Newton St NR10 ....53 D4
Newtown IP24 ....176 C3
Neylond Cres NR6 ...157 C6
Nicholas Ave PE14 ...145 C6
Nicholas Hamond Way 4
 PE37 ....153 C3
Nicholas Mews 8 NR2 .162 B7
Nicholls Way IP22 ....177 A5
Nick's La IP23 ....130 B2
Nicolson Ave NR20 ....50 B5
Nightingale Cl
 Denver PE38 ....172 D2
 Fakenham NR21 .....141 F4
 Hemsby NR29 ....167 E4
 Mulbarton NR14 ......89 A3
Nightingale Dr NR8 ..155 B1
Nightingale La
 Denver PE38 ....172 D3
 8 Feltwell IP26 ....98 E1
 1 Feltwell IP26 ....98 E1
 Norwich NR3 ....162 E8

Nightingale Rd IP27 ..175 F3
Nightingale Way IP24 .176 D1
Nightingale Wlk PE38 .172 C2
Nightmarsh La PE31 ...27 C4
Nile Rd
 Downham Market PE38 ..172 D4
 Great Yarmouth NR31 .170 D4
Nile St 1 NR2 ....162 B7
Nine Acre La NR24 ....19 C4
Ninham St NR1 ....162 E3
Nobb's Loke NR12 .....38 F4
Nobel Cres NR12 .....164 B4
Noble Cl NR7 ....159 D1
Noel Cl NR31 ....171 D6
Nordelph Cnr NR9 .....86 D6
Norfolk & Norwich Hospl
 NR1 ....178 A1
Norfolk & Norwich Univ
 Hospl NR4 ....161 A3
Norfolk & Suffolk Aviation
 Mus* NR35 ....123 D6
Norfolk Athletics Tk
 NR4 ....161 C4
Norfolk Dr NR17 .....176 C4
Norfolk Lavender Visitor
 Ctr* PE31 ....133 C6
Norfolk Motor Cycle Mus*
 NR28 ....151 C4
Norfolk Rd
 10 Honington PE31 ...126 B1
 10 Marham PE33 ......63 B4
 Norwich NR1 ....161 B3
 Sheringham NR26 ....138 C6
 Thetford IP24 ....176 E4
Norfolk Rural Life Mus*
 PE32 ....47 A6
Norfolk Ski Club*
 ....163 B3
Norfolk Sq PE38 .....172 B5
Norfolk St
 4 King's Lynn PE30 ..146 E5
 Norwich NR2 ....162 C5
 Wisbech PE13 ....152 C4
Norfolk Wildlife Hospl
 (RSPCA)* PE32 ....44 F3
Norfolk Wildlife Pk*
 NR9 ....51 C6
Norgate La IP20 .....130 E6
Norgate Rd NR4 .....161 E3
Norgate Way NR4 ...156 E8
Norman CE Prim Sch
 NR6 ....99 C7
Norman Cl
 East Dereham NR19 .154 C5
 Fakenham NR21 .....141 B6
Norman Dr
 Northwold PE33 ....81 B2
 Norwich NR4 ....158 F7
Norman Fst Sch NR13 .158 B2
Norman Rd
 Flitcham with Appleton
 PE31 ....28 E1
 Norwich NR3 ....158 E1
Norman Way PE31 .....15 B3
Normandy Cl IP20 .....99 C7
Normans Bldgs NR1 .178 B2
Norman's Burrow Rd
 NR21 ....31 B3
Normans La NR21 ....4 D1
North Ave NR29 ....50 B5
North Beach
 Heacham PE36 ....132 B1
 Wisbech PE13 ....152 A4
North Brink PE13 ....152 A4
North Cambridgeshire Hospl
 PE13 ....152 D5
North Denes Airfield
 NR30 ....168 D2
North Denes Mid Sch
 NR30 ....169 D8
North Denes Rd NR30 .169 C4
North Dr
 Fakenham NR21 .....141 C5
 Great Yarmouth NR30 .169 C4
North Elmham Prim Sch
 NR20 ....49 E8
North End
 Haddiscoe NR14 ......93 B1
 Stoke Holy Cross NR14 ..89 E5
 Wisbech PE13 ....152 B6
North Everard St
 PE30 ....146 E5
North Gage Cl NR7 ...159 C4
North Gn NR9 ....68 B1
North Gn Rd IP21 ...122 A4
North La NR21 ....17 E5
North Lawn PE38 .....97 B6
North Lopham Rd
 NR16 ....119 A3
North Lynn Ind Est
 PE30 ....147 A8
North Mkt Rd
 7 Great Yarmouth NR30 .169 D4
 Winterton-on-Sea NR29 .58 B6
North Norfolk Coast Nature
 Reserve* NR25 ....7 B8
North Norfolk Rly*
 ....9 B6
North Pickenham Rd
 PE37 ....153 D4
North Pk NR21 ....141 B6
North Pk Ave NR4 ...161 E6
North Pk Dr NR4 .....161 F4
North Quay NR30 ....169 C4
North Rd Bunwell NR16 .105 C4

North Rd continued
- 4 Great Yarmouth NR30 ....**169** D5
- Great Yarmouth NR31 .....**170** D4
- Hemsby NR29 ....**167** A7
- Ormesby St Margaret
  with Scratby NR29 ....**167** A4
- Watton IP25 ....**84** D3

North River Rd NR30 ...**169** C6

North St Brundall NR13 ..**165** E6
- Burnham Market PE31 ...**135** C3
- 6 Castle Acre PE32 ......**46** F2
- Great Dunham PE32 ......**47** E2
- King's Lynn PE30 ....**146** D6
- Langham NR25 ....**7** A4
- North Walsham NR28 ...**151** C5
- Sheringham NR26 ....**138** C7
- Wisbech PE13 ....**152** C5

North View NR21 ....**17** F3

North Walsham Cottage
  Hospl NR28 ....**151** C4

North Walsham Jun Sch
  NR28 ....**151** D5

North Walsham Rd
- Bacton NR28 ....**23** C3
- Coltishall NR12 ....**54** D7
- Crostwick NR12 ....**54** B2
- Felmingham NR28 ....**37** B8
- Happisburgh NR12 ....**23** F2
- Happisburgh NR12 ....**24** A6
- Northrepps NR27 ....**10** E1
- Norwich NR6 ....**159** A5
- Paston NR28 ....**151** F7
- Sprowston NR6 ....**159** B6
- Swafield NR28 ....**22** E4
- Thorpe Market NR11 .....**22** A7
- Witton NR28 ....**38** B8

North Walsham RUFC
  NR10 ....**37** E3

North Walsham Sta
  NR28 ....**151** C4

North Wootton Prim Sch
  PE30 ....**148** D8

Northcote Rd 11 NR3 .....**162** E8

Northern CI NR30 ....**168** F5

Northfield Ave NR23 ....**136** D6

Northfield CI NR18 ....**173** B6

Northfield Cres NR18 ....**136** E5

Northfield Gdns NR18 ...**136** D5

Northfield La
- Plumstead NR11 ....**20** B6
- Wells-next-the-Sea
  NR13 ....**136** E6
- **Northfield Loke** NR18 ..**173** B6

Northfield Rd
- Forncett NR16 ....**106** A4
- Mundesley NR11 ....**143** C5
- North Walsham NR28 ....**151** B6
- Swaffham PE37 ....**153** C6

Northfield Way NR23 ...**136** E6

Northfields NR4 ....**161** E4

Northfields Fst Sch
  NR4 ....**161** E4

Northgate
- Beccles NR34 ....**110** D1
- 11 Harleston IP20 ....**122** D1
- Hunstanton PE36 ....**132** C5
- Norwich NR6 ....**157** F5
- 3 Thorpe End NR13 .....**72** D6

Northgate C'ty High Sch
  NR19 ....**154** D6

Northgate Hospl
  NR30 ....**169** D6

Northgate St NR30 ....**169** C5

Northgate St Andrews Fst
  Sch NR30 ....**169** C6

Northgate Way PE34 ....**144** D6

Northmead Dr NR28 .....**151** C6

Northolt Rd IP25 ....**85** A3

Northrepps Prim Sch
  NR27 ....**11** A2

Northrepps Rd NR27 ...**139** E3

Northside NR7~ **72** E3

Northumberland St
  NR2 ....**162** B7

Northview Rd NR5 ......**157** C1

Northwell Pool Rd
  PE37 ....**153** C5

North-West Twr*
  NR30 ....**169** C5

Northwold Rd IP26 ......**99** A6

Norton Dr 2 Norwich NR4 **89** D8
- Norwich NR4 ....**162** A1

Norton Hill NR13 ....**74** A8

Norton Rd NR14 ....**92** B1

Norvic Dr NR4 NR5 .....**161** A7

Norvic Dr NR4 ....**161** E1

Norway CI PE31 ....**133** C6

Norwich Arts Ctr*
  NR2 ....**178** A3

Norwich Bsns Pk NR6 ..**158** D2

Norwich Cath NR1 ......**178** B3

Norwich City FC NR1 ...**163** A4

Norwich Comm NR18 ...**173** F6

Norwich Dr NR2 ....**32** E4

Norwich Gates PE35 ...**140** E1

Norwich High Sch for Girls
  NR2 ....**162** B3

Norwich Int Airport
  NR6 ....**158** B7

Norwich La IP27 ....**127** A4

Norwich Rd Acle NR13 ...**166** A4
- Ashmanhaugh NR12 ......**55** C7
- Attleborough NR17 .....**174** E6
- Aylsham NR11 ....**150** C3
- Barnham Broom NR9 .....**69** D2

Norwich Rd continued
- Bawdeswell NR20 ....**50** E7
- Bracon Ash NR14 ....**89** E3
- Briston NR24 ....**142** E5
- Brooke NR15 ....**90** E3
- Burgh & Tuttington NR11 ..**36** E6
- Caister-on-Sea NR30 ....**168** C5
- Cantley NR13 ....**92** D7
- Carbrooke IP25 ....**85** B3
- Cawston NR10 ....**35** B2
- Chedgrave NR14 ....**92** F7
- Cromer NR27 ....**139** C5
- Denton IP20 ....**123** B7
- Dickleburgh & Rushall
  IP21 ....**130** D6
- Ditchingham NR35 ....**109** A2
- Earsham NR35 ....**108** E1
- East Dereham NR20 .....**154** F5
- East Tuddenham NR20 ...**69** C6
- Edgefield NR24 ....**19** D6
- Fakenham NR21 ....**141** C4
- Foxley NR20 ....**50** D8
- Gillingham NR14 ....**110** C2

Great & Little Plumstead
- NR13 ....**73** A7
- Guist NR20 ....**33** A4
- Hardingham NR9 ....**86** E8
- 9 Hethersett NR9 ....**88** D7
- Hingham NR9 ....**86** A4
- Hingham NR9 ....**86** D5
- Holt NR25 ....**137** B5
- Horning NR12 ....**55** E4
- Horsham St Faith NR10 ..**53** D2
- Horstead with Stanninghall
  NR12 ....**54** C4
- Ingworth NR11 ....**36** B8
- Kimberley NR18 ....**87** B7
- Langley with Hardley
  NR14 ....**91** F6
- Lingwood & Burlingham
  NR13 ....**74** A2
- 12 Loddon NR14 ....**92** A2
- Long Stratton NR15 .....**106** F5
- Ludham NR29 ....**56** C5
- Marlingford NR9 ....**69** F4
- Mattishall NR20 ....**68** F6
- Mulbarton NR14 ....**89** B4
- Neatishead NR12 ....**164** F8
- North Walsham NR28 ...**151** B3
- Norwich NR5 ....**157** B2
- Poringland NR14 ....**90** B6
- Pulham St Mary IP21 ....**121** F4
- Rackheath NR13 ....**72** F8
- Reepham NR10 ....**149** C5
- Roughton NR11 ....**21** D8
- Salhouse NR13 ....**55** B1
- Saxlingham Nethergate
  NR15 ....**107** B8
- Scole IP21 ....**121** B1
- Shotesham NR15 ....**89** F2
- Shouldham PE33 ....**62** F3
- Smallburgh NR12 ....**38** D2
- Stockton NR34 ....**109** F5
- Strumpshaw NR13 ......**73** F2
- Swaffham PE37 ....**153** D4
- Swanton Morley NR20 ...**50** B2
- 4 Tacolneston NR16 ....**105** F5
- Tacolneston NR16 ....**106** A6
- Tharston & Hapton
  NR15 ....**106** C7
- Thetford IP24 ....**176** D4
- Thurton NR14 ....**91** C3
- Tivetshall St Mary NR15 ..**121** D4
- West Caister NR30 ......**168** B6
- Weston Longville NR9 ...**51** E5
- Wisbech PE13 ....**152** E5
- Woodton NR35 ....**108** C6
- Wroxham/Hoveton
  NR12 ....**164** B3
- Wymondham NR18 ......**173** D5
- Yaxham NR19 ....**68** C3

Norwich Rd Bsns Pk NR4 **176** D4

Norwich RFC NR12 ......**159** B8

Norwich Riverside
  NR1 ....**178** C2

Norwich Sch NR1 ....**178** B3

Norwich Sch of Art & Design
  NR1 ....**178** B3

Norwich St
- East Dereham NR19 ......**154** E5
- Fakenham NR21 ....**141** B4
- Hingham NR9 ....**86** D5
- Mundesley NR11 ....**143** A7

Norwich Sta NR1 ....**178** C2

Norwood Rd IP27 ....**175** A1

Notre Dame High Sch
  NR1 ....**178** B1

Notre Dame Prep Sch
  NR2 ....**162** B7

Nottingham Rd PE30 ...**146** E8

Nottingham Way
  NR30 ....**169** C3

Notykin St NR5 ....**161** A8

Nourse Dr PE31 ....**133** E5

Nova Scotia Rd
- Filby NR30 ....**168** A7
- Ormesby St Margaret
  with Scratby NR29 ......**167** B1

Nowhere La PE33 ....**80** D4

Nuffield CI NR31 ....**170** B4

Nuffield Cres NR31 .....**170** B4

Nunnery Dr IP24 ....**176** D1

Nunnery PI IP24 ....**176** D2

Nunnery Rd NR10 ......**154** D5

Nuns' Bridges Rd
  IP24 ....**176** C2

Nunsgate IP24 ....**176** D2

Nurseries Ave NR13 ...**165** E4

Nursery CI Acle NR13 ...**166** B4
- 7 Belton NR31 ....**94** A5
- King's Lynn PE30 ....**148** C2
- 3 Marthan NR29 ....**57** D5
- Norwich NR6 ....**157** E5
- 3 Roydon PE32 ....**28** A1

Nursery Dr
- Hunstanton PE36 ....**132** D4
- North Walsham NR28 ...**151** B3
- Wisbech PE13 ....**152** E8

Nursery Gdns NR13 ....**165** F6

Nursery La
- Brancaster PE31 ....**3** E6
- Costessey NR8 ....**156** F3
- Hockwold cum Wilton
  IP26 ....**114** A6
- 3 Norwich NR6 ....**148** C3
- **Nursery Rd** PE38 ......**172** C6
- Norwich NR6 ....**169** C6

Nursery Way PE32 .....**28** A1

Nursey CI NR35 ....**109** D3

Nut La NR27 ....**139** F3

Nutfield CI 7 NR4 ......**161** F1

Nuthall Cres PE30 ......**147** A8

Nuttele CI NR15 ....**107** C6

Nuttery Vale IP23 ......**130** F2

Nutwood CI NR8 ....**155** D2

O

Oak Ave
- 14 Great Yarmouth NR31 ..**94** C7
- King's Lynn PE30 ....**148** D2
- Marham PE33 ....**63** B4
- North Elmham NR20 .....**49** E7
- Norwich NR7 ....**163** F8
- 9 Poringland NR14 ......**90** C5
- West Winch PE33 ....**43** F2

Oak CI 4 Hethersett NR9 ..**88** D8
- Norwich NR5 ....**156** F2
- 14 Tasburgh NR15 ......**106** F6
- Thetford IP24 ....**176** A1

Oak Cres IP23 ....**130** D4

Oak Dr PE14 ....**77** F7

Oak Gr 7 Horsford NR10 ..**53** B3
- Sheringham NR26 ....**138** D5

Oak La East Ruston NR12 ..**38** E7
- 2 Hingham NR9 ....**86** D5
- Norwich NR3 ....**158** D3

Oak Lodge NR7 ....**163** C5

Oak Rd Dilham NR28 ....**38** D4
- Great Yarmouth NR31 ...**170** B6
- East Dereham NR19 .....**151** B4
- 3 Gorleston NR31 ......**170** C2
- Fettwell IP26 ....**98** E1

Oak St Fakenham NR21 ..**141** B4
- Norwich NR3 ....**178** A4

Oak Tree Bsns Pk NR18 ..**72** E8

Oak Tree CI 3 NR29 ....**57** D5

Oak Tree Way 8 IP20 ..**122** D1

Oak View Dr PE38 ......**172** C6

Oak Wood NR13 ....**165** E5

Oakapple Dr NR19 ......**154** D8

Oakcroft Dr NR14 ......**90** C5

Oakdale Rd NR13 ....**165** D5

Oakdene NR21 ....**15** C2

Oakfield CI 3 NR8 ......**172** C4

Oakfield Dr 8 NR13 .....**74** B8

Oakfield Rd
- Aylsham NR11 ....**150** C6
- Long Stratton NR15 .....**106** F3
- **Oakfields** NR14 ....**91** F2
- **Oakfields CI** 1 NR4 .....**89** C8
- **Oakhall** NR13 ....**165** D3

Oaklands
- Little Snoring NR21 ......**17** C3
- 4 Old Buckenham NR17 ..**104** D2
- Poringland NR14 ....**90** C6
- 6 Taverham NR8 ....**155** B2

Oaklands CI
- Attleborough NR17 ......**174** C3
- Halvergate NR13 ....**74** F2

Oaklands Dr
- Brandon IP27 ....**114** D4
- Cringleford NR4 ....**161** C1
- Walsoken PE13 ....**152** F7

Oaklands La 2 PE33 ...**61** D3

Oaklands The PE33 .....**153** C3

Oakley Church La
  IP21 ....**130** D4

Oakley CI PE13 ....**152** E4

Oakroyd Cres PE13 ....**152** C6

Oaks CI PE37 ....**153** C3

Oaks Dr Necton PE37 ...**65** F4
- Swaffham PE37 ....**153** C3

Oak's La NR13 ....**72** F2

Oaks The Ashill IP25 ....**84** A7
- Mattishall NR20 ....**68** F5

Oaktree Dr NR7 ....**159** B2

Oakwood CI NR10 ......**154** D8

Oakwood Dr NR10 ......**173** E6

Oakwood Rd NR19 .....**154** D8

Oasis Leisure Ctr
  PE36 ....**132** C4

Oasis Sport & Leisure Ctr
  NR1 ....**72** D5

Oasis Way PE36 ....**132** C2

Oatfield CI 7 NR10 .....**53** A3

Obelisk La NR8 ....**88** F5

Obelisk Plain NR25 .....**137** A6

Occupation Rd 10 NR30 ..**169** D8

Octagon Dr 4 PE33 ...**152** A6

Octavia CI NR13 ....**152** F6

Octavia Hill Birthplace Mus*
  PE13 ....**152** C5

Oddfellows Field 4 NR25 ..**7** C6

Offley Ct 7 NR5 ....**161** A8

Ogden CI NR18 ....**173** C4

Oil Mill La PE13 ....**152** B5

Old Barge Yd NR1 ......**178** C2

Old Becclesgate NR19 ..**154** D5

Old Brandon Rd IP26 ...**98** F1

Old Brewery La NR19 ..**154** D5

Old Buckenham High Sch
  NR17 ....**104** D2

Old Buckenham Prim Sch
  NR17 ....**104** D3

Old Buckenham Rd
  NR16 ....**105** A4

Old Bungay Rd NR35 ...**109** D4

Old Bury Rd
- Palgrave IP22 ....**129** E4
- Stanton IP21 ....**177** F1
- Thetford IP22 ....**176** C4
- Wortham IP22 ....**129** D4

Old Catton Mid Sch
  NR6 ....**158** E5

Old Chapel Rd
- Cantley NR13 ....**92** E7
- 2 Hemsby NR29 ....**58** B6

Old Chapel Way NR7 ...**72** E3

Old Church CI NR14 ....**89** F6

Old Church Rd
- Hainford NR10 ....**53** E6
- Hopton on Sea NR31 ....**171** D4
- Snettisham PE31 ....**12** E5

Old Coach Rd NR27 ....**139** C6

Old Coast Rd NR29 ....**167** E2

Old Fakenham Rd
- Attlebridge NR9 ....**52** B3
- Foxley NR20 ....**50** D8

Old Farm La NR8 ....**158** B1

Old Feltwell Rd IP26 ...**99** A5

Old Forge CI IP22 ......**129** B4

Old Forge CI NR14 .....**166** C4

Old Friendship La
  NR10 ....**35** C2

Old Gr Ct NR3 ....**158** D2

Old Hall CI
- Ashwellthorpe NR16 .....**105** F8
- 1 Norwich NR14 ....**163** B2
- Saham Toney IP25 ....**84** B5

Old Hall Dr PE31 ....**140** E3

Old Hall Gdns
- Brooke NR15 ....**90** F2
- Buxton with Lammas
  NR10 ....**37** A2

Old Hall La 7 NR4 ......**81** F8

Old Hall Rd
- East Dereham NR19 .....**154** D2
- Mattishall NR20 ....**68** D5
- Witton NR28 ....**38** B8

Old Hall The NR1 ....**27** C3

Old Harleston Rd
  NR35 ....**123** E7

Old High Rd IP22 ....**177** A5

Old Hithe Rd NR26 .....**138** A6

Old Hunstanton Rd
  PE36 ....**132** E7

Old Kiln 10 PE33 ....**43** F2

Old La East Ruston NR12 ..**24** A5
- Happisburgh NR12 ......**23** F1
- Reepham NR10 ....**34** B1
- Thelnetham IP22 ....**128** A2

Old Lakenham Hall Dr 6 ....

Old Laundry CI 3 NR2 ..**162** B8

Old Laundry Mews
  NR1 ....**163** A5

Old Liby Mews NR1 .....**178** C2

Old Lynn Rd PE13 ......**152** E7

Old Manor CI PE30 .....**148** C1

Old Methwold Rd
- Feltwell IP26 ....**98** E2
- Northwold PE33 ....**81** B2
- **Old Mill Dr** IP21 ....**121** F4

Old Mill Rd
- Caister-on-Sea NR30 ....**168** F5
- 3 Poringland NR14 .....**90** C5
- Roughton NR11 ....**139** B1

Old Mill Terr NR34 .....**110** D1

Old Mkt PE13 ....**152** C5

Old Mkt CI NR13 ....**166** C3

Old Mkt Gn 3 NR14 ...**92** A1

Old Mkt Pl 21 IP20 ....**122** D2

Old Mkt St
- 12 King's Lynn PE30 ....**146** E5
- 7 Thetford IP24 ....**176** D3
- **Old Mkt Way** NR15 ....**107** C5

Old Norwich Rd
- Horsham St Faith &
  Newton St Faith NR10 ..**53** D1
- Yaxley IP23 ....**130** A1

Old Pal Rd NR2 ....**162** B7

Old Pools Dro CB6 .....**95** F1

Old Post Office La
  NR35 ....**109** C3

Old Post Office St
- Fakenham NR21 ....**141** B4
- 2 Shipdham IP25 ....**67** B2
- **Old Post Rd** NR24 .....**142** C4
- **Old Rd** Acle NR13 ......**166** C4
- Acle NR13 ....**166** E5

Old Rectory CI
- King's Lynn PE30 ....**148** D5
- 4 Mulbarton NR14 .....**89** B3
- Norwich NR7 ....**163** E6
- **Old Rectory Rd** NR14 ..**91** D1
- **Old Reepham Rd** 4 ......

Old Roman Bank
  PE34 ....**144** A7

Old Sch Ct NR1 ....**178** C1

Old Sch Rd
- East Ruston NR12 ....**38** F8
- Guestwick NR20 ....**33** F5
- **Old Severalls Rd** IP26 ..**98** E6

Old Southwood Rd
  NR13 ....**74** B2

Old St
- 1 Newton Flotman NR15 ..**89** D1
- 3 Newton Flotman NR15 ..**107** A8
- **Old Sta Way** 6 NR25 ..**137** C5
- **Old Town Way** PE36 ..**132** D6
- **Old Turnpike Rd** NR11 ..**21** D7

Old Vicarage Gdn*
- NR21 ....**24** A3
- **Old Vicarage Pk** PE32 ..**63** E7
- **Old Warren** NR8 ....**155** D2
- **Old Watton Rd** NR4 ...**161** A5

Old Wells Rd
- Sculthorpe NR21 ....**16** A2
- Walsingham NR22 ......**16** E8
- **Old Woman's La** NR25 ..**7** F4
- **Old Yarmouth Rd** NR12 ..**39** C2
- **Oldfield Ave** PE14 ......**59** B1
- **Oldfield La** NR10 ....**154** E6
- **Oldfield La** PE13 ....**152** B3
- **Oldhall La** NR16 ....**118** C5
- **Oldhall Rd** NR4 ....**89** E8
- **Oldmedow Rd** PE30 ...**147** A2
- **Oldsunway** PE30 ......**146** D5
- **Oldwash La** NR16 .....**105** D3
- **Olive Ave** NR5 ....**89** D1
- **Olive CI** NR5 ....**157** C1
- **Olive Cres** NR10 ....**53** A4
- **Olive Rd** NR5 ....**157** C1
- **Oliver CI** 6 NR27 ....**139** C6
- **Oliver Mews** 4 NR30 ...**169** D4
- **Olivia CI** NR21 ....**141** A5

Ollands Rd
- Attleborough NR17 .....**174** C3
- Reepham NR10 ....**149** C4
- **Ollard Ave** PE13 ......**152** C7
- **Olley Rd** 8 NR27 ......**10** A5
- **Olney Rd** NR19 ....**154** D5
- **Onedine CI** PE31 ......**140** C5
- **Onley St** NR2 ....**162** B4
- **Onslow Ave** NR30 .....**169** D7
- **Onyx Ct** 10 PE13 ......**152** C4
- **Opie St** NR2 ....**178** B3
- **Opportune Rd** PE13 ...**152** C4
- **Orange Gr** 1 PE13 ....**152** C4
- **Orange Row** PE34 .....**144** A5
- **Orange Row Rd** PE34 ..**144** A6
- **Orch The** 4 Belton NR31 ..**94** A6
- Brandon IP27 ....**175** C3
- **Orchard Bank** NR8 ....**156** E8
- **Orchard CI** Acle NR13 ..**166** B4
- Ashill IP25 ....**84** A6
- Attleborough NR17 .....**174** C5
- Blofield Heath NR13 ....**73** C6
- Brancaster Staithe PE31 ..**3** C7
- Briston NR24 ....**142** D4
- Caister-on-Sea NR30 ...**168** C5
- Dersingham PE31 ....**140** D4
- Downham Market PE38 ..**172** D5
- Fakenham NR21 ....**141** D4
- Holt NR25 ....**137** E7
- 1 Ixworth NR19 ....**69** F2
- Mundesley NR11 ....**143** B7
- North Elmham NR20 .....**49** E7
- North Walsham NR28 ...**151** D6
- Norwich NR7 ....**163** C8
- Roughton NR11 ....**21** D7
- Sheringham NR26 ....**138** C6
- Tacolneston NR16 ......**105** F4
- Wattington PE33 ....**61** E5
- 19 Watton IP25 ....**84** D3
- 6 Wisbech PE14 ....**59** A1
- **Orchard Cres** 4 NR15 ..**106** B1
- **Orchard Ct** NR29 ......**167** A3

Orchard Dr
- Hellesdon NR6 ....**157** D3
- 5 Potter Heigham NR29 ..**56** F6
- West Walton PE14 ......**59** C8
- Wisbech PE13 ....**152** E4
- **Orchard Gdns** 3 PE30 ..**147** B6
- **Orchard Gr** Diss IP22 ..**177** C5
- Kettlestone NR21 ......**17** C5
- 6 King's Lynn PE34 ....**146** C3

Orchard La
- Aylsham NR11 ....**150** D4
- Castle Acre PE32 ....**46** F2
- King's Lynn PE30 ......**147** B5
- Reepham NR10 ....**149** D5
- Shouldham PE33 ....**62** D4

Orchard Pl
- Swaffham PE37 ....**153** B4
- Thompson IP24 ....**102** A7

Orchard Rd
- 8 Gayton PE32 ....**45** C6
- Lingwood NR13 ....**73** F3
- 2 Mattishall NR20 .....**68** E6
- 2 Spixworth NR10 .....**54** A2
- Wiggenhall St Germans
  PE34 ....**43** B1
- Wiggenhall St Germans
  PE34 ....**88** B8
- **Orchard St** NR2 ....**162** C7

Orchard Way
- Banham NR16 ....**119** D7
- 5 Burgh St Margaret
  (Fleggburgh) NR29 ......**57** C1
- 8 Hethersett NR9 ......**88** D8
- 7 Tasburgh NR15 ......**106** F6
- Terrington St John PE14 ..**42** B1
- Thetford IP24 ....**176** D5

Orchard Way continued
Wymondham NR18 . . . . . . .173 C4
Orchid Ave NR19 . . . . . . .154 D1
Orde Ave NR31 . . . . .170 C2
Ordnance Rd NR30 . . . . . .169 D1
Orford Cl **1** NR30 . . . . . .169 D3
Orford Pl Norwich NR1 . . . .178 B2
7 West Winch PE33 . . . . . .43 F2
Orford St NR1 . . . . .178 B2
Orford Gr NR13 . . . . .43 E2
Oriel Ave NR31 . . . . .170 A3
Oriel Cty High Sch
NR31 . . . . .170 A3
Ormesby Fst Sch
NR29 . . . . .167 A2
Ormesby La NR29 . . . . . . .76 A8
Ormesby Mid Sch
NR29 . . . . .167 A3
Ormesby Rd
Caister-on-Sea NR30 . . . . .168 D7
Ormesby NR29 . . . . .167 A6
Ormesby St Margaret
with Scratby NR29 . . . . . .168 C8
Scottow NR10 . . . . .37 B2
Ormond Rd NR30 . . . . . . .169 C5
Orwell Cl
King's Lynn PE30 . . . . . . .147 D4
2 Wymondham NR18 . . . .173 D5
Orwell Cres NR31 . . . . .94 A6
Orwell Rd NR2 . . . . .162 C3
Osbert Cl **4** NR1 . . . . . . .162 E1
Osborne Ave NR30 . . . . . .169 C7
Osborne Cl **1** NR28 . . . . .151 C7
Osborne Pk PE13 . . . . . . .152 C8
Osborne Rd
Norwich NR4 . . . . .161 D2
Wisbech PE13 . . . . .152 B7
Osier Cl NR19 . . . . .154 B4
Osier La NR15 . . . . .9 C1
Osprey Cl NR12 . . . . .164 D5
Ostend Gap NR12 . . . . . . .24 A7
Ostend Pl NR12 . . . . .24 A7
Ostend Rd NR12 . . . . .24 A6
Ostrich La NR19 . . . . .49 A3
Otter Cl **5** NR13 . . . . . . .55 A1
Otter Dr **17** NR14 . . . . . . .89 B3
Oulton Cl PE37 . . . . .153 C2
Oulton Rd NR6 . . . . .158 C5
Ouse Ave PE30 . . . . .146 D2
Ouse Ave The IP24 . . . . . .176 C3
Ouse La NR12 . . . . .39 F1
Out S Gates PE30 . . . . . . .146 E3
Outney Rd NR35 . . . . . . .124 A8
Outwell Rd Emneth PE14 . . .59 B2
Stow Bardolph PE34 . . . . . .78 E8
Oval Ave NR5 . . . . .161 C8
Oval Rd NR5 . . . . .157 C1
Over Cross NR14 . . . . . . .119 C8
Overbury Rd NR6 . . . . . . .158 A4
Overstone Ct NR6 . . . . . .158 F5
Overstrand Belfry VA Prim
Sch NR27 . . . . .11 A3
Overstrand Rd NR27 . . . . .139 C6
Overstrand Sports Club
NR27 . . . . .11 A3
Overwood La NR16 . . . . . .106 A3
Overy Rd PE31 . . . . .135 D3
Ovington Rd IP25 . . . . .84 C4
Owen Rd Diss IP22 . . . . . .177 F4
Great Yarmouth NR31 . . . . .169 B1
Owen's Cl **13** NR16 . . . . . .106 D3
Owl Dr **3** NR14 . . . . .89 B3
Oxborough Dr PE30 . . . . .148 E1
Oxborough La NR21 . . . . .141 C4
Oxborough Rd
Oxborough PE33 . . . . .81 D3
Stoke Ferry PE33 . . . . .81 A2
Oxburgh Cl **1** PE13 . . . . .152 A7
Oxburgh Hall (National
Trust) * PE33 . . . . .81 E4
Oxcroft NR13 . . . . .166 C4
Oxford Ave NR31 . . . . . . .170 B3
Oxford Pl PE34 . . . . .144 F6
Oxford Rd **2** Feltwell IP26 . .98 E1
2 Feltwell IP26 . . . . .98 E1
Oxford St NR2 . . . . .162 C5
Oxford Way **11** NR29 . . . . .57 D4
Oxnead Dr NR30 . . . . . . .168 D2
Oxnead La NR35 . . . . . . .107 F4
Oxnead Rd NR3 . . . . .158 B2

P

Pack La Briston NR24 . . . . .142 F3
East Carleton NR14 . . . . . . .89 A6
Strumpshaw NR13 . . . . . . .73 F3
Packway The IP20 . . . . . . .123 A3
Paddock Cl Belton NR31 . . . .93 F6
3 Fakenham NR21 . . . . . .141 E4
Paddock Farm IP31 . . . . . .127 B4
Paddock Farm Dr NR29 . . . .75 F8
Paddock Gdns NR27 . . . . .174 E5
Paddock Rd **13** IP20 . . . . . .122 D2
Paddock St NR21 . . . . . . .162 C8
Paddock The
3 Cromer NR27 . . . . .10 B5
Hemsby NR29 . . . . .167 A8
Trowse with Newton
NR14 . . . . .163 A2
Paddocks The
Bacton/Walcott NR12 . . . . . .23 E4
Beetley NR20 . . . . .49 D4
Brandon IP27 . . . . .175 E4
Downham Market PE38 . . . .172 B5
Griston IP25 . . . . .85 A1

Paddocks The continued
Norwich NR6 . . . . .158 F6
Swaffham PE37 . . . . .153 B3
Paddy's La NR9 . . . . .51 E1
Paddys Loke NR30 . . . . . .169 A7
Padgate NR13 . . . . .72 D6
Padgett's Rd PE14 . . . . . . .95 A6
Page Cl
3 North Walsham NR28 . .151 C6
Poringland NR14 . . . . .90 C5
Page Rd Brundall NR13 . . . .165 C4
Norwich NR5 . . . . .157 F1
Page Stair La PE30 . . . . . .146 D5
Pages Cl NR18 . . . . .173 B3
Pages La IP27 . . . . .84 B5
Paget Adams Dr **4** NR20 . .68 A8
Paget Rd NR30 . . . . .169 D3
Paige Cl **8** PE33 . . . . .61 D5
Paine Cl IP22 . . . . .177 B5
Paine Rd NR7 . . . . .163 D8
Painter St IP24 . . . . .176 C4
Palace St NR1 . . . . .178 B3
Pales Gn **4** PE32 . . . . .46 F2
Palgrave Cl NR8 . . . . .155 B1
Palgrave Rd
Great Dunham PE32 . . . . . .47 E1
Great Dunham PE32 . . . . .169 C5
Little Dunham PE32 . . . . . .65 D8
Palgrave VC Prim Sch
IP22 . . . . .177 D2
Palling Rd NR12 . . . . .24 D1
Palm Cl NR18 . . . . .173 B5
Palmer Rd
Great Yarmouth NR31 . . . . .170 D5
8 New Rackheath NR13 . . .72 E7
Norwich NR3 . . . . .158 C3
Palmer's La
Aylsham NR11 . . . . .150 C6
Freethorpe NR13 . . . . .92 F8
Palmers La NR17 . . . . .55 C5
Pansey Dr PE31 . . . . .140 C4
Panton Cl PE30 . . . . .146 D2
Panxworth Church Rd
NR13 . . . . .73 E8
Panxworth Rd NR13 . . . . . .73 F7
Paper St NR19 . . . . .68 C6
Paradise La
6 Bawdeswell NR20 . . . . .50 E7
8 King's Lynn PE30 . . . . .146 D5
Paradise Par **8** PE30 . . . . .146 D5
Paradise Rd
7 Bawdeswell NR20 . . . . .50 E7
Downham Market PE38 . . . .172 B5
11 King's Lynn PE30 . . . . .146 D5
Paragon Pl NR2 . . . . .162 C6
Parana Cl NR7 . . . . .159 C5
Parana Ct NR7 . . . . .159 C5
Parana Rd NR7 . . . . .159 C5
Parish Rd NR10 . . . . .53 D7
Park Ave **3** Barford NR9 . . .69 F2
King's Lynn PE30 . . . . . . .146 F4
North Walsham NR28 . . . . .151 D5
Scottow NR10 . . . . .37 D2
Wisbech PE13 . . . . .152 C6
Park Cl **1** Hethersett NR9 . . .88 D7
Holt NR25 . . . . .137 D5
Norwich NR6 . . . . .158 C5
Thurton NR14 . . . . .91 C4
Wymondham NR18 . . . . . .173 D1
Park Comm La NR16 . . . . .119 B5
Park Cres PE34 . . . . .61 B5
Park Ct NR16 . . . . .118 C5
Park Dr NR7 . . . . .88 C7
Park East **3** IP25 . . . . . . .67 B2
Park Farm La
Euston IP24 . . . . .126 C4
Hoxne IP21 . . . . .131 C2
Park High Sch PE30 . . . . .147 A4
Park Highatt Dr **2** IP25 . . . .67 B2
Park Hill PE31 . . . . .140 D5
Park La Blofield NR13 . . . . .165 B8
Cromer NR27 . . . . .139 D4
Deopham NR18 . . . . .87 A4
Downham Market PE38 . . . .172 B3
Hellhoughton NR21 . . . . . . .30 E5
Hockering NR20 . . . . .69 C8
North Walsham NR28 . . . . .151 A5
Norwich NR2 . . . . .162 B5
Reepham NR10 . . . . .149 B4
Scarning NR19 . . . . .67 R6
Snettisham PE31 . . . . .12 E4
Park St **3** PE13 . . . . .152 D5
Park The NR16 . . . . .118 B5
Park View
Botesdale IP22 . . . . .128 F3
Brandon IP27 . . . . .175 B2
Weeting IP27 . . . . .175 A7
Park View Ave NR29 . . . . . .57 D3
Park Way NR6 . . . . .157 E5
Parker Cl NR13 . . . . .165 B4

Parker Dr NR21 . . . . .141 D4
Parker Rd NR2 . . . . .162 B5
Parkers Cl NR18 . . . . .173 B6
Parker's La NR15 . . . . . . .106 F2
Parkers Prim Sch IP25 . . . . .84 C5
Parker's Rd NR20 . . . . .68 F6
Parkhill **8** PE32 . . . . .44 B3
Parkland Cl NR13 . . . . .55 E4
Parkland Cres
9 Horning NR12 . . . . . . .55 F3
Parkland Dr NR31 . . . . . . .158 F3
Parkland Est NR29 . . . . . .167 A8
Parkland Rd NR8 . . . . . . .158 F3
Parklands NR8 . . . . .156 D4
Parklands Ave IP25 . . . . . . .67 B2
Parklands Way **41** IP20 . . . .122 D2
Parkside PE26 . . . . .13 A7
Parkside Cl IP22 . . . . .177 C4
Parkside Dr NR6 . . . . .158 E5
Parkview IP24 . . . . .176 C4
Parkway NR30 . . . . .169 B5
Parliament Ct **5** NR7 . . . . .72 D4
Parliament La IP24 . . . . . .102 E3
Parmenter Rd NR4 . . . . . .161 F3
Parmeter Cl NR11 . . . . . . .150 D6
Parr Rd NR3 . . . . .158 A1
Parrow La NR11 . . . . .21 C6
Parsons Cl IP27 . . . . .175 B2
Parsons La **8** IP27 . . . . . . .14 D8
Parsons Mead NR4 . . . . . .161 F1
Partridge Dr
Mulbarton NR14 . . . . .89 A3
4 Thetford IP24 . . . . . . .176 D2
Partridge Rd NR11 . . . . . .150 B6
Partridge Way NR6 . . . . . .158 D4
Partridge Wlk IP27 . . . . . .175 F3
Parva Cl NR11 . . . . .20 B4
Pasteur Rd NR30 . . . . . . .169 B2
Paston Cl **4** NR30 . . . . .9 F1
Paston Coll NR28 . . . . . . .151 C5
Paston Ct **8** NR4 . . . . .89 B8
Paston Dr **3** NR30 . . . . . .168 DR
Paston Rd
Great Yarmouth NR31 . . . . .170 C6
Mundesley NR11 . . . . .143 D5
Paston Way NR27 . . . . . . .159 C2
Pasture Cl NR31 . . . . .28 R4
Pastures The
5 Blakeney NR25 . . . . .7 C6
Great Yarmouth NR31 . . . . .170 B7
Hemsby NR29 . . . . .167 A8
Little Snoring NR21 . . . . . . .17 B3
Patricia Ave NR12 . . . . . . .54 C6
Patricia Rd NR1 . . . . .162 D3
Patrick Rd **4** NR15 . . . . . .106 D3
Patten La NR15 . . . . .121 B3
Patterson Cl **3** NR20 . . . .169 C4
Patteson Cl **8** NR4 . . . . . . .89 B8
Pattison Rd NR3 . . . . .162 D8
Paul Dr PE32 . . . . .44 B3
Pauls La NR27 . . . . .11 A3
Pavilion Cl **5** IP22 . . . . . .177 A5
Pavilion Rd NR1 . . . . .170 D4
Paxman Rd PE30 . . . . . . .146 F2
Paxton Terr PE30 . . . . . . .146 E5
Payne Ave PE13 . . . . .152 D7
Paynes Hill PE30 . . . . . . .122 F6
Payne's La IP20 . . . . .98 E1
Peachtree St **6** NR21 . . . . .15 C2
Peacock Chase NR8 . . . . .173 D4
Peacock Cl PE26 . . . . .113 F6
Peacock La
Beetley NR20 . . . . .49 E5
Holt NR25 . . . . .137 B7
Peacock Rd NR8 . . . . .178 B4
Peacock Way NR4 . . . . . .142 A4
Peakhall Rd PE32 . . . . .48 F8
Peakwell Cl NR8 . . . . .155 C2
Pear Tree Cl NR20 . . . . . . .68 C6
Pear Tree Cnr NR21 . . . . . .31 C7
Pearce Rd IP22 . . . . .177 E4
Pearcefield NR1 . . . . .158 F2
Pearce's Cl **1** IP26 . . . . . .114 A7
Pearmain Rd IP22 . . . . . . .177 C5
Pearsons Cl
Freethorpe NR13 . . . . .92 E7
Holt NR25 . . . . .137 C6
Pearson's Rd NR3 . . . . . . .158 C4
Peartree Ave **2** NR29 . . . . .57 C4
Peartree Way **5** NR29 . . . . .59 A1
Peatlings La PE13 . . . . . . .152 A7
Pebble Cl **3** PE12 . . . . . . .41 B8
Pebble View Wlk
NR31 . . . . .171 E4
Peck Cl NR5 . . . . .160 E8
Peckover Cty Prim Sch
PE13 . . . . .152 B6
Peckover Cl **3** PE13 . . . . .152 E4
Peckover House *
PE13 . . . . .152 B5
Peckover Rd
Fakenham NR21 . . . . .141 A6
Norwich NR1 . . . . .161 E3
Peckover Way PE30 . . . . .147 E8
Peddars Cl PE36 . . . . .132 D6
Peddars Dr PE36 . . . . .132 D6
Peddars' La NR34 . . . . . . .110 C6
Peddars Vale PE37 . . . . . .153 D4
Peddars Way N PE36 . . . . .155 D2
Peddars Way N PE36 . . . . . .2 A4
Peddlars Turnpike
NR20 . . . . .33 F3
Pedham Rd NR13 . . . . .73 E7

Pedlars Croft **2** NR29 . . . .167 A8
Pedlar's Gr PE37 . . . . .153 C5
Pedlar's La NR21 . . . . .17 F1
Pedley La PE13 . . . . .152 A6
Peel St PE30 . . . . .146 F4
Pegasus Cl NR30 . . . . . . .168 D7
Pegg Rd NR26 . . . . .138 C5
Peggotty Rd NR30 . . . . . .170 D8
Peggy's La NR16 . . . . .105 E6
Peldon Dr PE13 . . . . .152 E5
Pelham Rd NR3 . . . . .158 D1
Pell Pl **2** PE33 . . . . .43 F2
Pell Rd PE31 . . . . .140 D4
Pemberton Rd **8** IP20 . . . .122 D1
Pembrey Cl NR31 . . . . . . .170 A5
Pembroke Ave NR31 . . . . .170 B4
Pembroke Rd NR2 . . . . . . .162 B5
Pendlesham Rise NR8 . . . .155 E2
Pendula Rd PE13 . . . . . . .152 B7
Penfold Dr NR18 . . . . .173 E5
Penfold St NR11 . . . . .150 C6
Penguin Rd PE30 . . . . . . .147 D4
Penhill La NR17 . . . . .103 D7
Penn Cl NR8 . . . . .156 D6
Penn Gr NR3 . . . . .158 C1
Penn Rd NR8 . . . . .156 D6
Pennington Way NR1 . . . . .140 A1
Penny Crest **3** NR21 . . . . .15 C2
Pennygate La NR12 . . . . . .38 F1
Pennyroyal Rd NR6 . . . . . .158 D5
Penrose Cl PE30 . . . . .147 B8
Penrose Gdns PE13 . . . . . .152 E4
Penryn Cl NR4 . . . . .161 E5
Penshurst Mews **8**
NR4 . . . . .161 F1
Pentney Abbey Leisure Ctr
PE32 . . . . .63 A7
Pentney Dro PE33 . . . . . . .62 E6
Pepper Cl **6** NR3 . . . . . . .158 C8
Peppers Cl IP27 . . . . .175 B7
Pepper's Gn PE30 . . . . . . .148 E8
Perebrown Ave NR30 . . . . .169 D7
Pereers Cl NR31 . . . . .170 A4
Peregrine Cl Diss IP22 . . . .177 F5
Norwich NR7 . . . . .159 C4
Peregrine Mews NR7 . . . . .159 C4
Peregrine Rd NR7 . . . . . . .159 C4
Perkin Field NR7 . . . . .144 B4
Perrings NR18 . . . . .173 B6
Perrys La NR10 . . . . .149 C4
Peter Ave NR8 . . . . .166 B3
Peter Cl NR29 . . . . .168 D8
Peterhouse Ave NR7 . . . . .159 C4
Peterhouse Fst Sch
NR31 . . . . .170 C4
Peterhouse Mid Sch
NR31 . . . . .170 B4
Peterkin Rd **3** NR4 . . . . . . .89 E8
Peters Cl NR19 . . . . .154 C1
Peter's Dro PE34 . . . . .61 C4
Peterscourt PE30 . . . . . . .147 D6
Petersfield Cl NR15 . . . . . .106 F4
Peterson Rd **8** NR4 . . . . . .89 B8
Peterson's La NR11 . . . . . .150 B7
Peto Cl NR5 . . . . .161 C7
Peto's Cnr NR33 . . . . .111 F8
Petre Cl **3** NR28 . . . . .151 C7
Petticoat Dro PE32 . . . . . . .64 E8
Petticoat La PE33 . . . . .62 D6
Pettingales **8** NR14 . . . . . .89 F4
Pettit La NR28 . . . . .38 C6
Petts Cl **3** PE13 . . . . .152 E7
Pettus Rd NR4 . . . . .161 E3
Petunia Way IP27 . . . . . . .175 A2
Pevcrell Rd NR5 . . . . .160 D8
Pheasant Cl NR14 . . . . .89 A3
Pheasant Wlk **2** NR12 . . . . .54 A2
Pheasants Wlk NR35 . . . . .123 E8
Phelps Rd NR7 . . . . .163 F7
Philadelphia La NR3 . . . . .158 D3
Philip Ford Way NR18 . . . .173 C2
Philip Nurse Rd PE31 . . . . .140 B3
Philip Pl NR19 . . . . .154 D2
Philip Rudd Ct PE32 . . . . . .45 A8
Philips' Chase PE30 . . . . .147 D7
Phillippo Cl **2** IP22 . . . . . . .28 A1
Pickards Way PE13 . . . . . .152 A6
Pickford Cl NR28 . . . . . . .151 E6
Picton Rd NR15 . . . . .106 E3
Pier Gdns NR31 . . . . .170 E4
Pier Plain NR31 . . . . .169 D2
Pier Rd NR31 . . . . .170 D3
Pier Wlk NR31 . . . . .170 E4
Pigeon St PE14 . . . . .41 D3
Pightle The IP27 . . . . .114 C8
Pightle Way Lyng NR9 . . . . .51 A4
Reepham NR10 . . . . .149 C5
Pigot La NR14 . . . . .90 C6
Pike La IP24 . . . . .176 D4
Pikeman Rd NR13 . . . . .72 E8
Pikes Nursery **4** NR29 . . . .56 C5
Pilgrim's Way **7** IP20 . . . .122 D2
Pilgrims Way
Little Cressingham IP25 . . . .83 F3
Weeting IP27 . . . . .175 C8
Pilling Pk Rd NR1 . . . . . . .163 B7
Pilling Rd NR7 . . . . .163 D7
Pilot St **3** PE30 . . . . .146 D5
Pimpernel Rd NR10 . . . . . .53 A8
Pincushion Dro PE14 . . . . . .78 B5
Pine Ave
Cockley Cley PE37 . . . . . . .82 D7

Orc - Plu **203**

Pine Ave continued
Marham PE33 . . . . .63 B4
Pine Cl
5 Downham Market
PE38 . . . . .172 C6
3 Eye IP23 . . . . .130 C1
4 Harleston IP20 . . . . . .122 D1
Hunstanton PE36 . . . . . . .132 D4
17 Marham NR29 . . . . . . .57 D4
Norwich NR4 . . . . .162 A3
Ormesby St Margaret
NR29 . . . . .167 A3
3 Snettisham PE31 . . . . . .12 E4
Thetford IP24 . . . . .176 B1
Pine Coombe **1** NR21 . . . . .15 C2
Pine Ct
East Dereham NR19 . . . . . .154 D2
Sheringham NR26 . . . . . . .138 E6
Pine Lake NR14 . . . . .90 B5
Pine Mall PE31 . . . . .133 C4
Pine Rd
King's Lynn PE30 . . . . . . .148 D2
Norwich NR7 . . . . .159 E1
Pine Tree Chase PE33 . . . . .43 F1
Pine Tree Cl IP22 . . . . . . .127 F5
Pine Trees Bsns Pk
NR7 . . . . .159 D3
Pine Wlk **6** NR25 . . . . .8 F5
Pinecot Ave **7** NR31 . . . . . .94 C6
Pineheath Rd NR25 . . . . . . .8 E3
Pinelodges The NR7 . . . . .163 C6
Pinetrees NR31 . . . . .93 E3
Pinetrees Rd NR7 . . . . . . .159 D3
Pinewood Cl NR6 . . . . . . .157 F4
Pinewood Dr
8 Horning NR12 . . . . . . .55 E4
Pinewood Leisure Ctr
NR25 . . . . .9 B3
Pinfold La
Hindolveston NR20 . . . . . . .33 D8
Northwold IP26 . . . . .99 A6
Pinfold Rd PE14 . . . . .77 E5
Pingle Rd PE14 . . . . .78 A4
Pingles Dr NR29 . . . . .148 C4
Pinkney La NR24 . . . . .18 E6
Pintail Dr **2** Blakeney NR25 . .7 C6
Great Yarmouth NR31 . . . . .170 A6
Pioneer Rd NR6 . . . . .159 A6
Piper Rd
King's Lynn PE30 . . . . . . .146 F1
Norwich NR7 . . . . .159 E1
Pipit's Mew NR17 . . . . .71 A4
Pippin Cl NR20 . . . . .167 A2
Pippin Pl PE13 . . . . .152 F7
Pirnhow St NR35 . . . . . . .109 B3
Pit La PE37 . . . . .153 C4
Pit Rd
Aldeby, Wheatacre,
Burgh St Peter NR34 . . . . .111 B4
Hemsby NR29 . . . . .167 A7
Northrepps NR27 . . . . .11 A1
Woodbastwick NR13 . . . . . .55 D1
Pit St NR11 . . . . .22 C6
Pitchford Rd NR5 . . . . . . .161 C6
Pitt Sq NR9 . . . . .86 C4
Pitt St NR3 . . . . .178 A4
Pitt's Hill NR15 . . . . .107 B8
Pitts Hill Cl NR15 . . . . . . .107 B8
Pitts Wlk PE37 . . . .
Plaford Rd NR7 . . . . .159 E1
Plane Rd NR31 . . . . .170 B6
Plantation Cl NR17 . . . . . .174 B4
Plantation Dr NR7 . . . . . . .159 D3
Plantation Rd
Aslacton NR15 . . . . .121 A7
Blofield NR13 . . . . .165 A7
4 Fakenham NR21 . . . . .141 F4
North Walsham NR28 . . . . .151 C5
Norwich NR6 . . . . .157 F6
Plantation The NR2 . . . . . .162 B4
Plantsman Cl NR4 . . . . . . .162 B3
Plasset Dr NR17 . . . . .174 F7
Platten's Cl **1** NR11 . . . . . .19 F1
Platteris Cl NR12 . . . . .54 A2
Players Way NR6 . . . . .158 E6
Playing Field La **18** NR29 . . .57 D4
Pleasance Cl PE30 . . . . . .147 A5
Pleasant Cl NR6 . . . . .157 D5
Pleasant Pl NR6 . . . . .157 D5
Pleasant Row **1** PE37 . . . .153 C3
Plough La
Hardingham NR9 . . . . .86 D6
Watlington PE33 . . . . .61 E5
Ploughboy La IP20 . . . . . . .54 D4
Ploughman Rd PE30 . . . . .147 C4
Ploughman's Dro IP26 . . . . .98 B1
Ploughman's La NR21 . . . . .17 E6
Ploughman's Piece PE36 . . .2 E6
Plover Cl
Great Yarmouth NR31 . . . . .170 A7
3 Thetford IP24 . . . . . . .176 D2
Plover Rd **12** IP25 . . . . .84 C3
Plovers Ct PE13 . . . . .175 F3
Plovers Way IP26 . . . . . . .113 F7
Plum La NR11 . . . . .20 C8
Plumbly Cl NR28 . . . . . . .151 C3
Plumb's Cl NR14 . . . . . . .142 E4
Plummer's La NR15 . . . . . .107 C7
Plump Rd NR15 . . . . .106 D5
Plumsgate Rd NR12 . . . . . .39 C1
Plumstead Rd NR13 . . . . . .73 D6
Plumstead Rd
Baconsthorpe NR25 . . . . . .20 A7
Edgefield NR24 . . . . .19 E5

Plumstead Rd continued
Great & Little Plumstead
NR13 .72 E6
4 Norwich NR1 . . . . .163 C8
Thorpe End NR13 . . . . .73 D6
Woodbastwick NR13 . . . . .73 D7
Plumstead Rd E NR7 . . . . .163 D8
Plymouth Cl **3** NR30 . .168 C6
Plymouth Rd **2** IP31 . . .126 B1
Pocahontas Way PE31 . .133 E5
Pockthorpe Gate NR9 . .163 A7
Pockthorpe La IP24 . . . .102 A7
Pockthorpe Loke
Barnham Broom NR9 . . . . . . .69 D2
Hickling NR12 . . . . .39 F7
Pockthorpe Rd NR9 . . . . .88 A8
Podmore La NR19 . . . . . . .67 C8
Point Dr **2** PE37 . . . . . .153 C3
Police Rd PE14 . . . . .41 D4
Polka Rd NR23 . . . . .136 D5
Pollard Rd NR10 . . . . .53 E6
Pommer's La NR30 . . . . .170 D8
Pond Cl **1** NR9 . . . . .88 C7
Pond Hills Rd NR25 . . . . .19 E7
Pond La Brandon IP27 . . .175 A2
Knapton NR28 . . . . .143 B2
Surlingham NR14 . . . . .73 B1
Taverham NR8 . . . . .156 F8
Pond Rd
Antingham NR28 . . . . .22 B4
East Dereham NR19 . . . . . . .154 C2
3 Horsford NR10 . . . . .53 A3
Swafield NR28 . . . . .22 C3
Ponds End La IP22 . . . . .127 E4
Pooley St IP22 . . . . .128 F7
Poorhouse La NR14 . . . . . .89 A2
Pope's La PE34 . . . . .144 A4
Poplar Ave
Great Yarmouth NR31 . . . . .170 C3
Heacham NR12 . . . . .133 C5
King's Lynn PE34 . . . . .43 D4
5 Marham PE33 . . . . .63 B4
Norwich NR4 . . . . .161 E1
Poplar Cl
Downham Market PE38 . . . .172 B6
Honington IP31 . . . . .126 B1
12 Horsford NR10 . . . . .53 A3
Norwich NR7 . . . . .72 D4
Poplar Dr Filby NR29 . . . .75 F8
Happisburgh NR12 . . . . .23 F3
King's Lynn PE30 . . . . .148 D2
Poplar Gr NR26 . . . . .138 E5
Poplar Rd
Attleborough NR17 . . . . . . .174 B2
West Winch PE33 . . . . .43 F1
Poplar Way NR17 . . . . . .174 C2
Poplars The Hilgay PE38 . .96 F8
Spexhall IP19 . . . . .124 F1
Swanton Abbott NR10 . . . . .37 C4
Tacolneston NR16 . . . . .105 F4
Pople St NR18 . . . . .173 B4
Poppy Cl
Chedgrave NR14 . . . . .91 F2
North Walsham NR28 . . . . .151 E5
4 Thetford IP24 . . . . .176 F4
Poppy Dr **5** NR26 . . . . .138 B6
Poppyfields La NR10 . . . .53 A3
Poppy's La IP21 . . . . .121 F5
Poringland Prim Sch
NR14 . . . . .90 D5
Poringland Rd NR14 . . . . .90 B5
Porson Rd NR7 . . . . .159 C1
Port Rd NR15 . . . . .122 B8
Port Row NR9 . . . . .51 B4
Portal Ave IP25 . . . . .84 F3
Portal Cl
4 Barnham IP24 . . . . .125 F6
2 Feltwell IP26 . . . . .98 D1
Portalfield **10** NR12 . . . .39 B4
Porter Rd **8** NR15 . . . . .106 E3
Porter St PE38 . . . . .172 A5
Porter's La NR9 . . . . .51 E5
Porter's Loke
1 Belton NR31 . . . . .94 A6
Burgh Castle NR31 . . . . . . .93 F6
Norwich NR7 . . . . .159 A3
Porter's Rd
Beighton NR13 . . . . .74 E1
Freethorpe NR13 . . . . .92 E8
Portersfield Rd NR2 . . . .162 B5
Porthole Cl NR13 . . . . . . .111 F1
Portland Cl NR13 . . . . . . .169 C3
Portland Pl
Great Yarmouth NR30 . . . . .169 E3
King's Lynn PE30 . . . . .146 D2
3 Thetford IP24 . . . . .116 A1
Portland St
3 King's Lynn PE30 . . . . .146 E5
Norwich NR2 . . . . .162 B5
Portsmouth Rd **3** IP31 . .126 B1
Portway Pl **6** NR2 . . . . .162 C7
Post Mill PE30 . . . . .147 C5
Post Mill Cl NR7 . . . . .72 D4
Post Office Cl **8** NR23 . .74 A3
Post Office La
Corpusty NR11 . . . . .34 F8
Garvestone NR9 . . . . .86 B8
Weston Longville NR9 . . . . .51 E2
11 Wisbech PE13 . . . . . . .152 C5
Post Office Rd
Dersingham PE31 . . . . .140 D3
Frettenham NR12 . . . . .54 A4
Great & Little Plumstead
NR13 . . . . .73 B7
Lingwood NR13 . . . . .74 A3

Post Office Rd continued
Lingwood & Burlingham
NR13 . . . . .73 F3
Toft Monks NR34 . . . . .110 E5
Postmill Cl NR18 . . . . . . .173 C4
Postwick La NR13 . . . . . .165 A4
Postwick Sta NR7 . . . . . . .72 E3
Potash La
Bracon Ash NR16 . . . . .88 D2
Eye IP21 . . . . .130 B2
Potato Dro PE14 . . . . .60 B4
Potspoon Hole
Coltishall NR12 . . . . .54 D8
Tunstead NR12 . . . . .37 D1
Potter Heigham Rd
NR29 . . . . .56 D8
Pottergate NR2 . . . . .178 A3
Pottergate St NR15 . . . . .106 A2
Potters Cres NR15 . . . . . .121 C8
Potters Dr NR31 . . . . .171 D5
Potters Field NR31 . . . . . .170 B2
Potter's La
Rickinghall Superior
IP22 . . . . .128 F1
Wymondham NR18 . . . . . . .105 B6
Potters Vale IP22 . . . . . . .128 C3
Pottles Alley **4** NR9 . . . .86 C5
Pottle's La NR13 . . . . .92 F5
Poulter's Dro PE14 . . . . . .77 D1
Poultry Rd IP27 . . . . .113 A3
Pound Cl
4 Harleston IP20 . . . . . . .122 D2
Hevingham NR10 . . . . .53 C8
Pound Gn La IP25 . . . . . . .67 C2
Pound Hill IP25 . . . . .84 B5
Pound La
Aylsham NR11 . . . . .150 B6
Brundall NR13 . . . . .165 F5
Burgh St Margaret (Fleggburgh)
NR29 . . . . .75 C8
Ditchingham NR35 . . . . . . .108 E2
Docking PE31 . . . . .134 D5
Filby NR29 . . . . .75 F8
Great Yarmouth NR31 . . . . .170 C3
Heacham NR12 . . . . .133 D6
Litcham PE32 . . . . .48 C6
Loddon NR14 . . . . .109 C8
North Tuddenham NR20 . . . .50 D2
Norwich NR7 . . . . .72 D4
Runhall NR20 . . . . .69 A4
Sloley NR12 . . . . .37 F2
Toft Monks NR34 . . . . .110 D6
Pound Rd
East Ruston NR12 . . . . .38 F7
Hevingham NR10 . . . . .53 C8
Ludham NR29 . . . . .56 C5
North Walsham NR28 . . . . .151 D5
Powell Cl **5** NR19 . . . . . .154 C6
Power's Pl PE38 . . . . .79 D1
Poynt Cl NR18 . . . . .173 B5
Pratts Hill NR14 . . . . .73 A1
Press La NR3 . . . . .158 C1
Preston Ave NR18 . . . . . .173 A2
Preston Cl
Freethorpe NR13 . . . . .92 E7
Wroxham/Hoveton
NR12 . . . . .164 B2
Preston La NR14 . . . . .109 F8
Preston Rd NR28 . . . . . . .151 D5
Preston VC Prim Sch
NR15 . . . . .106 F7
Pretty Dr IP21 . . . . .130 D6
Pride Way NR13 . . . . .72 E5
Primrose Cl
Attleborough NR17 . . . . . . .174 B5
East Dereham NR19 . . . . . .154 B4
16 Mulbarton NR14 . . . . . .89 B3
Mundesley NR11 . . . . .143 B5
Thetford IP24 . . . . .176 F4
Trunch NR28 . . . . .22 E5
Primrose Cres **2** NR7 . . .72 D3
Primrose Ct **3** NR7 . . . . .72 D3
Primrose Dr NR27 . . . . . .175 A2
Primrose Hill NR20 . . . . . .50 B4
Primrose La
Crostwick NR12 . . . . .54 C3
Sheringham NR26 . . . . .138 B5
Swanton Morley NR20 . . . . .50 B4
Primrose Rd
Hingham NR9 . . . . .86 B5
Norwich NR1 . . . . .163 A6
Primrose Sq NR20 . . . . . . .50 B4
Primrose Way
1 Great Yarmouth NR31 . . .94 C6
10 Horsford NR10 . . . . . . .53 A3
Primrose Wlk NR28 . . . . .151 E4
Primula Dr NR4 . . . . .161 D5
Prince Andrew Dr
PE31 . . . . .140 D3
Prince Andrew's Cl
1 Aldborough NR11 . . . . . .21 A5
Norwich NR6 . . . . .158 B5
Prince Andrew's Rd
NR6 . . . . .158 B5
Prince Charles Cl
PE31 . . . . .140 D3
Prince Edward Cl NR7 . .163 F7
Prince Henry Pl PE38 . . .172 D4
Prince of Wales Cl
PE13 . . . . .152 D8
Prince of Wales Rd
Caister-on-Sea NR30 . . . . .168 C6
Cromer NR27 . . . . .139 B7
Norwich NR1 . . . . .178 B3
Upton with Fishley NR13 . .166 B8
Prince Regent Way
IP22 . . . . .177 F3

Prince Rupert Way
NR13 . . . . .72 D5
Prince St PE13 . . . . .152 D5
Prince William Cl
PE36 . . . . .132 C3
Princes Cl IP27 . . . . .175 A2
Prince's Rd
Bungay NR35 . . . . .124 A7
Great Yarmouth NR30 . . . . .169 D4
Princes Rd IP13 . . . . .152 C4
Prince's St PE12 . . . . .41 B8
Princes St
North Walsham NR28 . . . . .151 A5
Norwich NR1 . . . . .178 B3
Swaffham PE37 . . . . .153 B4
Princes Way PE30 . . . . . .146 F5
Princess Beatrice Cl
PE36 . . . . .157 D2
Princess Cl **7** IP25 . . . . . .84 D3
Princess Ct **3** NR35 . . . .137 C5
Princess Dr PE36 . . . . . . .137 C5
Princess Way NR35 . . . . .123 F8
Princess's Dr
Dersingham PE35 . . . . .140 C1
Sandringham PE35 . . . . .27 D7
Pringle Way **5** PE37 . . . .98 F5
Prins Ave PE13 . . . . .152 D7
Prins Ct **3** PE13 . . . . . . .152 D7
Printing Mus* NR34 . . . .110 D1
Prior Bank Orch **3**
NR27 . . . . .139 C6
Prior Cl **5** NR15 . . . . . . .106 F6
Prior Rd NR7 . . . . .72 D5
Prior's Dr NR6 . . . . .158 E6
Priorswood NR8 . . . . .155 E3
Priory Chase
Downham Market PE38 . . . .172 B5
Wormegay PE33 . . . . .61 F8
Priory Cl Acle NR13 . . . . .166 C3
Alpington NR14 . . . . .90 F5
Caister-on-Sea NR30 . . . . .168 E4
2 Fritton & St Olaves
NR31 . . . . .93 D2
7 Hethersett NR9 . . . . .88 D7
Palgrave IP22 . . . . .177 D1
Sheringham NR26 . . . . .138 F5
Sporle with Palgrave
PE32 . . . . .65 D6
Priory Cres NR21 . . . . .6 E2
Priory Dro IP25 . . . . .83 D4
Priory Gdns
8 Fritton & St Olaves
NR31 . . . . .93 D2
12 Great Yarmouth NR30 . .168 D4
5 King's Lynn PE30 . . . . .146 D4
King's Lynn PE30 . . . . .148 C5
Shotesham NR15 . . . . .90 A2
Priory Maze & Gdns*
NR26 . . . . .138 F6
Priory Pk IP24 . . . . .176 C5
Priory Pl PE32 . . . . .46 C2
Priory Plain **18** NR30 . . .169 C4
Priory Rd Bacton NR12 . . .23 E4
Castle Acre PE32 . . . . .46 F1
Downham Market PE38 . . . .172 B5
Fritton & St Olaves NR31 . . .93 D2
Great Cressingham IP25 . . .83 D5
Hethersett NR9 . . . . .88 D7
King's Lynn PE30 . . . . .148 C5
Palgrave IP22 . . . . .177 C1
Watton IP25 . . . . .84 E3
Woodbastwick NR13 . . . . . .55 F1
Priory Row **11** NR30 . . . .169 C4
Priory St NR31 . . . . .170 D6
Priory Terr PE38 . . . . .172 B5
Priscilla Cl NR5 . . . . .161 D5
Pristow Gn La NR16 . . . .120 E7
Private Rd
Earsham NR35 . . . . .123 D8
Ormesby St Margaret
NR29 . . . . .167 A3
Procession La PE32 . . . . .153 F8
Proctor Ave **3** NR14 . . . .92 A2
Proctor Cl **4** NR14 . . . . .92 A2
Proctor Rd
Chedgrave NR14 . . . . .91 F2
8 Loddon NR14 . . . . .92 A2
Norwich NR6 . . . . .158 F6
Proctors Cl PE30 . . . . . . .146 D2
Progress Way IP23 . . . . . .130 B1
Prom The NR29 . . . . .167 E4
Promenade
Overstrand NR27 . . . . .11 A4
Sheringham NR26 . . . . .138 D7
Prophets Alley PE34 . . . . .61 C8
Prospect Pl PE13 . . . . . . .152 C3
Provan Cres **6** NR31 . . . .94 A5
Provence Pl **2** PE13 . . . .152 E3
Providence NR31 . . . . .94 A6
Providence St **5** PE30 . . .146 E4
Provost Rd PE20 . . . . .98 D1
**Pudding Norton Medieval
Village of*** PE31 . . . . .4 A3
Puddingmoor NR34 . . . . .110 C1
Pug St IP21 . . . . .121 B2
Pulham CE Prim Sch
IP21 . . . . .121 E5
Pulham Rd IP21 . . . . .121 D2
Pullover Rd PE34 . . . . . . .144 A7
Pump La NR30 . . . . .168 D3
Punsfer Way PE34 . . . . . . .60 C8
Purdance Cl NR5 . . . . . . .160 D8
Purdy St NR25 . . . . .8 E4
Purdy Way NR11 . . . . . . .150 B6
Purfleet PE30 . . . . .146 D5
Purfleet Pl **9** PE30 . . . . .146 D5

Purfleet St **8** PE30 . . . . .146 D5
Purland Rd NR7 . . . . .159 D2
Purley Ct NR31 . . . . .170 A4
Pursehouse Way IP22 . . .177 E4
Purtingay Cl **3** NR4 . . . .162 A1
Putney Cl IP27 . . . . .175 A1
Pye La Cranworth IP25 . . .86 A6
Deopham NR18 . . . . .86 E2
Pyebush La NR13 . . . . . . .166 B5
Pyecroft Rd PE14 . . . . . . .41 E3
Pyehurn La NR10 . . . . . . .53 A3
Pyehurn Mews NR8 . . . . .155 E3
Pyes Cl **1** NR25 . . . . .7 C6
Pye's La Castle Acre PE32 . .46 F2
Swanton Morley NR20 . . . . .50 C3
Pyes Mill Rd NR14 . . . . . .92 A1
Pyghtle The **4** NR16 . . . .118 C5
Pyke Cl NR30 . . . . .168 D7
Pyrl Cl NR13 . . . . .72 E5
Pymar's La **8** NR15 . . . . .107 B5
Pyrford Dr NR4 . . . . .161 F1

Q

Quaker La
Fakenham NR21 . . . . .141 B4
Norwich NR6 . . . . .53 E1
8 Spixworth NR12 . . . . . . .54 A1
Tasburgh NR15 . . . . .106 F6
Wisbech PE13 . . . . .152 E3
Quarry La NR9 . . . . .51 A5
Quay La NR25 . . . . .7 A7
Quay Mill Wlk **3** NR30 . .169 C4
Quay Rd NR31 . . . . .170 D4
Quay Side NR3 . . . . .178 B4
Quay The Blakeney NR25 . . .7 C6
Wells-next-the-Sea
NR23 . . . . .136 D6
Wiveton NR25 . . . . .7 E7
Quebec Cl **13** NR4 . . . . . . .89 B8
Quebec Rd
Dereham NR19 . . . . .154 D7
Norwich NR1 . . . . .163 A6
Quebec St NR19 . . . . .154 D5
Queen Anne's Rd
NR31 . . . . .170 C8
Queen Elizabeth Ave
PE30 . . . . .147 B7
Queen Elizabeth Dr
Dersingham PE31 . . . . .140 D3
Wisbech PE13 . . . . .152 D3
Queen Elizabeth Hospl
PE30 . . . . .147 E5
Queen Elizabeth Way
Bawsey PE30 . . . . .147 F6
Castle Rising PE30 . . . . .27 C1
4 Mundham NR18 . . . . . . .105 A8
Wymondham NR18 . . . . . . .173 C3
Queens Ave PE30 . . . . . . .146 D2
Queens Cl
8 Blakeney NR25 . . . . .7 C6
Norwich NR4 . . . . .162 A3
Queen's Cl PE33 . . . . .80 E4
Queen's Cres
Bircham PE31 . . . . .14 A3
Great Yarmouth NR31 . . . . .170 B3
Queen's Ct NR17 . . . . . . .174 D6
Queens Ct **1** NR15 . . . . .106 E3
Queens Dr PE30 . . . . .132 C6
Queen's Dr PE14 . . . . .77 A7
Queens Gdns PE36 . . . . . .132 D6
Queen's Pl **2** PE34 . . . . . .43 B1
Queens Rd
Brandon IP27 . . . . .175 D2
Cromer NR27 . . . . .139 D4
Norwich NR1 . . . . .178 A1
Wisbech PE13 . . . . .152 C4
Queen's Rd
Attleborough NR17 . . . . . . .174 C6
Clenchwarton PE34 . . . . . . .146 A5
Fakenham NR21 . . . . .141 C4
Great Yarmouth NR30 . . . . .169 D2
Hethersett NR9 . . . . .88 D8
Holt NR25 . . . . .137 C5
Queens Sch The PE13 . . .152 D3
Queen's Sq NR17 . . . . . . .174 D5
Queensway
Caister-on-Sea NR30 . . . . .168 E4
2 Earsham NR35 . . . . . . .123 F8
King's Lynn PE30 . . . . .147 C6
North Walsham NR28 . . . . .151 A5
Roydon IP22 . . . . .177 A4
Thetford IP24 . . . . .176 C2
Watton IP25 . . . . .84 D3
Wymondham NR18 . . . . . . .173 B5
Queensway Inf Sch
IP24 . . . . .176 C2
Queensway Mid Sch
IP24 . . . . .176 C2
Quidenham Rd
Harling NR16 . . . . .118 D5
Kenninghall NR16 . . . . .119 A5
Quidenham NR16 . . . . .118 F8

R

Rabbit La
Downham Market PE38 . . . .172 D6
Great Witchingham NR9 . . . .51 E6
Raby Ave PE30 . . . . .147 B6
Racecourse Rd NR7 . . . . .159 E1
Raceys Cl **4** PE14 . . . . . . .59 D2
Rachel Cl **7** NR5 . . . . . . .161 C5
Rackham Cl NR3 . . . . .162 D2
Rackham Rd NR3 . . . . . . .158 D2
Rackheath La NR13 . . . . . .54 B2
Rackheath Prim Sch
NR13 . . . . .54 D1
Radcliffe Rd NR8 . . . . . . .155 E2
RAF Air Defence Radar Mus*
NR13 . . . . .72 C8
Rafeman Cl NR5 . . . . .160 E7
Raglan St NR2 . . . . .162 C6
Ragmere Rd NR17 . . . . . .104 D1
Railway App **2** NR26 . . . .138 D7
Railway Hill IP20 . . . . . . .122 C2
Railway La PE31 . . . . .4 B7
Railway Rd
Downham Market PE38 . . . .172 A5
King's Lynn PE30 . . . . .146 E5
Wisbech PE13 . . . . .152 C3
Rainey Ct **13** IP20 . . . . . .122 D2
Rainsborough Rise
NR13 . . . . .72 D5
Rainsthorpe PE30 . . . . . . .147 D8
Rainthorpe Hall & Gdns*
NR15 . . . . .106 F8
Rainthorpe Hall*
NR15 . . . . .106 F8
Raleigh Ave NR30 . . . . . .169 D7
Raleigh Rd PE30 . . . . .147 B4
Raleigh Way NR14 . . . . . .90 B6
Ram La NR15 . . . . .121 C4
Ramblers The NR14 . . . . .90 B6
Rambouillet Cl NR31 . . . .170 A4
Ramms Ct NR23 . . . . .136 D6
Ramm's La PE37 . . . . .66 A4
Ramnoth Cty Jun Sch
PE13 . . . . .152 D4
Ramnoth Rd PE13 . . . . . .152 D4
Rampant Horse St
NR2 . . . . .178 A2
Rampart Rd NR30 . . . . . .169 C5
Rampart Way IP24 . . . . . .176 D3
Ramsay Gdns PE36 . . . . .132 D3
Ramsey Cl
Norwich NR4 . . . . .161 E3
Thetford IP24 . . . . .176 E6
Randall Cl **8** NR31 . . . . . .171 D5
Randell Cl NR18 . . . . .151 D4
Randle Gn NR5 . . . . .161 C8
Randolf Rd NR1 . . . . .162 E2
Rands Rd PE14 . . . . .59 C4
Rangoon Cl NR7 . . . . .159 C4
Ransome Ave IP21 . . . . . .130 D6
Ransome's Cl PE14 . . . . . .77 E5
Ranson Rd NR1 . . . . .163 B5
Ranworth Cl
Norwich NR4 . . . . .94 A6
Swaffham PE37 . . . . .153 B1
Ranworth Dr NR29 . . . . . .167 B2
Ranworth Fst Sch
NR5 . . . . .161 E7
Ranworth Rd
Blofield NR13 . . . . .165 F8
Norwich NR5 . . . . .161 D7
South Walsham NR13 . . . . .74 A8
Rash's Cres IP22 . . . . .129 C6
Rash's Gn NR19 . . . . .154 F2
Ratcliffe Rd NR21 . . . . . . .141 C4
Rattle Row
Mileham PE32 . . . . .48 C6
Wymondham NR18 . . . . . . .173 B4
Rattlerow Hill IP21 . . . . . .131 F2
Rattler's Rd IP27 . . . . . . .175 C3
Raven Cl NR31 . . . . .170 A7
Raveningham Gdns*
NR14 . . . . .110 A7
Raveningham Rd
Haddiscoe NR14 . . . . .110 C4
Stockton NR34 . . . . .110 A5
Raven's La PE31 . . . . .29 C5
Ravensway PE38 . . . . .172 C3
Ravine Rd NR31 . . . . .93 E1
Rawhall La NR20 . . . . .49 B5
Rawley Rd NR5 . . . . .161 B8
Rawlings Way **2** IP26 . . .98 E1
Rawlinsons La NR11 . . . .150 C7
Ray Bond Way NR11 . . . .150 C4
Raymond Cl NR6 . . . . . . .157 E7
Raymond Rd NR6 . . . . . . .157 F7
Raymond St
Thetford IP24 . . . . .176 D3
14 Wisbech PE13 . . . . . . .152 C4
Rayner's Cl **6** NR20 . . . . .68 C6
Rayner's La NR35 . . . . . . .109 D6
Rayner's Way NR20 . . . . . .68 E6
Raynham Cl PE30 . . . . . . .147 B4
Raynham Rd
Dunton NR21 . . . . .31 C6
Hempton NR21 . . . . .141 A3
Whissonsett NR20 . . . . .31 C2
Raynham St NR2 . . . . . . .162 B7
Rayns Cl NR5 . . . . .158 F5
Read's Cross NR14 . . . . . .109 E8
Readscross La NR14 . . . . .108 D8
Recorder Rd NR1 . . . . . . .178 C3
Recreation Dr PE38 . . . . . .97 A5
Recreation Gd Rd
NR7 . . . . .159 A4

Recreation Rd
East Dereham NR19 . . . . . . .154 C1
Great Yarmouth NR31 . . . . . .170 C5
Hethersett NR9 . . . . .88 C7
North Walsham NR28 . . . . .151 B4
Norwich NR2 . . . . .162 A5
Stalham NR12 . . . . .39 A4

Rectory Cl
Caister-on-Sea NR30 . . . . . .168 E5
Coltishall NR12 . . . . .54 D7
21 Long Stratton NR15 . . . .106 E3
2 Newton Flotman NR15 . . .89 D1
Rollesby NR29 . . . . .57 C2
Roydon PE32 . . . . .27 F2
Rectory Ct NR3 . . . . .158 D2
Rectory Dr PE34 . . . . .145 E5
Rectory Gdns NR9 . . . . . . .86 B5
Rectory Hill PE22 . . . . . . .128 D2
Rectory La
Bracon Ash NR14 . . . . .88 C3
Bunwell NR16 . . . . .105 C4
Great Ellingham NR17 . . . . .103 E8
Haddiscoe NR14 . . . . .110 F7
Hedenham NR35 . . . . .108 D4
Little Melton NR9 . . . . .160 A3
Loddon NR14 . . . . .92 A2
Mattingham NR35 . . . . .124 D8
Mulbarton NR14 . . . . .89 B3
North Runcton PE33 . . . . . . .44 A3
Poringland NR14 . . . . .90 D5
Scole IP21 . . . . .121 C1
Stuston IP21 . . . . .130 B4
Watlington PE33 . . . . .61 D5
Weeting IP27 . . . . .175 B7
West Winch PE33 . . . . .43 F3
Rectory Mdw
Diss NR29 . . . . .177 E4
Litcham PE32 . . . . .48 A4
Rectory Rd
Aldeby, Wheatacre,
Burgh St Peter NR34 . . . . . .111 A4
Bacton NR28 . . . . .23 C3
Brome & Oakley IP23 . . . . .130 B3
Broome NR35 . . . . .109 B3
Burston & Shimpling
IP22 . . . . .120 E2
2 Coltishall NR12 . . . . . . .54 C6
Coltishall NR12 . . . . .54 D7
Dickleburgh IP21 . . . . .121 B1
East Carleton NR14 . . . . . . .89 A4
Edgefield NR24 . . . . .19 D5
Elsing NR20 . . . . .50 F4
Gillingham NR34 . . . . .110 B3
Gissing IP22 . . . . .120 F4
Haddiscoe NR14 . . . . .110 F7
Hockering NR20 . . . . .69 B8
Hoveton NR12 . . . . .55 A7
Lyng NR9 . . . . .51 B4
Northrepps NR27 . . . . .11 A1
Outwell PE14 . . . . .77 F6
Rocklands NR17 . . . . .103 B7
Shelfanger IP22 . . . . .120 B2
Sutton NR12 . . . . .39 C3
Swanton Morley NR20 . . . . .50 B4
Tivetshall St Mary NR15 . . .121 C4
Topcroft NR35 . . . . .107 F4
Weston Longville NR9 . . . . .51 D2
Whissonsett NR20 . . . . .31 E2
Wood Norton NR20 . . . . .33 A7
Wortham IP22 . . . . .129 D6
Red Admiral Cl **1** NR18 .173 E4
Red Barn La NR11 . . . . .9 D1
Red Bridge La NR5 . . . . . .157 C2
Red Cottage Cl NR3 . . . . .158 A2
Red Lion Cl
Holme Hale IP25 . . . . .66 B2
Hoxne IP21 . . . . .131 A3
Red Lion St
3 Aylsham NR11 . . . . . . .150 C7
Norwich NR1 . . . . .178 B2
Red Lion Yd NR23 . . . . . . .136 D6
Redcastle Furze Prim Sch
IP24 . . . . .176 B3
Redcastle Rd IP24 . . . . . . .176 A4
Redcliffe Way NR13 . . . . .165 B4
Redell Cl **3** NR13 . . . . . . .55 A1
Redenhall Rd IP20 . . . . . .122 D2
Redfern Cl
East Dereham NR19 . . . . . .154 B4
King's Lynn PE30 . . . . .147 E8
Redfern Rd NR1 . . . . .159 D1
Redgate IP24 . . . . .176 E4
Redgate Hill PE36 . . . . . .132 D2
Redgate Rd PE13 . . . . .41 A4
Redgrave Rd
South Lopham IP22 . . . . . . .128 E7
Wortham IP22 . . . . .129 A5
Redman Rd NR28 . . . . . . .151 D3
Redmere Cl **4** NR12 . . . . .54 A4
Redmere Dro CB7 . . . . . . .112 D5
Redwell St NR2 . . . . .178 B3
Redwing Dr
1 Great Yarmouth NR31 . . .94 C7
5 Wisbech PE14 . . . . .152 D2
Redwing Gdns **7** NR10 . .54 A1
Redwings Visitor Ctr*
NR13 . . . . .93 F4
Reed La NR10 . . . . .48 F3
Reeder Cl NR19 . . . . .154 C5
Reeder's La NR14 . . . . .90 C6
Reedham Prim Sch
NR13 . . . . .93 A4
Reedham Rd
Acle NR13 . . . . .166 B1
Beighton NR13 . . . . .74 E1
Cantley NR13 . . . . .92 D6
Reedham Sta NR13 . . . . . . .92 F5

Reepham High Sch
NR10 . . . . .149 B3
Reepham Prim Sch
NR10 . . . . .149 B4
Reepham Rd
Bawdeswell NR20 . . . . .50 F8
Bricton NR20 . . . . .147 F7
Felthorpe NR10 . . . . .155 D5
Foulsham NR20 . . . . .33 D3
Guestwick NR20 . . . . .34 A1
Horsford NR10 . . . . .157 D7
Swannington NR9 . . . . .52 B5
Thurning NR20 . . . . .34 B8
Wood Dalling NR11 . . . . . . .34 D5
Reeve Cl Cromer NR27 . . .139 D4
Scole IP21 . . . . .130 D6
Reeves Ave PE30 . . . . . . .147 B8
Reeves La IP26 . . . . .114 A7
Reffley La PE30 . . . . .147 D8
Reffley Prim Sch
PE30 . . . . .147 D8
Reg Houchen Rd
PE31 . . . . .140 C3
Regal Cl IP25 . . . . .84 D3
Regal Rd PE13 . . . . .152 B2
Regency Ave PE30 . . . . . .147 C5
Regent Rvrl NR30 . . . . . . .169 D4
Regent Cl NR19 . . . . .154 D1
Regent Pl **1** PE30 . . . . . .146 E4
Regent Rd
Downham Market PE38 . . . .172 A4
8 Great Yarmouth NR30 . .169 D4
Regent St
1 Great Yarmouth NR30 . .169 C3
Wickmere NR11 . . . . .20 E4
Regent Way **6** NR20 . . . .146 D4
Regents Cl NR25 . . . . .137 B5
Regents Ct NR28 . . . . .151 B5
Regents Pk PE30 . . . . .147 C5
Regina Rd NR1 . . . . .178 A1
Regis Ave **4** NR2/ 9 F5
Regis Pl NR26 . . . . .138 D2
Reid Way PE30 . . . . .147 A8
Renowood Cl PE32 . . . . . . .48 B8
Renson Cl NR3 . . . . .158 C4
Renwick P k E NR27 . . . . .10 A4
Renwick By W NR27 . . . . .10 A4
Repps Rd
Ashby with Oby NR29 . . . . .56 F2
Ashby with Oby NR29 . . . . .57 B3
1 Martham NR29 . . . . .57 D4
Thurne NR29 . . . . .56 E3
Repton Ave NR6 . . . . .158 D2
Repton La PE31 . . . . .150 D5
Reve Cres **5** NR13 . . . . . .73 C6
Revell Rd PE38 . . . . .172 B4
Reydon Cl **10** NR5 . . . . . .161 A7
Reymerston Rd NR9 . . . . . .68 B2
Reynolds Ave NR3 . . . . . .168 C8
Reynolds La NR29 . . . . . . .56 E7
Reynolds Way PE31 . . . . .140 C3
Rhond The NR12 . . . . .164 C5
Rhone Pl **8** PE13 . . . . . . .152 E3
Rhoon Rd PE34 . . . . .144 E8
Rice Way NR7 . . . . .159 C2
Richard Haggard Cl **3**
IP25 .67 C2
Richard Hicks Dr **9**
NR19 . . . . .154 C4
Richard Young Cl **2**
PE13 . . . . .152 C8
Rickards Rd NR21 . . . . .15 C2
Richardson Cres NR9 . . . . .88 C8
Richenda Cl **2** NR5 . . . . .161 C5
Riches Cl NR15 . . . . .106 F6
Richmond Cl
Honingham NR9 . . . . .69 C6
Lyng NR9 . . . . .51 A5
Richmond Ct PE13 . . . . . .152 A4
Richmond Pk NR21 . . . . . .106 B8
Richmond Pk Golf Course
IP25 .84 D4
Richmond Pl NR9 . . . . .51 A4
Richmond Rd
Brandon IP27 . . . . .175 A1
Downham Market PE38 . . . .172 B4
4 Long Stratton NR15 . . . .106 E3
Norwich NR5 . . . . .156 E1
Saham Toney IP25 . . . . .84 C4
Richmond Rise NR10 . . . .149 C5
Rickinghall Dr PE22 . . . . .128 C3
Riddlesworth Hall Sch
IP22 . . . . .127 C8
Rider Haggard Rd
NR7 . . . . .159 D1
Ridgeway
Caister-on-Sea NR30 . . . . . .168 D8
Cromer NR27 . . . . .139 C4
Ridgeway The NR1 . . . . . .163 B8
Ridings The
5 Cringleford NR4 . . . . . . .89 B8
Fakenham NR21 . . . . .141 E4
2 Poringland NR14 . . . . . . .90 C5
Ridland's Rd
Briston NR24 . . . . .142 D2
Melton Constable NR24 . . .142 C1
Rigby Cl **1** NR14 . . . . . . .90 D5
Rigg Cl 2 PE13 . . . . .152 B3
Rightup Dro IP27 . . . . .113 C5
Rightup La NR18 . . . . .173 D2
Riley Cl NR7 . . . . .159 D1
Rill Cl PE30 . . . . .148 C2
Ring Rd NR7 . . . . .163 F7
Ringbank La NR11 . . . . .21 A6
Ringers Cl **4** NR18 . . . . . .173 D5
Ringers La NR9 . . . . .86 C5
Ringland La
Costessey NR8 . . . . .156 B6

Ringland La continued
Morton on the Hill NR9 . . . . .52 A2
Weston Longville NR9 . . . . . .51 F3
Ringland Rd NR8 . . . . .155 A1
Ringmer Dr 2 IP25 . . . . . . .84 C3
Ringmere Rd 2 IP25 . . . . . .84 C3
Ringmore Rd PE38 . . . . . . .97 B4
Ringsfield Rd NR34 . . . . . .124 F5
**Ringstead Downs Nature
Reserve*** PE36 . . . . .1 F2
Ringstead Rd
Burnham Market PE31 . . . .135 A2
Docking PE31 . . . . .134 A6
Heacham PE31 . . . . .133 E6
Ringstead PE36 . . . . .2 A2
Sedgeford PE36 . . . . .13 B8
Thornham PE36 . . . . .2 D6
Ringwood Cl NR9 . . . . . . .160 B2
Ripley Cl NR2 . . . . .161 F5
Ripon Way IP24 . . . . .176 B5
Rippingall Cl 6 NR27 . . . .150 D6
Rippingall Rd NR11 . . . . .150 D6
Rise The 10 Loddon NR14 . .92 A2
Sheringham NR26 . . . . .138 E6
Riseway Cl NR1 . . . . .163 B8
Rising Way 8 NR30 . . . . . .57 C4
Risley Ct NR16 . . . . .117 E5
River Cl PE32 . . . . .63 E8
River Ct NR21 . . . . .141 A3
River Dro PE33 . . . . .80 F2
River La Cranworth IP25 . . .85 F7
King's Lynn PE30 . . . . .147 A6
River Rd West Acre PE32 . . .46 B1
West Walton PE14 . . . . .59 A8
River Terr NR1 . . . . .152 A8
River Way NR11 . . . . .93 F6
River Wlk
Great Yarmouth NR30 . . . . .169 C8
King's Lynn PE30 . . . . .146 C6
Riverdale Cl NR13 . . . . . . .165 D3
Riverdene Mews NR8 . . . .155 E3
Rivermead NR12 . . . . .39 B3
Riverside
Cockley Cley PE37 . . . . .02 D7
Diss IP22 . . . . .177 B3
King's Lynn PE30 . . . . .147 B7
Norwich NR1 . . . . .178 C2
Reedham NR13 . . . . .92 F4
Riverside Cl NR6 . . . . .157 D2
Riverside Dyke NR12 . . . . .45 C6
Riverside Ind Ctr
NR31 . . . . .170 D5
Riverside Ind Est
PE30 . . . . .146 D7
Riverside Maltings
IP22 . . . . .177 F3
Riverside Rd
Great Yarmouth NR31 . . . . .170 D6
Holt NR25 . . . . .8 A1
Norwich NR1 . . . . .178 C3
Wroxham/Hoveton
NR12 . . . . .164 C4
Riverside Swimming Ctr
NR1 . . . . .178 C1
Riverside Way
Brandon IP27 . . . . .175 C5
1 Wisbech PE13 . . . . .152 B3
Riverside Wlk IP24 . . . . . .176 C4
Riverview Rd NR9 . . . . . . .146 E7
Riverview Dr NR13 . . . . . . .166 B8
RNLI Henry Bloggs Mus*
NR27 . . . . .139 D7
Robberds Way NR5 . . . . . .160 FR
Robert Andrew Cl
NR18 . . . . .87 B2
Robert Balding Rd
PE31 . . . . .140 C3
Robert Cl Trunch NR28 . . . .22 E5
7 Wymondham NR18 . . . .173 C6
Robert Gybson Way
NR2 . . . . .178 A3
Robert Herb Way 3
NR18 . . . . .173 E4
Robert Kett Jun Sch
NR18 . . . . .173 C5
Robert Key Dr 2 NR20 . . .68 E6
Robert St PE30 . . . . .146 E3
Roberts Cl 3 NR15 . . . . . .107 C5
Robertson Cl NR26 . . . . . .138 E6
Robin Cl
Great Yarmouth NR31 . . . . .170 A5
Mulbarton NR14 . . . . .89 A3
Robin Hill NR31 . . . . .133 D8
Robin Hood Rd
7 Norwich NR4 . . . . .89 E8
Norwich NR4 . . . . .162 C1
Robin Kerkham Way
PE34 . . . . .145 E6
Robin Mews 4 PE14 . . . . .152 D2
Robin Wlk IP27 . . . . .175 F3
Robin's La NR10 . . . . .149 B4
Robinson Rd IP21 . . . . . . .130 C5
Robson Rd NR5 . . . . .161 B6
Robyns Rd
3 Sheringham NR26 . . . . . .9 F5
Sheringham NR26 . . . . .138 F5
Rochester La NR18 . . . . . .173 C6
Rochford Rd 4 NR29 . . . . .57 C4
Rochford Wlk 5 PE13 . . . .152 E5
Rockall Way 6 NR30 . . . .168 C6
Rockingham Rd NR5 . . . . .161 C6
Rockland Cres PE37 . . . . .153 B2
Rockland Dr NR7 . . . . .163 C6
Rockland La NR14 . . . . .85 F1
Rockland Rd NR14 . . . . .90 F7
Rockland St Mary Prim Sch
NR14 . . . . .91 B6

Rocklands Prim Sch
NR17 . . . . .103 B7
Rocklands Rd NR17 . . . . . .103 B4
Rode La NR16 . . . . .105 B3
Rodham Rd PE33 . . . . .77 A1
Rodinghead 8 PE30 . . . . .147 D5
Rodney Rd NR30 . . . . .169 D3
Rodwell Cnr NR17 . . . . .35 C1
Roedich Dr NR8 . . . . .155 C3
Roger Ride 3 NR19 . . . . . .154 D2
Roger's Cl NR3 . . . . .171 D5
Rogers Cl 4 NR5 . . . . .161 B7
Roger's La NR15 . . . . .89 F1
Roland Dr NR15 . . . . .107 D5
Rolfe Cres PE31 . . . . .133 E5
Rollesby Jun Sch NR29 . . .57 D3
Rollesby Gdns 9 NR29 . . .57 D2
Rollesby Pl NR10 . . . . .37 B2
Rollesby Rd
Fleggburgh NR29 . . . . .57 C1
King's Lynn PE30 . . . . .147 A3
Martham NR29 . . . . .57 D4
Swaffham PE37 . . . . .153 B2
Rolleston Cl NR5 . . . . .161 B7
Rollingpin La NR19 . . . . . .154 D4
Roman Cres PE37 . . . . . . .153 D2
Roman Rd NR29 . . . . .133 B3
Roman Pl 8 NR30 . . . . . . .169 D4
Roman Way
Brancaster PE31 . . . . .3 C3
Caister-on-Sea NR30 . . . . . .168 C5
Thetford IP24 . . . . .176 C2
Romany Cl 8 NR29 . . . . . . .57 D2
Romany Rd NR3 . . . . .158 B2
Romany Wlk 6 NR14 . . . . .90 C5
Romer Dro PE33 . . . . .81 B3
Rook Dr NR8 . . . . .155 E3
Rookery Cl PE34 . . . . .145 C5
Rookery Farm Rd NR28 . . .23 F2
Rookery Hill NR14 . . . . . . .91 B7
Rookery La NR35 . . . . .108 C1
Rookery Pk Golf Club
NR33 . . . . .111 F1
Rookery Rd PE14 . . . . .145 E4
Rookery The IP27 . . . . . . .114 D5
Room La NR15 . . . . .122 D8
Ropemakers Row 6
NR3 . . . . .158 C1
Ropes Hill NR12 . . . . .55 D4
Ropes Hill Dyke NR12 . . . .55 D4
Ropes Wlk NR13 . . . . .165 F6
Rosa Cl NR14 . . . . .54 B1
Rosa Vella Dr 3 NR20 . . . .68 A8
Rosalie Cl NR6 . . . . .158 B4
Rosary Cl 9 NR14 . . . . . . .89 F3
Rosary Rd NR1 . . . . .163 A6
Rose Ave IP22 . . . . .129 D7
Rose Cottage's NR19 . . . . .66 D8
Rose Dr NR20 . . . . .68 A8
Rose La Botesdale IP22 . . .128 E3
Diss IP22 . . . . .177 F3
8 Elm PE13 . . . . .59 A1
Norwich NR1 . . . . .178 C3
Palgrave IP22 . . . . .177 D3
Rose La Cl IP22 . . . . .177 D2
Rose Valley NR4 . . . . .162 B5
Rose Wlk
Sculthorpe Airfield NR21 . . .15 C2
4 Wisbech PE13 . . . . .152 A8
Rose Yd NR3 . . . . .178 A4
Roseacre Cl NR2 . . . . .162 C2
Roseacre Est NR25 . . . . . . .9 A2
Rosebay Cl NR6 . . . . .158 D5
Roseberry Rd PE14 . . . . . . .59 B1
Rosebery Ave
King's Lynn PE30 . . . . .147 B6
7 Poringland NR14 . . . . . .90 D5
Rosebery Rd
Cromer NR27 . . . . .139 C5
Great & Little Plumstead
NR13 . . . . .73 A4
Norwich NR3 . . . . .158 D1
3 Sheringham NR27 . . . . .10 A5
Norwich NR3 . . . . .158 C1
Roscroft Way IP24 . . . . . . .176 C4
Roscroft Way IP24 . . . . . . .176 F2
Rosedale Cres NR1 . . . . . .163 A6
Rosedale Gdns NR31 . . . . .94 A5
Rosefields NR13 . . . . .165 C4
Rosemary La
1 Gayton PE32 . . . . .45 C6
2 New Buckenham NR16 . .104 F1
Norwich NR3 . . . . .178 B4
**Rosemary Musker Cty High
Sch** IP24 . . . . .176 F7
Rosemary Rd
Blofield NR13 . . . . .73 C6
Norwich NR7 . . . . .159 B4
Rosemary Terr NR21 . . . . .141 B5
Rosemary Way PE38 . . . . .172 D6
Rosery The NR14 . . . . .89 C3
Rosetta Rd NR10 . . . . .54 A2
Roseville Cl 8 NR1 . . . . . .163 B5
Rosewood NR28 . . . . .151 E5
Roslyn Rd NR11 . . . . .170 C5
Rosslare 1 NR4 . . . . .162 A1
Rossons Rd NR8 . . . . .155 C1
Rostwold Way NR21 . . . . .176 F2
Rosyth Rd 4 PE31 . . . . . . .126 B1
Rothbury Cl NR18 . . . . . . .173 B4
Rothbury Rd NR18 . . . . . .173 C4
Rotherstone La PE29 . . . . .179 E4
Roudham Junc NR16 . . . . .117 A6
Roudham Rd NR16 . . . . . .117 F6
Rouen Rd NR1 . . . . .178 B2
Rougham Cnr IP26 . . . . . . .99 F3
Rougham End PE32 . . . . . .47 C8
Rougham Hall PE32 . . . . . .47 A7

Rougham Rd PE32 . . . . . . .29 E1
Roughlands IP27 . . . . .113 E1
Rought Ave IP27 . . . . .175 D2
Roughton Rd
Roughton NR27 . . . . .139 B2
Thorpe Market NR11 . . . . . .21 F7
Roughton Rd Sta
NR27 . . . . .139 B4
Round Well Rd NR5 . . . . . .156 D1
Roundabout La NR14 . . . . .109 B8
**Roundham Medieval Village
of*** NR16 . . . . .117 E6
Roundhead Ct 8 NR7 . . . . .72 D4
Roundtree Cl NR7 . . . . . . .159 B2
Roundtree Way NR7 . . . . .159 B2
Roundway Down 17 NR7 . .72 D4
Rouse's La PE38 . . . . .172 D4
Row Hill 6 PE33 . . . . .43 F2
Row The Wereham PE33 . . .80 D3
West Dereham PE33 . . . . . . .80 B4

Rowan Cl
10 Great Yarmouth NR31 . .94 C7
Thetford IP24 . . . . .176 B1
7 Watlington PE33 . . . . . .61 D5
Wisbech PE13 . . . . .152 F7
Rowan Ct NR5 . . . . .156 F1
Rowan Dr
Brandon IP27 . . . . .175 C3
Gayton PE32 . . . . .45 C6
Rowan Rd
King's Lynn PE34 . . . . .43 D4
Marham PE33 . . . . .57 D4
Rowan Way
Fakenham NR21 . . . . .141 F4
Holt NR25 . . . . .9 F2
Rowington Rd NR1 . . . . . .178 A1
Rowland Ct NR1 . . . . .178 B1
Rowley Cnr IP26 . . . . .83 A5
Row's Mdw 1 NR15 . . . . .107 C5
Rowton Heath 8 NR7 . . . . .72 D4
Roxley Cl NR7 . . . . .163 F5
Royal Albert Ct 5 NR31 . .170 D4
Royal Ave NR30 . . . . .169 D7
Royal Cl 11 PE12 . . . . .41 B8
Royal Cromer Golf Course
NR27 . . . . .139 F5
**Royal Norfolk Regimental
Mus*** NR1 . . . . .178 B3
Royal Norwich Golf Course
NR6 . . . . .157 E3
Royal Pl 2 PE13 . . . . .152 C4
Royal Thames Rd
NR30 . . . . .168 D7
Royal W Norfolk Golf Club
PE31 .3 C8
Royalist Dr 28 NR7 . . . . . . .72 D4
Royden Way 5 NR27 . . . . .57 C1
Roydon Fen IP22 . . . . .177 A4
Roydon Prim Sch
IP22 . . . . .177 B5
Roydon Rd IP22 . . . . .177 C5
Royston Gn NR28 . . . . .151 D6
Rudd's Drif PE32 . . . . .48 E5
Rudds La NR10 . . . . .149 B3
Rudham Rd
Great Massingham PE32 . . .29 D2
Syderstone PE31 . . . . .15 A3
Rudham Stile La NR21 . . .141 B6
Rudolf Steiner Sch
NR12 . . . . .164 B3
Rugge Dr NR4 . . . . .161 E2
Rugg's La NR29 . . . . .75 C8
Ruin Rd NR28 . . . . .30 A5
Rumburgh La NR35 . . . . . .124 D7
Rump Cl 10 NR20 . . . . .50 B3
Run La NR14 . . . . .91 B6
Runcton Cl NR5 . . . . .161 B7
**Runcton Holme CE VA Prim
Sch** PE33 . . . . .61 E3
Runcton Rd PE33 . . . . .61 F2
Runhall Rd NR9 . . . . .69 A2
Runham Rd
Great Yarmouth NR30 . . . . .169 B5
Stokesby with Herringby
NR29 . . . . .75 C5
Runnel The NR5 . . . . .160 F6
Runton House Cl NR27 . . .10 A5
Runton Rd NR27 . . . . .139 A7
Rupert St NR2 . . . . .162 C4
Rushall Rd IP20 . . . . .122 B2
Rushford Rd
Coney Weston IP31 . . . . . . .127 B5
Euston IP24 . . . . .126 D7
Thetford IP24 . . . . .148 C3
Rushmeadow Rd
NR19 . . . . .154 A5
Rushmer Way NR26 . . . . .138 C5
Rushmore Rd NR7 . . . . . . .159 A4
Ruskin Ave NR31 . . . . .170 B2
Ruskin Cl PE13 . . . . .152 F7
Ruskin Rd Norwich NR5 . . .153 E5
Norwich NR4 . . . . .161 E4
Russell Ave
Caister-on-Sea NR30 . . . . . .168 E5
Great Yarmouth NR31 . . . . .170 C3
Norwich NR7 . . . . .159 B3
9 Spixworth NR10 . . . . . . .54 A2
Russell Cl NR13 . . . . .136 C6
Russell Ct NR13 . . . . .136 D6
Russell Rd NR30 . . . . .169 D4
Russell Sq 4 NR30 . . . . . .169 D4
Russell St
King's Lynn PE30 . . . . .146 F3
Norwich NR2 . . . . .162 C7
Wisbech PE13 . . . . .152 C6

Russell Terr NR11 .....143 C6
Russell Way NR18 .....173 C4
Russet CI NR17 .....174 E4
Russet Gr NR4 .....161 E5
Russet Rd IP22 .....177 C5
Russets The PE14 .....77 E6
Russett CI PE30 .....147 C8
Rustens Manor Rd 2 NR18 .....173 C5
Rustons Rd 59 F3
Ruthen Pl 1 NR19 .....154 D5
Rutherford Way IP24 .....176 C6
Rutland St NR2 .....162 C4
Ryalla Drift PE30 .....148 B4
Ryburgh Dr NR20 .....32 D5
Rydal CI NR5 .....161 C6
Ryders Way IP22 .....128 E2
Rye Ave NR3 .....158 B3
Rye CI
  North Walsham NR28 .....151 E6
  Norwich NR3 .....158 B2
Rye La NR17 .....174 C4
Ryeland Rd 2 NR29 .....148 C4
Ryelands 5 NR29 .....167 A7
Rye's CI PE33 .....62 D3
Ryley CI PE30 .....147 E8
Ryston CI PE38 .....172 C4
Ryston End PE38 .....172 C4
Ryston Pk PE38 .....172 F1
Ryston Pk Golf Course
  PE38 .....172 E1
Ryston Rd Denver PE38 .....172 D2
  West Dereham PE33 .....80 B4

S

Sackville CI 4 NR30 .....169 C3
Sacred Heart Convent Sch
  PE37 .....153 C5
Saddlebow Rd PE30 .....146 D1
Sadler CI PE30 .....146 F7
Sadler Rd NR6 .....157 F7
Sadlers Way NR28 .....151 E5
Saffron CI IP27 .....175 E2
Saham Rd IP25 .....84 C4
Sainsbury Ctr for the Visual
  Arts* NR4 .....161 C3
St Alban's Rd NR1 .....162 D3
St Albans Way IP24 .....176 B5
St Andrew Ct 1 NR31 .....171 E5
St Andrews Way 5 NR7 .....72 D3
St Andrews CE VA Prim Sch
  IP22 .....119 A1
St Andrews CI
  Barningham IP31 .....127 C3
  Buxton with Lammas NR10 .....36 E1
  Framingham Earl NR14 .....90 D5
  1 Hingham NR9 .....86 C4
  Long Stratton NR15 .....106 E4
  Poringland NR14 .....90 D5
  West Dereham PE33 .....80 C4
  Worstead NR28 .....38 A4
St Andrew's CI
  Blofield NR13 .....165 E5
  Caister-on-Sea NR30 .....168 D7
  Holme Hale PE32 .....66 A2
  Holt NR25 .....137 C6
  Northwold IP26 .....99 C8
  3 Old Buckenham NR17 .....104 D2
St Andrews Dr
  3 Norwich NR4 .....89 C8
  Quidenham NR16 .....103 E1
St Andrews Drift 2 NR25 .....7 A4
St Andrews Hill NR2 .....178 B3
St Andrew's Hospl NR7 .....72 E4
St Andrews La
  Necton PE37 .....65 F5
  Roydon PE32 .....28 A2
St Andrews Rd
  North Runcton PE30 .....147 B3
  Norwich NR7 .....157 D6
  Scole IP21 .....130 D5
St Andrew's Rd
  Great Yarmouth NR31 .....170 C6
  Lingwood NR13 .....73 F3
  Sheringham NR26 .....138 D6
St Andrews St NR2 .....178 B3
St Andrew's Way
  NR13 .....165 E5
St Andrews Way PE37 .....65 F5
St Andrews Wlk PE13 .....80 C5
St Ann La NR1 .....178 C2
St Anne's Cres
  Clenchwarton PE34 .....145 D6
  Great Yarmouth NR31 .....170 B4
St Annes Rd 4 NR14 .....90 D5
St Ann's St PE30 .....146 D5
St Anthony's Way
  IP27 .....175 E4
St Antony's Ave NR31 .....170 B2
St Audreys IP24 .....176 D3
St Augustine's CE Sch
  PE13 .....152 D8
St Augustines Rd
  PE13 .....152 C5
St Augustines St 3 NR3 .....162 D8
St Augustines Way 1
  PE30 .....148 C4
St Austin's Gr NR26 .....138 E7
St Barnabas CI IP24 .....176 C1

St Bartholomews CI 4
  NR2 .....162 B8
St Benedicts CI NR34 .....110 D5
St Benedicts Rd IP27 .....175 E4
St Benedicts St NR2 .....178 A3
St Benet's Abbey*
  NR12 .....56 C2
St Benets Ave NR28 .....151 E4
St Benet's CI 9 NR12 .....39 B4
St Benets Gr PE30 .....148 D3
St Benets Rd NR29 .....56 C3
St Benet's Rd
  Great Yarmouth NR31 .....170 B3
  Stalham NR12 .....39 E4
St Botolph's CI 3 PE30 .....148 C3
St Botolphs Prim Sch
  IP22 .....128 F3
St Catherine's Ave 5
  NR29 .....56 C8
St Catherines Rd NR7 .....163 F8
St Catherine's Way
  NR31 .....170 B4
St Christopher 2
  18 Belton NR31 .....94 A6
  6 Caister-on-Sea NR30 .....168 D7
St Christophers CI
  NR5 .....108 C7
St Christophers St
  NR6 .....158 E4
St Clare CI 6 NR31 .....171 D5
St Clement CI 2 PE14 .....77 F6
St Clement Mews 7
  NR3 .....171 D5
St Clements Dr 4 PE38 .....172 C6
St Clements High Sch
  PE34 .....144 C6
St Clements Hill NR3 .....158 E2
St Clements Way
  NR13 .....165 C4
St Crispins Dr NR3 .....178 A4
St Cross Rd IP20 .....123 B4
St David's CI 17 NR31 .....94 A6
St Davids CI
  Brandon IP27 .....175 D3
  Long Stratton NR15 .....106 E4
St Davids Dr 6 NR31 .....73 D6
St David's Rd NR9 .....88 C7
St Domonic's Dr IP27 .....175 E4
St Edmund CI
  Attleborough NR17 .....174 C5
  Great Yarmouth NR31 .....170 B3
  Poringland NR14 .....90 B6
St Edmund Rd IP27 .....114 E8
St Edmunds NR17 .....174 E5
St Edmund's Ave
  PE36 .....132 D5
St Edmunds CI
  Costessey NR8 .....156 F5
  Norwich NR6 .....157 E1
St Edmunds Com Sch
  PE30 .....146 E8
St Edmunds Dr PE14 .....59 D1
St Edmunds Gate
  Attleborough NR17 .....174 B4
  18 Hormington NR31 .....126 B1
St Edmunds Prim Sch
  IP21 .....131 A2
St Edmunds RC Prim Sch
  NR35 .....124 B8
St Edmunds Rd NR13 .....166 B3
St Edmund's Rd
  Downham Market PE38 .....172 D5
  Lingwood NR13 .....73 F3
  Taverham NR8 .....155 C1
St Edmunds Rise 2
  NR8 .....155 C1
St Edmunds Sq 18 IP31 .....126 B1
St Edmund's Terr
  Hunstanton PE36 .....132 C4
  King's Lynn PE30 .....146 C7
St Edmundsbury Rd
  PE30 .....146 E7
St Ethelberts CI PE31 .....133 C6
St Faith's Church*
  NR9 .....51 F7
St Faith's CI NR9 .....51 E5
St Faith's Dr PE30 .....147 A6
St Faiths La NR1 .....178 C3
St Faith's Rd NR6 .....158 D6
St Francis CI IP27 .....175 E4
St Francis Way 2 NR31 .....169 C4
St Furzers' Way 2 NR31 .....94 A6
St George's CI
  Saham Toney IP25 .....84 B5
  Thurton NR14 .....91 C4
St George's Dr
  Caister-on-Sea NR30 .....168 D7
  East Dereham NR19 .....154 D1
St Georges Mid Sch
  PE31 .....13 A1
St Georges Rd NR31 .....94 A6
St George's Rd NR30 .....169 D3
St Georges St NR3 .....178 A4
St Giles Cr PE14 .....59 B1
St Giles' La IP24 .....176 D4
St Giles Rd NR24 .....18 B2
St Giles St NR2 .....178 A2
St Guthlac CI PE37 .....153 C6
St Helena Way NR10 .....53 A3
St Helens CI 1 IP24 .....176 D6
St Helens Rd 23 F3
St Helens Way IP24 .....176 D6
St Hilda CI NR19 .....154 C6
St Hilda Rd
  Caister-on-Sea NR30 .....168 D7
  East Dereham NR19 .....154 C6
St Hilda's Cres NR31 .....170 B5
St Hugh's Gn NR31 .....170 B3

St James CI NR3 .....178 C4
St James Cres 18 NR31 .....94 A6
St James Dr 38 B8
St James Rd IP19 .....124 A1
St James' Rd PE30 .....146 D4
St James St PE30 .....146 D4
St James's Way NR15 .....106 E4
St James's Rd PE32 .....47 A2
St John Madder Mkt
  NR2 .....178 A3
St John St NR31 .....178 C2
St John the Baptist Cath*
  NR2 .....162 C5
St John's Ave NR31 .....170 C4
St Johns CI
  2 Norwich NR1 .....162 E2
  Swaffham PE37 .....153 C4
St John's CI
  Coltishall NR12 .....54 D7
  1 Hethersett NR9 .....88 D7
  Oxborough PE33 .....81 E4
St Johns La NR14 .....109 A8
St Johns Prim Sch
  NR12 .....164 D5
St Johns Rd Belton NR31 .....93 F6
  Stalham NR12 .....39 B4
St John's Rd
  Bungay NR35 .....124 A8
  Terrington St John PE34 .....60 C8
St John's Terr
  8 Great Yarmouth NR30 .....169 D3
  King's Lynn PE30 .....146 E4
St Johns Way PE38 .....172 A4
St John's Way
  1 Feltwell IP26 .....98 E1
  Thetford IP24 .....176 D5
St Joseph's Rd NR26 .....138 D6
St Julian Rd NR30 .....168 E4
St Julians Alley NR1 .....178 B2
St Laurence Ave NR13 .....165 C4
St Laurence Dr NR4 .....161 C1
St Laurence La NR31 .....178 A3
St Laurence Prim Sch
  NR34 .....124 F2
St Leger NR15 .....106 E3
St Leonards CI
  Scole IP21 .....130 D5
  Wymondham NR18 .....173 C6
St Leonards Rd NR1 .....163 A6
St Leonards St IP26 .....100 B4
St Luke's Terr NR30 .....169 D2
St Margarets Ave 8
  NR3 .....63 B4
St Margaret's CI 3 NR12 .....54 C6
St Margarets CI 2
  NR1 .....155 F3
St Margaret's CI IP16 .....166 B8
St Margaret's Dr NR27 .....139 C5
St Margaret's Dr NR7 .....159 C5
St Margarets Gdns
  NR12 .....164 D6
St Margaret's La
  2 Cromer NR27 .....139 C6
  6 King's Lynn PE30 .....146 D4
St Margarets La 8
  PE30 .....146 D4
St Margaret's Pl NR12 .....40 A5
St Margaret's Rd
  Bungay NR35 .....124 A6
  2 Cromer NR27 .....139 C6
St Margaret's St NR2 .....178 A3
St Margaret's Way
  1 Burgh St Margaret
   (Fleggburgh) NR29 .....57 C1
  6 Hopton-on-Sea NR31 .....171 D5
St Marthas RC Prim Sch
  PE30 .....146 C4
St Martin-at-Palace Plain
  NR3 .....178 B4
St Martins at Oak Wall La 7
  NR3 .....162 D8
St Martins CI NR27 .....139 C5
St Martins CI 4 NR3 .....162 D8
St Martin's Gdns 1
  NR16 .....104 F1
St Martin's La PE14 .....125 E6
St Martins La NR34 .....111 E2
St Martin's Rd
  2 Norwich NR3 .....162 D8
  Wisbech PE13 .....152 E7
St Martin's Way IP24 .....176 B2
St Mary CI NR17 .....174 C6
St Mary's 4 NR16 .....104 F1
St Mary's CI
  Alpington NR14 .....90 F5
  Flixton NR35 .....123 E5
  Harleston IP20 .....122 E2
  Heacham NR29 .....133 E6
  Hemsby NR29 .....167 A7
  Horsham St Faith &
   Newton St Faith NR10 .....53 E2
  Newton Flotman NR15 .....89 C1
  12 Snettisham PE31 .....12 E5
  1 Watton IP25 .....84 E3
  Wroxham/Hoveton
   NR12 .....164 B4
St Mary's Cres 6 IP19 .....124 F1
St Mary's Cres 2 IP24 .....176 C3
St Mary's Dr IP22 .....177 E4
St Marys Endowed Prim Sch
  NR11 .....21 E8
St Marys Gr NR7 .....159 C5
St Mary's La NR31 .....169 C3
St Marys La 1 NR25 .....7 A4

St Marys Mid Sch
  NR15 .....106 E4
St Marys Plain NR3 .....178 A4
St Marys Prim Sch
  NR2 .....49 D4
St Marys RC Prim Sch
  NR31 .....170 C6
St Marys Rd
  Ashby St Mary NR14 .....91 C4
  Hemsby NR29 .....167 D6
  3 Norwich NR1 .....162 D8
  12 Snettisham PE31 .....39 B4
St Mary's Rd
  Aldeby NR34 .....111 A3
  Cromer NR27 .....139 B6
  10 Long Stratton NR15 .....106 E3
  Poringland NR14 .....90 D5
  West Walton PE14 .....59 B8
St Mary's Way 5 NR15 .....131 C5
St Marys Wlk NR15 .....89 D1
St Matthew's Dr PE12 .....41 B8
St Matthews Rd NR1 .....178 C3
St Michaels NR12 .....39 C2
St Michael's Ave PE13 .....152 C7
St Michaels CE Prim Sch
  Gillingham NR34 .....110 B2
  King's Lynn PE30 .....146 D1
St Michaels CI NR20 .....50 B5
St Michael's CI
  Aylsham NR11 .....150 C7
  Thetford IP24 .....176 D4
St Michael's Cres IP25 .....83 D4
St Michael's Hospl
  NR11 .....150 C7
St Michaels Inf Sch
  NR11 .....150 C7
St Michaels Mid Sch
  NR5 .....160 F8
St Michael's Rd NR30 .....168 E4
St Michaels Way NR13 .....165 F2
St Michels Rd NR1 .....178 A3
St Mildreds Rd 3 NR5 .....161 B7
St Nicholas CI
  Dersingham PE31 .....140 E7
  6 Gayton PE32 .....45 C6
St Nicholas Ct 1 NR31 .....94 C6
St Nicholas Dr
  Caister-on-Sea NR30 .....168 D6
  Feltwell IP26 .....98 E2
St Nicholas Gdns 6
  NR3 .....169 D3
St Nicholas PI 4 NR26 .....138 D7
St Nicholas Priory Mid Sch
  NR30 .....169 D3
St Nicholas Rd
  Great Yarmouth NR30 .....169 D3
  North Walsham NR28 .....151 D5
St Nicholas Sch NR28 .....151 D4
St Nicholas St
  East Dereham NR19 .....154 D6
  2 King's Lynn PE30 .....146 D5
  Thetford IP24 .....176 C4
St Nicholas Wlk IP27 .....175 E4
St Nicholas's NR14 .....88 F3
St Nicholas's St 2 NR30 .....169 D3
St Olaves Rd NR3 .....162 E8
St Omer CI NR14 .....89 B4
St Pauls CI NR6 .....158 A5
St Paul's CI
  Brockdish IP21 .....131 C6
  4 Horsford NR10 .....53 B3
  5 Wisbech PE13 .....152 C4
St Paul's Rd S PE14 .....59 D8
St Paul's Way NR30 .....169 C7
St Peter & St Paul Prim Sch
  IP25 .....85 A5
St Peter's App IP27 .....175 B3
St Peters Ave NR11 .....150 C7
St Peters CE Jun Sch
  NR9 .....70 B5
St Peters CI 3 NR4 .....89 B8
St Peter's CI
  Brockdish IP21 .....131 C6
  King's Lynn PE34 .....146 B4
  Strumpshaw NR13 .....73 F2
  Yaxham NR19 .....68 A5
St Peters Hill NR18 .....87 A2
St Peter's La NR12 .....164 E8
St Peters PI IP27 .....175 B2
St Peters' Prim Sch NR30 .....169 C7
St Peters Rd
  Outwell PE14 .....77 E5
  Watlington PE34 .....61 C7
  Wiggenhall St Germans
   PE34 .....61 B8
St Peter's Rd
  Brooke NR15 .....90 F2
  Fakenham NR21 .....141 B6
  Great Yarmouth NR30 .....169 D3
  King's Lynn PE34 .....146 B4
  Lingwood NR13 .....73 F3
  Sheringham NR26 .....138 D7
  4 Wisbech PE13 .....152 C4
St Peters St IP27 .....178 A2
St Peter's Way 8 NR10 .....53 B3
St Peter's Wlk IP26 .....113 F7
St Philips Rd NR2 .....162 B6
St Roberts Way 15 NR31 .....94 A6
St Saviors La NR3 .....178 B4
St Stephen NR2 .....178 A2
St Stephens Rd NR1 .....175 A1
St Stephens Sq NR1 .....178 A1
St Stephens St NR1 .....178 A2
St Swithins Rd NR2 .....178 A3
St Thomas Dr IP27 .....175 E4

St Thomas Dr NR18 .....173 C2
St Thomas' La NR18 .....88 C4
St Thomas More RC Mid Sch
  NR2 .....162 A5
St Thomas Rd NR2 .....162 A6
St Thomas's La
  Ingoldisthorpe PE31 .....140 D8
  .....12 F4
St Thomas's Rd NR29 .....167 C7
St Valery La PE30 .....146 D2
St Vedast St NR1 .....178 C2
St Vincent Wlk NR31 .....171 E5
St Walstan's CI
  Norwich NR5 .....156 D1
  Taverham NR8 .....155 D1
St Williams Prim Sch
  NR7 .....163 D8
St Williams Way NR7 .....163 C7
St Winnold CI PE38 .....172 B4
St Withburga La 3
  NR19 .....154 D5
Saker CI 11 NR7 .....72 D4
Salamanca Rd 7 NR15 .....106 D3
Salcott Dr PE32 .....152 E5
Sale CI 8 NR14 .....92 A1
Sale Rd NR7 .....159 D2
Salhouse Dr PE37 .....153 B4
Salhouse Prim Sch
  NR13 .....55 B1
Salhouse Rd
  Great & Little Plumstead
   NR13 .....73 B6
  New Rackheath NR13 .....72 E7
  Norwich NR7 .....159 C2
  Sprowston NR13 .....72 D6
  Woodbastwick NR13 .....55 C1
  Wroxham NR12 .....164 B2
Salhouse Sta NR13 .....54 F1
Salisbury Rd
  Cromer NR27 .....139 D4
  Great Yarmouth NR30 .....169 D6
  Norwich NR1 .....163 B5
  Sheringham NR26 .....138 E7
Salisbury Way IP24 .....176 B4
Sallow La
  Framingham Pigot NR14 .....90 E7
  Snetterton NR16 .....118 D8
Salmon Rd NR30 .....170 D8
Salmon Dr 1 IP24 .....125 F6
Salmond Rd 11 NR25 .....84 F3
Salmon's Way NR21 .....141 F5
Salter Ave NR4 .....161 E5
Salter's La PE32 .....48 E4
Salter's Rd
  King's Lynn PE30 .....146 E7
  King's Lynn PE30 .....147 A6
Salters Way PE13 .....152 A2
Saltings The PE34 .....144 A5
Salts Rd PE14 .....59 C8
Sampson Rd NR28 .....151 C3
Samson Rd NR6 .....157 F4
Samson's La IP22 .....129 C4
Samuel Rd 1 NR1 .....163 B7
Sancroft Way IP20 .....123 A3
Sand Stone Way IP22 .....177 B4
Sandall Rd PE13 .....152 C3
Sandfield Rd 8 PE28 .....172 C6
Sandhole La NR13 .....73 A7
Sandhole Rd NR13 .....74 F1
Sandholme CI NR1 .....163 B8
Sandover CI NR7 PE33 .....43 F2
Sandown Golf Course
  NR29 .....167 C6
Sandown Rd
  Great Yarmouth NR30 .....169 D5
  Wisbech PE13 .....152 A2
Sandpiper CI 1 NR31 .....170 A5
Sandpit La
  Gimingham NR11 .....22 E8
  Saxlingham Nethergate
   NR15 .....107 A8
  Thorpe Market NR11 .....21 F7
Sandringham & W Newton CE
  Sch PE31 .....27 F6
Sandringham Ave
  Great Yarmouth NR30 .....169 D7
  12 Marham PE33 .....63 B4
  Wisbech PE13 .....152 D6
Sandringham Cres
  PE30 .....148 D5
Sandringham Ct S PE33 .....84 D3
Sandringham Ctry Pk*
  PE35 .....27 E5
Sandringham Dr
  Downham Market PE38 .....172 E5
  Heacham PE31 .....133 C4
Sandringham Private Hospl
  PE30 .....147 E6
Sandringham Rd
  Dersingham PE31 .....140 E2
  Hunstanton PE36 .....132 D4
  King's Lynn PE30 .....147 C7
  Norwich NR2 .....162 B6
Sandringham Way
  PE31 .....153 C2
Sandy CI NR31 .....171 E4
Sandy CI PE31 .....140 C7
Sandy Cres PE31 .....140 C7
Sandy Hill La NR25 .....150 B6
Sandy La Aylsham NR11 .....150 B6
  Bacton NR12 .....23 D3
  Barningham IP31 .....127 C4
  Beighton NR13 .....74 D2
  Belton with Browston
   NR31 .....93 F5
  Blackborough End PE32 .....44 C2

Sandy La *continued*
Bradwell NR31 .....94 C8
Buxton with Lammas
 NR10 ....53 F8
Canadas NR11 ......10 A3
Cantley NR13 ....92 E6
Castle Acre PE32 ...47 A2
Cromer NR27 ....139 A6
Denver PE38 ....172 C2
Dereham NR19 .....154 C8
Diss IP22 ....177 F4
Docking PE31 ......134 D6
East Dereham NR19 ...154 C6
East Tuddenham NR20 ...69 D8
Fakenham NR21 ....141 A5
Flegburgh NR29 ....75 B8
Great Massingham PE32 ...46 E8
Grimston PE32 .....44 C8
Hardingham NR9 ...86 D7
Hilgay PE38 ....97 C8
Hoveton NR12 .....54 D4
Ingoldisthorpe PE31 ...140 C7
King's Lynn PE30 ...148 F1
Loddon NR14 ....92 B1
Mundham NR14 ....109 A7
Norwich NR4 ....162 D1
Old Hunstanton PE36 ...133 F8
Oulton NR11 ....35 B7
Raveningham NR14 ...110 B8
Rocklands NR17 ....103 A6
Runton NR27 ....10 C4
St Mary, South Elmham
 otherwise Homersfield
 IP20 ....123 B3
Sheringham NR27 ...10 A5
Somerton NR29 ....57 E6
Smith Wroxton PE30 ...27 C1
Southrepps NR11 ...22 B7
Taverham NR8 ......156 C8
Thurning NR20 .....34 C8
West Acre PE32 ....46 B2
Weston Longville NR9 ...51 D4
Wisbech PE13 ......152 F4
Sandy La E NR19 ...154 C6
Sandy Way PE31 ...140 C7
Sandygate La PE34 ...144 F5
Sandyland PE13 ....152 B5
Sankence La NR11 ...35 E5
Santon Cl IP24 .....176 A3
Sapiston Rd IP31 ...126 D1
Sapwell Cl NR11 ...150 A6
Saracen Rd NR6 ....157 F6
Sarah Williman Cl 2
 NR4 ....161 C5
Sarah Rd NR19 .....132 F7
Sardis Way NR19 ...154 D4
Saturday Mkt Pl PE30 ...146 D4
Savery Cl NR5 ......161 B6
Savory Rd PE13 ....152 B7
Saw Mill La
 Brancaster PE31 ...3 B6
 7 Great Yarmouth NR31 ...169 B4
Sawston 1 PE30 ...147 D6
Sawyers Cl NR5 ....156 C1
Sawyer's La NR16 ...87 D7
Saxlingham La NR15 ...106 F7
Saxlingham Prim Sch
 NR15 ....107 B7
Saxlingham Rd
 Blakeney NR25 .....7 C5
 Saxlingham Nethergate
 NR15 ....107 C8
 Shotesham NR15 ...09 F1
Saxon Cres 3 IP31 ...126 B1
Saxon Ct PE37 .....153 D2
Saxon Gdns NR30 ...168 D5
Saxon Pl
 3 Thetford IP24 ...176 C3
 Weeting IP27 ......175 A8
Saxon Rd NR30 ....169 D4
Saxon Way
 Dersingham PE31 ...140 D4
 Wormegay PE33 ...62 C6
Saxon Wlk IP26 ....100 A4
Sayer Ct NR25 .....14 C4
Sayers St 8 NR2 ...162 C7
Scama La IP24 .....129 A2
Scania Way PE30 ...147 A1
Scarborough Rd NR22 ...17 A8
Scarfield La PE14 ...59 C2
Scarlet Rd NR4 ....162 D1
Scarnell Rd NR5 ...161 C6
Scarning Prim Sch
 NR19 ....154 A4
Scarrow Beck La NR11 ...21 A7
Sceptre Cl NR6 .....158 A3
Scholars Wlk IP22 ...177 C5
Schole Ave NR17 ...163 F6
School Cl
 Kenninghall NR16 ...119 A4
 Knapton NR28 .....143 A1
 2 Ludham NR29 ...56 C5
 Northrepps NR27 ...11 A2
 4 Rollesby NR29 ...57 D2
School Comm Rd .24 C3
School Hill
 Reedham NR13 ....93 A4
 Tasburgh NR15 ....106 E6
School La
 Brandon IP27 ......175 C3
 Cantley NR13 ......92 E6
 Colney NR4 ....160 E3
 East Dereham NR19 ...154 E1
 East Harling NR16 ...118 C5
 Gimingham NR11 ...22 E8
 Great Yarmouth NR31 ...170 D6
 17 Harleston IP20 ...122 D2

School La *continued*
 Heckingham NR14 ...109 F8
 Little Dunham PE32 ...65 E7
 Little Melton NR9 ...160 C2
 Neatishead NR12 ...55 D7
 North Runcton PE33 ...44 A2
 Northwold IP26 ....99 C7
 Norwich NR7 ......158 F3
 Norwich NR7 ......163 D6
 Rockland St Mary NR14 ...91 B7
 Runhall NR9 ....68 F1
 Runhall NR20 .....69 A4
 Skeyton NR10 .....37 A5
 Smallburgh NR12 ...38 D3
 Stoke Ferry PE33 ...80 F2
 Surlingham NR14 ...73 B1
 Thetford IP24 .....176 D3
 Walpole St Andrew PE14 ...41 E3
 Wereham PE33 ....80 E4
 1 Wisbech PE13 ...152 C5
 Wramplingham NR18 ...69 F1
 Wymondham NR18 ...105 A8
School Loke
 Bodham NR25 .....9 A2
 Hemsby NR29 .....167 A7
School Pastures PE31 ...3 E7
School Rd
 Alburgh IP20 ......123 A5
 Aldborough NR11 ...21 A5
 Ashmanhaugh NR12 ...55 B7
 Bacton NR28 ......23 B4
 Barton Turf NR12 ...38 E1
 Bedingham NR35 ...108 B3
 Beetley NR20 ......49 C5
 Blofield NR13 .....165 B8
 Bracon Ash NR14 ...89 A3
 Bradenham IP25 ...66 D3
 Bressingham IP22 ...129 D8
 Brisley NR20 ......49 A8
 Catfield NR29 .....56 C8
 Colkirk NR21 ......31 D5
 Earsham NR35 .....123 F8
 East Ruston NR12 ...38 E7
 Erpingham NR11 ...21 B2
 Foulden IP26 ......82 A1
 Freethorpe NR14 ...92 F7
 Frettenham NR12 ...54 A4
 Great Massingham PE32 ...29 D1
 Great Yarmouth NR30 ...169 B5
 Haveringland NR10 ...52 D7
 Heacham PE31 ....133 D5
 Hinderclay IP22 ...128 C3
 Holme Hale IP25 ...66 A2
 Horning NR12 .....55 A3
 Kirby Cane NR35 ...109 C4
 Lessingham NR12 ...24 D3
 Lingwood NR13 ...74 A3
 Little Cressingham IP25 ...83 F2
 Little Plumstead NR13 ...73 B6
 Ludham NR29 .....56 B5
 Marshland St James PE14 ...60 B4
 Mautby NR29 .....75 E5
 Middleton PE32 ...44 C2
 Morning Thorpe NR15 ...107 B3
 Neatishead NR12 ...55 E7
 1 Necton PE37 ...65 F4
 Newton Flotman NR15 ...89 D1
 Outwell PE14 .....77 D4
 Potter Heigham NR29 ...56 F6
 Roepham NR10 ...149 R4
 Runcton Holme PE33 ...61 E3
 St Andrew, Ilketshall
 NR34 ....124 E6
 Sculthorpe Airfield NR21 ...15 C3
 Seething NR15 ....108 E8
 10 Snettisham NR21 ...12 E5
 South Walsham NR13 ...74 A8
 Strumpshaw NR13 ...73 F1
 Swannington NR9 ...52 B5
 Taverham NR8 .....155 F1
 Terrington St John PE14 ...60 B7
 Thompson IP24 ...102 B7
 Tilney All Saints PE34 ...42 E4
 Tilney St Lawrence PE14 ...60 C7
 Tivetshall St Mary NR15 ...121 B5
 Walpole Highway PE14 ...59 C8
 Walton Highway PE14 ...59 C8
 Watlington PE33 ...61 D6
 Weasenham All Saints
 PE32 ....47 D8
 Weasenham St Peter
 PE32 ....30 D1
 West Rudham PE31 ...29 F6
 West Walton PE14 ...59 B8
 Whissonsett NR20 ...31 E2
 Wiggenhall St Germans
 PE34 ....61 B8
 Worstead NR28 ...38 A5
School Rd Back 4
 NR30 ....169 C5
School Sq IP24 .....102 E3
Schoolfield NR14 ...124 F1
Schoolfield NR10 ...155 C8
Schoolhouse La 1
 NR11 ....150 C7
Scole Comm IP21 ...130 C6
Scole Comm Rd IP21 ...130 D6
Scole Prim Sch IP22 ...130 D6
Scole Rd IP21 .....131 C6
Sconch Beck Rd IP20 ...123 A2
Scotch Hill Rd NR8 ...155 B1
Scotgate Cl IP24 ...102 E3
Scott Cl IP24 ......176 A6
Scott Rd NR1 ......163 B5
Scotter Rise 2 NR26 ...138 C5
Scottow Rd NR10 ...37 B2
Scott's Cnr NR16 ...105 B4
Scott's Hill NR14 ...89 A4

Scott's La IP26 ....99 A7
Scoulton Rd NR17 ...85 F2
Scratby Cres NR29 ...167 F3
Scratby Rd NR29 ...167 D3
Scrumpy Way NR16 ...119 D7
Sculthorpe Airfield
 NR21 ....15 E2
Sculthorpe Rd PE34 ...146 B5
Sculthorpe Bvd 7 NR21 ...15 C2
Sculthorpe CE Prim Sch
 NR21 ....16 C2
Sculthorpe Eastgate
 NR21 ....141 A5
Sculthorpe Rd NR21 ...141 A5
Sea Cl PE31 ....133 B6
Sea La PE36 ....132 E7
Sea Life Ctr* NR30 ...169 E2
Sea Palling Rd NR12 ...40 F5
Sea View Rd
 Hemsby NR29 .....167 D7
 Mundesley NR11 ...143 B7
Sea View Rise NR31 ...171 E4
Seabank Rd
 Heacham PE31 ....133 B6
 Wisbech PE13 .....152 F6
Seabank Way PE32 ...146 E7
Seabird Cl 1 NR30 ...168 D7
Seabrook Cl 3 NR5 ...161 A7
Seafield Cl NR30 ...169 D2
Seafield Rd N NR30 ...168 E6
Seafield Rd S NR30 ...168 D6
Seaforth Dr NR8 ...156 E2
Seagate PE36 ......132 C3
Seagate Rd PE36 ...132 B3
Seagull Rd NR29 ...167 E5
Seamere Rd NR9 ...86 D4
Searle Cl NR21 ....141 F5
Scaries Golf Course
 PE36 ....132 B1
Sears Cl NR11 .....150 C6
Seaside La NR12 ...24 E4
Seates The 6 NR8 ...155 D2
Scathwaite Rd NR30 ...147 D8
Seaview Cres NR26 ...136 D5
Seawake Cl NR31 ...170 A4
Seaward Cres NR11 ...143 B6
Seaward Wlk NR30 ...168 E8
Seckar Dr NR19 ...154 C4
Second Ave
 Caister-on-Sea NR30 ...168 D8
 Wisbech PE13 .....152 D4
Second Dro IP27 ...113 C3
Second Marsh Rd PE14 ...59 A7
Sedge Cl NR11 ....143 E4
Sedge Dro NR28 ...96 C7
Sedge Fen Rd PE38 ...97 B3
Sedge Rd NR19 ....154 B4
Sedgefen Dro PE38 ...112 E7
Sedgefen Rd IP27 ...112 F3
Sedgeford Fst Sch
 PE36 ....13 B7
Sedgeford La PE30 ...146 D4
Sedgeford Rd
 Docking PE31 .....134 B4
 Snettisham PE31 ...12 F5
Seeche Abbey PE34 ...43 D1
Seething CP Sch
 NR15 ....108 E8
Seething Old Hall Pk
 NR15 ....91 B1
Seething Rd NR35 ...108 D5
Seething St NR15 ...108 E8
Seaview Cres NR12 ...24 A7
Sefton Ave PE13 ...152 E6
Sefton La NR31 ...169 C3
Sego Vale NR6 ....156 E8
Segrave Rd 6 PE30 ...147 A8
Selby Pl 11 NR30 ...169 D2
Self's La IP22 .....128 C7
Selwyn Dr 8 NR11 ...94 A5
Selwyn Gdns IP21 ...121 E5
Selwyn Rd NR31 ...170 A5
Semere La NR21 ...121 D4
Sendall Rd NR29 ...151 B3
Sennowe Rd NR20 ...32 F4
Senter's Rd PE31 ...140 D2
Seppings Rd NR21 ...141 A6
Seppings Way NR14 ...72 E6
Serpentine La NR10 ...152 C6
Setch Rd Middleton PE33 ...44 A1
 West Winch PE33 ...43 F1
Seton Rd NR8 .....155 E1
Setons Halt Sta NR23 ...5 F2
Seventh Ave PE13 ...152 E4
Severalls Rd IP26 ...98 D5
Sewell Rd Lamas NR10 ...37 A2
 Norwich NR1 .....163 B4
Sewells Cl 5 NR15 ...89 C1
Sewell's La NR15 ...90 D3
Sexton Rd NR35 ...108 D2
Seymour Ave
 Brandon IP27 .....114 D4
 Great Yarmouth NR30 ...168 D6
Shack La NR13 ....165 D6
Shadingfield Cl 16
 NR30 ....169 D2
Shadwell Cl IP27 ...175 B7
Shakers' Rd
 Brandon IP27 .....115 A1
 Wangford IP27 ...114 C4
Shakespeare Rd NR30 ...169 E8
Shakespeare Way
 Taverham NR8 ....156 E8
 Thetford IP24 .....176 E6
Shannon Dr 4 NR31 ...94 A8
Shannons Cl NR17 ...174 C4
Sharman Ave IP25 ...84 D4
Sharmans Loke NR31 ...93 F5

Sharon Cl
 2 East Dereham NR19 ...154 D1
 Felmingham NR28 ...37 A8
Sharp St NR29 ....56 C7
Sharpe Way NR29 ...167 B2
Sharper's Cnr IP27 ...113 D2
Sharrington Rd
 Gunthorpe NR21 ...18 A7
 Gunthorpe NR21 ...18 B5
Shawcross Rd NR27 ...10 A4
Shaw's Yd PE31 ...30 B7
Shearwater Dr
 8 Great Yarmouth NR31 ...94 C8
 2 Great Yarmouth NR31 ...170 A7
Sheddick Ct NR19 ...154 D6
Sheffield Rd NR18 ...173 C5
Sheldrake Cl NR21 ...141 F5
Sheldrick Pl NR19 ...154 E2
Shelduck Dr 7 PE31 ...12 E5
Shelfanger Rd IP22 ...177 C7
Shelford Dr PE30 ...147 B8
Shelley Cl NR30 ...168 D6
Shelley Dr NR8 ...156 D8
Shelley Way IP24 ...176 E6
Shelterhouse Cnr
 IP24 ....125 A4
Sheldon with Hardwick Sch
 NR15 ....107 B2
Shephard Cl 1 NR28 ...151 C6
Shepheards Cl NR11 ...150 E8
Shepherd Cl 2 NR4 ...161 D5
Shepherd Way NR8 ...155 C2
Shepherds Cl
 Cromer NR27 .....10 B5
 11 Hexford NR10 ...53 A3
 Runton NR27 .....10 B5
Shepherd's Fold PE37 ...153 D7
Shepherds La IP22 ...129 B3
Shepherd's La NR10 ...36 A2
Shepherds La NR11 ...35 B6
Shepherds Pightle PE36 ...2 D6
Shepherdsgate Rd
 PE34 ....144 C1
Shepley Cnr 2 NR30 ...147 D5
Sheppard Way NR17 ...174 C5
Shereford Rd
 Fakenham NR21 ...141 A3
 Hempton NR21 ...141 A2
Sheridan Cl NR8 ...156 F8
Sheringham Com Prim Sch
 NR26 ....138 C5
Sheringham High Sch
 NR26 ....138 C5
Sheringham Mus* NR26 ...138 D7
Sheringham Pk (National
 Trust)* NR26 .....9 B6
Sheringham Rd
 West Beckham NR25 ...9 B3
 Weybourne NR25 ...8 F5
Sheringham Sta NR26 ...138 C7
Shernborne Rd PE31 ...140 E7
Sheringham Golf Course
 NR26 ....138 A7
Sherwood Ave PE13 ...152 D7
Sherwood Rd NR4 ...162 C1
Sheval Cl NR15 ....121 A8
Shickle Pl IP27 ....127 F6
Shillgate Way NR8 ...155 B2
Shillito Rd NR13 ...165 F6
Shimpling Rd IP21 ...121 B1
Ship La PE36 ......2 C6
Shipden Ave NR27 ...10 A4
Shipden Ct NR27 ...139 A7
Shipdham Airfield IP25 ...67 E2
Shipdham Airfield Ind Est
 IP25 ....67 F2
Shipdham Rd
 Carbrooke IP25 ...85 A5
 East Dereham NR19 ...154 D1
 Scarning NR19 ...67 B6
 Shipdham NR19 ...67 E5
Shipgate Rd PE31 ...29 B5
Shippea Hill Sta CB7 ...112 C3
Shipstone Rd 11 NR3 ...162 D8
Shire Ave NR30 ...94 C8
Shire House Ctr* NR27 ...9 F5
Shirehall Mus & TIC*
 IP26 ....16 F7
Shires The NR8 ...155 F2
Shirley Cl 3 NR12 ...54 A4
Shoe Devil La NR35 ...124 C4
Shoemakers La PE37 ...64 E3
Shooters Cl NR8 ...155 E1
Shop La Hellesdon NR5 ...88 C8
 Tunstead NR12 ...38 A3
Shop St NR19 .....67 A5
Shorncliffe Ave NR3 ...158 C1
Shorncliffe Cl 1 NR3 ...158 C1
Short Beck 8 IP20 ...99 E1
Short Cl PE38 .....172 C6
Short Dro IP27 ....112 D2
Short Gn IP22 .....120 B5
Short La Billingford NR20 ...50 A8
 Fellwell IP26 .....92 D2
 Hapisburgh NR12 ...24 B3
 Harpley PE31 ....29 D4
 Mautby NR29 .....75 E6
 Swardeston NR14 ...89 D5
Short Rd
 8 Attleborough NR17 ...174 C5
 Belton with Browston
 NR31 ....94 A4
Short St NR15 ....89 D1
Short-Thorn Rd NR10 ...52 F5

Shotesham La NR15 ...107 C8
Shotesham Rd
 Howe NR15 ....90 C2
 Poringland NR14 ...90 B3
 Woodton NR35 ...108 A4
Shotford Rd IP20 ...122 D1
Shouldham Cl PE31 ...140 C3
Shouldham La PE37 ...153 A4
Shouldham Rd
 Marham PE33 ....63 A3
 Shouldham Thorpe PE33 ...62 C2
Shreeves Rd IP22 ...177 E4
Shropham Rd IP24 ...102 E3
Shrub Dro PE38 ...112 F6
Shrub Hill PE38 ...112 F7
Shrublands The NR10 ...53 B4
Shrublands Way NR31 ...170 B5
Shuttleworth Cl NR31 ...170 A8
Sidegate Rd
 Great Yarmouth NR30 ...169 C5
 Hopton on Sea NR31 ...171 B7
Sidell Cl 11 NR4 ...89 B8
Siding Rd NR14 ...111 C1
Sidings The IP24 ...176 C5
Sidney Cl
 2 Great Yarmouth NR30 ...169 D2
 8 Marham NR29 ...57 C4
Sidney Rd
 Costessey NR8 ...156 F4
 Ingham NR12 .....24 D1
 Ingham NR12 .....39 D4
Sidney St PE30 ...146 F3
Sienna Mews 3 NR1 ...163 B7
Sigismund Rd NR1 ...162 D3
Silfield La NR10 ...173 D1
Silfield Gdn PE36 ...132 D4
Silfield Rd NR18 ...173 C2
Silfield St PE30 ...147 C6
Silfield St NR18 ...88 A2
Silkmill Rd 2 NR30 ...169 D4
Silt Rd Nordelph PE38 ...78 R7
 Runcton Holme PE33 ...61 C4
 Terrington St Clement
 PE34 ....25 F3
 Upwell PE14 .....77 F1
Silver Coar NR27 ...11 C2
Silver Dr PE31 ....140 C4
Silver Drif PE37 ...64 E5
Silver End NR10 ...149 B5
Silver Gdns 5 NR11 ...94 A5
Silver Hill PE30 ...147 D6
Silver Rd NR1 ....178 C4
Silver St
 Attleborough NR17 ...174 F6
 Besthorpe NR17 ...104 D7
 Flegburgh NR29 ...75 C8
 Garvestone NR9 ...86 C6
 Norwich NR3 .....162 E8
 South Lopham IP22 ...128 F7
 Wisbech PE13 .....152 C6
Silvergate La NR11 ...35 F6
Silvertree's Way PE33 ...43 E1
Simon Scotland Rd
 PE30 ....146 F2
Simpson Cl NR28 ...151 B5
Sinclair Ct NR31 ...170 A8
Sir Edward Stracey Rd
 NR11 ....72 U8
Sir Lewis St PE30 ...146 E6
Sir William's Cl NR11 ...150 D6
Sir William's La NR11 ...150 D7
Siskin Cl NR31 ...170 A6
Sitka Cl NR21 .....133 C6
Six Crossways NR14 ...91 D3
Sixteen Foot Bank
 PE14 ....77 D1
Sixth Ave PE13 ...152 E4
Skedge Way 13 NR13 ...73 C6
Skelton Cl 14 IP22 ...177 E4
Skelton Rd Diss IP22 ...177 E4
 Norwich NR7 .....163 C8
Skeeton View NR28 ...151 B3
Skeyton Cnr NR10 ...37 B6
Skeyton New Rd NR10 ...151 B5
Skeyton Rd
 North Walsham NR28 ...151 A4
 Skinner's La IP20 ...122 B4
Skinners La NR12 ...164 B2
Skipping Block Row
 NR18 ....88 B6
Skippon Way NR13 ...72 D5
Skitfield Rd NR20 ...33 C6
Skoner Rd NR5 ...161 B8
Skoyles' La NR9 ...88 A8
Skye Cl NR5 ......161 A8
Slade La
 Framingham Pigot NR14 ...90 E6
 Old Buckenham NR17 ...104 B1
 Shropham NR17 ...129 B6
 Yelverton NR14 ...90 F6
Slade Rd NR21 ....18 B7
Sleaford Gn NR3 ...158 C2
Sleigh La IP25 ....84 E2
Sleights Dr PE14 ...59 C5
Slessor Cl 2 IP25 ...84 F3
Slip Rd NR14 .....93 A1
Slip The PE36 .....2 C3
Slipshoe La NR15 ...122 B7
Sloane Way IP24 ...176 B2
Sloe La NR13 .....72 D8
Sloley Rd NR28 ...38 A3
Slopers Rd NR18 ...87 F7

Slough La
Attleborough NR17 ....174 E3
North Tuddenham NR20 ...68 E8
Slough Rd IP22 ....29 A1
Slugs La NR12 ....111 C8
Sluice Dro IP26 ....113 E7
Sluice Rd Denver PE38 ..172 B1
Wiggenhall St Germans
PE34 ....61 A8
Slutshole La NR17 .....105 A7
Small Lode PE14 ....77 F5
Smallbrough Rd
Barton Turf NR12 ......55 E8
Smallbrough NR12 .....38 D2
Smallholdings Rd
PE34 ....145 D4
Smallworth La IP22 ....128 B7
Smea The NR12 ....39 E1
Smeat St **2** NR5 .....161 B7
Smee La NR13 ....72 E4
Smee St NR3 ....72 F4
Smeeth Rd Emneth PE14 ..59 F2
St John's Fen End PE14 ...60 A5
Smith Ave PE30 ....146 E6
Smithdale Rd NR5 .....157 B1
Smithdon Cty High Sch
PE36 ....132 D4
Smithfield Rd NR1 .....162 E3
Smiths Dr IP21 ....121 B1
Smith's Dro PE38 ......112 C8
Smiths La NR21 ....141 E5
Smith's Loke NR13 ....170 A6
Smithson Cl NR18 .....173 C4
Smithson Dr NR20 .....68 F5
Smithyne Ave
Dereham NR19 ....68 A7
3 East Dereham NR19 ..154 F3
Smithy Cl PE31 ....133 D5
Smithy Rd PE31 ....140 D8
Smock Mill Loke
NR18 ....173 B5
Smuggler's Cl PE36 ...132 F8
Smuggler's La NR10 ...149 B4
Smugglers' Rd IP26 ...100 F8
Snaefell Pk NR26 .....138 D6
Snake's La Lound NR32 ..94 C2
Topcroft NR35 ....108 A4
Snape Hall Rd **4** NR15 .106 E3
Snape Hill IP22 ....128 C2
Snape La PE38 ....172 B5
Sneath Rd NR15 ......121 A8
Snetterton Circuit
......................118 D8
Snettisham Beach
PE31 ....12 A3
Snettisham Fst Sch
PE31 ....12 E5
Snettisham Nature Reserve*
PE31 ....11 C3
Snoring Rd NR21 ......17 C3
Snow St IP22 ....177 A6
Snowberry Cl **4** NR6 ..155 B2
Snowdrop Cl **2** NR13 ..94 C6
Snowdrop Dr NR17 ....174 B4
Snowhill Drift NR19 ...154 D6
Snow's Hill **6** NR14 ..92 A2
Snow's La NR14 ......92 A2
Soame Cl NR11 ....150 D5
Soames Pl NR4 ....67 B7
Soanes Ct NR9 ....51 A5
Softley Dr NR4 ....161 C2
Sole Cl NR10 ....53 B3
Soleme Rd NR3 ....158 B1
Solent Cl NR10 ....168 E5
Somerleyton Hall* 111 E8
NR32
Somerleyton Prim Sch
NR32 ....111 D8
Somerleyton St **2** NR2 .162 C5
Somerleyton Sta
NR32 ....111 C7
Somers Rd PE13 ......152 B4
Somersby Cl **2** PE30 ..147 A8
Somerset Ave NR20 ...169 D4
Somerset Way NR8 ...155 A1
Somerton Rd
Martham NR29 ....57 D5
Somerton NR29 ....58 A6
Somerville Ave NR13 ..170 B3
Somerville Rd **1** PE30 .146 E3
Sorrel Cl PE30 ....147 C8
Sorrel Dr NR17 ....174 B4
Sorrel La NR20 ....49 D5
Sorrel Rd **25** NR31 ....94 C6
Sotherton Rd NR31 ...161 F3
Soudan Cl **3** NR30 ...168 D7
South Acre Hall PE32 ..46 E1
South Acre Rd PE32 ..46 F1
South Ave Norwich NR7 .163 E5
Swanton Morley Airfield
......................50 B5
South Beach PE31 ....133 A3
South Beach Par
NR30 ....170 E6
South Beach Pl NR30 ..169 E2
South Beach Rd
Heacham PE31 ....133 A4
Hunstanton PE36 .....132 B3
South Brink PE13 .....152 A3
South Burlingham Rd
NR13 ....74 B3
South Cl NR25 ....7 A4
South Cnr NR20 ......3 B7
South Croft NR9 .....88 C7
South Denes Rd NR30 .169 D1

South Everard St
PE30 ....146 E3
South Gage Cl NR7 ...159 C4
South Gn NR19 ....154 E3
South Gn Gdns NR19 ..154 E3
South Harford Mid Sch
NR4 ....89 E8
South Hill Cl NR7 .....163 F8
South Hill Rd NR7 ....163 F8
South Icehouse Hill
NR31 ....170 D6
South Lynn Plain
PE30 ....146 E4
South Mkt Rd NR30 ...169 D4
South Moor Dr PE31 ..133 D4
South Pk IP27 ....175 B7
South Pk Ave
Norwich NR1 ....161 E3
2 Norwich NR1 ......162 A4
South Quay NR30 .....169 C3
South St
Great Dunham PE32 ..47 F1
Hockwold cum Wilton
......................113 F6
2 King's Lynn PE30 ..146 E4
Sheringham NR26 ....138 C7
South Walsham Rd
Acle NR13 ....166 A5
South Walsham NR13 ..74 B5
South Wlk NR13 .....72 E5
South Wood Dr NR14 ..90 B6
South Wootton Fst Sch
PE30 ....148 C2
South Wootton Jun Sch
PE30 ....148 B1
South Wootton La
NR18 ....148 C1
Southacre Rd PE32 ...65 C7
Southampton Pl **1**
NR30 ....169 D4
Southburgh La NR9 ...86 A5
Southburgh Rd NR9 ...86 A7
Southend
Bradenham IP25 ......66 D3
East Dereham NR19 ..154 D4
Southend Rd PE36 ....132 C3
Southern La IP22 .....128 D5
Southern Reach **7** NR4 .89 B3
Southernwood **4** NR6 .158 D5
Southery Prim Sch
PE38 ....97 A5
Southery Rd
Feltwell IP26 ....98 B2
Methwold IP26 ....97 F3
Southfield PE32 ......45 D5
Southfield Dr **8** PE35 .43 F7
Southfield La NR15 ...55 C1
Southfields **1** PE30 ..147 B6
Southgate **9** IP20 ....122 D1
Southgate Cl NR21 ...136 C5
Southgate La
Norwich NR1 ....178 C1
Snettisham PE31 .....12 E4
Southgate St PE30 ...146 D4
Southgates Dr NR21 ..141 B5
Southgates Rd NR30 ..169 D2
Southlands PE37 .....153 B2
Southrepps Rd
Antingham NR28 .....22 B4
Gimingham NR11 .....22 E6
Southside PE34 ......79 D8
Southtown Fst Sch
NR31 ....169 B2
Southtown Rd NR31 ...169 C2
Southwell Rd
5 Horsham St Faith &
Newton St Faith NR10 ..53 D2
Norwich NR1 ....178 A1
Wisbech PE13 ....152 C7
Southwood Rd
Beighton NR13 ....74 C1
Cantley NR13 ....92 C8
Sovereign Cl **2** PE13 ..152 A6
Sovereign Way PE38 ..172 A4
Sow's Loke NR12 .....55 E6
Spa La Aylsham NR11 .150 B3
Oulton NR11 ....35 B8
Spalding's Chair Hill
IP24 ....126 E8
Spar Rd NR6 ....158 C5
Sparhawk Ave NR7 ...159 C4
Sparhawk Cl NR7 ....159 C4
Sparhawk Fst Sch
NR7 ....159 C4
Sparrow Cl **4** NR31 ..94 C7
Sparrowgate Rd PE14 .59 C5
Speedwell Cl **6** NR17 .174 B4
Speedwell Rd NR18 ..173 D4
Speedwell Way
Norwich NR5 ....160 F5
16 Redenhall with Harleston
IP20 ....122 D1
Speke St NR2 ....162 A2
Spelman Rd NR2 .....162 A4
Spencer Ave NR19 ...170 C6
Spencer Cl
Great & Little Plumstead
NR13 ....73 B7
1 Lingwood NR13 ...74 A3
West Walton PE14 ...59 B8
Spencer Ct **12** IP25 ..84 D3
Spencer Rd NR6 .....158 C5

Spencer St NR3 ......162 E8
Spencers Cl NR20 ....49 E7
Spens Ave NR31 .....170 B3
Spenser Ave NR28 ...151 D4
Spenser Rd PE30 ....148 B1
Spice Chase PE34 ...60 C7
Spicer's La NR16 ....106 B5
Spiers Way PE37 ....177 B4
Spindle Cl NR18 .....173 D4
Spindle Rd NR6 .....158 D4
Spindrift Cl **8** NR29 ..58 B6
Spinks' La NR15 .....108 D2
Spinks La NR18 .....88 B4
Spink's La NR18 .....173 F6
Spinners Cl PE37 ....153 B5
Spinners La PE37 ....153 B5
Spinney Cl Beetley NR20 ..49 D4
Brandon IP27 ....175 C2
King's Lynn PE30 ....148 B4
8 Long Stratton NR15 .106 E3
Norwich NR7 ....163 F8
Spinney Rd NR17 ....163 E8
Spinney The NR14 ...110 B7
Spirkett's La IP20 ....122 D1
Spitalfields NR1 .....163 A7
Spitfire Rd NR6 ......158 C6
Spixworth Fst Sch
NR10 ....54 A2
Spixworth Rd
Hainford NR10 ....53 F4
Horsham St Faith &
Newton St Faith NR10 ..53 E2
Splash Leisure Complex
NR26 ....138 B7
Splashes The PE37 ..153 B7
Spong La
Carleton St Peter NR14 ..91 D5
East Carleton NR14 ..88 F4
Shropham NR17 ......103 C4
Spooner Row Prim Sch
NR18 ....105 A8
Spooner Row Sta
NR18 ....105 A8
Sporle Fst Sch PE32 ..65 D6
Sporle Rd
Little Dunham PE32 ..65 D7
Swaffham PE37 ......153 C5
Spring Cl PE30 ......148 C1
Spring Gr PE34 ......144 B4
Spring La
Forncett NR16 ....106 B5
Hempnall NR15 ......107 E3
King's Lynn PE30 ....147 C7
Shouldham PE33 .....62 D4
South Creake NR22 ..16 A6
Yaxham NR19 ....68 B6
Spring Rd IP31 ......127 A7
Springbank Cres NR13 .165 B4
Springdale Cres NR13 ..165 B4
Springdale Rd NR13 ..165 B4
Springfield NR18 ....166 C3
Springfield Cl
Crimplesham PE33 ...80 B6
Norwich NR29 ....58 A4
Springfield N NR29 ..58 A4
Springfield Rd
Great Yarmouth NR31 .170 D4
Hemsby NR29 ....58 A4
Norwich NR2 ....162 B4
Taverham NR8 ....155 D2
Walpole St Andrew PE14 .41 D4
Springfield Wlk IP21 ..121 E5
Springfields
Attleborough NR17 ...174 B5
P Poringland NR14 ..90 C5
Springfield Cl **8** NR25 ..8 F5
Springles The **6** NR27 ..10 B5
Springvale **3** PE32 ..45 C6
Springwell La NR17 ..51 F6
Springwell Rd NR20 ..31 D2
Springwood
Taverham NR8 ....155 E1
Woodton NR35 ....108 A6
Springwood High Sch
PE30 ....147 C6
Sprowston Fst & Mid Sch
NR7 ....159 A4
Sprowston High Sch
NR7 ....159 A4
Sprowston Pk Golf Course
NR7 ....159 E5
Sprowston Rd NR3 ...158 F2
Sprowston Ret Pk
NR7 ....159 C2
Spruce Ave **2** NR29 ..167 A2
Spruce Cl NR31 .....94 C8
Spruce Cres **4** NR14 ..90 C5
Spruce Dr IP27 ......175 D2
Spruce Rd PE38 .....172 B6
Spur La NR14 ....90 C6
Spur Rd NR9 ....69 C2
Spurdens Cres NR8 ..158 C3
Spurge Sq **3** NR18 ..173 E4
Spynke Rd NR3 .....158 B1
Squire's Dr Upwell PE14 .77 E3
Upwell PE14 ....78 A3
Squire's Dro PE14 ...78 A3
Squires Hill NR13 ....165 C4
Squire's Rd NR13 ...75 A2
Stablefields IP26 ....99 C7
Stacy Rd NR3 ....162 E8
Staden Pk NR11 .....11 D1
Stafford Ave NR3 ...156 F1
Stafford Rd NR31 ...169 B2
Stafford St NR2 .....162 B6
Stainsby Cl PE31 ....133 D4
Staithe Cl **3** NR12 ..55 E4

Staithe La PE36 ......2 C7
Staithe Rd
Barton Turf NR12 .....38 F1
Burgh St Peter NR34 ..111 C3
Catfield NR29 ....56 D8
Halvergate NR13 .....146 F1
Heacham PE31 ......133 C5
Hickling NR12 ....39 E1
Langley with Hardley
NR14 ....91 F4
Ludham NR29 ....56 C5
Marsham NR29 ......57 D5
Repps with Bastwick
NR29 ....56 F4
Somerton NR29 ......57 E6
Stalham NR12 ....39 B3
Stalham NR12 ....152 E5
Staithe Stree NR23 ..136 D6
Staitheway Rd NR12 ..164 C4
Stalham Cty High Sch
NR12 ....39 B4
Stalham Mid Sch NR12 .39 B3
Stalham Rd
Ashmanhaugh NR12 ..55 C8
Hickling NR12 ....39 E2
Sea Palling NR12 ....24 F1
Wroxham/Hoveton
NR12 ....164 D6
Stalland La NR18 ....86 D2
Stalland The NR18 ...86 D2
Stallett Way PE34 ...60 C8
Stan Petersen Cl NR1 .163 A6
Standard Pl **8** NR30 .169 D3
Standard Rd
Great Yarmouth NR30 .169 E3
Wells-next-the-Sea
NR23 ....136 D6
Standley Ct NR18 ...173 B4
Stanfield Rd
Mileham PE32 ....48 E6
Tittleshall PE32 .....48 C7
Wymondham NR18 ..173 F3
Stanford Cres NR13 ..73 B7
Stanford Tuck Rd
NR28 ....151 B7
Stanhoe Rd NR31 ...134 E4
Staniforth Rd IP24 ...176 B2
Stanley Ave
Great Yarmouth NR31 .170 D2
Neatishead NR12 ....55 E7
Norwich NR7 ....163 C5
Stanley Cl NR13 .....92 B6
Stanley Dr PE12 .....41 A8
Stanley Rd Diss IP22 .177 B4
Great Yarmouth NR30 .169 C5
North Walsham NR28 .151 D6
Stanley St **7** PE30 ..146 E5
Stanleys La NR18 ...173 C2
Stanmore Rd NR7 ...163 E6
Stannard Cl **4** NR27 .177 C4
Stannard Rd NR4 ...161 F5
Stanninghall Rd NR12 .54 B4
Stanton Rd
Barningham IP31 ....127 C2
Dersingham PE31 ...140 C3
Star Farm Cl **2** NR31 .94 C6
Star Hill NR12 ....24 C3
Star La
Long Stratton NR15 ..106 E3
1 Thetford IP24 ....176 C3
Tivetshall St Margaret
NR15 ....121 C5
Star Mdw NR21 .....141 B4
Stark Cl IP22 ....177 C4
Starling Cl NR11 ....150 C5
Starling Rd NR3 .....162 D8
Starling Rise NR27 ..11 B2
Starston La PE20 ...122 C1
Statham Cl NR4 .....162 B2
Station App NR1 .....178 C2
Station Cl
East Dereham NR19 ..154 D6
4 Lingwood NR13 ...74 A3
3 Marham NR29 ....57 D4
Sheringham NR27 ...10 A5
Swainsthorpe NR14 ..89 D4
Station Dr
Fransham NR19 ......66 A8
Reedham NR13 ......92 F5
Wisbech PE13 ....152 C4
Station Hill IP20 .....122 D2
Station La
Garvestone NR9 .....68 D1
Hethersett NR9 ......88 E7
Thetford IP24 ....176 C5
Thornham PE36 .....2 C6
Station New Rd NR13 .165 D3
Station Rd Acle NR13 .166 B2
Alburgh IP20 ....123 A5
Aldeby NR34 ....110 B4
Attleborough NR17 ..174 E5
Attlebridge NR9 .....50 D6
Aylsham NR11 ......150 B6
Barnham IP24 ....125 E6
Beccles NR34 ....110 D1
Brundall NR13 ......165 D2
Burnham Market PE31 .135 C3
Burston & Shimpling
IP21 ....120 F2
Cantley NR13 ....92 C8
Clenchwarton PE34 ..145 B4
Coltishall NR12 .....54 C7
Congham PE32 .....27 F3
Corpusty NR11 ......19 F1
Cromer NR27 ....139 C4
Dersingham PE31 ...140 B4
Diss IP22 ....177 F3
Ditchingham NR35 ..109 B2

Station Rd continued
Docking PE31 ....134 D5
Downham Market PE38 ..172 A5
2 Earsham NR35 ...123 F8
East Dereham NR19 ..154 E4
East Rudham PE31 ..30 B5
East Winch PE32 ....44 F3
Ellingham NR35 .....109 D3
Flordon NR15 ....106 C4
Forncett NR16 ......106 C4
Foulsham NR20 .....33 C3
Fransham NR19 .....66 B7
Fulmodeston NR21 ..17 F4
Geldeston NR34 ....109 F2
Great Moulton NR15 ..121 A7
Great Ryburgh NR21 ..32 A6
Great Yarmouth NR31 .169 B3
Guestwick NR20 ....33 F5
Haddiscoe NR14 ....93 D1
Hardingham NR9 ...86 E8
Harleston IP20 ......122 D2
Hilgay PE38 ....96 C6
Hindolveston NR20 ..33 E8
Holme Hale IP25 ....65 F2
Holt NR25 ....137 C6
Honing NR28 ....38 C6
Hopton on Sea NR31 .171 D4
Kimberley NR18 ....87 A6
King's Lynn PE30 ...148 B5
Lakenheath IP27 ....112 E3
Lenwade NR9 ....51 E5
Lingwood & Burlingham
NR13 ....74 A3
Middleton PE32 .....44 C4
Mundesley NR11 ...143 B6
North Elmham NR20 ..49 F7
North Walsham NR28 .151 B4
Ormesby St Margaret
with Scratby NR29 ...167 B2
5 Potter Heigham NR29 .56 F6
Pulham Market NR15 ..121 E4
Pulham St Mary IP21 ..122 A4
Quidenham NR16 ...118 C8
Rackheath/Salhouse
NR13 ....72 F8
Reedham NR13 .....92 F5
Reepham NR10 .....149 C5
Roydon PE32 ....28 A2
6 Sheringham NR27 ..10 A5
Sheringham NR26 ...138 D7
Snettisham PE31 ...12 D4
Somerleyton, Ashby &
Herringfleet NR32 ...111 C7
Stanhoe PE31 ....14 E8
Strumpshaw NR13 ..91 F8
Taverham NR8 ......156 F8
Terrington St Clement
PE34 ....144 C2
Thetford IP24 ....176 C5
Thorpe Market NR11 ..22 A6
Tilney All Saints PE34 .144 F2
Tivetshall St Margaret
NR15 ....121 B7
Walpole Cross Keys PE14 ..41 F5
Walsingham NR22 ..16 F7
Walsoken PE14 .....59 E4
Watlington PE33 ....61 C6
Wells-next-the-Sea
NR23 ....136 D5
Wendling NR19 .....66 F7
West Dereham PE33 ..80 B3
Weybourne NR25 ...8 F5
Whinburgh & Westfield
NR19 ....68 A5
Worstead NR28 .....37 F3
Wroxham/Hoveton
NR12 ....164 C5
Wymondham NR18 ..104 F8
Station Rd N NR31 ...93 F6
Station Rd S NR31 ...93 F5
Station St PE37 .....153 B5
Station Way PE27 ...175 C5
Steam Mill La NR31 ..169 B4
Stearne Cl IP24 .....176 B2
Stebbings Cl **3** PE32 .28 A1
Steel's Dro PE38 ....79 C1
Steepgreen Cl NR1 ..163 C8
Steeple Chase NR8 ..155 F2
Steeple La NR15 ....106 A4
Steer Rd PE31 ....27 B8
Steggles Dr IP22 ....177 C5
Stegg's La NR19 ....67 F4
Stephen Beaumont Way
NR19 ....154 F2
Stephenson Cl
1 Great Yarmouth NR30 .169 D5
West Raynham Airfield
PE31 ....30 B3
Stephenson Way IP24 ..176 A2
Stephenson Way Ind Est
IP24 ....176 A2
Stepping La NR1 ....178 B2
Stepping Stone La
NR12 ....39 A4
Stepshort NR31 .....94 A6
Stermyn St **16** PE13 ..152 C5
Stevens Cl IP25 .....84 D4
Steven's La
Ashwellthorpe NR16 ..106 B8
Bunwell NR16 ....88 E1
Stevens Rd
Cromer NR27 ....139 C4
2 Little Snoring NR21 ..17 B3
Stevenson Rd NR5 ..161 B7
Steward Pl **1** NR18 ..173 D5

Steward St 4 NR3 ....162 E8
Steward Way NR19 ....154 C5
Stewards Cl NR10 ....149 C4
Stewks Hall Drift NR9 ....51 B6
Stibbard Rd NR21 ....17 F1
Stickfer La NR16 ....106 A6
Stiffkey Ct 11 PE31 ....61 D6
Stiffkey Rd Warham NR21 ...5 F5
Weils next-the-sea
NR23 ....136 F5
Stigand's Gate NR19 .....154 D7
Stile Cl 12 NR14 ....89 B3
Stile La NR18 ....173 B5
Stileman Way 11 PE31 ....12 E4
Stillington Cl NR7 ....159 B3
Stilwell Dr NR19 ....154 B6
Stirling Cl
Downham Market PE38 .172 D6
Taverham NR8 ....155 F3
Stirling Rd NR21 ....15 C5
Stirrups La NR17 ....171 E1
Stitch The PE14 ....77 B8
Stock Lea Rd PE30 ....148 C4
Stocks Hill NR9 ....160 B5
Stocks La NR13 ....165 E5
Stockton Rd NR34 ....110 A3
Stody Dr PE30 ....148 E1
Stody Rd NR22 ....18 D6
Stoke Holy Cross Prim Sch
NR14 ....89 F4
Stoke La NR14 ....89 F5
Stoke Rd
Barton Bendish PE33 .....81 C5
Bixley NR14 ....162 F1
Boughton PE33 ....81 A4
Caistor St Edmund NR14 ..89 F7
Methwold IP26 ....79 A6
Poringland NR14 ....90 B5
Wereham PE33 ....80 E4
Wormegay PE33 ....62 A5
Stokes Ave IP25 ....84 C3
Stokesby New Rd
NR13 ....166 F6
Stokesby Rd NR29 ....75 D6
Stone Breck NR5 ....156 E2
Stone Cl 2 PE33 ....61 D5
Stone Hill Rd NR30 ....168 D6
Stone La Bintree NR20 .....33 B3
Bressingham IP22 ....119 F7
3 Hingham NR9 ....86 C4
Hoveton NR12 ....164 D8
Runhall NR9 ....68 F6
Stonebridge Rd NR28 ....23 D2
Stonecross Rd PE38 ......172 D5
Stonecutters Way
NR30 ....169 C4
Stonefield Rd NR25 ....20 A8
Stonegate
Aylsham NR11 ....150 A3
Morley NR18 ....87 A3
Stonegate St PE30 ....146 D4
Stonehill Way NR27 ....10 C4
Stonehouse Rd
Norwich NR7 ....159 B4
Upwell PE14 ....54 F2
Upwell PE14 ....77 E5
Stoney End 7 NR20 ....68 F6
Stoney La Beetley NR20 ...49 B4
Reepham NR10 ....149 B6
Stow Rd PE32 ....27 F2
Stony La
Attleborough NR17 ....174 B6
Pulham Market IP21 .....121 E7
Raveningham NR14 ....110 A6
Tivetshall St Margaret
NR15 ....121 B5
Wortwell IP20 ....122 F4
Storbeck Rd 2 PE13 ......152 D7
Stores St IP27 ....175 C3
Store's St IP22 ....177 C6
Story's La NR16 ....165 B5
Stow Barn Rd PE33 ....80 A7
Stow Bedon Rd IP24 ......102 C7
Stow Bridge Rd
Stow Bardolph PE34 ......61 D1
Wimbotsham PE34 ....79 E8
Stow Gdns PE33 ....152 E4
Stow La PE13 ....152 E4
Stow Mill* NR28 ....143 D4
Stow Rd Outwell PE14 ....78 A7
Runcton Holme PE33 ......61 A3
Wiggenhall St Mary Magdalen
PE34 ....61 B5
Wisbech PE13 ....152 F5
Stowlay La NR17 ....103 B6
Stracey Rd Lamas NR10 ..36 F1
Norwich NR1 ....163 A5
Strachan Cl PE31 ....133 E5
Stradbroke CE Prim Sch
IP21 ....131 E1
Stradbroke Fst Sch
NR31 ....170 D5
Stradbroke Rd NR31 ......170 C5
Straight La 10 IP20 ....122 D2
Strangers Hall Folk Mus*
NR2 ....178 A3
Stranton Ave NR19 ....68 A5
Strasbourg Way NR19 ...154 B1

Stratford Cl
Dersingham PE31 ....140 E3
Norwich NR1 ....162 F2
Stratford Cres NR4 ....161 C1
Stratford Dr NR1 ....162 E3
Stratton Cl 6 PE37 ....153 C3
Stratton Rd
Hainford NR10 ....53 E6
Stratton Strawless NR10 ..53 E8
Wacton NR15 ....106 D2
Strawberry Cl 3 PE13 ...152 A6
Strawberry Fields NR12 ..39 B3
Strayground La NR18 .....173 B2
Street Hill NR12 ....55 E7
Street The Acle NR13 ....166 C3
Alburgh IP20 ....122 F6
Aldborough NR11 ....20 F5
Aldeby NR34 ....110 F4
Ashby St Mary NR14 ......91 C5
Ashwellthorpe NR16 .....106 A8
Ashwellthorpe NR16 .....106 A8
Aslacton NR15 ....106 A1
Aylmerton NR11 ....10 A2
Baconsthorpe NR25 ....19 F8
Bacton NR28 ....23 B2
Barnham IP24 ....125 E6
Barton Turf NR17 ....9 A7
Bawdeswell NR20 ....50 E7
Beachamwell PE37 ....81 E8
Beeston with Bittering
PE32 ....48 C2
Belaugh NR12 ....164 A6
Bergh Apton NR15 ....91 A3
Billingford NR20 ....50 B7
Bintree NR20 ....33 B2
Blo' Norton IP22 ....128 B6
Booton NR10 ....149 C4
Botesdale IP22 ....128 B2
Bracon Ash NR14 ....89 A3
Bramerton NR14 ....90 F7
Brampton NR10 ....36 E3
Brandon IP27 ....175 A4
Bressingham IP22 ....119 D2
Bridgham NR16 ....117 E4
Brinton NR24 ....18 D6
Brinton NR24 ....18 D8
Brockdish IP21 ....131 B6
Brockdish IP21 ....131 D6
Brome & Oakley IP23 ....130 C3
Brooke NR15 ....90 E2
Brundall NR13 ....165 C4
Brundall NR13 ....165 C4
Burgh & Tuttington NR11 .36 E4
Caston NR17 ....84 E8
Catfield NR29 ....56 C8
Claxton NR14 ....91 D6
Coltishall NR12 ....54 E7
Coney Weston IP31 ....127 B4
Corpusty NR11 ....19 F1
Costessey NR8 ....156 E5
Croxton IP24 ....116 C6
Dickleburgh IP21 ....121 B1
Dilham NR28 ....38 D4
Earsham NR35 ....123 F8
East Tuddenham NR20 ...69 C6
Erpingham NR11 ....21 A2
Felthorpe NR10 ....155 C8
Flixton NR35 ....123 E6
Flordon NR15 ....106 D8
Puxley NR20 ....50 D8
Framingham Pigot NR14 ..90 D6
Fulmodeston NR21 ....17 F3
Garvestone NR9 ....68 E1
Geldeston NR34 ....109 F2
Gooderstone PE33 ....81 F5
Great Cressingham PE25 ..83 C4
Great Snoring NR21 ....17 A3
Great Yarmouth NR30 .....76 F5
Halvergate NR13 ....174 F1
Hempnall NR15 ....107 C5
Hemsby NR29 ....167 A7
Hevingham NR10 ....53 C8
Heydon NR11 ....34 F6
Hickling NR12 ....39 F4
Hinderclay IP22 ....128 C3
Hindolveston NR20 ....33 D8
Hindringham NR17 ....17 E7
Hockering NR20 ....69 B8
Honingham NR9 ....69 E6
Horsey NR29 ....40 E1
Kelling NR25 ....8 C5
Ketteringham NR18 ....88 E6
Kettlestone NR21 ....17 C2
Knapton NR28 ....143 B1
Lamas NR10 ....36 D1
Lenwade NR9 ....51 D5
Lessingham NR12 ....24 D1
Little Barningham NR11 ...20 B4
Little Snoring NR21 ....17 B3
Long Stratton NR15 ......106 E3
Lound NR32 ....94 C4
Marham PE33 ....63 B5
Market Weston IP22 ......127 E4
Marlingford NR9 ....69 E4
Mautby NR29 ....75 E5
Melton Constable NR24 ..142 A5
Mileham PE32 ....48 B6
Morning Thorpe NR15 ...107 C4
Morston NR25 ....7 A6
Morton on the Hill NR9 ....52 A3
North Lopham IP22 ....119 A2
North Pickenham PE37 ....84 B7
Ovington IP25 ....84 E5
Poringland NR14 ....90 C5
Pulham St Mary IP21 .....122 A3
Redenhall with Harleston
IP20 ....122 F1

Street The continued
Redgrave IP22 ....128 E5
Reepham NR10 ....149 C3
Riddlesworth IP22 ....127 D7
Ringland NR8 ....70 B8
Rockland St Mary NR14 ..91 B7
Rocklands NR17 ....103 C7
Rougham PE32 ....47 B7
Ryburgh NR21 ....32 C2
St Margaret, South Elmham
IP20 ....123 E2
Salle NR10 ....149 D8
Saxlingham Nethergate
NR15 ....107 B8
Scoulton NR9 ....85 D3
Sculthorpe NR21 ....16 B1
Sculthorpe Airfield PE31 ..15 B3
Sea Palling NR12 ....40 A5
Seething NR15 ....108 E6
Shelton NR15 ....122 B8
Shotesham NR15 ....90 A2
Somerleyton, Ashby &
Herringfleet NR32 ....111 D8
Somerton NR29 ....57 F6
South Lopham IP22 ....128 D8
South Pickenham PE37 ...83 D7
South Walsham NR13 .....74 A8
Sparham NR9 ....51 B4
Sparham NR9 ....51 B6
Sporle with Palgrave
PE32 ....65 C7
Starston IP20 ....122 C3
Surlingham NR14 ....165 B1
Sustead NR11 ....20 E7
Swafield NR28 ....151 D8
Swanton Abbott NR10 ....37 C4
Swanton Novers NR24 ...18 C2
Taverham NR8 ....156 B8
Tharston & Hapton
NR15 ....106 C7
Tharston & Hapton
NR15 ....106 D5
Themelthorpe NR20 ....33 F2
Thornage NR25 ....18 E6
Thurlton NR14 ....92 F1
Thurne NR29 ....56 E2
Thurton NR14 ....91 C3
Tibenham NR16 ....120 E8
Tivetshall St Mary NR15 ..121 B5
Topcroft NR35 ....107 F3
Warham NR23 ....6 A4
Wattisfield IP22 ....128 A1
Wellingham PE32 ....47 F8
West Rexham NR25 ....9 B2
Weybourne NR25 ....8 E5
Winfarthing IP22 ....118 G4
Witton NR28 ....23 E1
Woodton NR35 ....7 E6
Wootton NR35 ....108 C5
Stretton Sch NR2 ....162 C3
Strickland Ave 3 PE31 ....12 E4
Strickland Cl 6 PE31 ......12 E4
Stringside Dro PE33 ....81 B3
Strumpshaw Rd NR13 ....165 E3
Strumpshaw Steam Mus*
NR13 ....165 C5
Stuart Cl Brandon IP27 ..175 C3
8 Hethersett NR9 ....88 D8
7 Hethersett NR9 ....88 D8
Stuart Gdns NR1 ....178 C3
Stuart Rd
Aylsham NR11 ....150 C7
Norwich NR1 ....178 C1
Stubb Rd NR12 ....39 F2
Stubbs Gn La NR14 ....109 C8
Sturdee Ave NR30 ....169 D8
Sturdee Cl IP24 ....176 F6
Sturmy Cl 13 NR15 ....106 E3
Sturston La IP21 ....130 B4
Sturston Rd IP21 ....130 B5
Style Loke NR9 ....69 F2
Styles Cl NR31 ....170 A4
Stylman Rd NR5 ....161 A7
Suckling Ave NR3 ....158 B3
Suckling Dro PE14 ....78 C5
Suckling La
Framingham Pigot NR14 ..90 D6
Hickling NR12 ....39 F3
Suckling Pl NR35 ....108 C5
Suffield Cl
1 Cringleford NR4 ....89 B8
8 Long Stratton NR15 ...106 D3
North Walsham NR28 ....151 A6
Suffield Rd NR31 ....170 C4
Suffield Way PE30 ....147 B8
Suffling Rd NR30 ....170 D8
Suffolk Ave NR31 ....126 B1
Suffolk Pl NR19 ....154 C1
Suffolk Rd
Great Yarmouth NR31 ...170 C8
King's Lynn PE30 ....147 C6
Norwich NR4 ....161 C3
Sheringham NR26 ....138 D6
Sugar La PE31 ....140 E4
Sukey Way NR5 ....160 F6
Summer Cl PE14 ....41 B4
Summer Dr NR14 ....164 D6
Summer La IP25 ....85 A4
Summerfield PE13 ....152 A6
Summerfield Rd NR29 ....58 A4
Summerhouse Cl
NR27 ....139 A6
Sumpter Rd NR4 ....161 E3
Sun Barn Rd NR10 ....149 B4
Sun La
Great Yarmouth NR30 .....94 C4
Norwich NR3 ....158 D1
Sun Rd NR35 ....109 B2

Suncroft NR1 ....162 F2
Sundew Cl 6 IP24 ....176 F4
Sunk Rd NR30 ....16 F7
Sunley Cl NR35 ....109 C2
Sunningdale NR4 ....162 A2
Sunninghill Cl 14 NR31 ...94 C8
Sunny Cl NR5 ....157 B1
Sunny Gr NR3 ....161 B8
Sunny Hill NR1 ....162 E2
Sunnyside
Bedingham NR35 ....108 C4
Diss IP22 ....177 D5
Heacham PE31 ....133 D5
Sunnyside Ave 10 NR4 ..90 C5
Sunnyside Cl PE31 ....133 D5
Sunnyside Rd PE32 ....29 D2
Sunsalve Ride NR19 .....154 C1
Sunset Wlk NR22 ....24 E4
Supple Cl NR1 ....163 C7
Surlingham Dr PE37 .....153 B1
Surlingham La
Bramerton NR14 ....90 F8
Rockland St Mary NR14 ..91 B8
Surlingham Prim Sch
NR14 ....73 B1
Surrey Cl NR7 ....159 C5
Surrey Gr NR1 ....178 B1
Surrey Mount 4 NR18 ...73 C6
Surrey St Cromer NR27 ..139 C7
5 King's Lynn PE30 .....146 D5
Norwich NR1 ....178 B2
Surrogate St NR17 ....174 D5
Sursham Ave NR10 ....158 F4
Sussex Rd NR11 ....90 C5
Sussex St NR3 ....178 A4
Sustead La NR11 ....9 F1
Suters Dr NR8 ....155 E2
Sutherland Ave NR6 .....156 A4
Suton La NR18 ....173 A1
Sutton Cres NR13 ....92 F8
Sutton Fst Sch NR12 ......39 C2
Sutton Mdws PE13 ....152 A8
Sutton Rd Catfield NR29 ..39 C1
Great Yarmouth NR30 ...169 D7
Hickling NR12 ....39 D1
Swaffham PE37 ....153 B1
Terrington St Clement
PE34 ....144 A4
Wisbech PE13 ....153 A7
Sutton Windmill & Broads
Mus* NR12 ....39 D2
Suttons Cl 1 PE14 ....77 F6
Swaffham Com Hospl
PE37 ....153 C5
Swaffham Gap IP26 ....82 C1
Swaffham Golf Course
PE37 ....64 E1
Swaffham Leisure Ctr
PE37 ....153 C2
Swaffham Raceway
PE37 ....64 C4
Swaffham Rd
Ashill IP25 ....84 A7
Barton Bendish PE33 .....63 C2
Cockley Cley PE37 ....82 D7
East Dereham NR19 ......154 D6
Mundford IP26 ....100 B1
Narborough PE32 ....63 F7
Oxborough PE33 ....81 E4
Raynham NR21 ....30 F2
Swaffham PE37 ....84 E4
Wotton IP25 ....84 C4
Swaffham S Greenhoe
VC Prim Sch *
PE37 ....153 B2
Swaffham VC Nursery Sch
PE37 ....153 B2
Swafield Rise NR28 ....151 D7
Swafield St NR5 ....160 F7
Swale The NR5 ....160 F6
Swallow Cl 8 NR31 ......170 A7
Swallow Dr IP27 ....175 E3
Swallowfield Rd PE30 ...147 C4
Swamp La
Great Ellingham NR17 ...103 F7
Roydon IP22 ....177 A6
Swan Cl Aylsham NR11 ..150 C6
Swannington NR9 ....52 B5
Swan Cotts PE32 ....47 D5
Swan Dr NR20 ....49 C3
Swan Entry 2 NR22 ......16 F7
Swan La
Coney Weston IP31 ....127 B4
Fincham PE33 ....62 E1
King's Lynn PE30 ....147 A6
Redenhall with Harleston
IP20 ....122 D2
Shipdham IP25 ....67 C3
Tharston & Hapton
NR15 ....106 E4
Swan Loke NR15 ....151 C5
Swan Rd
Dersingham PE31 ....133 C5
Shouldham Thorpe PE33 ..62 C5

Swanton Ave NR19 ....154 E7
Swanton Cl NR19 ....154 E7
Swanton Dr NR20 ....154 E6
Swanton Gr NR19 ....154 E6
Swanton Morley Airfield
(Dis) NR20 ....50 A5
Swanton Morley Prim Sch
NR20 ....50 B4
Swanton Morley Rd
Hoe NR20 ....50 A6
North Elmham NR20 ....49 F6
Swanton Rd
Dereham NR20 ....50 A1
East Dereham NR19 .....154 E6
Foxley NR20 ....18 B5
Norwich NR3 ....162 B8
Swardeston La NR14 ......89 B6
Swargate La NR15 ....108 E8
Swash La NR13 ....54 D2
Sweden Pl IP27 ....175 B2
Sweet Briar Rd
7 Long Stratton NR15 ..106 E3
Norwich NR6 ....161 F8
Sweet Briar Rd Ind Est
NR3 ....157 F1
Sweetacres 7 NR20 .....167 B6
Sweetbriar Gdns NR20 ..49 C4
Sweetbriar La
Edgefield NR24 ....19 D5
Sheringham NR26 ....138 C7
Sweyn Cl IP24 ....176 B2
Swim Rd NR29 ....75 F6
Swinbourne Cl NR6 ......158 C3
Swindells Cl NR5 ....157 A2
Swiney La NR18 ....87 A3
Swirle's Pl 6 NR30 ....169 C4
Sybil Rd PE13 ....152 C6
Sybil Wheeler Cl
6 Thetford IP24 ....176 D6
2 Thetford IP24 ....176 D6
Sycamore Ave
10 Great Yarmouth NR31 ..94 C7
Wymondham NR18 ....173 C6
Sycamore Cl
Attleborough NR17 ....174 C4
King's Lynn PE30 ....148 D2
6 Loddon NR14 ....91 F1
North Walsham NR28 ...151 D6
Thompson IP24 ....102 A7
Sycamore Cres NR2 .....161 F7
Sycamore Gr 2 NR31 ...170 B6
Sycamore Gr NR26 ....138 D5
Sycamore Way IP22 .....177 E5
Sycamores The NR19 ...154 E3
Sydenham Cl NR13 ......166 B4
Syderstone Rd NR21 .....15 B3
Sydney Dye Ct PE32 ......65 C5
Sydney Rd 11 NR10 ....54 A2
Sydney Terr 2 PE30 .....146 D1
Syers La IP32 ....48 D2
Syleham Hall La IP21 ....131 F5
Syleham Rd
Syleham IP21 ....131 B4
Syleham IP21 ....131 D4
Sylvan Cl 6 NR16 ....157 E6
Sylvan Way
2 Blofield Heath NR13 ...73 C6
Taverham NR8 ....156 E8
Sylvden Dr PE13 ....152 F6
Symonds Ave NR29 ......167 C2
Gyon Cl PE38 ....172 B4
Sywell Cl NR6 ....158 F6
Sywell Gr 5 PE14 ....59 A1

T

Tabernacle La NR16 ....105 F4
Tacolneston VC Prim Sch
NR16 ....105 F6
Tagg Way 3 NR13 ....72 E7
Talbot Cl NR18 ....173 C6
Talbot Sq NR3 ....178 A4
Tales of the Old Gaol
House* PE30 ....146 D4
Tallon Ave NR29 ....02 A2
Tamworth La NR31 ....169 B2
Tan La NR30 ....168 E4
Tanager Cl NR3 ....158 D3
Tanner St 4 IP24 ....176 C4
Tanners Gn NR9 ....68 C3
Tanning La 1 NR16 ....104 F1
Tanns La IP22 ....119 A2
Tansy Cl NR6 ....158 D4
Tar Works Rd NR30 ......169 C6
Target Hill IP20 ....123 B2
Tarragon Cl 11 NR31 ......94 C6
Tasburgh Rd NR15 ....106 F8
Tasman Dr NR11 ....22 F8
Tatterford Dr NR17 ....30 E7
Tatterscott Pk Bsns Ctr
NR11 ....15 C1
Tattersett Rd IP24 ....15 B2
Tattleport Rd IP21 ....121 E5
Taverham Chase NR8 ...156 D8
Taverham Cty High Sch
NR8 ....155 B2
Taverham Hall Sch
NR8 ....156 A8
Taverham La NR8 ....156 C8
Taverham Mid Sch
NR8 ....156 C8
Taverham Rd
Felthorpe NR10 ....155 C7

Taverham Rd continued
Honingham NR9 ....69 F6
Taverham NR8 ....156 D8
Tavern Cl NR20 ....49 D4
Tavern La Diss IP22 ...177 F3
East Dereham NR19 ...154 E2
Tavistock Rd PE13 ...152 D5
Taylor Ave 9 NR4 ....89 B8
Taylor Rd Diss IP22 ...177 B4
Norwich NR5 ....161 C6
Taylor's La
Gressenhall NR20 ....49 C3
Norwich NR6 ....158 D6
Trimingham NR11 ....11 E1
Taylors Loke
1 Cley next the Sea NR25 ...7 E6
1 Hemsby NR29 ....167 A8
Taymor Pl NR4 ....95 D4
Teal Cl 3 PE31 ....12 E5
Teal Wlk 16 NR31 ....94 C8
Teasel Cl NR20 ....68 A8
Teasel Dr IP24 ....176 E5
Teasel Rd NR17 ....174 B4
Teasel Rise 4 NR26 ...138 B6
Tebbutt Ave 6 NR19 ...154 C3
Ted Ellis Nature Reserve*
NR14 ....91 D8
Tedder Cl
6 Barnham IP24 ....125 F6
16 Watton IP25 ....84 E3
Tee Cl 1 NR14 ....89 B2
Telegraph La E NR1 ...163 B6
Telegraph La W 4 NR1 ...163 B6
Telford Cl
King's Lynn PE30 ....147 D4
2 Norwich NR3 ....157 F1
Telford Way IP24 ...176 B6
Temple Cl NR25 ....8 F6
Temple Dr NR25 ....8 F6
Temple Rd
Great Yarmouth NR30 ...169 D4
King's Lynn PE30 ....148 D1
North Walsham NR28 ...151 A8
Templemere NR3 ....159 A2
Templewood La NR25 ...137 F8
Ten Bell La NR2 ....178 A3
Ten Mile Bank
Hilgay PE38 ....96 F6
Littleport CB6 ....96 E1
Ten Mile Bank Prim Sch
PE38 ....96 F7
Tennyson Ave PE30 ...146 F4
Tennyson Rd
3 Diss IP22 ....177 E4
3 Great Yarmouth NR30 ...169 D8
King's Lynn PE30 ....146 F4
Tennyson Way IP24 ...176 E6
Tensing St NR5 ....108 C5
Terence Airey Ct 25
IP20 ....122 D2
Terence Ave NR7 ....159 A4
Teresa Rd 6 NR12 ....39 B4
Tern Cl 9 IP25 ....84 C3
Tern Gdns NR31 ....170 A6
Tern Rd NR29 ....167 E5
Terrington Cl 3 PE14 ...77 A4
Terrington St Clements Sch
PE34 ....144 C6
Terrington St John Prim Sch
PE14 ....60 B8
Testerton Cotts NR21 ...32 A6
Texas Ave NR21 ....15 C2
Texel Way NR11 ....143 A7
Thain's La NR27 ....10 B5
Thames Way 8 NR30 ...168 C6
Thamesfield Way
NR31 ....169 B2
Thatchwood Ave PE14 ...59 C2
Theatre Plain NR30 ...169 C4
Theatre Rd NR23 ...136 C6
Theatre St
East Dereham NR19 ...154 D6
Norwich NR2 ....178 A2
Swaffham PE37 ....153 B4
Thelnetham Rd
Blo' Norton IP22 ....128 B6
Hopton IP22 ....127 F5
Themelthorpe Rd NR20 ...33 E1
Theobald Rd NR1 ....89 E8
Thetford Ancient House
Mus* IP24 ....176 C4
Thetford Cottage Hospl
IP24 ....176 D4
Thetford Gram Sch
IP24 ....176 C4
Thetford Priory (English
Heritage)* IP24 ...176 C4
Thetford Rd
Brandon IP27 ....175 E3
Coney Weston IP31 ...127 B4
Euston IP24 ....126 B6
Garboldisham IP22 ...127 F8
Northwold IP26 ....99 B8
Santon Downham IP27 ...115 B5
Watton IP25 ....84 D3
Wretham IP24 ....117 A7
Thetford Sta IP24 ...176 C5
Thetford Warren Lodge
(English Heritage)*
IP24 ....115 C3
Thetford Way PE30 ...148 C3
Thiefgate La PE34 ....43 D2
Thieves' Bridge Rd
PE33 ....61 E5

Thieves' La
Attleborough NR17 ...174 E5
Burgh & Tuttington NR11 ...36 E6
Little Ellingham NR17 ...103 C8
Thieves La NR13 ....55 A1
Third Ave PE13 ....152 E5
Third Marsh Rd PE14 ...59 A7
Thirlby Rd NR8 ....151 D3
Thirlmere 16 NR9 ....88 D8
Thistle Cl Norwich NR5 ...160 F5
Thetford IP24 ....176 F5
Thistledown Rd NR10 ...53 B2
Thomas Bole Cl IP22 ...128 A8
Thomas Bullock Prim Sch
IP25 ....67 C2
Thomas Cl 4 PE33 ....61 D5
Thomas Manning Rd
IP22 ....177 E4
Thomas Paine Ave 3
PE34 ....176 C4
Thomas St PE30 ....146 E3
Thomas Vere Rd NR7 ...163 F7
Thompson Ave 7 NR25 ...137 C5
Thompson Cl NR20 ....50 B4
Thompson Prim Sch
IP24 ....102 B7
Thompson Rd
Griston IP25 ....85 A1
Norwich NR7 ....163 F8
Thompson's La PE33 ...81 A2
Thompsons Yd NR3 ...178 B4
Thor Cl NR7 ....163 E7
Thor Loke NR7 ....163 E7
Thor Rd NR7 ....163 E7
Thoresby Ave PE30 ...147 B4
Thoresby Coll PE30 ...146 D4
Thorn La NR1 ....178 B2
Thorn Rd Catfield NR29 ...56 C8
Fakenham NR21 ....141 D4
Thornage Rd NR25 ...137 A5
Thornham Cl NR7 ...159 B2
Thornham Cnr PE36 ...2 E2
Thornham Rd
Methwold IP26 ....98 E7
Methwold IP26 ....99 A6
Norwich NR7 ....159 B2
Thornton Cl NR24 ...142 E4
Thoroughfare La
NR29 ....167 B4
Thoroughfare The
IP20 ....122 D2
Thorpe Abbots Rd
IP21 ....131 A8
Thorpe Ave NR7 ....163 E8
Thorpe Cl NR7 ....163 F7
Thorpe Dr NR17 ....174 D4
Thorpe Hall Cl NR7 ...163 C5
Thorpe Hamlet Fst Sch
NR1 ....163 B6
Thorpe Hamlet Mid Sch
NR1 ....163 B6
Thorpe House Sch
NR7 ....163 C6
Thorpe Mews NR7 ...163 F6
Thorpe Mkt Rd NR11 ...21 E7
Thorpe Rd
Haddiscoe NR14 ....110 F8
Norwich NR1 ....178 C2
Southrepps NR11 ....22 A7
Thorpe St Andrew Sch
NR7 ....72 D4
Thorpeland Cl 4 PE33 ...61 D3
Thorpeland La 3 PE33 ...61 D3
Thorpland Rd NR21 ...141 E6
Threadneedle St NR15 ...91 A4
Three Acre Cl NR12 ...164 C6
Three Cnr Dr NR6 ...158 F6
Three King La NR2 ...178 A2
Three Mile La NR5 ...156 F1
Three Post Rd 5 IP25 ...84 C3
Three Score Rd
Colney NR5 ....161 A5
Norwich NR5 ....160 F4
Threxton Rd IP25 ....84 C3
Thrigby Rd NR29 ....75 E6
Thrush Cl 2 NR14 ....89 B3
Thumb La NR7 ....31 F2
Thunder La NR7 ....163 E7
Thurgarton Rd NR11 ...21 A5
Thurland's Dro PE14 ...77 D5
Thurlby Rd NR5 ....160 E8
Thurlin Rd PE30 ....147 B4
Thurling Plain NR7 ...159 E1
Thurlow Cl NR5 ....160 E8
Thurlton Prim Sch
NR14 ....92 F1
Thurlton Rd NR14 ...110 B7
Thurne Rd NR29 ....57 A2
Thurne Rise 2 NR29 ...57 D5
Thurne Way NR29 ....57 A2
Thurning Rd NR20 ....33 E8
Thursford Mus* NR21 ...17 D5
Thursford Rd
Great Snoring NR21 ...17 A5
Hindringham NR21 ...17 E1
1 Little Snoring NR21 ...17 B3
Thurst Rd NR27 ....11 A3
Thurston Cl 3 NR5 ...160 F8
Thurton Prim Sch
NR14 ....91 D4
Thuxton Sta NR9 ....68 C2
Thwaite Rd NR35 ....109 A2
Thyme Cl
Attleborough NR17 ...174 B4
2 Thetford IP24 ...176 F5
Thynne's La NR26 ....68 E5
Tibenham Rd NR15 ...121 A8

Tiercel Ave NR7 ....159 C4
Tillett Cl NR29 ....167 C2
Tillett Rd NR3 ....158 E2
Tillett Rd NR29 ....167 C2
Tills Cl NR6 ....158 F4
Tills Rd NR6 ....159 A4
Tilney All Saints Prim Sch
PE34 ....42 E4
Tilney Rd NR20 ....69 C6
Tilney St Lawrence CP Sch
PE34 ....60 C8
Timberhill NR1 ....178 B2
Timothy Cl NR1 ....163 B8
Timperley Est NR21 ...31 D5
Tinker's Dro PE13 ...152 C8
Tinker's Dro PE13 ...152 D7
Tinkers' La
Garvestone NR9 ....68 C1
Strumpshaw NR13 ....73 D1
Tinker's La NR15 ....121 C4
Tintern Gr 4 PE30 ...148 C4
Tippett Cl NR5 ....160 F6
Tipton Cl NR19 ....154 D2
Titchwell Marsh Nature
Reserve* PE31 ....2 F7
Tithe Barn Cl IP26 ...100 C5
Tithe Barn La NR24 ...142 F3
Titheborn La
Marham PE33 ....63 D6
2 Thurlton NR14 ....92 F1
Titlow Rd 22 IP20 ...122 D2
Tittleshall Rd
Litcham PE32 ....48 A5
Mileham NR20 ....48 E8
Tittleshall PE32 ....48 A5
Tivetshall Cty Prim Sch
NR15 ....121 B5
Toad Hole Cottage Mus*
NR29 ....56 A6
Toad La
Ditchingham NR35 ...108 F5
Great & Little Plumstead
NR13 ....72 F5
Thwaite NR35 ....109 A5
Todhunter Ave NR34 ...110 C2
Todkill's La PE12 ....41 C8
Toftes Pl 4 NR5 ....161 B8
Toftwood Jun Sch
NR19 ....154 C2
Tolhouse Mus The*
NR30 ....169 C3
Tolhouse St NR30 ...169 C3
Toll Bar NR21 ....141 A6
Tollgate Rd NR31 ...169 C1
Tollgate Way NR5 ...161 A5
Tollhouse Rd NR5 ...161 E7
Tolye Rd NR5 ....160 F7
Tombland NR1 ....178 B3
Tooks Comm La NR34 ...124 F5
Top Driftway IP24 ...117 C8
Top Rd Belaugh NR12 ...164 A6
St Andrew, Ilketshall
NR34 ....124 E5
Wicklewood NR18 ....87 B4
Wingfield IP21 ....131 E3
Topcliffe Ave 3 NR15 ...55 A1
Topshill Rd NR11 ....21 E6
Torrey Cl PE31 ....133 E5
Tortoiseshell Way NR18 ...173 E4
Tottenham St 3 NR30 ...169 D5
Tottenhill Row NR31 ...61 F6
Tottington Cl 6 NR5 ...160 F8
Tottington La IP22 ...177 B4
Tottington Rd
Little Cressingham IP25 ...101 C8
Thompson IP24 ....102 A7
Tottington IP24 ....101 F7
Tower Cl Brandon IP27 ...175 B3
Costessey NR8 ....156 C4
Tower Hill
Costessey NR8 ....156 C4
Norwich NR3 ....163 B6
Tower La
Middleton PE32 ....44 D4
Sidestrand NR27 ....11 B3
Tower Mdw PE37 ...153 C5
Tower Mill Rd NR35 ...124 A8
Tower Pl 10 PE30 ...146 D4
Tower Rd
Burgh St Margaret (Fleggburgh)
NR29 ....57 C1
Burnham Overy PE31 ...135 E7
Canadas NR11 ....10 A4
Elm PE14 ....77 A7
Hilgay PE38 ....97 A8
Repps with Bastwick
NR29 ....57 A5
Terrington St Clement
PE34 ....144 C7
Tower St PE30 ....146 D4
Town Bridge PE13 ...152 B5
Town Cl Corpusty NR11 ...19 E6
East Winch PE32 ....44 F3
North Elmham NR20 ...49 C5
Tower Rd NR35 ....137 B6
Town Cl House Prep Sch
NR2 ....162 C3
Town Cl Rd NR2 ....162 C3
Town Cnr NR10 ....53 C8
Town End NR11 ....143 C6
Town Est PE38 ....172 B5
Town Gn NR18 ....173 B4
Town House La IP22 ...128 B2
Town House Mus*
PE30 ....146 D4
Town House Rd NR8 ...156 F4
Town La Aylsham NR11 ...150 C7
Brancaster Staithe PE31 ...3 D7
Castle Acre PE32 ....46 F2

Town La continued
Garvestone NR9 ....68 C2
Town Lands Trading Est
NR81 ....170 B7
Town Rd
Burgh St Margaret (Fleggburgh)
NR29 ....57 C1
Ingham NR12 ....39 C4
Town St Outwell PE14 ...77 D5
Swanton Morley NR20 ...50 B4
Town Wall Rd NR30 ...169 C5
Town Yd 4 NR25 ....7 E6
Townlands NR11 ....170 B7
Townley Cl PE14 ....77 E5
Townley Prim Sch
PE14 ....95 A7
Townsend Gn N NR21 ...141 F5
Townsend Rd
Norwich NR4 ....162 C1
Upwell PE14 ....77 E3
Townshend Cl 8 NR30 ...169 D3
Townshend Gn E
NR21 ....141 F5
Townshend Gn W
NR21 ....141 F5
Townshend Pl 4 IP25 ...67 C2
Townshend Rd
Dereham NR19 ....154 D7
Wisbech PE13 ....152 D6
Townshend Terr 2
PE30 ....146 E6
Tracey Rd NR7 ....159 E1
Trafalgar Ind Est
PE38 ....172 C4
Trafalgar Rd
Downham Market PE38 ...172 B4
8 Great Yarmouth NR30 ...169 D3
Trafalgar Rd E NR31 ...170 D6
Trafalgar Rd W NR31 ...170 C6
Trafalgar Sq NR30 ...169 D3
Trafalgar Sq NR30 ...169 D3
Trafalgar St NR1 ...178 B1
Trafford Pk 1 PE13 ...152 E6
Trafford Rd
Norwich NR1 ....178 A1
Wisbech PE13 ....152 D5
Traice Rd NR16 ....105 D7
Transport La NR14 ...109 D7
Trap La NR21 ....141 B6
Trelawny Rd 8 NR29 ...57 D4
Tremaine Cl NR6 ....157 E1
Trenchard Cres 4 IP25 ...84 F3
Trenchard Sq IP26 ...98 D1
Trendall Rd NR7 ...159 C4
Trenowaths Pl 7 PE30 ...146 D5
Trent V C CI IP20 ....99 A5
Tretts Loke NR29 ....57 C1
Trident Dr NR1 ....163 A7
Trimingham Rd
Gimingham NR11 ....22 E8
Trimingham NR11 ....11 E1
Trimming Wlk NR8 ...156 E8
Trinity Ave NR31 ....170 B4
Trinity Cl NR19 ....154 D6
Trinity Hospl (Bede House)*
PE31 ....27 C3
Trinity Pl NR30 ....169 D4
Trinity Rd
Walpole Highway PE14 ...59 F8
Wisbech PE13 ....152 B6
Trinity Sq 1 NR30 ...169 D1
Trinity St NR22 ....16 F1
Triple Plea La NR35 ...108 B4
Triple Plea Rd NR35 ...108 A8
Trix Rd NR2 ....162 C4
Tropical Butterfly World*
NR17 ....103 F5
Trory St NR2 ....162 C5
Troston Rd IP31 ....126 C1
Troutbeck 8 NR9 ....88 D8
Trowse Prim Sch
NR14 ....163 B2
True's Yd Fishing Heritage
Mus* PE30 ....146 D6
Truman Cl
8 Norwich NR4 ....161 C5
Rackheath/Salhouse
NR13 ....72 F8
Trumpery La NR14 ...90 C8
Trunch Hill IP20 ...123 A7
Trunch Rd Denton IP20 ...123 B6
Mundesley NR11 ...143 B4
Swafield NR28 ....22 E4
Tucker St NR27 ....139 B7
Tucks Rd NR28 ....38 A5
Tuckswood Ctr 2 NR4 ...162 C1
Tuckswood Fst Sch
NR4 ....162 D1
Tuckswood La NR4 ...162 D1
Tud La NR9 ....69 E6
Tuddenham Rd NR11 ...150 B6
Tudor Ave IP22 ....177 A5
Tudor Cl IP24 ....176 C2
Tudor Cres PE36 ....132 D2
Tudor Way
Dersingham PE31 ....140 D4
8 Hellesdon NR14 ....89 B3
Tudor Wlk
Great Yarmouth NR31 ...170 C1
12 Honington IP31 ...126 B1
Tuesday Mkt Pl 4 PE30 ...146 D5
Tuffen La IP22 ....128 B2
Tulip Cl NR17 ....174 C5
Tulip Tree Dr 5 NR4 ...89 F7
Tumbler Hill PE37 ...153 C6
Tumbleyhill Rd PE32 ...46 C2
Tumbril La IP21 ....131 D7
Tunbeck Cl IP20 ....123 A3
Tunbeck Rd IP20 ....123 A4

Tungate Cres NR4 ....89 B8
Tungate Rd NR28 ....151 A5
Tungate Way 6 NR12 ...54 C6
Tunneys La NR35 ....109 B2
Tunns Yd NR23 ....136 D6
Tuns Rd PE37 ....65 F4
Tunstall Cl 5 NR5 ...161 A7
Tunstall Rd NR13 ....74 F2
Tunstead La NR12 ...164 D6
Tunstead Prim Sch
NR12 ....37 F1
Tunstead Rd
Tunstead NR12 ....37 E1
1 Wroxham/Hoveton
NR12 ....164 B3
Turbine Way PE37 ...153 B6
Turbo Rd NR21 ....15 D2
Turbus Rd PE30 ....146 E7
Turf Fen La NR29 ....56 B5
Turf Lot Dro PE14 ....95 B5
Turin Way NR31 ....171 E4
Turkey La NR24 ....19 D6
Turn The NR10 ....53 A8
Turner Cl
5 Great Yarmouth NR31 ...170 A7
Wymondham NR18 ...173 E5
Turner Rd NR2 ....162 A7
Turner's Cl PE34 ....79 E8
Turnham Gn 10 NR7 ...72 D4
Turning The NR26 ...138 C6
Turnpike Cl Foxley NR20 ...50 D8
Turnpike The NR13 ...152 E6
Turnpike The
Ashwellthorpe NR16 ...106 A7
Carleton Rode NR16 ...105 D2
Tusser Rd NR8 ....156 E8
Tusting Cl NR7 ....158 F4
Tuttington Rd NR11 ...150 F8
Tuttles La E NR18 ...173 D6
Tuttles La W NR18 ...173 B6
Tuxhill Chase PE34 ...42 B4
Tuxhill Rd PE34 ....42 B5
Twickenham Ave IP27 ...175 B1
Twickenham Rd NR6 ...158 B5
Twiss Cl 5 IP22 ....129 D7
Two Acres 6 PE22 ...44 B3
Two Fields Way 11 NR20 ...50 C7
Two Saints Cl NR12 ...146 D7
Two Sisters Cl 6 PE12 ...41 B8
Twrs The PE38 ....172 C5
Twyford La NR20 ....33 C3
Twyford Rd NR20 ....33 A6
Tyburn PE30 ....148 C5
Tyne Mews NR10 ....168 C5
Tyrrell's Rd 2 NR31 ...169 B4

U

Ulfkell Rd IP24 ....176 B2
Ulleswater Ave
Castle Rising PE30 ....27 C1
3 King's Lynn PE30 ...148 F1
Ullswater Ave 4 PE30 ...148 F1
Ullswater Dr 22 NR9 ...88 D8
Ulph Pl PE31 ....135 D3
Uncle's La IP19 ....124 B2
Unicorn Yd 2 NR11 ...150 C6
Union Dritt NR20 ....68 A8
Union La
4 King's Lynn PE30 ...146 D4
Wortham IP22 ....129 D5
Union Pl 19 PE13 ....152 C5
Union Rd
8 Great Yarmouth NR30 ...169 D4
Smallburgh NR12 ....38 C3
Union St Norwich NR2 ...178 A2
4 Wisbech PE13 ....152 C5
Univ of E Anglia NR4 ...161 C3
University Cres NR13 ...170 B4
University Dr NR4 ....161 B4
Unthank Rd NR4 ....161 F2
Upgate Rd NR4 ....90 D5
Upgate Rd NR15 ...108 E7
Upgate St
Carleton Rode NR16 ...105 A4
Southery PE38 ....97 B5
Uphalle NR18 ....155 D1
Uplands Ave NR30 ...168 D5
Uplands Pk NR26 ...138 C6
Uplands Way IP22 ...177 D5
Upper Breckland Rd
NR5 ....156 F1
Upper Brook La IP20 ...131 E8
Upper Burnthouse La
IP20 ....131 E8
Upper Cliff Rd NR31 ...170 D4
Upper Goat La NR2 ...178 A3
Upper Grange Cres
NR30 ....168 D5
Upper Hall La NR24 ...18 D8
Upper Harmans La
IP20 ....122 B1
Upper Kiln La NR15 ...90 F4
Upper King St NR2 ...178 B3
Upper Oakley IP21 ...130 D4
Upper Olland St NR35 ...124 A8
Upper Rose La IP22 ...177 E2
Upper St Gissing IP22 ...120 F4
Salhouse NR13 ....55 B2
Upper St Giles St NR2 ...178 A3
Upper Stafford Ave
NR5 ....156 F1
Upper Tumbril La
Brockdish IP20 ...131 D8
Needham IP20 ...122 A1
Scole IP20 ....131 D8
Upton Cl NR4 ....162 A3

Upton Dr PE37 ....153 B2
Upton Rd Norwich NR4 ..162 A3
  South Walsham NR13 ....74 B8
Upton Way NR12 ....24 C5
Uptons Way IP26 ....82 A2
Upwell Prim Sch PE14 ..77 D4
Upwell Rd PE14 ....95 A7
Utopia Way NR12 ....39 B3

V

Vale Cl 8 NR10 ....53 B3
Vale Rd High Kelling NR25 ..8 E2
  Mundesley NR11 ....143 A8
  Thurlton NR14 ....91 C3
Valentine Ct PE36 ....132 D5
Valentine Rd PE36 ....132 D4
Valentine St NR2 ....162 C6
Valinger's Pl 7 PE30 ..146 E4
Valingers Rd PE30 ....146 E3
Valley Dr The NR1 ....163 B8
Valley Gdns 1 NR28 ....151 E5
Valley La NR25 ....137 D8
Valley Rd Norwich NR5 ..157 C1
  Bunton PE32 ....106 F6
Valley Rise PE31 ....140 C4
Valley Side Rd 1 NR1 ..163 C8
Valley View NR19 ....154 C6
Valley View Cres NR5 ..157 A1
Valpy Ave NR3 ....158 A1
Vancouver Ave PE30 ..146 E3
Vancouver Rd 2 NR7 ..163 C8
Vane Cl NR7 ....72 D4
Vanguard Rd
  2 Great Yarmouth NR31 ..94 C8
  Great Yarmouth NR31 ..170 A8
Varsity Rd IP25 ....84 F3
Varvel Ave NR7 ....159 C4
Vassar Ct 6 NR20 ....68 F6
Vaunces La IP21 ....131 B8
Vaunce's La IP21 ....131 B8
Vauxhall St NR2 ....162 C5
Vauxhall Terr NR20 ....169 C6
Vawdrey Rd NR8 ....155 F1
Veltshaw Cl PE31 ....133 B4
Venables Cl NR1 ....163 B7
Ventura Cl IP26 ....98 F5
Vera Cl 10 NR13 ....72 E7
Vera Rd
  New Rackheath NR13 ..72 E7
  Norwich NR6 ....158 B4
Verdon's La NR18 ....87 F2
Verdun Rd PE13 ....152 D5
Vervain Cl 26 NR31 ....94 C6
Vicar St NR18 ....173 B4
Vicarage Cl
  Costessey NR8 ....156 F5
  Foulden IP26 ....82 A1
  1 Potter Heigham NR29 ..56 F6
Vicarage La
  Bungay NR35 ....124 C8
  Hoveton NR12 ....164 F5
Vicarage Mdws NR19 ..154 D4
Vicarage Rd
  Cromer NR27 ....139 B6
  Deopham NR18 ....86 D3
  East Ruston NR12 ....24 A3
  Foulden IP26 ....82 A2
  Hockham IP24 ....102 D3
  Norwich NR3 ....158 C1
  Paston NR28 ....143 D2
  Salhouse NR13 ....55 A2
  Sheringham NR26 ....138 C6
  Thetford IP24 ....176 D5
  Wingfield IP21 ....131 E3
  Worstead NR28 ....38 A5
Vicarage St NR28 ....151 C5
Vicarage Wlk 11 IP25 ..84 E3
Viceroy Cl PE31 ....140 C4
Victoria Ave PE36 ....132 D5
Victoria Cl Diss IP22 ..177 E3
  Heacham PE31 ....133 E6
  Taverham NR8 ....156 C8
Victoria Ct 20 IP25 ....84 D3
Victoria Gdns 7 NR30 ..169 D2
Victoria Hill IP23 ....130 C1
Victoria La
  Caister-on-Sea NR30 ..168 F4
  2 Downham Market
  PE38 ....172 A5
  Great Yarmouth NR30 ..169 D6
  Norwich NR1 ....178 A2
  Sheringham NR26 ....138 C7
Victoria Terr PE34 ....146 C4
Victoria Way NR5 ....157 B2
Victory La PE34 ....61 B8
Victory Rd
  Downham Market PE38 ..172 B4
  Wisbech PE13 ....152 B3
Viking Cl
  Great Yarmouth NR31 ..170 D2
  Swaffham PE37 ....153 D2
Viking Rd 1 NR30 ....169 C7
Village Cl 4 NR4 ....161 C5

Villarome NR30 ....168 C5
Villavon Way 4 NR13 ..73 D6
Villebois Rd NR30 ....63 B4
Vimy Dr NR18 ....173 D4
Vimy Ridge NR18 ....173 D4
Vincent J 17 IP26 ....98 E1
Vincent Pl 16 IP25 ....84 D3
Vincent Rd
  Norwich NR1 ....163 A7
  Sheringham NR26 ....138 E7
Vincents Rd NR9 ....69 A4
Vince's Rd IP22 ....177 F4
Vine Cl
  Coney Weston IP31 ....127 B5
  Hemsby NR29 ....167 B8
Vine Hill PE34 ....61 C2
Vinery Cl 1 PE34 ....146 C5
Violet Cl
  Attleborough NR17 ....174 C5
  16 Great Yarmouth NR31 ..94 C6
Violet Dr NR26 ....138 B6
Violet Rd NR18 ....158 F1
Violet Way NR19 ....154 C4
Virginia Cl NR7 ....159 C4
Vong La Grimston PE32 ..28 B1
  Roydon PE32 ....45 A8
Vulcan Rd N NR6 ....158 C5
Vulcan Rd S NR6 ....158 C4

W

Waddington St NR2 ..162 B7
Waddling La NR27 ....111 F7
Wade Cl NR11 ....150 C5
Wadehall La NR14 ....111 B1
Wades Way NR20 ....22 F5
Wadham Cl NR11 ....170 D3
Wadham Rd NR11 ....173 D4
Waggon & Horses La
  NR3 ....178 B3
Wagtail Cl 2 NR31 ....170 A6
Wagtail Way IP24 ....176 D1
Wainford Rd NR35 ....124 C8
Wakefield Rd NR5 ....161 C5
Wakehurst Cl 6 NR4 ..161 F1
Wakes La NR19 ....154 D5
Walcot Cl NR5 ....161 A7
Walcot Rd IP22 ....177 E6
Walcot Rise IP22 ....177 F5
Walcup's La PE32 ....29 D2
Waldeck Rd NR4 ....162 A3
Waldegrave 8 NR5 ....161 A8
Waldeman Ave NR8 ..158 A5
Waldemar Pk NR8 ....158 A5
Wales Bank PE14 ....59 A1
Wales Ct PE38 ....172 C5
Walk The
  Great Yarmouth NR31 ..170 B6
  Hickling NR12 ....39 F3
  Dulton NR13 ....35 A8
Walker St 1 PE30 ....146 E6
Walks The NR14 ....111 A4
Walkway The NR12 ....24 A7
Wall La PE31 ....29 C4
Wall Rd Erpingham NR11 ..20 F3
  Norwich NR3 ....158 E2
Wallace Cl
  Dereham NR19 ....154 B6
  King's Lynn PE30 ....147 D4
Wallace Iwite Way
  PE31 ....140 C3
Waller Cl NR13 ....72 D5
Wallers La NR20 ....33 C3
Wallgate La NR11 ....17 D5
Wall's La NR11 ....20 F3
Walnut Ave 5 PE33 ....43 E2
Walnut Ave N 1 PE33 ..43 E2
Walnut Cl
  Brandon IP27 ....175 E2
  Foulden IP26 ....82 A2
  Hopton IP22 ....127 F5
  Iaverham NR8 ....155 D2
Walnut Gr
  1 Fakenham NR21 ....141 E4
  Watton IP25 ....84 D4
Walnut Hill NR14 ....73 A1
Walnut Pl PE33 ....82 A5
Walnut Rd PE14 ....41 E3
Walnut Row NR18 ....63 B4
Walnuts The
  Grimston PE32 ....28 B1
  Norwich NR4 ....162 A2
Walpole Bank PE14 ....41 C3
Walpole Cross Keys Prim Sch
  PE34 ....42 A6
Walpole Highway Prim Sch
  PE14 ....59 F8
Walpole La PE14 ....41 F4
Walpole Rd
  Great Yarmouth NR30 ..169 D7
  King's Lynn PE30 ....146 E7
Walpole St NR2 ....178 A2
Walpole Way 8 PE33 ..43 E2
Walpole Wr Gdns* ....
Walsham Cl PE30 ....147 D5
Walsingham Ct 2 PE13 ..152 A7
Walsingham Dr NR8 ..155 E3
Walsingham Prim Sch
  NR22 ....16 F8
Walsingham Rd
  Binham NR21 ....6 D3
  Burnham Thorpe PE31 ..135 F2
Walsoken Rd PE14 ....59 F8
Walter Howes Cres
  PE32 ....44 C3
Walters Cl NR31 ....171 D5

Walters Rd NR8 ....156 C8
Walton Cl PE30 ....148 C4
Walton Rd
  Norwich NR1 ....162 E3
  St John's Fen End PE14 ..60 A5
  West Walton PE14 ....59 F5
  Wisbech PE13 ....152 E7
Waltons Way IP27 ....175 D2
Wangford Rd IP27 ....113 F3
Wansbrough Rd 10
  NR15 ....106 E3
Wanson La PE34 ....144 A5
Waples Way NR15 ....154 D3
Wapping NR29 ....167 A2
Warbler Cl 3 NR31 ....94 C7
Ward Rd NR13 ....55 B1
Wardley Hill Rd NR35 ..109 D4
Ward's Chase PE34 ....79 B8
Warham Rd Binham NR21 ..6 E2
  Wells-next-the-Sea
  NR23 ....136 E4
Warham St Mary's Halt Sta
  NR23 ....5 F4
Waring Rd NR5 ....161 B6
Warner Ave NR19 ....154 E7
Warner Cl NR31 ....94 C6
Warnett Rd NR7 ....159 D1
Warren Ave
  Fakenham NR21 ....141 F4
  Norwich NR6 ....158 A5
Warren Cl
  Brandon IP27 ....175 D3
  High Kelling NR25 ....8 E3
  15 Horsford NR10 ....53 A3
  Thetford IP24 ....176 A3
  Watlington PE33 ....61 D5
Warren Ct 1 NR27 ....139 C6
Warren Dr NR11 ....143 B3
Warren Gn NR11 ....72 F8
Warren Loke NR31 ....93 E3
Warren Pl 4 NR19 ....154 D5
Warren Rd
  Great Yarmouth NR31 ..171 D8
  High Kelling NR25 ....8 E3
  Hopton on Sea NR31 ..171 D6
  Shouldham PE33 ....62 D4
  Southrepps NR11 ....22 C6
Warren The
  Cromer NR27 ....139 C6
  Horsham St Faith &
  Newton St Faith NR10 ..53 D2
  Little Snoring NR21 ....17 C7
  Norwich NR6 ....158 E4
Warren View NR4 ....109 D8
Warren's La NR1/ 174 C6
Warren's Rd PE34 ....145 D6
Warren's Way 5 NR16 ..105 F5
Warstade Way PE37 ..153 B4
Warwick Dr NR18 ....173 C5
Warwick St NR2 ....162 B5
Wash La Alburgh IP20 ..122 E2
  Aslacton NR15 ....106 A1
  Barnham Broom NR9 ..119 D6
  Burgh St Peter NR34 ..111 C4
  Clenchwarton PE34 ..144 C6
  Gissing IP22 ....120 E5
  Hales NR14 ....109 E6
  Hinderclay IP22 ....128 C4
  Howe NR15 ....90 C2
  Hedgrave IP22 ....129 A5
  St Peter, South Elmham
  NR35 ....123 F3
  Saxlingham Nethergate
  NR15 ....107 B7
  Saxlingham Nethergate
  NR15 ....107 D8
  Shelfanger IP22 ....120 B2
  Shotesham NR15 ....89 F1
  Topcroft NR35 ....108 A4
  Wacton NR15 ....106 B2
  Whissonsett NR20 ....31 E2
Wash Rd PE14 ....95 E4
Washpit Dro
  South Acre PE32 ....64 U8
  Swaffham PE37 ....153 C8
  West Rudham PE31 ....29 F6
Watch House Hill
  NR35 ....124 C8
Watch House La NR12 ..23 E4
Water End La PE32 ....48 D2
Water Gdns The PE13 ..152 A5
Water La Barnham IP24 ..125 E6
  Barsham NR21 ....16 F4
  Botesdale IP22 ....128 D1
  Cringleford NR4 ....161 D1
  Garboldisham IP22 ....128 A8
  Great & Little Plumstead
  NR13 ....73 A5
  Ingham NR12 ....24 D2
  1 King's Lynn PE30 ..146 D5
  Letheringsett with Glandford
  NR25 ....8 A2
  Middleton PE32 ....44 C1
  Mundesley NR11 ....143 C4
  Neatishead NR12 ....55 E7
  Runton NR27 ....10 A5
  Thelnetham IP22 ....128 B5
  Thetford IP24 ....176 C4
Water Mdw Cl NR29 ..167 A3
Water Mill La IP21 ....131 A4
Water Moor La NR21 ..141 C6
Water Sports Ctr PE34 ..43 C5
Water The NR14 ....88 C4
Waterbank Rd NR26 ..138 D7
Watercress La NR20 ..28 E6
Waterden Cl 5 PE30 ..147 A8
Waterfield Ave NR21 ..141 D5
Waterfield Cl 2 NR21 ..141 D5

Waterfield Mdws
  NR28 ....151 E5
Waterheath Rd NR34 ..110 E5
Watering La PE33 ....43 E2
Watering Piece La
  NR29 ....56 C7
Watering Rd IP21 ....131 B1
Watering The 3 NR3 ..162 U6
Waterland Cl NR12 ....55 A8
Waterland Cl NR30 ....168 C7
Waterlees Rd
  Walsoken PE13 ....59 A6
  2 Wisbech PE13 ....152 E7
Waterloo Ave 4 IP22 ..129 D7
Waterloo Cl 3 NR10 ..53 A3
Waterloo Pk Ave NR3 ..158 C1
Waterloo Pk Cl 6 NR3 ..158 C1
Waterloo Rd
  Great Yarmouth NR30 ..169 E2
  Hainford NR10 ....53 D6
  Wells-next-the-Sea
  NR23 ....136 D6
  Norwich NR3 ....162 D8
Waterloo St 13 PE30 ..146 E5
Waterlow Rd PE34 ....42 C4
Waterman Rd NR2 ....161 F7
Waterman's La PE38 ..79 D1
Waterman's Way PE38 ..79 A4
Watermeadow Cl 3
  NR14 ....91 F1
Watermill Cl NR11 ....9 F1
Watermill Gn IP24 ....176 C3
Watermill La PE37 ....82 A6
Waters La NR27 ....167 A7
Watersfield Way
  NR19 ....154 D2
Waterside PE30 ....146 F7
Waterside The NR4 ..157 D3
Waterworks Rd
  Norwich NR2 ....162 A7
  Old Hunstanton PE36 ..132 F7
Watery La
  Beeston with Bittering
  PE32 ....48 B3
  Grimston PE32 ....45 B8
  Necton PE37 ....66 A8
  Quiet NR30 ....33 A4
  Matlask NR11 ....20 D5
  Necton PE37 ....66 A8
  Scarning NR19 ....154 A1
  Shipdham IP25 ....67 C2
Wathen Way NR10 ....150 C1
Watkin Rd NR4 ....89 E8
Watling Cl NR30 ....168 E6
Watling Rd
  Attleborough NR17 ....174 C4
  Norwich NR1/ 159 D1
Watlings The NR19 ....67 B6
Watlington Prim Sch
  PE33 ....61 D5
Watlington Rd
  Tottenhill PE33 ....61 F6
  Watlington PE33 ....61 F5
Wattlefield Rd
  Tacolneston NR16 ....105 C6
  Wymondham NR18 ....88 A1
  Wymondham NR18 ....105 C6
Watton Jun Sch IP25 ..84 D3
Watton Rd Ashill IP25 ..84 A6
  Barford NR9 ....69 E2
  Colney NR4 ....160 F4
  Great Cressingham IP25 ..83 D4
  Great Ellingham NR17 ..103 D8
  Great Melton NR9 ....70 B2
  Griston IP25 ....85 A2
  Ingham NR9 ....86 B5
  Hockham IP24 ....102 E4
  Little Cressingham IP25 ..83 F2
  Little Melton NR9 ....160 B4
  North Pickenham PE37 ..83 C8
  Shipdham PE37 ....67 R1
  Shropham NR17 ....103 A4
  Stow Bedon NR17 ....102 D7
  Swaffham PE37 ....153 D2
  Thompson IP25 ....102 A8
Wauncl Cres NR31 ....170 D2
Wavell Rd NR19 ....154 C7
Wavency Ct
  Hoveton NR12 ....164 E6
  Hunstanton PE36 ....132 D3
Wavency Dr
  10 Belton NR31 ....94 A6
  Wroxham/Hovelon
  NR12 ....164 D5
Waveney Fst Sch NR31 ..94 A5
Waveney Hill NR12 ....111 F3
Waveney Hts IP21 ....131 C6
Waveney Rd
  Bungay NR35 ....124 B8
  Diss IP22 ....177 E3
  Ditchingham NR35 ....109 B2
  Great Yarmouth NR31 ..169 C1
  Hunstanton PE36 ....132 C3
  King's Lynn PE30 ....147 D5
Waveney Valley Swimming
  Pool NR35 ....124 A7
Waxham Cl NR11 ....143 A8
Waxham Ct NR12 ....40 A5
Waxham Rd NR12 ....40 B5
Wayford Rd NR12 ....38 F4
Wayland Ave 1 IP25 ..84 C3
Wayland Cl NR17 ....174 D5

Wayland Com High Sch
  IP25 ....84 D3
Wayland Hospl NR17 ..174 A7
Wayland Rd NR17 ....103 C8
Wayland Way NR16 ..119 D7
Wayland Wlk NR28 ....172 B7
Wayland Wlk PE38 ....172 B7
Weasenham Hall PE32 ..27 C2
Weasenham La 1 PE13 ..152 D2
Weasenham Prim Sch
  PE32 ....47 D8
Weasenham Rd
  Great Massingham PE32 ..29 E1
  Litcham PE32 ....47 E7
Weavers Cl 1 NR10 ..53 D2
Weavers Croft 8 IP20 ..122 D2
Weavers Ct IP22 ....177 D5
Weavers View NR12 ....37 F1
Webb Dr 4 NR28 ....151 E5
Webbs Cl 2 NR28 ....151 E5
Webdell Cl 3 NR1 ....162 E1
Webster Cl
  5 Norwich NR5 ....161 B8
  3 Stoke Holy Cross NR14 ..89 F4
Webster Way NR30 ....168 D6
Wedgewood Ct NR31 ..170 C3
Wedgwood Dr PE13 ..152 D5
Weedon Way NR30 ....147 D4
Weeting Castle (English
  Heritage)* IP27 ....114 E8
Weeting Heath National
  Nature Reserve*
  IP27 ....114 C7
Weeting Prim Sch
  IP27 ....175 B8
Welbeck Ave 8 NR29 ..57 D4
Welbeck Rd PE13 ....152 E4
Welborne Rd NR20 ....68 F5
Welden Rd NR19 ....154 B4
Welgate Cl 3 NR20 ....68 E6
Welhome's Cl 13 NR15 ..106 E3
Well Cl NR9 ....51 A6
Well Creek Rd PE14 ....77 F6
Well End PE34 ....77 A7
Well Hall La NR20 ....45 A6
Well Hill NR19 ....68 C5
Well La NR19 ....51 A6
Well Loke NR3 ....158 B3
Well Medieval Village of*
  PE32 ....45 B7
Well Rd Cantley NR13 ..92 D6
  Great Yarmouth NR30 ..169 D2
Well St Docking PE31 ..134 C5
  Great Yarmouth NR30 ..169 D3
  Thetford IP24 ....176 D3
  Witton NR28 ....23 D3
Wellbeck NR15 ....90 F2
Wellbeck Rd NR15 ....91 A2
Wellesley Ave NR1 ....163 B7
Wellesley Ave N 4 NR1 ..163 B7
Wellesley Ave S NR1 ..163 B6
Wellesley Fst Sch
  NR1 ....163 B7
Wellesley Rd
  Great Yarmouth NR30 ..169 D5
  8 Long Stratton NR15 ..106 D3
Wellesley St 8 PE30 ..146 E5
Wellingham Rd
  Litcham PE32 ....47 E7
  Tittleshall PE32 ....48 A8
Wellington Cl
  Brandon IP27 ....175 D3
  Gimingham NR11 ....22 F8
Wellington Cres NR21 ..15 C3
Wellington La NR2 ....162 C6
Wellington Pl 12 NR30 ..169 C4
Wellington Rd
  Briston NR24 ....142 B4
  East Dereham NR19 ..154 D5
  4 Feltwell IP26 ....98 E1
  Great Yarmouth NR30 ..169 E2
  King's Lynn PE30 ....146 E5
  King's Lynn PE30 ....147 A5
  Norwich NR2 ....162 B6
Wells Ave NR28 ....151 A3
Wells Cl 1 NR10 ....53 E5
Wells Cottage Hospl
  NR23 ....136 E5
Wells La IP20 ....122 D1
Wells Maritime Mus*
  NR23 ....136 D6
Wells next the Sea Prim &
  Nursery Sch NR23 ..136 E5
Wells next the Sea Sta
  NR23 ....136 F4
Wells Rd
  Burnham Overy Staithe
  PE31 ....135 E2
  Fakenham NR21 ....141 B4
  Hindringham NR21 ....17 D6
  Needham IP20 ....122 C1
  North Creake NR21 ....4 D1
  Stiffkey NR23 ....6 C6
  Walsingham NR22 ....16 F8
Wellspring Rd NR13 ....92 C8
Welsford Rd
  3 Norwich NR8 ....89 D8
  Norwich NR4 ....162 B1
Weltons Loke NR9 ....52 A6
Wendene NR5 ....160 F7
Wendling Rd NR19 ....48 F2
Wendover Rd NR13 ....72 D8
Wenman Ct 5 NR5 ....160 F8

Wensom Cl 3 PE33 . . . . .61 D6
Wensum Cres NR6 . . . . .157 D3
Wensum Cl NR21 . . . . .32 C6
Wensum Dr NR20 . . . . .49 F7
Wensum Gdns 1 NR20 . . . .50 B3
**Wensum Mdws Mental
Health Hospl** NR6 . .157 D4
Wensum Rd NR9 . . . . .51 A4
Wensum St NR3 . . . . .178 B3
Wensum Valley Cl
NR6 . . . . .157 D4
Wensum Valley Golf Course
NR8 . . . . .155 A2
Wensum Way
1 Belton NR31 . . . . .94 A6
2 Fakenham NR21 . . . . . .141 E4
Wensum Wlk NR8 . . . . .155 F3
Wentworth Gn NR4 . . . . . .161 F2
Wereham Row PE33 . . . . . .80 D2
Wesley Ave PE34 . . . . .144 B5
Wesley Cl
Downham Market PE38 . . . .172 B5
4 Mattishall NR20 . . . . . . .68 E6
Terrington St Clement
PE34 . . . . .144 B5
Wesley Rd
King's Lynn PE30 . . . . .148 C5
Terrington St Clement
PE34 . . . . .144 B5
Wessex St NR2 . . . . .178 A1
West Acre Rd PE37 . . . . . .153 A6
West Ave
Great Yarmouth NR31 . . . .170 C3
Ormesby St Margaret
NR29 . . . . .167 A3
West Carr Rd NR17 . . . . . .174 A4
West Cl NR15 . . . . .157 A2
West Cliff
Cromer NR27 . . . . .139 B7
Sheringham NR26 . . . . . . .138 D7
West Cres NR20 . . . . .50 A5
West Croft NR9 . . . . .88 C7
West Dereham Rd
PE33 . . . . .80 D3
West Dr IP27 . . . . .175 A2
West Dro N PE14 . . . . .59 D8
West Dro S PE14 . . . . .59 E8
West Earlham Fst Sch
NR5 . . . . .161 D6
West Earlham Mid Sch
NR5 . . . . .161 D6
West End Briston NR24 . .142 F5
Costessey NR8 . . . . .156 C4
Hilgay PE38 . . . . .79 D1
Northwold IP26 . . . . .99 B8
West End Ave
Brundall NR13 . . . . .165 A4
Costessey NR8 . . . . .156 C5
West End Ct 6 IP25 . . . . . .84 C3
West End Rd NR12 . . . . . . .89 B7
West Flegg Mid Sch
NR29 . . . . .57 D5
West Gate NR18 . . . . .173 B4
West Hall Rd
Dersingham PE31 . . . . .140 D3
Mundford IP26 . . . . .100 B5
West Harling Rd NR16 . . . .118 A4
West Head Rd PE34 . . . . . .79 C2
West Herne La IP22 . . . . . .128 D5
West La NR10 . . . . .53 D1
West Lexham Hall
PE32 . . . . .47 C4
West Lynn Cty Prim Sch
PE34 . . . . .146 C5
West Norwich Hospl
NR21 . . . . .161 F7
West Par Norwich NR2 . . .162 B6
Wisbech PE13 . . . . .152 B7
West Pottergate NR2 . . . .162 B6
West Raynham Airfield (dis)
PE31 . . . . .30 C3
West Raynham Rd
NR21 . . . . .30 F4
West Rd
Caister-on-Sea NR30 . . . . .168 D4
Dersingham PE31 . . . . .140 D3
Great Yarmouth NR30 . . . .168 F1
3 Great Yarmouth NR30 .169 D5
Norwich NR5 . . . . .157 A2
Ormesby St Margaret
NR29 . . . . .167 A2
Shouldham Thorpe PE33 . . .62 C2
Tacolneston NR16 . . . . . . .105 F4
Watton IP25 . . . . .84 D3
West Caister NR30 . . . . . . .168 B4
West Runton Sta NR27 . . . .10 A5
West St
North Creake NR21 . . . . .4 D1
Wisbech PE13 . . . . .152 C4
West Stree 15 NR30 . . . . .169 D2
West Tofts Rd IP26 . . . . . .100 D3
West View PE37 . . . . .83 D7
West View Rd NR13 . . . . . . .74 A2
West View Rd NR13 . . . . . .165 E6
West Way
Downham Market PE38 . . . .172 B4
Stow Bardolph PE34 . . . . . .61 D1
Tacolneston NR16 . . . . . . .105 E5
Whissonsett PE34 . . . . .79 D8
West Winch Prim Sch
PE33 . . . . .43 E2
West Winch Rd PE33 . . . . .43 F4
West Wood Cotts NR21 . . .32 B5
Westacre Dr NR2 . . . . .158 E7
Westbourne Rd NR12 . . . . .54 D7

Westbriggs Dro PE33 . . . . . .62 B5
Westbrook Ave 1 NR31 . . .170 B6
Westcliff Ave NR27 . . . . . .139 A7
Westerley Cl NR20 . . . . . . .168 D4
Westerley Way NR30 . . . . .168 D4
Western Ave NR7 . . . . .163 E6
Western Bypass NR11 . . . .150 B5
Western Cl 4 IP26 . . . . .98 D1
Western Ct NR29 . . . . .57 C1
Westfield Ave NR23 . . . . . .136 C6
Westfield Cl 2 NR29 . . . . . .57 C1
Westfield La NR19 . . . . . . .154 F1
Westfield Rd
Brundall NR13 . . . . .165 D4
East Dereham NR19 . . . . . .154 E2
Swaffham PE37 . . . . .153 B4
Wisbech PE13 . . . . .152 E7
Westfields
Attleborough NR17 . . . . . .174 B4
Narborough PE32 . . . . .63 E7
Westfields Cl
Terrington St John PE14 . . . .60 C8
Tilney St Lawrence PE34 . . .42 C1
Westgate
Hevingham NR10 . . . . .53 B8
Hunstanton PE36 . . . . .132 C4
Norwich NR6 . . . . .157 F5
Shropham NR17 . . . . .103 B4
Walsingham NR22 . . . . .16 F8
Westgate Cl NR2 . . . . .162 A4
Westgate Rd NR10 . . . . .53 B8
Westgate Rd
Holme next the Sea PE36 . . .2 A6
Hunstanton PE36 . . . . .1 F6
Westgate St
Hilborough IP26 . . . . .83 A3
Shouldham PE33 . . . . .62 D4
Southery PE38 . . . . .97 A5
Westhall IP21 . . . . .131 F1
Westhorpe Cl 3 PE30 . . . .147 A8
Westland Chase PE33 . . . .43 F1
Westlegate NR1 . . . . .178 B2
Westmead Ave PE13 . . . . .152 E2
Westmead Rd NR21 . . . . . .141 C4
Weston Cl 1 NR13 . . . . . . .73 C6
Weston Ct NR6 . . . . .158 F6
Weston Miller Dr
PE13 . . . . .152 C7
Weston Rd Easton NR9 . . . .70 A7
Norwich NR3 . . . . .158 C3
17 Wisbech PE13 . . . . . . .152 C4
Weston Rise NR20 . . . . . . .168 D5
Weston Sq Yd NR13 . . . . . .137 B6
Weston Terr NR26 . . . . . . .138 E7
Weston Wood Cl NR7 . . . . .163 E7
Weston Wood Rd NR7 . . . .163 D7
Westry Cl PE13 . . . . .59 C5
Westwick Dr NR28 . . . . . . .151 A4
Westwick Rd NR28 . . . . . . .37 F5
Westwick St NR2 . . . . .178 A3
Westwood Dr NR6 . . . . . . .157 D6
Westwood Gdns NR18 . . . .173 A6
Westwood La NR21 . . . . . . .32 B5
Weybourne Rd
Bodham NR25 . . . . .9 A3
Sheringham NR26 . . . . . . .138 B7
Weybourne Sta NR25 . . . . . .8 F5
Weymer Gdns NR25 . . . . . . .8 E5
Wharf St PE12 . . . . .41 B8
Wharton Dr NR28 . . . . . . .151 E7
Whartons La NR18 . . . . . . .173 B2
Wheat Fields NR8 . . . . . . .155 F2
Wheatacre Cl 3 NR14 . . . . .53 A3
Wheatacres IP24 . . . . .176 D5
Wheatcroft Way NR20 . . . .68 A8
Wheatfield Way NR15 . . . .106 F4
Wheatfields
Hillington PE31 . . . . .28 B4
Rickinghall Superior
IP22 . . . . .128 E2
Wheatley Bank PE14 . . . . .59 C5
Wheatley Dr PE30 . . . . . . .148 B4
Wheatley Rd NR21 . . . . . . .161 F7
Wheat Rd NR14 . . . . .90 F4
Wheelbarrow La IP20 . . . .123 F1
Wheeler Rd NR3 . . . . .158 A1
Wheelers La NR15 . . . . . . .108 E8
Wheelwright Rd PE30 . . . .147 C5
Wheelwrights Cl NR13 . . . .92 E8
Wherry Cl NR29 . . . . .57 D6
Wherry Rd NR1 . . . . .178 C1
Wherry Reach 2 NR13 . . .166 D4
Wherry Way NR30 . . . . . . .169 C2
Whiffler Rd NR3 . . . . .157 F2
Whimbrel Dr
1 Great Yarmouth NR31 . . .94 C8
2 Great Yarmouth NR31 . .170 A7
Whin Comm Rd
Denver PE38 . . . . .172 D1
Tottenhill PE33 . . . . .61 F6
Whinburgh Rd NR19 . . . . . .67 F3
Whinchat Way 3 NR11 . . . .94 C7
Whinmere Rd NR12 . . . . . . .39 E3
Whipp's La NR16 . . . . .105 F7
Whissom Cl 1 PE30 . . . . . .147 A8
Whissonsett Rd NR20 . . . . .48 E8
Whitby St 3 PE13 . . . . . . .152 C5
White City Rd PE14 . . . . . .178 D6
White Clover Rd 26 NR31 .94 C6
White Cross
Burgh & Tuttington NR11 . . .36 E4
Hardingham NR9 . . . . .86 E8
White Cross Rd PE37 . . . . .153 C4
White Farm La NR17 . . . . .163 C6
White Gate La NR11 . . . . . .11 D2
White Gates NR15 . . . . . . .121 D5
White Hall Dr PE34 . . . . . .146 C4

White Hart St
2 Aylsham NR11 . . . . .150 C7
East Harling NR16 . . . . . . .118 C5
Foulden IP26 . . . . .82 A2
White Heath Rd NR15 . . . . .91 B3
White Horse Dr PE31 . . . . .140 C4
White Horse La
Bixley NR14 . . . . .89 F8
Trowse with Newton
NR14 . . . . .163 A1
Worstead NR28 . . . . .38 B6
White Horse St IP27 . . . . . .175 A2
White House Cl NR3 . . . . . .158 B3
White House Dr 28
NR15 . . . . .106 E3
White House Est
NR27 . . . . .139 D4
White House Farm La
IP21 . . . . .122 B2
White House Gdns 12
NR14 . . . . .90 D5
White House La NR17 . . . .174 F5
White House Rd CB7 . . . . .112 A7
White La PE33 . . . . .63 A3
White Lion Rd
Coltishall NR12 . . . . .54 D6
Wheatacre NR34 . . . . .111 B4
White Lion St
Holt NR25 . . . . .137 B6
Norwich NR2 . . . . .178 A2
White Lodge Bsns Est
NR4 . . . . .89 E8
White Oaks PE37 . . . . .65 E2
White Post Rd NR11 . . . . . .21 D5
White Rd
Barton Bendish PE33 . . . . . .63 D1
Methwold IP26 . . . . .99 A5
White Rose Cl NR5 . . . . . . .161 D8
White St NR29 . . . . .57 D5
White Woman La NR6 . . . .159 A6
White Woman La Mid Sch
NR6 . . . . .158 F6
Whitecross La PE34 . . . . . .144 E4
Whitedike Dro IP26 . . . . . .113 B8
Whitefriars NR3 . . . . .178 B4
Whitefriars CE Prim Sch
PE13 . . . . .146 D3
Whitefriars Rd NR30 . . . . .146 D3
Whitefriars Terr PE30 . . . .146 D3
Whitegate Rd NR11 . . . . . . .22 B7
Whitegates Cl 6 NR9 . . . . .88 D7
Whitehall Rd NR2 . . . . . . .162 B5
Whitehart Cl NR26 . . . . . . .138 D7
Whitehart La IP27 . . . . . . .175 C4
Whitehart St 6 IP24 . . . . .176 C4
Whitehorse La NR17 . . . . . .174 C5
Whitehorse Plain 7
NR30 . . . . .169 C5
Whitehorse St
1 Fakenham NR21 . . . . . .141 C3
Wymondham NR18 . . . . . .173 B3
Whitehouse La
Earsham NR35 . . . . .108 C1
Wicklewood NR18 . . . . .87 C4
Whitelands NR21 . . . . .141 D5
Whiteplot Rd IP26 . . . . .98 D5
Whitethorn Cl 8 NR6 . . . .158 D5
Whiteway Rd PE31 . . . . . . .135 B3
Whiting Rd NR4 . . . . .162 D1
Whiting's La NR17 . . . . . . .103 A6
Whitlingham La NR14 . . . .163 C4
Whitsands Rd PE37 . . . . . .153 A5
Whittington Hill PE33 . . . . .81 B2
Whittome Mill PE38 . . . . . . .79 D1
Whitwell Rd
Norwich NR1 . . . . .163 A7
Reepham NR10 . . . . .149 A2
Sparham NR9 . . . . .51 B6
Whitwell St NR10 . . . . . . .149 C2
Whitworth Ave 1 NR17 . . .174 C5
Wick Farm Cl 3 IP25 . . . . .84 D3
Wick La NR29 . . . . .57 D2
Wickhampton Rd NR13 . . . .93 A8
Wicklewood Prim Sch
NR18 . . . . .87 B5
Wicklewood Rd NR18 . . . . .87 B6
Wickmere Rd NR11 . . . . . . .20 C5
Wicks Yd 7 NR19 . . . . . . .154 D5
Wiclewood Way PE31 . . . .140 C3
Widgeon Cl NR31 . . . . .170 A6
Wier Ave NR20 . . . . .68 F6
Wigg Rd NR21 . . . . .141 B6
Wiggenhall Rd PE34 . . . . . .42 E3
**Wiggenhall St Mary
Magdalen Sch** PE34 . . . .61 B5
Wiggs Rd NR14 . . . . .110 F7
Wighton Halt Sta NR23 . . . .5 F3
Wigmam Hill IP22 . . . . . . .129 C5
Wilberforce Rd
Norwich NR5 . . . . .161 B6
Wisbech PE13 . . . . .152 D5
**Wild Flower Ctr* NR25 . . . .7 E3
Wild Radish Cl 16 NR14 . . .89 B3
Wild Rd NR3 . . . . .158 D1
Wildbriar Cl PE33 . . . . .43 E1
Wilde Rd 1 NR13 . . . . .72 E7
Wilderness Cl NR13 . . . . . .165 F4
Wilderness La IP20 . . . . . .122 D2
Wildfields Cl PE34 . . . . . . .145 D5
Wildfields Rd PE34 . . . . . . .145 C6
Wildflower Way NR35 . . . .109 A2
Williamson Cl IP22 . . . . . .177 D6
Wilkins Ct NR5 . . . . .161 C7
Wilkins Pl PE14 . . . . .59 D3

Wilkinson Rd NR13 . . . . . . .72 E7
Wilkinson Way NR28 . . . . .151 D4
Wilks Farm Dr NR7 . . . . . .159 A5
William Booth Rd
PE30 . . . . .147 D5
William Booth St NR2 . . . .178 A2
William Brown Way 1
IP22 . . . . .177 A5
William Bush Cl NR10 . . . . .35 B2
William Cl 5 Watton IP25 . .84 D3
6 Wymondham NR18 . . . .173 C6
William Cowper Cl
East Dereham NR19 . . . . . .154 C1
East Dereham NR19 . . . . . .154 E1
William Marshall CE Prim
Sch PE14 . . . . .95 D4
William Mear Gdns
NR1 . . . . .163 B6
William Paston Rd
PE38 . . . . .151 D6
William Peck Rd 7 NR10 .54 A2
William Rd
Fakenham NR21 . . . . .141 F5
Wisbech PE13 . . . . .152 C6
William St 9 PE30 . . . . . . .146 E3
William Way NR13 . . . . . . .154 C1
Williams Loke NR7 . . . . . . .163 D8
Williams Way
3 Holt NR25 . . . . .137 C5
North Walsham NR28 . . . . .151 C6
Williamson Cl NR7 . . . . . . .159 C2
Williamson Cres 4
IP24 . . . . .176 C2
Willis St NR2 . . . . .178 B4
Willoway Ave 1 NR31 . . . .72 E7
Willow Ave NR31 . . . . .94 C7
Willow Cl
Brandon IP27 . . . . .175 D2
Lingwood NR13 . . . . .74 A2
Long Stratton NR15 . . . . . .106 E2
6 Mattishall NR20 . . . . . .68 E6
Middleton PE32 . . . . .44 B4
North Walsham NR28 . . . . .151 D7
10 Tasburgh NR15 . . . . . .106 F6
Wortwell IP20 . . . . .123 A4
Wymondham NR18 . . . . . .173 D5
Willow Cres 3 PE33 . . . . . .63 B4
Willow Ct
3 Attleborough NR17 . . . .174 B5
Beetley NR20 . . . . .49 D4
Willow Dr
Clenchwarton PE34 . . . . . .145 E5
Dersingham PE31 . . . . .140 D3
King's Lynn PE33 . . . . .43 F4
Tilney All Saints PE34 . . . . .42 E4
West Winch PE33 . . . . .43 F1
Willow Gr
East Dereham NR19 . . . . . .154 D2
Sheringham NR26 . . . . . . .138 E5
King's Lynn PE30 . . . . .148 D2
Willow Heath Rd PE33 . . . .80 B7
Willow Herb Wlk 4
NR18 . . . . .173 E4
Willow La
Bedingham NR35 . . . . .108 B3
Broome NR35 . . . . .109 C3
Carbrooke IP25 . . . . .85 B5
Norwich NR2 . . . . .178 A3
Willow Pk PE30 . . . . .147 C8
Willow Pl PE33 . . . . .62 A5
Willow Rd
Downham Market PE38 . . . .172 B6
East Dereham NR19 . . . . . .154 B4
Hunstanton PE36 . . . . .132 C3
King's Lynn PE30 . . . . .148 D2
Willow Way
2 Ludham NR29 . . . . .56 C5
18 Marsham NR29 . . . . . .57 D4
Wisbech PE13 . . . . .152 D3
Willow Wlk 9 SP20 . . . . . .122 D1
Willows Ct 10 NR29 . . . . . .57 D4
Wilshere Ct 11 NR30 . . . . .169 D3
Wilson Dr PE32 . . . . .44 F3
Wilson Rd 6 NR1 . . . . .163 B5
Wilson's Dro PE32 . . . . .45 E3
Wilson's Way NR25 . . . . . . .7 D6
Wilton Cres 2 NR20 . . . . . .148 C5
Wilton Rd Feltwell IP26 . . .98 E1
Heacham PE31 . . . . .133 C6
Wilton View NR28 . . . . . . .151 D5
Wimbledon Ave IP27 . . . . .175 A1
Wimbledon Way 2
PE38 . . . . .172 B4
Wimbotsham Rd PE38 . . . .172 C6
Wimpole Dr PE30 . . . . .148 E1
Winceby Cl 5 NR7 . . . . . . .159 C2
Winch Rd PE32 . . . . .45 C5
Winchcomb Rd NR7 . . . . . .161 F7
Winchester Way IP24 . . . . .176 B5
Windermere Cl NR15 . . . . . .90 E2
Windermere Rd PE30 . . . . .148 F2
Windle Twr NR13 . . . . .74 C5
Windmill Ave NR30 . . . . . . .68 A8
Windmill Cl
Poringland NR14 . . . . .90 C4
Thetford IP24 . . . . .176 D5
Windmill Hill NR11 . . . . .14 A3
Windmill La
Costessey NR8 . . . . .157 A4
Syleham IP21 . . . . .131 D4
Wretham IP24 . . . . .102 B1
Windmill Rd
Gimingham NR11 . . . . .22 F8
1 Marham PE33 . . . . .63 B4
Norwich NR3 . . . . .158 F2
Worstead NR28 . . . . .38 A6
Wortwell IP20 . . . . .123 A4
Windsor Ave NR30 . . . . . . .169 D7

Windsor Chase NR8 . . . . . .155 D1
Windsor Cl 7 IP24 . . . . . . .125 F6
Windsor Cres PE13 . . . . . .133 C5
Windsor Ct IP25 . . . . .84 D3
Windsor Dr
Dersingham PE31 . . . . .140 D3
Wisbech PE13 . . . . .152 D8
Windsor Pk
East Dereham NR19 . . . . . .154 D8
8 King's Lynn PE30 . . . . .146 E3
Windsor Rd
Caister-on-Sea NR30 . . . . .168 E6
Cantley NR13 . . . . .92 C6
King's Lynn PE30 . . . . .146 E3
Norwich NR6 . . . . .158 A5
Windsor Rise PE36 . . . . . . .132 C2
Windsor St 1 PE38 . . . . . . .172 A5
Windsor Terr NR30 . . . . . . .146 E3
Windsor Way NR31 . . . . . . .170 B4
Windy La NR15 . . . . .107 B8
Windy Ridge PE33 . . . . .43 E2
Winfarthing Ave PE30 . . . .146 D3
Winfarthing Rd
Banham NR16 . . . . .119 D6
Shelfanger IP22 . . . . .120 B2
Wingate Way NR2 . . . . .162 C7
Wingfield Rd
Lakenheath IP27 . . . . .113 E2
Norwich NR3 . . . . .162 D8
Syleham IP21 . . . . .131 D5
Weybread IP21 . . . . .131 F6
Wing's La NR20 . . . . .33 B7
Wings Rd IP27 . . . . .113 E1
Winifred Rd NR31 . . . . .169 B3
Winifred Way NR10 . . . . . .168 D8
Winmer Ave 8 NR30 . . . . . .58 B6
Winners Wlk NR8 . . . . .155 E3
Winn's Ct NR25 . . . . .137 A7
Winsford Way NR5 . . . . . . .157 C1
Winstanley Rd 21 NR7 . . . .72 D4
Winston Churchill Dr
PE30 . . . . .147 C4
Winston Dr NR21 . . . . .15 E6
Winter Rd NR2 . . . . .162 A6
Winterton Fst Sch
NR29 . . . . .58 B6
Winterton Rd
Hemsby NR29 . . . . .167 B8
Somerton NR29 . . . . .57 F6
Wisbech & Fenland Mus*
PE13 . . . . .152 C4
Wisbech Castle*
PE13 . . . . .152 C4
Wisbech Gram Sch
PE13 . . . . .152 B5
Wisbech Rd
King's Lynn PE30 . . . . .146 D3
Manea PE15 . . . . .95 A2
Nordelph PE38 . . . . .78 D4
Outwell PE14 . . . . .77 F7
Walpole PE14 . . . . .41 D4
Wisbech PE13 . . . . .152 E8
Welney PE14 . . . . .95 E6
Wissey View IP26 . . . . .100 B4
Wissington Sugar Factory
PE33 . . . . .97 E8
Wistaria Rd PE13 . . . . .152 F7
Wisteria Cl NR10 . . . . .154 F4
Witard Cl NR7 . . . . .159 D1
Witard Rd NR7 . . . . .163 D8
Withersdale Rd IP20 . . . . .123 A1
Withington St 1 PE12 . . . . .41 A8
Withy Way NR8 . . . . .155 E1
Witton Cl
Heacham PE31 . . . . .133 C5
Reedham NR13 . . . . .92 F5
Witton Gn NR13 . . . . .92 F5
Witton La NR13 . . . . .165 A8
Wittons La IP21 . . . . .131 A3
Wiveton Rd NR25 . . . . .7 D6
Woburn St NR2 . . . . .162 C5
Wodehouse Cl 1 NR20 . . . .39 B4
Wodehouse Cl 1 IP25 . . . . .84 D3
Wodehouse Rd
Bacton NR12 . . . . .23 D4
Old Hunstanton PE36 . . . . .132 E7
Wodehouse St NR3 . . . . . .162 E8
Wolfe Rd NR1 . . . . .163 B7
Wolferton Dr PE32 . . . . . . .153 B2
Wolfaston Ave NR14 . . . . .154 D7
Wolseley Rd NR31 . . . . . . .169 B2
Wolterton Pk* NR11 . . . . . .20 C3
Wolterton Rd NR11 . . . . . . .20 C2
Womersley Rd 6 NR1 . . . .163 B7
Womersley Rd NR1 . . . . . .163 B7
Wood Avens Way
NR18 . . . . .173 E4
Wood Cl Brandon IP27 . . . .175 D2
Kenninghall NR16 . . . . . . .119 A4
Wood Dalling Rd
Guestwick NR20 . . . . .34 A6
Reepham NR10 . . . . .149 C6
Wood Dene Sch NR11 . . . . . .9 F3
Wood Gn NR13 . . . . .72 F8
Wood Hill NR8 . . . . .154 D8
Wood La Aldeby NR34 . . . .110 E5
Bedingham NR35 . . . . .108 C2
Bradenham IP25 . . . . .66 D4
Bressingham IP22 . . . . . . .119 E2
Burwell NR14 . . . . .91 A3
Burgh & Tuttington NR11 . . .36 C5
Dickleburgh & Rushall
IP21 . . . . .130 F6
Great Ellingham NR17 . . . .103 D8
Hepworth IP22 . . . . .127 C2
Holme Hale PE35 . . . . .66 B1
Honingham NR9 . . . . .69 E8

Wood La *continued*
Kelling NR25 . . . . .8 C5
Little Ellingham NR17 . . . . .86 B1
Long Stratton NR15 . . . . . .107 A2
Morley NR18 . . . . .87 A1
Pulham Market IP21 . . . .121 C8
Scole IP21 . . . . .130 F8
Starston IP20 . . . . .122 C3
Strumpshaw NR13 . . . . .73 F2
Swardeston NR14 . . . . .89 C5
Thelnetham IP22 . . . . . . .128 A2
Wicklewood NR18 . . . . .87 B4
Wood Norton Rd
Foulsham NR20 . . . . .33 C5
Stibbard NR21 . . . . .32 E7
Wood Rising Rd NR9 . .86 A5
Wood St Norwich NR1 . .178 A1
Wisbech PE13 . . . . .152 B6
Wood St Rd NR29 . . . . .56 B8
Wood View NR28 . . . . .151 A4
Wood View Ct NR5 . . . .157 A2
Wood View Rd NR6 . . .157 E5
Woodbastwick Rd
Blofield NR13 . . . . .165 C7
Blofield Heath NR13 . . . . .73 C6
Woodbastwick NR13 . . . . .55 C1
Woodbine Cl
North Walsham NR20 . . . .151 C5
Potter Heigham NR29 . . . . .56 F7
Woodcock Cl NR3 . . . .158 D3
Woodcock La PE34 . . . .61 B7
Woodcock Mews 4
NR31 . . . . .170 A6
Woodcock Rd NR3 . . .158 C3
Woodcock's La NR9 . . .88 A8
Woodcote Pk PE13 . . . .152 A4
Woodcroft Ct NR7 . . . .159 E2
Woodend Rd PE31 . . . .133 E5
Woodfarm La NR31 . . .170 A2
Woodfield
Briston NR24 . . . . .142 C4
1 East Dereham NR19 . . .154 C1
Woodfield Rd NR25 . . .137 C7
Woodforde Rd NR7 . . .159 D2
Woodgate 12 NR4 . . . . .89 B8
Woodgate La NR20 . . . .50 B3
Woodgate Rd NR20 . . . .50 A2
Woodgate Way PE31 . .134 F4
Woodhall Rd PE38 . . . . .97 B8
Woodham Leas NR6 . . .158 E6
Woodhill Rise NR5 . . . .161 C8
Woodhouse Cl 1 NR26 .138 B6
Woodland Dr
Bungay NR35 . . . . .124 A7
Fllingham NR35 . . . . .109 E3
Norwich NR6 . . . . .158 E4
Thorpe End NR13 . . . . .72 C7
Woodland Farm Ind Units
NR10 . . . . .53 A6
Woodland Gdns PE30 . .148 D5
Woodland La NK24 . . .142 F2
Woodland Rd NR6 . . . .157 E6
Woodland Rise
Sheringham NR26 . . . . . .138 E5
12 Tasburgh NR15 . . . . . .106 F6

Woodland Rise W
NR26 . . . . .138 D4
Woodland View Mid Sch
NR10 . . . . .54 A2
Woodland View Mobile Home
Pk NR10 . . . . .53 D6
Woodlands 58 IP20 . . . .122 D2
Woodlands Cl
Holt NR25 . . . . .137 D7
4 Thetford IP24 . . . . . . .176 E6
Woodlands Cres 1 NR7 .72 D5
Woodlands Dr IP24 . . .176 D6
Woodlands Mid Sch
NR31 . . . . .94 C6
Woodlands Rd NR5 . . .157 A2
Woodlands Rise IP27 . .175 A2
Woodlands The IP25 . . .84 A7
Woodlands Way Rd
NR12 . . . . .55 D4
Woodlark Cl 2 IP24 . . .176 D2
Woodpecker Dr 8 IP25 .84 C3
Woodpecker Mews 5
NR31 . . . . .170 A6
Woodrising Rd NR9 . . . .85 D4
Woodrow Ave NR25 . . .137 B5
Woodrow La NR15 . . . .121 A8
Woodrow Pl NR1 . . . . .163 B6
Woodruff Cl 3 NR6 . . .158 D5
Woods Cl 8 NR9 . . . . . . .88 C7
Woods End NR17 . . . . .174 C4
Wood's La NR20 . . . . . .49 B8
Woodside
Burnham Market PE31 . . .135 A2
North Walsham NR28 . . .151 E4
Woodside Ave
Dersingham PE31 . . . . . .140 C5
Heacham PE31 . . . . .133 D4
Woodside Cl
Attleborough NR17 . . . . .174 C4
Dersingham PE31 . . . . . .140 C5
1 Taverham NR8 . . . . . .155 C1
Woodside Fst Sch
NR7 . . . . .159 E1
Woodside Pk NR17 . . . .174 C3
Woodside Prim Sch
NR9 . . . . .00 D7
Woodside Rd NR7 . . . .159 E1
Woodstock La NR15 . . .120 F8
Woodstock Way 3 NR29 .57 D4
Woodton Prim Sch
NR35 . . . . .108 C5
Woodton Rd NR35 . . . .108 A7
Woodview NR28 . . . . .38 A4
Woodview Cl IP25 . . . . .84 C4
Woodview Rd NR9 . . . . .70 B5
Woodward Cl IP27 . . . .60 D8
Woodward Rd NR3 . . . .158 B2
Woodwark Ave 3 PE30 .146 E6
Woodyard Cl 9 NR14 . . .89 B3
Woodyard Sq The
NR35 . . . . .108 C5
Wooll Dr NR28 . . . . . . .151 D7
Woolner's La NR14 . . . . .90 E7
Woolstencroft Ave
PE30 . . . . .146 F7
Wootton Rd PE30 . . . .147 B7

Worcester Cl 3 NR29 . .167 A2
Worcester Rd PE13 . . .152 C7
Worcester Way
Attleborough NR17 . . . . .174 E4
Great Yarmouth NR31 . . .170 B4
Wordsworth Cl PE38 . . .172 D5
Wordsworth Gn IP24 . .176 E7
Wordsworth Rd
2 Diss IP22 . . . . .177 E4
Norwich NR5 . . . . .161 C6
Workhouse La
Foulsham NR20 . . . . .33 D4
Tilney St Lawrence PE34 . . .42 C1
Upwell PE14 . . . . .77 D4
Workhouse Rd NR12 . . .38 C3
Worlds End NR13 . . . . .74 C1
Wormegay Rd
Blackborough End PE32 . . .44 C1
Wormegay PE32 . . . . .62 D8
Worstead Prim Sch
NR28 . . . . .38 A5
Worstead Rd NR28 . . . .38 B4
Worstead Sta NR28 . . . .37 F4
Wortham Cl 3 NR5 . . .161 A8
Wortham Prim Sch
IP22 . . . . .129 C4
Worthing Rd
North Elmham NR20 . . . . .49 F7
Swanton Morley NR20 . . .50 B6
Wramplingham Rd
NR18 . . . . .173 D8
Wren Cl Brandon IP27 . .175 E3
Norwich NR4 . . . . .161 E2
Wren Dr
2 Great Yarmouth NR31 . .94 C7
Great Yarmouth NR31 . . .170 A6
Wrench Cl 4 NR11 . . . .150 D6
Wrench Rd NR5 . . . . . .161 D6
Wreningham Fst Sch
NR16 . . . . .88 D1
Wrens The 1 IP24 . . . .176 D2
Wretton Fen Dro PE33 . .80 D1
Wretton Rd PE33 . . . . . .80 F2
Wretton Row PE33 . . . .80 C3
Wright Ave NR19 . . . . .154 D1
Wright Cl NR30 . . . . . . .168 E7
Wright Dr NR19 . . . . . .154 C4
Wrights Cl NR11 . . . . . .150 C7
Wright's La PE12 . . . . . .41 B8
Wright's Loke NR28 . . . .22 E5
Wroe The PE14 . . . . . . .59 C1
Wroo Rd NR17 . . . . . . .103 F5
Wroughton Fst Sch
NR31 . . . . .170 B6
Wroughton Mid Sch
NR31 . . . . .170 B7
Wroxham Ave PE37 . . .153 C2
Wroxham Rd
Coltishall NR12 . . . . .54 E6
Rackheath NR13 . . . . .72 D8
Salhouse NR13 . . . . .54 E2
Sprowston NR7 . . . . .159 C5
Wroxham Sta NR12 . . . .164 C6
Wyatt Way IP24 . . . . . .176 B7
Wycliffe Rd NR4 . . . . . .161 D3
Wylde Croft NR8 . . . . .155 D2

Wymer Dr NR11 . . . . . .150 C4
Wymer St NR2 . . . . . . .162 B6
Wymers La NR13 . . . . . .74 B8
Wymondham Abbey Sta
NR18 . . . . .173 A3
Wymondham Coll NR18 . .87 B1
Wymondham Heritage Mus*
NR18 . . . . .173 C4
Wymondham High Sch
NR18 . . . . .173 C5
Wymondham Leisure Ctr
NR18 . . . . .173 C4
Wymondham Rd
Bracon Ash NR14 . . . . . . .88 E2
Bunwell NR16 . . . . .105 B5
East Carleton NR14 . . . . . .88 F4
Flordon NR15 . . . . .106 C8
Kimberley NR18 . . . . .87 B6
Morley NR18 . . . . .87 A3
Wreningham NR16 . . . . . .88 B2
Wymondham NR18 . . . . .105 A8
Wymondham Sta
NR18 . . . . .173 C2
Wyndfields 10 PE37 . . . .65 F4
Wyndham Pk NR27 . . . .10 C5
Wyndham St NR26 . . . .138 D7
Wyngates NR13 . . . . . . .165 F6
Wynne's La PE34 . . . . .145 C4

Y

Yallop Ave NR31 . . . . . .171 D8
Yare Cl
Caister-on-Sea NR30 . . . .168 D6
Great Yarmouth NR30 . . .169 C6
Yare Rd NR31 . . . . .94 A6
Yare Valley Dr NR4 . . .161 C2
Yare View Cl NR13 . . . . .92 F1
Yarmouth Bsns Pk
NR31 . . . . .169 B2
Yarmouth Rd
Blofield NR13 . . . . .165 F6
Broome NR35 . . . . .109 B1
Brundall NR13 . . . . .165 C5
Caister-on-Sea NR30 . . . .168 F7
Corton NR32 . . . . .171 D1
Dilham NR28 . . . . .38 C4
Geldeston NR34 . . . . . . .110 A3
Hales NR14 . . . . .109 F8
Hemsby NR29 . . . . .167 A6
Kirby Cane NR35 . . . . . . .109 E3
Lound NR32 . . . . .94 B3
Ludham NR29 . . . . .56 C5
North Walsham NR28 . . .151 C4
Norwich NR7 . . . . .163 E5
Ormesby St Margaret
NR29 . . . . .167 C1
Postwick with Witton
NR13 . . . . .165 A5
Raveningham NR14 . . . . .110 A8
Stalham NR12 . . . . .39 B3
Thurlton NR14 . . . . .93 A1
Toft Monks NR34 . . . . . .110 E5
Worstead NR28 . . . . .38 A6

Woo - Zur 213

Yarmouth Stadium
NR30 . . . . .168 E2
Yarmouth Way NR30 . .169 C3
Yarrow Cl IP24 . . . . . . .176 F5
Yarrow Rd Bintree NR20 . .33 B2
2 Dereham NR20 . . . . . . .68 A8
Yaxham CE Prim Sch
NR19 . . . . .68 C6
Yaxham Rd
East Dereham NR19 . . . .154 E4
Mattishall NR20 . . . . .68 C6
Yaxham Sta NR19 . . . . .68 A4
Yaxley Way NR5 . . . . . .161 A8
Yaxley's La NR11 . . . . . .150 C6
Yaxley's Rd NR30 . . . . .169 B6
Yelverton Cl NR6 . . . . . .157 D5
Yelverton Rd NR14 . . . . .90 E5
Yesmere 10 NR14 . . . . . .89 B3
Yew Ct NR7 . . . . .159 D4
Yew Tree Cl 24 NR31 . . . .94 C7
Yew Tree Ct NR20 . . . . . .69 B7
Yew Tree Rd NR17 . . . .174 C5
York Ave PE36 . . . . .132 D5
York Gdns PE13 . . . . . .152 D6
York La 13 NR12 . . . . . . .39 B4
York Rd Cromer NR27 . .139 D5
Great Yarmouth NR30 . . .169 D3
King's Lynn PE30 . . . . . .146 E3
Wisbech PE13 . . . . .152 D6
York St NR2 . . . . .162 B4
York Villa Cl NR29 . . . . .75 E8
York Way IP24 . . . . . . .176 B5
Youell Ave NR31 . . . . . .170 D1
Youngmans Cl NR28 . . .151 D3
Youngmans La NR12 . . . .38 E6
Youngman's La NR10 . . .37 C5
Youngmans Rd NR18 . . .173 C8
Young's Cres NR13 . . . . .92 E7
Young's Row PE12 . . . . .41 A8

Z

Zara Way NR19 . . . . . . .154 C1
Zephyr Cl NR30 . . . . . .168 D7
Zig-Zag La NR15 . . . . .108 C8
Zobel Cl NR3 . . . . .157 F2
Zurich Cl NR31 . . . . . . .171 E4